The GoodFood COOK BOOK

The GoodFood COOK BOOK

Over 650 triple-tested recipes for every occasion

Edited by Jane Hornby

BBC
BOOKS

Contents

Foreword
by Gillian Carter

This book is for everyone who wants reliable recipes and practical help for their everyday cooking as well as for special occasions. It really is like having a friend in the kitchen whose advice you can trust.

The recipes were originally produced for *Good Food* magazine, and have been selected by food writer Jane Hornby. Jane worked on *Good Food* magazine for 5 years, and is a truly natural and creative cook who has the knack of showing others how to get as much pleasure out of cooking as she does.

As you'd expect from *Good Food*, this book is packed with easy-to-follow information, so first timers can confidently follow instructions and get great results. More experienced and adventurous cooks, cake makers, and those of you who love to entertain, will find plenty to inspire you, so you can take your cooking to a new level.

I hope you enjoy using this fantastic book.

Editor, *Good Food* magazine

PAGE 1 *Iberico ham with slow-roast tomatoes and artichokes (page 153)* **PAGE 2** *Strawberries and cream layer (page 281)* **OPPOSITE Clockwise from top left** *Walker's mushroom, bacon and barley broth (page 25); Ham, leek and potato pie (page 418); Mango and cardamom syllabub (page 354); Sticky thyme and mustard bacon chops (page 139)*

Introduction

Welcome to *The Good Food Cook Book*, the biggest and best-ever collection of recipes from BBC *Good Food* magazine. We hope this book will become your friend in the kitchen no matter what kind of cook you are.

With literally thousands of great recipes to choose from, picking the definitive 650 recipes wasn't easy. The final cut consists of a fabulous range of recipes for any occasion you'd care to mention, with a helpful and practical stance that will neither alienate you nor bog you down with too much information. Expect to find everything from how to boil an egg to making a wedding cake – and all that's in between.

There's more to good cooking than just a good recipe, of course – confidence is key. We've poured all our experience from the *Good Food* test kitchen, plus useful reader feedback, into this book to create something that is as helpful and practical as possible and gives you all the information you need to get cooking.

How to use the book

Whatever you want to cook, we're confident you'll find it here. With a clear design, this book is easy to dip in and out of when you're busy, whilst containing the knowledge behind more in-depth techniques, should you need it.

The recipes are split into 18 intuitive chapters. Experience tells us that most people look for quick and simple recipes to cook throughout the week, and save more complicated or lengthy cooking for the weekend. So with that in mind, the savoury meal ideas in the first half of the book are split between 'Everyday ideas' and 'Weekend cooking', to spare you the search. Of course, it's up to you what you cook and when, but the recipes marked as everyday ideas will have shorter methods, fewer ingredients, and on the whole are family friendly and make good use of storecupboard ingredients. Weekend recipes are that little bit more special, sometimes with more involved cooking, and ideal for informal entertaining.

But it's not just great ideas for lunch and dinner that you'll find amongst these pages, Chapters 9–18 are each carefully chosen collections of recipes for when you want to cook something special or more unusual - one of our famous bakes perhaps, your own homemade bread or preserves, or maybe even a celebration cake. And each chapter has plenty of supporting information to make your dish a success. If you need guidance in cooking for big occasions, we have two whole chapters dedicated to Christmas and cooking for crowds, complete with menu ideas.

Each chapter begins with a few reference-style pages, covering shopping, storage and preparation and other useful information on the ingredients featured, plus illustrated step-by-step guides to give you real confidence with new techniques. Chapters also include guidance on such kitchen quandaries as how to know when a steak is ready, how to rescue a split sauce and how to make ice cream without a special machine. Page by page, we've really tried to answer all your culinary questions.

Many of the recipes have helpful hints and tricks alongside, which we've called 'tips', 'know-how' and 'try this…' and we've also flagged recipes that can be classed as 'superhealthy', 'low-fat' and 'good-for-you', as well as labelling recipes that are meat-free or suitable for freezing. For more information on what these labels mean and how to spot them, have a look at the key on page 10.

Although we don't have a chapter especially for vegetarians, many of the recipes in this book are vegetarian or meat-free. Recipes marked with the meat-free sign might include cheese or other diary products. We don't specify vegetarian cheese in these recipes but there are a number of veggie-friendly cheeses readily available these days, which you can substitute for regular cheese.

At the start of every recipe the prep and cook time is given, plus helpful information on the numbers it serves. Many recipes can be scaled up or down easily, and this too is indicated. The given prep time includes gathering ingredients and any chopping; cook time includes any step in which heat is used. Often you will be able to continue prepping as you cook, making best use of your time.

Where overnight soaking, marinating, cooling or any other lengthy prep is needed, we've let you know from the outset, so there are no nasty surprises. And don't be too quick to dismiss a recipe because it has a long cook time; it might include a 'walk-away time', for example, when a stew needs long, slow simmering, but no involvement from you, allowing you to get on with something else as it cooks.

The indices at the back of the book work hard for you too – the recipe index flags up recipes that are family friendly, meat-free, healthy, ideal for two, suitable for freezing ahead, one-pots and ready in 30 minutes or less, while the main index allows you to find recipes quickly by ingredient.

Cooking on a budget

Another concern for many of us, especially in these financially challenging times, is how to make delicious and nutritious food on a budget. The good news is that creating your own home-cooked family food needn't cost the earth, and eating on a budget certainly shouldn't mean having less interesting food on your plate. Within this book you'll find affordable, delicious ideas for day-in, day-out meals, plus ideas for entertaining without breaking the bank.

A few tips toward cooking on a budget:

- Make a list before you go shopping and stick to it.
- Switch to own-brand products in the supermarket, such as canned tomatoes, curry pastes, etc – they are often every bit as good as branded products and will save you a great deal of money.
- Try using cheaper cuts of meat and types of fish, and use canned or frozen alternatives to fresh where appropriate. Ask yourself: do you even need to use meat for every meal? There are plenty of other delicious ways to add protein to your meal with pulses, grains and dairy products to name a few.
- Buy in season. Seasonal fruit and veg will always be the cheapest option as they are the most plentiful – there's a seasonal table on page 471 if you're not sure what's good when.
- Batch-cooking soups, stews and pie fillings and then freezing half is a great way to make use of offers instore and saves overall cooking time.
- Before buying in bulk, make sure that you will be able to use all of the food before it reaches its use-by date. Buy one get one free offers often end up as buy one, put one in the bin. Be realistic about how much value they are really offering.
- Jointing a whole chicken into legs, thighs and breasts is far better value than buying chicken breasts alone.
- We aim to use full packs, cans and jars of perishable ingredients in our recipes, to save you wasting food.

And finally, whatever you do, don't keep this book pristine on your shelf. Make it an essential part of your kitchen kit; write in it, add to it, adorn the pages with splashes and streaks. The best-loved cook books bear the patina of family life – we hope *The Good Food Cook Book* earns it place at the heart of yours.

Happy cooking!

Cook's notes

Many of the recipes will have healthy benefits, such as high levels of omega 3 or fibre, and this will often be mentioned in the recipe introduction.

All of the recipes are sent to a qualified nutritionist to be analysed – each analysis includes main ingredients but does not include optional extras – it's up to you to use your common sense here. Remember that making simple changes to a recipe can make a dramatic difference to the fat content of a recipe, such as removing the skin from chicken breasts or using semi-skimmed milk instead of full-fat.

Throughout our recipes we recommend using salt 'to taste'. We add it to water for boiling pasta and vegetables, but if you don't want to, it's not essential for recipe success.

- Where possible we use humanely reared meat, free-range chickens and eggs and sustainably-sourced fish and unrefined sugar.
- Eggs are large in the UK and Australia and extra large in America unless stated otherwise.
- We use lightly salted butter and semi-skimmed milk, unless otherwise stated.
- Wash fresh produce before preparation
- Recipes contain nutritional analyses for 'sugar', which means the total sugar content including all natural sugars in the ingredients, unless otherwise stated.
- All the recipes in this book list both imperial and metric measurements. Conversions are approximate and have been rounded up or down. Follow one set of measurements only; do not mix the two.
- Cup measurements, which are used by cooks in Australia and America, have not been listed here as they vary from ingredient to ingredient.
- Kitchen scales should be used to measure dry/solid ingredients

Guideline daily amounts (GDA)*

	Women	Men
Kcalories	2000	2,500
Fat	70g (no more than 20g should be saturated)	95g (no more than 30g should be saturated)
Salt	Maximum 6g for adults and 11–14-year-olds, 5g for 7–10-year-olds (5g is 1 tsp)	
Sugar	90g	120g

*correct at time of press

A key to the symbols used

V *Meat-free recipes or suitable for vegetarians*
Always check the labels on shop-bought ingredients such as cheese, pesto and curry sauces to ensure they are suitable.

❋ *Can be frozen*
Unless otherwise stated, freeze for up to 3 months. Defrost thoroughly and heat until piping hot.

 super healthy These recipes are low in saturated fat (5g or less per portion), low in salt (1.5g or less) and at least one of the following: provides one-third or more of your daily requirement of fibre, iron, calcium, folic acid and/or vitamin C or contains at least one portion of 5-a-day fruit and veg.

low fat Recipes contain 12g or less fat per portion

good for you Recipes are low in saturated fat and salt

 Advice on cooking techniques, preparation and background on any unfamiliar ingredient.

 tip Information on substituting ingredients, adding extra flavours, using leftovers and make-ahead instructions.

 try this... Suggests how to give a meal a twist or gives a quick, additional recipe for you to try.

Conversion tables

WEIGHT

Metric	Imperial	Metric	Imperial	Metric	Imperial	Metric	Imperial	Metric	Imperial
25g	1oz	200g	7oz	425g	15oz	800g	1lb 12oz	1.6kg	3lb 8oz
50g	2oz	225g	8oz	450g	1lb	850g	1lb 14oz	1.8kg	4lb
75g	2½oz	250g	9oz	500g	1lb 2oz	900g	2lb	2kg	4lb 8oz
85g	3oz	280g	10oz	550g	1lb 4oz	950g	2lb 2oz	2.25kg	5lb
100g	4oz	300g	11oz	600g	1lb 5oz	1kg	2lb 4oz	2.5kg	5lb 8oz
125g	4½oz	350g	12oz	650g	1lb 7oz	1.25 kg	2lb 12oz	2.7kg	6lb
140g	5oz	375g	13oz	700g	1lb 9oz	1.3kg	3lb	3kg	6lb 8oz
175g	6oz	400g	14oz	750g	1lb 10oz	1.5kg	3lb 5oz		

For measurements under 25g /1 oz use spoons

VOLUME

Metric	Imperial	Metric	Imperial	Metric	Imperial	Metric	Imperial	Metric	Imperial
30ml	1 fl oz	175ml	6 fl oz	400ml	14 fl oz	850ml	1½ pints	1.7 litres	3 pints
50ml	2 fl oz	200ml	7 fl oz	425ml	¾ pint	1 litre	1¾ pints	2 litres	3½ pints
75ml	2½ fl oz	225ml	8 fl oz	450ml	16 fl oz	1.2 litres	2 pints	2.5 litres	4½ pints
100ml	3½ fl oz	250ml	9 fl oz	500ml	18 fl oz	1.3 litres	2¼ pints	2.8 litres	5 pints
125ml	4 fl oz	300ml	½ pint	600ml	1 pint	1.4 litres	2½ pints	3 litres	5¼ pints
150ml	¼ pint	350ml	12 fl oz	700ml	1¼ pints	1.5 litres	2¾ pints		

LINEAR

Metric	Imperial	Metric	Imperial	Metric	Imperial	Metric	Imperial	Metric	Imperial	Metric	Imperial
2mm	1/16in	4cm	1½in	9.5cm	3¾in	18cm	7in	28cm	11in	39cm	15½in
3mm	1/8in	4.5cm	1¾in	10cm	4in	19cm	7½in	29cm	11½in	40cm	16in
5mm	¼in	5cm	2in	11cm	4¼in	20cm	8in	30cm	12in	42cm	16½in
8mm	⅜in	5.5cm	2¼in	12cm	4½in	22cm	8½in	31cm	12½in	43cm	17in
1cm	½in	6cm	2½in	13cm	5in	23cm	9in	33cm	13in	44cm	17½in
1.5cm	⅝in	7cm	2¾in	14cm	5½in	24cm	9½in	34cm	13½in	46cm	18in
2cm	¾in	7.5cm	3in	15cm	6in	25cm	10in	35cm	14in	48cm	19in
2.5cm	1in	8cm	3¼in	16cm	6¼in	26cm	10½in	37cm	14½in	50cm	20in
3cm	1¼in	9cm	3½in	17cm	6½in	27cm	10¾in	38cm	15in		

SPOON MEASURES

Metric	Imperial
5ml	1tsp
10ml	2tsp
15ml	1tbsp
30ml	2tbsp
45ml	3tbsp
60ml	4tbsp
75ml	5tbsp

Over 5 tbsp, use fl oz measure

OVEN TEMP

	C	Fan oven	Gas
Very cool	110	90	¼
	120	100	½
Cool	140	120	1
	150	130	2
Moderate	160	140	3
	180	160	4
Moderately hot	190	170	5
	200	180	6
Hot	220	200	7
	230	210	8
Very hot	240	220	9

MICROWAVE

1	95 watts	Low
2	120 watts	Low
3	285 watts	Low
4	380 watts	Med
5	475 watts	Med
6	570 watts	Med
7	665 watts	High
8	760 watts	High
9	850 watts	High

SUGAR TEMPERATURE

	C	F
Thread	107	225
Soft Ball	119	238
Firm Ball	125	256
Hard Ball	138	280
Soft Crack	151	304
Hard Crack	168	336

Soups

If there's one thing every cuisine has in common it's soup. Cooks the world over have been simmering up this most basic of meals for centuries. From cleansing broths to creamy chowders, there's really nothing more satisfying than producing a homemade and warming bowlful. Bring a crusty loaf to the table and you've a meal fit for a king, without the royal price tag. As a bonus, few foods can beat soup as a healthy and filling option, often packed with your 5-a-day veg.

Home cooks hold their favourite soups close to their hearts; comforting, easy to make and, perhaps most importantly, the ultimate in good-value meals. There are, of course, good fresh soups available in cartons from any supermarket, but making your own and perhaps freezing in batches really makes kitchen sense – especially if you need to use up vegetables sooner rather than later.

There's so much choice available too, with a soup to suit every occasion; be it a family meal, quick lunch or smart starter. And if you're keen on cooking seasonally, soups are a lifesaver. The starchy winter stalwarts potatoes, celeriac, parsnips and swede can all be transformed into comfort food with a little persuasion. Then, of course, there are the wonderful soups of spring, summer and autumn too – vibrant pea and mint, fresh gazpacho or silky pumpkin or mushroom anyone?

Whatever soup you decide to make, it will call on stock as one of the main ingredients. Using ready-made stock will do the job just fine, but if you would like to try making your own (and it's worth it), then you'll find recipes on page 28–29.

FROM HUMBLE BEGINNINGS

Many soups begin with sweating vegetables in a little oil or butter until softened, but not golden. Cooking the vegetables this way before adding liquid makes an excellent backbone of flavour for the soup, and should not be rushed.

Butter gives the best flavour when softening vegetables, but oil will help you to keep the saturated fat down; or use half and half if you like. By the time the vegetables are sweated, they will be soft through – the rest of the cooking will be fairly quick.

If you have some baking parchment to hand, try fitting a piece snugly over the surface of the vegetables. The paper (called a cartouche) traps the steam in the pan, helping the vegetables to soften more quickly and evenly.

What you add next determines the character of your soup – a tomato-based soup will offer a tasty base for Mediterranean or spicy flavours.

OPPOSITE *Rich tomato soup with pesto (page 15)*

Creamy soups, made with stock and milk, cream or perhaps crème fraîche, are normally thickened by blending the ingredients with a roux base, made with flour. Thinner broths rely on a good-quality stock and plenty of flavour from aromatic herbs and spices – and tend to be a low-fat option.

USEFUL EQUIPMENT

Use a large pan, with enough surface area on the base to soften any vegetables in a shallow layer. Once the liquid has gone into the pan, stir now and again as it simmers, as the solids can catch on the bottom without you realising.

For a smooth soup, either use a hand-held blender, food processor or jug blender. Fill processors or blenders no more than half full and hold the lid down with a clean tea towel, just in case of eruptions! For a super-smooth result, pass the soup through a sieve and into a clean pan.

GETTING AHEAD

Soup is a flexible friend, and can be frozen or made well ahead. To preserve its flavour, bring it slowly to a simmer until piping hot, rather than boiling it hard.

Starchy soups containing pulses or root veg can also thicken up considerably as they cool and may need a splash of hot stock or water added to the soup to loosen.

Don't re-heat soups that have had yogurt or other low-fat dairy products added as they can easily split when reheated. Instead, stir through the finished soup just before serving and warm through gently.

Pasta and rice in soups will drink up lots of the surrounding liquid as it cools. Consider boiling pasta or rice separately and add it to the reheated soup.

Lots of people enjoy soup at lunchtime – so why not make a batch then freeze or chill individual portions ready to microwave. As when freezing soups (as with any liquid), make sure that you give it room to expand as it freezes. Leave a few cms at the top of plastic containers or bags before sealing. To freeze soup (and stocks) into freezer-friendly blocks, put a freezer bag into a container, fill with the soup and tie the top. Once frozen, lift out of the container and voila – a perfectly square block of soup, easily stacked.

STOCKS

Stock-making is a great habit to get into. Think of stock as a something-from-nothing bonus and, rather than binning or composting veg trimmings and old bones, add them to a stockpot instead.

Meat stocks are usually made with beef, lamb or veal. Poultry stocks can be made with chicken, turkey, duck, goose or even game bird carcasses and giblets while fish stock needs raw bones from white fish or shellfish shells. If you're asking a butcher or fishmonger to prepare meat or fish, ask them for the bones too. These can always be frozen for another time; if you have the freezer space and providing you have a very large pan, it makes good sense to stockpile bones and giblets in the freezer, ready to make one large batch of stock. This also helps with fuel economy too.

Where meat stock is concerned, both raw and cooked bones are suitable for use. Roasting raw bones, any giblets (but not the liver) and vegetables in a little fat before putting them into the stock pot will give a stock a rich brown colour and flavour, however cooked bones, such as a roast chicken carcass, will still give good results.

To give all stocks a little more personality, tuck in a few 'aromatics' – a few peppercorns plus a few parsley stalks, bay leaves and thyme sprigs, tied together with a piece of string (known as a *bouquet garni*).

Stocks are always started cold and then, for food safety reasons, brought to a full boil before simmering. If the water level drops as the stock simmers, top it up with just-boiled water from the kettle. Bones should remain submerged as the stock cooks. Skim away any scum that rises to the surface every now and then.

Once your stock is made, it can be seasoned and chilled or frozen as is, or reduced down. We wouldn't recommend adding salt to the stock before it's reduced or used in cooking; instead, season your final dish to taste.

Chill the stock or freeze it as soon as possible once cool. Once chilled, meat stock will become slightly jelly-like. This is perfectly normal and will give your finished recipe a delicious richness.

Chicken noodle soup

Fast, full of flavour and low in fat, this aromatic Asian-style soup will keep away winter chills.

**SERVES 2 (EASILY DOUBLED) • PREP 10 MINS
COOK 30 MINS**

900ml/1½pint chicken or vegetable stock
1 skinless chicken breast, about 175g/6oz
1 tsp chopped fresh root ginger
1 garlic clove, finely chopped
50g/2oz rice or wheat noodles
2 tbsp sweetcorn, canned or frozen
2-3 mushrooms, thinly sliced
2 spring onions, shredded
2 tsp soy sauce, plus extra for serving
mint or basil leaves and a little shredded chilli (optional),
    to serve

1 Pour the stock into a pan and add the chicken, ginger and garlic. Bring to the boil, then reduce the heat, partly cover and simmer for 20 minutes, until the chicken is tender. Remove the chicken to a board and shred into bite-size pieces using a couple of forks.
2 Return the chicken to the stock with the noodles, corn, mushrooms, half the spring onions and the soy sauce. Simmer for 3-4 minutes until the noodles are tender. Ladle into two bowls and scatter over the remaining spring onions, herbs and chilli shreds, if using. Serve with extra soy sauce, for sprinkling.

PER SERVING 217 kcals, carbs 26g, fat 2g, sat fat 0.4g, salt 2.52g

try this...

For a vegetarian alternative, replace the chicken with 175g/6oz firm tofu cut into cubes, simmer for 5 minutes, then add the other ingredients as before.

Rich tomato soup with pesto

You'll find it hard to go back to shop-bought tomato soup once you've tried this flavoursome recipe. Choose a fresh pesto to finish the dish off – it's worth it. (See photo on page 12.)

SERVES 4 • PREP 10 MINS • COOK 15 MINS

1 tbsp butter or olive oil
2 garlic cloves, crushed
5 soft sun-dried or sunblushed tomatoes in oil, drained
    and roughly chopped
3 x 400g cans plum tomatoes
500ml/18fl oz chicken or vegetable stock
1 tsp sugar, any type, or more to taste
142ml pot soured cream
125g pot fresh basil pesto
basil leaves, to serve, optional

1 Heat the butter or oil in a large pan, then add the garlic and soften for a few minutes over a low heat. Add the sun-dried or sunblushed tomatoes, canned tomatoes, stock, sugar and seasoning, then bring to a simmer. Let the soup bubble for 10 minutes until the tomatoes have broken down a little.
2 Whizz with a hand blender, adding half the pot of soured cream as you go, until smooth. Taste and adjust the seasoning – add more sugar if you need to. Serve in bowls with 1 tbsp of the pesto swirled on top, a little more soured cream and scattering of basil leaves.

PER SERVING 213 kcals, carbs 14g, fat 14g, sat fat 7g, salt 1.15g

tip Adding a pinch of sugar to tomato-based soups and sauces takes away any acidity from the tomatoes and really rounds out the flavour.

Spiced carrot and lentil soup

 Warm up with this low-fat, super-tasty storecupboard soup. For a dairy-free alternative, use reduced-fat coconut milk instead of the milk.

SERVES 4 ● PREP 10 MINS ● COOK 15 MINS
V ❄

2 tsp cumin seeds
pinch dried chilli flakes
2 tbsp olive oil
600g/1lb 5oz carrots, washed and coarsely grated
    (no need to peel)
140g/5oz split red lentils
1 litre/1¾ pints vegetable stock
125ml/4fl oz milk
plain yogurt and naan breads, to serve

1 Heat a large saucepan and dry-fry the cumin seeds and chilli flakes for 1 minute, or until they start to jump around the pan and release their aromas. Scoop out about half of the seeds with a spoon and set aside. Add the oil, carrots, lentils, stock and milk to the pan and bring to the boil. Simmer for 15 minutes until the lentils have swollen and softened.
2 Whizz the soup with a hand blender or in a food processor until smooth (or leave it chunky if you prefer). Season to taste and finish with a dollop of yogurt and a sprinkling of the reserved toasted spices. Serve with warmed naan breads.

PER SERVING 238 kcals, carbs 34g, fat 7g, sat fat 1g, salt 0.25g

try this...

Substitute the chilli flakes and cumin seeds for ras el hanout, if you have some in the cupboard. You could add cooked shredded chicken at the end of cooking, too.

Moroccan chickpea soup

 Based on a classic North African soup called 'harira', this aromatic and easy bowlful contains 2 of your 5-a-day, and re-heats brilliantly.

SERVES 4 ● PREP 10 MINS ● COOK 20 MINS
V ❄

1 tbsp olive oil
1 medium onion, chopped
2 celery sticks, chopped
2 tsp ground cumin
600ml/1pint vegetable stock
400g can chopped plum tomatoes with garlic
400g can chickpeas, rinsed and drained
100g/4oz frozen broad beans
zest and juice ½ lemon
large handful coriander or parsley and flatbread,
    to serve

1 Heat the oil in a large saucepan, then gently fry the onion and celery for 10 minutes until softened, stirring frequently. Tip in the cumin, then fry for another minute.
2 Turn up the heat, then add the stock, tomatoes and chickpeas, plus a good grind of black pepper. Simmer for 8 minutes. Throw in the broad beans and lemon juice, then cook for 2 minutes more. Season to taste, then spoon into bowls and sprinkle over a little lemon zest and herbs. Serve with flatbread.

PER SERVING 148 kcals, carbs 17g, fat 5g, sat fat 1g, salt 1.07g

tip Spice up the soup further with a spoonful of harissa paste. Curry lovers can swap the cumin for 1 tsp garam marsala.

Hearty pasta soup

 A new way with filled pasta, this soup is a meal in a bowl.

SERVES 4 • PREP 5 MINS • COOK 25 MINS
V ❄ BEFORE ADDING PASTA

1 tbsp olive oil
2 carrots, chopped
1 large onion, finely chopped
1 litre/1¾ pints vegetable stock
400g can chopped tomatoes with garlic
200g/7oz frozen mixed peas and beans
250g pack fresh filled pasta (we used tortellini
    with ricotta and spinach)
handful basil leaves, chopped (optional)
grated Parmesan and garlic bread, to serve

1 Heat the oil in a pan. Fry the carrots and onion for 5 minutes until starting to soften. Add the stock and tomatoes, then simmer for 10 minutes.
2 Add the peas and beans with 5 minutes to go. Once the vegetables are is tender, stir in the pasta. Return to the boil and simmer for 2 minutes until the pasta is just cooked.
3 Stir in the basil, if using. Season, then serve in bowls topped with a sprinkling of Parmesan and slices of garlic bread.

PER SERVING 286 kcals, carbs 44g, fat 9g, sat fat 3g, salt 0.88g

tip Can't get hold of fresh basil? If you've got a tub of pesto in the fridge, stir a spoonful into the soup just before you serve it.

Polish sausage soup

Almost a one-pot stew, this satisfying sausage soup is sure to be a hit with the whole family.

SERVES 4 • PREP 10 MINS • COOK 30 MINS
❄

2 large onions, thinly sliced
2 tbsp olive oil
2 garlic cloves, thinly sliced
200g Kabanos, chopped
1 tsp paprika, sweet or smoked
85g/3oz brown basmati rice
1 tbsp chopped thyme
2 litres/3½ pints strong-flavoured beef stock
3 carrots, thickly sliced
100g/4oz shredded kale

1 Fry the onions in the oil for 5 minutes. Add the garlic and sausage, fry for a few minutes more, then stir in the paprika, rice and thyme.
2 Pour in the stock, bring to the boil, then add the carrots and some salt and pepper. Cover and then simmer for 20 minutes. Stir in the kale, then cook 10 minutes more. Serve with crusty bread.

PER SERVING 433 kcals, carbs 34g, fat 24g, sat fat 6g, salt 3.83g

 Kabanos are Polish sausages, firm in texture and with a smoky taste. They're widely available in supermarkets. You could also use chorizo in this recipe.

Leek and potato soup with mustard toasts

Mustard toasts give this classic soup a modern twist – if you like, bake them earlier in the day and warm them through in the oven to make life easier.

**SERVES 8 EASILY HALVED • PREP 15 MINS
COOK 25 MINS**
❄

50g/2oz butter
8 rashers streaky bacon, chopped
5 large leeks, sliced
2 large potatoes, cubed
1.2litres/2 pints vegetable stock
2 bay leaves
300ml/½ pint milk
handful chopped parsley
FOR THE TOASTS
1 long, thin baguette
4 tbsp olive oil
1 tbsp wholegrain mustard

1 Melt the butter in a large pan, add the bacon and fry until just starting to colour. Add the leeks and potatoes, then stir well until they are glistening.
2 Add the stock and bay leaves, season and bring to the boil. Partly cover and simmer for 15 minutes, until everything is tender. Remove the bay leaves, then whizz the soup in batches in a food processor or blender. Return to the pan and stir in the milk. Reheat gently and season to taste. Add more stock or water if the soup seems too thick (this will depend on the size of your potatoes).
3 While the soup cooks, make the toasts. Heat oven to 200C/180C fan/gas 6. Cut the baguette into thin diagonal slices. Mix the oil and mustard together, then brush over both sides of the bread. Spread them on a large baking sheet and bake for 10 minutes. Scatter the parsley over the soup and serve with the toasts for dipping.

PER SERVING 314 kcals, carbs 31g, fat 17g, sat fat 6g, salt 2g

Butternut squash soup with chilli and crème fraîche

Come in from the cold to a warming bowl, full of the taste of autumn.

SERVES 4 • PREP 15 MINS • COOK 45-50 MINS
Ⓥ ❄

1 butternut squash, about 1kg/2lb 4oz, peeled and
    deseeded
2 tbsp olive oil
1 tbsp butter
2 onions, diced
1 garlic clove, thinly sliced
2 mild red chillies, deseeded and finely chopped
850ml/1½pints hot vegetable stock
4 tbsp crème fraîche, plus more to serve

 Chillies vary dramatically in heat, sometimes even within the same pack. To gauge what you're dealing with, touch the cut edge of the chilli, then touch the tip of your tongue with your finger. If it's fiercely hot, add less. Barely there? Add more.

1 Heat oven to 200C/180C fan/gas 6. Cut the squash into large cubes, about 4cm/1½in across, then toss in a large roasting tin with half the olive oil. Roast for 30 minutes, turning once during cooking, until golden and soft.
2 While the squash cooks, melt the butter with the remaining oil in a large saucepan, then add the onions, garlic and ¾ of the chilli. Cover and cook on a very low heat for 15–20 minutes until the onions are completely soft.
3 Tip the squash into the pan, add the stock and the crème fraîche, then whizz with a hand blender until smooth. For a really silky soup, put the soup into a liquidiser and blitz it in batches. Return to the pan, gently reheat, then season to taste. Serve the soup in bowls with swirls of crème fraîche and a scattering of the remaining chopped chilli.

PER SERVING 264 kcals, carbs 28g, fat 15g, sat fat 7g, salt 0.61g

Gazpacho

Dazzling red, smooth enough to drink from a glass but with a bit of texture to keep you interested, this no-cook soup makes an ideal start to a summer meal.

SERVES 6-8 ● PREP 25 MINS, PLUS CHILLING TIME NO COOK
Ⓥ

1 red onion, chopped
2 garlic cloves, finely chopped
red pepper, chopped
4 ripe tomatoes, chopped
1 slice white bread, torn and crusts removed
500ml jar passata
5 tbsp olive oil, plus extra to serve
4 tbsp wine vinegar
1 tsp Tabasco or harissa
300ml/½pint vegetable stock
1 tsp sugar
basil leaves, to serve

1 Put the onion, garlic, red pepper, tomatoes and bread in the food processor and blend until finely chopped but not too smooth. Transfer to a large bowl with the passata, oil, vinegar, Tabasco or harissa, stock, sugar, salt and pepper. Mix thoroughly, cover the bowl with cling film or foil and put in the fridge for at least 2 hours or overnight.

2 To serve, pour into small bowls or glasses, drizzle over a little olive oil and sprinkle with a few torn basil leaves.

PER SERVING 288 kcals, carbs 38.3g, fat 12.9g, sat fat 1.8g, salt 0.89g

Pea and mint soup

A quick simmer brings out the best in the new season's peas. To find out what's in season when, turn to page 471.

SERVES 4 ● PREP 10 MINS ● COOK 20 MINS
Ⓥ ❄ **COUNTS AS 1 OF 5-A-DAY**

1 bunch spring onions, roughly chopped
1 medium potato, diced
1 garlic clove, crushed
850ml/1½pints vegetable stock
900g/2lb young peas in the pod (or use 250g frozen petits pois)
4 tbsp chopped mint
large pinch caster sugar
1 tbsp lemon or lime juice
150ml/¼pint buttermilk or soured cream

1 Put the spring onions into a large pan with the potato, garlic and stock. Bring to the boil, turn down the heat, then simmer for 15 minutes. Meanwhile, blanch 3 tbsp of the peas in boiling water for 2–3 minutes. Drain then put in a bowl of ice-cold water and set aside. Add the remaining peas to the soup base, then simmer for just 5 minutes – no longer, or you will lose their fresh flavour.

2 Stir in the mint, sugar and lemon or lime juice, cool slightly, pour into a food processor or liquidiser. Whizz until smooth. Stir in half the buttermilk or soured cream and season.

3 To serve the soup cold, cool quickly by tipping into a shallow container, then chill. You may need to add more stock to the soup before serving as it will thicken as it cools. To serve hot, return the soup to the rinsed-out pan and reheat without boiling.

4 Drain the reserved peas then scatter over the soup in bowls. Finish with a swirl of buttermilk or soured cream.

PER SERVING 108 kcals, carbs 17g, fat 1g, sat fat 1g, salt 0.84g

Chilli beef noodle soup

Reviving and spicy noodle soups make fantastic after-work food.

SERVES 2 • PREP 10 MINS • COOK 15 MINS

1.5 litres/2¾ pints vegetable or beef stock
6 thin slices peeled fresh ginger
1 large red chilli, halved lengthways
1 bunch spring onions, finely sliced
1 sirloin steak, trimmed
1 tbsp sunflower oil
250g pack pak choi, quartered
300g/11oz thin egg noodles

1 Place the stock, ginger, chilli and spring onions in a large saucepan and bring to the boil. Meanwhile, heat a griddle pan until very hot and brush the steak with the oil. Griddle the steak for 2 minutes each side for medium-rare. Transfer to a board and leave to rest for 1 min, then thinly slice.
2 Add the pak choi and noodles to the stock. Bring to the boil then simmer for 3 minutes until tender. Ladle the stock, noodles and pak choi into large serving bowls and top with thin slices of steak.

PER SERVING 815 kcals, carbs 114g, fat 23g, sat fat 3g, salt 3.98g

> If you don't have a griddle pan, use an ordinary frying pan. Cooking the steak whole, rather than stir-frying in pieces means that the meat will stay juicy and can be cooked just how you like it.

Spicy prawn laksa

Laksa is a tasty noodle soup popular in Malaysia and Singapore. If you see laksa paste in your supermarket, grab a jar and use that instead of the Thai paste.

SERVES 4 EASILY HALVED • PREP 5 MINS COOK 15 MINS

1 tbsp sunflower oil
300g bag crunchy stir-fry vegetables
140g/5oz shiitake mushrooms, sliced
2 tbsp Thai green curry paste
400g can reduced-fat coconut milk
200ml/7fl oz vegetable or fish stock
300g/11oz medium straight-to-wok noodles
200g bag large, raw peeled prawns

1 Heat a wok, add the oil, then stir-fry the veg and mushrooms for 2-3 minutes. Take out and set aside, then tip the curry paste into the pan and fry for 1 minute. Pour in the coconut milk and stock. Bring to the boil, drop in the noodles and prawns, then reduce the heat and simmer for 4 minutes until the prawns are cooked through. Stir in the veg, then serve.

PER SERVING 327 kcals, carbs 32g, fat 17g, sat fat 10g, salt 0.97g

> *tip* To use dried noodles for this recipe, boil 100g medium egg, wheat or rice noodles in a separate pan of water, following the pack instructions. Drain, then add to the soup at the end of cooking.

OPPOSITE Clockwise from top left Creamy chicken soup (page 22), Pea and mint soup (page 19), Spicy prawn laksa (page 20), Spring vegetable soup (page 24), Silky pumpkin soup (page 25), Polish sausage soup (page 17)

French onion soup

A perfect dish for entertaining, the soup will keep in the fridge for several days.

SERVES 6 • PREP 25-35 MINS • COOK 1½ HRS
V ❄

50g/2oz butter
2 tbsp olive oil
1 tsp sugar
900g/2lb Spanish yellow onions (about 4 large),
    thinly sliced
2 x 295g cans beef consommé
300ml/½ pint white wine
1 bay leaf, optional
½ beef stock cube, crumbled
2 tbsp Cognac
FOR THE TOPPING
6 diagonal slices French baguette bread
generous knob soft butter
1 small garlic clove, crushed
140g/5oz Gruyère, coarsely grated

1 Heat the butter and oil in a large saucepan. Stir in the sugar and onions, then cook uncovered and over a low heat for 20 minutes, stirring often until softened. Now leave the onions to cook for another 20–25 minutes, stirring only a few times, giving a dark, crispy caramelised layer on the base of the pan.
2 Pour a little of the consommé into the onions and scrape all the caramelised bits from the bottom of the pan. Pour in the rest of the consommé, two tins of water and the wine. Drop in the bay leaf (if using), bring to the boil then turn down the heat, cover the pan and simmer for 45 minutes.
3 Toast the bread. Blend the butter and garlic, and spread over the toasted bread. Scatter most of the cheese over, pressing it on lightly. Set aside.
4 Stir the stock into the soup until dissolved. Pour in the cognac and cook for a couple of minutes. Season to taste, then discard the bay leaf. Ladle the soup into 6 heatproof bowls and put on a baking sheet. Lay a slice of bread on the top of each bowl, then scatter a little more cheese over the surface of the soup. Put under a heated grill for a few minutes until the cheese is bubbling and golden. Be careful when eating, as the soup will be very hot from the grilling.

PER SERVING 520 kcals, carbs 24g, fat 26g, sat fat 14g, salt 4.06g

Creamy chicken soup

Although creamy in both name and texture, this soup actually has no cream added.

SERVES 4 • PREP 15 MINS • COOK 25 MINS
❄

85g/3oz butter
1 small onion, roughly chopped
1 large carrot, cut in small chunks
2 small King Edward or red-skinned potatoes (about
    300g/11oz), cut into small chunks (no need to peel)
1 large leek, trimmed and thinly sliced
1 heaped tbsp fresh thyme leaves, plus extra to serve
50g/2oz plain flour
1.3 litres/2¼ pints hot chicken stock
200g/7oz cooked chicken, torn into big chunks
⅛-¼ tsp freshly grated nutmeg
crusty bread, to serve

1 Melt 25g of the butter in a large wide pan. Add the onion and fry for 3–4 minutes until just starting to colour. Stir in the carrot and potatoes and fry for 4 minutes, then add the leek and thyme and cook for 3 more minutes. Set aside.
2 Melt the remaining butter in a medium non-stick pan. Stir in the flour and stir for 3–4 minutes until pale golden. With the pan still on the heat, pour in the hot stock, about 150ml at a time, continuing to stir as you do so and beating well between each addition. When all the stock has been added, stir it into the vegetables, bring to a simmer, then cook very gently for 8–10 minutes to finish cooking them, giving it all an occasional stir.
3 Stir in the chicken and enough nutmeg, salt and pepper to suit your taste. Warm through, then serve piping hot with a grinding of pepper, a scattering of extra thyme leaves and some chunks of bread.

PER SERVING 449 kcals, carbs 32g, fat 24g, sat fat 13g, salt 1.10g

Broccoli soup with croûtons and goat's cheese

This is ideal for a warming lunch or starter. If you are not a fan of goat's cheese, try Brie instead.

**SERVES 4 OR 6 AS A STARTER • PREP 10 MINS
COOK 15 MINS**
V ❄

2 thick, crustless slices of bread, cubed
1 tbsp olive oil
900g/2lb broccoli
50g/2oz butter
1 large onion, finely chopped
generous grating fresh nutmeg
1 litre/1¾ pints vegetable or chicken stock
600ml/1 pint full-cream milk
100g/4oz medium-soft goat's cheese,
    chopped (rind and all)

1 Heat oven to 200C/180C fan/gas 6. Put the bread in a bowl and add the oil and a little salt. Mix well to coat the bread, then tip onto a baking tray. Bake for 10–12 minutes until crunchy and golden.

2 Meanwhile, chop the broccoli stalks and florets, keeping them separate. Melt the butter in a pan, then add the onion, broccoli stalks and nutmeg and fry for 5 minutes until soft. Add the broccoli florets and stock, then the milk. Cover and simmer gently for 8 minutes until the broccoli is tender.

3 Take out about 4 ladles of broccoli, then blend the rest in a food processor or with a hand blender, until smooth. Return the reserved broccoli to the soup and check for seasoning. (The soup will keep in the fridge for 2 days or you can cool and freeze it and keep the croutons in a plastic food bag.)

4 To serve, reheat if necessary and scatter with the croûtons and goat's cheese.

PER SERVING 435 kcals, carbs 24g, fat 28g, sat fat 15g, salt 1.99g

Cream of wild mushroom soup

This rich and filling dish is the perfect way to use up end-of-season mushrooms on the cheap.

SERVES 4 • PREP 30 MINS • COOK 40 MINS
V ❄

25g/1oz dried porcini mushrooms
50g/2oz butter
1 onion, finely chopped
1 garlic clove, sliced
few thyme sprigs
400g/14oz mixed wild mushrooms
850ml/1½ pints vegetable stock
200ml pot crème fraîche
4 slices white bread, about 100g/4oz, cubed
chives and truffle oil, to serve

1 Bring a kettle to the boil, then pour enough water over the dried porcini just to cover. Heat half the butter in a saucepan, then gently sizzle the onion, garlic and thyme for 5 minutes until softened and starting to brown. Drain the porcini, reserving the juice, then add to the onion with the mixed wild mushrooms.

2 Leave to cook for 5 minutes until the fresh mushrooms go limp. Pour over the stock and the reserved juices (avoiding the last drops as they can be gritty). Bring to the boil, then simmer for 20 minutes. Stir in the crème fraîche, then simmer for a few minutes more. Blitz the soup with a hand blender or liquidiser, pass through a fine sieve, then set aside.

3 Heat the remaining butter in a frying pan, fry the bread cubes until golden, then drain on kitchen paper. To serve, heat the soup and froth up with a hand blender, if you like. Ladle the soup into bowls, scatter over the croûtons and chives and drizzle with truffle oil.

PER SERVING 347 kcals, carbs 20g, fat 27g, sat fat 16g, salt 0.89g

Spring vegetable soup

Soup can be both satisfying and special, as this dish proves.

**SERVES 2 EASILY DOUBLED • PREP 10 MINS
COOK 15 MINS**

V ❄

1 tbsp olive oil
2 leeks, washed and finely chopped
100g/4oz green beans, cut into short lengths
1 large courgette, diced
1.2 litre/2 pints vegetable stock
3 vine-ripened tomatoes, deseeded and chopped
400g can cannellini beans
1 nest of vermicelli (about 35g)
FOR THE PISTACHIO PESTO
25g pack basil
1 garlic clove, crushed
25g/1oz pistachio nuts
25g/1oz Parmesan, finely grated
2 tbsp olive oil

1 Heat the oil, then fry the leeks until softened. Add the green beans and courgette, then pour in the stock and season to taste. Cover and simmer for 5 minutes.
2 Meanwhile, make the pesto: put the basil, garlic, nuts, Parmesan, oil and ½ tsp salt in a food processor, then blitz until smooth.
3 Stir the tomatoes, cannellini beans and vermicelli into the soup pan, then simmer for 5 minutes more until the veg and vermicelli are just tender.
4 Stir in half the pesto. Ladle into bowls and serve with the rest of the pesto spooned on top.

PER SERVING 594 kcals, carbs 56g, fat 31g, sat fat 6g, salt 2.35g

Winter minestrone with pesto croûtes

*The trinity of onion, carrot and celery gives this soup its heart, then add what you will.
Instead of cabbage, use any winter greens.*

**SERVES 4 EASILY HALVED OR DOUBLED • PREP 15 MINS
COOK 40 MINS**

❄ V

2 tbsp olive oil
1 onion, chopped
100g/4oz unsmoked lardons or chopped streaky bacon
2 large carrots, chopped
2 sticks celery, chopped
1 medium potato, chopped
2 garlic cloves, finely chopped or crushed
400g can chopped tomatoes
1 litre/1¾ pints vegetable stock
2 tsp chopped sage leaves, or 1 tsp dried
few cabbage leaves, shredded
400g can haricot beans
handful chopped parsley

1 Heat the olive oil in a large pan, add the onion and lardons or bacon and fry for about 5 minutes until the onion is starting to brown. Tip in the carrots, celery, potato and garlic, stir well and cook for a few minutes.
2 Add the tomatoes, stock and sage, and bring to the boil, stirring. Reduce heat to simmer and cook partly covered for 30 minutes, stirring in the cabbage after 15 minutes. Drain and rinse the beans and add to the pan with the parsley. Season and serve with pesto croûtes, or crusty bread.

PER SERVING (SOUP) 274 kcals, carbs 28g, fat 13g, sat fat 3g, salt 2.56g

Pesto croûtes

Cut 3–4 slices crusty bread into chunks, about 2cm thick. Tip into an ovenproof pan. Mix 3 tbsp olive oil and 1 tbsp pesto, then add to the bread, tossing it with your hands until the croûtes are evenly coated. Bake in a moderate oven for about 10 minutes until crisp.

tip To make it veggie, leave out the bacon and use 100g/4oz sliced chestnut mushrooms instead.

Silky pumpkin soup

When pureéd, pumpkin makes one of the smoothest soups going. This is a special autumn starter or lunch.

SERVES 6 ● PREP 20 MINS ● COOK 25 MINS
❄ Ⓥ IF USING VEGETABLE STOCK

4 tbsp olive oil
2 onions, finely chopped
1 kg/2lb 4oz pumpkin or squash (try kabocha), peeled,
    deseeded and chopped into chunks
700ml/1¼pint vegetable or chicken stock
142ml pot double cream
4 slices wholemeal seeded bread, (crusts cut off)
    cubed
handful pumpkin seeds

1 Heat 2 tbsp oil in a large saucepan, then soften the onions for 4 minutes. Add the pumpkin or squash to the pan and cook for 8–10 minutes, stirring occasionally until it starts to soften and turn golden.
2 Pour the stock into the pan, then season. Bring to the boil, then simmer for 10 minutes until the squash is very soft. Pour the cream into the pan, bring back to the boil, then whizz with a hand blender. For an extra-velvety consistency you can now push the soup through a fine sieve into another pan. (The soup can now be frozen for up to 1 month.)
3 Heat the remaining oil in a frying pan, then fry the bread until it starts to become crisp. Add the seeds to the pan, then cook for a few minutes more until they are toasted. (These can be made a day ahead and stored in an airtight container.) Reheat the soup if needed, taste for seasoning, then serve scattered with croûtons and seeds and drizzled with more olive oil, if you want.

PER SERVING 317 kcals, carbs 20g, fat 24g, sat fat 9g, salt 0.54g

Walkers' mushroom, bacon and barley broth

 Dried porcini mushrooms give this soup a rich flavour, which the barley and veg soak up. (See photo on page 6)

SERVES 6 ● PREP 20 MINS ● COOK 1 HR 15 MINS
❄

200g pack lardons or rashers bacon, cut into
    small pieces
2 onions, chopped
4 medium carrots, chopped
3 celery sticks, finely chopped
2 garlic cloves, crushed
1 sprig each rosemary and thyme
30g pack dried porcini or dried mixed wild mushrooms
1 glass dry white wine
1.5 litres/2¾ pints chicken stock
175g/6oz pearl barley, well rinsed
1 small head spring greens or chunk of Savoy cabbage
Parmesan or any strong hard cheese, grated, to serve

1 Sizzle the lardons or bacon in a dry pan for 10 minutes until golden, stirring now and then. When the bacon is ready, stir in the veg, garlic and herbs, cover and gently cook for 10 minutes.
2 Meanwhile, put the mushrooms into a jug, then fill up to the 600ml mark with boiling water. Soak for 10 minutes.
3 Lift the mushrooms out of their juice with a slotted spoon and roughly chop. Turn up the heat under the pan, add the mushrooms, fry for 1 minute, then pour in the wine. Let it evaporate right down, then add the mushroom liquid, avoiding the last drops, as they can be gritty. Add the stock and barley. Simmer for 40 minutes until the barley is tender. Lift out the thyme and rosemary stalks. (The soup can be made up to 2 days ahead or frozen for up to 1 month.)
4 When ready to serve, finely shred the greens and simmer in the soup for 5 minutes until tender. Season to taste, then serve with cheese for sprinkling and crusty bread and butter.

PER SERVING 290 kcals, carbs 35g, fat 9g, sat fat 3g, salt 1.75g

tip If you make ahead, loosen the soup with a little more stock as the barley will thicken it over time.

Prawn and fennel bisque

 Prawn shells give a deep seafood flavour to this luxurious soup. It's quite a rich dish, so serve in small bowls or cute teacups.

SERVES 8 AS A STARTER • PREP 30 MINS COOK 55 MINS

❄

450g/1lb raw tiger prawns in their shells
4 tbsp olive oil
1 large onion, chopped
1 large fennel bulb, chopped, fronds reserved
2 carrots, chopped
150ml/¼pint dry white wine
1 tbsp brandy
400g can chopped tomatoes
1 litre/1¾ pints fish stock
2 generous pinches paprika
TO SERVE
150ml pot double cream
8 tiger prawns, shelled but tail tips left on (optional)
fennel fronds (optional)

1 Shell the prawns, then fry the shells in the oil in a pan for about 5 minutes. Add the onion, fennel and carrots and cook for about 10 minutes until the veg start to soften. Pour in the wine and brandy, bubble hard for about 1 minute to drive off the alcohol, then add the tomatoes, stock and paprika. Cover and simmer for 30 minutes. Meanwhile, chop the prawns.
2 Blitz the soup as finely as you can with a hand blender or food processor, then press through a sieve into a bowl. Spend a bit of time really working the mixture through the sieve as this will give the soup its velvety texture.
3 Tip back into a clean pan, add the prawns and cook for 10 minutes, then blitz again until smooth. (You can make and chill this a day ahead or freeze it for 1 month. Thaw overnight in the fridge.) To serve, gently reheat in a pan with the cream. If garnishing, cook the 8 prawns in a little butter. Spoon the soup into small bowls and top with the prawns and snipped fennel fronds.

PER SERVING 120 kcals, carbs 7g, fat 6g, sat fat 1g, salt 1.17g

Silky celeriac soup with smoked haddock

As the haddock is just flaked over to finish, you can leave it out if any of your guests aren't keen.

SERVES 6 • PREP 10 MINS • COOK 40 MINS

❄

50g/2oz unsalted butter
1 onion, chopped
1 leek, finely chopped
1 garlic bulb, cut through the middle
few thyme sprigs, plus extra to serve
4 bay leaves
1 celeriac, peeled and diced
2 medium potatoes, diced
1 litre/1¾ pints chicken stock
500ml/18fl oz milk
2 fillets natural smoked haddock
500ml/18fl oz double cream

1 Heat the butter in a large saucepan until foaming, then lower the heat a little. Sweat the onion and leek with the garlic, thyme and 2 bay leaves. Add the celeriac and potatoes and cook for 10 minutes, stirring frequently so the vegetables don't stick to the pan. Pour over the stock to just about cover, bring to the boil, then simmer gently for 20 minutes.
2 Meanwhile, in a deep frying pan, bring the milk and remaining bay leaves to the boil. Lower to a very gentle simmer, slide in the haddock and cover with baking paper. Cook for 3–4 minutes until the fish flakes easily. Remove the fish from the milk and flake into a bowl; cover to keep warm.
3 When the celeriac is tender, pour in the cream, bring back to the boil and remove from the heat. Remove the garlic and herb stalks, then blitz until silky smooth using a hand blender. (If you want to freeze the soup, stir through the fish now. Serve scattered with the flaked haddock and thyme leaves.)

PER SERVING 636 kcals, carbs 16g, fat 54g, sat fat 30g, salt 1.87g

OPPOSITE Prawn and fennel bisque

Chunky fish chowder

 super healthy *This is perfect for weekend lunchtimes served by itself, or with a quick soda bread or cheese scones (see pages 250 and 317).*

SERVES 4 ● PREP 15 MINS ● COOK 25 MINS

2 tsp olive oil
2 leeks, finely sliced
550g/1lb 4oz potatoes, cut into small cubes
1 litre/1¾ pints fish stock
zest 1 lemon
300ml/½pint whole milk
330g can sweetcorn, rinsed and drained
250g/9oz skinless, boneless salmon, cut into chunks
250g/9oz skinless, boneless white fish, cut into chunks
handful chives, snipped with scissors
2 tbsp double cream, optional

1 Heat the oil in a large saucepan, tip in the leeks and fry gently for 5 minutes until softened, but not coloured. Add the potatoes and cook for a further minute. Pour in stock and lemon zest, cover and simmer for 12–15 minutes or until the potatoes are tender. With a slotted spoon, remove half the potatoes and leeks from the stock and set aside.
2 Transfer the remaining potatoes, leeks, stock and milk into a blender or food processor and whizz until smooth. Pour back into the pan, add the sweetcorn, fish and reserved vegetables. Cover and gently heat for 3–4 minutes until the fish is just cooked through – don't boil. Stir in the chives and cream, if using, then season to taste.

PER SERVING 425 kcals, carbs 47g, fat 13g, sat fat 4g, salt 0.82g

Homemade stock

A good stock is incredibly easy to make when you have a bit of extra time, and a really thrifty way to make the most of a roast, spare vegetables and fish trimmings. If you need to watch your salt intake then making stock at home is also a great way to reduce the amount of salt in your cooking.

Chicken giblet stock

**MAKES ABOUT 1 LITRE/1¾ PINTS ● PREP 10 MINS
COOK 1¼HRS-1½HRS**

giblets from 1 chicken (or turkey)
1 stick celery, halved (use the leaves too, if you have them)
2 large carrots, halved
1 onion, sliced
2 leeks, roughly chopped
1 tsp peppercorns, about 12–14
2 bay leaves
small handful parsley stalks
2 sprigs rosemary or thyme (optional)

1 Put all the ingredients into a large pan. Cover with 1 litre water then bring to the boil. Simmer for 1¼ hours, making sure that the giblets are always covered. Top up with boiling water from the kettle if you need to. Skim the surface as it simmers to remove any scum.
2 Strain the stock, discarding the chicken and veg. You can now boil the stock down to concentrate the flavour, if you like. Cool if not using straight away, and freeze if you like.

> **If you've bought a chicken without giblets, you can use the carcass. This will make a bigger batch of stock. Follow the recipe above but add enough water to cover the carcass. This works as well with turkey too.**

Brown beef stock

MAKES ABOUT 1 LITRE/1¾ PINTS • PREP 10 MINS
COOK 4-6 HRS
❄

1.5kg/3lb 5oz beef or veal bones
2 onions, quartered
2 carrots, very roughly chopped
2 celery sticks, very roughly chopped
1 tsp peppercorns
2 bay leaves
small handful parsley stalks
2 sprigs rosemary or thyme (optional)

1 Heat oven to 220C/200C fan/gas 7. Spread the bones, onions, carrots and celery over a large roasting tray, then roast for about 45 minutes, turning half way through, until golden. Tip everything into a large pan, add the peppercorns and herbs then enough cold water just to cover. Bring to the boil then simmer for between 4 and 6 hours (the longer the better really), topping up the water level with water from the kettle if you need to. Skim the surface as it simmers to remove any scum.
2 Strain the stock, discarding the bones and veg. You can now boil the stock down to concentrate the flavour, if you like. Cool, if not using straight away. This is helpful as it will allow you to scoop away any excess fat from the surface, and give a clearer end result. Freeze, if you like.

Fish stock

MAKES ABOUT 600ML/1 PINT • PREP 5 MINS
COOK 30-40 MINS
❄

450g/1lb fish bones or trimmings, from white fish is best
a small glass white wine, dry is best
1 leek, thickly sliced
2 sticks celery or 1 fennel bulb, roughly chopped
1 carrot
½ tsp black peppercorns, about 5–6
small handful parsley stalks
1 large or 2 small bay leaves
few peppercorns

1 Put all the ingredients into a pan then cover with 700ml water or enough to cover completely. Bring to the boil then simmer for 30 minutes, skimming the surface once or twice to remove any scum.
2 Strain, discarding all the other ingredients, then season to taste if you like. Cool, if not using straight away, and freeze if you like.

Vegetable stock

MAKES ABOUT 600ML/1 PINT • PREP 5 MINS
COOK 30-40 MINS
Ⓥ ❄

2 sticks celery, roughly chopped (use the leaves too, if you have them)
2 large carrots, roughly chopped
1 large onion, or 2 small, sliced
1-2 leeks, roughly chopped
1 tsp black peppercorns, about 12-14
2 bay leaves
small handful parsley stalks

1 Put all the ingredients into a pan with a pinch of salt and cover with 850ml water or enough water to cover completely. Put a lid on the pan, bring to the boil and simmer briskly for 30-40 minutes.
2 Strain, discarding the veg and cool, if not using straight away. To freeze, carry on boiling to reduce the stock down further, then decant into freezer bags or containers, ice-cube trays work well too. Remember to dilute them with boiling water before using.

Eggs and cheese

Nutritious and full of flavour, eggs are the ultimate fast food and a key ingredient. From hollandaise to quiches, in baking and desserts, meringues and custards, many dishes rely on the remarkable ability of an egg to add lightness, richness or structure. As for cheese and dairy products, not only are we lucky enough to have wonderful British cheeses, butters, yogurts and creams, but also cheeses from around the world such as Greek feta, Italian Parmesan and buffalo mozzarella and creamy French Brie, Camembert and goat's cheese, which are as likely to find their way into our shopping baskets as a block of Cheddar.

EGGS – THE FRESHER THE BETTER

Around 30 million eggs are eaten every day in the UK, and, chances are, you'll be cooking with chicken's eggs. However, depending on where you'll shop and the season, you'll find quail eggs, duck eggs, even sometimes pheasant eggs.

Whatever you plan to do with them, buy the best you can afford. The colour of the egg doesn't have anything to do with its quality, but rather the breed of hen that laid it and the type of diet the bird enjoyed. Yolks vary from pale yellow to deep orange; a diet rich in green vegetation will give a deep golden yolk.

Depending on what you're cooking, the age of an egg can be crucial to the success of your recipe. As a general rule, the more simply you serve them, the fresher they should be. This is especially important for poached and fried eggs – the white, or albumen, will still be thick and jelly-like, and should cling to the yolk and hold its shape well. Older eggs are fine for baking and actually better for meringue-making. If you're not sure of the age of an egg, pop it in a glass of water; the older the egg is, the higher it will float.

When buying in a supermarket, delve to the back of the shelf and choose eggs with the longest use-by date, then keep the eggs in the fridge. Room-temperature eggs are best for baking, so be sure to take them out of the fridge a good few hours before using.

Eggs stamped with the Lion quality mark are produced to the highest standards of food safety and are laid by hens vaccinated against salmonella. However, eating raw or undercooked egg isn't recommended for some people – particularly pregnant women, the elderly, babies and toddlers and people who are generally unwell.

WHAT DOES THE LABEL MEAN?

Even the most savvy of shoppers can find egg labelling confusing:
- Free-range eggs are laid by hens with constant access to outdoor runs and vegetation.
- Organic eggs are free-range, but reared on certified organic feed and land. (Not all free-range eggs are organic, but all organic eggs are free-range.)

OPPOSITE Croque madame (page 40)

- Barn (or perchery) eggs are laid by hens kept indoors with access to the floor and a perch.
- Cage system (battery) eggs are laid by hens kept in tiered cages with sloping mesh floors so that the eggs roll forward out of the reach of the birds to await collection. This is the most intensive and controversial method of egg production.

If you're not sure what size your egg is, large British eggs are now defined as weighing between 63g and 73g, medium eggs between 53g and 63g and small eggs under 53g.

Boiling an egg

Put room-temperature eggs into a large pan of cold water. If the eggs are in too small a pan, they can bump together. Bring the pan to the boil then, once the first big bubble rises from the bottom, start timing and reduce the heat to a simmer rather than a rolling boil.

- 4 minutes will give you the perfect **dipping egg**.
- A **just set yolk** will take 6 minutes.
- For a **slightly wobbly white**, simmer for 3 minutes.
- **Hard-boiled** eggs take 10 minutes.
- For **smaller or larger** eggs reduce or increase cooking times by 1 minute.
- For **canapés and salads**, drop quail's eggs into simmering water and leave for 1 minute for a runny yolk, or 1½ minutes for a just-set yolk.
- Putting the eggs into cold water and bringing them to the boil, rather than lowering them into already boiling water, prevents the shells from cracking.
- It's important to **cool hard-boiled** or **salad eggs** under cold running water to arrest the cooking and prevent a green ring from appearing around the edge of its yolk.

Poaching

Many cooks, including good ones, claim not to be able to poach an egg – but poaching directly in water is simple and requires no added fat, unlike cooking in a poaching pan.

Start with a large saucepan or deep frying pan – you need plenty of room for manoeuvre. Bring the water up to the gentlest of simmers (some recipes call for a little vinegar at this point, to help the white to set), then crack the egg into a cup. Very gently swirl the water and, once it has slowed to a very lazy whirlpool, carefully slide the egg into the middle of the pan. As the water turns, the thinner layer of white will knit itself to the rest of the egg. Leave the egg for 3 minutes then gently lift it out with a slotted

spoon. Eggs can be poached in advanced; as soon as the egg is set, put it into a bowl of iced water to cool. Chill for up to a day. Reheat in simmering water for 1 minute.

Frying

The best-tasting eggs are cooked in butter, but a thin layer of vegetable or sunflower oil (not extra virgin olive) works too.

Heat on a low to medium heat until the fat starts to shimmer, but don't overheat – frying at a lower temperature prevents overly rubbery whites and spitting fat. Break the egg into a cup or jug then slide the egg into the oil and leave it alone, no lifting or moving it about, until the white is set. Once most of the white has set, carefully spoon some of the hot fat over the remaining soft white until it sets. Alternatively, cover the pan with a lid to set the top. Cooking should take about 4 minutes in total.

For eggs over easy, lever a fish-slice under the egg and turn it over in one quick movement. A non-stick pan is definitely an advantage for this. Leave the eggs for 30 seconds, or longer if you want to cook the yolk through.

Scrambling

Scrambled eggs should be creamy and soft, rather than bouncy and dry (for perfect scrambled eggs see page 37). Perhaps scrambled eggs should be renamed folded eggs, as that far better describes how to create the perfect panful. Folding the eggs over themselves as they set, rather than stirring the pan madly, will reward you with thick creamy curds.

Always take the pan off the heat while the eggs still look a little too runny; by the time you've buttered your toast, they will have set. Beware very hot plates when serving eggs as they can easily overcook as they wait on the plate.

Omelettes and more

A basic French omelette can be one of the most satisfying suppers. The best are made from fresh eggs, seasoned and cooked quickly in a little butter until just set. The right sized pan is essential; a 20cm/8in pan is about right for a three-egg omelette – too large and the omelette will be thin, too small and it will be too thick.

Spanish omelettes are a whole different pan of eggs! Thick cakes of egg, with potato, onion and other flavourings, they are cooked for a longer time, then turned in the pan during cooking, to set the egg right through and create a golden crust all over.

A frittata is a very similar dish from Italy but it is often thinner than a Spanish omelette, and flashed under a hot grill to set, rather than being turned in the pan. If you're daunted by cooking an omelette the Spanish way, grill the top instead and call it a frittata.

Storing eggs

Egg shells are highly porous and can absorb all sorts of smells from your fridge so keep them in their box in the fridge and away from strong-smelling food such as onions.

Eggs can be frozen raw and beaten. You can also freeze whites and yolks separately. Freeze for up to a month and allow them to defrost completely in the fridge before use.

Separating eggs

Crack the egg against the side of a bowl. Carefully pull the two halves of shell apart, tipping the yolk into one half. The white will start to leak out into the bowl below. Pass the yolk between the two shell halves, until the white has drained away. Always separate eggs one at a time, tipping the white into another bowl before starting the next. Then, if a yolk does burst, you won't contaminate all the whites.

Whisking egg whites

Some recipes, such as a soufflé, will call for egg whisking. To get the best volume to your egg whites, take note of these following pointers:
• Older eggs will whisk up to a greater volume.
• Always use a large spotlessly clean bowl, ideally glass or copper and not plastic. To be super sure that your bowl is grease-free, rub around the inside with a little lemon juice or vinegar.
• Whisk the whites at room temperature.
• Use electric hand beaters or a stand mixer, if possible.
• Once you've reached the correct consistency, use the whites as soon as possible.
• Avoid over-whisking; the whites should never look dry.
For more information about meringues, see page 353.

TYPES OF CHEESE

There is so much to say about cheese that we could fill this whole book. Top line is that all cheese starts with milk – usually cow's, sheep's, goat's or buffalo's. Pasteurised or raw milk is then 'ripened' with lactic acid-producing bacteria to sour it. Nowadays, most cheese is made with pasteurised milk, then cultures are added to give the cheese its distinctive flavour (unpasteurised milk already contains the bacteria). This milk is then mixed with rennet or a vegetarian alternative. Rennet contains an enzyme, which breaks the milk into solid and liquid components; the curds and whey. The curds are cut, drained, then shaped to make the cheese. The whey is discarded or is sometimes reheated again, as with ricotta.

What follows is a quick guide to *Good Food*'s favourite and most used cheeses – it's by no means an exhaustive list, but all the cheeses mentioned will be widely available and useful to home cooks.

Brie originated in North-eastern France, but is now made all over the world. The large, flat wheels of cheese have a white rind and a paste that changes from chalky and mild to runny and almost mushroomy as it matures. Great for melting.

Camembert is a soft cow's milk cheese with a furry white rind speckled with beige. When mature, the cheese will have a strongly-flavoured and runny yellow paste. Camembert is made in individual cheeses about 11cm/4.5in in diameter, and is often baked in its box.

Cheddar, the real thing, still made with unpasteurised milk, comes from just a few farms around the village of Cheddar, in Somerset, but the cheese is now made all over the UK and the world. A good mature Cheddar is rich and tangy, with a dry almost flaky paste and has many uses in the kitchen.

Cheshire cheese, when young, is crumbly, white and with a fresh, milky flavour. As it matures, Cheshire takes on a mature character, but keeps its special texture.

Comté is a hard cheese from France, with a delicious depth of flavour, and melting qualities similar to that of Gruyère. It makes a great croque monsieur.

Cottage cheese is made from skimmed milk, and so is low in fat and high in protein and is popular with people watching their weight. It can be a little bland by itself, so pep up the flavour with some chopped chives, or buy a flavoured variety.

Double Gloucester is a hard cow's cheese with a smooth texture, milky, nutty flavour and peachy colour, thanks to the addition of annatto, which is a natural colouring.

Dolcelatte is a creamy and soft blue cheese from Italy and makes a great, milder alternative to Gorgonzola.

Emmental is the Swiss one with the holes. It has a subtle fruity flavour, a smooth texture and melts very well.

Feta is a semi-hard Greek cheese and the perfect partner for lamb, mint, lemon and watermelon. It's very salty with a sharp character. Traditionally made with goat's or sheep's milk, it is now often made with cow's milk too. The best feta is labelled 'barrel aged'.

Goat's cheese can be hard or soft. Mild, rinded goat's cheeses are often sold in slices from a larger log and are great for grilling. Soft, mild cheeses without a rind are good for stuffing and spreading and are delicious with honey too. Some goat's cheese such as Valençay, are dusted in ash or rolled in leaves, or matured in little rounds known as 'crottins', often topped with herbs. These cheeses are best saved for eating, rather than cooking. (Some people who have an intolerance to cow's milk may find goat's milk cheeses easier to digest.)

Gorgonzola is an Italian blue cheese, which can be mild or strong, depending on its age. Try it tossed through pasta or gnocchi, or served with soft, ripe fruit as a dessert cheese.

Gruyère is sweet and tangy and more flavourful than its Swiss sister, Emmental. It's predominantly used in cooking, for its brilliant melting texture, and is popularly used in dishes such as fondues and gratins.

Halloumi is firm, salty but mild and doesn't really come alive until it's cooked. Once it's grilled, griddled or fried, it turns golden on the outside and oozes within. Like feta, it goes fantastically with Mediterranean flavours.

Lancashire is a mild and tangy, crumbly-textured white cheese that melts well.

Manchego, a Spanish sheep's milk cheese, is often served with 'membrillo', or quince paste, and is good as part of a tapas menu, with a glass of cold dry sherry.

Mascarpone, almost like thick cream without any real cheesy flavour, is as at home in savoury recipes as it is in sweet, such as the Italian classic tiramisu. It can be lightened by being beaten together with fromage frais or yogurt and makes a delicious filling for cakes. Due to its high fat content, mascarpone is excellent for sauces.

Mozzarella is shaped and pulled in a bath of hot water, creating that characteristic smooth, ribbony structure.

Choose less expensive blocks for melting over pizzas and in pasta and save delicate buffalo mozzarella for tearing over salads or enjoying on its own. As an aside, **Provolone** is made in much the same way as mozzarella, then salted and matured.

Parmigiano Reggiano is a storecupboard staple these days, and it adds savouriness and bite to so many dishes. It can be finely grated, shaved thinly or even broken into chunks and enjoyed by itself as a canapé, with a little balsamic vinegar drizzled over. Pick cheeses aged for more than 24 months for the strongest flavour and driest texture and use younger cheeses for cooking. Grana Padano can be used in much the same way.

Pecorino is a sheep's cheese with a sharp, salty flavour. It is usually grated or shaved. Try it as an alternative to Parmesan.

Paneer is a vegetarian Indian cheese, which is made using lemon juice instead of rennet. Paneer is firm, and can be fried until golden then added to curries or grilled on skewers.

Quark is a very low-fat, smooth creamy cheese. Use it in place of thick yogurt, cream or crème fraîche. **Fromage frais** is much the same, though not all of it is low in fat, so check the label if that's what you're after.

Red Leicester is a cow's milk cheese with a crumbly texture and mild flavour and is coloured with annatto. Use it as you would Cheddar.

Ricotta, or 're-cooked', is made from the whey left over from the production of cow's cheese or, traditionally, Pecorino made with sheep's milk. The whey is reheated and, as a result, leftover solids can be collected to make this soft, lower-fat cheese. It can then be baked and used as a stuffing for pasta.

Roquefort is a soft French blue cheese with a slightly granular, crumbly texture and a strong flavour. It is fabulous crumbled through salads.

Soft or cream cheese is so versatile – excellent for creamy sauces, cheesecakes and frostings. Full-fat soft and cream cheese have a very high fat content. Be careful to choose full-fat versions if you intend to use them in cooking, as lower-fat types can easily split when heated.

Stilton, the king of blue cheeses, is full flavoured and smooth. Its intense savouriness makes it a perfect partner to mushrooms and chestnuts, as well as apples and pears.

Taleggio, an Italian washed-rind cheese, has a pale pinky rind and a fruity, almost apricotty flavour within. Delicious melted over polenta or potatoes.

Vacherin is a highly seasonal cow's milk cheese made during the winter months in France and Switzerland and packaged in round spruce boxes. When fully ripe, after two to three months, the cheese is mild and creamy within, and is often eaten with a spoon.

Wensleydale is a cow's milk cheese named after its Yorkshire home. It has a delicate, slightly sour flavour and distinctive moist, flaky texture. There is also a blue version.

The perfect cheeseboard

The cheeseboard can be every bit as exciting as the other courses, if you choose correctly. We'd recommend that you theme your cheeseboard by country and offer just three or four cheeses – something creamy and light (a young goat's cheese is ideal), a punchy semi-hard cheese (such as Cheddar), a perfectly-ripe semi-soft cheese, and then a magnificent chunk of blue cheese.

Make sure that whenever you plan to enjoy cheese by itself, you take it out of the fridge for at least an hour, to let it acclimatize.

When shopping for Christmas cheeses, use your eyes as well as your palate, aiming to select contrasting shapes and textures: one large wedge of a fabulous cheese is far more tempting than an array of mean slices. Three to five cheeses (350-600g each) is the ideal number for eight guests if you want to have plenty left for the rest of the holiday.

Grapes, cold from the fridge, are a great accompaniment, but why not try something more unusual too, such as quince or plum paste, or even our dried fig cake (page 438) with homemade oatcakes (page 439).

Storage

Ideally cheeses should be kept in a cool larder, but not many of us have those these days. Keep cheese wrapped in greaseproof paper, inside a plastic food bag or box and use within a week. Parmesan wrapped tightly in clingfilm will last for several months.

OTHER DAIRY PRODUCTS

Unsalted butter is best for cooking, as it contains few solids that can burn when melted. The saltiness of **salted butter** can skew the seasoning of a dish. Best instead to use unsalted butter and season it with salt to taste. Salted butter will keep longer, as the salt acts as preservative.

Single cream is thin and runny, and is used mainly for pouring over desserts. It can also be used in cooking, such as in custards and to enrich sauces, but take care not to let it boil. Single cream has 18 per cent fat.

Double cream is thicker, richer and can be whipped to one and a half times its original volume. It is good for cooking as the level of fat (48 per cent) keeps the cream stable at high temperatures. You can freeze double cream when it is lightly whipped, then defrost it when needed. Extra-thick double cream has the same level of fat but has a thick spoonable consistency and won't whip.

Whipping cream is lighter than double cream, with 38 per cent fat, and will whip up to twice its original volume. Use for filling cakes, mousses and soufflés.

Soured cream is made with single cream, so is lower in fat, but is thick and spoonable – perfect with baked potatoes or as the base of a dip. The sour flavour comes from cultures similar to those used to make yogurt.

Crème fraîche originates from Northern france, and has a slightly tangy soured flavour. It is good for spooning and also cooking as it won't split. Half-fat crème fraîche is excellent if you're looking for a healthier option, but take care when heating it.

Clotted cream contains a whopping 55 per cent fat, but has a wonderful, unique flavour and texture. Double cream is heated (and essentially reduced down as some of the liquid evaporates), then cooled to a thick cream with a buttery crust. Perfect for a cream tea.

Buttermilk used to be a by-product of butter-making, but it is now made from milk, thickened with a culture. Its slightly acidic nature helps flours with an added raising agent to rise particularly well, giving the lightest scones, thick pancakes and muffins. If a recipe calls for buttermilk but you can't find it in the shops, simply substitute with a low-fat, mild natural yogurt (or add a squeeze of lemon to the same volume of whole milk. It will go a little lumpy but that won't affect the end result).

Yogurt is made with milk (usually whole milk but often semi-skimmed or skimmed), which is pasteurised then has cultures added. Kept at just the right temperature, the cultures cause the milk to thicken, and gives the yogurt its tangy flavour. Greek yogurt is made in the same way but with reduced-down milk, to give it its lovely thick consistency. It can be used in place of whipped cream. Yogurt can be used instead of cream at the very end of cooking, but take care not to let it boil, as it will split.

A simple omelette

A well-made omelette, perhaps flavoured with a few herbs or filled with your favourite filling, is one of life's simple pleasures.

SERVES 1 • PREP 2 MINS • COOK 1–2 MINS
V

3 eggs, as fresh as possible, room temperature
2 knobs unsalted butter
1 tsp finely grated Parmesan

> ### Goat's cheese and chorizo omelette
> Beat a handful snipped chives into the eggs. Fry a few slices chorizo or salami and a pinch chilli flakes in a little oil until the meat crisps. Mix with 1 crumbled slice goat's cheese. Cook the omelette as above, spoon the chorizo mixture over one half of the omelette once it is ready, then fold and serve.

1 Warm a 20cm non-stick frying pan on a medium heat. Beat the eggs loosely so that you can still see a little distinction between yolk and white. Drop a knob of butter into the pan. Don't let it brown. Season the eggs with the Parmesan, salt and pepper, then pour into the pan.
2 Let the eggs bubble slightly for a couple of seconds, then take a wooden fork or spatula and gently draw the mixture in from the sides of the pan a few times, so it gathers in folds in the centre. Leave for a few seconds, then stir again to lightly combine the uncooked egg with the cooked. Leave briefly again, then repeat until most of the egg is set.
3 With the pan flat on the heat, shake it back and forth a few times to settle the mixture. It should slide easily in the pan and look soft and moist on top. A quick burst of heat will brown the underside. Fold the omelette over, rub the other knob of butter over to glaze and serve immediately.

PER SERVING 396 kcals, carbs none, fat 33g, sat fat 14g, salt 0.95g

Spicy tomato baked eggs

Vary this dish by flavouring the simple tomato sauce with whatever you have to hand – curry powder, pesto or fresh herbs, for example.

SERVES 2 • PREP 5 MINS • COOK ABOUT 20 MINS
V ▦ SAUCE ONLY

1 tbsp olive oil
2 red onions, chopped
1 red chilli, deseeded and finely chopped
1 garlic clove, sliced
small bunch coriander, stalks and leaves chopped
    separately
2 x 400g cans cherry tomatoes
1 tsp caster sugar
4 eggs

1 Heat the oil in a frying pan that has a lid, then soften the onions, chilli, garlic and coriander stalks for 5 minutes until soft. Stir in the tomatoes and sugar, then bubble for 8-10 minutes until thick. (Can be frozen for 1 month at this point.)
2 Using the back of a large spoon, make 4 dips in the sauce, then crack an egg into each one. Put a lid on the pan, then cook over a low heat for 6–8 minutes, until the eggs are done to your liking. Scatter with the coriander leaves and serve with crusty bread.

PER SERVING 340 kcals, carbs 21g, fat 20g, sat fat 5g, salt 1.25g

Perfect scrambled eggs

Fast food at its best; use a non-stick pan with a wooden spoon, folding the eggs as they cook rather than stirring.

SERVES 1 (EASILY DOUBLED) • **PREP 1 MIN**
COOK 2 MINS
V

2 large free-range eggs
6 tbsp single cream or full-fat milk
knob of butter

Smoked salmon and lemon eggs
Halve, toast and butter a bagel. Drape a slice of smoked salmon on each half and spoon over the scrambled egg. Grind over black pepper and serve with a wedge of lemon on the side.

Spinach and ham eggs
Add baby spinach leaves to the scrambled egg at the last moment and fold in until just wilted. Top a toasted muffin with a slice of ham or prosciutto, then pile on the scrambled eggs.

1 Lightly whisk the eggs, cream or milk and a pinch of salt together until all the ingredients are just combined and the mixture has one consistency.
2 Heat a small non-stick frying pan for 1 minute or so, then add the butter and let it melt. Don't allow the butter to brown or it will discolour the eggs. Pour in the egg mixture and let it sit, without stirring, for 20 seconds. Stir with a wooden spoon, lifting and folding it over from the bottom of the pan. Let it sit for another 10 seconds then stir and fold again.
3 Repeat until the eggs are softly set and slightly runny in places, then remove from the heat and leave for a few seconds to finish cooking. Give a final stir and serve.

PER SERVING With cream: 373 kcals, carbs 4g, fat 32g, sat fat 16g, salt 0.59g

Cheese, bacon and onion puff

Bake a basic batter mixture with a few added ingredients for a simple family supper.

SERVES 4 • **PREP 15 MINS** • **COOK 40 MINS**

140g/5oz plain flour
4 eggs
200ml/7fl oz milk
small knob of butter, plus extra for greasing
2 tbsp finely grated Parmesan
8 rashers smoked streaky bacon, chopped
4 spring onions, thinly sliced
140g/5oz mature Cheddar, grated

1 Heat oven to 230C/210C fan/gas 8. To make the batter, tip the flour into a bowl and beat in the eggs until smooth. Gradually add the milk and carry on beating until the mixture is completely lump-free. Grease a large, round ceramic dish, about 22cm wide, and dust it with the grated Parmesan.
2 Heat the butter in a frying pan. Sizzle the bacon for about 5 minutes until crisp, then cool. Tip the bacon, onions and Cheddar into the batter and stir until completely combined.
3 Tip into the prepared dish so it comes almost to the top, then bake for 30–35 minutes until puffed up and golden. Bring to the table piping hot and serve straight from the dish with a crisp salad.

PER SERVING 680 kcals, carbs 30g, fat 51g, sat fat 18g, salt 2.15g

Real Spanish omelette

Make an omelette the Catalonian way; a classic dish made simple with only 5 ingredients.

SERVES 4 • PREP 10 MINS • COOK 50 MINS
V

150ml/¼ pint extra virgin olive oil
500g/1lb 2oz new potatoes, skins scraped and
    thickly sliced
1 onion, chopped
6 eggs
3 tbsp chopped flat-leaf parsley

> *tip* Serving tapas? Make the omelette, leave it to cool, then cut into bite-size squares.

1 Heat the oil in a large frying pan, add the potatoes and onion and stew gently, partially covered, for 30 minutes, stirring occasionally until the potatoes are softened. Strain the potatoes and onion through a colander, reserving the oil, then tip them into a large bowl. Set aside the strained oil.
2 Beat the eggs in a separate bowl, then stir into the potatoes with the parsley and plenty of salt and pepper. Heat a little of the strained oil in a smaller frying pan. Tip everything into the pan and cook on a moderate heat, using a spatula to shape the omelette into a cushion.
3 When almost set, invert on a plate and slide back into the pan and cook for a few more minutes. Invert twice more, cooking the omelette briefly each time and pressing the edges to keep the 'cushion' shape. Slide onto a plate and cool for 10 minutes before serving.

PER SERVING 516 kcals, carbs 23g, fat 43g, sat fat 7g, salt 0.31g

Potato, spring onion, dill and cheese frittata

 If you like, make this the night before and leave it in the fridge. For a non-veggie option, add a couple of slices of ham.

SERVES 4 • PREP 10 MINS • COOK 20 MINS
V

2 tbsp olive oil
400g/14oz leftover cooked new potatoes, sliced
4 eggs, beaten
4 spring onions, finely sliced
small bunch dill, roughly chopped
25g/1oz Cheddar, grated

1 Heat the oil in a small non-stick frying pan (that can go under the grill) over a medium heat. Add the potatoes, then fry until beginning to crisp, about 8 minutes. In a bowl, whisk together the eggs, spring onions, dill and some seasoning. Heat the grill.
2 Tip the eggs into the frying pan, mix quickly, lower the heat, then sprinkle over the cheese. After about 8 minutes, when the almost set through, pop the pan under the grill for 2–3 minutes or until firm and golden. Slide the frittata out of the pan. Eat straight away or allow to cool then chill.

PER SERVING 244 kcals, carbs 18g, fat 15g, sat fat 4g, salt 0.40g

OPPOSITE Clockwise from top left Potato, spring onion, dill and cheese frittata, Simple Greek salad (page 41), Real Spanish omelette, Goat's cheese and chorizo omelette (page 36), Cheese and onion pork chops (page 44), Spicy tomato baked eggs (page 36).

Croque madame with spinach salad

This is a twist on croque monsieur, the ubiquitous French café snack. To make your Mrs a Mr, simply omit the egg. (See photo on page 30.)

**SERVES 1 EASILY DOUBLED • PREP 5 MINS
COOK 10 MINS**

1 thick slice crusty white bread or sourdough
1½ tsp wholegrain or Dijon mustard
2 thin slices ham, trimmed of excess fat
50g/2oz mature Cheddar or other melting cheese, grated
½ tsp cider or white wine vinegar
1 tsp olive oil, plus a little to fry the egg
1 very fresh egg
big handful baby leaf spinach
a few cornichons, to serve (optional)

1 Heat grill to High. Put the bread onto a baking sheet and lightly toast it on both sides. Spread 1 tsp mustard over one side, then top with the ham and cheese. Whisk the remaining mustard and the vinegar with 1 tsp oil then season, ready to dress the spinach.
2 Grill the croque for 3 minutes, or until the cheese is bubbling and turning golden.
3 Meanwhile, put a non-stick frying pan over a low heat. Add a little oil, then crack in the egg and let it gently fry. When the egg is cooked to your liking, lift it on top of the toast. Toss the dressing with the spinach (and cornichons, if using) and serve.

PER SERVING 548 kcals, carbs 31.7g, fat 33.4g, sat fat 13.9g, salt 3.19g

Quick cheese and onion rarebit

Make a meal out of cheese on toast. A little mustard or chutney spread on the toast is good, too.

SERVES 4 AS A SNACK • PREP 5 MINS • COOK 5 MINS

4 slices thick white bread
350g tub four-cheese sauce
3 spring onions, sliced
100g/4oz (or 4 slices) good-quality ham, torn into
    large strips
50g/2oz mature Cheddar, grated

1 Toast the bread in the toaster while you heat the grill to High. Mix the cheese sauce, onions and a grind of pepper together in a small bowl.
2 Transfer the toast to the grill rack and drape some ham over each slice. Next, spoon the cheese sauce onto the ham and spread it around with the back of the spoon. Scatter the grated cheese over the sauce, then pop the rarebit under the grill until the cheese turns bubbly and golden. Cut each slice in half and serve while still hot.

PER SERVING 367 kcals, carbs 29g, fat 20g, sat fat 10g, salt 2.14g

tip A ready-grated bag of cheese, bunged in the freezer, will save you time when making rarebits, pizzas and omelettes. Use it by the handful from frozen.

Simple Greek salad

This recipe serves 4 as a main, but also makes a great supporting act for the lamb souvlaki skewers on page 464.

SERVES 4 • PREP 20 MINS • NO COOK

450g/1lb best ripe tomatoes, cored and cut into
    chunks
1 red onion, cut into chunks
6 tbsp olive oil
juice 1 lemon
handful each flat-leaf parsley leaves and mint leaves,
    kept whole
200g feta cheese, broken into large chunks
20 black olives, preferably Kalamata
warmed pitta bread, to serve (optional)

1 Gently mix together all the ingredients, trying not to break up the feta too much, then season and serve.

PER SERVING 324 kcals, carbs 7g, fat 29g, sat fat 9g, salt 2.72g

> *tip* Get ahead: mix the tomatoes, onion, oil and lemon and olives and set aside for up to 2 hours or over night in the fridge. The juices will soften the onion ever so slightly as everything marries together. Bring back to room temperature to serve then finish with the cheese and herbs.

Bacon, blue cheese and walnut salad

In winter months, replace the cherry tomatoes with slices of ripe pear or crisp apple for a very special starter.

SERVES 6 • PREP 15 MINS • COOK 15 MINS

500g punnet cherry tomatoes, halved
1 garlic clove, crushed
drizzle extra virgin olive oil
5 tbsp walnuts
3 large handfuls baby spinach or other salad leaves
large handful basil leaves
200g lardons
100g/4oz Roquefort, cut into chunks
FOR THE DRESSING
2 tbsp sherry vinegar
4 tbsp olive oil

1 Heat oven to 190C/170C fan/gas 5. Put the tomatoes in a small roasting tin or dish and scatter with the garlic. Season, drizzle with oil and roast for about 15 minutes, until slightly shrivelled. At the same time and temperature, toast the walnuts until fragrant, about 10 minutes, then chop them roughly. Cover the tomatoes and walnuts with foil then turn the oven down to 110C/90C fan/gas ½ to keep them warm. Toss the spinach and basil together in a large bowl and season lightly.
2 Heat a little oil in a pan and sizzle the lardons for 3–4 minutes until lightly browned. Tip on to a sheet of foil and keep these warm in the oven too.
3 Bring the dressing ingredients to a boil in a small pan (the vinegar will smell very strong, so stand back), then pour the dressing over the salad and toss again to wilt slightly. Add the tomatoes and most of the nuts with most of the cheese, then toss. Serve on plates, scattered with the remaining cheese and nuts.

PER SERVING 297 kcals, carbs 4g, fat 27 g, sat fat 8g, salt 2g

> *tip* To make this salad into more of a main, try tossing in 1kg cooked sliced new potatoes.

Halloumi, watermelon and mint salad

This salad is equally good with feta cheese. There's no need to cook feta; simply cube or crumble it and plate up the salad.

SERVES 4 • PREP 10 MINS • COOK 5 MINS
V

250g/9oz halloumi, thinly sliced
flesh from 1kg/2lb 4oz chunk watermelon, sliced
200g/7oz fine green beans, raw or blanched and refreshed
small bunch mint, finely shredded
juice 1 lemon
1 tbsp extra virgin olive oil, plus extra to drizzle (optional)
toasted pitta bread, to serve

1 Heat grill to High. Lay the cheese on a baking sheet in a single layer, then grill for 2 minutes on each side until golden. Toss the watermelon, beans and mint together with the lemon juice and olive oil, season well, then layer on plates with the slices of halloumi.
2 Drizzle with a little more oil, if you like, then serve with warm pittas.

PER SERVING 287 kcals, carbs 12g, fat 20g, sat fat 10g, salt 2.29g

Summer couscous salad

Turn courgettes into something really special with this simple summer salad. Great as a side for barbecue parties too.

SERVES 4 EASILY HALVED OR DOUBLED • PREP 20 MINS COOK 10 MINS
V

250g/9oz couscous
250ml/9fl oz hot vegetable stock
400g can chickpeas, drained and rinsed
1-2 tbsp vegetable or olive oil
300g/11oz courgettes, sliced on the slant
300g/11oz small vine-ripened tomatoes, halved
250g pack halloumi, thickly sliced and then halved
    lengthways
FOR THE DRESSING
125ml/4fl oz olive oil
3 tbsp lime juice
2 large garlic cloves, finely chopped
2 tbsp chopped fresh mint
½ tsp sugar

1 Tip the couscous into a bowl, pour the hot stock over and mix well with a fork. Cover with a plate and leave for 4 minutes.
2 Meanwhile, tip all the dressing ingredients into a bowl and mix well. Fluff up the couscous with a fork, stir in the chickpeas and follow with half the dressing. Mix well and pile onto a large serving dish.
3 Heat 1 tbsp oil in a large frying pan and fry the courgette slices over a high heat for 2–3 minutes until dark golden brown. Lift out onto kitchen paper. Now put the tomatoes, cut-side down, into the pan, and cook for another couple of minutes until tinged brown on the underside. Top the couscous with the courgettes and then the tomatoes.
4 If the pan is dry, pour in a little more oil, then add the halloumi strips and fry for 2–3 minutes, turning them over from time to time, until crisp and sizzled brown. Pile on top of the tomatoes and drizzle with the remaining dressing.

PER SERVING 721 kcals, carbs 47g, fat 50g, sat fat 14g, salt 2.86g

tip You could add 1 tsp harissa to the dressing, if you like a little spice

OPPOSITE *Halloumi, watermelon and mint salad*

Paneer in herby tomato sauce

This healthier take on a tikka masala sauce uses yogurt instead of cream.

SERVES 2 • PREP 15 MINS • COOK 15 MINS
V

½ tsp cumin seeds
1 green chilli, chopped and seeded
3cm piece fresh root ginger, peeled and chopped
150g Greek yogurt
1 tsp light muscovado sugar
½ tsp garam masala
2 tbsp chopped fresh coriander leaves and stems
juice ½ lime
3 tbsp tomato purée
250g/9oz frozen peas
227g pack paneer, cut into 1cm cubes
2–3 ripe tomatoes, cut into wedges
handful roasted cashew nuts, chopped, to serve

1 Toast the cumin seeds in a dry heavy pan until fragrant – about 30 seconds. Crush roughly in a mortar and pestle, then tip into a blender with the chilli, ginger, yogurt, sugar, garam masala, coriander, lime juice, tomato purée and 200ml water. Blitz until smooth.
2 Pour the sauce into a saucepan. Cook for 5 minutes, stirring often. Add the peas and simmer for 3-5 minutes until almost cooked.
3 Stir in the paneer and tomatoes and heat through for 2–3 minutes. Scatter with cashews to serve.

PER SERVING 607 kcals, carbs 24g, fat 38g, sat fat 23g, salt 3.26g

Cheese and onion pork chops

A tangy combination of cheese, onions and mustard brings out the best in British pork chops.

SERVES 4 • PREP 5 MINS • COOK 15 MINS

4 pork chops or loin steaks
2 tsp olive oil
1 tsp English mustard
4 tbsp caramelized onions, from a jar
50g/2oz Cheshire cheese, crumbled
1 tsp chopped thyme or ½ tsp dried

1 Heat grill to High, then place the chops on a grill pan, rub with oil and season. Grill for about 6 minutes on each side, until golden.
2 Spread a little mustard over one side of each chop, then top with 1 tbsp onions. Combine the cheese and thyme, sprinkle over the chops, then grill until golden and bubbly.

PER SERVING 378 kcals, carbs 8g, fat 23g, sat fat 9g, salt 0.56g

Sticky stuffed chicken
Cut pockets in 4 skinless chicken breasts. Mix the onions, cheese and thyme with 50g/2oz breadcrumbs, then divide between the pockets. Brush the chicken with mustard and oil, season, then bake at 200C/180C fan/gas 6 for 20–25 minutes until cooked through. Serve with a crisp green salad.

10 ways to use up...
Cheese and eggs

CHEESE

1 **Tasty risotto** Don't throw away Parmesan rinds; save them for the next time you make risotto instead. Dropped into the rice as it simmers, the rinds will infuse Parmesan flavour right through the dish.

2 **Cheat's cheese sauce** Melt 200ml crème fraîche with 140g crumbled cheese (any type) until smooth. Pour over cooked cauliflower or vegetables as a side dish.

3 **Tasty cheese spread** Mash leftover cheese (traditionally Cheshire or another sharp, crumbly cheese) with a little soft butter, then season with a pinch of ground mace and cayenne. Great spread over hot fingers of toast.

4 **Cheesy pastry** Add a handful of grated Cheddar or other hard, strong cheese to the rubbed-in ingredients when making pastry from scratch. See page 262 for a simple shortcrust recipe which you can adapt.

5 **Make it a dip** Stir a little olive oil, chopped basil or dill and some seasoning through leftover ricotta or soft goat's cheese and enjoy with breadsticks or crudités.

6 **Pep up your coleslaw** Stir in a handful of grated cheese and some snipped chives.

7 **Try a melt** Turn an open sandwich into a melt; scatter with grated cheese and flash it under a hot grill until oozing.

8 **Go Mexican** Quesadillas (Mexican toasted tortilla sandwiches) can be made with any melting cheese. Scatter cheese over one half of a flour tortilla, then top with ham, chopped spring onions, chicken, tomatoes, jalapenos – whatever you have in the fridge. Scatter with a little more cheese, fold the tortilla in half, then cook in a dry pan for 3 minutes on each side until crisp and melting.

9 **Finish off the cheeseboard** Make a white sauce (see page 76 for a basic recipe) then stir in 250g mixed, crumbled cheese. Add some torn ham if you have any. Boil 400g pasta, drain, mix with the sauce then bake for 30 minutes or until golden on top for a filling, family-friendly meal.

EGGS

10 Leftover tortilla, frittata and quiche make excellent snacks or lunchbox fillers, but most egg dishes are best eaten straight away. Leftover egg whites can be used to make meringues, soufflés and mousses. Leftover yolks are ideal for making ice cream or custard (see pages 373 and 381).

Eggs Benedict

Eggs Benedict are traditionally served as two per person, but one makes a perfect brunch
or light lunch portion – it really depends on how hungry you feel.

SERVES 2 • PREP 10 MINS • COOK 20 MINS

1 tbsp white wine vinegar
4 of the freshest eggs you can get
2 muffins, split
25g/1oz butter, for spreading
2 slices thick-cut ham, halved
FOR THE HOLLANDAISE SAUCE
2 egg yolks
140g/5oz butter, melted
juice ½ lemon
pinch cayenne pepper

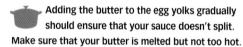 Adding the butter to the egg yolks gradually should ensure that your sauce doesn't split. Make sure that your butter is melted but not too hot.

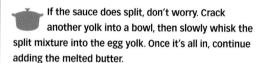 If the sauce does split, don't worry. Crack another yolk into a bowl, then slowly whisk the split mixture into the egg yolk. Once it's all in, continue adding the melted butter.

1 To make the hollandaise, sit a large bowl over a pan of hot water and whisk the egg yolks with 2 tbsp hot water. Very gradually, add the melted butter until it has all been incorporated. Once you have added half of the butter, you will be able to start adding it a little faster. Whisk in the lemon juice and season with the cayenne pepper and some salt to taste, then cover the surface of the sauce with clingfilm and set aside.
2 Heat the grill to high. Heat a pan of water with the vinegar until gently boiling, then poach the eggs for 2 minutes until just under-done. Set aside in the pan while you prepare the muffins.
3 Lay the muffins on a flat baking sheet, cut-side up, then toast under the grill until brown. Butter the muffins lightly, then top each with a piece of ham and then an egg. Use a slotted spoon to remove the egg from the pan and dab away any excess water from under the spoon with kitchen paper. Spoon a quarter of the hollandaise over each egg, then return the sheet to the grill to brown for a minute, if you like. Serve immediately.

PER SERVING 1093 kcals, carbs 31.9g, fat 91.8g, sat fat 49.7g, salt 4.04g

Spinach and smoked salmon egg muffins

If you prefer smoked salmon to ham, try this classic variation on eggs Benedict, also known as 'eggs royale'.

SERVES 4 • PREP 10 MINS • COOK 20 MINS

1 tbsp white wine vinegar
4 of the freshest eggs you can get
300g/11oz spinach
25g/1oz butter, for frying and spreading
2 muffins, split
4 long slices good-quality smoked salmon
FOR THE HOLLANDAISE SAUCE
2 egg yolks
140g/5oz butter, melted
juice ½ lemon
pinch cayenne pepper

1 Make the hollandaise sauce as above.
2 Heat the grill to high. Poach the eggs in pan of water with the vinegar. Meanwhile, fry the spinach in a wok with a knob of butter until wilted, then drain and season.
3 To serve, lay the muffins on a flat baking sheet, cut-side up, then toast until brown. Butter the muffins lightly, then top each with a ruffle of smoked salmon. Divide the spinach between the muffins, leaving a slight dip in the middle to sit the eggs in. Spoon a quarter of the sauce over each egg, then return the tray to the grill to brown for a minute. Serve immediately.

PER SERVING 626 kcals, carbs 17g, fat 51g, sat fat 28g, salt 3.5g

Spinach-baked eggs with Parmesan and tomato toasts

Eggs and spinach (such good bedfellows) baked with a flavoured butter are simple to do, and make a really good summery lunch for friends.

SERVES 4 • PREP 15 MINS • COOK 20 MINS
V

400g/14oz fresh spinach
100g/4oz basil, Parmesan and tomato butter
  (see below)
4 eggs
8–12 slices French bread

1 Heat oven to 190C/170C fan/gas 5. Wash the spinach and trim off any thick stalks. Put into a large pan then cook, covered, until the spinach is wilted, about 2–3 minutes. Drain well, pressing out all excess water, then return to the pan with about a quarter of the basil butter, stirring until the spinach is glistening.
2 Heat grill to High. Divide the spinach between 4 buttered ramekins, then break an egg into each. Season with salt and pepper, then top each with a slice of butter. Bake for 10–12 minutes, until the eggs are just set.
3 Meanwhile, grill the bread on one side until crisp, then spread the untoasted side with the remaining butter and grill again until crisp. Serve the eggs with the toast on the side.

PER SERVING 494 kcals, carbs 31g, fat 33g, sat fat 18g, salt 2.23g

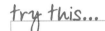

try this...

Basil and tomato butter
Beat 100g/4oz unsalted butter until soft and creamy, then add 4 rounded tbsp finely grated Parmesan, 10 shredded basil leaves and 1 tbsp finely chopped sun-dried tomatoes. Roll into a log shape in a sheet of cling film then chill until firm. Can be made up to 3 days ahead and kept chilled, or frozen for up to a month.

Baked ricotta with tomato, olive and basil salad

A great entertaining idea for summer, this ricotta can be baked up to a day ahead and the salad dressing made in advance.

SERVES 6 • PREP 15 MINS • COOK 35 MINS
V

3 x 250g tubs ricotta
2 eggs
100g/4oz Parmesan, finely grated
4 large tomatoes – a mix of colours looks good
handful good-quality black olives, stones removed
2 tbsp olive oil
1 tbsp extra virgin olive oil
1 tbsp red wine vinegar
¼ tsp caster sugar
1 garlic clove, crushed
small bunch basil, leaves only

1 Heat oven to 200C/180C fan/gas 6. Beat the ricotta and eggs together, fold in most of the Parmesan, then season to taste. Line a 900g loaf tin with parchment, then scoop the ricotta into the tin. Level the top, scatter with the remaining cheese, then bake for 35 minutes or until set and golden. Leave to cool, then turn it out.
2 Slice the tomatoes fairly thickly, then very roughly chop the olives. Whisk the olive oils, vinegar, sugar, garlic, olives and seasoning together. Just before you serve, roughly chop a few of the basil leaves and stir most into the dressing.
3 To serve, slice the ricotta and put it onto plates. Toss the tomatoes with a little dressing. Serve alongside the ricotta with the dressing drizzled over and the remaining basil scattered on top.

PER SERVING 354 kcals, carbs 6g, fat 28g, sat fat 13g, salt 0.82g

Marinated fig and mozzarella salad

A sourish marinade works really well with sweet figs and creamy, rich mozzarella. For a change, you could try crumbled goat's cheese.

SERVES 4 AS A MAIN, 6 AS A STARTER • PREP 15 MINS, PLUS MARINATING

V

8 ripe figs, stalks trimmed
4 tbsp balsamic vinegar
2 tbsp extra virgin olive oil, plus extra for drizzling
zest and juice 1 lemon
1 tbsp chopped fresh thyme
handful fresh mint leaves
2 x 150g packs mozzarella cheese
50g wild rocket

tip Another great way with this recipe is to pile the marinated figs and mozzarella on a piece of crusty bread and grill until the cheese melts and the toast is crisp. Top with rocket and serve as a bruschetta.

1 Cut each fig lengthways into four wedges. Make a marinade by whisking together the vinegar, oil and lemon juice with some salt and pepper to taste.
2 Stand the fig wedges up in the middle of a large shallow serving dish, keeping them close together. Scatter the lemon zest and thyme on top, then drizzle with the marinade. Leave to stand at room temperature for 30 minutes.
3 Roughly chop the mint. Drain and slice the mozzarella, toss with half the mint and season to taste.
4 To serve, arrange the mozzarella and mint mixture round the figs, scatter with lightly torn rocket leaves and the remaining mint, then drizzle with a little olive oil.

PER SERVING 364 kcals, carbs 14g, fat 25g, sat fat 11g, salt 1.18g

Roquefort toasts with peppered pears

Peppering the pears gives this dish a little bit of attitude without being overpowering. Dip into the cheese as you would pâté, and enjoy with a glass of good wine.

SERVES 2, EASILY DOUBLED • PREP 20 MINS • COOK 5 MINS

V

2 just-ripe pears, cored, then each cut into 8
1 tsp mild olive oil
¼ tsp mixed peppercorns, crushed
85g/3oz Roquefort
5 tbsp double or whipping cream
2 handfuls baby salad leaves
slices from sourdough loaf, halved and toasted just
    before serving
FOR THE DRESSING
1 tsp walnut oil
2 tsp olive oil
1½ tsp red or white wine vinegar
½ tsp honey

1 Heat a griddle pan until very hot, brush or toss the pear chunks with a little oil, sprinkle with the crushed pepper, then griddle for 1–2 minutes on each side until nicely striped.
2 Put the cheese into a mixing bowl, break it up a little with a wooden spoon, then beat it until almost smooth. Very softly whip the cream in a small bowl, then fold it into the cheese. Spoon the mixture into 2 small ramekins or pots.
3 Whisk the dressing ingredients together with some seasoning, turn the salad leaves in the dressing a few times to coat, then serve with the toasted sourdough, griddled pears and the cheese mixture.

PER SERVING 644 kcals, carbs 57g, fat 42g, sat fat 21g, salt 2.65g

OPPOSITE Clockwise from top left Baked ricotta with tomato, olive and basil salad (page 47), Spinach-baked eggs with Parmesan and tomato toasts (page 47), Smoked salmon soufflés (page 50), Roasted tomato, basil and Parmesan quiche (page 52) Cheesy Swiss bake (page 51), Roquefort toasts with peppered pears (page 48).

Smoked salmon soufflés

These non-scary soufflés are baked ahead then reheated in the oven just before serving.

SERVES 6 • PREP 30 MINS • COOK 25–30 MINS
❄

40g/1½oz butter, plus extra for greasing
25g/1oz plain flour
300ml/½ pint milk
85g/3oz full-fat soft cheese
2 tsp chopped dill
3 eggs, separated
85g/3oz smoked salmon, chopped
zest ½ lemon
TO SERVE
6 tsp crème fraîche
2 large slices smoked salmon
dill sprigs

tip To freeze, cool completely at the end of Step 2, then overwrap the dishes with baking parchment and foil. They will keep in the freezer for 6 weeks. Thaw for 5 hours in the fridge before continuing with Step 3.

1 Put the butter, flour and milk in a pan and cook, stirring, over a medium heat until thickened. Stir in the cheese, in small spoonfuls, and the dill; season to taste, then beat to incorporate.
2 Heat oven to 200C/180C fan/gas 6. Butter 6 x 150ml soufflé dishes and line the bases with baking paper. Stir the egg yolks into the sauce, add the chopped salmon and lemon zest. Whisk the egg whites until stiff, then carefully fold into the salmon mixture. Spoon into the dishes and bake in a roasting tin half-filled with cold water for 15 minutes, until risen and golden. Cool – don't worry if they sink.
3 When ready to serve, heat oven to 200C/180C fan/gas 6. Very carefully turn the soufflés out of their dishes, peel off the lining paper and place on squares of baking parchment on a baking sheet. Top each with 1 tsp crème fraîche and bake for 10–15 minutes until the soufflés start to puff up. Quickly top each with a frill of salmon and a dill sprig. Serve on their own or with some dressed salad leaves.

PER SERVING 237 kcals, carbs 6g, fat 19g, sat fat 11g, salt 1.17g

Cheddar soufflé

Didn't think you could manage to make a soufflé? Try this simple recipe and conquer a classic.

SERVES 4 • PREP 15 MINS, PLUS COOLING COOK 25–30 MINS
Ⓥ

50g/2oz butter, plus extra for greasing
25g/1oz breadcrumbs
50g/2oz plain flour
1 tsp mustard powder
300ml/½ pint milk
4 eggs, separated
100g/4oz extra-strong Cheddar, grated

tip For individual soufflés, fill six small ramekins up to three-quarters full, run a knife around the edges and then bake as before for 10-15 minutes. For a sweet soufflé idea, turn to page 369.

1 Heat oven to 200C/180C fan/gas 6 and place a baking sheet on the middle shelf. Butter a 15cm soufflé dish generously, then sprinkle in the breadcrumbs and rotate the dish to ensure the butter is evenly coated. Tip out the excess crumbs.
2 Melt the butter in a pan then stir in the flour and mustard. Cook, stirring, for 1 minute. Take the pan off the heat and gradually stir in the milk. Return to the heat and stir continuously until very thick – around 10 minutes. Transfer to a bowl and cool. Stir in the yolks and Cheddar and season well.
3 Whisk the egg whites into soft peaks in a clean bowl. Using a large metal spoon, gently fold the whites into the cheese sauce in a figure of eight.
4 Spoon the mixture into the dish. Run a knife around the edge to create a gap between the mix and the dish (this ensures the soufflé rises above the rim and doesn't stick). Place on the baking sheet and bake for 25 minutes until the top is golden, risen and has a slight wobble. Serve immediately.

PER SERVING 402 kcals, carbs 18g, fat 29g, sat fat 15g, salt 1.02g

Baked goat's cheese with beetroot, honey and thyme

This veggie main can be prepared ahead – giving you more time to relax before supper.

**SERVES 2 EASILY DOUBLED • PREP 20 MINS
COOK 10 MINS**
V

2 eggs, beaten
100g/4oz breadcrumbs (use Japanese panko crumbs
    if you can find them)
2 x 100g soft, rindless mild goat's cheeses
1 tbsp olive oil
2 cooked beetroot either from a pack (unvinegared),
    or home cooked
2 small thyme sprigs
FOR THE DRESSING
small bunch thyme, leaves removed
2 tsp red wine vinegar
2 tsp honey
2 tbsp olive oil

1 Heat oven to 220C/200C fan/gas 7. Make the dressing: mash the thyme leaves with a pinch of salt using a mortar and pestle, stir in the other dressing ingredients, then set aside.
2 Tip the eggs and breadcrumbs into separate shallow dishes. Dip the cheeses into the egg, then roll in the breadcrumbs. Repeat so they are completely coated. Put the cheeses on an oiled baking sheet, then drizzle a little oil over. Bake for 10 minutes until they are golden.
3 While the cheese cooks, finely slice the beetroot, then arrange on plates. When the cheese is cooked, place on top of the beetroot and top with thyme sprigs. Drizzle the dressing over the beetroot and serve.

PER SERVING 672 kcals, carbs 53g, fat 40g, sat fat 14g, salt 2.63g

> To cook beetroot, bring a pan of water to the boil with a splash of vinegar in it, then add the beets and simmer for 30–40 minutes until tender. Or rub the beetroots with a little oil and salt, wrap in foil and bake at 160C/140C fan/gas 4 for up to 2 hours until tender, depending on their size. Peel after cooking.

Cheesy Swiss bake

An Alpine speciality best enjoyed on a cold winter's day. If you can't find raclette, use jarlberg or gruyère.

SERVES 4 • PREP 20 MINS • COOK 45 MINS

1kg/2lb 4oz floury potatoes, cut into bite-size chunks
knob of butter
1 onion, chopped
200g/7oz smoked bacon, cut into small pieces
125ml/4fl oz dry white wine
142ml pot double cream
350g/12oz raclette cheese, grated
½ tsp smoked paprika

1 Heat oven to 200C/180C fan/gas 6. In a large pan, boil the potatoes for 5 minutes, then drain and tip into a large bowl.
2 Melt the butter in a saucepan and gently fry the onion until soft. Add the bacon and cook for a further 5 minutes. Mix the bacon and onion with the potatoes in the bowl.
3 Stir in the wine, cream, most of the cheese and a little paprika. Season and mix together, then spread over a large, buttered baking dish. Sprinkle with the remaining cheese, cover with foil and cook for 25 minutes. Remove the foil, sprinkle a little more paprika over the top and cook for a further 20 minutes until the cheese is golden brown.

PER SERVING 889 kcals, carbs 46g, fat 60g, sat fat 34g, salt 3.57g

Roasted tomato, basil and Parmesan quiche

A taste of summer, this quiche is full of Italian flavours and is perfect for dinner in the garden.
See below for more classic combinations. See page 263 for a step-by-step guide to lining the tin.

CUTS INTO 8 SLICES • PREP 40 MINS, PLUS CHILLING
COOK 40 MINS

300g/11oz cherry tomatoes
drizzle of olive oil
2 eggs
284ml pot double cream
handful basil leaves, shredded, plus a few small ones
    left whole for scattering
50g/2oz Parmesan, grated
FOR THE PASTRY
280g/10oz plain flour, plus extra for dusting
140g/5oz cold butter, cut into pieces

1 Heat oven to 200C/180C fan/gas 6. To make the pastry, tip the flour and butter into a bowl, then rub together with your fingertips until completely mixed and crumbly. Add 8 tbsp cold water, then bring everything together with your hands until just combined. Roll into a ball and use straight away or chill for up to 2 days. (The pastry can also be frozen for up to a month.)

2 Roll out the pastry on a lightly floured surface to a round about 5cm larger than a 25cm tin. Use your rolling pin to lift it up, then drape it over the greased tart case so there is an overhang of pastry. Using a small ball of pastry scraps, push the pastry into the corners of the tin. Chill in the fridge or freezer for 20 minutes.

3 In a small roasting tin, drizzle the tomatoes with olive oil and season with salt and pepper. Put the tomatoes in a low shelf of the oven.

4 Lightly prick the base of the tart with a fork, line the tart case with a large circle of greaseproof paper or foil, then fill with baking beans. Blind-bake the tart for 20 minutes, remove the paper and beans, then continue to cook for 5–10 minutes until biscuit brown. When you remove the tart case from the oven, take out the tomatoes, too.

5 While the pastry is cooking, beat the eggs in a large bowl. Gradually add the cream, then stir in the basil and season. When the case is ready, sprinkle half the cheese over the base, scatter over the tomatoes, pour over the cream mix, then finally scatter over the rest of the cheese. Bake for 20–25 minutes until set and golden brown. Leave to cool in the case, trim the edges of the pastry, then remove from the tin. Scatter over the remaining basil and serve in slices.

PER SERVING 494 kcals, carbs 29g, fat 39g, sat fat 22g, salt 0.48g

try this...

Quiche Lorraine

Part-bake the pastry case as above. Gently fry 200g lardons until pale golden. Cut most of 85g Gruyère into small cubes, then grate the rest. Scatter the bacon and cubed cheese over the pastry, then fill with the egg mix. Scatter with the grated cheese, then bake.

Sticky onion and Cheddar quiche

Part-bake the pastry case as above. Heat 25g butter in a pan and cook 500g finely sliced onions for 30 minutes, stirring occasionally, until they become sticky and dark golden brown. Beat these and 140g grated mature Cheddar into the egg and cream mix and bake as before.

Leek and mushroom quiche

Finely slice 4 leeks and soften in 25g butter, then turn up the heat and add 250g sliced chestnut mushrooms and cook for 5 minutes until tender. Cool, then beat into the egg and cream mix, along with 140g Gruyère, coarsely grated. Bake as before.

Pea, mint and goat's cheese quiche

Boil 300g frozen peas for 3 minutes then drain and cool under cold running water. Purée with 3 tbsp olive oil and a handful chopped mint leaves and season well. Spoon over the pastry case. Add 4 finely sliced spring onions to the cream and egg mix, then scatter over 200g crumbled goat's cheese and bake.

Thyme potatoes with Camembert fondue

Baking a cheese whole and still in its box is a fantastic way to share it with friends – and so much easier than making proper fondue!

SERVES 10 AS A NIBBLE • PREP 10 MINS COOK 45 MINS

V

500g/1lb 2oz small waxy potatoes, such as Charlotte
2 tbsp olive oil
few thyme sprigs, leaves stripped
1 whole Camembert, in its wooden box

1 Heat oven to 200C/180C fan/gas 6. Halve the potatoes and arrange over a baking sheet in one layer. Brush the cut sides with olive oil and sprinkle with salt, pepper and thyme leaves. Bake for 45 minutes until golden and crisp.
2 Unwrap the Camembert, put it back in its box and wrap the box in foil. Bake in the oven for the final 10 minutes. Remove the lid and serve with the potatoes for dipping.

PER SERVING 128 kcals, carbs 8g, fat 8g, sat fat 4g, salt 0.4g

Herby cheese roulade

This herb-speckled cheese roulade with a tasty filling of garlicky greens can be made up to 12 hours ahead.

SERVES 6 • PREP 20 MINS • COOK 25 MINS

V

FOR THE ROULADE
vegetable oil, for greasing
50g/2oz butter
3 garlic cloves, crushed
50g/2oz plain flour
300ml/½ pint milk
75g/2¾oz Parmesan, finely grated
4 medium eggs, separated
small pack fresh flat-leaf parsley, chopped
FOR THE FILLING
1 tbsp olive oil
25g/1oz butter
200g/7oz spring greens, shredded
1 garlic clove, crushed

tip Get ahead. Make up to the end of Step 2, turn out onto the paper and trim off the crisp edges. Cover with a damp cloth and leave for up to 12 hours. Continue as from Step 3. To reheat, fill with the garlicky greens and roll up. Wrap tightly in greaseproof paper, then foil, to help hold its shape. Lift onto a baking sheet, then cook for 15 minutes at 190C/170C fan/gas 5. Discard the foil and paper and serve immediately.

1 Heat oven to 190C/170C fan/gas 5. Oil a 23 x 33cm Swiss roll tin and line with baking parchment.
2 For the roulade, melt the butter in a large pan. Add the garlic and fry for 1 minute. Add the flour, cook for 1 minute, stirring constantly, then gradually stir in the milk. Boil, stirring, until the sauce is thick and smooth. Remove from the heat and stir in half the cheese. Season, then allow to cool slightly. Beat in the egg yolks and parsley. Whisk the egg whites to stiff, but not dry, peaks in a clean bowl, then gently fold into the cheese sauce. Pour into the tin, tipping it so that the mixture fills all the corners. Bake for 15 minutes until risen and golden.
3 Meanwhile, for the filling, heat the oil and butter in a large wok or frying pan and stir-fry the spring greens and garlic for 4–5 minutes until tender. Season.
4 Sprinkle the remaining cheese over a sheet of baking parchment just larger than the tin. Turn the roulade out onto the parchment, then peel off the lining paper. Trim the crispy edges. Use a slotted spoon to remove the spring greens from the butter, then spread over the roulade leaving a 2.5cm space at one short end uncovered. Roll up the roulade from that short end, using the paper to help. Serve the roulade immediately, drizzled with the garlicky butter.

PER SERVING 297 kcals, carbs 10g, fat 23g, sat fat 12g, salt 0.81g

3

Pasta, polenta, gnocchi and noodles

No wonder pasta and noodles have become so popular – they require no prep, cook quickly and make an economical choice. Versatility is key – make it low fat, make it indulgent, make it for the kids, make it with a simple sauce or dress it up with special seafood – whatever your mood there's a pasta, or a noodle dish to suit. Gnocchi and polenta, two other Italian staples, are worth adding to your repertoire if you haven't done so already.

OPPOSITE *Sweet potato and goat's cheese ravioli (page 78)*

TYPES OF PASTA

With spaghetti bolognese named as one of the nation's favourite foods, we can be sure that pasta is here to stay. But there's a whole lot more to it than white spaghetti.

Most Italians favour dried pasta to fresh for all the same reasons as us Brits: it's easy to store, economical and simple to cook. Most of the dried pasta we buy in the UK is durum wheat pasta, made with white durum wheat flour and water. Dried egg pasta is, as the same suggests, made with durum wheat flour and eggs or egg yolks. Egg pasta has a richer flavour.

As with wholewheat bread, wholewheat pasta is made with unrefined flour, which gives it a higher fibre content and nuttier taste. You'll need to cook wholewheat pasta a little longer than white.

If you or someone you know can't tolerate gluten, there are now plenty of gluten-free pastas to choose from. Look for buckwheat, corn and rice pastas, available in special diet sections of all supermarkets, and make sure you follow the cooking instructions carefully as they often need less time to cook.

Fresh and frozen filled pastas make an interesting change and are also extremely quick to cook for weeknight suppers. Most are fairly delicate, so don't be tempted to overcook or boil them too hard, or they will split open.

WHAT SHAPE?

There are around 350 different shapes of pasta available in Italy and, although you won't find quite so many on our supermarket shelves, there's still plenty of choice here too. Far from being simply decorative, pasta is made in different shapes for a very practical reason – to go with a particular texture or sauce and to help the sauce cling to the pasta, rather than stay on the plate.

Long pasta shapes are best for lighter or creamier sauces or simple tomato-based sauces. Look for linguine, spaghetti, fettuccine and tagliatelle.

Shorter shapes tend to be good with chunky, more robust sauces, as the sauce gets scooped up by the pasta. Look for penne (quills), rigatoni (tubes), fusilli (twists) and conchiglie (shells).

Stuff big shapes like cannelloni and giant conchiglie, and use tiny ones such as stelline (little stars) in soups.

Filled pastas such as ravioli and tortellini make a quick-and-easy option too, and, depending on the filling, require only a simple knob of butter or scattering of Parmesan to make a meal.

Essentially, if you don't have the right pasta for the right sauce, it won't be the end of the world, but keeping a pack of each kind of pasta as mentioned above – long, short, big and tiny – will leave you able to cook almost any pasta dish.

COOKING PASTA

Pasta needs one thing to cook well: plenty of boiling water, salted if you like. Tip in the pasta, stir it to separate the pieces then boil for 8–10 minutes, depending on the pack instructions (and the type of pasta), until just tender. Don't cover the pan with a lid. Stir the pasta now and again to prevent it sticking together or to the base of the pan. (If cooking spaghetti, gently push the strands into the water as they soften, then stir and leave to boil.)

The pasta is ready when it is floppy but not overly so. The best way to test if it's ready is to eat a bit; lift a piece out, cool for a few seconds then bite it – there should be some resistance without the pasta being chewy. This perfectly cooked pasta is called al dente, or 'to the tooth'.

Reserve some of the cooking water in a cup (many recipes call for this as, when added to the pasta and its sauce, it helps to marry the two together), then drain well in a colander. A pair of tongs will help you to manoeuvre pasta, but if you don't have any, simply use two forks instead.

Pasta is always best eaten straight away, however, if you need to leave it for a few minutes, either toss it with a little olive oil, or boil the kettle and run the water through the pasta to loosen the pieces.

For salads, undercook the pasta slightly, cool under running water then add a little olive oil to keep the strands separate.

MAKING YOUR OWN PASTA

Pasta-making is hugely satisfying, but it is still one of those jobs that really is made easier with a little mechanical help. A food processor will quickly and evenly bind the liquid and dry ingredients and a pasta machine, with its heavy rollers, will make rolling out the dough a breeze compared to using a rolling pin. If you're new to pasta making, try to borrow a pasta machine for your first few attempts – most machines end up gathering dust in the cupboard!

Homemade 'long' pastas, such as spaghetti and tagliatelle, although impressive, can be tricky not to over cook. However, where homemade pasta really comes into its own is for making filled shapes like tortellini or ravioli (see page 78).

Much like bread, pasta dough needs kneading until silky smooth, to lengthen the strands of gluten within the flour. If you have a dough attachment in your food processor, use that to help.

The type of flour used is important. Ideally, use '00' ('doppio zero') flour, which is now available in larger supermarkets (you can use strong white bread flour at a push). The 00 flour is made from durum wheat and is milled until superfine to give your pasta the correct smooth texture. Durum wheat is a particularly gluten-packed variety, which gives the dough elasticity and strength.

NOODLES

Noodles are Asia's answer to pasta: most countries, from Vietnam to Japan have their own speciality. But we no longer have to look far afield for somewhere to buy our rice or buckwheat noodles as supermarkets are now stocked with all kinds for every use.

Yellow dried egg noodles are widely available in various thicknesses. Some brands come in handy portion-sized nests, some in larger, flatter sheets. What thickness you choose depends on your taste really, although a medium-thickness noodle is probably the most handy size thickness to keep in the storecupboard.

Wheat noodles come in many different shapes and sizes – from thick, substantial Japanese udon to the fine, Vietnamese mi chay, which are sold coiled in nests. Some chefs recommend cooking them until al dente so that they still retain a little bite.

Rice noodles are mainly sold as thread noodles portioned in little bundles, which are ideal for soups, salads and for filling spring rolls. The wider, tagliatelle-like rice noodles are traditionally used in pad thai. Rice noodles are delicate and normally require just soaking in boiling water until tender, rather than boiling in a pan.

Japanese soba noodles are ideal for soupy ramen and salads. Made from buckwheat, they have a nutty flavour and firm texture. You'll find lots of soba to choose from in Japanese and Chinese stores and some brands in larger supermarkets.

Aside from rice noodles, most noodles are boiled before frying or putting into soups and salads. So-called 'straight-to-wok' noodles save you the hassle as they are pre-cooked and can go straight into the pan. Although convenient, they can break easily and are coated in oil.

To prep noodles ahead, cook or soak the noodles until a little underdone, then drain and cool them under the cold tap. Run a little sunflower or vegetable oil through the noodles, cover and chill until needed.

POLENTA

Polenta is the Italian word for a cooked dish made from ground maize or corn, but it is often used to describe the uncooked grain as well. Made from finely ground maize, polenta is a fine, free-running and sandy-like ingredient which, when mixed with water and simmered until thickened, is used all over Italy as an alternative to bread, pasta, rice or potatoes. Italians sometimes spread the uncooked grains under fresh pasta, to help the pasta dry out, and under bread to prevent it from sticking and to give it a crunchy crust. They also use polenta in baking, in moist citrussy or nutty cakes, for example, which is a particularly useful option if you are avoiding gluten.

Regular polenta is sold in Italian delis (usually labelled 'farina gialla', 'per polenta' or 'di granturco') and some large supermarkets. Some brands will tell you this is the only polenta worth buying, but it takes about 40 minutes of constant supervision to cook; these types are also more likely to go lumpy than instant, so you may have difficulty getting it smooth if you haven't used it before.

Instant or quick-cook polenta, sometimes called fine cornmeal, has already been cooked but still looks like a grain. Cook this with stock, stirring, and within 5–8 minutes and it will thicken to a smooth, lump-free, mash-like texture.

Once your polenta is made, choose to serve it 'wet' or let it set. Wet polenta is a great alternative to mashed potatoes, spooned into a mound and eaten with stews, casseroles or ragús. It goes particularly well with sausages, beef and game. For a finishing touch, sizzle butter or oil (add some chopped garlic or a few sage leaves if you like) in a small pan and drizzle it over the polenta to serve.

For set polenta, tip the soft polenta into an oiled baking sheet, or even just onto an oiled board, smooth it out, then let it cool until set. You can then slice the polenta, ready to grill, griddle, fry, bake, or barbecue. This makes a great topping for pies and it's a useful gluten-free alternative to bread.

Pre-cooked polenta is a handy alternative – this has already been cooked and set in a block, ready to slice. It's convenient, but more expensive than cooking it yourself.

GNOCCHI

These little potato and flour dumplings are another Italian staple, usually made with potatoes and wheat flour. They are delicious baked under, or tossed with, a sauce – in fact they are more or less interchangeable with pasta.

Making homemade gnocchi is great fun, however mastering a perfect, light-as-air batch of gnocchi can take practice. The potatoes need to be as fluffy and aerated as possible, ideally passed through a potato ricer rather than being mashed. Making the dough requires a certain lightness of touch too.

Gnocchi are best eaten on the day they are made, or frozen flat on sheets, then packed up into bags or boxes. They can be boiled from frozen.

Sounds too complicated? Don't worry, there's a recipe for quick and easy ricotta gnocchi on page 72 and also plenty of ideas for usinf ready-made gnocchi, which are usually very good.

Macaroni cheese

An old favourite that's comforting to eat and easy on the wallet.

SERVES 4 • PREP 15 MINS, PLUS INFUSING • COOK 30 MINS
V

700ml/1¼ pints full-fat milk
1 onion, peeled and halved
1 garlic clove, peeled
1 bay leaf
350g/12oz macaroni
50g/2oz butter, plus extra for greasing
50g/2oz plain flour
175g/6oz mature Cheddar, grated
1 tsp English mustard powder
50g/2oz Parmesan, finely grated
50g/2oz coarse white breadcrumbs

---

tip Macaroni cheese is a very versatile dish – you can add extra flavours you love or use up leftover ingredients. Try a creamy Gorgonzola, or try using some nutty-tasting Gruyère instead of Cheddar.

Carbonara For a smoky kick, add a little cooked chopped smoked bacon or pancetta to the sauce.

Creamy veg Gently fry some leeks and mushrooms in a little butter, then stir into the pasta along with sauce. Top with a layer of thinly sliced tomatoes instead of Parmesan and breadcrumbs.

---

1 In a small pan, warm the milk, onion, garlic and bay leaf until almost boiling. Remove from the heat, leave to infuse for 10 minutes, then strain.
2 Cook the macaroni following the pack instructions. Drain, then run under the cold tap and stir to stop the pasta sticking together.
3 Heat oven to 190C/170C fan/gas 5 and butter a 25 x 18cm ovenproof dish. Melt the butter in a medium pan. When foaming, add the flour, and cook, stirring constantly, for 1 minute on a low heat.
4 Slowly stir the warm infused milk into the pan until smooth. Simmer for 3–4 minutes, stirring, until the sauce has thickened. Remove the pan from the heat, then add the Cheddar and mustard powder. Season, then stir until the cheese has melted.
5 Mix with the macaroni, tip into the baking dish, sprinkle the Parmesan and breadcrumbs over the top, then bake for 15–20 minutes until golden brown and bubbling.

PER SERVING 860 kcals, carbs 97g, fat 40g, sat fat 24g, salt 1.72g

Must-make tuna pasta bake

Whip up a bargain meal for 6 using storecupboard ingredients.

SERVES 6 • PREP 10 MINS • COOK 40 MINS

600g/1lb 5oz rigatoni, penne or macaroni
50g/2oz butter
50g/2oz plain flour
600ml/1 pint milk
250g/9oz mature Cheddar, grated
2 x 160g cans tuna steaks in spring water, drained
330g can sweetcorn, drained
large handful chopped parsley

1 Heat oven to 180C/160C fan/gas 4. Boil the pasta for 2 minutes less than the time stated on the pack.
2 To make the sauce, melt the butter in a saucepan and stir in the flour. Cook for 1 minute, then gradually stir in the milk. Simmer, stirring, until the mixture thickens. Remove from the heat and stir in all but a handful of cheese.
3 Drain the pasta, mix with the white sauce, tuna, sweetcorn and parsley, then season. Transfer to a baking dish and top with the rest of the grated cheese. Bake for 15–20 minutes until the cheese on top is golden and starting to brown.

PER SERVING 752 kcals, carbs 99g, fat 26g, sat fat 15g, salt 1.43g

Spaghetti carbonara

Master this hearty pasta dish and you'll never be stuck for a quick supper.

SERVES 4 • PREP 10 MINS • COOK ABOUT 12 MINS

400g/14oz spaghetti
1 tbsp olive oil
200g/7oz smoked pancetta cubes or streaky bacon, chopped
3 eggs
½ x 142ml pot double cream
50g/2oz Grana Padano or Parmesan, finely grated, plus extra to serve
2 garlic cloves, crushed

Herby mushroom spaghetti
Substitute the pancetta for sliced mushrooms and add leaves from a sprig of thyme for a vegetarian alternative.

Lower-in-fat carbonara
Omit the extra egg yolk and replace double cream with low-fat crème fraîche.

1 Boil the pasta following the pack instructions. Meanwhile, put the oil in a frying pan over a medium heat then add the pancetta or streaky bacon. Fry until the fat in the meat has melted down and the meat is golden. Remove from the heat and set aside.

2 Crack 2 of the eggs into a mixing bowl. Separate the yolk from the third egg and add it to the bowl (you won't need the white). Beat the eggs together with the cream and cheese.

3 Add the garlic to the pancetta and return the frying pan to the hob. Fry over a high heat for 1 minute or until the garlic is cooked and the pancetta warmed through.

4 Drain the pasta and tip it back into the hot saucepan off the heat. Pour the egg mixture over the pasta, followed by the hot pancetta, garlic, and any fat and oils. Toss quickly and thoroughly with a spaghetti spoon or tongs. Keep stirring until the sauce thickens slightly. Serve with extra cheese and freshly ground pepper.

PER SERVING 734 kcals, carbs 75g, fat 36g, sat fat 15g, salt 2.95g

Classic spaghetti with tomato sauce

A basic pasta sauce that should be in everyone's repertoire.

SERVES 4 • PREP 10 MINS • COOK 20 MINS
V ❄ SAUCE ONLY

3 tbsp olive oil
1 medium onion, chopped
2 garlic cloves, crushed
400g can chopped tomatoes
small bunch basil leaves, chopped
400g/14oz dried spaghetti
150g ball mozzarella

1 Heat the oil in a large frying pan, then add the onion and cook for 5 minutes, stirring occasionally, until starting to soften. Add the garlic, then cook for 2 minutes more until the onion starts to turn golden. Tip in the tomatoes and half the basil. Leave to gently bubble for 15 minutes until the sauce has thickened and looks pulpy. Stir occasionally and break up any large clumps of tomato with the back of your spoon.

2 Meanwhile, boil the pasta following the pack instructions. Reserve a little of the pasta cooking water then drain. Toss the pasta with the sauce, adding a few spoons of the pasta water if the sauce looks dry. Tear over the mozzarella and the rest of the basil, then serve.

PER SERVING 542 kcals, carbs 79.5g, fat 17.8g, sat fat 6.2g, salt 0.51g

Spaghetti Genovese

This is a typical dish from Genoa in northern Italy. Making your own pesto makes it that little bit more special.

SERVES 4 • PREP 5 MINS • COOK 10 MINS
V

300g/11oz new potatoes, sliced
300g/11oz spaghetti
200g/7oz trimmed green beans, cut in half
125g/4½oz fresh pesto, from a tub or homemade
　(see below)
extra virgin olive oil, for drizzling

1 Bring a large pan of salted water to the boil, then add the potatoes and spaghetti together. Boil for 10 minutes until the potatoes and pasta are almost tender. Tip in the green beans halfway through the cooking time.
2 Reserve 4 tbsp of the cooking liquid then drain everything together. Return the potatoes, pasta and beans to the pan, then stir in the fresh pesto and reserved cooking liquid. Season to taste, divide between four serving plates and drizzle with a little extra virgin olive oil.

PER SERVING 330 kcals, carbs 8g, fat 23g, sat fat 9g, salt 0.5g

Homemade pesto sauce

So much more lively-tasting than shop bought, homemade pesto is worth making in big batches.

MAKES 250ML • PREP 10 MINS • COOK 5 MINS
V

50g/2oz pine nuts
large bunch basil
50g/2oz Parmesan
150ml/¼ pint extra virgin olive oil, plus extra for storing
2 garlic cloves

1 Heat a small frying pan over a low heat. Cook the pine nuts until golden, shaking occasionally. Put them into a food processor with the remaining ingredients and process until smooth, then season.
2 Pour the pesto into a jar and cover with a little extra oil, then seal and store in the fridge. The pesto will keep there for up to 2 weeks.

PER TBSP 105 kcals, carbs none, fat 11g, sat fat 2g, salt 0.06g

20-minute spaghetti marinara

 Keep a bag of frozen seafood in the freezer, ready to whip up a meal in no time.

SERVES 4 • PREP 5 MINS • COOK 15 MINS

1 tbsp olive oil
1 onion, chopped
1 garlic clove, chopped
1 tsp paprika
400g can chopped tomatoes
1 litre/1¾ pints chicken stock
300g/11oz spaghetti, roughly broken
240g pack mixed frozen seafood, defrosted
handful parsley leaves, chopped
lemon wedges, to serve

1 Heat the oil in a large frying pan, then cook the onion and garlic over a medium heat for 5 minutes until soft. Add the paprika, tomatoes and stock, then bring to the boil.
2 Turn down the heat to a simmer. Stir in the pasta and cook for 7 minutes, stirring occasionally to stop the pasta from sticking. Stir in the seafood, cook for 3 minutes more until it's all heated through and the pasta is cooked, then season to taste. Sprinkle with parsley and serve with lemon wedges.

PER SERVING 370 kcals, carbs 62g, fat 5g, sat fat 1g, salt 1.4g

tip To make this Spanish-style, add a pinch of saffron and a little white wine along with the tomatoes.

Gnocchi and tomato bake

 Maximum Italian flavour for very little effort.

SERVES 4 • PREP 5 MINS • COOK 25 MINS
V ❄

1 tbsp olive oil
1 onion, chopped
1 red pepper, deseeded and finely chopped
1 garlic clove, crushed
400g can chopped tomatoes
500g pack gnocchi
handful basil leaves, torn
60g mozzarella, torn into chunks

1 Heat the oil in a large frying pan, then soften the onion and pepper for 5 minutes. Stir in the garlic, fry for 1 minute, then tip in the tomatoes and gnocchi. Bring to a simmer.
2 Heat the grill to High. Bubble the sauce for 10–15 minutes, stirring occasionally, until the gnocchi are soft and the sauce has thickened. Season, stir through the basil, then transfer to a large ovenproof dish.
3 Scatter with the mozzarella, then grill for 5–6 minutes until the cheese is bubbling and golden.

PER SERVING 285 kcals, carbs 50g, fat 7g, sat fat 3g, salt 1.64g

Gnocchi with roasted squash and goat's cheese

 Just like pasta, gnocchi pair wonderfully with goat's cheese. Add a sprinkling of dried crushed chilli if you like a little spice.

SERVES 4 • PREP 15 MINS • COOK 20 MINS
V

450g/1lb butternut squash, peeled and cut into
    small chunks
1 garlic clove, left whole
2 tbsp olive oil
500g pack gnocchi
200g/7oz young leaf spinach
100g/4oz goat's cheese

1 Heat oven to 200C/180C fan/gas 6. Tip the squash into a roasting tin with the garlic and oil, salt and pepper and mix well. Roast for 20 minutes, shaking the pan halfway through, until tender and golden.
2 Meanwhile, cook the gnocchi according to the pack instructions. With a few seconds to go, throw in the spinach, then drain the gnocchi and spinach together. Tip into the roasting tin, then mix everything together well, mashing the softened garlic. Spoon onto warm serving plates, then crumble over the cheese to serve.

PER SERVING 333 kcals, carbs 53g, fat 10g, sat fat 4g, salt 1.76g

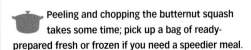 **Peeling and chopping the butternut squash takes some time; pick up a bag of ready-prepared fresh or frozen if you need a speedier meal.**

Creamy courgette lasagne

A lighter lasagne for summer – ideal for using up home-grown courgettes.

SERVES 4 • PREP 10 MINS • COOK 10 MINS
V

9 dried lasagne sheets
1 tbsp sunflower or olive oil, plus a little extra
    for drizzling
1 onion, finely chopped
700g/1lb 9oz courgettes (about 6), coarsely grated
2 garlic cloves, crushed
250g tub ricotta
50g/2oz mature Cheddar
350g jar tomato sauce for pasta

For homemade tomato sauce, follow step 1 in the Classic spaghetti with tomato sauce recipe on page 59. To make it speedier, forget the onion and simply soften the garlic in the oil for 2 mins before adding the tomatoes and basil. Season with a pinch of sugar, salt and pepper.

---

1 Heat oven to 220C/200C fan/gas 7. Put a pan of water on to boil, then cook the lasagne sheets for about 5 minutes until softened, but not cooked through. Rinse in cold water, then drizzle with a little oil to stop them sticking together.
2 Meanwhile, heat the oil in a large frying pan, then fry the onion. After 3 minutes, add the courgettes and garlic and continue to fry until the courgette has softened and turned bright green. Stir in two-thirds of both the ricotta and the Cheddar, then season to taste.
3 Heat the tomato sauce in the microwave for 2 minutes on High until hot.
4 In a large baking dish, layer up the lasagne, starting with half the courgette mix, then the pasta, then tomato sauce. Repeat, then top with blobs of the remaining ricotta and scatter with the rest of the Cheddar. Bake on the top shelf for about 10 minutes until the pasta is tender and the cheese is golden.

PER SERVING 405 kcals, carbs 38g, fat 21g, sat fat 8g, salt 1.36g

Creamy polenta with spinach

So much quicker to make than mashed potatoes, you could use soft cheese or Greek yogurt instead of the mascarpone.

SERVES 4 • PREP NONE • COOK ABOUT 10 MINS

175g/6oz quick-cook polenta
5 tbsp mascarpone
100g bag young leaf spinach

1 Cook the polenta according to the pack instructions. When the polenta is softened and smooth, stir through the mascarpone and spinach. Leave for 30 seconds until the spinach has just begun to wilt, then stir again, season generously and serve.

PER SERVING 240 kcals, carbs 33g, fat 10g, sat fat 6g, salt 0.14g

OPPOSITE Clockwise from top left *Griddled polenta with corn and green salsa (page 79), Asparagus cream pasta (page 71), Gnocchi and tomato bake (page 61), 30-minute chicken and tarragon pasta (page 65), Must-make tuna pasta bake (page 58), Thai rice noodle salad with pork (page 66).*

Tortellini with ricotta, spinach and bacon

 A warm pasta salad full of texture and flavour. To make it vegetarian, simply omit the bacon.

SERVES 4 • PREP 10 MINS • COOK ABOUT 5 MINS

250g pack filled tortellini (we used ricotta and spinach)
2 rashers lean back bacon
25g/1oz walnut pieces
zest ½ lemon, juice 1
1 tbsp finely grated Parmesan, plus extra for serving (optional)
1 tbsp extra virgin olive oil, plus extra for serving (optional)
100g bag baby spinach
2 tbsp ricotta

1 Heat the grill. Cook the pasta according to the pack instructions, then drain in a colander and cool under gently running water.
2 Meanwhile, grill the bacon on a baking sheet until golden and crisp at the edges. When almost ready, tip the walnuts onto the sheet to toast a little. Snip the bacon into strips.
3 Mix the lemon zest and juice, Parmesan and oil in a large bowl. Season with pepper, then tip in the spinach, tortellini, bacon and walnuts. Toss well, add the ricotta in small blobs, then gently toss again. Season to taste, then serve with a drizzle more oil and more Parmesan, if you like.

PER SERVING 285 kcals, carbs 30g, fat 14g, sat fat 5g, salt 1.13g

Saucy sausage pasta

A basic tomato, onion and garlic sauce is the starting point for loads of pasta dishes. You could use tuna, ham, bacon or vegetarian sausages if you prefer.

SERVES 4 • PREP 10 MINS • COOK 15 MINS

1 tbsp olive oil
8 pork sausages (the best your budget will allow), cut into chunky pieces
1 large onion, chopped
2 garlic cloves, crushed
½–1 tsp chilli powder, depending on your taste
400g can chopped tomatoes
300g/11oz short pasta, such as fusilli or farfalle

1 Put a large pan of water on to boil. Heat the oil in a large frying pan and fry the sausage chunks on a fairly high heat until golden brown. Now turn the heat down, add the onion and garlic, and cook for 5 minutes or until the onion is soft.
2 Stir in the chilli powder and tomatoes, bring to the boil, then simmer for 10 minutes while you cook the pasta according to the pack instructions.
3 Drain the pasta, then tip it into the sausage sauce, mixing well to coat. Serve with crusty bread.

PER SERVING 645 kcals, carbs 74g, fat 30g, sat fat 10g, salt 2.77g

tip To boost your 5-a-day, try adding broccoli florets to the pasta water for the last few minutes of cooking, then drain them with the pasta and stir them into the sauce.

30-minute chicken and tarragon pasta

Tarragon and chicken are perfect partners in this sophisticated midweek supper treat.

SERVES 3 • PREP 5 MINS • COOK 10 MINS

250g/9oz long, wide dried pasta, such as pappardelle
   or tagliatelle
2 tbsp olive oil
2 skinless chicken breasts, cut into small pieces
2 garlic cloves, chopped
142ml pot single cream
3–4 tbsp roughly chopped fresh tarragon leaves
100g/4oz spinach, any thick stems removed
lemon wedges, to serve

1 Cook the pasta following the pack instructions. Meanwhile, heat the oil and fry the chicken over a high heat for 4–5 minutes, stirring, until golden and cooked. Add the garlic, cream, tarragon and 3 tbsp of the pasta cooking liquid. Gently heat through.
2 When the pasta is cooked, stir in the spinach (it will immediately wilt in the hot water). Drain well, then toss into the creamy chicken. Season to taste then serve with the lemon for squeezing.

PER SERVING 560 kcals, carbs 65g, fat 19g, sat fat 7g, salt 0.58g

Crisp Italian chicken and polenta

This one-pot supper takes good advantage of the pre-cooked blocks of polenta you can find in the pasta aisle. You could use small chunks of unpeeled potato instead of polenta.

**SERVES 2 EASILY DOUBLED • PREP 5 MINS
COOK 25 MINS**

500g pack ready-to-use polenta
25g/1oz Parmesan, grated
2 skin-on boneless chicken breasts
250g pack cherry tomatoes
leaves from a few sprigs rosemary, torn
1 garlic clove, sliced
2 tbsp olive oil

1 Heat oven to 220C/200C fan/gas 7. Using your fingers, roughly break up the polenta into small chunks and scatter it in the bottom of a small roasting tin. Tip in the Parmesan and mix. Sit the chicken breasts, cherry tomatoes, rosemary and garlic on top of the polenta, drizzle with olive oil, then season to taste.
2 Roast for 25 minutes until the chicken skin is crisp and golden and the polenta and cheese are turning crusty around the edges. Serve with a green salad.

PER SERVING 513 kcals, carbs 47g, fat 20g, sat fat 5g, salt 4.63g

try this...

Polenta chips
Heat oven to 200C/180C fan/gas 6. Cut a 500g pack ready-to-use polenta into thick chips and rub all over with a little oil. Spread out over a baking sheet and cook for 20 minutes until golden.

Thai rice noodle salad with pork

A fresh new meal with mince for the whole family to enjoy.

SERVES 4 • PREP 10 MINS • COOK 10 MINS

sunflower oil, for frying
500g/1lb 2oz pork mince
small knob fresh root ginger, grated
pinch cayenne pepper or chilli powder
125g pack fine vermicelli rice noodles
200g/7oz beansprouts
zest and juice 2 limes
2–3 tbsp fish or soy sauce, to taste
1 tsp muscovado or soft brown sugar
1 red onion, halved and thinly sliced
2 Little Gem lettuce hearts, leaves separated and roughly torn

1 Heat a little oil in a non-stick frying pan and stir-fry the pork, ginger and cayenne or chilli for 10 minutes, until the mince is browned and cooked through.
2 As it cooks, place the noodles and beansprouts in a heatproof bowl and cover with boiling water. Leave for 4 minutes or until the noodles are tender. Drain, then cool under cold running water and drain again. Return to the bowl.
3 Stir together the lime zest and juice, fish or soy sauce and sugar. Stir into the noodles with the red onion and lettuce. Mix into the noodles, divide between four bowls and serve warm.

PER SERVING 384 kcals, carbs 34g, fat 16g, sat fat 5g, salt 1.70g

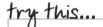

try this...

Sesame steak noodles

Follow steps 2 and 3 as above. Heat 1 tsp sunflower oil in a frying pan. Tip 2 tbsp sesame seeds onto a plate. Rub 1 tsp oil into 4 x 175g sirloin steaks and press into the sesame seeds. Fry for 5 minutes for medium rare, turning halfway through. Leave to rest for 5 minutes, then thinly slice. Toss 1 deseeded and shredded red chilli, and a handful of mint leaves into the noodles. Top with the steak to serve.

Chicken chow mein

Top up your 5-a-day with this speedy midweek supper, full of fresh veg.

**SERVES 4 • PREP 10 MINS, PLUS MARINATING
COOK 10 MINS**

3 garlic cloves, crushed
thumb-size piece fresh root ginger, grated
1 red chilli, deseeded and chopped
1 tbsp soy sauce
2 tbsp tomato purée
2 chicken breasts, cut into chunky strips
3 blocks dried egg noodles
½ head broccoli, broken into florets
3 carrots, cut into thin sticks
1 tbsp vegetable oil
300g pack beansprouts
3 spring onions, halved and sliced into long strips
1 tbsp oyster sauce

1 Mix together the garlic, ginger, chilli, soy sauce and tomato purée, then add the chicken and leave it to marinate while you prep the rest of the ingredients.
2 Boil a large pan of water, add the noodles, broccoli and carrots, then cook for 4 minutes before draining.
3 Heat the vegetable oil in a wok, tip in the chicken and its marinade, then stir-fry for 4–5 minutes until cooked. Toss in the noodles, vegetables, beansprouts and spring onions to warm through, then mix the oyster sauce with 2 tbsp water and stir this in just before serving.

PER SERVING 545 kcals, carbs 80g, fat 12g, sat fat 1g, salt 1.98g

Prawn, mango and soba salad with ginger dressing

 Asian-style cold noodle salads are ideal for suppers during hot weather, and make an interesting lunchbox choice too.

SERVES 4 • PREP 15 MINS • COOK 5 MINS

250g pack soba noodles
½ cucumber, cut into fingers
1 large mango, peeled and cut into chunks
6 spring onions, finely sliced
200g/7oz large cooked prawns
2 tbsp toasted sesame seeds, to serve
FOR THE DRESSING
juice 2 limes
2 tbsp soy sauce
1 tbsp chilli garlic sauce
1 tbsp chopped pickled ginger
1 tbsp vegetable oil

1 Boil the soba noodles in plenty of salted water for about 5 minutes or according to the pack instructions – they are very starchy, so use a lot of water. Drain and rinse with cold water, pat dry with some kitchen paper, then tip into a large bowl. Add the cucumber, mango, onions and prawns.
2 Mix the dressing ingredients together, pour half over the salad, then gently toss together – using a couple of forks or a pair of tongs will make this job easier. Sprinkle with sesame seeds and serve with the remaining dressing.

PER SERVING 360 kcals, carbs 63g, fat 4g, sat fat none, salt 3.56g

tip If you want to pack the salad up for later, keep the dressing separate then toss together just before you eat.

Malaysian rice noodles with prawns

A hot, well-seasoned wok is a must for this Malaysian speciality, known as char kway teow.

SERVES 2 • PREP 10 MINS • COOK 10 MINS

1 tbsp light soy sauce
2 tbsp sweet soy sauce
200g/7oz raw, peeled prawns
3 tbsp groundnut or vegetable oil
2 garlic cloves, chopped
1 tsp sambal oelek, or 1 chopped chilli
400g/14oz fresh flat rice noodles (or 140g/5oz dried
    rice noodles, soaked for 5 minutes in boiling water,
    then drained)
2 eggs, beaten
140g/5oz beansprouts
bunch spring onions, cut into finger lengths

1 In a small bowl, mix together the soy sauces and 1 tbsp water. Season the prawns with salt and pepper.
2 Heat a large wok over a medium heat. Add 1 tbsp oil and the garlic, and stir-fry briefly until light golden and fragrant. Stir in the prawns, then the sambal oelek or chilli and cook for 2 minutes until just cooked and pink. Set the prawns aside on a plate.
3 Increase the heat to High. Add the remaining oil and tip in the noodles. Pour 2 tbsp of the soy sauce mixture over the noodles and season to taste with black pepper. Keep stirring the noodles for 2–3 minutes until slightly charred. Using a ladle, push the noodles around the outer edges of the wok. Pour in the eggs and quickly scramble. Fold over the noodles and add the remaining sauce mixture, the beansprouts and spring onions, stirring continuously. Return the prawns to the wok, mix well, then serve immediately.

PER SERVING 598 kcals, carbs 65g, fat 25g, sat fat 5g, salt 4.81g

A well-seasoned wok acts like a non-stick pan, enabling food to be cooked over a high heat without sticking. Season a wok by heating it with a generous mixture of groundnut or vegetable oil and table salt. Swirl the mixture around to coat the wok and heat until smoking. Allow to cool, then wipe off the salt crust with kitchen paper before using.

tip To make this veggie, replace the prawns with slices of firm tofu.

Singapore noodles with tofu

You'll love the combination of fresh tastes and textures in this traditional spicy stir-fry dish.

SERVES 2 • PREP 15 MINS • COOK 10-12 MINS
V

100g/4oz fine rice noodles
140g/5oz firm tofu
2 tbsp sunflower oil
1 tsp tikka masala curry paste
2 tsp reduced-salt soy sauce
1 tbsp sweet chilli sauce
3 spring onions, shredded
1 small chunk fresh root ginger, finely chopped
1 red pepper, deseeded and thinly sliced
100g/4oz mangetout
100g/4oz beansprouts
roughly chopped coriander and lime wedges, to serve

1 Put the noodles in a bowl and pour over boiling water to cover. Leave for 4 minutes, then drain and rinse under cold running water until cold. Drain well, then snip into short lengths with scissors.
2 Rinse the tofu in cold water, then cut into small chunks. Pat dry with kitchen paper. Heat 1 tbsp of the oil in a wok or large frying pan, add the tofu, then stir-fry for 2–3 minutes, stirring until lightly browned. Drain on kitchen paper. Blend together the curry paste, soy, chilli sauce and 1 tbsp water.
3 Add the remaining oil to the wok and heat it up. Add the spring onions, ginger, pepper and mangetout, then stir-fry for 1 minute. Add the noodles and beansprouts, then stir to mix. Tip in the sauce mix, stirring until everything is well coated. Serve sprinkled with coriander and with lime wedges on the side for squeezing over.

PER SERVING 391 kcals, carbs 57g, fat 15g, sat fat 9g, salt 0.99g

Pad Thai

We've simplified this Thai street food classic to make your life easier, but the flavour is still very authentic.

SERVES 2–3 • PREP 10 MINS • COOK 5 MINS

125g/4½oz thick rice noodles
3 tbsp lime juice (about 2 limes)
½ tsp cayenne pepper
2 tsp light muscovado sugar
2 tbsp fish sauce
2 tbsp vegetable oil
200g/7oz cooked and peeled tiger prawns
4 spring onions, sliced
140g/5oz beansprouts
25g/1oz salted peanuts, finely chopped
small handful coriander leaves
TO SERVE
1 or 2 limes, cut into wedges
sweet chilli sauce

1 Put the noodles in a large heatproof bowl, cover with boiling water and leave for 4 minutes, then drain and refresh under cold running water.
2 Put the lime juice, cayenne, sugar and fish sauce in a bowl and mix well. Have all the other ingredients ready by the hob.
3 Heat the oil and fry the prawns until warmed through. Add the spring onions and noodles and toss around. Tip in the lime juice mixture, then stir in the beansprouts and half the peanuts and coriander. Cook for 1 minute until everything is heated through.
4 Pile into a large dish, scatter with the rest of the peanuts and coriander, and serve with lime wedges and sweet chilli sauce.

PER SERVING 531 kcals, carbs 62g, fat 20g, sat fat 3g, salt 3g

OPPOSITE *Singapore noodles with tofu*

Goat's cheese, garlic and pancetta linguine

Squidgy, sweet roast garlic and caramelised onions make an unusual, but utterly irresistible base to this pasta dish.

SERVES 4 • PREP 5 MINS • COOK 30 MINS

1 garlic bulb, broken into cloves, unpeeled
4 tbsp extra virgin olive oil, plus extra for drizzling
3 onions, finely sliced
2 tbsp fresh thyme leaves
12 slices pancetta
400g/14oz linguine
200g/7oz firm goat's cheese
handful chopped parsley, to serve

> **Linguini looks like flattened spaghetti and is more delicate to eat than tagliatelle. The name means 'little tongues' – and this recipe will certainly have you licking your lips.**

1 Heat oven to 200C/180C fan/gas 6. Loosely wrap the garlic cloves in some foil with 1 tsp oil. Place in a roasting tin and cook for about 20 minutes until soft.
2 Meanwhile, heat 2 tbsp oil and fry the onions until golden brown and soft, about 15 minutes, adding the thyme for the final 5 minutes. In a separate pan, dry-fry the pancetta until golden and crisp, then set aside. Cook the pasta according to the pack instructions.
3 Pop the roasted garlic out of their skins, add to the onions, then stir in the remaining oil. Drain the pasta, reserving a little of the cooking water, then toss through the onions, adding a good splash of the reserved water.
4 Crumble over the cheese and lightly stir. Season, then pile onto plates. Scatter with parsley, drizzle with some more oil and top with the pancetta slices.

PER SERVING 740 kcals, carbs 83g, fat 34g, sat fat 13g, salt 2.23g

Pasta with creamy walnut pesto

Our walnut pesto makes a great wintry change to green or red pesto. Try it spread over crostini or stirred into a risotto at the end of cooking too.

SERVES 4 WITH LEFTOVER PESTO FOR 2 • PREP 15 MINS COOK 12 MINS
V ❄ PESTO ONLY

400g/14oz pasta (we used orecchiette)
175g/6oz walnut halves or pieces
1 garlic clove
handful fresh basil, leaves roughly torn, plus extra
    to serve (optional)
100g/4oz Parmesan, finely grated, plus extra
    to serve (optional)
50g/2oz butter
4 tbsp extra virgin olive oil
50ml/2fl oz double cream

1 Cook the pasta according to the pack instructions. Meanwhile, put the walnuts and garlic in a food processor and whizz until finely chopped. Add the basil, cheese, butter and oil and pulse a few more times. Season.
2 Pour the cream into a pan and warm through. Add two-thirds of the pesto, then gently heat to loosen it. When the pasta is ready, drain, reserving 2 tbsp of the cooking water, then mix both with the sauce. Serve immediately, sprinkled with the extra Parmesan and basil, if using. The leftover pesto will keep in the fridge for up to a week, or can be frozen for up to a month.

PER SERVING 805 kcals, carbs 77g, fat 47g, sat fat 15g, salt 0.48g

try this...

> Mature Pecorino, a sheep's cheese, is often less expensive than Parmesan, and offers a similar tangy flavour and dry texture.

Hot-smoked salmon pasta with pine nuts

A few special ingredients turn pasta into a dish ideal for entertaining friends.

SERVES 6 • PREP 5 MINS • COOK 10 MINS

600g/1lb 5oz trofie pasta, or other smallish shape
100ml/3½fl oz white wine
142ml pot double cream
2 tbsp finely grated Parmesan
450g/1lb hot-smoked salmon, skin removed
   and flaked
85g/3oz toasted pine nuts

1 Cook the pasta according to the pack instructions. Meanwhile, bring the wine to the boil in a large frying pan, then let it simmer for 1 minute. Reduce the heat, stir in the cream and season well.

2 When the pasta is cooked, drain briefly and tip into the frying pan with the sauce. Add the Parmesan and flaked salmon pieces, then mix gently together. Pile into bowls, sprinkle with pine nuts and serve with a simple salad alongside.

PER SERVING 702 kcals, carbs 78g, fat 30g, sat fat 10g, salt 2g

Asparagus cream pasta

Making a creamy sauce with the asparagus stalks gives every bite of this pasta the delicate flavour of spring.

**SERVES 2 EASILY DOUBLED • PREP 10 MINS
COOK 30 MINS**
V

142ml tub double cream
2 garlic cloves, peeled, but left whole
1 bunch asparagus
50g/2oz Parmesan, half grated, half shaved
250g/9oz tagliatelle

1 In a small saucepan, bring the cream and garlic to the boil. Take off the heat, remove the garlic, then set the pan aside.

2 To prepare the asparagus, cut off and discard the woody ends, then neatly cut the tips away from the stalks. Keep the tips and stalks separate. Cook the stalks in boiling salted water for about 4–5 minutes until tender, drain, then tip into the cream with the grated Parmesan. Blitz with a hand blender until smooth.

3 Cook the pasta according to the pack instructions, then throw in the tips 2 minutes before the end of the cooking time. Gently reheat the cream, drain the pasta, then tip it into a bowl with the cream. Toss, divide into pasta bowls and serve topped with Parmesan shavings.

PER SERVING 913 kcals, carbs 100g, fat 47g, sat fat 26g, salt 0.53g

Stir-fried scallops and chorizo with spaghetti

Friends will love sharing this smart pasta supper.

**SERVES 4 EASILY HALVED • PREP 15 MINS
COOK 12 MINS**

12 scallops, with or without roe
500g pack fresh spaghetti
3 tbsp extra virgin olive oil
¼ tsp dried chilli flakes
85g/3oz chorizo, cut in small chunks
1 red and 1 orange pepper, halved and cut into
     big chunks
2 garlic cloves, thinly sliced
small bunch flat-leaf parsley, roughly chopped

1 Trim the scallops, removing the small piece of white, opaque muscle. Detach the roes from the white meat, if they have them.
2 Cook the spaghetti according to the pack instructions, then drain and toss with the olive oil, chilli and seasoning. Pile into a big, deep serving dish and keep warm.
3 Heat a frying pan and add the chorizo. Cook over a low to medium heat until the fat runs, then turn up the heat, add the peppers and garlic and stir-fry for 3–4 minutes. Season and pile on top of the spaghetti.
4 Place the pan back on a high heat, add the scallops and roe, if using, and fry for 1–2 minutes on each side until the white meat is lightly browned and the meat and roe are both firm. Add the scallops and parsley to the spaghetti, season, and toss to mix everything together. Serve in bowls, giving each person three scallops.

PER SERVING 584 kcals, carbs 75g, fat 17g, sat fat 3g, salt 0.93g

Spinach and ricotta gnocchi

These luxurious gnocchi are light but decadent at the same time. They are quicker to make than the classic gnocchi on page 77, as there are no potatoes to boil beforehand.

**SERVES 4 • PREP 40 MINS, PLUS CHILLING
COOK 10 MINS**
V

200g/7oz young spinach, washed
small handful parsley leaves, finely chopped
1 garlic clove, crushed
140g/5oz ricotta
85g/3oz plain flour
2 eggs
100g/4oz Parmesan, finely grated, plus extra
     to serve
freshly grated nutmeg
olive oil and rocket, to serve

1 Boil the kettle. Place the spinach in a large bowl and pour boiling water over it. Leave for 2 minutes until wilted, then drain thoroughly. Leave to cool, then wrap in a clean tea towel and hold it over the sink and squeeze out as much water as possible. Finely chop.
2 Place the spinach, parsley, garlic, ricotta, flour, eggs, cheese and a generous grating of nutmeg into a large bowl and season with salt and pepper. Use a fork to stir very thoroughly until everything is completely mixed. With dampened hands, shape the mix into walnut-size balls. Place on a large plate or baking sheet and chill for at least 30 minutes.
3 When ready to cook, heat the oven to warm and bring a large pan of water to the boil. Reduce the heat to medium and drop in batches of about 8–10 gnocchi at a time. They will sink to the bottom at first. When they rise to the top, give them about 1 minute more, then remove with a slotted spoon and keep warm while you cook the rest. Serve the gnocchi on warm plates drizzled with olive oil and scattered with rocket and more cheese.

PER SERVING 287 kcals, carbs 19g, fat 15g, sat fat 8g, salt 0.86g

Spaghetti alle vongole

A glass of cold white wine, such as a Sancerre, is the perfect accompaniment to this classy dish of pasta with clams.

SERVES 2 • PREP 15 MINS • COOK 10–12 MINS

140g/5oz spaghetti
500g/1lb 2oz fresh clams in their shells
2 ripe tomatoes
2 tbsp olive oil
1 fat garlic clove, chopped
1 small or ½ large fresh red chilli, finely chopped
75ml/2½fl oz white wine
2 tbsp chopped flat-leaf parsley

1 Put a large pan of water on to boil, ready for the pasta. Rinse the clams in several changes of cold water. Discard any that are open or damaged. Cover the tomatoes with boiling water, leave for 1 minute, then drain and slip off the skins. Remove the seeds and chop the flesh.
2 Cook the pasta according to the pack instructions. Meanwhile, heat the oil in a large pan, add the garlic and chilli, then fry gently for a few seconds. Stir in the tomatoes, then add the clams and a splash of wine, salt and pepper and bring to the boil. Cover the pan and cook for 3–4 minutes, until the clams are open.
3 Drain the pasta, then tip it into the pan with the parsley and toss everything together. Serve in bowls with bread for mopping up the juices.

PER SERVING 409 kcals, carbs 56g, fat 13g, sat fat 2g, salt 0.10g

Greek lamb with orzo

Orzo looks like large grains of rice, but is in fact a form of small pasta shapes. Together with meltingly tender herby lamb, it makes for a very handsome one-pot dish.

SERVES 6 • PREP 20 MINS • COOK 2 HOURS 35 MINS
❄ **AT END OF STEP 2**

1kg/2lb 4oz boned shoulder of lamb
2 onions, sliced
1 tbsp chopped oregano, or 1 tsp dried
2 cinnamon sticks, broken in half
½ tsp ground cinnamon
2 tbsp olive oil
400g can chopped tomatoes
1.2 litres/2 pints hot vegetable or chicken stock
400g/14oz orzo
freshly grated Parmesan, to serve

1 Heat oven to 180C/160C fan/gas 4. Cut the lamb into 4cm chunks, then spread them over the base of a large wide casserole dish. Add the onions, oregano, cinnamon sticks, ground cinnamon and olive oil, then stir well. Bake, uncovered, for 45 minutes, stirring halfway through.
2 Pour over the chopped tomatoes and stock, cover tightly, then return to the oven for 1½ hours, until the lamb is very tender.
3 Remove the cinnamon sticks, then stir in the orzo. Cover again, then cook for a further 20 minutes, stirring halfway through. The orzo should be cooked and the sauce thickened. Sprinkle with Parmesan and serve.

PER SERVING 696 kcals, carbs 58g, fat 36g, sat fat 16g, salt 0.68g

The Italian word 'orzo' means barley. When cooked, it has a texture similar to risotto rice. Look for it in the specialist sections of supermarkets, or in Greek, Italian and Middle Eastern delis. It can go by a variety of other names including 'puntaletti' and 'romarino'. If you can't find it, use another small pasta, such as trofie.

Pasta with lemon butter prawns

Five-ingredient entertaining – now that's what we call clever.

**SERVES 4 • PREP 5 MINS, PLUS INFUSING
COOK 10 MINS**

100g/4oz unsalted butter
zest 3 lemons
200g/7oz large peeled raw prawns
350g/12oz tagliatelle
100g bag rocket

1 Melt the butter in a small pan, then add the zest and leave to infuse for about 15 minutes. Add a little of the butter to a small frying pan, then fry the prawns for 2–3 minutes.
2 Meanwhile, cook the tagliatelle according to the pack instructions. Drain, return to the pan, then add the butter, prawns and rocket. Toss together, season and serve immediately.

PER SERVING 531 kcals, carbs 68g, fat 22g, sat fat 13g, salt 0.65g

Spinach and three-cheese cannelloni

Scrumptious filled pasta topped with a rich tomato sauce that's ideal for freezing. Pasta heaven!

**SERVES 4 • PREP 25 MINS • COOK 1 HOUR
V ❄ UNCOOKED**

FOR THE TOMATO SAUCE
1 tbsp olive oil
3 garlic cloves, finely sliced
pinch golden caster sugar
1 tbsp red wine vinegar
1 tsp dried oregano
2 x 400g cans chopped tomatoes
FOR THE FILLING
500g/1lb 2oz spinach, washed
300g/11oz soft, rindless goat's cheese, crumbled
100g/4oz Parmesan, finely grated
pinch grated nutmeg
200g/7oz dried cannelloni tubes
1 ball mozzarella, sliced

1 First make the tomato sauce. Heat the oil in a shallow pan, then fry the garlic for 1 minute until fragrant. Add the sugar, vinegar, oregano and tomatoes then season. Simmer the sauce for 20 minutes, stirring occasionally, until thick and rich.
2 Heat oven to 200C/180C fan/gas 6. Put the spinach in a large colander, then pour over a kettle of hot water to wilt it (you may need to do this twice). Cool with cold water, then wring out the water really well using a tea towel.
3 Roughly chop the spinach in a food processor, then add the goat's cheese and half the Parmesan. Season with salt, pepper and nutmeg, then whizz until finely chopped. Spoon the mixture into a plastic food bag with the corner cut off and use this to squeeze the filling into the cannelloni tubes. Lay the tubes in the bottom of a baking dish then top with the tomato sauce, mozzarella and remaining Parmesan. (Can be frozen for up to 1 month at this point – defrost before cooking.) Bake for 25–30 minutes until golden and bubbling, then leave to stand for 5 minutes before serving.

PER SERVING 660 kcals, carbs 49g, fat 39g, sat fat 22g, salt 2.32g

tip Choose larger-leafed spinach, as opposed to baby leaf, for this dish. Wash it very well in a bowl of cold water – then lift out and drain; spinach is notoriously gritty.

OPPOSITE Clockwise from top left Greek lamb with orzo (page 73), Classic lasagne (page 76), Pasta with creamy walnut pesto (page 70), Spinach and ricotta gnocchi (page 72), Spaghetti alle vongole (page 73), Pasta with lemon butter prawns

Classic lasagne

Everyone's favourite, and so easy to make. Why not make double for the freezer?

**SERVES 6 ● PREP 20 MINS, PLUS MAKING WHITE SAUCE
COOK 1 HOUR 40 MINS**
❄ **IF SAUCE NOT PREVIOUSLY FROZEN**

3 tbsp olive oil, plus a little for greasing
1 onion, finely chopped
1 garlic clove, sliced
1 carrot, roughly chopped
1 tbsp tomato purée
100ml/3½fl oz white wine
1 x 400g can plus 1 x 200g can chopped tomatoes
handful basil leaves
750g/1lb 10oz lean beef mince
90g pack prosciutto
200ml/7fl oz hot beef stock
little grated nutmeg
300g pack fresh lasagne sheets
1 quantity white sauce (see below)
125g ball mozzarella

tip Try freezing the uncooked lasagne. Defrost
in the fridge overnight, then cook for an extra
10 minutes, or cook from frozen for 1½ hours at
180C/160C fan/gas 4.

1 Heat 2 tbsp oil in a saucepan, then add the onion, garlic
and carrot. Cook for 5–7 minutes over a medium heat until
softened. Turn up the heat a little and stir in the purée. Cook
for 1 minute, pour in the wine, then bubble until reduced by
two-thirds. Stir in the tomatoes and basil. Bring to the boil,
then simmer for 20 minutes. Leave to cool a little, then whizz
in a food processor.
2 While the sauce simmers, heat the remaining 1 tbsp oil in
a frying pan, then cook the beef in two batches for about 10
minutes until browned all over. Finely chop 4 slices of
prosciutto, then stir them through the meat mixture.
3 Pour over the tomato sauce and stock, add the nutmeg,
then season. Bring to the boil, then simmer for 30 minutes
until the ragú looks rich and is well coated in sauce. (The ragú
can be left for 3 days in the fridge or frozen for 3 months.)
4 Heat oven to 180C/160C fan/gas 4. To assemble the
lasagne, lightly oil an ovenproof serving dish (30 x 20cm).
Spoon over a third of the ragú sauce, then cover with
lasagne sheets. Drizzle over about one quarter of the white
sauce. Repeat until you have 3 layers of pasta. Cover with
the remaining quantity of white sauce, making sure you can't
see any pasta poking through.
5 Tear the mozzarella into thin strips, then scatter over the
top. Arrange the rest of the prosciutto on top. Bake for 45
minutes until the top is bubbling and lightly browned.

PER SERVING 580 kcals, carbs 31g, fat 32g, sat fat 14g, salt 1.71g

All-in-one white sauce

**MAKES 500ML/18 FL OZ ● PREP 5 MINS
COOK 10 MINS**
Ⓥ ❄

1 Melt 50g/2oz butter in a saucepan, stir in 50g/2oz plain
flour, then cook for 2 minutes. Slowly whisk in 600ml/1 pint
milk, then bring to the boil, stirring. Turn down the heat and
cook until the sauce starts to thicken and coats the back of
a wooden spoon. The sauce can now be cooled and kept
in the fridge for up to 3 days or frozen for 3 months.

PER 100ML 164 kcals, carbs 13.5g, fat 10.4g, sat fat 6.4g, salt 0.31g

try this...

For Bolognese sauce to serve with pasta, follow the
lasage recipe up to Step 3, then simmer the sauce for
1 hour, adding a splash of water if needed, until the
meat is tender and the sauce rich and thick.

Step-by-step: Homemade potato gnocchi

This is a classic gnocchi recipe – fluffy little pillows of potato and flour, ready to serve with your favourite sauce.

**SERVES 6 ● PREP 20 MINS
COOK ABOUT 25 MINS**
V

1kg/2lb 4oz floury potatoes
(Marfona are best but you
can use King Edward)
3 large eggs, beaten
about 300g/11oz plain flour,
depending on the texture
of the potatoes, plus extra
for dusting

1 Lower the whole potatoes (still in their skins) into a pan of salted boiling water. Simmer for 10–15 minutes until just soft. Peel quickly, holding the hot potatoes in a tea towel to protect your hands.

2 Pass the potatoes thorough a potato ricer. Repeat to add lightness. Make a hollow in the pile of potatoes, pour in the eggs and sprinkle over a little flour. Add more flour if needed but not too much as you want the gnocchi to taste of potatoes not flour.

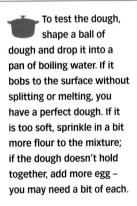

To test the dough, shape a ball of dough and drop it into a pan of boiling water. If it bobs to the surface without splitting or melting, you have a perfect dough. If it is too soft, sprinkle in a bit more flour to the mixture; if the dough doesn't hold together, add more egg – you may need a bit of each.

To keep the gnocchi warm as you go along, put them in a large dish over a pan of simmering water, coating them with a little sauce or dressing.

The only way to make gnocchi ahead of time is to cook them and put them in a buttered dish, then cover them in a sauce and chill for up to 24 hours. Heat through in the oven until bubbling and brown.

3 Blend everything with your hands, working quickly. You should have a soft dough that holds together, doesn't feel sticky and can be easily shaped. Test a piece of dough now (see know-how, left).

4 Divide the dough into 3 equal pieces. Roll a piece at a time into long, thumb-width cylinders on a lightly floured surface, again working lightly and quickly. Keep the surface well floured.

5 Cut the dough into short lengths then roll the gnocchi in a little flour. Press lines into one side of each gnocchi using the tines of a fork. Lay them out on a large board until required.

6 Bring a large, deep pot of salted water to the boil. Cook 8–10 gnocchi at a time for 2 minutes, during which time they will bob back up to the surface. Scoop them out with a slotted spoon. Taste – they should be soft and light.

Homemade ravioli

Fresh ravioli are incredibly satisfying to make and far easier than you may think. (See the finished dish on page 54.)

**SERVES 4 • PREP 30 MINS, PLUS 30 MINS RESTING TIME
COOK 5 MINS**

V

300g/11oz '00' pasta flour, plus extra for kneading and rolling
pinch fine salt
3 eggs
semolina, for dusting
1 quantity of filling (see below)

try this...

Sweet potato and goat's cheese filling
Bake or steam 2 sweet potatoes then mash roughly.
Mix with 125g/4½oz crumbled goat's cheese. Cook the
ravioli and dress with chilli oil, toasted pumpkin
seeds, Parmesan and freshly ground black pepper.

Parma ham and pesto filling
Roughly tear 70g/3oz Parma ham and mix with
250g/9oz diced mozzarella and 4 tbsp fresh pesto.
Cook the ravioli and serve with butter, toasted pine
nuts and freshly grated Parmesan.

Ricotta, pea and mint filling
Mix together 100g/4oz peas (thawed if frozen), 2 tbsp
chopped fresh mint, 250g/9oz ricotta and the zest
1 lemon. Cook and serve with butter, a squeeze of
lemon juice and freshly grated Parmesan.

1 Place the flour and salt in a food processor and crack
in the eggs. Pulse until the mixture forms sticky-looking
crumbs. Turn the mixture out onto a lightly floured surface
and bring together to form a firm dough. Knead for
5 minutes until the dough feels smooth then wrap in cling
film and chill for 30 minutes or so. This allows the dough to
relax and soften.

2 Cut the pasta into quarters then roll out each piece using
a pasta machine. Dust with flour or semolina as you go and
move it down a notch on to a thinner setting every second
roll. Continue until you get to the penultimate setting. If you
like your ravioli very thin, go for the thinnest setting.

3 Quickly stamp out rounds using a ravioli cutter or a 6cm
biscuit cutter before the dough has chance to dry out and
become brittle (photo 1). Lay the circles on a semolina-
dusted plate or baking sheet and cover with cling film as
you cut the remainder.

▶

1

2

3

4 Place a small teaspoonful of filling in the centre of each round (photo 2). Dampen the edges with water then sandwich another round on top. Use your fingertips to seal the edges, trying to expel all the air as you go (photo 3). Lay the ravioli on a semolina-dusted tea towel to dry for a few minutes.

5 Cook the pasta in a large pan of gently boiling salted water for 4–5 minutes until tender. Do not use a full rolling boil as you would for dried pasta as it is likely to cause the ravioli to split open. Drain, dress and serve.

PER SERVING 507 kcals, carbs 80g, fat 14g, sat fat 5g, salt 1.02g

---

Semolina is made from durum wheat and is quite coarse so it acts as an abrasive and prevents the pasta sticking to the surface more effectively than flour. It also adds a little bite to the finished ravioli.

Ravioli trays are a great way to make several ravioli in one go and are particularly good for softer fillings such as those made with ricotta or mascarpone. Remember to dust the tray with semolina or flour before laying in the pasta or they can be tricky to get out.

Griddled polenta with corn and green salsa

A great vegetarian main course, full of flavour and texture.

**SERVES 6 • PREP 25 MINS, PLUS CHILLING
COOK 25 MINS**
V

375g pack polenta
398g can sweetcorn, drained
1 red chilli, deseeded and finely chopped
50g/2oz Parmesan, finely grated
2 avocados, peeled and cut into chunks
FOR THE SALSA
1 cucumber, cut into chunks
4 spring onions, sliced
small bunch coriander, leaves roughly chopped
juice 2 limes
4 tbsp olive oil

1 Bring 1.5 litres water to the boil in a large saucepan. While stirring the water constantly with a wooden spoon, tip in the polenta in a steady stream. Lower the heat so the polenta isn't spluttering too much, then cook, stirring occasionally, for 10 minutes.

2 Meanwhile, line a 40 x 30cm baking sheet with baking parchment. Stir the corn, chilli and grated cheese into the polenta with 2 tsp salt, then spoon out onto the sheet. Spread to a rough rectangle, making sure the polenta is packed tightly. Cover with another sheet of baking parchment and a flat baking sheet, then top with some cans or jars to press and flatten the polenta while you chill it in the fridge for at least 2 hours, or up to a day.

3 Mix together the avocados, cucumber, spring onions, coriander, lime juice and 2 tbsp of the oil with some seasoning.

4 Heat a griddle pan or the barbecue, trim the edges off the set polenta to neaten, then slice it into 12 wedges. Brush both sides of each wedge with a little of the remaining oil then cook for 5 minutes on each side until charred and hot through. Serve a couple of wedges per person, topped with a generous spoon of the chunky green salsa.

PER SERVING 473 kcals, carbs 62g, fat 21g, sat fat 4g, salt 0.54g

4

Pulses, rice and grains

Nutritionists have long preached the fantastic benefits of pulses, rice and whole grains, but, until recently, they were largely viewed as a mainstay for vegetarians. Over the past few years, all these have grown increasingly fashionable. Not only do pulses and grains taste great and do you good, but they are also easy to use, cheap to buy and keep well. From spicy Indian dhal to houmous to a pearl barley risotto, there's always something you'll want to make – and we don't mean opening a can of baked beans!

PULSES

Pulse is the word used to describe any seed that grows inside a pod. So, that covers all beans, lentils and peas.

Pulses are high in fibre and are also one of the richest plant sources of protein. They count towards your 5-a-day, but only one portion of them, no matter how many you eat. A 5-a-day portion is 80g – roughly three heaped tablespoons. In this chapter we'll concentrate on pulses from the storecupboard, leaving fresh, green beans, broad beans, garden peas and the like until the vegetables chapter (page 200).

BEANS AND PEAS

All canned or dried beans have more or less the same uses, whether cooked in soups and stews, dressed in salads or mashed.

Black beans are a staple of Latin American and Caribbean cuisine. They have an earthy flavour and are good in strong, spicy dishes.

Black eye beans/peas are cream-coloured beans with a black eye. They have a good creamy texture and are traditionally partnered with rice.

Borlotti beans are creamy or pale brown and flecked with pink. These are similar to pinto beans and popular in hearty Italian soups and stews.

Butter beans are large, flat white beans with a creamy buttery flavour and mealy texture. They are very good with vegetables or creamy sauces.

Cannellini beans are slightly longer and fatter than haricot beans but similar in taste and texture. They hold their shape well after cooking, which makes them good in salads and soups.

Chickpeas are a popular choice for countless dishes and the traditional base for houmous. Dried split chickpeas are treated as lentils to make the classic Indian dish chana dhal.

Flageolet beans are a pretty, pale green long bean, much loved by the French and particularly good with roast lamb.

Haricot beans are simple white beans used in earthy one-pots, gutsy salads and soups. Try whizzing them with olive oil and garlic to make bean mash.

OPPOSITE Quinoa, lentil and feta salad (page 86)

Pinto beans are similar in taste and texture to borlotti, with a slightly darker colour. A favourite in Mexican dishes.
Yellow split peas are used to make pease pudding, some Indian dhals and also thick creamy pea and ham soup.

Dried or canned?

Buying dried pulses can be better value but you do need to do a bit of forward planning. They have a harder texture and need to be soaked before use. Although pulses last seemingly forever in the storecupboard, they can become overly hard, so check the date on the pack before cooking.

The general rule when it comes to cooking is to cover soaked dried beans or peas with cold water in a pan, bring to the boil, then simmer; the length of time will depend on the pulse. Don't add salt as this toughens the skins.

If you want to swap dried for canned, you will need to cook 100g dried beans instead of using a 400g can.

LENTILS

Most lentils need no soaking and take only about 20 minutes to cook. They work well with assertive flavours such as bacon, smoked fish, chilli and garlic.
Green lentil varieties include the prized Puy lentil from France, which stay firm when cooked. **Red lentils** are quick-cooking lentils. They also cook right down, which makes them great for thickening soups. Other types include **beluga lentils**, so called because they glisten like caviar and **brown lentils**, which are mild and often a little soft.

RICE

You can choose from a variety of rices to give your everyday meals different tastes and textures.
Basmati rice has long, slender grains and a fragrant taste and aroma. it can be used for plain boiled rice, in pilau, biryani and stir-fries. For perfectly fluffy rice, rinse until the water runs clear before cooking.
Brown rice is a firm and nutty whole long grain. It takes longer to cook than white rice, but contains more fibre and B vitamins. Choose brown basmati, if there's a choice.
Carmargue red rice is vibrant and full-flavoured with a short grain and a rich, nutty taste. Great in salads or stuffing.
Long grain rice lacks in flavour but is an economical choice. Easy cook rice has been steamed, making the grain harder and less easy to overcook at home.

Ready-cooked rice pouches can make a handy stand-by, but the texture and flavour can't rival freshly cooked rice. Frozen cooked rice is also available in some supermarkets.
Risotto rice is rich and creamy. As they cook, the grains swell and release their starch to create the risotto texture. Arborio and Carnaroli and Vialone Nano are the most common varieties. Paella rice, labeled bomba, is similar.
Thai or fragrant jasmine rice has a soft and slightly sticky texture when cooked. Good with Chinese and South-east Asian food.

Food safety

If you are cooking rice ahead of time, it is very important to cool the rice as quickly as possible (spread it over a tray or large plate), then chill it. A bacteria particular to cereals can quickly proliferate in rice, and can lead to upset stomachs or worse. Use within one day and, if reheating, always reheat to piping hot.

GRAINS AND SEEDS

Grains and seeds are an essential part of a healthy and balanced diet. Wholegrains are particularly beneficial because they retain their bran and germ (the outer coating), in which 90 per cent of their nutrients are found. Wholegrain foods can have a protective effect against heart disease, strokes and type-2 diabetes; plus, as complex carbohydrates, they give a steady release of energy.
Bulghar wheat is a cracked (but not whole) grain with a nutty flavour and makes a healthy alternative to rice.
Pearl barley is far too interesting a grain to be used solely to thicken the odd stew or soup – pearl barley also makes great risottos, pilaus and salads.
Spelt is a member of the wheat family, but some people with a wheat intolerance are able to eat it. Farro is a similar Italian grain. Use as you would barley.
Quinoa, pronounced 'keenwa', is seed remarkably rich in protein. It's a nutritious and gluten-free alternative to pasta or rice, and is perfect for salads, soups, stews and pilaus.
Couscous isn't strictly a grain, but a type of tiny pasta made from semolina (durum wheat flour). It is good for salads or as a starchy side, and is ready in 10 minutes.
Oats are loaded with goodness, helping to lower cholesterol levels and also lowering the glycaemic index (GI) of foods. Put them into homemade granola, cereal bars, add to crumb toppings or work them into breads.

Spicy chicken couscous

 This quick one-pot Moroccan dish is perfect for a summer supper.

SERVES 4 • PREP 10 MINS • COOK 10 MINS

250g/9oz couscous
300ml/½ pint hot chicken stock
3 tbsp olive oil
1 onion, chopped
2 skinless chicken breasts, sliced
85g/3oz blanched almonds
1 tbsp hot curry paste
100g/4oz ready-to-eat apricots, halved
small bunch coriander
natural yogurt, to serve

1 Put the couscous into a large bowl. Pour over the stock and stir. Cover with a plate or cling film and leave to stand for 5 minutes until all the liquid has been absorbed. Separate the grains by roughing them up with a fork.
2 Heat the oil in a pan and the fry the onion for 2–3 minutes until softened. Toss in the chicken and stir-fry for 5–6 minutes until tender. Add the almonds and, when golden, stir in the curry paste and cook for 1 minute more. Tip in the couscous, apricots and coriander, then toss well. Serve with a dollop of yogurt.

PER SERVING 486 kcals, carbs 45g, fat 23g, sat fat 2g, salt 0.56g

Grilled aubergines with spicy chickpeas and walnut sauce

With creamy smoky aubergine, nutty chickpeas and earthy walnuts, this meal will keep you interested to the last mouthful.

SERVES 2 • PREP 20 MINS • COOK 30 MINS
V

4 tbsp olive oil
1 onion, finely chopped
1 red chilli, deseeded and finely chopped
2cm/¾in piece fresh ginger, finely chopped
½ tsp each ground cumin, coriander and cinnamon
400g can chickpeas, rinsed and drained
200g/7oz tomatoes, chopped
juice ½ lemon
2 aubergines, sliced lengthways
FOR THE WALNUT SAUCE
200g tub Greek yogurt (use reduced-fat if you like)
1 garlic clove, crushed
25g/1oz walnuts, chopped
handful coriander leaves, roughly chopped

1 Heat 2 tbsp oil in a pan, add the onion and fry until soft and lightly browned, about 10 minutes. Add the chilli, ginger and spices and mix well. Stir in the chickpeas, tomatoes and 5 tbsp water, bring to the boil, then simmer for 10 minutes. Season and add the lemon juice.
2 Heat the grill to High. Spread the aubergines over a grill pan, brush lightly with the remaining oil, sprinkle with salt and pepper, then grill until golden. Flip them over, brush again with oil, season and grill again until tender and golden.
3 Mix the yogurt with the garlic, most of the walnuts and coriander and a little salt and pepper. Arrange the aubergine slices over a warm platter and spoon over the chickpea mix. Drizzle with the walnut sauce and scatter with the remaining walnuts and coriander.

PER SERVING 640 kcals, carbs 39g, fat 45g, sat fat 10g, salt 0.9g

Spiced bulghar, chickpea and squash salad

If satisfying and salad aren't two words you'd put together, this warmly spiced dish might change your mind.

SERVES 4 • PREP 15 MINS • COOK 20 MINS
V

1 butternut squash, about 1kg/2lb 4oz peeled, deseeded
    and cut into small chunks
2 red peppers, deseeded and sliced
2 tbsp harissa paste
1 tbsp olive oil
140g/5oz bulghar wheat
600ml/1 pint hot vegetable stock
1 garlic clove, crushed
juice ½ lemon
150g pot natural bio-yogurt
400g can chickpeas, drained and rinsed
180g bag baby leaf spinach

1 Heat oven to 200C/180C fan/gas 6. Toss the squash and red pepper in the harissa paste and oil. Spread the chunks out on a large baking sheet and roast for 20 minutes until softened and the edges of the vegetables are starting to char.
2 Meanwhile, put the bulghar wheat in a large bowl and pour over the hot stock, then cover tightly with cling film and leave to absorb the liquid for 15 minutes until the grains are tender but still have a little bite. In a separate bowl, mix the garlic and lemon juice into the yogurt and season to taste.
3 Let the bulghar wheat cool slightly then toss in the roasted vegetables, chickpeas and spinach – the leaves may wilt a little. Season, drizzle with the garlicky yogurt and serve warm.

PER SERVING 388 kcals, carbs 66g, fat 9g, sat fat 1g, salt 1.18g

 Bio-yogurt is a good choice for dressings as it tends to be much less sharp in flavour than ordinary natural yogurt.

Biryani-stuffed peppers

This Indian-inspired rice stuffing can also be used in large beefsteak tomatoes, but they will take less time to cook than the peppers. Enjoy warm or cold.

SERVES 6 • PREP 15 MINS • COOK ABOUT 1 HR
V

4 tbsp olive oil
1 onion, chopped
2 garlic cloves, chopped
1 cinnamon stick
1 tsp each turmeric, ground cumin, ground coriander,
    cardamom pods
250g/9oz basmati rice
handful parsley leaves, roughly chopped
handful coriander leaves, roughly chopped
zest and juice 1 lemon
50g/2oz each pine nuts and raisins
6 red peppers

1 Heat oven to 200C/fan 180C/gas 6. Heat half the oil in a saucepan and fry the onion and garlic. Add the spices and cook for a few mins more. Stir the rice through. Add enough cold water to cover the rice, cover pan with a lid and bring to the boil. Turn down the heat and cook for 10 mins until just tender. Stir the herbs, lemon zest and juice, pine nuts and raisins through the rice.
2 Cut around the stalks of the peppers and discard. Use a teaspoon to scrape away the pith and seeds. Stuff the peppers with rice and sit in a small roasting tray. Pour 100ml water into the tin and drizzle with the remaining oil. Cover the tin with foil, then roast for 20 minutes. Remove the foil, then continue to cook for 20 minutes until the peppers are soft and just starting to fall apart.

PER SERVING 274 kcals, carbs 46g, fat 9g, sat fat 1g, salt 0.02g

Falafel burgers

 Storecupboard chickpeas make the basis of these gently spiced, filling burgers. Stuff into pittas with salad and salsa for a hunger-busting and healthy supper.

SERVES 4 • PREP 10 MINS • COOK 6 MINS
V ❄

400g can chickpeas, rinsed and drained
1 small red onion, roughly chopped
1 garlic clove, chopped
handful flat-leaf or curly parsley
1 tsp each ground cumin and coriander
½ tsp harissa paste or chilli powder
2 tbsp plain flour
2 tbsp sunflower oil
toasted pittas, 200g tub tomato salsa and green salad,
    to serve

1 Pat the chickpeas dry with kitchen paper. Tip into a food processor along with the onion, garlic, parsley, spices, flour and a little salt. Blend until fairly smooth, then shape into four patties with your hands.
2 Heat the oil in a non-stick frying pan, add the burgers, then quickly fry for 3 minutes on each side until lightly golden. Serve with toasted pittas, tomato salsa and green salad.

PER SERVING 161 kcals, carbs 18g, fat 8g, sat fat 1g, salt 0.36g

try this...

Falafel can be eaten cold for lunch too. Shape and cook the mix in mini patties. Pack up with houmous, veg sticks, pitta and shop-bought or homemade tzatsiki.

Quick bean and chorizo chilli

This is great with rice and natural yogurt but also delicious piled onto a baked potato and served with a dollop of soured cream.

SERVES 2 GENEROUSLY • PREP 5 MINS • COOK 15 MINS
❄

100g/4oz chorizo, sliced
350g tub fresh tomato and chilli sauce
400g can kidney beans, rinsed and drained
400g can chickpeas, rinsed and drained

1 Dry-fry the chorizo for a few minutes in a non-stick frying pan until crisp. Carefully pour off any fat from the pan, then tip in the sauce and beans with 100ml water. Bring to a simmer, cover, then lower the heat and bubble for 10 minutes.

PER SERVING 463 kcals, carbs 50g, fat 18g, sat fat 6g, salt 6.32g

try this...

Spicy shepherd's pie for four
Cook the chilli using 200g/7oz chorizo. Boil 750g/1¾lb floury potatoes until tender then mash with ½ tsp paprika, 1 crushed garlic clove, a splash of milk and a little olive oil. Spoon the chilli into a baking dish, top with the mash and grill until golden.

Mexican bean salad

Not one to leave your tummy rumbling, this filling salad really hits the spot and has a spicy kick.

**SERVES 4 • PREP 10 MINS, PLUS COOLING
COOK 10 MINS**
V

4 eggs
2 ripe avocados
2 x 400g cans beans (kidney beans and pinto beans are
    a good mix), rinsed and drained
1 small red onion, finely sliced
large bunch coriander, leaves only, roughly chopped
250g/9oz cherry tomatoes, halved
3 tbsp good-quality lime and coriander dressing
1 red chilli, deseeded and finely sliced
½ tsp ground cumin

1 Put the eggs into a pan of cold water, bring to the boil and cook for 6 minutes. Cool under cold water.
2 Slice the avocados and place them in a large bowl with the beans, onion, coriander and tomatoes. In a small bowl, mix the dressing with the chilli and cumin.
3 Once the eggs are cool enough to handle, peel off the shells and cut into quarters. Toss the salad with the dressing and nestle in the eggs. Serve straight away – it is delicious with toasted tortillas.

PER SERVING 430 kcals, carbs 25g, fat 29g, sat fat 3g, salt 1.61g

tip For a tasty supper or lunchbox snack, pile the Mexican bean salad into the centre of flour tortillas or stuff into a pittas, then grate over some Cheddar and add a dollop of natural yogurt. Roll up the tortillas or close over the pittas tightly and eat.

Quinoa, lentil and feta salad

Quinoa is a 'superfood' and makes a great substitute for rice or couscous. You know it's cooked when the seed unfurls to reveal a little tail and has a tender texture.

SERVES 4 • PREP 15 MINS • COOK 15 MINS
V

200g/7oz quinoa
1 tsp olive oil
1 shallot or ½ onion, finely chopped
2 tbsp tarragon, roughly chopped
400g can Puy or green lentils, rinsed and drained
¼ cucumber, lightly peeled and diced
100g/4oz feta, crumbled
bunch spring onions, thinly sliced
zest and juice 1 orange
1 tbsp red or white wine vinegar

1 Cook the quinoa in a large pan of boiling water for 10–15 minutes until tender, drain well, then set aside to cool.
2 Meanwhile, heat the oil in a small pan and cook the shallot or onion for a few minutes until softened. Add the tarragon, stir well, then remove from the heat.
3 Stir the softened shallot and tarragon into the cooled quinoa along with the lentils, cucumber, feta, spring onions, orange zest and juice and vinegar. Toss well together and chill until ready to serve.

PER SERVING 286 kcals, carbs 39g, fat 9g, sat fat 3g, salt 1.48g

tip For extra flavour, try cooking the quinoa in stock rather than plain water.

Chicken, green bean and barley salad

When tossed with dressing and served warm or cold, pearl barley is nutty and satisfying and easily rivals lentils, bulghar or couscous.

SERVES 4 • PREP 25 MINS • COOK 25 MINS

1 small rotisserie chicken (or roast your own)
100g/4oz pearl barley
200g/7oz green beans, trimmed
1 yellow pepper, cut into matchsticks
1 small red onion, cut into thin half-moon slices
50g/2oz flaked almonds, toasted
zest 1 lemon
handful flat-leaf parsley, finely chopped
FOR THE DRESSING
3 tbsp red wine vinegar
5 tbsp extra virgin olive oil
1 tsp Dijon mustard
1 tsp smoked paprika

1 Cook the pearl barley in boiling, salted water until tender, but not too soft, about 20 minutes. Drain well, then tip into a large bowl. Meanwhile, remove the skin from the chicken and shred the meat off the bones into bite-size pieces.
2 Boil the green beans in salted water for about 5 minutes, until just tender. Drain, rinse with cold water to cool, then pat dry. Add to the barley along with the pepper, onion, almonds, lemon zest and parsley.
3 Whisk together the dressing ingredients with some seasoning. Pour over the salad, toss everything together and serve.

PER SERVING 624 kcals, carbs 27g, fat 42g, sat fat 9g, salt 0.45g

Tricolore couscous salad

A beautiful red, white and green supper that's also great for lunchboxes; just pack it into a tub with the leaves on the top, ready to toss through.

SERVES 4 • PREP 15 MINS • NO COOK
V

200g/7oz couscous
2 tsp vegetable stock powder (or use a cube)
250g/9oz cherry tomatoes, halved
2 ripe avocados, peeled, stoned and chopped
150g ball buffalo mozzarella, drained and chopped
handful rocket or young spinach leaves
FOR THE DRESSING
1 rounded tbsp pesto
1 tbsp lemon juice
3 tbsp olive oil

1 Mix the couscous and stock in a bowl, pour over 300ml boiling water, then cover with a plate and leave for 5 minutes.
2 For the dressing, mix the pesto with the lemon juice and some seasoning, then gradually mix in the oil. Pour over the couscous and mix with a fork.
3 Mix the tomatoes, avocados and mozzarella into the couscous, then lightly stir in the rocket or spinach to serve.

PER SERVING 456 kcals, carbs 30g, fat 32g, sat fat 8g, salt 0.60g

Warm lentil salad with Serrano ham, chicken and rocket

You can make this salad for four with just two chicken breasts, as the lentils and ham are very satisfying.

SERVES 4 • PREP 15 MINS • NO COOK

1 red onion, halved and very thinly sliced
1 tbsp sherry vinegar, plus extra for drizzling (optional)
handful flat-leaf parsley, roughly chopped
4 ripe tomatoes, roughly chopped
2 tsp small capers, drained
250g/9oz ready-cooked Puy lentils (or cook your own)
2 tbsp extra virgin olive oil, plus extra for drizzling (optional)
8 slices Serrano ham
2 cooked chicken breasts, torn into pieces
100g/4oz wild rocket

1 Put the onion in a bowl, drizzle over the vinegar, then season with salt and pepper. Set aside for 10 minutes or so until the onion has softened slightly.
2 Meanwhile, in another large bowl, mix the parsley and tomatoes with the capers. When ready to serve, tip the lentils into a sieve and rinse with boiling water from the kettle. Drain. Toss the onion and its juices into the lentils, then add the olive oil and carefully mix everything together.
3 Scoop the mixture onto a large serving platter, then top with the ham, chicken and rocket. Drizzle with more olive oil and a little more vinegar, if you like, then serve.

PER SERVING 320 kcals, carbs 20g, fat 12g, sat fat 3g, salt 2.3g

White bean, parsley and garlic mash

 Canned beans and chickpeas are perfect for mashing when you need a speedy side dish.

SERVES 4 • PREP 5 MINS • COOK 10 MINS

2 tbsp olive oil
2 shallots or ½ small onion, finely chopped
2 chopped garlic cloves, chopped
2 x 400g cans cannellini beans, drained
50ml/2fl oz stock or water
handful flat-leaf parsley, leaves roughly chopped

1 Heat the oil in a saucepan and tip in the shallots or onion. Gently cook for 5 minutes, add the garlic, then give it another 2 minutes until soft.
2 Tip the beans into the pan and roughly mash with the other ingredients. Add enough stock or water to loosen the mash, stir in the parsley, then season.

PER SERVING 189 kcals, carbs 23g, fat 7g, sat fat 1g, salt 1.34g

try this...

Bean mash with lemon & feta
Follow the recipe as above, adding the grated zest
1 lemon, 100g/4oz crumbled feta and a handful of
chopped black olives during step 2. Perfect with
griddled lamb.

OPPOSITE Clockwise from top left *Quick bean and chorizo chilli (page 85), Falafel burgers (page 85), Warm lentil salad with Serrano ham, chicken and rocket, Stuffed tomatoes with lamb mince, dill and rice (page 97), Grilled aubergine with spicy chickpeas and walnut sauce (page 83), Garlic prawns with Asian puy lentils (page 91).*

Jambalaya

 Here's some spicy inspiration for your storecupboard rice, corn and tomatoes.

SERVES 4 GENEROUSLY • PREP 10 MINS PLUS STANDING COOK 25 MINS

about 200g/7oz chorizo or other spicy sausage, skinned and chunkily chopped
1 red pepper, deseeded and roughly chopped
400g can chopped tomatoes with garlic
300g/11oz easy-cook long grain rice
2 handfuls of frozen sweetcorn kernels, or 1 small can, drained
a large sprinkling Cajun seasoning
TO SERVE
small handful parsley, chopped
142ml pot soured cream

1 Heat a large frying pan then dry-fry the chorizo for a few minutes until the fat starts to run and the meat crisps a little. Add the pepper, fry for 2 minutes to soften a little, then add the rest of the ingredients plus 400ml water and some salt and pepper.
2 Bring to the boil then turn down to a simmer and cover with a lid. Simmer for 15 minutes until most of the liquid has been absorbed. Set aside off the heat for another 5 minutes then scatter with the parsley and serve with dollops of soured cream.

PER SERVING 537 kcals, carbs 87g, fat 16g, sat fat 5g, salt 0.94g

Oven-baked risotto

Cook this risotto in the oven while you get on with something else. It doesn't need stirring but the result is still wonderfully creamy.

SERVES 4 • PREP 5-10 MINS • COOK 25 MINS

250g/9oz smoked back bacon, chopped into small pieces
1 onion, chopped
25g/1oz butter
300g/11oz risotto rice
75ml/2½fl oz dry white wine
150g pack cherry tomatoes, halved
700ml/1¼ pints hot chicken stock
50g/2oz Parmesan, finely grated

1 Heat oven to 200C/180C fan/gas 6. Fry the bacon pieces in an ovenproof pan or casserole dish for 3–5 minutes until golden and crisp. Stir in the onion and butter and cook for a further 3–4 minutes until soft. Tip in the rice and mix well until coated. Pour over the wine and cook for 2 minutes until absorbed.
2 Add the cherry tomatoes and the hot stock, then give the rice a quick stir. Cover with a tightly fitting lid and bake for 18 minutes until just cooked. Stir through most of the Parmesan and serve sprinkled with the remainder.

PER SERVING 517 kcals, carbs 63g, fat 20g, sat fat 10g, salt 3.38g

Egg-fried rice with prawns and peas

Make your own takeaway favourite with storecupboard ingredients and a few bits from the freezer.

**SERVES 4 EASILY HALVED • PREP 5 MINS
COOK 20 MINS
❄ IF PRAWNS NOT PREVIOUSLY FROZEN**

250g/9oz basmati rice, rinsed
2 tbsp vegetable oil
2 garlic cloves, finely chopped
1 red chilli, deseeded and shredded
2 eggs, beaten
200g/7oz frozen peas
1 bunch spring onions, finely sliced
300g/11oz cooked small prawns
1 tbsp soy sauce, plus extra for serving (optional)

1 Put the rice in a saucepan with 500ml water. Bring to the boil, cover, then simmer for 10 minutes or until almost all the water has gone. Leave off the heat, covered, for 5 minutes more.

2 Heat the oil in wok or large frying pan. Add the garlic and chilli, then cook for 10 seconds – making sure it doesn't burn. Throw in the cooked rice, stir-fry for 1 minute, then push it to the side of the pan. Pour the eggs into the empty side of the pan, then scramble them, stirring. Once just set, stir the peas and spring onions into the rice and egg and cook for 2 minutes until the peas are tender. Add the prawns and soy sauce, heat through, then serve with extra soy sauce on the side, if you like.

PER SERVING 416 kcals, carbs 56g, fat 10g, sat fat 2g, salt 2.06g

Garlic prawns with Asian puy lentils

 Liven up lentils with a zesty dressing and juicy prawns.

**SERVES 4 • PREP 15 MINS, PLUS MARINATING
COOK 20 MINS**

400g/14oz raw peeled tiger prawns, defrosted if frozen
zest and juice 1 lime
2 large garlic cloves, crushed
2 tbsp oil
2 red chillies, deseeded and finely chopped
200g/7oz dried Puy lentils
FOR THE DRESSING
2 tbsp soy sauce
1 tbsp clear honey
1 tbsp rice wine vinegar
3 tbsp sesame seeds, toasted
small bunch coriander, leaves roughly chopped

1 Place the prawns in a shallow dish. Mix together the lime zest and juice, garlic and oil and half of the chillies, then pour this over the prawns. Cover and chill for 20 minutes to marinate.

2 Meanwhile, put the lentils in a pan, cover with twice their depth in water, bring to the boil, and simmer for 15–20 minutes until tender. Top up the water if you need to.

3 To make the dressing, put the remaining chilli, soy sauce, honey and vinegar into a small bowl and stir together. Drain the lentils, then tip them into a large bowl. Spoon over almost all the dressing while the lentils are hot, then tip in the sesame seeds and mix well.

4 Heat a frying pan until really hot. Lift the prawns out of the marinade, then fry them for about 4 minutes until pink through and turning golden. Pour in the marinade and bring to the boil.

5 Fold the chopped coriander through the lentils, then spoon onto serving plates. Top with the prawns and any pan juices.

PER SERVING 349 kcals, carbs 29g, fat 12g, sat fat 2g, salt 1.89g

try this...

Italian-style salad

Toss together equal quantities of leftover cooked pasta and Puy lentils. Stir through spoonfuls ready-made pesto, a handful of rocket leaves and top with Parmesan shavings.

Spiced chicken and quinoa balti

Quinoa makes a great alternative to rice – in this recipe it's used exactly as you would rice in a pilau.

SERVES 4 • PREP 5 MINS • COOK 30 MINS

1 tbsp sunflower oil
2 large onions, thickly sliced
4 skinless chicken breasts
4 tbsp balti paste
200g/7oz quinoa
400g can chopped tomatoes
1 litre/1¾ pints chicken stock
50g/2oz roasted salted cashews
small bunch coriander, leaves chopped

1 Heat the oil in a large pan, fry the onions for 5 minutes until golden and softened, then tip onto a plate. Add the chicken breasts, browning for a few minutes on each side, then stir in the balti paste, quinoa and onions. Sizzle for a few minutes, then pour in the tomatoes and stock and give everything a good mix. Bubble for 25 minutes until the quinoa is tender.
2 Stir in the cashews and most of the coriander with some seasoning, then pile into bowls and scatter over the rest of the coriander to serve.

PER SERVING 527 kcals, carbs 45g, fat 19g, sat fat 3g, salt 1.83g

Jollof rice with chicken

Jollof rice is a traditional one-pot rice dish, popular all over West Africa. It's made with either vegetables, meat or fish and is always flavoured with ginger, garlic and chillies.

SERVES 4 • PREP 10 MINS • COOK 1 HOUR

8 skinless boneless chicken thighs, cut into large pieces
3 tbsp vegetable or sunflower oil
1 large onion, halved and sliced
3 tbsp tomato purée
600ml/1 pint chicken stock
400g/14oz basmati rice, rinsed
1 red pepper, deseeded and thickly sliced
1 yellow pepper, deseeded and thickly sliced
100g/4oz okra, halved (see below)
bunch coriander, roughly chopped, to serve
FOR THE GINGER AND CHILLI BASE
2 garlic cloves
2 x 400g cans plum tomatoes
thumb-size piece fresh root ginger
1 Scotch bonnet or other hot chilli, deseeded

1 Season the chicken then brown it in 2 tbsp of the oil in a large deep frying pan. Lift onto a plate. Add the rest of the oil to the pan and fry the onion for 5 minutes until soft. Meanwhile put the garlic, tomatoes, ginger and chilli into a food processor or blender and whizz until smooth.
2 Add the tomato purée to the onions, fry for 2 minutes then add the ginger and chilli mixture. Stir in the stock and chicken, bring to the boil then simmer for 15 minutes.
3 Add the rice to the pan, turn the heat down to a simmer then cover with foil and a lid (so no steam can escape) and cook for 20 minutes.
4 Take the lid off (the rice won't be cooked yet) then scatter the peppers and okra over the rice. Re-cover and cook for 10 minutes until the veg is softened and the rice tender. Just before serving, mix the veg through and scatter over the coriander.

PER SERVING 705 kcals, carbs 98g, fat 15g, sat fat 3g, salt 1.73g

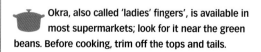 Okra, also called 'ladies' fingers', is available in most supermarkets; look for it near the green beans. Before cooking, trim off the tops and tails.

Japanese salmon and avocado rice

This dish contains the omega-3 goodness of sushi but saves you the painstaking rolling and shaping. The salmon is marinated in lemon juice and soy, which 'cooks' and flavours the fish.

**SERVES 4 • PREP 15 MINS, PLUS MARINATING
COOK 15 MINS**

300g/11oz sushi rice (or use basmati), rinsed
350g/12oz skinless salmon fillet
2 small, ripe avocados, sliced
juice 1 lemon
4 tsp light soy sauce
4 tsp toasted sesame seeds
2 spring onions, thinly sliced
1 red chilli, deseeded and thinly sliced
small handful coriander leaves

1 Put the rice into a pan with 400ml water. Bring to the boil, turn the heat to low, cover, then simmer for 10–12 minutes until the rice is almost cooked. Remove from the heat then leave, covered, for another 10 minutes.
2 Thinly slice the salmon and arrange on a platter with the sliced avocado. Drizzle over the lemon juice and soy, making sure everything is evenly covered. Leave in the fridge to marinate for 10 minutes.
3 Carefully tip the juices from the salmon platter into the rice, then stir in a little salt. Divide the rice between 4 bowls. Scatter the sesame seeds, spring onions, chilli and coriander over the salmon and avocado, then serve with the rice.

PER SERVING 519 kcals, carbs 59g, fat 22g, sat fat 3g, salt 1.02g

Easy salmon sushi

low fat *No need to worry about shaping your sushi here either – this recipe is made simply on a baking sheet, ready to slice.*

**SERVES 6 AS A STARTER OR NIBBLE • PREP 20 MINS,
PLUS COOLING • COOK 20 MINS**

300g/11oz sushi rice, rinsed
4 tbsp rice wine vinegar
1 tbsp caster sugar
200g/7oz smoked salmon slices

1 Put the rice into a pan with 400ml water. Bring to the boil, turn the heat to low, cover, then simmer for 10–12 minutes until the rice is almost cooked. Remove from the heat then leave, covered, for another 10 minutes.
2 Heat the rice wine vinegar, sugar and a pinch of salt together in the microwave for about 30 seconds until the sugar dissolves. Tip the cooked rice into a large bowl. Pour over the warm rice wine mixture and stir. Leave to cool.
3 Line a 20 x 20cm baking sheet with a double layer of cling film. Dampen your hands with water then press the sushi rice over the bottom of the sheet. Cover the rice completely with smoked salmon slices. Fold the cling film over the salmon to cover, pressing down well with your hands to mould everything together. Chill for up to 3 hours.
4 To serve, dip a sharp knife into a little hot water to stop the rice from sticking to the blade, then cut into 16 rectangles.

PER SERVING 216 kcals, carbs 41g, fat 2g, sat fat none, salt 1.6g

 Sushi rice is Japanese short grain rice. It looks like pudding, or risotto rice, with a pearly, round grain. When cooked, the starch in and around the grain thickens, causing the grains to stick together. This is why it's so good for shaping into blocks for sushi. It's also much easier to pick up with chopsticks when served as a side – logical really!

Vegetable tagine with almond and chickpea couscous

A take on a traditional Moroccan dish, this tagine won't take all day to make.

SERVES 4 • PREP 20 MINS • COOK 15 MINS
V ❄ TAGINE ONLY

400g/14oz shallots, peeled (see Know how)

2 tbsp olive oil

1 large butternut squash, about 1.25kg/2lb 12oz, peeled,
    deseeded and cut into bite-size chunks

1 tsp ground cinnamon

½ tsp ground ginger

450ml/16fl oz strong-flavoured vegetable stock

12 small, pitted prunes

2 tsp clear honey

2 red peppers, deseeded and cut chunks

3 tbsp chopped coriander

2 tbsp chopped mint, plus extra for sprinkling

FOR THE COUSCOUS

250g/9oz couscous

1 tbsp harissa paste

400g can chickpeas, rinsed and drained

handful toasted flaked almonds

1 Fry the shallots in the oil in a large pan for 5 minutes until they are softening and browned. Add the squash and spices, and stir for 1 minute. Pour in the stock, season well, then add the prunes and honey. Cover and simmer for 8 minutes.
2 Add the peppers and cook for 8–10 minutes until just tender. Stir in the coriander and mint.
3 Pour 400ml boiling water over the couscous in a bowl, then stir in the harissa with ½ tsp salt. Tip in the chickpeas, then cover and leave for 5 minutes. Fluff up with a fork and serve with the tagine, flaked almonds and extra mint.

PER SERVING 483 kcals, carbs 85g, fat 11g, sat fat 1g, salt 0.61g

 To peel shallots without tears, tip them into a bowl and pour over boiling water. Leave for 10 minutes, then drain – the skins will peel away easily, without stinging your eyes.

Pumpkin curry with chickpeas

Make this vegetarian one-pot a day ahead and let the flavours improve, ready for serving with naans and piles of fluffy rice.

SERVES 4 • PREP 20 MINS • COOK 20 MINS
V ❄

1 tbsp sunflower oil

3 tbsp Thai yellow curry paste

2 onions, finely chopped

3 large stalks of lemongrass, bashed with the back
    of a knife

6 cardamom pods

1 tbsp mustard seed

1kg/2lb 4oz pumpkin or a small squash, cut into chunks

250ml/9fl oz vegetable stock

400ml can reduced-fat coconut milk

400g can chickpeas, drained and rinsed

2 limes

large handful mint leaves

naan bread, to serve

1 Heat the oil in a sauté pan, then gently fry the curry paste with the onions, lemongrass, cardamom and mustard seed for 2–3 minutes until fragrant. Stir the pumpkin or squash into the pan and coat in the paste, then pour in the stock and coconut milk. Bring everything to a simmer, add the chickpeas, then cook for about 10 minutes until the pumpkin is tender. (The curry can now be cooled and chilled for 24 hours or frozen for up to 1 month.)
2 Squeeze the juice of 1 lime into the curry, then cut the other lime into wedges to serve alongside. Just before serving, tear over the mint leaves, then bring the curry to the table with the lime wedges and warm naan breads.

PER SERVING 293 kcals, carbs 26g, fat 18g, sat fat 10g, salt 1.32g

Golden veggie shepherd's pie

This recipe makes enough for two pies or one large and several individual portions for the freezer.

SERVES 10 • PREP 30 MINS • COOK A STAGGERED 1¾ HOURS
V ❄

FOR THE LENTIL SAUCE
50g/2oz butter
2 onions, chopped
4 carrots, diced
1 head celery, chopped
4 garlic cloves, finely chopped
200g/7oz chestnut mushrooms, sliced
2 bay leaves
1 tbsp dried thyme
500g/1lb 2oz dried green lentils
100ml/3½fl oz red wine (optional)
1.7 litres/3 pints vegetable stock
3 tbsp tomato purée

FOR THE TOPPING
2kg/4lb 8oz floury potatoes, such as King Edward,
   cut into chunks
85g/3oz butter
100ml/3½fl oz milk
50g/2oz mature Cheddar, grated

1 To make the sauce, heat the butter in a pan, then gently fry the onions, carrots, celery and garlic for 15 minutes until soft and golden. Turn up the heat, add the mushrooms, then cook for 4 minutes more. Stir in the herbs, then add the lentils. Pour over the wine (if using) and stock – it's important that you do not season with salt at this stage. Simmer for 40–50 minutes until the lentils are very soft. Now season to taste, take off the heat, then stir in the tomato purée.
2 While the lentils are cooking, boil the potatoes for about 15 minutes until tender. Drain well, mash with the butter and milk, then season.
3 Heat oven to 190C/170C fan/gas 5. To assemble the pies, divide the lentil mixture between all the dishes that you are using, then top with mash. Scatter over the cheese and either bake for 30 minutes until the topping is golden, or freeze for up to 3 months.

PER SERVING 449 kcals, carbs 68g, fat 13g, sat fat 7g, salt 0.59g

Lincolnshire sausage and lentil simmer

This big one-pot will have everyone asking for more.

SERVES 6 • PREP 10 MINS COOK ABOUT 1 HOUR 10 MINS
❄

1 tbsp vegetable oil
130g pack cubed pancetta or diced bacon
12 Lincolnshire or other good pork sausages
2 onions, roughly chopped
1 large carrot, chopped into small pieces
4 garlic cloves, roughly chopped
3 sprigs rosemary
300g/11oz Puy lentils
850ml/1½ pints hot chicken stock
1 tbsp white wine vinegar
400g can chopped tomatoes
2 tbsp chopped flat-leaf parsley

1 Heat the oil in a large casserole or very large frying pan with a lid. Add the pancetta and sausages and sizzle for 10 minutes, turning the sausages occasionally until nicely browned and sticky. Scoop the sausages out onto a plate.
2 Add the onions, carrot and garlic to the pancetta and continue to cook for 3–4 minutes until the onions soften. Return the sausages to the pan and add the rosemary, lentils, stock, vinegar and tomatoes, then season with salt and pepper. Bring to the boil and simmer rapidly for 5 minutes, then lower the heat, cover and simmer for 45 minutes, stirring every so often until the lentils are tender. (It can now be chilled and frozen for up to 1 month.) Check the seasoning, scatter over the parsley and serve from the pan.

PER SERVING 640 kcals, carbs 37g, fat 37g, sat fat 13g, salt 4.24g

Kedgeree

Treat yourself to a special brunch.

SERVES 4 • PREP 10 MINS • COOK 35 MINS

FOR THE CRISP ONIONS
2 tbsp vegetable or sunflower oil
2 medium onions, halved and very thinly sliced
FOR THE KEDGEREE
350g/12oz undyed smoked haddock
175g/6oz lightly smoked salmon fillet
1 dried red chilli
300ml/½ pint full-fat milk
3 tbsp vegetable or sunflower oil
1 medium onion, chopped
about 14 fresh or freeze-dried curry leaves
4 cardamom pods, split
1 cinnamon stick, broken into pieces
280g/10oz basmati rice, rinsed
½ tsp turmeric
50g/2oz butter
2 eggs
handful coriander leaves and some lime wedges,
    to serve

1 Heat the oil in a large pan and cook the onions for about 20–25 minutes, stirring once or twice until deep golden brown. Spread them over kitchen paper and leave to crisp up. Meanwhile, put the fish in a frying pan with the chilli. Cover with milk and simmer for 4 minutes. Take off the heat and stand, covered, for 10 minutes to finish cooking the fish.
2 Heat the oil in a deep-frying or sauté pan (with a lid). Add the onion and whole spices and fry until the onion is soft and golden, about 7–8 minutes, stirring often. Lift the fish from the milk, discard the skin and any bones, cover and keep warm. Stir the rice into the onion for 1 minute then add the milk, 300ml water and the turmeric. Boil, then cover and simmer for 10 minutes until tender.
3 Dot with the butter then top with the fish. Take off the heat and keep covered. Meanwhile, put the eggs in a pan of cold water, time for 6 minutes once boiling, then cool under cold water. Peel and quarter.
4 To serve, break the fish into big pieces with a fork, throw in the coriander and stir gently to mix, adding the eggs at the end. Season, scatter crisp onions on top and serve with lime wedges for squeezing.

PER SERVING 714 kcals, carbs 67g, fat 33g, sat fat 11g, salt 4.42g

Easiest-ever paella

 A few simple ingredients come together brilliantly in this Spanish-style supper.

SERVES 4 • PREP 5 MINS • COOK 25 MINS

1 tbsp olive oil
1 leek or onion, sliced
110g pack chorizo sausage, chopped
1 tsp turmeric
300g/11oz long grain rice
1 litre/1¾ pints hot fish or chicken stock
200g/7oz frozen peas
400g bag frozen seafood mixed, defrosted
lemon wedges, to serve

1 Heat the oil in a deep frying pan, then soften the leek or onion for 5 minutes without browning. Add the chorizo and fry until it releases its oils. Stir in the turmeric and rice until coated by the oils, then pour in the stock. Bring to the boil, then simmer for 15 minutes, stirring occasionally.
2 Tip in the peas and cook for 5 minutes, then stir in the seafood to heat through for a final 1–2 minutes cooking or until the rice is cooked. Check for seasoning and serve immediately with lemon wedges.

PER SERVING 518 kcals, carbs 75g, fat 12g, sat fat 4g, salt 1.29g

Stuffed tomatoes with lamb mince, dill and rice

These tomatoes improve in flavour if you cook them the day before you plan to eat. Add a drop of water and cover with foil when reheating, or simply serve at room temperature.

SERVES 4 • PREP 20 MINS • COOK 45 MINS

4 beef tomatoes
pinch sugar
4 tbsp Greek extra virgin olive oil, plus extra to drizzle
1 Spanish onion, finely chopped
2 garlic cloves, finely chopped
200g/7oz minced lamb
1 tsp ground cinnamon
2 tbsp tomato purée
50g/2oz long grain rice
100ml/3½fl oz chicken stock
4 tbsp chopped dill
2 tbsp chopped flat-leaf parsley
1 tbsp chopped mint

1 Heat oven to 180C/160C fan/gas 4. Slice the tops off the tomatoes and reserve. Scoop out most of the pulp with a teaspoon, being careful not to break the skin. Finely chop the pulp, and keep any juices. Sprinkle the insides of the tomatoes with a little sugar, then place them on a baking tray.
2 Heat 2 tbsp olive oil in a large frying pan, add the onion and garlic, then gently cook for about 10 minutes until soft but not coloured. Add the lamb, cinnamon and tomato purée, turn up the heat, then fry until the meat is browned. Add the tomato pulp and juice, the rice and the stock. Season generously. Bring to the boil, then simmer for 15 minutes or until the rice is tender and the liquid has been absorbed. Set aside to cool a little, then stir in the herbs.
3 Stuff the tomatoes up to the brim, top with their lids, drizzle with 2 tbsp more olive oil, sprinkle 3 tbsp water onto the baking tray, then bake for 35 minutes. Serve with salad and crusty bread, hot or warm.

PER SERVING 300 kcals, carbs 21g, fat 19g, sat fat 5g, salt 0.30g

Quinoa rice pilau with dill and roasted tomatoes

 If you need convincing about quinoa then try this – it partners perfectly with simply cooked fish or chicken.

SERVES 4–6 • PREP 10 MINS • COOK 25 MINS

250g/9oz cherry tomatoes, halved
4 tbsp olive oil
1 onion, thinly sliced
3 sticks celery, sliced
½ tsp cumin seeds
2 garlic cloves, finely chopped
100g/4oz basmati rice (brown or white)
140g/5oz quinoa
large bunch dill, chopped
500ml/18fl oz chicken or vegetable stock
50g/2oz pine nuts, toasted

1 Heat oven to 180C/160C fan/gas 4. Put the tomatoes on a baking sheet and drizzle with 2 tbsp olive oil and some seasoning. Roast for 15 minutes, remove and set aside.
2 Heat the remaining olive oil in a large pan. Add the onion, celery, cumin and garlic, then season to taste. Fry on a medium heat for 10 minutes until golden. Add the rice, quinoa, dill and stock. Cover with a lid and cook for 12–15 minutes or until the rice is soft. Add the tomatoes and pine nuts, and gently stir through.

PER SERVING 412 kcals, carbs 45g, fat 22g, sat fat 3g, salt 0.54g

Mushroom risotto

Making risotto the traditional way does require your undivided attention, but follow our step-by-step recipe and you'll find it simple – even relaxing – and delicious!

SERVES 4 ● PREP 10 MINS ● COOK ABOUT 20 MINS
V

50g/2oz dried porcini mushrooms
1 vegetable stock cube
2 tbsp olive oil
1 onion, finely chopped
2 garlic cloves, finely chopped
250g pack chestnut mushrooms, sliced
300g/11oz risotto rice, such as arborio
175ml/6fl oz white wine
25g/1oz butter
50g/2oz Parmesan or Grana Padano, freshly grated
handful parsley leaves, chopped

Butternut squash and sage risotto
Peel a 1kg/2½lb butternut squash and cut into bite-size chunks, toss with 1 tbsp olive oil and 1 tbsp chopped sage and roast for 30 minutes until golden and soft. Gently fry a handful of sage leaves in a little more oil until crisp. Make the risotto as above, ignoring the mushrooms and using 1.2 litres/2 pints veg or chicken stock. Stir the squash through the risotto, add the cheese and butter then serve topped with the sage leaves.

Risotto primavera
Make the risotto as above, ignoring the mushroom, and using a bunch of spring onions instead of the onion. When the risotto has been cooking for about 15 minutes, stir in 200g/7oz peas or shelled broad beans and 250g/9oz asparagus, trimmed and cut into short lengths. Keep adding the stock and stirring; the vegetables will be tender at the end of cooking. Add the cheese and butter, let the risotto rest, then serve.

1 Put the dried mushrooms into a large bowl and pour over 1.2 litres boiling water. Soak for 20 minutes, then strain into a bowl, discarding the last few tablespoons of liquid left in the bowl, as this can be gritty. Crumble the stock cube into the mushroom liquid, then squeeze the mushrooms gently to remove any liquid. Chop the mushrooms.

2 Heat the oil in a shallow saucepan or deep frying pan over a medium flame. Add the onion and garlic, then fry for about 5 minutes until soft. Stir in the fresh and soaked mushrooms, season with salt and pepper and continue to cook for 8 minutes until the fresh mushrooms have softened.

3 Tip the rice into the pan and cook for 1 minute. Pour over the wine and let it bubble to nothing so the alcohol evaporates. Keep the pan over a medium heat and pour in a quarter of the mushroom stock. Simmer the rice, stirring often, until the rice has absorbed all the liquid. Add about the same amount of stock again and continue to simmer and stir. Repeat until all the stock has been used and the rice is creamy, plump and just tender.

4 Take the pan off the heat, add the butter and scatter over half the cheese and the parsley. Cover and leave for a few minutes to let the rice rest. Give the risotto a final stir, spoon into bowls and scatter with the remaining cheese and parsley.

PER SERVING 445 kcals, carbs 63g, fat 17g, sat fat 7g, salt 1.45g

OPPOSITE Clockwise from top left Boston baked beans (page 100), Gigantes plaki (page 100), Pumpkin curry with chickpeas (page 94), Easy salmon sushi (page 93), Spiced chicken and quinoa balti (page 92), Japanese salmon with avocado rice (page 93).

Gigantes plaki

*These baked butter beans are most tasty served at room temperature the day after cooking,
drizzled with olive oil as part of a meze, or to accompany lamb.*

**SERVES 4 ● PREP 20 MINS, PLUS OVERNIGHT SOAKING
COOK ABOUT 2 HOURS**

V ❄

400g/14oz dried butter beans
3 tbsp extra virgin olive oil, plus extra to serve
1 Spanish onion, finely chopped
2 garlic cloves, finely chopped
2 tbsp tomato purée
800g/1lb 12oz ripe tomatoes, skins removed and roughly
    chopped (see below)
1 tsp sugar
1 tsp dried oregano
pinch ground cinnamon
2 tbsp chopped flat-leaf parsley, plus extra to serve

1 Soak the beans overnight in plenty of water. Drain, rinse, and put into a large pan of cold water. Bring to the boil, then simmer for about 50 minutes until slightly tender but not soft. Drain, then set aside.

2 Heat oven to 180C/160C fan/gas 4. Heat the olive oil in a large frying pan, tip in the onion and garlic, then cook over a medium heat for 10 minutes until softened but not browned. Add the tomato purée, cook for a further minute, add the remaining ingredients, then simmer for 2–3 minutes. Season generously, then stir in the beans. Tip into a large ovenproof dish, then bake for approximately 1 hour, uncovered, so the sauce thickens. Allow to cool, then scatter with parsley and drizzle with a little more olive oil to serve.

PER SERVING 431 kcals, carbs 66g, fat 11g, sat fat 1g, salt 0.2g

 To remove the skin from a tomato, score a small cross at the rounded end. Put it into a bowl and pour over boiling water, leaving it for a few seconds, then dunk into cold water. The tomato skin will have started to peel where you cut the cross – so simply peel away with your fingers.

tip If you like, use 3 x 400g cans butter beans. Make the sauce as above, tip in the drained and rinsed beans and continue as before. Whatever you use, this recipe contains an amazing 5 of your 5-a-day.

Boston baked beans

Haricot beans take very well to the sweetly spiced flavours of this dish. This is perfect family fare – kids will love it.

**SERVES 6 ● PREP 20 MINS, PLUS SOAKING
COOK 2–2½ HOURS**

❄

500g/1lb 2oz dried haricot beans
2 onions, roughly chopped
2 celery sticks, roughly chopped
2 carrots, roughly chopped
2 tbsp Dijon mustard
2 tbsp light muscovado sugar
½ tbsp black treacle or molasses
2 tbsp tomato purée
800g/1lb 12oz piece belly pork
handful parsley, roughly chopped

1 Soak the beans in a large bowl of cold water for at least 4 hours or overnight. Heat oven to 180C/160C fan/gas 4. Drain and rinse the beans and put in a large flameproof casserole with 1.5 litres water. Boil for 10 minutes, skimming off any scum that appears on the surface.

2 Add the onions, celery, carrots, mustard, sugar, treacle or molasses and tomato purée. Stir until everything is well mixed, then bury the piece of pork in among the beans. Cover tightly and cook in the oven for 2–2½ hours until the beans and pork are very tender. Check halfway through the cooking time and top up with hot water from the kettle, if necessary.

3 Take the pork out of the pot. Cut into large chunks and serve with the beans, sprinkled with parsley.

PER SERVING 615 kcals, carbs 54g, fat 27g, sat fat 10g, salt 0.8g

Makhani dhal

Dhal, made from either lentils, peas or beans, is eaten all over India, with bread or rice. It's a good source of protein for vegetarians, and makes a great side dish with one of the other curries in this book.

SERVES 8 • PREP 10 MINS • COOK 45 MINS
❄ **BEFORE ADDING THE CREAM**

225g/8oz black lentils
2 onions, finely chopped
2 green chillies, deseeded and sliced
50g/2oz butter, plus a small knob
1 tbsp grated fresh root ginger
3 garlic cloves, thinly sliced
1 tsp ground turmeric
½ tsp hot chilli powder (optional)
2 tsp ground cumin
2 tsp ground coriander
2 bay leaves
2 x 400g cans red kidney beans, rinsed
142ml pot double cream
½ tsp garam masala
handful chopped coriander

1 Boil the lentils in 800ml water for 15 minutes until almost tender. Meanwhile, fry the onions and chillies in 50g butter for about 7 minutes until starting to soften. Stir in the ginger, garlic and spices and cook over a low heat for 1 minute more.
2 Pour in 800ml boiling water followed by the cooked lentils and any liquid. Add the bay leaves and beans, then simmer for 20 minutes more until thickened. (This can be made 2 days ahead and chilled, or frozen for up to 1 month.)
3 To serve, return to the heat if necessary and stir in the cream. Season well. Pour into a bowl, dot with the remaining butter, dust with garam masala and scatter with coriander.

PER SERVING 317 kcals, carbs 30g, fat 17g, sat fat 9g, salt 0.78g

tip For perfectly fluffy basmati rice, wash the rice in a sieve under running water until the water runs clear. Allow 75g/2½oz per serving. Tip the rice into a saucepan with double the amount of liquid (e.g. 75g rice would need 150ml salted water). Bring to the boil, put on a tight fitting lid, turn down the heat and cook for 10 minutes. Turn off the heat and leave for 10 minutes before serving. All the water should have absorbed and the grains should be tender.

Squash and barley salad with balsamic vinaigrette

Set this colourful, healthy platter on the table and watch it disappear.

SERVES 8 • PREP 5 MINS, PLUS COOLING • COOK 25 MINS
V

1 butternut squash, peeled and cut into long pieces
1 tbsp olive oil
250g/9oz pearl barley
300g/11oz tenderstem broccoli, cut into
    medium-size pieces
100g/4oz sunblushed tomatoes, sliced
1 small red onion, diced
2 tbsp pumpkin seeds
1 tbsp small capers, rinsed
15 black olives, pitted
small bunch basil, chopped
FOR THE DRESSING
5 tbsp balsamic vinegar
6 tbsp extra virgin olive oil
1 tbsp Dijon mustard
1 garlic clove, finely chopped

1 Heat oven to 200C/180C fan/gas 6. Place the squash on a baking sheet and toss with olive oil. Roast for 20 minutes.
2 Meanwhile, boil the barley for about 25 minutes in salted water until tender, but al dente. While this is happening, whisk the dressing ingredients in a small bowl, then season with salt and pepper. Drain the barley, then tip it into a bowl and pour over the dressing. Mix well and let it cool.
3 Boil the broccoli in salted water until just tender, then drain and rinse in cold water. Drain and pat dry. Add the broccoli and remaining ingredients to the barley and mix well. This will keep for 3 days in the fridge and is delicious warm or cold.

PER SERVING 301 kcals, carbs 40g, fat 14g, sat fat 2g, salt 0.55g

Poultry and game birds

Over the last few decades, chicken has gone from being a relative luxury to a commodity, which has been reflected directly in the quality of some extremely cheap chicken that is on sale in supermarkets. Happily, food campaigners have worked to open our eyes to the welfare issues surrounding intensive poultry farming and now our shopping habits are changing. Although a good chicken is a wonderful thing and a safe bet for most dinner guests, it's good to try something new – perhaps duck for a supper for two, or a guinea fowl or pheasants in season.

CHICKEN

For the best value, buy a whole bird, which can be jointed into portions (see page 105), or pick up packs of legs or thighs and drumsticks as these are far more reasonable (and tastier) than breast meat. On that note, let's discuss the difference between white and brown meat.

Chicken breasts are white meat, and are most people's first choice when looking for a quick supper option. They can easily dry out and become tough, though, so wrapping them in bacon or stuffing them will help to keep the meat moist – as will cooking it fast in stir-fries or on the griddle. Depending on the recipe, you'll see that we'll call for chicken breasts with or without skin in this book. Keeping the skin on helps to protect the meat from fierce heat, however it will increase the amount of fat in the finished recipe. When griddling chicken, always remove the skin.

Thighs and drumsticks are brown meat, full-flavoured and moist, but need longer cooking; it usually takes about 40 minutes until these become tender. A whole leg portion is the ideal size for one – and even organic and free-range chicken legs are very good value. Chicken wings are amazingly good value, too, but they are fairly small and vary in size. You'll need 3–4 per portion as a starter and a few more as a main course.

With all chicken, look for plump, blemish-free meat and skin, without any discoloured patches. The skin will normally be a whitish pink, except for corn-fed chickens, which have a golden yellow hue to their flesh and skin. The flavour isn't markedly different, but they do look impressively golden when roasted. A poussin is a young chicken which will feed two people.

TURKEY

Turkey breast or steaks offer a low-fat alternative to chicken and pork, especially when making meatballs and burgers, and are often very good value but, again, they do need careful cooking as they can easily dry out.

Most of us cook a whole turkey once, maybe twice, a year at Christmas or Easter. Be it a bronze or white-feathered breed, the important thing is that your turkey has been allowed to grow at a natural rate, giving the meat

OPPOSITE Summer-in-winter chicken (page 115)

a chance to develop a definite flavour. Be careful about what turkey you choose (very cheap meat can only be produced by means of intense farming) and how you cook it, and you'll be rewarded with a fantastically succulent centrepiece. For more about turkey, turn to page 389.

DUCK AND GOOSE

Farmed duck, domesticated from the wild mallard, is the most common kind of duck available, but wild duck is also available in season (from August to January). Geese are only available fresh at Christmas time, as they are fattened up through the year for this date.

Both duck and goose consist of brown meat throughout and hold a great deal of fat under the skin and within their bodies. The flesh is rich in flavour and goes particularly well with slightly tart tastes such as apples, oranges, cherries or cranberries. Although the fat is wonderful for roasting potatoes, it isn't great to eat while it's still on the meat.

To release the fat from the skin on duck breasts, score the skin (taking care not to cut through to the flesh) before frying. Cook the skin side gently, so that the fat runs away, before turning the meat over. Duck legs are usually roasted or 'confited', which involves slow-cooking in fat then roasting until tender and crisp. Goose is best roasted, with the fat being drained away every now and then during cooking. The extra fat layer, and the fact that it's bonier, with a large ribcage, means that, weight for weight, a goose will feed fewer people than a turkey.

QUAIL AND GUINEA FOWL

You will need one quail per person as a starter and two per person as a main course. They have a fairly high proportion of lean, meaty flesh to bone and a delicate flavour. Quail are now reared on a mass scale. Guinea fowl are somewhat similar to chicken or pheasant but have a darker, slightly drier and gamier-tasting flesh. The meat can dry out very quickly, which makes this type of bird a great candidate for pot-roasting.

GAME BIRDS

Game refers to birds and animals shot from the wild for food during a season which runs from autumn to mid-winter. Game is free-range and a healthy option – often low in fat and cholesterol and rich in vitamins. The flesh of game birds is delicate and easily overcooked – which explains why often they are cooked 'pink' rather than well done. Game can be an acquired taste, so if you haven't cooked with it before, start with pheasant and work up to partridge and grouse as you become familiar with the taste.

Pheasant is probably the best-known game bird and the easiest to buy. The birds are sold as a brace (a male and a female) or singly (females are said to be more tender, if you have the choice). Pheasants usually come oven-ready, but if they are still in feather, ask your butcher to prepare them. The male has beautiful long tail feathers, whereas the female is brown and more dowdy. Pheasant can be hung for anything from a few days to two weeks – the longer it hangs, the stronger the flavour. Pheasant is in season from October to February.

Partridge is a smaller relative of the pheasant and there are two varieties: French and grey. They are usually hung for a week, and one bird serves one person. Partridge is in season from September to February.

Grouse is considered the king of all the feathered game; so much so that the first day of the grouse season, 12 August, is known as 'The Glorious Twelfth'. Grouse is native to Scotland but is found elsewhere in the UK, too. Its flesh is rich, with a distinctive red colour and a gamey flavour, and the bird is small enough to feed one person nicely. Young birds are best roasted, while older birds work well cooked in a casserole.

Wood pigeon has beautiful dark red meat with a sweet, nutty flavour. The breasts are ideal for pan-frying, and particularly good with tart berries and citrus flavours. A **squab** is a young pigeon.

BUYING AND STORING POULTRY

It's important to buy the best-quality poultry you can afford – at the very least buy free range. Organic poultry really is worth the extra cost, not only for the excellent levels of welfare involved in its production but also because you get a fuller-flavoured meat on your plate.

Unwrap poultry from its packaging, put it onto a plate or a tray with a lip, wrap well and keep it in the bottom of the fridge to prevent raw meat juices dripping over other foods. Keep in the fridge for up to 2 days. For whole birds, remove the giblets (usually a bag containing the neck, heart, liver and kidneys) and keep these separately in the fridge.

Step-by-step: Jointing a whole chicken

When you consider that a whole chicken is not much more expensive than two breasts sold in a pack, it's clear that jointing a chicken is a skill worth learning. It also allows you to keep the breast meat on the bone, if you like, which will help the meat to stay moist as it cooks.

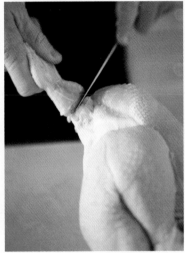

1 Pull out one of the wing joints. Using a small knife, cut round the skin and flesh around the joint nearest the breast. Scrape back the flesh. Using a large knife, smash through the bone halfway along and detach. Repeat on the other side.

2 Detach the scaly leg bone at the drumstick with a hefty thump of the large knife. Slash through the skin where the thigh joins the body and pull the leg firmly from the socket to dislocate the thigh bone. Press down and pull to expose the 'oyster' muscle underneath the bird. Slice the thigh away from the back of the body.

3 Lay the whole leg joint out on the board, find the mid-point socket joint and simply cut straight through it for neat thigh and leg joints.

4 Using poultry scissors or heavy kitchen scissors, cut away the back half of the breast carcass to leave a 'crown' of chicken breast and wing joint. Cut through the top of the crown to divide it in half, producing two breasts.

5 Lay each breast joint on the board, then cut in half again at right angles so you have one portion with a wing joint and one without. You should now have eight neat joints of chicken.

Chicken Caesar salad

Crisp croûtons, creamy dressing and chargrilled chicken, ready in under half an hour.

SERVES 4 ● PREP 10 MINS ● COOK 15 MINS

1 medium ciabatta loaf (or 4 thick slices crusty white bread), cut into cubes
3 tbsp olive oil
2 skinless, boneless chicken breasts
1 large cos or romaine lettuce, leaves separated
FOR THE DRESSING
1 garlic clove, crushed
2 anchovies from a can, mashed to a paste
5 tbsp mayonnaise
1 tbsp white wine vinegar
handful grated Parmesan or Grano Padano, plus extra for shaving

try this...

Grill or fry 6 rashers of bacon until crisp and leave to cool. Break into bite-size pieces, then toss through the salad, or swap the chicken for 2 x 185g cans tuna steak. Drain and flake the fish over the dressed salad.

1 Heat oven to 200C/180C fan/gas 6. Spread the bread over a large baking sheet and toss with 2 tbsp of the oil. Season with sea salt flakes. Bake for 8–10 minutes, turning occasionally, until golden and crisp.
2 Rub the chicken with the remaining oil and season. Heat a griddle pan then cook the chicken for 5–7 minutes on each side. Check if it's cooked by poking the tip of a sharp knife into the thickest part; there should be no sign of pink and the juices will run clear.
3 Combine all of the dressing ingredients except for the cheese shavings, then season to taste. The dressing should be the consistency of yogurt – stir in a few teaspoons of water to thin it if needed.
4 Tear the lettuce into a large bowl. Pull the chicken into bite-size strips and scatter half over the leaves, along with half the croûtons. Add most of the dressing and toss with your fingers. Add the rest of the chicken and croûtons, then drizzle with the remaining dressing. Scatter the Parmesan on top and serve straight away.

PER SERVING 453 kcals, carbs 27.4g, fat 27.8g, sat fat 5.3g, salt 1.37g

Smoky maple duck salad

Roasting the duck skin-side down is less smoky for your kitchen than pan-frying; just make sure the roasting tin is really hot before adding the duck.

SERVES 2 ● PREP 10 MINS ● COOK 20 MINS

2 duck breasts, skin on
3 tbsp maple syrup
1 garlic clove, crushed
1 tbsp chipotle chilli paste (see below), or try harissa for a hotter flavour
160g bag bistro salad (the kind with shredded beetroot)
bunch radishes, about 200g/7oz, thinly sliced or grated
1 tbsp sherry vinegar

Chipotle paste is a smoky, slightly sweet and spicy chilli paste. If you can't find it, stir together equal quantities smoked paprika, tomato purée and dark brown sugar and use as above.

1 Heat oven to 220C/200C fan/gas 7. Score criss-crossed lines into the duck skin almost all the way down to the flesh. Put a small roasting tin in the oven and let it heat up. Season the duck all over then put into the tin, skin-side down, and roast for 10 minutes until the skin is golden and the fat has run out. Roast for 15 minutes if you like your duck well done.
2 Meanwhile, mix 2 tbsp maple syrup with the garlic and chilli paste. Tip the fat out from the pan, turn the duck skin-side up, then roast for another 5 minutes, basting with the maple syrup mix once or twice until the duck is sticky, glazed and pink in the middle. Remove and let the duck rest for 5 minutes; reserve the cooking juices.
3 Pile the salad and the radishes onto two serving plates. Slice the duck at an angle and nestle it into the salad. Stir the rest of the maple syrup and the sherry vinegar into the pan juices, then drizzle it over the salad, season, and serve straight away.

PER SERVING 527 kcals, carbs 20g, fat 36g, sat fat 10g, salt 0.54g

Thai chicken curry

Invest in a Thai brand of paste and your curry will rival the real thing.

SERVES 4 • PREP 10 MINS • COOK 20 MINS

1 tbsp vegetable oil
2 shallots or 1 small onion, thinly sliced
1 stalk lemongrass, thinly sliced *(see below)*
3–4 tsp red Thai curry paste
4 skinless, boneless chicken breasts, cut into bite-size
   pieces
1 tbsp fish sauce
1 tsp sugar (brown sugar is best)
4 freeze-dried kaffir lime leaves
400ml can coconut milk
small bunch fresh coriander

1 Heat the oil in a wok or large saucepan for a couple of minutes then add the shallots or onion and lemongrass. Fry for 3–5 minutes until soft and translucent. Stir in the curry paste and cook for 1 minute, stirring all the time.

2 Add the chicken pieces and stir until they are coated. Add the fish sauce, sugar, lime leaves and coconut milk. Bring slowly to the boil, then reduce heat and simmer, uncovered, for 15 minutes until the chicken is cooked. Stir the curry a few times while it cooks to stop it sticking and to keep the chicken submerged.

3 While the chicken is cooking, strip the leaves from the coriander stalks, gather into a pile and chop them very roughly. Taste the curry and season with salt, if you think it needs it. Stir half the coriander into the curry and sprinkle the rest over the top. Serve with Thai jasmine or basmati rice.

PER SERVING 348 kcals, carbs 4.6g, fat 20.9g, sat fat 14.9g, salt 1.44g

 Peeling away the slightly tougher outer leaves from the lemongrass will make it easier to slice, and eat. Bash the lemongrass a little first with a rolling pin or saucepan to bruise it a little and release even more of its wonderful aromatic scent and flavour.

Chicken tikka skewers with cucumber salad

low fat *This Indian favourite is easy to prepare at home. The juicy skewers are grilled, too, for maximum flavour and minimum calories.*

SERVES 4 • PREP 20 MINS • COOK 15–20 MINS

150g pot low-fat natural yogurt
2 tbsp hot curry paste
4 skinless, boneless chicken breasts, cubed
250g pack cherry tomatoes
4 wholemeal chapatis, warmed, to serve
FOR THE CUCUMBER SALAD
½ cucumber, halved lengthways, deseeded and sliced
1 red onion, thinly sliced
handful chopped coriander leaves
juice 1 lemon
50g pack lamb's lettuce or pea shoots

1 Put 8 wooden skewers in a bowl of water to soak. Mix the yogurt and curry paste together in a bowl, then add the chicken (if you have time, leave to marinate for an hour or so). In a large bowl, toss together the cucumber, red onion, coriander and lemon juice. Chill until ready to serve.

2 Heat the grill to Medium. Shake off any excess marinade, then thread the chicken pieces and cherry tomatoes onto the pre-soaked skewers. Cook under the grill for 15–20 minutes, turning from time to time, until cooked through and nicely browned.

3 Stir the lettuce or pea shoots into the salad, then divide between 4 plates. Top each serving with 2 chicken tikka skewers and serve with the warm chapatis.

PER SERVING 214 kcals, carbs 8g, fat 4g, sat fat 1g, salt 0.61g

Chicken tikka masala

This takeaway favourite is freezer-friendly and quick to reheat, giving you the chance to get ahead and save money.

MAKES 10 SERVINGS • **PREP 15 MINS** • **COOK 45–50 MINS**
❄

4 tbsp vegetable oil
25g/1oz butter
4 onions, roughly chopped
6 tbsp chicken tikka masala curry paste (use shop-bought
    or make your own – see recipe below)
2 red peppers, deseeded and cut into chunks
8 skinless, boneless chicken breasts, cut into chunks
2 x 400g cans chopped tomatoes
4 tbsp tomato purée
2–3 tbsp mango chutney
150ml/¼ pint double cream
150ml/¼ pint natural yogurt
chopped coriander, to serve

1 Heat the oil and butter in a large casserole, then add the onions and a pinch of salt. Cook gently for 15–20 minutes until soft and golden. Add the paste and peppers, then cook for 5 minutes more to cook out the rawness of the spices.
2 Add the chicken and stir well to coat in the paste. Cook for 2 minutes, then tip in the tomatoes, purée and 200ml water. Cover with a lid and gently simmer for 15 minutes, stirring occasionally, until the chicken is cooked through.
3 Remove the lid, stir through the mango chutney, cream and yogurt, then gently warm through and season. (At this point some or all of the dish can be frozen for up to 1 month. Once defrosted, reheat very gently to avoid splitting the yogurt.) Scatter the curry with coriander leaves and serve with basmati rice and naan bread.

PER SERVING 345 kcals, carbs 13g, fat 19g, sat fat 8g, salt 1.04g

try this...

To make your own curry paste, whizz together 5 garlic cloves, 1 large piece fresh root ginger, roughly chopped, 1 red chilli, deseeded and roughly chopped, 2 tsp each ground cumin and coriander, 1 tsp each turmeric, paprika and garam masala, and the seeds from 4 cardamom pods. Add a little water or mild oil to bring the paste together. (Store in the fridge for up to 1 week or freeze for 1 month.)

Jerk chicken with beans

Served with mounds of fluffy rice, this makes a perfect family meal. It's great made with pork, too; just brown off sliced tenderloin then return to the pan when you add the beans.

SERVES 4 • **PREP 5 MINS** • **COOK 40 MINS**
❄

8 chicken drumsticks
4 tsp jerk seasoning
4 tsp olive oil
2 red onions, sliced
small bunch coriander, stalks finely chopped,
    leaves reserved
2 x 400g cans chopped tomatoes
400g can kidney beans, drained

1 Toss the chicken in 1 tsp jerk seasoning and a little salt and pepper. Heat half the oil in a large frying pan, quickly brown the chicken, then remove. Tip in the remaining oil, onions and coriander stalks, then soften for 5 minutes, stirring in the remaining jerk seasoning for the final minute.
2 Return the drumsticks to the pan, pour over the tomatoes, then bring to a simmer. Cover, then cook for 20 minutes. Remove the lid, stir in the beans, then cook for 10 minutes more. Scatter with the coriander leaves and serve with rice.

PER SERVING 438 kcals, carbs 23g, fat 19g, sat fat 5g, salt 1.68g

Fragrant duck with wild rice pilau

Make a smart Indian-inspired supper for two using storecupboard ingredients.

SERVES 2 • PREP 10 MINS, PLUS MARINATING COOK 20 MINS
❄️ **PILAU ONLY**

2 duck breasts, skin on
1½ tsp garam masala
1 tsp grated fresh root ginger
FOR THE PILAU
1 tbsp butter
1 tsp cumin seeds
100g/4oz mixed basmati and wild rice
300ml/½ pint chicken or vegetable stock
85g/3oz frozen peas
bunch spring onions, finely sliced
2 tbsp mango chutney, to serve

tip For a healthier alternative, you can make this with chicken breasts. Brown the chicken, skin-side down, for 5 minutes, then roast for 15 minutes until cooked through. Leave to rest before serving as above.

1 Score criss-crossed lines into the duck skin almost all the way down to the flesh, then rub in the garam masala and ginger. Chill for 30 minutes, if you have time.
2 Heat oven to 200C/180C fan/gas 6. Heat a heavy, non-stick pan, then gently fry the duck, skin-side down, for 10 minutes until the fat runs out. Pour off the excess fat halfway through. Transfer to a roasting tin and cook in the oven, skin-side up, for 10 minutes, then remove and set aside to rest.
3 While the duck is cooking, melt the butter in a pan. Add the cumin seeds, fry for 2–3 minutes, then stir in the rice for another few minutes. Pour over the stock, cover partly with a lid, then simmer for 10–12 minutes, adding the peas for the final 4 minutes. When the rice is cooked and all the liquid has been absorbed, fork through the spring onions and some seasoning to taste. Slice the duck and serve with the rice and a spoonful of chutney.

PER SERVING 894 kcals, carbs 47g, fat 57g, sat fat 17g, salt 1.37g

Caribbean chicken

 Try with the coconut rice and peas on page 215 – it's a classic combo, then serve the chicken on a platter with the rice and wedges of lime for everyone to dig in.

SERVES 4 EASILY DOUBLED • PREP 10 MINS, PLUS MARINATING • COOK 25 MINS
❄️

1 tbsp ground allspice
2 tsp ground cinnamon
4 spring onions, chopped
2 red chillies, seeded and chopped
½ tsp dried thyme
2 tsp light muscovado sugar
1 tbsp sunflower oil
4 skinless, boneless chicken breasts
2 limes
fresh coriander, to serve

1 Tip the spices, onions, chillies, thyme, sugar and oil into a food processor or blender and blend until fairly smooth. Add a little salt if you like. You could use a pestle and mortar, but it's harder work.
2 Spread the marinade evenly over the chicken in a shallow dish. Cover and leave in the fridge to marinate for at least 30 minutes.
3 Squeeze the juice of one of the limes, then sprinkle over the chicken. Heat a griddle pan or barbecue and cook the chicken slowly for 25–30 minutes, turning once. Scatter with coriander and serve with the remaining lime cut into wedges and plain rice or coconut rice and peas.

PER SERVING 207 kcals, carbs 7g, fat 5g, sat fat 1g, salt 0.2g

Easy sweet and sour chicken

 This homemade sweet and sour stir-fry is so much better than a takeaway version.

SERVES 4 ● PREP 10 MINS ● COOK 10 MINS

150ml/¼ pint tomato ketchup
3 tbsp malt vinegar
4 tbsp dark muscovado sugar
2 garlic cloves, crushed
1 tsp vegetable or sunflower oil
4 skinless, boneless chicken breasts, cut into chunks
1 small onion, roughly chopped
2 red peppers, deseeded and cut into chunks
227g can pineapple pieces in juice, drained
100g/4oz sugar snap peas, roughly sliced
handful salted, roasted cashew nuts (optional)

1 Mix the ketchup, vinegar, sugar and garlic in a bowl. Heat the oil in a wok or frying pan then add the chicken, onion and peppers. Stir-fry for 5 minutes until the chicken is turning golden and the veg are starting to soften.
2 Stir in the pineapple pieces and sugar snap peas, fry for another 3 minutes or until the chicken is completely cooked, then toss in the sauce. Heat through, then serve scattered with the cashew nuts.

PER SERVING 305 kcals, carbs 38g, fat 2g, sat fat none, salt 1.63g

Sticky lemon chicken

 With just four ingredients, this low-fat grill recipe couldn't be simpler.

SERVES 4 ● PREP 5 MINS ● COOK 15 MINS

a little vegetable or sunflower oil
4 boneless chicken breasts, skin on, about 140g/5oz each
1 large lemon
2 tsp fresh thyme leaves or a generous sprinkling of dried
1½ tbsp clear honey

1 Heat grill to High and lightly oil a shallow heatproof dish. Put the chicken in the dish, skin-side down, and season with salt and pepper. Grill for 5 minutes. While the chicken is grilling, cut four thin slices from the lemon.
2 Turn the chicken fillets over and put a slice of lemon on top of each one. Sprinkle over the thyme and a little more seasoning, then drizzle with the honey. Squeeze over the juice from the remaining lemon and spoon round 2 tbsp water. Return to the grill for 10 minutes more, until the chicken is golden and cooked all the way through. Serve the chicken and the sticky juices with rice or potatoes and a green vegetable – broccoli or leeks are good.

PER SERVING 193 kcals, carbs 6g, fat 4g, sat fat 1g, salt 0.83g

OPPOSITE Clockwise from top left Italian-style chicken burger (page 113); Cheat's chicken Kiev (page 113); Smoky maple duck salad (page 106); French-style chicken with peas and bacon (page 112); Chicken tikka skewers with cucumber salad (page 107); Parmesan spring chicken (page 114).

Rosemary chicken with tomato sauce

 Anchovies are often used in Italian meat recipes to add a deeply savoury edge. This is a perfect one-pot for the freezer and to serve with mash.

SERVES 4 ● PREP 5 MINS ● COOK 30 MINS
❄

1 tbsp olive oil
8 skinless, boneless chicken thighs
1 rosemary sprig, leaves finely chopped
1 red onion, finely sliced
3 garlic cloves, sliced
2 anchovy fillets, chopped
400g can chopped tomatoes
1 tbsp capers, drained
75ml/2½fl oz red wine (optional)

1 Heat half the oil in a non-stick pan, then brown the chicken all over. Add half the chopped rosemary, stir to coat, then set aside on a plate.
2 In the same pan, heat the rest of the oil, then gently cook the onion for about 5 minutes until soft. Add the garlic, anchovies and remaining rosemary, then fry for a few minutes more until fragrant.
3 Pour in the tomatoes and capers with the wine, if using, or 75ml water if not. Bring to the boil, then return the chicken pieces to the pan. Cover, then simmer for 20 minutes until the chicken is cooked through. Season and serve with a crisp green salad and crusty bread.

PER SERVING 275 kcals, carbs 5g, fat 9g, sat fat 3g, salt 1.09g

French-style chicken with peas and bacon

This creamy one-pot chicken dish is a great-value way of feeding the whole family.

SERVES 4 ● PREP 10 MINS ● COOK 30 MINS

6 rashers smoked streaky bacon, chopped
8 skinless, boneless chicken thighs
2 garlic cloves, thinly sliced
1 bunch spring onions, roughly chopped
300ml/½ pint hot chicken stock
250g/9oz frozen peas
1 Little Gem lettuce, roughly shredded
2 tbsp crème fraîche

1 In a large frying pan, dry-fry the bacon over a medium heat for 3 minutes until the fat is released and the bacon is golden. Transfer the bacon to a bowl, leaving the fat in the pan. Add the chicken and brown for 4 minutes on each side.
2 Push the chicken to one side of the pan and tip in the garlic and spring onions, cooking for about 30 seconds, just until the spring onion stalks are bright green. Pour in the stock, return the bacon to the pan, cover and simmer for 15 minutes.
3 Increase the heat under the pan. Tip the peas and lettuce into the sauce and cook for 4 minutes, covered, until the peas are tender and the lettuce has just wilted. Check that the chicken is cooked through. Stir in the crème fraîche just before serving.

PER SERVING 379 kcals, carbs 7g, fat 16g, sat fat 7g, salt 1.6g

tip Make the chicken dish healthier by using half the bacon, half-fat crème fraîche and skinless chicken breasts.

Italian-style chicken burgers

These are great served with the chunky oven chips on page 214.

SERVES 4 ● **PREP 10 MINS** ● **COOK 20 MINS**
❄ **CRUMBED CHICKEN, RAW**

2 skinless, boneless chicken breasts
2 tbsp olive oil
25g/1oz dried breadcrumbs
25g/1oz Parmesan, finely grated
125g ball mozzarella, sliced
4 burger or ciabatta buns, split and lightly toasted
salad leaves, sunblushed tomatoes and fresh basil pesto,
    to serve

1 Heat oven to 200C/180C fan/gas 6. Cut each chicken breast in half, lightly flatten using a rolling pin or heavy can, then rub all over with oil. Spread out the breadcrumbs and Parmesan on a plate, then dip the chicken in to coat.
2 Place the chicken on another baking sheet and cook for 10–12 minutes until just crisp and cooked through. Place a mozzarella slice on top and return to the oven until starting to melt. Pile the burgers onto buns with some salad leaves, tomatoes and a dollop of pesto.

PER SERVING 410 kcals, carbs 34g, fat 17.6g, sat fat 6.9g, salt 1.44g

Cheat's chicken Kiev

 Easy garlicky chicken that isn't dripping with butter.

SERVES 4 ● **PREP 15 MINS** ● **COOK 20–25 MINS**

6 garlic cloves, 2 peeled
small bunch flat-leaf parsley
4 tsp olive oil
85g/3oz fresh breadcrumbs
4 skinless, boneless chicken breasts
4 tbsp garlic and herb soft cheese

1 Heat oven to 200C/180C fan/gas 6. Whizz together the 2 peeled garlic cloves, parsley and 1 tsp of the oil in a food processor. Add the breadcrumbs and seasoning before pulsing briefly to mix. Tip onto a plate.
2 Cut a slit (roughly thumb-length) in the side of each chicken breast, at the plump end. Spoon a quarter of the soft cheese into each hole and press the edges together to seal. Rub 2 tsp oil over all the chicken breasts before pressing into the herby crumbs to coat.
3 Place the coated chicken in a shallow roasting tin. Scatter round the remaining unpeeled garlic cloves and drizzle with the rest of the oil. Bake for 20–25 minutes until the chicken is cooked and the crumbs are crisp and golden. Squeeze out the soft roasted garlic from the skins and serve with the chicken.

PER SERVING 327 kcals, carbs 18g, fat 12g, sat fat 5g, salt 0.78g

try this...

For a crunchy and creamy chicken pasta bake, make the breadcrumbs as above, leaving out the parsley and adding just 1 garlic clove. Cook 300g wholemeal pasta shapes. Thinly slice the chicken and fry in oil for 5 minutes. Add the soft cheese and 200ml double cream and bubble for 1 minute. Stir in the chopped parsley and drained pasta. Season, then tip into an ovenproof dish. Sprinkle with crumbs and grill for 3–4 minutes. Just add salad.

Parmesan spring chicken

 Parmesan sizzles around skinless chicken to make this a deliciously savoury yet low-fat dish.

SERVES 4 • PREP 10 MINS • COOK 10 MINS

1 egg white
5 tbsp finely grated Parmesan
4 skinless, boneless chicken breasts
400g/14oz new potatoes, cut into small cubes
140g/5oz frozen peas
good handful baby spinach leaves
1 tbsp white wine vinegar
2 tbsp olive oil

1 Heat grill to Medium and line the grill pan with foil. Beat the egg white on a plate with a little salt and pepper. Tip the Parmesan onto another plate. Dip the chicken first in egg white, then roll in the cheese. Grill the coated chicken for 10–12 minutes, turning once, until browned and crisp.
2 Boil the potatoes for 10 minutes, adding the peas for the final 3 minutes, then drain. Toss the vegetables with the spinach leaves, vinegar, oil and seasoning to taste. Divide between four warm plates, then serve with the chicken.

PER SERVING 339 kcals, carbs 20g, fat 11g, sat fat 3g, salt 0.53g

Chicken with herby mascarpone

Try this fast supper for a Friday night in. Serve with potatoes and green beans.

SERVES 2 EASILY DOUBLED • PREP 5 MINS COOK 20 MINS

3 tbsp mascarpone
1 tbsp finely chopped rosemary
1 garlic clove, crushed
2 boneless chicken breasts, skin on
4 slices prosciutto
splash olive oil
juice ½ lemon

1 Heat oven to 200C/180C fan/gas 6. Mix the mascarpone with the rosemary, garlic and seasoning. Place the chicken breasts on a board and lift, but don't detach, the skin. Put a spoonful of the mascarpone mix under the skin of each breast. Wrap 2 slices of prosciutto around each, as neatly and tightly as you can, to keep the filling enclosed.
2 Heat a non-stick frying pan, add the olive oil and quickly brown the chicken on both sides. Transfer to a roasting tin, then finish off in the oven for 15–20 minutes until just cooked through. Add the lemon juice to the roasting tin and stir over the heat, scraping off any crispy bits. Spoon the juices over the chicken and serve with potatoes and green beans.

PER SERVING 339 kcals, carbs 3g, fat 20g, sat fat 9g, salt 1.24g

tip You can use streaky bacon instead of the proscuitto, if you have some in the fridge. Stretch the rashers using a knife to make them a little thinner, then wrap them around the chicken.

Chicken, fennel and tomato ragú

 A nutritious, low-fat feast that provides a satisfying four of your five-a-day. The chicken is a good source of protein and selenium, while the fennel is rich in B vitamins.

SERVES 2 • PREP 5 MINS • COOK 30 MINS

1 large fennel bulb
1 tbsp olive oil
2 boneless skinless chicken breasts, cut into chunks
1 garlic clove, peeled and chopped
200g/7oz new potatoes, cut into chunks
400g can chopped tomatoes
150ml/¼ pint chicken or vegetable stock
3 roasted red peppers in brine, from a jar or deli counter, chopped
crusty bread, to serve

1 Trim the green tops from the fennel and reserve. Halve, then quarter the fennel, cut out the core, then cut lengthways into slices. Heat the oil in a pan, add the chicken and fry quickly until lightly coloured. Add the fennel and garlic, then stir briefly until the fennel is glistening.

2 Tip in the potatoes, tomatoes, stock and a little seasoning and bring to the boil. Cover and simmer for 20 minutes until the potatoes are tender. Stir in the peppers and heat through. Roughly chop the reserved fennel fronds and sprinkle them over the ragout. Serve with crusty bread to mop up the juices.

PER SERVING 351 kcals, carbs 28g, fat 9g, sat fat 1g, salt 1.43g

Summer-in-winter chicken

 Come winter-time this cheering little one-pot really does the trick.

SERVES 4 • PREP 5 MINS • COOK 20 MINS

1 tbsp olive oil
4 skinless, boneless chicken breasts
200g/7oz cherry tomatoes, halved
3 tbsp fresh basil pesto (see page 60 for a recipe)
3 tbsp crème fraîche (half-fat is fine)
small handful fresh basil (optional)

1 Heat the oil in a frying pan, preferably non-stick. Add the chicken and fry without moving it until it takes on a bit of colour. Turn the chicken and cook on the other side. Continue cooking for about 12–15 minutes until the chicken is cooked through. Season all over with a little salt and pepper.

2 Throw the tomatoes into the pan and stir them around for a couple of minutes until they start to soften. Reduce the heat and stir in the pesto and crème fraîche until it makes a sauce. Scatter with a few basil leaves, if you have them, then serve with rice and salad or mash and broccoli.

PER SERVING 262 kcals, carbs 2g, fat 12g, sat fat 5g, salt 0.37g

tip To make this into a vegetarian supper, fry the tomatoes in the oil, add the pesto and crème fraîche and serve over griddled halloumi slices or spoon over some spinach and ricotta-stuffed ravioli

Herbed turkey meatballs

 Turkey mince means these meatballs are low in fat, while the herbs and sauce ensure they're not lacking in flavour.

SERVES 5 • PREP 15 MINS, PLUS CHILLING COOK 15 MINS
❄

85g/3oz breadcrumbs
75ml/2½fl oz semi-skimmed milk
350g/12oz turkey mince
2 tsp dried oregano
small bunch flat-leaf parsley, chopped
2 tsp olive oil
680g bottle onion and garlic passata
4 tsp sugar
500g pack pasta, any shape

1 Tip the crumbs into a large bowl, then stir in the milk until the crumbs have absorbed the liquid. Add the mince, 1 tsp oregano and half the parsley, then season and mix with a fork. Use wet hands to shape into 30 meatballs. Chill the meatballs for up to 30 minutes, if you have time, as this will help them to hold together as they cook.

2 Heat the oil in a large non-stick pan, then brown the meatballs for 5 minutes, turning to cook all over. Pour in the passata, sugar, remaining oregano and most of the remaining parsley. Stir well, then simmer for 8–10 minutes until the meatballs are just cooked through.

3 Meanwhile, cook the pasta according to the pack instructions. Season the sauce, spoon the meatballs and sauce over the pasta, then sprinkle over any remaining parsley.

PER SERVING 260 kcals, carbs 33g, fat 4g, sat fat 1g, salt 1.45g

One-pan duck with Savoy cabbage

Duck breast is perfect for weeknight entertaining – it's easy to cook and readily available.

SERVES 4 • PREP 10 MINS • COOK 30 MINS

2 duck breasts, skin on
1 tsp black peppercorns, crushed
600g/1lb 5oz cooked new potatoes, thickly sliced
small bunch flat-leaf parsley, roughly chopped
1 garlic clove, finely chopped
6 rashers smoked streaky bacon, chopped
1 Savoy cabbage, trimmed, quartered, cored and finely sliced
1 tbsp balsamic vinegar
2 tbsp olive oil

1 Score criss-crossed lines into the duck skin almost all the way down to the flesh then season generously with the peppercorns and some salt. Cook the duck gently, skin side down in a non-stick sauté pan for 15 minutes to brown and release its fat, then flip over onto the flesh side for 5 minutes.

2 Remove the duck from the pan, then turn up the heat. Add the potatoes to the pan, fry until brown and crisp, then scatter over the parsley and garlic. Scoop out with a slotted spoon onto a plate, then season with salt.

3 Keep the pan on the heat. Fry the bacon until crisp, then add the cabbage. Cook for 1 minute, add a splash of water, then fry for 2 minutes, just until the cabbage is wilted. While the cabbage is cooking, whisk any juices from the duck with the vinegar and olive oil. To serve, carve the duck breast into slices. Fan out on plates, spoon a neat bundle of cabbage on one side, then pile a serving of potatoes on the other. Drizzle over the dressing and serve.

PER SERVING 504 kcals, carbs 33g, fat 31g, sat fat 8g, salt 1.16g

*OPPOSITE **Clockwise from top left** Pigeon and hedgerow salad (page 119); Buffalo wings with blue cheese dip (page 118); Chilli chicken one-pot (page 121); Herbed turkey meatballs; One-pan duck with Savoy cabbage; Chicken and mushroom puff pie (page 122).*

Avocado, chicken and bacon salad

 Everyone loves this combination – adding a little chopped tarragon pulls the whole dish together.

**SERVES 8–10 AS PART OF A BUFFET • PREP 20 MINS
COOK 10 MINS**

FOR THE DRESSING
1 tbsp sherry vinegar
1 tbsp sherry (optional)
4 tbsp olive oil
small bunch fresh tarragon, roughly chopped
FOR THE SALAD
6 rashers smoked streaky bacon
1 large or 2 small rotisserie chickens, about 1.8kg/4lb
    in total
2 large, ripe avocados
squeeze lemon juice
100g bag baby leaf spinach

1 Make the dressing by whisking together the sherry vinegar, sherry (if using), oil, tarragon and seasoning. Grill or dry-fry the bacon until crisp. Pull the chicken meat into bite-size pieces, discarding the skin and bones.
2 Just before serving, peel the avocados and slice into thick wedges. Toss in a little lemon juice to prevent them discolouring. Put the spinach in a large bowl and pile the chicken and avocados on top. Trickle over the dressing and toss together. Crumble the bacon over and serve.

PER SERVING 298 kcals, carbs 1g, fat 19g, sat fat 4g, salt 0.79g

Buffalo wings with blue cheese dip

Finger bowls and napkins are essential for these fiery American-style wings and their cooling dipping sauce.

SERVES 6 • PREP 30 MINS • COOK 30 MINS

4 tbsp butter
5 tbsp hot chilli sauce
1 tbsp white wine vinegar
900g–1kg (2lb–2lb 4oz) chicken wings
¼ tsp celery salt
plain flour, for dusting
sunflower oil, for frying
celery sticks, to serve
FOR THE BLUE CHEESE DIP
150ml/¼ pint buttermilk (or mild natural yogurt)
150ml/¼ pint soured cream
85g/3oz blue cheese, crumbled
1 garlic clove, crushed
¼ tsp sweet paprika

1 Slowly melt the butter, chilli sauce and vinegar in a medium-sized saucepan, then pour into a large bowl.
2 Mix all the ingredients for the blue cheese dip together with a pinch of salt. Cover and chill until needed.
3 Trim the end off each chicken wing, then cut each in half through the joint. Tip the wings into a bowl. Add the celery salt, seasoning and enough flour so they're all evenly coated.
4 Heat 4 tbsp oil in a large, deep frying pan and add the wings (do this in 2 batches if your pan isn't big enough). Fry them, stirring frequently, until they are cooked through and browned all over, about 10 minutes for each batch. Keep them warm in a low oven. As soon as they're all cooked, transfer them to the bowl of butter sauce and stir well. Repeat with the second batch. Serve the wings on a platter with any extra buttery sauce poured over and the blue cheese dip and celery sticks on the side.

PER SERVING 411 kcals, carbs 5g, fat 36g, sat fat 15g, salt 1.26g

Pigeon and hedgerow salad

Traditionally, berries served with game are cooked down to a rich sauce, but here they're
tossed into a light, seasonal salad for autumn.

SERVES 2 • PREP 10 MINS • COOK 10 MINS

2 pigeon breasts, skin removed
2 tbsp olive oil
FOR THE DRESSING
3 tbsp olive oil
2 tsp Dijon mustard
1 tbsp cider vinegar
1 bunch chives, half snipped, half finely chopped
FOR THE SALAD
handful shelled hazelnuts, roughly chopped
2 large handfuls mixed salad leaves
small handful parsley leaves
100g/4oz blackberries

1 Toss the pigeon in the olive oil and some cracked black pepper, then set aside until ready to cook. Make the dressing by mixing the oil, mustard and vinegar with the finely chopped chives, a little water and some seasoning then set aside.
2 Heat a dry frying pan, then toast the hazelnuts until golden and set aside. Place the pan back on the heat, then pan-fry the pigeon breasts for 2–3 minutes on each side until plump. Leave to rest in the pan for 5 minutes.
3 When the pigeon has rested, remove to a chopping board. Toss the salad ingredients together in a bowl with the snipped chives and a drizzle of dressing, then pile in the centre of 2 plates. Finely slice the pigeon breasts and arrange around the salads. Spoon over the rest of the dressing and serve.

PER SERVING 411 kcals, carbs 5g, fat 36g, sat fat 5g, salt 0.51g

Velvety duck liver parfait

A parfait always goes down well as a smart starter with plenty of toast, sliced gherkins
and chutney. Any leftovers are always a welcome lunch, spread over crusty bread.

SERVES 6 WITH LEFTOVERS • PREP 30 MINS, PLUS SETTING • COOK 15 MINS
❄

250g pack butter, diced and slightly softened
2 shallots, finely sliced
1 garlic clove, sliced
600g/1lb 7oz duck or chicken livers, or a mix of both, trimmed (see below)
splash each brandy and port
1 tbsp tomato purée
FOR THE TOPPING
100g/4oz butter
1 tbsp thyme leaves
1 tsp cracked black peppercorns
toast, gherkins and chutney, to serve

1 Heat 85g of the butter in a large frying pan, then gently soften the shallots and garlic for 3–4 minutes. Turn up the heat, add the livers, then fry until just browned. Add the brandy and port and boil down as quickly as possible – if the sauce catches light for an instant, all the better. Cool completely.
2 Season the livers generously, then tip the contents of the pan into a food processor with the tomato purée and remaining butter; blitz until smooth. Pass through a fine sieve into a bowl, taste for seasoning, then tip into a serving dish. Level the top then chill to set.
3 Make the topping by melting the butter and leaving it for a minute to settle and separate. Pour the yellow butter that has risen to the top into another bowl and discard the milky liquid. Leave the butter to cool slightly, then mix in the thyme and peppercorns. Pour over the parfait and set in the fridge. (Will keep for 2 days in the fridge.)

PER SERVING 535 kcals, carbs 2g, fat 50g, sat fat 31g, salt 1.11g

 Before cooking, rinse the livers in cold water. Pat dry and then, using a small sharp knife, cut away any sinews and discard.

Confit of duck

A classic, hugely popular recipe from France that never fails to impress. Serve with roast or sauté potatoes and dressed leaves.

SERVES 4 EASILY DOUBLED • PREP 20 MINS, PLUS SALTING COOK A STAGGERED 2½ HOURS
❄

handful coarse sea salt
4 garlic cloves, roughly chopped
4 bay leaves, roughly torn
handful thyme sprigs, roughly torn
4 duck legs, skin on
100ml/3½fl oz white wine

If you are preparing ahead, pack the duck legs tightly into a plastic container or jar at the end of Step 2, then pour over the fat – but not the liquid at the bottom of the pan. Cover and leave in the fridge for up to a month, or freeze for up to 3 months. The liquid you are left with makes a tasty gravy, which can be chilled or frozen until needed.

1 The day before cooking, scatter half the salt, half the garlic and herbs over the base of a small shallow dish. Lay the duck legs, skin-side up, on top, then scatter over the remaining salt, garlic and herbs (photo 1). Cover and chill overnight or up to 2 days ahead.

2 Pour the wine into a saucepan that will snugly fit the duck legs in a single layer (photo 2). Brush the salt off the duck and put it skin-side down in the wine. Cover, bring to the boil over a medium heat then cook as gently as possible for 2 hours, checking occasionally that the liquid is just barely simmering. After 2 hours the duck legs should be submerged in their own fat and the meat should be very tender when prodded (photo 3). Leave to cool.

3 To crisp up, heat oven to 220C/200C fan/gas 7. Remove the legs from the fat and place, skin-side down, in an ovenproof frying pan. Roast for 30–40 minutes, turning halfway, until brown and crisp (photo 4).

PER SERVING 636 kcals, carbs none, fat 57g, sat fat 16g, salt 2.83g

1 2 3 4

Italian chicken with ham, basil and beans

Another great one-pot that makes the best of great-value chicken thighs. Try this at the end of summer,
when tomatoes are at their most flavourful.

SERVES 4 • PREP 15 MINS • COOK 1 HOUR 15 MINS

8 skinless chicken thighs, bone in
large bunch basil
8 slices prosciutto or other dry-cured ham
2 tbsp olive oil
2 whole heads garlic, halved across the middle
800g/1lb 12oz mix of yellow and red tomatoes, halved or
 quartered if large
175ml/6oz dry white wine (a crisp Italian would be ideal)
400g can cannellini or other white beans, rinsed and
 drained

1 Season the chicken thighs. Pinch off 8 sprigs basil and lay one on top of each chicken thigh. Wrap each thigh in a piece of ham, with the ends tucked underneath.
2 Heat oven to 160C/140C fan/gas 3. Heat the oil in a large roasting tin. Add the chicken and fry for 4 minutes each side or until the ham is just crisped and the chicken lightly golden.
3 Add the tomatoes, garlic, half the remaining basil leaves and the wine. Cover with foil then bake for 40 minutes.
4 Take out of the oven; turn it up to 220C/200C fan/gas 7. Remove the foil then stir the beans into the tomatoey juices. Return to the oven, uncovered, for 30 minutes until the tomatoes, chicken and garlic are starting to crisp and chicken is very tender. Just before serving, tear the remaining basil roughly then scatter over the pan.

PER SERVING 455 kcals, carbs 22g, fat 16g, sat fat 4g, salt 1.79g

Chilli chicken one-pot

This tasty chicken one-pot with chorizo and beans reheats perfectly – all it needs
is garlic bread and a big salad.

SERVES 8 • PREP 20 MINS • COOK 1 HOUR 5 MINS
❄

2 large onions, halved and sliced
2 tbsp olive oil
250g/9oz chorizo, skinned and thickly sliced
4 red peppers, deseeded and cut into large chunks
2 x 400g cans chopped tomatoes
2 chicken stock cubes, crumbled
½–1 tsp dried chilli flakes
2 tsp dried oregano
16 large skinless, boneless chicken thighs
3 x 400g cans red kidney beans, drained
TO SERVE
small bunch coriander, chopped
2–3 avocados, stoned and sliced
good squeeze lime juice

1 Heat oven to 180C/160C fan/gas 4. Fry the onions in the oil for 5 minutes until they become soft and start to colour. Add the chorizo and fry for a few minutes more. Stir in the peppers, then pour in the tomatoes, followed by a can of water, the stock cubes, chilli and oregano.
2 Nestle the chicken into the sauce, pushing them under the liquid. Bring to a simmer, cover, then cook in the oven for 40 minutes. Add the beans, stir, then cook for 20 minutes more. (You can make this up to 2 days ahead and keep chilled.) Stir in most of the coriander and toss the rest with the avocados, lime and a little salt, then pile this on top of the chilli.

PER SERVING 501 kcals, carbs 30g, fat 18g, sat fat 6g, salt 3.16g

try this...

For a tasty side, beat 250g soft salted butter with an electric hand whisk until creamy, then beat in 6 crushed garlic cloves and 2 tsp dried oregano. Thickly slice 2 long French sticks on the diagonal, then sandwich the slices back together with the garlic butter to re-form the loaf. Wrap each loaf in foil. Bake alongside the chicken for 30 minutes or until the bread is crisp and the butter has melted.

Pan-fried chicken in mushroom sauce

A creamy, comforting French dish for easy autumn entertaining. Make sure you've plenty of crusty bread to mop up the sauce.

SERVES 6 • PREP 10 MINS • COOK 1 HOUR 10 MINS
❄

2 tbsp sunflower oil
6 large chicken legs, halved at the joint to give 6 thighs
    and 6 drumsticks
700ml/1¼ pints chicken stock
50g/2oz butter
1 onion, finely diced
400g/14oz mixed wild mushrooms
300ml/½ pint dry white wine
300ml/½ pint double cream

1 Heat the oil in a large non-stick frying pan. Fry the chicken in two batches, 8–10 minutes each time, then lift into a casserole dish.

2 Pour over enough stock just to cover the chicken. Bring to the boil, then part-cover the pan and simmer for 30 minutes or until the chicken is tender.

3 Meanwhile, drain the oil from the frying pan then add the butter and soften the onion for 5 minutes. Turn up the heat, add the mushrooms, then fry for 3 minutes until they soften. Pour over the wine, turn up the heat then boil rapidly for 6–8 minutes until reduced by two-thirds.

4 Once the chicken is cooked, strain the stock into the pan with the onion, mushrooms and white wine, bring back to the boil and reduce again by two- thirds until it is thick and syrupy. Pour in the cream, bring it to the boil and season if you want. Heat the chicken through in the sauce for 2–3 minutes then turn off the heat and leave to rest for a few minutes before serving.

PER SERVING 600 kcals, carbs 3g, fat 40g, sat fat 22g, salt 0.8g

Chicken and mushroom puff pie

A proper crowd-pleasing pie, easily made ahead ready for when the family are all together. Serve with creamy mashed potatoes.

**SERVES 4–6 EASILY DOUBLED • PREP 15 MINS
COOK 1 HOUR**
❄ **(FILLING ONLY, OR WHOLE PIE IF USING FRESH PASTRY)**

1 tbsp vegetable oil
8 skinless, boneless chicken thighs
8 rashers smoked streaky bacon, cut into large pieces
1 onion, halved and sliced
250g pack baby button mushrooms
handful thyme sprigs
2 tbsp plain flour
400ml/14fl oz chicken stock
200ml/7fl oz milk
500g pack fresh puff pastry, or frozen and defrosted
1 egg, beaten

1 Heat the oil in a large, non-stick frying pan. Season the chicken, then fry in two batches for 5–8 minutes until browned. Set aside. Fry the bacon for 5 minutes until crisp. Add the onion, mushrooms and thyme, then cook on high for 3 minutes until starting to colour.

2 Tip in the flour and stir for 1 minute. Off the heat, slowly stir in the stock and milk, then add the chicken. Simmer for 30 minutes. Spoon into a large pie dish (about 20 x 30cm) with a lip and leave to cool.

3 Heat oven to 220C/200C fan/gas 7. On a floured surface, roll the pastry to the thickness of two £1 coins. Cut a long strip as wide as the rim of the pie dish and, using a little of the egg, fix to the edge of the pie dish. Brush with egg, then cover the pie with the pastry. Gently press the edges with your fingers and trim with a sharp knife. Brush with egg to glaze. (Can now be chilled for up to 2 days.) Bake for 30 minutes or until the pastry has risen and is dark golden brown.

PER SERVING 855 kcals, carbs 57g, fat 47g, sat fat 17g, salt 2.73g

Easy chicken tagine

 Try this fragrant North African speciality with the Harissa couscous on page 215.

SERVES 4 • PREP 10 MINS • COOK 40 MINS

2 tbsp olive oil
8 skinless, boneless chicken thighs, halved if large
1 onion, chopped
2 tsp grated fresh root ginger
pinch saffron or turmeric
1 tbsp honey
400g/14oz carrots, cut into sticks
small bunch parsley, roughly chopped
lemon wedges, to serve

1 Heat the oil in a large wide pan with a lid, add the chicken, then fry quickly until lightly coloured. Add the onion and ginger, then fry for a further 2 minutes. Add 150ml water, the saffron, honey and carrots, season, then stir well.

2 Bring the tagine to the boil, cover tightly, then simmer for 30 minutes until the chicken is tender. Uncover and increase the heat for about 5 minutes to reduce the sauce a little. Sprinkle with parsley and serve with lemon wedges for squeezing over.

PER SERVING 304 kcals, carbs 14g, fat 11g, sat fat 3g, salt 0.48g

Classic coq au vin

A proper coq au vin can't be rushed. Soak up the rich, intense red-wine sauce with boiled potatoes or pasta.

SERVES 6 • PREP 1 HOUR, PLUS MARINATING COOK ABOUT 1 HOUR 30 MINS

2.25kg/5lb chicken pieces
175g/6oz chopped smoked bacon or lardons
500ml/16fl oz chicken stock, plus more if needed
2 shallots, chopped
2 garlic cloves, chopped
bouquet garni (tied sprigs of bay leaves, thyme
   and parsley)
50g/2oz butter
18–20 baby onions or small shallots, peeled
250g/8oz button mushrooms, trimmed and quartered
1 tbsp chopped parsley
25g/1oz plain flour
FOR THE MARINADE
1 onion, sliced
1 carrot, sliced
2 stalks celery, sliced
1 garlic clove
1 tsp black peppercorns
750ml bottle red wine
3 tbsp olive oil

1 Combine all the marinade ingredients, except the oil, in a saucepan and simmer for 5 minutes. Cool completely then pour over the chicken in a deep, non-metallic bowl. Drizzle with 2 tbsp oil. Cover and chill for 1–3 days, turning the pieces from time to time.

2 Pat the chicken dry with kitchen paper. Strain and reserve the liquid, reserving the vegetables separately. Heat the remaining oil in a casserole and fry the bacon until golden. Scoop out then fry the chicken in batches over a medium heat for at least 10 minutes until browned all over.

3 Add the reserved vegetables and cook for 5–7 minutes. Pour in the marinade liquid. Boil, then simmer for 5 minutes. Add the stock, shallots, garlic, bouquet garni, seasoning and chicken. Cover and simmer until tender for 45–60 minutes.

4 Melt 25g of the butter in a pan and brown the baby onions for a few minutes. Remove, then brown the mushrooms for 3–5 minutes. Set aside. Mash together the remaining butter and flour until smooth, to make a beurre manié.

5 When cooked, remove the chicken. Strain the sauce and discard the vegetables. Bring the sauce to a simmer and whisk in the beurre manié a little at a time. Add the baby onions, simmer for 5–8 minutes, until almost tender. Add the bacon, mushrooms and chicken and simmer for 5 minutes. Season to taste then serve scattered with parsley.

PER SERVING (for 6) 764 kcals, carbs 9.3g, fat 49g, sat fat 16, salt 1.85g

Ginger chicken

Unlike some curries made from scratch, this is simple to put together but still tastes authentic.

SERVES 6 • PREP 20 MINS, PLUS MARINATING COOK 30 MINS
❄

1kg/2lb 4oz skinless, boneless chicken thighs, cut into large chunks
1 thumb-size piece fresh ginger, peeled and very finely chopped
4 garlic cloves, finely chopped
1 tsp chilli powder
juice 1 lime
2 tbsp sunflower oil
small bunch coriander, chopped
2 medium onions
1 tsp ground turmeric
400ml can reduced-fat coconut milk
1 fresh red chilli, seeded and sliced
1 chicken stock cube, crumbled

1 Put the chicken in a bowl with the ginger, garlic, chilli powder, lime juice, 1 tbsp of the oil and half the coriander. Stir well, then cover and leave in the fridge to marinate until ready to cook. For the best flavour, do this in the morning or, better still, the night before.
2 Peel and quarter the onions, then very finely chop them in a food processor; for this curry you want the onion really fine. Heat the remaining oil in a wok or large frying pan, then add the onion and stir-fry for about 8 minutes until soft. Stir in the turmeric and cook for 1 minute more, stirring well.
3 Tip in the chicken mixture with the marinade and cook over a high heat until the chicken changes colour. Pour in the coconut milk, add the chilli and stock cube, then cover and simmer for 20 minutes until the chicken is tender. Stir in the remaining coriander, then serve with pilau rice, a bowl of mango chutney and some poppadoms or naan bread.

PER SERVING 310 kcals, carbs 6g, fat 16g, sat fat 8g, salt 1.29g

French bean and duck Thai curry

Duck makes a more unusual and luxurious alternative to chicken in this slow-cooked curry.

PREP 20 MINS • COOK 1 HOUR 45 MINS • SERVES 4
❄ **BEFORE ADDING BEANS**

3–4 duck breasts, skin on, about 700g/1lb 9oz in total
6 tbsp Thai green curry paste
1 tbsp light brown sugar
400ml can coconut milk
2 tbsp fish sauce
juice 2 limes
6 kaffir lime leaves, 3 left whole and 3 finely shredded
200g/7oz French beans, trimmed
2 handfuls beansprouts
handful coriander leaves
1 red chilli, deseeded and sliced

1 Place a deep frying pan over a low heat and add the duck breasts, skin-side down. Slowly fry until the skin is golden and there's a pool of fat in the bottom of the pan; about 20 minutes. Flip onto the other side for 1 minute, then remove.
2 Pour all but 2 tbsp of the fat from the pan. Fry the curry paste and sugar for 1–2 minutes then tip in the coconut milk, a can of water, fish sauce, half the lime juice and the whole lime leaves. Simmer, then slice the duck breasts and tip into the curry. Cover the pan, then cook on the lowest heat for 1 hour.
3 Add the beans then simmer, covered, for 10 minutes. Taste and add more lime juice, fish sauce or sugar to season. Stir in the beansprouts, cook for 1 minute more, then serve topped with coriander, shredded lime leaves and sliced chilli.

PER SERVING 638 kcals, carbs 11g, fat 57g, sat fat 26g, salt 2.32g

OPPOSITE French bean and duck Thai curry

Massaman curry roast chicken

This full-flavoured chicken would make a great one-pan alternative to your usual weekend roast. Massaman curry paste is mild, so it's perfect for all the family.

SERVES 4 • PREP 15 MINS • COOK 1½ HOURS

1 whole chicken, about 1.8kg/4lb
2 thumb-size pieces root ginger, one roughly chopped, one grated
1 stick lemongrass, bashed with a rolling pin
1 lime, cut into quarters
70g pack Massaman curry paste
1 tsp olive oil
450g/1lb baby new potatoes, any larger ones halved
400ml can coconut milk
1 tsp brown sugar, any type
200g/7oz green beans, trimmed
1 tsp fish sauce
2 tbsp roasted unsalted peanuts, crushed

1 Heat oven to 200C/180C fan/gas 6. Put the chicken into a medium roasting tin. Put the ginger chunks, the lemongrass and half the lime into the cavity. Tie the legs together with string. Mix 1 tsp curry paste with the oil, rub all over the chicken, then season.
2 Cover loosely with foil, then roast for 35 minutes. Uncover, add the potatoes and stir them around in any juices. Roast for 40 minutes more or until the chicken is cooked through and golden and the potatoes tender.
3 Rest the chicken, loosely covered. Meanwhile, add the remaining curry paste and grated ginger to the pan and fry for 2 minutes until fragrant. Stir in the coconut milk and sugar; boil for 5 minutes or until slightly thickened.
4 Tip in the beans, simmer for 4 minutes (or until tender) then splash in the fish sauce, resting juices and a squeeze of remaining lime, to taste. Scatter with peanuts to serve.

PER SERVING 895 kcals, carbs 25g, fat 62g, sat fat 27g, salt 1.75g

Mustard chicken with winter vegetables

This is a great way to make a whole chicken go further. It takes some time, but it is well worth it, as you'll get every single bit of flavour from the bird.

SERVES 4–6 • PREP 10 MINS • COOK 1½ HOURS
❄

1 whole chicken, about 1.8kg/4lb
2 onions
6 celery sticks
6 carrots
2 bay leaves
2 thyme sprigs
1 tsp black peppercorns
50g/2oz butter
100g/4oz smoked lardons
3 small turnips, peeled and cut into wedges
1 tbsp plain flour
2 tbsp wholegrain mustard
3 rounded tbsp crème fraîche
small bunch flat-leaf parsley, chopped

1 Put the chicken in a deep casserole. Halve 1 onion, 1 celery stick and 1 carrot. Add to the pot with the herbs, peppercorns and some salt. Add water to come halfway up the chicken, bring to the boil, then cover and simmer for 1½ hours. Cool slightly, remove the chicken, then strain the stock into a bowl.
2 As it cooks, chop the remaining onion, and slice the celery and carrots. Heat the butter in the pan, add the onion and lardons and fry for 5 minutes. Add the remaining veg and fry for 2 minutes. Stir in the flour, cook for 1 minute then stir in 900ml stock (make it up with water if you need to). Simmer, covered, for 20–25 minutes until the vegetables are tender.
3 When cool enough to handle, strip the meat from the chicken bones and tear into pieces. Add the chicken with the mustard and crème fraîche and simmer, stirring gently. Season and sprinkle with parsley.

PER SERVING 920 kcals, carbs 20g, fat 62g, sat fat 23g, salt 3.06g

Foolproof slow-roast chicken

Slow roasting is a great way to keep a chicken moist all the way through. Adding the potatoes to the roasting tin infuses them with plenty of flavour, too.

SERVES 4 • PREP 15 MINS • COOK 2 HOURS 20 MINS

butter, for greasing
1 whole chicken, about 1.6kg/3lb 8oz
1kg/2lb 4oz potatoes, halved or quartered if large
2 whole garlic heads, halved through the middle
100ml/3½fl oz white wine
100ml/3½fl oz chicken stock
2 stems rosemary, broken into sprigs
6 bay leaves
1 lemon, cut into wedges

1 Heat oven to 160C/140C fan/gas 3. Brush a large roasting tin all over with butter and smear some over the skin of the chicken.
2 Place the chicken in the tin and arrange the potatoes around it. Put the halved garlic heads in the tin, pour over the white wine and stock, then cover with foil and place in the oven. Cook for 1 hour then remove the foil and give the potatoes a shake. Add the herbs and lemon wedges, then cook, uncovered, for 50 minutes.
3 Turn the heat up to 220C/200C fan/gas 7. Roast for 30 minutes more, then remove the chicken and potatoes from the pan. Cover the chicken loosely with foil and leave to rest on a plate for at least 10 minutes before carving. Keep the potatoes warm. Serve with any pan juices.

PER SERVING 634 kcals, carbs 56g, fat 27g, sat fat 9g, salt 1.76g

Roast duck legs with red wine sauce

Duck legs love a long, slow roasting so that the flesh falls off the bones. At the same time, the juices build the basis of a tasty gravy.

SERVES 4 • PREP 10 MINS • COOK 1 HOUR 10 MINS

4 duck legs
bunch rosemary sprigs
4 fat garlic cloves
½ tsp five-spice powder
½ bottle red wine
2 tbsp redcurrant or quince jelly

1 Heat oven to 190C/170C fan/gas 5. Put the duck legs in one layer in a roasting tin on a bed of rosemary sprigs and garlic cloves. Sprinkle with salt and five-spice powder. Roast for 1 hour.
2 Bring the wine and jelly to a gentle simmer in a pan, stirring to dissolve the jelly, then continue to simmer for 5 minutes.
3 When the duck has been cooking for an hour, remove from the oven and spoon off almost all the fat (save it for roast potatoes), then pour the wine mixture around the duck and return it to the oven for 10–15 minutes to finish cooking and reduce the sauce. Serve with roast or new potatoes and a green vegetable.

PER SERVING 473 kcals, carbs 7g, fat 20g, sat fat 6g, salt 0.51g

Classic roast chicken and gravy

A family feast flavoured with traditional herbs to guarantee empty plates all round.

**SERVES 4 ● PREP 10 MINS, PLUS RESTING
COOK 1½ HOURS**

1 onion, roughly chopped
2 carrots, roughly chopped
1 whole chicken, about 1.6kg/3lb 8oz
1 lemon, halved
small bunch thyme (optional)
25g/1oz butter, softened
FOR THE GRAVY
1 tbsp plain flour
250ml/9fl oz chicken stock

1 Heat oven to 190C/170C fan/gas 5. Scatter the vegetables over the base of a roasting tin that fits the chicken, but doesn't swamp it. Season the cavity of the chicken liberally, then stuff with the lemon halves and thyme, if using. Sit the chicken on the vegetables, smother all over with the butter, then season the skin. Roast for 1 hour 20 minutes until golden and cooked. To check, pierce the thigh with a skewer and the juices should run clear.
2 Using a pair of tongs, lift the chicken to a dish or board to rest for 15–20 minutes. As you lift the dish, let any juices from the chicken pour out of the cavity into the roasting tin.
3 While it rests, make the gravy. Place the roasting tin over a low flame, then stir in the flour and sizzle to a light brown, sandy paste. Gradually pour in the stock, stirring, until you have a thickened sauce. Simmer for 2 minutes. Strain, if you like, then season to taste. When you carve the bird, add any extra resting juices to the gravy.

PER SERVING 567 kcals, carbs 4g, fat 40g, sat fat 13g, salt 0.84g

Roast poussin with oregano, orange and sherry

Try to pick smallish poussin as the larger ones can be a bit much to get through.
The orange and sherry make terrific pan juices to drizzle over the birds for serving.

**SERVES 4 EASILY DOUBLED ● PREP 5 MINS
COOK 35–40 MINS**

4 poussin
2 tbsp olive oil
2 tsp dried oregano
2 oranges
4 tbsp medium or dry sherry

1 Heat oven to 190C/170C fan/gas 5. Put the poussin in a roasting tin, drizzle with the oil, sprinkle over the oregano and season with some salt and pepper.
2 Meanwhile, finely grate the zest from one of the oranges, and squeeze the juice from both. Sprinkle over the birds with the sherry. Return to the oven and roast for a further 20–25 minutes.

PER SERVING 549 kcals, carbs 4g, fat 38g, sat fat 10g, salt 0.67g

OPPOSITE Clockwise from top left Roast duck legs with red wine sauce (page 127); Classic roast chicken and gravy; Ginger chicken (page 125); Partridge with wine and cinnamon (page 131); Roast pheasant with ricotta and Parma ham (page 131); Crispy duck and baked apples (page 130).

Guinea fowl with roast chestnuts

A rustic autumnal roast that's just as easily made with a chicken, if you like.

SERVES 4 EASILY DOUBLED • PREP 25 MINS
COOK 1½ HOURS

1 whole guinea fowl, about 1.3kg/3lb
1 lemon
2 bay leaves
several thyme sprigs
3 tbsp olive oil
500g/1lb 2oz potatoes, unpeeled, cut into chunks
3 garlic cloves, unpeeled and bruised
200g/7oz chestnut mushrooms, halved if large
200g/7oz vacuum-packed chestnuts
FOR THE SAUCE
150ml/¼ pint white wine
150ml/¼ pint chicken stock
1 tbsp bramble or redcurrant jelly

1 Heat oven to 190C/170C fan/gas 5. Season the guinea fowl inside and out, halve the lemon, then put inside the bird with the bay leaves and 2 of the thyme sprigs. Set in a roasting tin, drizzle with a little oil, then roast for 15 minutes.
2 Meanwhile, strip the remaining thyme leaves from their stalks. Mix the potatoes, thyme, garlic and remaining oil, then season. Put the potatoes around the bird, then return to the oven. After 45 minutes, stir the mushrooms into the potatoes along with the chestnuts. Roast for a further 15 minutes until the mushrooms are cooked. Spoon the vegetables onto a warm platter. Nestle the cooked bird back among the veg. Keep warm while you prepare the sauce.
3 Boil the pan juices on the hob, add the wine, stock and jelly, then bring to the boil, stirring to dissolve the jelly. Boil hard until the sauce is slightly thickened. Taste and add more seasoning if necessary, then pour into a jug and pass round for everyone to help themselves.

PER SERVING 633 kcals, carbs 45g, fat 24g, sat fat 6g, salt 0.56g

Crispy duck and baked apples

Don't be alarmed by the cooking time – it's mostly walk-away time, and essential for a delicious crisp-skinned result.

SERVES 4 • PREP 10 MINS • COOK 4 HOURS

1 large duck, weighing about 1.5kg/3lb 5oz
4 eating apples

1 Heat oven to 120C/100C fan/gas ½. Pull any excess fat from the duck's cavity and use a roasting fork or skewer to lightly prick the skin of the bird all over. Rub the duck generously inside and out with flaky sea salt, then lay it on a rack over a roasting tin, breast-down. Roast for 3 hours, pricking every now and then. While the duck is cooking, score a line gently around the middle of each apple and set aside (this stops them exploding when they cook).
2 After 3 hours, remove the duck from the oven and raise the heat to 180C/160C fan/gas 4. Sit the duck on a plate and carefully pour away most of the fat from the tin. Return the duck to the rack, right way up, and continue to roast for 30 minutes. Put the apples around the side of the duck and roast for a final 30 minutes. By now you should have the crispiest duck and apples on the verge of collapse. Leave the duck to rest for 10 minutes, then carve and serve with the apples.

PER SERVING 612 kcals, carbs 15g, fat 49g, sat fat 13g, salt 1.25g

Partridge with wine and cinnamon

A sauce of wine, honey and cinnamon make a very good balance for the gamey flavour of partridge. You could also try this with quail.

SERVES 2 • PREP 15 MINS • COOK 40 MINS

2 tbsp olive oil, plus extra for drizzling
2 oven-ready partridges
3 garlic cloves, sliced
100ml/3½fl oz white wine
2 tsp tomato purée
1 tbsp honey
1 tbsp concentrated chicken stock
good handful Kalamata olives
1 cinnamon stick, halved
200g/7oz cherry tomatoes
400g can borlotti beans in water, drained
handful flat-leaf parsley, roughly chopped, plus extra
    for sprinkling
baguette slices, toasted, rubbed with garlic and drizzled
    with olive oil, to serve

1 Heat the oil in a large, deep frying pan and quickly brown the partridges all over, then remove. Add the garlic and fry until softened. Pour in the wine, bubble over a high heat, then add the tomato purée, honey, stock, olives, cinnamon and seasoning, plus 150ml water. Return the birds to the pan, then cover and simmer over a low heat for 20 minutes.
2 Stir in the rest of the ingredients, plus a splash of water if the pan looks dry. Cover and simmer for 20 minutes until tender. Sprinkle with parsley. Serve with the toasts.

PER SERVING 667 kcals, carbs 34g, fat 28g, sat fat 5g, salt 0.71g

Roast pheasant with ricotta and Parma ham

Pheasant is often roasted with bacon as it helps to keep the breast meat moist. Here we've used Parma ham, which crisps up beautifully in the oven.

SERVES 6 • PREP 20 MINS • COOK 1 HOUR

90g pack Parma ham
140g/5oz ricotta
1 tbsp thyme leaves, plus some sprigs
3 tbsp freshly grated Parmesan
2 oven-ready pheasant
150ml/¼ pint extra dry vermouth
olive oil, for drizzling

1 Heat oven to 220C/200C fan/gas 7. Separate the layers of Parma ham, chop 2 of the slices then mix with the thyme, Parmesan and some seasoning.
2 Carefully ease the skin away from the breast meat of each pheasant and use half the stuffing per bird, pressing it into the contours of the breasts through the skin. This protects the meat from the heat and will stop it drying out. Poke some sprigs of thyme into the body cavity to add flavour.
3 Put the pheasants in a roasting tin and top each one with the remaining ham. Season with pepper, then pour over the vermouth and drizzle with oil.
4 Roast for 20 minutes, then turn down the heat to 180C/160C fan/gas 4 and cook for 40 minutes more, basting every now and then with the pan juices until the legs are no longer pink. Cover with foil and a tea towel and leave to stand for 10 minutes before carving.

PER SERVING 336 kcals, carbs 2g, fat 16g, sat fat 6g, salt 1.13g

Meat

Roast it, grill it, fry it, slow-cook it – as meat is often the main ingredient around which a meal hangs, it's quality has to be good. While chops, steaks, mince and sausages are handy for quick or family cooking, whole joints of good-quality meat are the crowning glory of a good roast or celebration dinner. And the less popular cuts are great value and have wonderful flavour too. All you need is the know-how to cook them.

BUYING MEAT

Always buy meat from a source that you trust – a good supermarket, local butcher, farmers' market or farm shop, or online mail-order company. Of those five sources, the last four will usually be able to tell you the most about the meat – where it comes from, how it was reared and slaughtered, as well as if it was hung, and for how long. All of these elements will have an impact on the meat's flavour and tenderness.

STORING RAW AND COOKED MEAT

Unless meat is vacuum-packed and you intend to keep it for a long time, or if your meat is going to be frozen, unwrap all meat and put it onto a plate or into a bowl, cover with clingfilm and keep it at the bottom of the fridge. Keep raw meat away from cooked foods or anything that will be eaten raw. Meat will keep in this way for between 2–4 days, depending on the cut.

COOKING TECHNIQUES

All meat should be allowed to come up to room temperature, or at least not be fridge cold, before cooking. This will ensure the meat cooks evenly.

Griddling Look for a heavy-based, cast-iron pan with even, deep ridges. Heat the pan on a hob until you can feel a good heat rising. Don't add oil to the pan as it will sit in the grooves and burn. Instead, brush the meat with oil. To ensure it doesn't stick to the pan, leave the meat for at least 2 minutes so that it seals before prodding or pushing it.

Frying To fry meat, add a little oil or clarified butter to a hot but not smoking heavy pan. The pan should give plenty of room – too crowded and the meat will sweat. It's a waste to fry with expensive extra virgin olive oil because the cooking process will destroy its flavour. It also has a lower 'smoking point' so you may end up with a smokey kitchen.

Grilling A cool grill can result in overcooked meat, so make sure it is properly preheated. Meat should be trimmed before cooking or the fat will spit. Don't prick sausages before grilling as this causes the skins to split.

OPPOSITE Roast lamb with rosemary and garlic (page 153)

Braising involves cooking meat in liquid, at a low-to-moderate temperature in a covered pan until meltingly tender. Stews and casseroles are braises. Sometimes the meat is browned before adding the liquid, but not always. **Slow-roasting** is a brilliant technique for stress-free cooking. Ideal for pork belly, lamb shoulder and whole ducks, it allows tough muscle fibres to cook to tenderness, for excess fat to melt away and for skin to remain crisp.

Choose the best cuts for roasting
On or off the bone is a matter of preference. Meat cooked on the bone has more flavour, but a boned, rolled joint is much easier to carve and great for stuffing. A covering of fat will baste the meat as it cooks.

Preparing a joint
If your joint is off the bone, you'll need to tie it together so the meat cooks evenly and is easy to carve. Simply loop some thick string around one end of the joint, tuck the end under twice and tie into a knot. Keep tying loops along the joint so the meat looks tidy and will not lose its shape and fall apart when cooking. Always let the meat come to room temperature before roasting.

How to cook
There are specific oven temperatures and timings within the roast recipes in this chapter. A general roasting method is to start large joints off at 230C/210 fan/gas 8 for 20 mins (or sear small joints all over in a pan with a little fat). Turn oven to 190C/170C fan/gas 5 then calculate 15 mins cooking per 450g/lb for rare, 20 mins for medium rare, 25 for medium and 30 mins for well done. Pork should always be cooked to well done.

Is it ready?
It's what everyone worries about when cooking a roast, but there are a couple of easy ways to check:
1 Use a meat thermometer For beef and lamb, look for about 50C for rare, 55C medium rare, 60C medium and 70C well done. Insert into the thickest part of the joint (avoiding any bones). As the meat rests, its temperature will continue to rise by 5–10 degrees, so it's best to take the meat out of the oven 5–10C before it reaches the required temperature.
2 Insert a metal skewer A cool skewer means the meat is rare, warm will give you a medium result, while hot is well done.

Finishing touches
Leave the joint to rest on a platter so the juices get a chance to settle and run back into the meat. Cover with foil to stop all the heat escaping. Leave for 10 mins for a small joint, 20–30 mins for larger ones.

Resting time
To make sure you get the perfect juicy roast, leave the joint to rest on a platter so the juices get a chance to settle and run back into the meat. Cover with foil to stop all the heat escaping. Leave for 10 minutes for a small joint, 20–30 minutes for larger ones.

BEEF
Be it mince for burgers, a whole rib for a roast or oxtail for a stew, beef is a good source of high-quality protein, iron and B vitamins. But that doesn't mean to say all beef is equal.

In order to be tender and full-flavoured, beef needs to be 'hung'. This can either mean hanging the meat in a chilled environment, or vacuum packing it then keeping it for anything from 10 days to six weeks. During this time enzymes within the meat makes the muscle fibres more tender. The longer the beef has been hung, the better the flavour and texture and the higher the price of it. Dry-aged beef is deemed to be the very best.

When choosing any cut of beef, look for firm, fine-grained meat; it should be moist, rather than dry or slimy, and with a light marbling of fat. Any fat on the outside of the beef should be creamy coloured. Properly hung beef should be deep burgundy in colour, rather than bright red. Go for cleanly cut, neatly trimmed pieces of beef, with no fragments of shattered bone. For roasting, buying meat on the bone will always give you the best flavour.

Which cut?
Fillet is an extremely lean and tender steak taken from the middle back of the cow. These muscles do very little work, so the meat's tenderness makes up for it slightly lacking in flavour. It is best served on the rare side, as it can easily dry out and is ideal for smart main courses, and also for rare beef salads. When cooking fillet whole, ask for a piece from the middle, not the end. Also ask the butcher to remove the sinewy fibre that runs down the side.

A **cote du boeuf** is also cut from the rib, but it has the bone attached and hence has a real depth of flavour to it.

Ribeye steak is the chef's favourite. This cut used to be quite cheap but is now creeping up in price. It has an open-fibre texture and a marbling of creamy fat.

Sirloin steaks are cut from the front end of the animal (rib) and have a tender texture yet great flavour.

Rump steaks are cut from the rear of the animal and tend to be cut thicker than sirloin steak, which makes them a little less tender, but with plenty of flavour. This cut is slightly less expensive than sirloin.

Skirt steak (or onglet) is a once forgotten, now newly fashionable, cut that is often used for mince, but can also be sliced and cooked quickly. Flank makes a good substitute. This cut must be cooked no more than medium rare or it will be just too tough.

Beef rib, on the bone or boned and rolled, is a famously delicious cut for roasting, with its marbled fat and generous size. It is expensive, however. Good alternatives are sirloin and top rump.

Brisket, topside and **silverside** are good value for money and ideal for pot roasts as they need longer cooking to become tender.

Mince is ideal for burgers and meat sauces. Choose good-quality mince for homemade burgers with 20 per cent fat – this will baste the burgers from within and drain away. A lower-fat mince is fine for chilli and bolognese sauces, etc.

Braising steak is a general term for meat taken from the top of the leg which needs to be cooked slowly in liquid – ideal for rich casseroles, curries and stews. Pre-packed braising steak is often cut into pieces that are so small they can break up by the time the meat is tender, so if you can, cut your own or ask your butcher to do it.

Chuck steak, feather steak, shin and **brisket** can all be used the same way. Ox cheek is a wonderfully flavourful piece of meat, which, if you're lucky enough to find it, needs longer cooking than most braising steak.

Veal

Controversy has raged around the production of veal for decades, but in recent years farming methods have become far more humane. Rose veal, for example, is produced on farms monitored by the RSPCA Freedom Food programme, which enforces strict welfare standards.

Cooking a steak

Here are some basic tips for quick-cooking cuts, which can be enjoyed from very rare to well done, depending on your taste:

- If you want a steak to be cooked **medium-rare** or less, choose a steak 2–3cm thick so that it can caramelize on the outside but stay pink in the middle.
- Start with a steak that has come to room temperature or has at least been out of the fridge long enough for the chill to come off it.
- Oil the meat and not the pan – this will stop the pan becoming overly smoky. Use groundnut, vegetable or sunflower oil as these can withstand high-temperature cooking without burning and spoiling the flavour. Finish with a little butter at the end of cooking, if you like.
- Have your pan very hot – almost smoking. This will give your meat a good crust.
- Turn the steaks once, rather than flipping them over and over. Doing this will only stall the cooking.
- **Rare steak** will take 1–2 minutes per side. For medium-rare steak cook for 2 minutes on each side. For medium add 1 minute each side and for well done, add 2. Use your fingers to prod the meat. When rare, it will feel soft; medium-rare should be only lightly bouncy; well done will feel much firmer.
- Let the steaks rest for a couple of minutes in a warm place. Make sure you do this on a clean plate, not the one that previously held the raw steak.
- If you want to slice the steak to serve it, cut against the grain. This makes it more tender.

PORK

One of the most versatile types of meat, pork is economical, tender if cooked correctly, and oozing with flavour. It is often thought of as a particularly fatty type of meat but some cuts, such as tenderloin, can be extremely lean. Pork is high in protein and is an excellent source of iron, zinc and B vitamins.

Look for firm, pale pink flesh, damp but not oily in texture and with white fat. Bones should be tinged with red; white bones indicate the animal is older and the meat less tender than it should be.

Whether you choose pork for a roast, a quick stir-fry or slow-cooked stew, the meat should always be cooked thoroughly.

Which cut?

Loin is the most common choice for a roast, as it is lean and tender with a good coating of fat. Chops are the loin cut into slices. Chump and loin chops are the most meaty.

Tenderloin (fillet) is the pig equivalent of fillet steak; tenderloin is very tender and needs only quick cooking (though pork should never be eaten raw).

Belly has become a gastropub classic; as one of the first re-discovered cheap cuts to hit menus. Ask for the 'thick end' if you're roasting it. It's vital that you score the skin very well, ideally with a craft knife, so that you can achieve good crackling, and easily cut the meat up once it's cooked. Also good braised in Asian dishes.

Shoulder is excellent for slow-roasting; properly cooked pork shoulder will pull apart and be supremely tender. It is usually boned out, rolled and scored for roasting.

Sausages – the good-quality ones – will be made with a combination of 50:50 minced meat from the shoulder and belly, plus seasonings. Most shop-bought sausages also contain some kind of binder, such as breadcrumbs or rusk. If you wish to cook with chorizo, do try to seek out the softer chorizo, which has not been cured. It is soft to the touch and, when cooked, releases a delicious, spicy red oil.

Leg meat mostly goes to make hams, but you will find gammon (see below) and also **pork leg steaks**. The latter are very lean; cook quickly to avoid drying out.

Spare ribs can be bought separated into ribs or as a whole rack. Look for ribs with plenty of meat and fat around the bones and cook them long and slow.

Pork mince can be made into burgers or used as an alternative to beef in meaty sauces. It can be very fatty, so be sure to drain off the excess.

Cured meats

Bacon is pork that has been cured in one of two ways: dry or wet. It can be bought as rashers or larger cuts. Dry-cure bacon has been rubbed with salt and flavourings and will have the best texture and flavour – it also won't leak water as it cooks. Bacon that isn't labelled as dry cure will have been soaked in brine, or even injected with it.

Streaky bacon comes from the belly of the pig, back bacon comes from the loin, and middle bacon is half and half. Gammon steaks are large slices of raw bacon from the hind leg of the pig. Lardons are cubes of streaky bacon; you can sometimes find whole pieces of streaky bacon and cut it into big cubes yourself (see the Boston baked beans recipe on page 100).

Pancetta is Italian cured pork belly - the equivalent of streaky bacon – and can be bought as cubetti (cubes) or rashers. Pancetta is cut more thinly than streaky bacon, so if you substitute it for bacon, reduce the cooking time.

Ham and gammon are both from the hind leg of a pig and will be cured in the same way as bacon and either smoked or unsmoked. Strictly speaking, a gammon is a joint or whole leg that has been cured while still on the pig, whereas a ham is a leg than has been cut away from the pig and then cured separately. Usually ham is boiled in a large pan (or cooked in a tent of foil in the oven), then drained, the fat scored, and then baked with a sticky or spicy glaze. Depending on the strength of its cure, a ham or gammon may need to be soaked before cooking, so check with your butcher. If you buy your ham bone-in, keep the bone for stock once the meat has all gone.

Prosciutto The name is widely used to describe Italian, seasoned, cured and air-dried ham intended to be eaten raw. Most famous is 'prosciutto di Parma' or Parma ham.

Serrano is the Spanish equivalent to prosciutto. Germany also has its own cured hams.

Salami, French garlic sausage and **chorizo** (not the soft kind) and other similar sausages have an intense flavour that arises from the long curing process, during which the sausage matures and dries in its skin. This process means that these sausages are ready to eat, despite being uncooked.

LAMB

Technically, lamb is a sheep that is under one year old, and is known for its delicate flavour and tender flesh. Young lamb come from an animal slaughtered between 6 and 8 weeks - it is the palest of all lamb. Spring lamb (also called early or summer lamb) is 3 to 5 months old. Lamb meaning meat from a 1–2 year old sheep is called 'hogget' - it has a stronger flavour and less tender flesh; any meat from a sheep over 2 years old is called 'mutton'. It has much more flavour, but a tougher flesh.

When choosing lamb, look for firm, fine-grained meat with a velvety texture; it should be moist, rather than dry or slimy and any fat on the outside of the meat should be white.

Properly hung lamb should have a deep red, rather than bright red, colour, although very young lamb will be paler than older lamb.

Which cut?

Leg of lamb is the classic roasting joint. Ask for a part-boned leg as this will be easier to carve. Legs can be boned entirely (butterflied) and cooked more quickly. Leg steaks are also available.

Breast of lamb is the lamb equivalent to pork belly. It is a fatty cut, but when rolled and slow-roasted it makes an excellent roast.

Best end of neck (rack of lamb) and fillet is the most tender meat and requires quick cooking.

Loin, together with the best end, makes a saddle of lamb, which can be boned and rolled as a superb, if expensive, roasting joint. The loin can also be cut into loin chops.

Mince can be seasoned and used for burgers, kofte kebabs, not to mention meat sauces for shepherd's pie and moussaka. It can be fatty, so drain off the excess. when cooking.

Neck fillet is a much underused cut, less expensive than fillet, but still suitable for quicker cooking and fairly tender. It has a fine marbling of fat, which melts as it cooks.

Shoulder can be cooked whole, or boned and rolled. Shoulder always needs to be slow-cooked or braised.

Chump is equivalent to the rump in beef and makes a good two-person roast. Chump chops are generous and make good eating. It is sometimes called lamb rump.

Shanks are the lower part of the leg and need long, slow cooking.

VENISON

A rich, dark red meat, venison is a good low-fat alternative to beef, very good value and widely available. Although classified as game, most of the meat you will find in supermarkets will have come from farmed deer.

As with any animal, it's the leg and shoulder muscles that do most of the work, so these will need long, slow cooking. The loin and fillet can be cooked quickly and are best served medium-rare, as you would a good steak. Left together, they are referred to as a saddle. As with fillet steak, the fillet is the narrow long muscle that runs just alongside the loins, and is the most tender cut. The flank or belly is the most fatty part and is great added to pork

mince for burgers. The neck is a favourite for stews and pie fillings. The haunch is the top of the animal's back legs. This cut can be cooked slowly for stews and pies, or marinated, sliced thinly and grilled.

RABBIT

Rabbit is abundant, available all year round, and is incredibly cheap. It has a mild flavour that is similar to chicken. Wild rabbits are smaller, leaner and tougher, and will take longer to cook than farmed, but both are butchered in the same way. When you buy rabbit pieces you will get a mix of small front legs, larger back legs and the saddle – which contains the loin. Rabbit meat is available from the butcher, online and at large supermarkets. The mild taste of rabbit pairs well with dominant flavours such as wine and garlic. Rabbit can be tough, but when braised the meat becomes deliciously tender.

OFFAL

In the true spirit of 'nose to tail eating', offal is having something of a resurgence. Love it or hate it, it is low in fat, nutritious and great value too. All offal should be kept in the fridge and used within a day of purchase.

Liver can be cooked by itself, or used to make pâtés, parfaits, terrines and warm salads. Calve's, lamb's and pig's liver can all be thinly-sliced and pan-fried, but calve's liver is the one to pick if you have a choice, for its pale colour and delicate texture and flavour. Look for even-coloured liver, without blemishes, and remove any tubes or sinews before cooking.

Kidneys can be sold loose, or still encased in their fat (suet). Calve's kidney are the best choice here too, for their superior flavour. They are good pan-fried or cooked in a quick pan sauce. Lamb's kidneys are the next best choice, followed by pig's kidneys, which are rather strong in flavour. Save ox kidney for cooking in pies – the flavour is too strong for them to be eaten by themselves. Look for smooth, plump kidneys without any blemishes. Before cooking, cut kidneys lengthways through the middle then snip out the white core with a pair of scissors.

Oxtail is very flavoursome, very bony, as you'd expect, but also contains wonderful nuggets of meat and marrowbone. When slow-cooked, the meat becomes very tender and the marrow helps to make a rich and glossy sauce.

Meatballs with spaghetti

Tuck into a family-size portion of meatballs, then stash the rest in the freezer.

**MAKES ABOUT 10 SERVINGS • PREP 30 MINS
COOK 30 MINS**
❄

8 good-quality pork sausages, split and meat squeezed out
1kg/2lb 4oz beef mince
1 onion, finely chopped
large bunch flat-leaf parsley, finely chopped
85g/3oz Parmesan, grated, plus extra to serve
100g/4oz fresh breadcrumbs
2 eggs, beaten
olive oil, for drizzling and cooking
4 garlic cloves, crushed
4 x 400g cans chopped tomatoes
125ml/4fl oz red wine (optional)
3 tbsp caster sugar
spaghetti, to serve (you will need 100g per portion)

try this...

> For Spanish-style meatballs, swap the Parmesan for
> 1 tbsp smoked paprika in the mince mixture, sizzle
> 140g finely diced chorizo in with the garlic for the
> sauce and leave out the basil. Serve with some roast
> potatoes and salad.

1 Use your hands to mix together the sausage meat, mince, onion, half of the parsley, the Parmesan, breadcrumbs, beaten eggs and lots of seasoning. The more you squeeze and mash the mince, the more tender the meatballs.

2 Heat oven to 220C/200C fan/gas 7. Roll the mince mixture into about 50 golf-ball-size meatballs. Set aside any meatballs for freezing, allowing about 5 per portion, then spread the rest out in a large roasting tin. Drizzle with a little oil (about 1 tsp per portion), shake to coat, then roast for 20–30 minutes until browned.

3 Meanwhile, make the sauce. Heat the oil in your largest pan. Add the garlic and sizzle for 1 minute. Stir in the tomatoes, wine (if using), sugar, remaining parsley and seasoning. Simmer for 15–20 minutes until slightly thickened.

4 Spoon out any portions for freezing, then add the cooked meatballs to the pan to keep warm while you cook some spaghetti. Spoon the sauce and meatballs over the spaghetti, and serve with extra Parmesan, if you like.

PER SERVING 870 kcals, carbs 95g, fat 37g, sat fat 13g, salt 1.34g

Lamb steaks with tomatoes and olives

*Italian flavours bring out the natural sweetness of lamb. Throw this together in five minutes
and serve with crusty bread.*

SERVES 4 • PREP 5 MINS • COOK 20 MINS

2 tbsp olive oil
4 lamb leg steaks (approx 140g/5oz each)
1 large red onion, cut into 8 wedges
2 tsp dried oregano
150ml/¼ pint dry white wine
400g pack cherry tomatoes
100g/4oz black olives
handful flat-leaf parsley, chopped

1 Heat oven to 200C/180C fan/gas 6. Heat the oil in a large roasting tin on the hob. Brown the lamb steaks in the tin over a high heat for about 1 minute each side.

2 Add the onion to the roasting tin with the oregano. Pour over the wine and throw in the tomatoes. Scatter the olives over the top, then place the tin in the oven for 15 minutes until the lamb is cooked. Scatter with flat-leaf parsley and serve with boiled new potatoes.

PER SERVING 322 kcals, carbs 7g, fat 21g, sat fat 7g, salt 1.84g

Italian pork patties with potato wedges

A clever new way with pork mince that the whole family will love.

SERVES 4 • PREP 15 MINS • COOK 35-45 MINS
❄

4 baking potatoes, unpeeled, each cut into
   8–10 wedges
2 tbsp olive oil
zest and juice 1 lemon
50g/2oz fresh breadcrumbs (see below)
500g pack pork mince
50g/2oz Parmesan, finely grated
2 tbsp chopped parsley
1 large garlic clove, crushed

1 Heat oven to 200C/180C fan/gas 6. Toss the potato wedges in a large roasting tin with 1 tbsp oil and the lemon juice. Spread out in a single layer. Bake for 35–45 minutes, turning halfway through cooking, until golden brown and crisp.
2 Meanwhile, place the breadcrumbs in a mixing bowl and moisten with 2 tbsp cold water. Add the mince, Parmesan, parsley, garlic and lemon zest. Season, mix well, then shape into 4 large flat patties.
3 Heat the remaining oil in a pan and cook the patties for 7 minutes on each side, or until they have a golden crust and are cooked through. Serve with the wedges and a tomato and rocket salad, if you like.

PER SERVING 503 kcals, carbs 45g, fat 22g, sat fat 8g, salt 1.73g

tip For a traditional Italian meatball sandwich, replace the lemon zest and parsley with a pinch of dried chilli flakes and 1 tsp fennel seeds. Shape into small meatballs and grill or fry until cooked through. Serve piled into ciabatta rolls with a spoonful of fried onions and peppers.

 Make fresh breadcrumbs whenever you have a couple of slightly stale slices of bread left over. Tear the bread into rough pieces and whizz in a food processor or mini processor. Store in a sealed plastic bag in the freezer and use from frozen.

Sticky thyme and mustard bacon chops

Just like roast ham at Christmas, bacon chops go fantastically with a sticky marmalade glaze.
For a satisfying and quick winter supper, tuck into this with mash and greens.

**SERVES 2 EASILY DOUBLED • PREP 5 MINS
COOK 25 MINS**

2 thick bacon loin chops, trimmed of excess fat
   (or use gammon steaks)
1 tsp olive oil
knob of butter
1 large onion, thinly sliced
1 tsp thyme leaves
2 tbsp Seville orange marmalade
1 tsp wholegrain mustard
300ml/½ pint chicken stock

1 Season the bacon chops with pepper (there's no need to add extra salt). Heat the oil in a non-stick frying pan, then sizzle and brown the chops over a medium heat for 5 minutes, turning once. Lift onto a plate.
2 Add the butter to the pan. Once it looks foamy, stir in the onion and thyme and fry very gently for 15 minutes until the onion is soft and golden. Stir in the marmalade, mustard and stock, then simmer for 2 minutes until it starts to thicken to a sauce. Return the chops to the pan, simmer for 3 minutes more, then serve.

PER SERVING 520 kcals, carbs 19g, fat 34g, sat fat 13g, salt 6.08g

Quick roast lamb

If you're in the mood for a roast but time is short, this quick recipe really hits the spot.
Serve with seasonal green vegetables.

SERVES 2 • PREP 5 MINS • COOK 25 MINS

400g/14oz new potatoes
250g/9oz Chantenay carrots, or large carrots cut into
    big chunks
1 tbsp oil, plus a little more for the lamb
1 sprig rosemary, leaves chopped
100ml/3½fl oz red wine
100ml/3½fl oz lamb stock
1–2 tsp redcurrant jelly
4 lamb chops or cutlets

1 Heat oven to 220C/200C fan/gas 7. Put the potatoes and carrots onto a baking sheet, toss with the oil and rosemary, then season well. Roast for 15 minutes on the top shelf until the veg are golden and almost tender.
2 Meanwhile, make the gravy. Put the wine and stock into a small pan, then boil until reduced by about two-thirds. Stir in the redcurrant jelly, season and keep warm.
3 Rub the lamb in a little oil, then season. Tuck the lamb in amongst the veg, then return to the oven for 8–10 minutes, turning the lamb halfway through. Serve with the redcurrant gravy.

PER SERVING 606 kcals, carbs 44g, fat 32g, sat fat 13g, salt 0.7g

Hob-to-table moussaka

A midweek moussaka with all the flavour but none of the fuss.

SERVES 4 • PREP 10 MINS • COOK 25 MINS
❄

2 tbsp olive oil
1 large onion, finely chopped
2 garlic cloves, finely chopped
500g/1lb 2oz minced lamb
400g can chopped plum tomatoes
2 tbsp tomato purée
2 tsp ground cinnamon
200g jar chargrilled aubergines in olive oil, drained
    and chopped
200g pack feta, crumbled
3 tbsp fresh mint, chopped

1 Heat the oil in a large, shallow pan. Toss in the onion and garlic and fry until soft. Add the mince and stir-fry for 3–4 minutes until browned. Spoon away any excess fat.
2 Tip the tomatoes into the pan and stir in the tomato purée and cinnamon, then season generously with salt and pepper. Leave the mince to simmer for 20 minutes, adding the aubergines halfway through the cooking time.
3 Sprinkle the feta and mint over the mince. Bring the moussaka to the table as the feta melts and serve it with a crunchy green salad and toasted pitta.

PER SERVING 529 kcals, carbs 11g, fat 39g, sat fat 16g, salt 2.31g

OPPOSITE Clockwise from top left *Irish coddled pork with cider (page 143), Italian pork patties with potato wedges (page 139), Quick roast lamb, Beef stroganoff with herby pasta (page 142), Sausages with oregano, mushrooms and olives (page 145), Meatballs with spaghetti (page 138).*

Beef stroganoff with herby pasta

Freezing the beef will ensure that you can get it super thin when it's time to slice it.

**SERVES 4 • PREP 10 MINS, PLUS FREEZING
COOK 20 MINS**

400g/14oz beef rump steak, trimmed
1 tbsp butter
1 tbsp olive oil
300g/11oz small button mushrooms
400g/14oz pappardelle pasta
3 shallots, finely chopped
1 tbsp plain flour
300ml/½ pint beef stock
1 tbsp Dijon mustard
1 tbsp tomato purée
3 tbsp crème fraîche
handful flat-leaf parsley, chopped

1 Freeze the beef for 45 minutes before you begin. Remove from the freezer and slice it as thinly as you can, then season.
2 In a large, non-stick frying pan, melt half the butter with half the oil. Increase the heat, then quickly sear the beef in batches until browned on both sides. Remove the meat and set aside. Repeat with the mushrooms, then set aside with the beef. Cook the pasta according to the pack instructions.
3 Add the remaining butter and oil to the pan and soften the shallots for a few minutes. Stir in the flour for 1 minute, then gradually stir in the stock. Bubble for 5 minutes until thickened, then stir in the mustard, purée, crème fraîche and seasoning. Bubble for 1 minute more, then return the beef and mushrooms to the pan.
4 Drain the pasta, toss with half the parsley and season. Serve with the creamy stroganoff and sprinkled with the remaining parsley.

PER SERVING 614 kcals, carbs 81g, fat 18g, sat fat 7g, salt 0.94g

try this...

For creamy beef curry, follow the recipe as above up to the end of step 2, boiling 300g basmati rice instead of the pasta. Soften the shallots in butter, then stir in 2 tbsp curry paste, the tomato purée and flour, then fry for 1 minute. Add the stock and bubble as before, then stir in crème fraîche or use natural yogurt instead. Serve with rice and scatter with chopped coriander.

Spiced pineapple pork

 The classic combination of pork and pineapple lives on in this slightly retro and irresistible sweet and sour one-pan recipe.

SERVES 4 • PREP 5 MINS • COOK 12 MINS

2 tsp vegetable oil
4 pork loin steaks, trimmed of excess fat
2 tbsp light muscovado sugar
1 tbsp dark soy sauce
1 tsp tomato purée
432g can pineapple rings in juice, drained but juice reserved
½ tsp chilli powder
1 tsp Chinese five-spice powder
handful coriander, to serve

1 Add the oil to a large non-stick pan, season the steaks well, then fry for 5 minutes on each side until golden and almost cooked through. Mix the sugar, soy, tomato purée and most of the pineapple juice in a bowl.
2 Add the pineapple rings to the pan and let them caramelise a little alongside the pork. Add the chilli and five-spice to the pan, then fry for 1 minute until aromatic. Tip in the soy mix and let it bubble around the pork and pineapple for a few minutes until slightly reduced and sticky. Sprinkle with coriander, then serve with rice and Chinese greens.

PER SERVING 315 kcals, carbs 22g, fat 9g, sat fat 3g, salt 1.25g

Irish coddled pork with cider

Host a private St Patrick's Day supper with this cider-infused Irish stew for two that's easily doubled.

SERVES 2 ● PREP 5 MINS ● COOK 30 MINS

small knob of butter
2 pork loin chops
4 rashers smoked bacon, cut into pieces
1 carrot, cut into large chunks
2 potatoes, cut into chunks
½ small swede, cut into chunks
¼ large cabbage, cut into smaller wedges
1 bay leaf
100ml/3½fl oz Irish cider
100ml/3½fl oz chicken stock

1 Heat the butter in a casserole dish until sizzling, then fry the pork for 2–3 minutes on each side until browned. Remove from the pan. Tip the bacon, carrot, potatoes and swede into the pan, then gently fry until slightly coloured.
2 Stir in the cabbage, sit the chops back on top, add the bay leaf, then pour over the cider and stock. Cover the pan, then leave everything to gently simmer for 20 minutes until the pork is cooked through and the vegetables are tender. Serve at the table spooned straight from the dish.

PER SERVING 717 kcals, carbs 37g, fat 44g, sat fat 17g, salt 2.59g

tip You could also use lamb chops for this recipe, if you'd prefer. Simply trim the excess fat from the chops before browning, and add them to the pan when the veg have simmered for 10 minutes.

Classic Swedish meatballs

Creamy and delicate, these meatballs are perfect with mash and a dollop of cranberry or, if you can find it, lingonberry sauce.

SERVES 4 ● PREP 15 MINS ● COOK 20 MINS

400g/14oz lean pork mince
1 egg, beaten
1 small onion, finely chopped or grated
85g/3oz fresh white breadcrumbs
1 tbsp finely chopped dill, plus extra to serve
1 tbsp olive oil
1 tbsp butter
2 tbsp plain flour
400ml/14fl oz hot beef stock (from a cube is fine)

1 In a bowl, mix the mince with the egg, onion, breadcrumbs, dill and seasoning. Form into small meatballs about the size of walnuts – you should get about 20.
2 Heat the olive oil in a large non-stick frying pan and brown the meatballs. You may have to do this in 2 batches. Remove from the pan, melt the butter, then sprinkle over the flour and stir well. Cook for 2 minutes, then slowly whisk in the stock. Keep whisking until it is a thick gravy, then return the meatballs to the pan and heat them through. Sprinkle with dill and serve with cranberry jelly, greens and mash.

PER SERVING 301 kcals, carbs 22g, fat 13g, sat fat 4g, salt 1.73g

Turkish lamb pilau

Aromatic rice and tender lamb, ideal for sharing with friends after work.

SERVES 4 • PREP 10 MINS • COOK 20 MINS

small handful pine nuts or flaked almonds
1 tbsp olive oil
1 large onion, halved and sliced
2 cinnamon sticks, broken in half
500g/1lb 2oz lean lamb neck fillet, cubed
250g/9oz basmati rice
500ml/18fl oz hot lamb or chicken stock
12 ready-to-eat-dried apricots
handful fresh mint leaves, roughly chopped

1 Dry-fry the pine nuts or almonds in a large pan until lightly toasted, then tip onto a plate. Add the oil to the pan, then fry the onion and cinnamon together until starting to turn golden. Turn up the heat and stir in the lamb, frying it until the meat changes colour, then tip in the rice and cook for 1 minute, stirring all the time.
2 Add the stock and apricots, then season to taste. Turn the heat down, cover and simmer for 12 minutes until the rice is tender and the stock has been absorbed. Toss in the nuts and mint and serve.

PER SERVING 584 kcals, carbs 65g, fat 24g, sat fat 9g, salt 1.4g

Thai beef stir-fry

 Make this one of your weeknight regulars – tasty, quick and just five ingredients to think about!

SERVES 4 • PREP 5 MINS • COOK 5 MINS

2 tbsp vegetable oil
400g/14oz beef strips or steak, cut into thin strips
1 red chilli, deseeded and finely sliced
2 tbsp oyster sauce
handful basil leaves (use holy basil – see below)

1 Heat a wok or large frying pan until smoking hot. Pour in the oil and swirl around the pan, then tip in the beef strips and chilli. Stir-fry until the meat is lightly browned, about 3 minutes, then pour over the oyster sauce. Heat through then stir in the basil leaves and serve with plain rice.

PER SERVING 178 kcals, carbs 1g, fat 10g, sat fat 2g, salt 0.55g

 Thai holy basil has an intense flavour that's more aniseedy than the usual Mediterranean-style basil. You'll find it in Asian stores and specialist grocers.

Steak and sticky red wine shallots

To turn this recipe into a quick coq au vin, make it with chicken breasts, leaving them in the pan as the wine reduces.

SERVES 2 • PREP 10 MINS • COOK 20 MINS

8 shallots, peeled and quartered but left whole
    at the root
2 sirloin steaks, about 175g/6oz each
crushed black peppercorns
25g/1oz butter
4 tbsp balsamic vinegar
175ml/6fl oz red wine
150ml/¼ pint beef stock

1 Simmer the shallots in a pan of water for 2–3 minutes, then drain and set aside. Season the steaks with a little salt and plenty of crushed peppercorns. Heat half the butter in a pan until sizzling, then cook the steaks for 3 minutes on each side for medium, or until done to your liking.

2 Remove the steaks and keep warm. While they rest, add the remaining butter to the pan, throw in the shallots, then sizzle in the sticky pan until starting to brown. Add the balsamic vinegar and bubble for a few minutes. Add the wine and boil down until sticky, then add the beef stock and simmer until everything comes together. Spoon the shallots over the steaks and serve with green beans and chips.

PER SERVING 524 kcals, carbs 10g, fat 33g, sat fat 16g, salt 1.87g

Sausages with oregano, mushrooms and olives

A quick stew for cold winter nights – great with a pile of pasta.

SERVES 4 • PREP 10 MINS • COOK 20 MINS

450g pack reduced-fat sausages
1 tsp sunflower oil
2 tsp dried oregano
2 garlic cloves, sliced
400g can cherry or chopped plum tomatoes
200ml/7fl oz beef stock
100g/4oz pitted black olives
500g pack mushrooms, thickly sliced

1 Using kitchen scissors, snip the sausages into meatball-size pieces. Heat a large pan and fry the pieces in the oil for about 5 minutes until golden all over. Add the oregano and garlic, fry for 1 minute more, then tip in the tomatoes, stock, olives and mushrooms. Simmer for 15 minutes until the sausages are cooked through and the sauce has reduced a little.

PER SERVING 264 kcals, carbs 12g, fat 16g, sat fat 4g, salt 2.19g

 When frying low-fat sausages, keep them on a gentle heat as they can burn easily.

Sticky maple pork with apples

 Pork fillet is surprisingly low in fat, making this comforting supper good for you too.

SERVES 4 • PREP 10 MINS • COOK 15 MINS

600g/1lb 5oz pork fillet
1 tbsp olive oil
2 eating apples, cored and cut into eighths
1 garlic clove, crushed
2 tbsp maple syrup
1 tbsp red or white wine vinegar
2 tbsp wholegrain mustard

tip For a great-value meal, replace the pork with a 400g pack pork sausages, cut into chunks. Cook for 10–12 minutes before adding the apple slices.

1 Cut the pork into 3cm-thick slices. Heat the oil in a large non-stick frying pan, add the pork, then fry on both sides until lightly browned, about 5 minutes in total. Lift out of the pan and set aside. Add the apples to the pan, then cook for 3–4 minutes until starting to soften.
2 Stir in the garlic, maple syrup, vinegar and 3 tbsp water, bring to the boil, then return the meat to the pan along with any juices. Simmer for a few more minutes, stirring until the pork is cooked through and the sauce is thick and sticky. Stir in the wholegrain mustard and serve with rice.

PER SERVING 303 kcals, carbs 13g, fat 13g, sat fat 4g, salt 0.52g

Liver and bacon sauté with potatoes and parsley

If you're not a liver lover, this tasty twist on classic liver and onions may just convert you.

SERVES 2 • PREP 5 MINS • COOK 25 MINS

400g/14oz new potatoes, halved
2 tbsp olive oil
4 spring onions, trimmed and each cut into 2–3 pieces
    on the diagonal
4 rashers of unsmoked bacon, snipped into pieces
1 tbsp plain flour
1 tsp paprika, plus extra for sprinkling
175g/6oz lamb's liver, sliced into thin strips
small bunch flat-leaf parsley, chopped
150ml/¼ pint hot vegetable stock
4 tbsp soured cream

1 Drop the potatoes into a pan of boiling salted water and cook for 12-15 minutes. Drain and set aside.
2 Heat the oil in a wok or large frying pan. Add the potatoes and fry them for 4–5 minutes over a high heat until browned and crispy. Remove from the pan and set aside.
3 Tip the spring onions and bacon into the pan, stir and sizzle for 3–4 minutes or until the bacon gets crisp. Meanwhile, season the flour with paprika, a little salt and plenty of black pepper, then use to coat the liver.
4 Stir the liver into the pan and cook for 2–3 minutes. Toss in the potatoes and quickly reheat. Stir in the chopped parsley, remove everything from the pan and divide between 2 plates. Keep warm.
5 Quickly pour the hot stock into the pan and scrape all the crispy bits up from the bottom. Bubble for 1–2 minutes, then pour around the liver and potatoes. Serve topped with soured cream and a sprinkling of paprika.

PER SERVING 570 kcals, carbs 41g, fat 32g, sat fat 10g, salt 2.5g

OPPOSITE *Sticky maple pork with apples.*

Toad in the hole with onion gravy

Crisp batter and meaty sausages combine in this great-value family classic. The rich homemade onion gravy is also good with grilled sausages and mounds of mash.

SERVES 4 • PREP 20 MINS • COOK 45 MINS

100g/4oz plain flour, plus 1 tbsp for the gravy
½ tsp English mustard powder
1 egg
300ml/½ pint milk
3 thyme sprigs, leaves only
8 plain pork sausages
2 tbsp sunflower oil
2 onions, peeled and sliced
1 tsp soft brown sugar
500ml/18fl oz beef stock

1 Heat oven to 220C/200C fan/gas 7. Tip the flour into a large mixing bowl and stir in the mustard powder with a good pinch of salt. Make a well in the centre, crack in the egg, then add a little milk. Stir with a wooden spoon, gradually incorporating some of the flour, until you have a smooth batter in the well. Add the rest of the milk gradually, stirring until all the milk and flour has been mixed together to a smooth batter. Tip it back into the jug you measured your milk in, for easier pouring later on, then stir in the thyme.
2 Put the sausages into a 20 x 30cm roasting tin. Add 1 tbsp of the oil, toss well, then roast for 15 minutes.
3 Carefully take the hot tin from the oven, then quickly pour in the batter – it should sizzle and bubble when it hits the hot fat. Cook for another 30–40 minutes until the batter is cooked through, well risen and crisp.
4 For the gravy, cook the onions with the remaining oil in a large non-stick frying pan for about 20 minutes, stirring often, until golden brown. Sprinkle in the sugar for the final 5 minutes. Add 1 tbsp flour, then cook, stirring constantly, for 2 minutes. Gradually pour in the stock, stirring well to make a smooth sauce. Bubble for 4–5 minutes to thicken, then season. Cut into large wedges and serve with the gravy spooned over.

PER SERVING 591 kcals, carbs 42.1g, fat 37.6g, sat fat 11.4g, salt 2.54g

try this...

For mini toads, divide 12 cocktail sausages between the 12 holes of a muffin tin. Roast for 5 minutes, then pour a little batter into each hole and cook for 15–20 minutes.

For a fruity accompaniment, peel and core 2 apples and peel a red onion. Cut into wedges and add to the roasting tin with the sausages.

Spice it up by using good chilli-flavoured sausages and stir 100g ready-roasted pepper strips into the batter.

Shepherd's pie

*You'll turn to this no-nonsense shepherd's pie again and again. To make it into
a cottage pie, just substitute beef mince for the lamb.*

SERVES 4 • PREP 15 MINS • COOK 1 HOUR
❄

1 tbsp sunflower oil
1 large onion, chopped
2 or 3 medium carrots, chopped
500g pack minced lamb
2 tbsp tomato purée
large splash Worcestershire sauce
500ml/18fl oz beef stock
900g/2lb potatoes, cut into chunks
85g/3oz butter
3 tbsp milk

1 Heat the oil in a large frying pan then soften the onion and carrots for a few minutes. Turn up the heat, crumble in the lamb and brown it, tipping away any excess fat. Add the tomato purée and Worcestershire sauce, fry for 2 minutes then add the stock. Simmer, then cover and cook for 40 minutes, uncovering halfway.

2 Meanwhile, heat oven to 180C/160C fan/ gas 4, then make the mash. Boil the potatoes in salted water for 10–15 minutes until tender. Drain, then mash with the butter and milk.

3 Put the mince into an ovenproof dish, top with the mash and ruffle with a fork. (The pie can now be chilled and frozen for up to a month.) Bake for 20–25 minutes until the top is starting to colour and the mince is bubbling through at the edges. Leave to stand for 5 minutes before serving.

PER SERVING 663 kcals, carbs 49g, fat 39g, sat fat 20g, salt 1.35g

Herby lamb cobbler

*This cobbler topping is light inside and crisp on the outside. It's great on top of chicken and
beef stews too.*

SERVES 6 • PREP 40 MINS • COOK 2½ HOURS
❄

200g/7oz smoked streaky bacon, in bite-size pieces
900g/2lb lamb neck fillets, cut into large chunks
350g/12oz baby onions, peeled
5 carrots, cut into large chunks
350g/12oz small button mushrooms
3 tbsp plain flour
3 bay leaves
small bunch thyme
350ml/12fl oz red wine
350ml/12fl oz lamb or beef stock
large splash Worcestershire sauce
FOR THE COBBLER TOPPING
350g/12oz self-raising flour
4 tbsp chopped mixed herbs, including thyme,
    rosemary and parsley
200g/7oz chilled butter, grated
juice 1 lemon
5 bay leaves
beaten egg, to glaze

1 Heat oven to 180C/160C fan/gas 4. In a flameproof casserole, sizzle the bacon for 5 minutes until the fat runs. Turn up the heat, then brown the lamb in batches. Remove with a slotted spoon then add the onions, carrots and mushrooms. Fry for 5 minutes, then stir in the flour. Return the meat to the pan with the herbs, wine, stock and Worcestershire sauce. Season, cover and braise for 1 hour 20 minutes.

2 Make the topping just before the cooking time is up. Tip the flour, herbs and seasoning into a large bowl. Rub in the butter. Make a well, then add the lemon juice and 3 tbsp water. Bring together to a soft dough, roll out to about 5mm thick, then cut into rounds with a 7cm cutter, re-rolling any trimmings. Overlap the circles of dough and bay leaves on the top of the stew. Brush with egg and bake for 45 minutes until golden.

PER SERVING 963 kcals, carbs 59g, fat 60g, sat fat 31g, salt 2.89g

Feta-crusted lamb with rich tomato sauce

If you're cooking for four, simply double the ingredients and make sure you use a pan large enough for the crust on the meat to stay above the tide of sauce.

SERVES 2 EASILY DOUBLED ● PREP 20 MINS, PLUS MARINATING AND RESTING ● COOK 30 MINS

7- or 8-bone rack of lamb, trimmed of fat then cut into
    two racks

FOR THE MARINADE
few thyme sprigs, left whole, plus extra sprigs to serve
1 tbsp extra virgin olive oil, plus extra for frying and drizzling
zest ½ lemon
2 garlic cloves, crushed
½ tsp dried oregano

FOR THE SAUCE
1 fat or 2 regular garlic cloves, crushed
small bunch flat-leaf parsley, stalks finely chopped
400g can cherry tomatoes
½ tsp dried oregano

FOR THE CRUST
50g/2oz feta, finely crumbled
zest ½ lemon
pinch dried oregano
½ slice white bread (day old, if possible), whizzed into crumbs

1 Put the racks into a food bag with all the marinade ingredients. Rub into the lamb, then leave for 30 minutes or up to 24 hours. It's important that you cook the lamb from room temperature.

2 Heat 1 tbsp oil in a wide casserole and soften the garlic and the parsley stalks for 1 minute. Add the tomatoes and oregano and simmer for 5 minutes, popping the cherry tomatoes. Roughly chop the parsley leaves and add half to the pan.

3 Heat oven to 230C/210C fan/gas 8. Combine the crust ingredients, adding the remaining parsley leaves.

4 Leave most of the marinade on the meat, season, then press the crust onto the lamb. Sit the racks in the sauce, crust-side up. Strew the thyme sprigs over, then drizzle with oil. Roast uncovered, for 20 minutes (for pink and juicy meat) until golden and the sauce thickened. Rest for 10 minutes, then carve. Serve with spoonfuls of sauce.

PER SERVING 582 kcals, carbs 12g, fat 48g, sat fat 18g, salt 1.47g

Ossobucco

This classic veal recipe provides the focus for a magnificent Italian Sunday lunch. Ask for hind-quarter shin bones (about 4 cm/1½in thick) as they are meatier and more tender than the front ones.

SERVES 6 ● PREP 30 MINS ● COOK ABOUT 2½ HOURS
❄

15g/½oz dried porcini mushrooms
6 thick slices of veal shin bone, complete with marrow
1 tbsp plain flour, seasoned
50g/2oz unsalted butter
3 tbsp olive oil
1 large carrot, diced
1 large celery stick, trimmed and diced
200ml/7fl oz dry white wine
225ml/8fl oz tomato sugocasa or passata
250ml/9fl oz hot vegetable stock

1 Soak the porcini in 200ml boiling water for at least 15 minutes. Dust the veal with the seasoned flour. Heat the butter and oil in a very large flameproof casserole over a medium-high heat. When the sizzling stops, fry the veal for 2–3 minutes on each side until golden. Transfer to a plate.

2 Tip the carrot and celery into the pan then fry gently until slightly softened. Turn up the heat, add the wine and boil hard for 2 minutes.

3 Lift the mushrooms from the soaking liquid and squeeze dry. Chop the porcini roughly and add to the pan, together with all but the last tablespoon of soaking liquid. Add the sugocasa or passata and stock, then stir.

4 Add the veal in a single layer, cover and bring to the boil. Immediately reduce the heat and simmer very gently for 2 hours, turning the veal slices halfway, until the meat is very soft. The liquid should reduce to a thickish sauce, but if it's still thin after 1¼–1½ hours, half-remove the lid to allow evaporation.

PER SERVING 383 kcals, carbs 7g, fat 23g, sat fat 10g, salt 1.15g

One-pan rogan josh

A restaurant classic that's just so easy to make yourself.

SERVES 6 • PREP 35 MINS • COOK 1 HOUR–1 HOUR 15 MINS
❄

2 onions, quartered
4 tbsp sunflower oil
4 garlic cloves, finely crushed
thumb-size piece fresh root ginger, peeled and very finely grated
2 tbsp Madras curry paste
2 tsp paprika
1 cinnamon stick
6 green cardamom pods, bashed to break the shells
4 cloves
2 bay leaves
1 tbsp tomato purée
1kg/2lb 4oz lean leg of lamb, cut into generous cubes
150ml/5fl oz Greek yogurt
chopped coriander, to serve

1 Put the onions in a food processor and whizz until very finely chopped. Heat the oil in a large heavy-based pan, then fry the onions with the lid on, stirring every now and then, until really golden and soft. Add the garlic and ginger, then fry for 5 minutes more.
2 Tip the curry paste, all the spices and the bay leaves into the pan, with the tomato purée. Stir well over the heat for about 30 seconds, then add the meat and 300ml water. Stir to mix, turn down the heat, then add the yogurt.
3 Cover the pan, then gently simmer for 40–60 minutes until the meat is tender and the sauce nice and thick. Serve scattered with coriander, with plain basmati or pilau rice.

PER SERVING 386 kcals, carbs 6g, fat 24g, sat fat 9g, salt 0.54g

Beef bourguignon

Rich with red wine and topped with sautéed vegetables, a good bourguignon never disappoints.

SERVES 6 • PREP 30 MINS, PLUS MARINATING COOK 2¾ HOURS
❄

1.6kg/3lb 8oz braising steak, cut into large chunks
3 bay leaves
small bunch thyme
2 bottles cheap red wine
2 tbsp vegetable or sunflower oil
3 large or 6 medium carrots, peeled and cut into large chunks
2 onions, roughly chopped
3 tbsp plain flour
1 tbsp tomato purée
TO SERVE
300g/11oz lardons
500g/1lb 2oz pearl onions or small shallots, peeled
small knob of butter
400g/14oz mushrooms
handful chopped parsley

1 Put the beef into a large bowl with the bay, thyme and wine. Cover and chill overnight. Strain the meat, keeping the wine.
2 Heat oven to 200C/180C fan/gas 6. Heat half the oil in a large frying pan until really hot, then brown the meat in batches. Deglaze the pan with a little wine and set aside.
3 Heat the rest of the oil in a large casserole and fry the vegetables until golden. Stir in the flour, cook until sandy, then stir in the purée and the beef with its juices, herbs and wine from the pan and the marinade. Season, simmer, then cover and cook in the oven for 2 hours until the meat is tender. (Can be made up to 2 days ahead or frozen for up to a month.)
4 Meanwhile, fry the lardons and onions in the butter for 10 minutes or until the lardons are starting to crisp and the onions are softening and colouring. Turn the heat up, add the mushrooms then fry everything together for another 5 minutes. When the beef is cooked, tip the mushrooms and bacon into the stew and simmer gently for 10 minutes. Serve scattered with chopped parsley.

PER SERVING 767 kcals, carbs 16.4g, fat 39.4g, sat fat 15.5g, salt 2.09g

Iberico ham with slow-roast tomatoes and artichokes

It's worth taking the time to slow-roast your own tomatoes for this full-flavoured starter or lunch.

SERVES 4 • PREP 20 MINS • COOK 3 HOURS

100g/4oz flaky sea salt
4–6 plum tomatoes, halved
8 slices Iberico ham or prosciutto
280g jar chargrilled artichokes
handful black olives, Spanish or Kalamata
handful small-leaved flat-leaf parsley
extra virgin olive oil, to serve

1 Heat oven to 140C/120C fan/gas 1. Make a thick layer of salt on a baking sheet, top with the tomatoes, cut-side up, then slowly roast for 3 hours until they are semi-dried. Remove from the salt. (If you are keeping them for longer than a day, store in a sterilised jar completely submerged in olive oil.)

2 To serve, arrange two slices of ham on each plate. Toss the tomatoes, artichokes, olives and parsley in a little oil, then arrange in the centre. Serve with some breadsticks.

PER SERVING 185 kcals, carbs 5g, fat 16g, sat fat 3g, salt 3g

Roast lamb with rosemary and garlic

If you have time, stud the lamb a day in advance as this allows the flavour of the garlic and rosemary to really permeate the meat.

SERVES 6–8 • PREP 15 MINS • COOK 2 HOURS

leg of lamb, about 2.5kg/5lb 8oz
1 garlic bulb, 4 cloves thinly sliced
1 bunch rosemary, pulled into small sprigs
1 tbsp vegetable oil
2 carrots, cut into large chunks
1 onion, cut into quarters
150ml/¼ pint red wine
1.2 litres/2 pints beef or lamb stock

try this...

Fresh mint sauce
Finely chop 2 bunches of mint leaves. Put the chopped leaves into a bowl with 3 tablespoons of caster sugar then pour over 3 tablespoons of boiling water. Stir until the sugar dissolves, then add 2 tbsp of vinegar. Let the sauce steep for at least 10 minutes before serving.

1 Using a sharp small knife, make at least 30 small incisions all over the meat. Poke a slice of garlic and a tuft of rosemary into each incision. (If done in advance, cover the lamb well and refrigerate. Remove from the fridge 1 hour before roasting.)

2 Heat oven to 190C/170C fan/gas 5. Heat a large frying pan, add a little oil and brown the lamb all over. Scatter the carrots, onion, remaining whole garlic cloves (in skins) and rosemary in a large roasting tin, pour in the wine and stock, then add the lamb.

3 Roast for about 1 hour 45 minutes. Turn the lamb halfway through cooking. Let the lamb rest in a warm place covered in foil for about 30 minutes.

4 For the gravy, strain the stock from the tin through a sieve into a saucepan. Reduce it a little on the hob if you want to concentrate the flavour, skimming off any fat that comes to the surface. Serve the lamb with the gravy and your choice of vegetables.

PER SERVING (6) 580 kcals, carbs 6g, fat 32g, sat fat 15g, salt 0.85g

OPPOSITE Clockwise from top left Chinese-style braised beef one-pot (page 156), Feta-crusted lamb with tomato sauce (page 150), Crisp roast pork with honey mustard gravy (page 165), Pan-fried venison with blackberry sauce (page 159), Slow-roast pork rolls with apple chilli chutney (page 155), Iberico ham with slow-roast tomatoes and artichokes.

Rabbit cacciatore (hunter's stew)

Cooking the rabbit slowly with a rich tomato sauce keeps the meat really tender.

SERVES 4 • PREP 30 MINS • COOK 1½ HOURS
❄

900g/2lb rabbit pieces
2 tbsp plain flour, seasoned
3 tbsp olive oil
2 onions, chopped
3 garlic cloves, chopped
large bunch parsley, most chopped
300ml/½ pint white wine
2 x 400g cans cherry tomatoes
1 tbsp sugar
about 20 large green olives

try this...

If you'd like to make this with chicken instead, use whole leg portions. The cooking time will be the same.

1 Toss the rabbit pieces in the seasoned flour. Heat 1 tbsp olive oil in a large shallow pan and brown the rabbit in 3 batches, adding another tbsp oil for each batch. Lift out all the rabbit onto a plate and set aside.
2 Add the onions and garlic to the pan with the remaining oil, then cook gently for 15 minutes until softened. Add the chopped parsley and cook for a few minutes more. Return the rabbit and splash in the wine. Turn up the heat and bubble the wine until it is half gone, then stir in the tomatoes. If the rabbit isn't completely covered, add a splash of water.
3 Cover the pan and simmer for 40 minutes until the rabbit is tender – the timing can vary, but if it's still tough just continue to cook, adding more water if needed, and the meat will eventually start to come away from the bone. When the meat is ready, throw in the olives, cover, and simmer for 5–10 minutes more. Season with sugar, salt and pepper then scatter with the remaining parsley to serve. Serve with polenta, mash or a buttery flat pasta such as tagliatelle.

PER SERVING 440 kcals, carbs 25.4g, fat 20.1g, sat fat 4.9g, salt 2.15g

Lamb cutlets with herb relish

Who needs cutlery anyway? The little bone attached to each of these tender cutlets makes a perfect handle.

SERVES 20 WITH OTHER DISHES • PREP 30 MINS COOK 30–40 MINS

4 x 7–8 bone racks of lamb, French-trimmed
FOR THE ALMOND CRUST
50g/2oz blanched almonds
1 garlic clove
1 tbsp Dijon mustard
FOR THE HERB RELISH
large bunch parsley (about 50g/2oz)
good handful mint
2 tbsp capers
3 anchovy fillets
1 garlic clove
1 tbsp red wine vinegar
200ml/7fl oz olive oil

1 Heat oven to 180C/160C fan/gas 4. Put the almonds and garlic in a food processor and process to a rough paste. Brush the fat side of the racks with a little mustard, then press the almond crust onto it. Roast for 30–40 minutes until the lamb is browned on the outside and pink inside. Leave to cool, then wrap in foil and chill for up to 24 hours.
2 Put all the herb relish ingredients in the food processor and whizz to a rough paste. Pour into a small bowl. When ready to serve, cut the lamb between the bones into little cutlets and arrange over a platter. Spoon a little herb relish onto each or serve separately in a small bowl.

PER SERVING 204 kcals, carbs 1g, fat 19g, sat fat 6g, salt 0.29g

Slow-roast pork rolls with apple chilli chutney

Rather like a homemade hog roast, this recipe is ideal for a bonfire party or any relaxed winter gathering.

SERVES 6–8 • PREP 15 MINS • COOK 6 HOURS
❄ **CHUTNEY ONLY**

2.5kg/5lb 8oz pork shoulder joint, skin scored and tied
2 tsp thyme leaves
1 tsp fennel seeds
1 tbsp olive oil
buttered soft bread rolls, to serve

FOR THE APPLE CHILLI CHUTNEY

1 tbsp olive oil
2 onions, finely chopped
1–2 red chillies, deseeded and finely chopped
4 eating apples, peeled, cored and chopped into
    small chunks
4 tbsp cider vinegar
4 tbsp golden caster sugar
leaves from 1 thyme sprig

1 Heat oven to 240C/220C fan/gas 9. Sit the pork in a large roasting tin. Mix together the thyme, fennel seeds, oil, some pepper and 1 tsp salt. Rub over the pork and into the skin. Roast for 30 minutes, then cover the whole tin with foil. Reduce the oven to 140C/120C fan/gas 1 and cook for 5 hours more.

2 For the chutney, heat the oil in a large pan. Soften the onions and chillies for 10–15 minutes. Stir in the apples, vinegar, sugar and 50ml water. Cover and cook gently for 15–20 minutes, stirring occasionally, until the apple is very soft. Blitz half of the apple mixture with a hand blender until smooth, then stir back into the pan with the thyme leaves.

3 Take the pork from the oven and raise the temperature to 240C/220C fan/gas 9. Uncover the pork and roast for 30 minutes to crisp the skin. Remove the crackling, let the meat rest wrapped in foil, then roast the crackling for another 30 minutes. Stuff the shredded pork into buns with some chutney and serve the crackling on the side.

PER SERVING 714 kcals, carbs 22g, fat 41g, sat fat 15g, salt 1.31g

Succulent braised venison

Long, slow cooking tenderizes tougher cuts of venison, and vegetables add an earthy sweetness. Don't be tempted to use a really lean cut of venison as this will overcook and become dry.

**SERVES 8 EASILY DOUBLED • PREP 15 MINS
COOK 1 HOUR 50 MINS**

2 carrots, roughly chopped
140g/5oz turnip or swede, roughly chopped
2 onions, roughly chopped
3 celery sticks, roughly chopped
olive oil and butter, for frying
1 garlic clove, crushed
1kg/2lb 4oz boned leg or shoulder of venison, cut into
    large chunks
5 tbsp plain flour, seasoned
2 tbsp redcurrant jelly
450ml/16fl oz dry red wine (Rioja is good)
450ml/16fl oz beef stock
2 thyme sprigs
1 bay leaf

1 Heat oven to 180C/160C fan/gas 4. Fry the vegetables in a little oil and butter in a heavy based casserole for 4–5 minutes until golden. Tip in the garlic and fry for a further minute, then set aside.

2 Put the venison into a plastic bag with the seasoned flour and shake to coat. Add a little more oil and butter to the pan, then fry the venison over a high heat, stirring now and then, until well browned. Don't crowd the pan – cook in batches if necessary. Set aside with the vegetables.

3 Add the redcurrant jelly and wine to the pan and bring to the boil, scraping up all the bits that have stuck to the bottom. Pour in the stock, then add the thyme, bay leaf, meat and vegetables. Bring to the boil. Cover and transfer to the oven for about 1½ hours or until tender. Season the sauce to taste and serve.

PER SERVING 277 kcals, carbs 18g, fat 10g, sat fat 2g, salt 0.7g

Chinese-style braised beef one-pot

If you can get it, ox cheek is fantastic value and rich in flavour – perfect for this dish. Serve with fluffy rice.

SERVES 6 • PREP 10 MINS • COOK 2–2½ HOURS

3–4 tbsp olive oil
6 garlic cloves, thinly sliced
good thumb-size piece fresh root ginger, peeled and shredded
1 bunch spring onions, sliced
1 red chilli, deseeded and thinly sliced
1.5kg/3lb 5oz braising beef, cut into large pieces (we used ox cheek)
2 tbsp plain flour, well seasoned
1 tsp Chinese five-spice powder
2 whole star anise
2 tsp light muscovado sugar (or use whatever you've got)
3 tbsp Chinese cooking wine or dry sherry
3 tbsp dark soy sauce, plus extra to serve
500ml/18fl oz beef stock
steamed bok choi and steamed basmati rice, to serve

1 Heat 2 tbsp of the oil in a large shallow casserole. Fry the garlic, ginger, onions and chilli for 3 minutes until soft and fragrant. Tip onto a plate. Toss the beef in the flour, add 1 tbsp oil to the pan, then brown the meat in batches, adding the final tbsp oil if you need to. It should take about 5 minutes to brown each batch.

2 Add the five-spice and star anise to the pan, tip in the gingery mix, then fry for 1 minute until fragrant. Turn up the heat, add the sugar and beef, stir, then splash in the wine or sherry, scraping up any meaty bits. Heat oven to 150C/130C fan/gas 2.

3 Pour in the soy and stock (it won't cover the meat completely), simmer, then cover and cook in the oven for 1½–2 hours, stirring halfway through cooking. The meat should be meltingly tender. Season with more soy. (Can be chilled and frozen for up to 1 month.)

4 Nestle the cooked bok choi into the pan, then bring to the table with the basmati rice and tuck in.

PER SERVING 513 kcals, carbs 9g, fat 29g, sat fat 10g, salt 2.39g

Crisp Chinese pork

Cut the pork into large chunks for a main course or smaller pieces for serving alongside other dishes.

**SERVES 4 • PREP 10 MINS, PLUS AT LEAST 2 HOURS SALTING
COOK 2 HOURS**

1.3kg/3lb piece boned pork belly, skin on and scored
2 tsp Chinese five-spice powder
FOR THE DIPPING SAUCE
4 tbsp soy sauce
small knob fresh root ginger, grated
1 tbsp Thai sweet chilli sauce
1 spring onion, finely chopped

1 Rub the pork with the five-spice and 2 tsp flaky sea salt then leave, uncovered, in the fridge for at least 2 hours, but preferably overnight.

2 When ready to cook, heat the oven to its maximum setting. Lay the pork on a rack over a roasting tin, skin uppermost. Roast for 10 minutes then lower the heat to 180C/160C fan/ gas 4 and cook for a further 1½ hours. If the skin isn't crisp by this point, turn up the heat to 220C/200C fan/gas 7 and cook for another 30 minutes until crisp. Leave to rest on a board for at least 10 minutes.

3 To make the dipping sauce, mix all the ingredients together with 2 tbsp water. Cut the pork into small pieces, then serve with the sauce, plus boiled rice and steamed greens, if you like.

PER SERVING 696 kcals, carbs 3g, fat 50g, sat fat 19g, salt 5.83g

Asian aubergine and pork hot pot

Slow-cooked aubergines become deliciously soft and absorb all the flavour of this fragrant Asian stew.

SERVES 4 • PREP 20 MINS • COOK 1 HOUR 20 MINS
❄

3 tbsp sunflower oil
750g/1lb 10oz fatty pork, such as shoulder or
    skinless belly, cut into large chunks
2 aubergines, cut into large chunks
2 tbsp dark muscovado sugar
5 star anise
1 cinnamon stick
2 onions, chopped
very large piece fresh root ginger, peeled and finely sliced
1 red chilli, deseeded and sliced
1 bunch coriander, leaves and stalks separated,
    stalks finely chopped
2 tbsp Thai fish sauce
juice 1 large lime

1 Heat oven to 200C/180C fan/gas 6. Heat 2 tbsp of the oil in an ovenproof sauté pan and brown the meat well (you may have to do this in batches), then scoop it out of the pan. Add the rest of the oil and the aubergines, brown them on all sides, scoop out and add to the pork. Tip the sugar into the pan and leave to caramelise slightly, then return the pork and aubergine to the pan with the star anise and cinnamon, and coat in the sticky caramel.

2 Add the onions, ginger and half the chilli, and cook for a few minutes with the pork. Add the coriander stalks and splash in the fish sauce and enough water to come about a third of the way up the side of the pan. Cover and place the pan, undisturbed, in the oven for 1 hour. (it can now be frozen for up to a month.)

3 Remove from the oven and add the lime juice and more fish sauce to taste. Stir through half the coriander leaves and the remaining chilli, and scatter over the rest of the coriander.

PER SERVING 574 kcals, carbs 18g, fat 40g, sat fat 13g, salt 1.81g

Beef Rendang

This slow-cooked Malaysian dish makes a great alternative to an Indian curry, but with every bit as much flavour.

SERVES 4 • PREP 15 MINS • COOK 2 HOURS

1 tbsp sunflower oil
750g/1lb 10oz stewing beef, cut into large chunks
1 large onion, quartered
3 garlic cloves
2cm piece root ginger, peeled
5-6 tbsp Rendang curry paste (see below)
400g can coconut milk
2 star anise
1 cinnamon stick
3 tbsp desiccated coconut, toasted

1 Heat a heavy pan over a medium heat. Add the oil and beef and cook for 10 minutes until brown. You may have to do this in two batches.

2 Meanwhile, blend the onion, garlic, ginger and curry paste in a food processor to make a wet paste.

3 Add the paste to the pan and stir to coat the meat. Cook for 2 minutes. Pour in the coconut milk and stir through. Add the star anise and cinnamon. Cover and simmer very gently for 1½ hours.

4 After this time, add the desiccated coconut and also a splash of water if the sauce seems too dry. Stir through and simmer for another 30 minutes until the beef is tender. Skim off any excess oil and season if needed, before serving with rice.

PER SERVING 570 kcals, carbs 9g, fat 40g, sat fat 23g, salt 1.33g

> **Rendang curry paste is a blend of coriander, cumin, dried shrimp paste, garlic, ginger, palm sugar, shallots, tamarind and turmeric. This forms the base of the Malaysian curry. Rendang paste is available in larger supermarkets and specialist shops.**

Proper beef, ale and mushroom pie

A rich beef stew that can be topped with pastry or simply served with mash and vegetables.
See page 264 for a step-by-step guide to lining and covering a pie.

SERVES 6 • PREP A STAGGERED 1 HOUR
COOK A STAGGERED 3 HOURS

FOR THE BEEF
small handful dried porcini mushrooms, about 15g/½oz
2 tbsp vegetable oil
1kg/2lb 4oz braising steak (buy as a whole piece and
    cut into large chunks)
2 large onions, roughly chopped
4 large carrots, chopped into large chunks
2 tsp golden caster sugar
4 tbsp plain flour
300ml/½ pint dark ale
2 beef stock cubes mixed with 400ml/14fl oz boiling water
small bunch each thyme, bay leaf and parsley,
    tied together
200g/7oz smoked bacon, lardons or chopped rashers
200g/7oz chestnut mushrooms, halved

FOR THE PASTRY
650g/1lb 7oz plain flour, plus extra for dusting
250g/9oz lard or cold butter, diced, plus extra for greasing
    (see below)
1 egg yolk, beaten, to glaze

1 Cover the porcini in boiling water for 20 minutes, then squeeze out but keep the soaking water. Heat oven to 160C/140C fan/gas 3.

2 Heat 1 tbsp oil in a large casserole, brown the meat in batches, then set aside. Add the onions and carrots to the pan, with a drizzle of oil, then cook on a low heat for 5 minutes until softened. Add the soaked mushrooms, sizzle for 1 minute more, then stir in the sugar and flour. Stir until the flour turns brown. Return the meat and any juices to the pan, add the ale, stock and porcini soaking liquid, discarding the last few drops. Season, add the herbs then bring to a simmer. Cover and cook in the oven for about 2 hours, until the meat is really tender.

3 Meanwhile, fry the bacon in a little more oil for 3 minutes until crisp. Turn up the heat, add the mushrooms and cook for 4 minutes until golden. Stir into the cooked stew. Cool completely – better still, make the stew up to 2 days in advance and chill. (Can also be frozen for up to 3 months and defrosted when needed.)

4 For the pastry, whizz the flour and lard or butter and a generous pinch salt in a processor until fine, then add up to 200ml ice-cold water to make a soft dough. Knead until smooth then wrap and chill for at least 1 hour.

5 Heat oven to 220C/200C fan/gas 7 and place a flat baking sheet in the oven. Heavily grease a 24–28cm pie dish and dust well with flour. Use two-thirds of the pastry to line the base, leaving the excess overhanging. Mound the beef in the dish, using a slotted spoon so that some gravy is left in the container.

6 Brush the edges of the pastry in the dish with egg yolk, then cover with the remaining pastry. Trim the edges, crimp the pastry, then re-roll your trimmings to make decorations, if you like. Brush heavily with egg. Make a few little slits in the centre of the pie, place on the hot baking sheet, then bake for 40 minutes until golden. Leave the pie to rest for 10 minutes while you heat up the leftover gravy.

PER SERVING 1,244 kcals, carbs 105g, fat 70g, sat fat 29g, salt 2.61g

> **Making pastry with lard gives a deliciously 'short' texture – crumbly and tender. The butter gives it a really good flavour. You can use whichever you prefer or, for the best texture and flavour, you can use half of each.**

Steamed steak pudding

This is a wonderful take on a classic steamed steak and kidney pudding. For more information on steaming and wrapping a pudding basin, see page 393.

SERVES 4–6 • PREP 30 MINS, PLUS CHILLING COOK 4½ HOURS

FOR THE PASTRY
450g/1lb self-raising flour
225g/8oz shredded beef suet

FOR THE FILLING
1 tbsp each butter and vegetable oil, plus extra oil
   and butter for greasing
2 large onions, thinly sliced
8 garlic cloves, thinly sliced
4 large field mushrooms, stems removed
500g/1lb 2oz braising steak, cut into large cubes
1 tbsp plain flour, seasoned
1 tsp tomato purée
200ml/7fl oz brown ale
1 tsp sugar
4 thyme sprigs, leaves picked

try this...

To make a steak and kidney pudding, omit the mushrooms. Cut 200g ox kidney into cubes, discarding any sinew. Coat in seasoned flour and brown in the pan until golden, then add to the rest of the filling.

1 To make the pastry, sift 1 tsp salt and the flour together. Add the suet then 300ml cold water. Work until it all comes together into a dough. Wrap in cling film and chill for 1 hour.
2 Heat the butter and oil in a large frying pan. Gently fry the onions and garlic for 10 minutes until soft. Tip out of the pan, then add a little more oil. Now fry the mushrooms until golden, then tip out. Toss the beef in the flour and fry in batches, adding more oil as you go, until really golden brown. Mix the purée, ale, sugar and thyme into the pan, then cool.
3 Now butter a 1.4-litre basin. Roll the suet pastry out to about 1cm thick and use to line the sides of the basin. Trim so that there's a little overhang. Re-roll what's left and cut out a lid 1cm wider than the top of the basin. Put the mushrooms around the sides of the basin, stalks facing in, then fill the basin with meat, onion and juices. (You might not need all the juices.)
4 Place the lid on top and crimp the edges together to seal. Make a double layer of buttered foil and baking paper, and pleat it in the centre. Scrunch this over the pudding, foil-side up, then tie with string under the rim of the basin. Trim to about 2cm under the string, then put into a steamer or sit on a saucer in a large pan of gently simmering water that's halfway up the sides of the bowl. Steam the pudding for 4 hours. Unwrap and turn out onto a big plate. Good with broccoli or cauliflower cheese.

PER SERVING (6) 777 kcals, carbs 71g, fat 44g, sat fat 18g, salt 2g

Pan-fried venison with blackberry sauce

 Blackberries are delicious in savoury sauces, and this version is the perfect match for the richly flavoured venison. Like steak, venison can be eaten rare.

SERVES 4 • PREP 10 MINS • COOK 15 MINS

1 tbsp olive oil
2 thick venison steaks or 4 medallions
1 tbsp balsamic vinegar
150ml/¼ pint strong beef stock
2 tbsp redcurrant jelly
1 garlic clove, crushed
85g/3oz fresh or frozen blackberries

1 Heat the oil in a frying pan, fry the venison for 5 minutes, then turn over and fry for 3–5 minutes more, depending on how rare you like it and on the thickness of the meat (cook for 5–6 minutes on each side for well done). Lift the meat from the pan and set aside to rest.
2 Add the balsamic vinegar to the pan, then pour in the stock, jelly and garlic. Stir over quite a high heat to blend everything together, then add the blackberries and carry on cooking until they soften. Serve with the venison and some mash potato and broccoli.

PER SERVING 182 kcals, carbs 7g, fat 5g, sat fat 1g, salt 0.24g

Chilli con carne

Warm your cockles on a winter weekend with a big pan of spicy con carne. Great with rice or baked potatoes and a pot of soured cream for dolloping.

**SERVES 4 • PREP 10 MINS, PLUS STANDING
COOK 1 HOUR 10 MINS**
❄

1 large onion, chopped
1 tbsp oil
1 red pepper, deseeded and sliced
1 heaped tsp hot chilli powder (or 1 level tbsp mild)
1 tsp paprika
1 tsp ground cumin
2 garlic cloves, crushed
500g/1lb 2oz lean minced beef
300ml/½ pint beef stock
400g can chopped tomatoes
½ tsp dried marjoram or dried mixed herbs
1 cube dark chocolate, or 1 tsp sugar
2 tbsp tomato purée
400g can red kidney beans, drained

1 Put a large frying pan or casserole over a medium heat then fry the onion in the oil for 5 minutes until softened. Tip in the red pepper, chilli, paprika and cumin. Stir, then leave to cook for another 5 minutes, stirring occasionally. Add the garlic for the final minute.
2 Increase the heat then add the meat and cook for at least 5 minutes, breaking it up with the wooden spoon. The meat should fry, rather than stew.
3 Add the stock, tomatoes, marjoram, chocolate, purée and seasoning then simmer for 45 minutes, stirring occasionally, until the mince is tender and the sauce is rich and thick. Add a splash of water if necessary.
4 Tip in the beans, simmer for another 10 minutes, then season to taste. Stir in the chocolate and let the chilli stand for 10 minutes off the heat before serving, to let the flavours mingle.

PER SERVING 387 kcals, carbs 25g, fat 17g, sat fat 6g, salt 2.32g

Pork with black pudding and roasted rhubarb

This is a great dinner party dish as you can prepare the stuffing, the pork and the rhubarb up to 24 hours ahead, leaving just a very simple sauce to make at the last minute.

**SERVES 6 EASILY HALVED • PREP 25 MINS
COOK 45-50 MINS**

2 pork tenderloin fillets, about 350g/12oz each
juice 1 lemon
250g/9oz black pudding, skinned and cut into slices
12 thin rashers streaky bacon, stretched with the back
    of a knife
1 tbsp olive oil
300g/11oz rhubarb, cut into 5cm lengths on
    the diagonal
1 tbsp clear honey, warmed
200ml/7fl oz vegetable stock
2 rounded tbsp crème fraîche

1 Heat oven to 190C/170C fan/gas 5. Split the pork fillets lengthwise almost in half and open out like a book. Bash with a rolling pin to flatten, then season all over with salt, pepper and lemon juice. Fill the pork with the black pudding, then close the fillets around it.
2 Wrap the bacon around the pork, tucking the ends under the pork where possible. Transfer to a large roasting tin, drizzle with the oil, then roast for 30 minutes.
3 Toss the rhubarb with the honey. Add to the roasting tin, then return to the oven for 10–12 more minutes until the rhubarb is tender and the bacon nicely browned. Transfer the pork and rhubarb to a warm plate and keep warm while you make the sauce.
4 Set the roasting tin on the hob and add the stock to the cooking juices. Boil, scraping all the pan juices from the base. Bubble for a few minutes, then stir in the crème fraîche and whisk. Taste for seasoning. Slice the pork and serve with the rhubarb and a little sauce. Serve the remaining sauce separately.

OPPOSITE Pork with black pudding and roasted rhubarb

PER SERVING 426 kcals, carbs 9g, fat 28g, sat fat 8g, salt 2g

Lamb tagine with dates and sweet potatoes

This is one of those wonderful dishes that improves with keeping. Try with the Harissa couscous on page 215.

SERVES 10 • PREP 30 MINS • COOK 2 HOURS
❄

6 tbsp olive oil
4 onions, thinly sliced
2 tbsp finely chopped fresh root ginger
2kg/4lb 8oz boneless lamb shoulder, cut into 5cm chunks
4 tsp ground cumin
2 tsp each paprika and ground coriander
2 cinnamon sticks
850ml/1½ pints passata
700g/1lb 9oz sweet potatoes, cut into chunks
350g/12oz pitted dates
TO SERVE
100g/4oz blanched almonds, toasted
good handful coriander, roughly

1 Heat the oil in a large deep pan. Add the onions, then gently fry until softened, about 5 minutes. Stir in the ginger, add the meat in batches, then fry on all sides until lightly coloured. Return all the meat to the pan, stir in the spices and cinnamon sticks, then cook for 1 minute.

2 Add the passata and 800ml water, then bring to the boil, stirring. Season well, then cover and simmer for 1½ hours, until the lamb is tender. (Can be frozen or chilled for up to 3 days at this stage.)

3 Add the sweet potatoes, stir well, cover again, then cook for 20 minutes or until the potatoes are just tender. Stir in the dates and heat through for 5 minutes. Taste and add more seasoning if necessary. To serve, spoon the tagine into a serving dish and scatter with the almonds and coriander.

PER SERVING 646 kcals, carbs 49g, fat 32g, sat fat 13g, salt 0.82g

Muffin-topped winter beef pot

A muffin topping is a much lighter alternative to traditional suet-style dumplings. A smaller quantity of good-quality braising beef and more sweet carrots and parsnips make this a great choice for the kids.

SERVES 2 ADULTS AND 2–3 CHILDREN • PREP 20 MINS COOK 2½ HOURS
❄ **WITHOUT TOPPING**

500g/1lb 2oz braising beef, cut into bite-size chunks
2 tbsp plain flour, seasoned
2 tbsp olive oil
1 large onion, finely chopped
450g/1lb carrots, cut into chunks
2 large parsnips, cut into chunks
1 bay leaf
2 tbsp sun-dried or regular tomato purée
300ml/½ pint red wine (or replace with stock)
450ml/16fl oz vegetable or beef stock
FOR THE TOPPING
225g/8oz plain flour
3 tsp baking powder
140g/5oz Cheddar, coarsely grated
2 tbsp olive oil
150ml/¼ pint milk

1 Heat oven to 150C/130C fan/gas 2. Toss the beef in the seasoned flour. Heat the oil in a casserole, brown the beef in batches then set aside.

2 Add 2 tbsp water and the onion to the casserole, scraping up the crusty bits from the bottom. Lower the heat and fry gently for 10 minutes, until the onion has softened.

3 Tip in the carrots, parsnips and bay leaf, then fry for 2 minutes more. Return the beef, stir in the purée, wine and stock, then boil. Cover, and cook in the oven for 1¾–2 hours until the meat is tender. (Can be made up to 2 days ahead or frozen for up to 1 month.) Take out of the oven and increase the temperature to 190C/170C fan/gas 5.

4 For the topping, sieve the flour and baking powder into a bowl and add half the cheese. Combine the oil and milk, then stir into the flour to make a soft, slightly sticky dough. Add more milk, if necessary. Spoon over the meat and vegetables, sprinkle with the remaining cheese and bake for about 15 minutes until golden, risen and cooked through.

PER ADULT SERVING 847 kcals, carbs 82g, fat 39g, sat fat 14g, salt 2.81g

Fillet of beef with peppercorn sauce

Best served traditionally with homemade chips, onion rings, watercress and slices of tomato.
Fillet is an expensive cut; for instructions on cooking sirloin or rump instead, turn to page 135.

**SERVES 2 EASILY DOUBLED OR HALVED • PREP 5 MINS
COOK 20 MINS**

1 tbsp vegetable oil
25g/1oz clarified butter (see below)
2 fillet steaks, about 140g/5oz each, at room temperature
knob of butter
2 large shallots, finely chopped
6 medium mushrooms, sliced
2 tsp green and pink peppercorns, crushed
3 tbsp brandy
100ml/3½fl oz red wine
200ml/7fl oz good-quality beef stock
3 tbsp double cream

1 Heat a frying pan over a medium-to-high heat, then pour in the oil and half of the clarified butter. Season the steaks generously then cook for 2 minutes each side for medium-rare, or 3 minutes each side for medium, depending on the thickness. Seal the rounded edges, too. Transfer to a plate.
2 Add the butter to the pan, then fry the shallots, mushrooms and peppercorns over a medium heat for 5 minutes, until the shallots have softened and the mushrooms browned. Return the steaks to the pan. Heat the brandy in a metal ladle, light with a match then carefully pour into the hot pan, standing well back. Once the pan has stopped flaming, remove the steaks again.
3 Pour in the wine, turn up the heat and boil rapidly until reduced by half. This will take about 5 minutes. Add the stock and reduce again, this time by two-thirds. Stir in the cream, bubble to thicken a little then check the seasoning. Return the fillets and any juices to the pan to warm through, spooning the sauce over.

PER SERVING 594 kcals, carbs 1g, fat 42g, sat fat 21g, salt 0.57g

try this...

To make Bearnaise sauce, finely chop 1 shallot and put into a saucepan with 3 tbsp white wine vinegar and a few peppercorns. Boil down to 1 tbsp then strain. Follow the recipe for Hollandaise sauce on page 46, adding the reduced vinegar to the egg yolks before whisking. Add a little chopped tarragon and parsley once the sauce is ready. You won't need the lemon juice.

Clarifying butter removes its milk solids, which burn easily when frying at high temperatures. To make your own clarified butter, melt a little more butter than you need in a small pan, then drain off the yellow part, discarding the white solids left at the bottom.

Flavoured butters to serve with steak

A great way to add flavour to a steak is with a little pat of tasty butter, melting over the steak as it rests.
Here are a few flavour ideas. For steak cooking times, see page 135.

Take 100g/4oz butter out of the fridge for an hour to soften. Flavour is key, so use good-quality butter. Beat the butter with a wooden spoon until it is soft and creamy, then beat in any flavourings you fancy. Tip the flavoured butter onto a square of baking parchment or cling film, roll it around the butter to form a sausage shape, then twist the ends to seal. The butter is now ready to be stored for up to 3 days in the fridge or up to a month in the freezer.

Garlic and parsley

Beat 2 tbsp finely chopped parsley and 1 crushed garlic clove into the butter. Add a little fine sea salt if using unsalted butter.

Chilli, coriander and lime

Beat in finely grated zest of 1 lime, ½ deseeded and very finely chopped red chilli and 2 tbsp chopped coriander. Add a little fine sea salt if using unsalted butter.

Horseradish and chive

Add 2 tbsp horseradish cream, 6 coarsely crushed black peppercorns, a little fine sea salt and 2 tbsp snipped chives.

Roast rib of beef with sweet red onions and roasted whole garlic

Just add some roast potatoes, Yorkshire pudding, Savoy cabbage, gravy and horseradish sauce and there you have it – the classic British roast.

SERVES 4 WITH LEFTOVERS • PREP 10 MINS • COOK ABOUT 2 HOURS FOR MEDIUM BEEF

2kg/4lb 8oz (2 ribs' worth) rib of beef on the bone
4 large red onions, peeled with the root left intact
4 tbsp olive oil, plus extra for the garlic
1 tbsp dark muscovado sugar
1 tbsp balsamic vinegar
2 large heads garlic, left whole but with the tops sliced off
FOR THE GRAVY
1 tbsp plain flour
600ml/1 pint fresh beef stock
2 tbsp balsamic vinegar

Horseradish cream

To make your own fiery horseradish cream, mix a 200g pot crème fraîche with 5 tbsp hot horseradish (or more or less, depending on how hot you like it). Season with salt and pepper and stir in a handful chopped chives, if you like.

1 Heat oven to 180C/160C fan/gas 4. Season the beef with salt and pepper, place in a roasting tin and roast for 20 minutes per 450g/lb for rare, 25 minutes per 450g/lb for medium, or 30 minutes per 450g/1lb for well done.
2 Quarter the onions and place in a small roasting tin. In a bowl, mix together the oil, sugar and balsamic vinegar, then coat the onions in it. Drizzle a little oil over the garlic and add to the roasting tin with the onions.
3 When the beef has 1¼ hours left to cook, put the onions and garlic on the shelf below and roast for the remaining cooking time, turning the onions occasionally until caramelised and softened, and the garlic cloves are soft.
4 Remove the meat from the oven and transfer to a carving board in a warm place. Cover with foil and rest for 20 minutes.
5 Meanwhile, make the gravy. Drain all but 1 tbsp of the fat from the roasting tin. Put the tin over a direct heat, tip in the flour and cook for 30 seconds. Gradually stir in the stock, scraping the bottom of the pan, until you have a smooth gravy. Keep stirring until it thickens slightly, then tip in the vinegar and bubble for 5 minutes. Season and tip in any juices from the resting meat before serving. Strain through a sieve, if you like. Serve with the sweet onions and softened garlic cloves.

PER SERVING 548 kcals, carbs 16g, fat 25g, sat fat 6.5g, salt 0.9g

Best Yorkshire puddings

The secret to getting gloriously puffed-up Yorkshires is to have the fat sizzling hot from the start.

MAKES 8 LARGE PUDS OR 24 SMALL • PREP 5 MINS COOK 25 MINS
❄

sunflower oil
140g/5oz plain flour
4 eggs
200ml/7fl oz semi-skimmed milk

1 Heat oven to 230C/210C fan/gas 8. Drizzle a little oil evenly into 2 x 4-hole Yorkshire pudding tins or a 12-hole non-stick muffin tin and place in the oven to heat through.
2 To make the batter, tip the flour into a bowl and beat in the eggs until smooth. Gradually add the milk and carry on beating until the mix is completely lump-free. Season with salt and pepper.
3 Pour the batter into a jug, then remove the hot tins from the oven. Carefully and evenly pour the batter into the holes. Place the tins back in the oven and leave undisturbed for 20–25 minutes until the puddings have puffed up and browned. Serve immediately. (You can now cool them and freeze for up to 1 month.)

PER PUD (8 large puds) 199 kcals, carbs 15g, fat 13g, sat fat 2g, salt 0.12g

Crisp roast pork with honey mustard gravy

This honey mustard gravy is light and easy; perfect with the delicate flavour of roast pork.
Keeping the bone in the meat will help the meat stay moist and lock in lots of flavour.

SERVES 4 WITH PLENTY OF LEFTOVERS • PREP 10 MINS
COOK 2 HOURS 20 MINS

2kg/4lb 8oz pork loin (bone in), skin and fat scored
1 tbsp olive oil
100ml/3½fl oz hot chicken stock
1 tbsp wholegrain mustard
1 tbsp clear honey
1 tsp finely chopped thyme leaves

1 Heat oven to 240C/220C fan/gas 9. Pat the pork all over with kitchen paper. Lightly rub all over with oil, place in a large roasting tin and sprinkle liberally with salt. Cook for 20 minutes, turn down the oven to 190C/170C fan/gas 5, then cook for 30 minutes per 450g/1lb (about 2 hours). Remove from the tin, place on a serving plate and loosely cover with foil.
2 Pour off excess fat from the tin. Add the stock to the tin, then stir to incorporate the meat juices and sticky bits at the bottom. Pour through a sieve into a small pan. Add the mustard, honey and thyme, plus juices from the resting meat, to the pan. Stir and simmer for 5 minutes until starting to turn syrupy. Serve alongside the pork.

PER SERVING 726 kcals, carbs 3g, fat 47g, sat fat 18g, salt 0.71g

try this...

If your crackling isn't as crisp as you'd like, cut it away from the pork and return to the oven at 230C/210C fan/gas 8 on a baking sheet and let it crisp up as you make the gravy. The pork can rest under a sheet of foil.

tip When you're at the butcher's, ask for the joint to be chined (cut through the bone) for easier carving. The butcher will also score the skin for you.

Bramley apple sauce

SERVES 6–8 • PREP 10 MINS • COOK 20 MINS
❅

3 Bramley apples, peeled, cored and sliced
50g/2oz golden caster sugar
50g/2oz butter

1 Tip all of the ingredients into a pan, then cover with a lid. Place the pan on a low heat, stirring occasionally, for about 15 minutes until the apples break down into a purée. Stir to knock out any lumps, then tip into a serving dish.

PER SERVING (6) 130 kcals, carbs 18g, fat 7g, sat fat 4g, salt 0.13g

Fish

Seawater fish, freshwater fish, delicious smoked and cured fish and seafood are all easy to cook with a little guidance. And fish is so good for you, too – we should all be eating more of it. Your fishmonger is your best friend here; he will gut, fillet, slice and chop away so you don't have to, and he will also guide you in making the right choice of fish that is in season and sustainably caught. There are only a few rules to follow: buy it fresh, and keep the cooking simple and the flavourings few.

BUYING FRESH FISH AND SEAFOOD

A fresh whole fish will be shiny and firm, with bright eyes and pink or red gills. Above all, it should not smell fishy. Fillets and steaks should have a shiny translucent flesh without blemishes, feel firm and also have no discernible smell. In fact, all fish or seafood should smell of sea air, nothing more.

Shellfish, aside from prawns and shelled scallops, are sold live and should smell fresh and clean. Always buy shellfish from a reliable source, as it can pose a health risk if it is not super-fresh. Frozen fish is a great option – fish and seafood frozen at sea can often be 'fresher' than fresh fish, and, of course, it is easy to store too.

STORING FISH AND SEAFOOD

Keep fish as cool and moist as possible for as short a time as you can – 24 hours at the most in a dish covered with clingfilm and placed in the coldest part of the fridge. Whole fish keep slightly longer than fillets, but in any case you should keep all fish well covered when storing it.

If you know that the fish is really fresh, it can be frozen immediately after purchase. Firm, white-fleshed fish can be frozen for up to 3 months, more delicate fish for up to 1 month. Many kinds of fish are frozen at sea and then defrosted for sale, and these should not be refrozen. Ask at the counter if you're not sure about how they were stored.

PREPARING FISH

Gutting fish is a messy job, so ask your fishmonger to do that for you. Skinning and scaling is easier though. Keeping the skin on helps the fish to stay together as it cooks and protects the delicate flesh from direct heat. It can, of course, be peeled away after cooking (when steaming a salmon fillet, for example). The scales need to be removed if you want to cook and serve your fish whole or as skin-on fillets.

To remove the skin from a fillet, put the fillet skinside-down on a chopping board. Grip the skin at the end nearest to you, then, holding a

OPPOSITE Smoked mackerel with herb and beetroot couscous (page 181).

sharp, thin-bladed knife at right angles to the fillet, with the blade almost upright, work in a gently sawing motion, pushing the flesh away from the skin rather than cutting it. Keep the skin taut as you go.

To remove scales, put the fish in a plastic bag (this prevents the scales flying everywhere), then rub against the grain of the scales (or from tail to head on a whole fish) with the back of a large knife. Rinse.

Always check fillets for bones by running your fingers along the flesh side. 'Pin bones' are the largest bones in the fillet and will be near the thickest end. A pair of tweezers makes pulling these out a simple job.

There are step-by-step pictures showing how to fillet a flat fish and round fish on pages 173 and 174.

WHAT IS SUSTAINABLE FISHING?

Sustainable fish comes from stocks that are not overfished and have been caught by environmentally friendly means that do not damage habitats and other creatures. There is no definitive list of fish that we should or shouldn't buy, as fish stocks do fluctuate, so for peace of mind choose fish approved by the Marine Stewardship Council – see their website www.msc.org for up-to-date information or check the Marine Conservation Society's good and bad fish ratings at www.fishonline.org. Ask your fishmonger which fish on his counter comes from a sustainable source and choose only from that selection. Keep an open mind to trying new fish too.

As a general rule, even when a species is not at risk from over fishing, we still need to be thoughtful about what we buy. So don't, for example, simply switch from eating cod to pollack. It's better from a sustainability and health point of view to eat as great a variety of fish and shellfish as you can, rather than sticking to the same favourites.

OILY FISH

Oily fish have oil-rich dark or pinky flesh and are a great source of omega 3 fatty acids and a good source of protein, vitamins A and D and minerals. Omega 3 acids are important for mental function and protecting the heart. Oily fish have a strong flavour and so they pair brilliantly with other punchy flavours such as chilli, spice and citrus, to mention just a few. They also tend to have a firm texture, making them ideal for most methods of cooking.

Debate continues over portion sizes – we hear about the health benefits of oily fish, yet we are told there could be health risks because of pollutants. At time of going to press, pregnant women, those intending to become pregnant and young girls should aim to eat 2–3 portions a week (one portion is 140g). Men and boys, and women beyond reproductive age, should aim to eat 4 portions a week.

Examples of oily fish are mackerel, sardines (pilchards), salmon, trout, tuna, herring and eel.

Smoked oily fish, such as smoked salmon, retains some omega 3, however their salt content tends to be quite high. If you're following a heart-healthy diet or just watching your salt intake, opt for fresh or frozen instead.

WHITE FISH

White fish can be either 'round', such as cod, haddock and sea bass, or 'flat', such as plaice and sole. Round fish are ideal prepared in fillets and cooked whole – often with aromatic ingredients stuffed into their bellies – and their flesh tends to cook to thick white flakes. Flat fish tend to be more delicate, with a finer texture, and can be served in fillets, or whole, or cut into pieces and fried as goujons. All white fish is very low in fat and contains some omega 3 acids, but at much lower levels than in oily fish. Other examples of white fish are tilapia, coley (saithe), pollack, bream, halibut, skate, monkfish and snapper.

SMOKED AND CANNED FISH

Before fridges came along, smoking and salting were essential ways of preserving fish. Hot smoking cooks the flesh through, whereas cold-smoked fish is salted and then smoked without heat. Smoked fish has a strong, distinctive flavour that goes brilliantly with eggs, potatoes and creamy ingredients, to name a few.

Hot-smoked fish (such as smoked mackerel) are excellent in salads and for whizzing into pâtés, whereas cold-smoked fish can be enjoyed as they are (smoked salmon, for example), or added to tarts, pies and soups (smoked haddock in particular).

Kippers are herring that have been split, salted then smoked. Bloaters are the same as kippers but are the whole fish. An Arbroath smokies is a haddock that has been beheaded, cleaned and then salted and hot smoked.

Canned fish is often seen as the poor relative of fresh,

but canned sardines, mackerel and other fish are actually high in nutrients. Choose fish in spring water or in a healthier oil such as olive, rather than in salty brine, as fish already has a high sodium content. Canned tuna is not counted as an oily fish as its levels of omega 3 are depleted through the canning process.

SEAFOOD

All live, 'in-shell' seafood (scallops, clams, mussels, oysters) should be bought on the day of cooking. Keep in a bowl lightly covered with damp kitchen paper (never under water), in the bottom of the fridge. They must be alive when you cook or open them.

Scallops

Ready-prepared scallops should be off-white; pure white flesh may indicate that they have been soaked in water to pump up their size and weight. The coral, or roe, should be a perky orange. There are two main types of scallop sold in the UK: large King scallops and Queenie scallops, which are about the size of a twenty-pence piece.

Diver-caught live scallops on the shell are the best you can get, but they do cost the most as they are hand-picked and are often firmer and sweeter. They also won't have been dredged – a practice that damages the seabed. Farmed scallops are fine.

Being meaty, scallops are ideal for stir-frying, pan-frying, grilling, steaming and skewering for a BBQ. Add to seafood stews for the last few minutes to avoid overcooking.

If you buy scallops still in the shell, discard any that don't close straight away after a sharp tap. To open, prise the shells apart then carefully release the muscle from the top and bottom shell. Once released, carefully pull away any part of the muscle that is not the white meat or orange roe, taking particular care to remove all traces of the stomach sac (this is virtually black). If you intend to serve scallops back in their shells, the shells must be well scrubbed with hot water first.

Clams

These simply need rinsing in a bowl of water several times to get rid of any grit. Discard any shells that are broken or damaged or feel particularly heavy (these could be full of sand). Discard any that don't close when tapped or that fail to open on cooking.

Mussels

Mussels are at their best during autumn and winter (traditionally when there is an 'r' in the month), but they are available throughout the year.

Wash them under cold running water until it runs clear, and scrub away any barnacles and weed, if needed. Pull the 'beard' away from each individual mussel. Tap open mussels sharply on the worktop; if they close, keep them. Discard any that don't close. Once cooked, any mussels that haven't opened should be discarded.

Oysters

The two main types of oyster available in the UK are the rock or Pacific oyster and the native. Rock oysters originate from the Pacific and although they won't breed in UK waters, they are farmed here. They grow quickly, making them less expensive than natives. Natives are in season only when there is an 'r' in the month and aren't available in such abundance. Rock oysters are a pointy teardrop shape, native oysters are a round shape. The flavour can vary through sharp, salty, sweet and metallic, the texture from firm to soft and creamy.

When choosing oysters, look for a very tightly shut undamaged shell. Store them at the bottom of the fridge for up to 24 hours, lightly covered and rounded-side down so that they don't lose any juice.

Oysters are usually enjoyed raw, however Pacific oysters can also be cooked – a few classics are Oysters Kilpatrick (with bacon and Worcestershire sauce), Oysters Rockefeller (with spinach and Parmesan) and deep-fried, breadcrumbed oysters, called Po'boys.

See page 186 for step-by-step instructions on how to open and serve oysters.

Prawns

Tiger, king and North Atlantic prawns are those most commonly sold in the UK. They are fished in both the ocean and fresh water, and are available farmed as well as wild. Fresh prawns should feel firm and have no discernible smell. They deteriorate quickly and don't store for more than a day. Frozen prawns are perfectly good – simply defrost them in the fridge before use. All prawns only need quick cooking, as they can quickly overcook and become tough.

Raw prawns are best for cooking, but they may need 'deveining' first. If the prawns are shell-on, twist off the heads and then peel away the shell and legs. If there is a blackish thread that runs along the length of its back, it should be removed. The neatest way to get rid of this vein is to poke a skewer or the tip of a small knife into the prawn mid-way along its back. Pull gently, and the thread should come up with the skewer.

To butterfly a prawn, peel and devein as above, leaving the tail on. Then make a deep cut along the belly of the prawn, open it out and press it down so that it's flat. The prawn will curl and open out as it cooks.

Lobster

Lobster at home is a real luxury, but a lot less expensive than in a restaurant – so why not give it a go? The flesh is white, sweet and succulent.

Generally speaking, the colder the waters in which the lobster was fished, the better the flavour. We mainly see Canadian or American lobsters, which have round, very fleshy claws, and European lobsters, which are fished around the UK, Brittany and Norway have smaller claws and are considered to have the best flavour.

Never buy a raw dead lobster – they must be live, or cooked. If buying ready-dressed lobster, all you have to do is check the use-by date, keep it chilled and enjoy it straight from the shell. If buying one to dress yourself, feel its weight. Choose a lobster that weighs 650–900g (1½–2lb) – much heavier than this and you'll pay more for shell than meat. To test if the lobster was fresh before it was cooked, ask your fishmonger to pull the tail outwards. If it was fresh, the tail will snap back into place.

Lobsters are blue/black when live and turn bright red when cooked. A live lobster should be spritely, with its tail tucked under its body and a hard shell. Mind your fingers!

The most humane way to cook a live lobster is to freeze it for two hours before cooking. Fill a very large pan with salted water (as salty as the sea) and bring it to the boil. Put the lobster into the vigorously boiling pan (Canadian and American lobsters tend to have a thinner shell and need around 10 minutes boiling time per 450g/1lb; European ones will cook in around 12 minutes per 450g/1lb), then plunge it straight into a sinkful of iced water to stop the cooking.

For full step-by-step instructions for preparing a cooked lobster, turn to page 199.

Crab

A number of crabs are indigenous to the British coastline, but the brown edible crab is the most popular. White crab meat comes from the legs and claws and the dark meat comes from within the body. White meat is delicate and light, whereas the dark meat is dense and spreadable, almost like pâté.

When buying ready-prepared crabmeat, the best choice is 'hand-picked', as it will have been prepared carefully, should contain no or very little shell and the meat will have retained its fresh quality. Most frozen and canned crabmeat tends to be watery, grey and lacking in flavour.

If you'd like to cook your own crab, then a live one should be fairly active when you buy it. Weigh it and jot the weight down. Keep it in the fridge for no longer than a day then, prior to cooking, give it a few hours in the freezer – they hibernate in the cold and will become comatose. Not doing this, apart from being cruel, means that the shock of sudden immersion into boiling water can cause the crab to 'shoot' (lose) its claws. Remove the crab from the freezer, drop it into a deep pan of boiling salted water, cook for 15 minutes per 450g/1lb, cool rapidly in iced water, then dress. There are step-by-step instructions for preparing a cooked crab on page 188.

Squid

A member of the family that includes octopus and cuttlefish, squid are available all year round and are totally delicious when cooked correctly. The golden rule is to either cook squid for seconds or hours, but never in-between – otherwise it will become tough.

Good-quality squid, whether fresh or frozen, should have virtually no aroma. Unprepared, it will have a delicate, purple brownish membrane. The body of the squid should be pearly white with no hint or tinge of pink.

You will need 750g/1lb 10oz uncleaned whole squid to get 450g/1lb squid rings. To prepare your own squid, it's best to go for the whole squid weighing 100–350g/4–12oz each. If you prefer not to clean the squid yourself, a good fishmonger will do it for you.

Step-by-step: Preparing squid

OK, so preparing a squid is never going to be a job for the faint of heart – it is slippery and a little messy, but, if you are mad about fish, the it's a skill worth knowing.

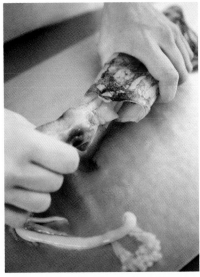

1 Gently pull the head away from the body, taking the intestines with it. Cut the tentacles away from the head just in front of the eyes. Squeeze out the beak-like mouth from the centre of the tentacles and cut this off too. Discard it along with the rest of the head and the intestines.

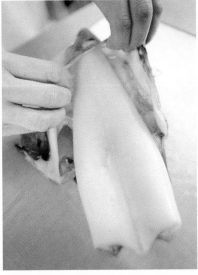

2 Pull the semi-transparent skin off the body, together with the fins from either side of the squid to reveal the milky white flesh underneath. Don't throw the fins away – they can be skinned and sliced into strips.

Often in restaurants, you'll see squid cut into rectangles and scored into diamonds before cooking. When you cook the squid, the squid will roll up attractively and the scored lines will catch any flavourings that the squid is cooked with (or give coatings a really good foothold). Open out the pouch as before, then, with the tip of a knife, score criss-crossed lines about 1cm apart all over what was the inner side of the pouch. Cut into 5cm pieces.

3 Pull out and discard the plastic-like quill from inside the body, then wash out the pouch with water.

4 Cut the body across into thin rings. Alternatively, slit the pouch open lengthways along one side and cut it into squares. Separate the tentacles into pairs if they are large, or leave them in a clump if small.

Step-by-step: Preparing a flat fish

Flat fish spend their days on the sea floor, feeding and trying to blend into the surroundings away from predators – hence their flat slipper shape, mottled colouring and eyes on one side of their head. Common, smaller types of flat fish include sole, plaice, dabs, flounder, witch and megrim. Larger flat fish including turbot, brill and halibut can get very big indeed.

1 Ask the fishmonger to gut the fish and remove the dark skin from the upper side of the fish. With a large knife, cut the head away cleanly, just behind the gills.

2 Using kitchen scissors, trim away the frills from either side of the fish.

tip
If you're keen on fish and want to prepare your own regularly, then invest in a fish knife. Fish knives have a much thinner, more flexible blade than ordinary knives, and allow you to fillet and remove skin neatly and swiftly. A pair of sturdy kitchen scissors or poultry shears are just the job for trimming away fins and frills.

3 Squeeze out any roe if necessary and wash away any blood from the cavity.

4 Pat dry with kitchen paper and set aside, or chill, ready for frying, grilling or roasting.

Step-by-step: Filleting a cooked flat fish

Rather than filleting small flat fish such as sole and dabs before cooking, it's simpler to leave them on the bone and serve them whole. If you want the fish filleted before eating, once cooked you can follow the clever method below, which removes all the bones in one go. This technique is most successful in Dover sole, which have firm flesh. Cooking makes the flesh shrink away from the bones, which makes them easier to see.

1 Sit the fish on a board, skinned-side up. Run a fine knife down the natural line in the centre of the fish.

2 Push the fillets away from bone, but leave them attached to the outside of the fish.

3 Working from the head end of the fish, slowly pull out the main skeleton, easing the fillets aside as the bone comes loose.

4 Carefully push the fillets back so it resembles the whole fish again.

try this...

If you want to remove the fillets from a whole, raw flat fish, leave the head and skin on and don't worry about trimming the frills.

1 Starting on the uppermost side of the fish, cut a line just behind the head, beyond the gills. Go all the way down to the bone. Cut a line at the top of the tail too, where the tail ends and the flesh starts.

2 Cut a line down one side of the backbone. Gently cut the flesh away, following the bones underneath the fillet closely. Brush your knife in small sweeping movements rather than sawing. Carry on until you have released the whole fillet.

3 Repeat on the other side, and on the second side of the fish. Trim away any frills then skin the fillet, if you like.

Step-by-step: Filleting a round fish

The fish in the following pictures is a large sea bass – a so-called 'round' fish because its body is round rather than flat. This method of filleting will work for other round fish, such as mackerel, salmon and mullet.

1 Start with the fins. Cut away any spiky fins with scissors. Then, using a sharp filleting knife, slice firmly across the back of the head just behind the small fin, cutting down to the bones.

2 Begin releasing the flesh. Insert the knife tip at the head end above the backbone. Run the knife down to the tail, working in small sweeping movements and releasing the flesh on top of the centre bones.

3 Peel off the fillet. Use your other hand to hold the flesh away from the bones and continue slicing until the fillet is released. Bend the tail round slightly to make the flesh taut, making slicing easier.

4 Remove the second fillet. Turn the fish over to cut away the second fillet just as you did the first, this time working from the tail to the head. Use your other hand to keep the sloping flesh firm.

5 Neaten up. Trim the ends and edges of both fillets. Use your fingertips to check the fish for stray bones and remove any with your fingers or tweezers.

6 Cut into portions. If you're filleting a large fish, cut each fillet into portions. Score the skin on each fillet a couple of times – this helps the skin to crisp as it cooks.

Hot-smoked salmon and egg Caesar

Caesar isn't just for chicken – make your own dressing or use 3–4 tablespoons of a shop-bought version.

**SERVES 2 EASILY DOUBLED • PREP 5 MINS
COOK 6 MINS**

2 eggs
2 Little Gem lettuces
150g pack hot-smoked salmon flakes
2 tsp capers
50g/2oz ready-made croûtons
FOR THE DRESSING
2 tbsp olive oil
1 small garlic clove, crushed
few shakes Worcestershire sauce
1 tbsp mayonnaise
1 tbsp white wine vinegar

1 Put the eggs in a small pan with enough water to cover, then bring to the boil. Boil for 6 minutes exactly, drain, cool under running cold water, then peel. Meanwhile, combine all the ingredients for the dressing.
2 Separate the leaves from the lettuces and divide between two bowls. Scatter over the salmon flakes, capers and croûtons. Quarter the eggs, add them to the salad, then drizzle over the Caesar dressing and serve at once.

PER SERVING 434 kcals, carbs 19g, fat 28g, sat fat 5g, salt 3.29g

Griddled tuna with parsley salad

Simple, fresh ingredients let the tuna's flavour shine through in this healthy dish for two.

SERVES 2 • PREP 15 MINS • COOK 2 MINS

2 line-caught yellowfin tuna steaks, about 140g/5oz each
1 tbsp olive oil
2 lemon wedges
FOR THE PARSLEY SALAD
2 handfuls (about 50g/2oz) flat-leaf parsley leaves,
    very roughly chopped
2 shallots, finely sliced
1 tbsp capers, roughly chopped
small handful green olives, stoned and roughly chopped
6 tbsp olive oil
1 tbsp Dijon mustard
juice ½ lemon

1 First make up the parsley salad by mixing all the ingredients together and stirring until completely combined. Set aside while you cook the tuna.
2 Heat a griddle or frying pan until practically smoking. Rub the tuna with the olive oil and season with salt and pepper. Griddle the tuna steaks for 1 minute on each side, turning them 90 degrees in the pan after 30 seconds if you want criss-cross patterns. This will give you tuna that is medium-rare; if you like it well cooked, give it a few more minutes on each side. It's important not to move the fish around the pan before it's seared as it will stick and break up. The steak will release itself from the pan once it's ready to be turned.
3 Serve each steak with half the salad, a lemon wedge for squeezing over and a few new potatoes, if you like.

PER SERVING 578 kcals, carbs 3g, fat 48g, sat fat 7g, salt 2.30g

try this...

Salsa verde
A dollop of this classic herby sauce is a natural partner for simply cooked fish. It's also very good with rare roast beef and grilled lamb. To make salsa verde, put 1 large bunch roughly chopped flat-leaf parsley, 1 crushed garlic clove, zest and juice 1 lemon, 2 tbsp capers and 3 tbsp extra virgin olive oil into a food processor and whizz to a chunky sauce. Season to taste.

Family fish pie

Fish pie just like you remember, and so easy to put together. Make up to a day ahead, chill, then bake for 40 minutes.

SERVES 4 • PREP 15 MINS • COOK 50 MINS
❄ **WITHOUT EGGS**

1kg/2lb 4oz floury potatoes, peeled and cut into
    even-size chunks
400g/14oz skinless white fish fillet
400g/14oz skinless smoked haddock fillet
1 small onion, quartered
4 cloves
2 bay leaves
600ml/1 pint full-fat milk
4 eggs
small bunch parsley, leaves only, chopped
100g/4oz butter
50g/2oz plain flour
pinch freshly grated nutmeg
50g/2oz mature Cheddar, grated

1 Boil the potatoes for 20 minutes. Meanwhile, put the fish, onion, cloves and bay leaves in a frying pan and pour over 500ml of the milk. Bring just to the boil, reduce the heat and simmer for 8 minutes. Lift the fish onto a plate and strain the milk into a jug to cool. Flake the fish into big pieces in a large baking dish.
2 Meanwhile, boil the eggs for 8 minutes, then cool in a bowl of cold water. Peel, quarter and scatter over the fish, then sprinkle with the chopped parsley.
3 Melt half the butter in a pan, stir in the flour and cook for 1 minute over a moderate heat. Whisk in the poaching milk gradually, then bring to the boil for about 5 minutes, whisking continuously, until thickened. Season with salt, pepper and nutmeg, then pour over the fish.
4 Heat oven to 200C/180C fan/gas 6. Drain, season and mash the potatoes with the remaining butter and milk then use to top the pie. Sprinkle with the cheese, then bake for 30 minutes.

PER SERVING 824 kcals, carbs 61g, fat 40g, sat fat 22g, salt 3.12g

Tex-Mex fish fillets

 Spice up your fish and serve with rice for something different midweek.

SERVES 4 • PREP 5 MINS • COOK 10 MINS

4 boneless white fish fillets, about 140g/5oz each
2 tbsp fajita or Tex-Mex seasoning
2 tbsp sunflower oil
200g pot guacamole (or see page 453 to make your own)
handful coriander leaves, roughly chopped
lime wedges, to serve

1 Dust the fish in the seasoning, then set aside. Heat the oil in a shallow frying pan, then fry for 3-4 minutes on each side until crisp. Serve each piece of fish with a spoonful of guacamole on top, a scattering of chopped coriander and a lime wedge for squeezing.

PER SERVING 245 kcals, carbs 2g, fat 14g, sat fat 2g, salt 0.54g

tip To make your own Tex-Mex seasoning, mix 3 tsp ground cumin, 3 tsp ground coriander and ½ tsp chilli powder with a large pinch of salt and a good grind of pepper.

Feel-good fishcakes

These budget-friendly fishcakes made with canned sardines are packed full of good stuff.

SERVES 4 • PREP 15 MINS • COOK 30-35 MINS
❄

600g/1lb 5oz floury potatoes, cut into chunks
2 x 120g cans sardines in spring water, drained
4 tbsp chopped parsley
zest and juice 1 small lemon
3 tbsp light mayonnaise
4 tbsp fat-free Greek yogurt
1 tbsp seasoned plain flour
4 tsp sunflower oil
green salad and lemon wedges, to serve

1 Cook the potatoes in boiling salted water until tender, 15–20 minutes. Meanwhile, coarsely mash the sardines in a bowl (there's no need to remove the calcium-rich bones as they are soft enough to eat). Mix in 3 tbsp chopped parsley and half the lemon zest and juice. Meanwhile, mix the mayonnaise and yogurt with the remaining parsley, lemon zest and juice and some seasoning.
2 Drain the potatoes, then mash until smooth. Gently mix into the sardine mixture and season. Shape into 8 fat fishcakes using floured hands, then dust lightly with the seasoned flour. (Can now be frozen for up to a month.)
3 Heat half the oil in a non-stick frying pan and fry half the fishcakes for 3–4 minutes on each side until golden and crisp. Keep warm; repeat with the remaining oil and fishcakes. Serve with the lemony mayonnaise, salad and lemon wedges.

PER SERVING 287 kcals, carbs 29g, fat 13g, sat fat 2g, salt 0.67g

Crunchy fish fingers

 Even the most finicky kids will want to try these healthy, low-fat fish fingers. Coat and freeze ahead, if you like.

SERVES 4 • PREP 10 MINS • COOK 15 MINS
❄ **RAW**

250g/9oz pollack fillets (or other sustainable white fish)
juice ½ lemon
½ tsp fish seasoning
50g/2oz polenta
50g/2oz dried breadcrumbs
1 egg, lightly beaten
2 tbsp olive oil

1 Heat oven to 200C/180C fan/gas 6. Cut the fish into 8 pieces, then squeeze over the lemon juice.
2 Line a baking sheet with baking parchment and mix the fish seasoning, polenta and breadcrumbs on it. Dip the fish into the egg, then turn several times in the polenta and breadcrumb mixture to coat. Repeat with all the pieces of fish. (Can now be frozen for up to a month.)
3 Drizzle with oil and bake for 15 minutes, turning halfway through cooking.

PER SERVING 205 kcals, carbs 20g, fat 8g, sat fat 1g, salt 0.32g

Super-quick fish curry

 Supper on the table in 15 minutes, and it's low fat to boot.

SERVES 4 • PREP 5 MINS • COOK 10 MINS

1 tbsp vegetable oil
1 large onion, chopped
1 garlic clove, chopped
1–2 tbsp madras curry paste (or use something milder
    if you like)
400g can chopped tomatoes
200ml/7fl oz vegetable stock
600g/1lb 5oz Icelandic cod fillet, skinned and
    cut into big chunks
rice or naan bread, to serve

1 Heat the oil in a deep pan and gently fry the onion and garlic for about 5 minutes until soft. Add the curry paste and stir-fry for 1–2 minutes, then tip in the tomatoes and stock.
2 Bring to a simmer, then add the fish. Gently cook for 4–5 minutes until the fish flakes easily. Serve immediately with rice or naan.

PER SERVING 191 kcals, carbs 8g, fat 5g, sat fat 1g, salt 0.54g

Pesto fish stew
Fry the onion and garlic until soft, then add the tomatoes and stock along with 2 tbsp red pesto. Bring to a simmer and cook the fish as before, throwing in a handful torn basil leaves just before serving with crusty French bread.

Grilled salmon teriyaki with cucumber salad

This sticky Japanese glaze helps to keep the fish moist while it cooks. It's also very good as a marinade for chicken.

SERVES 4 • PREP 10 MINS • COOK 20 MINS

1 tbsp sunflower oil
5 tbsp soy sauce
5 tbsp mirin or dry sherry
1 tbsp golden caster sugar
1 piece fresh root ginger, peeled and finely grated
2 garlic cloves, crushed to a paste
4 salmon fillets
FOR THE CUCUMBER SALAD
1 small cucumber
1 tbsp rice wine vinegar
1 tbsp soy sauce
½ tsp golden caster sugar
1 tbsp toasted sesame seeds

1 Heat the grill to High and brush a sturdy baking sheet with oil. In a large bowl, mix the soy, mirin, sugar, ginger and garlic together until the sugar has dissolved, then toss the salmon in the soy mix until coated. Tip the remaining marinade into a small saucepan and bring to a simmer.
2 Grill the salmon for about 15 minutes, brushing it every few minutes with the simmering marinade until cooked through and glazed. Remove from the grill. Simmer the marinade until sticky, then pour it over the cooked salmon.
3 For the cucumber salad, use a swivel-blade peeler to peel the cucumber into slices. Make the dressing by mixing the vinegar with the soy sauce, sugar and sesame seeds. Toss the cucumber with the dressing and serve with the salmon and boiled rice.

PER SERVING 340 kcals, carbs 18g, fat 18g, sat fat 3g, salt 4.23g

OPPOSITE Clockwise from top left Feel-good fishcakes (page 177); Hot-smoked salmon and egg Caesar (page 175); Mussels steamed with cider and bacon (page 185); Tex-Mex fish fillets (page 176), Grilled salmon teriyaki with cucumber salad; Griddle tuna with parsley salad (page 175).

Thai-style steamed fish

 Serve with Thai jasmine rice. If you've got some sesame seeds, toast a handful and toss them into the rice just before serving.

SERVES 2 • PREP 10 MINS • COOK 15 MINS

2 trout fillets, about 140g/5oz each
small knob fresh root ginger, peeled and chopped
1 small garlic clove, chopped
1 red chilli, deseeded and finely chopped
zest and juice 1 lime
3 baby pak choi, each quartered lengthways
2 tbsp soy sauce

1 Nestle the fish fillets side by side on a large square of foil and scatter the ginger, garlic, chilli and lime zest over them. Drizzle the lime juice on top then scatter the pieces of pak choi around and on top of the fish. Pour the soy sauce over the pak choi and loosely seal the foil to make a package, making sure you leave space at the top for the steam to circulate as the fish cooks.
2 Steam for 15 minutes. (If you haven't got a steamer, put the parcel on a heatproof plate over a pan of gently simmering water, cover with a lid and steam.)

PER SERVING 199 kcals, carbs 4g, fat 7g, sat fat 2g, salt 3.25g

Salmon and dill fishcakes

Pulled from the freezer, these fishcakes make a sophisticated and easy supper – for very little cost. Serve with lemon wedges and watercress.

MAKES 8 MAKE HALF, FREEZE HALF • PREP 30 MINS COOK 30 MINS

800g/1lb 12oz skinless salmon fillet
2 bay leaves
small bunch dill, stalks and fronds separated
500ml/18fl oz milk
600g/1lb 5oz floury potatoes, cut into small even-size
   chunks
zest 1 lemon
4 tbsp mayonnaise
1 tsp Dijon mustard
4 tbsp capers, rinsed and dried
plain flour, for dusting your hands
1 egg, beaten
100g/4oz breadcrumbs
4 tbsp vegetable or sunflower oil
lemon wedges and watercress, to serve

1 Put the salmon in a frying pan with the bay leaves and dill stalks. Pour over enough milk to cover the fish, bring to the boil, then lower the heat to a gentle simmer and leave to poach for 4 minutes. Turn off the heat, then set aside for 5 minutes. Lift out the salmon with a fish slice onto a plate. Flake into large pieces, then cool.
2 Meanwhile, boil the potatoes in salted water for about 10 minutes, or until tender. Drain well, then leave to steam in the colander for 2 minutes. Mash the potatoes. Stir in the lemon zest, mayonnaise, mustard, capers and some seasoning.
3 With your hands, gently mix the fish into the mash. Dust your hands and work surface with flour and shape the mix into 8 cakes. Dip into the egg, then press into the breadcrumbs. Heat half the oil in a frying pan until very hot. Fry 4 fishcakes for 5 minutes each side until golden. Remove; keep warm. Repeat with the rest, or freeze.

PER FISHCAKE 431 kcals, carbs 27g, fat 25g, sat fat 5g, salt 1.05g

try this...

For a fast watercress sauce to serve with your fishcakes,
whizz 50g/2oz watercress with 200ml/7fl oz crème fraîche
until smooth. Season to taste then heat until bubbling hot.

Dover sole with buttered leeks and shrimps

One of the easiest ways to cook fish it is to roast it with a splash of wine. This
keeps the flesh wonderfully moist and also half-makes the sauce for you.

SERVES 2 • PREP 10 MINS • COOK 30 MINS

50g/2oz butter
2 Dover sole or another flat fish, about 350g/12oz each,
    trimmed and top skin removed
125ml/4fl oz small glass white wine
4 leeks, cut into large chunks
100g tub potted shrimps
small bunch chives, snipped

1 Heat oven to 220C/200C fan/gas 7. Lightly butter a large
roasting tin and lay the fish in it, side by side. Pour over the
wine and dot the fish with any remaining butter. Season with
salt and pepper, then bake for 15–20 minutes or until the
flesh just starts to come away from the bone.
2 Meanwhile, cook the leeks in boiling salted water for 8–10
minutes until soft, then drain. When the fish is ready, carefully
lift onto a warm platter or plates. Place the roasting tin over
a low flame, then heat the leeks and potted shrimps with the
juices until the butter has melted. Stir through the chives,
then serve with the fish and a few buttered new potatoes.

PER SERVING 673 kcals, carbs 10g, fat 43g, sat fat 24g, salt 4.26g

Smoked mackerel with herb and beet couscous

 Beetroot and mackerel are a great combination, especially with a dollop of
horseradish yogurt. A no-cook treat. (See photo on page 166)

SERVES 3 • PREP 20 MINS • NO COOK

100g/4oz couscous
1 tsp hot horseradish, or horseradish sauce
150g pot 2% fat Greek yogurt
½ cucumber, deseeded and cut into cubes (see below)
small bunch dill, roughly chopped
small bunch mint, roughly chopped
small red onion, finely chopped
juice 1 lemon
1 tbsp extra virgin olive oil
250g pack cooked beetroot, cut into cubes
250g pack peppered smoked mackerel (this will normally
    contain 3 fillets)

1 Put the couscous into a large bowl, pour over 150ml
boiling water then cover with cling film and set aside for
10 minutes. Meanwhile, mix the horseradish into the yogurt
and season with salt and pepper.
2 When all of the liquid has been absorbed into the
couscous, remove the cling film then press the couscous
around the sides of the bowl to help it cool more quickly.
3 Put the cucumber, herbs, onion, lemon juice and oil into
the couscous, then toss well. Now add the beets and toss
briefly. Pile the couscous onto plates, flake a mackerel fillet
into a few big pieces alongside each serving (discard the
skin), then serve with a big dollop of the horseradish yogurt.

PER SERVING 489 kcals, carbs 30.3g, fat 30.8g, sat fat 7.5g, salt 1.91g

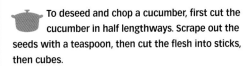 **To deseed and chop a cucumber, first cut the
cucumber in half lengthways. Scrape out the
seeds with a teaspoon, then cut the flesh into sticks,
then cubes.**

Pesto and olive-crusted fish

 Give fish a lift with a crunchy, zesty crust.

SERVES 4 • PREP 5 MINS • COOK 15 MINS

2 tbsp green pesto
finely grated zest 1 lemon
10 green olives, pitted and roughly chopped
85g/3oz fresh breadcrumbs
4 white fish fillets, such as cod or haddock

1 Heat oven to 200C/180C fan/gas 6. Mix the pesto, lemon zest and olives together, then stir in the breadcrumbs.
2 Lay the fish fillets on a baking sheet, skin-side down, then press the crumbs over the surface of each piece. Bake in the oven for 10–12 minutes until the fish is cooked through and the crust is crisp and brown.

PER SERVING 219 kcals, carbs 17g, fat 4g, sat fat 1g, salt 1.14g

> *tip* This pesto crumb mixture is also a fantastic topping for chicken breasts or lamb chops.

One-pan Spanish fish stew

 Sustainable white fish or salmon fillets work best for this sunshine meal in a bowl.

SERVES 4 • PREP 10 • MINS COOK 40 MINS

handful flat-leaf parsley leaves, chopped
2 garlic cloves, finely chopped
zest and juice 1 lemon
3 tbsp olive oil, plus extra to serve
1 medium onion, finely sliced
500g/1lb 2oz floury potatoes, cut into 2cm chunks
1 tsp paprika
pinch cayenne pepper
400g can chopped tomatoes
1 fish stock cube
200g/7oz raw peeled king prawns
½ x 400g can chickpeas, rinsed and drained
500g/1lb 2oz skinless white fish fillets, cut into very
    large chunks

1 In a small bowl, mix the parsley with half the garlic and the lemon zest, then set aside. Heat 2 tbsp oil in a large sauté pan. Throw in the onion and potatoes, cover the pan, then sweat everything for about 5 minutes until the onion has softened. Add the remaining oil, garlic and spices, then cook for 2 minutes more.
2 Pour over the lemon juice and sizzle for a moment. Add the tomatoes, half a can of water and crumble in the stock cube. Season with a little salt, then cover the pan. Simmer everything for 15–20 minutes until the potatoes are just cooked.
3 Stir through the prawns and chickpeas, then nestle the fish chunks into the top of the stew. Reduce the heat and recover the pan, then cook for about 8 minutes, stirring very gently once or twice. When the fish is just cooked through, remove from the heat, scatter with the parsley mixture, then bring the dish to the table with the bottle of olive oil for drizzling over and some crusty bread, if you want.

PER SERVING 382 kcals, carbs 33g, fat 11g, sat fat 2g, salt 1.92g

White fish with spicy beans and chorizo

 Storecupboard ingredients come together wonderfully in this quick, low-fat dish. It counts as 4 of your 5-a-day.

SERVES 4 • PREP 5 MINS • COOK 15 MINS
❄ **BEAN MIX ONLY**

1 tbsp olive oil
1 onion, chopped
small rosemary sprig, leaves finely chopped
25g/1oz chorizo or other spicy sausage, chopped
2 fat garlic cloves, crushed
700g bottle passata
410g can cannellini beans in water, drained
200g/7oz shredded green cabbage
pinch sugar
4 skinless chunky fillets haddock or cod

1 Heat the oil in a large frying pan, then soften the onion for 5 minutes. Add the rosemary, chorizo and garlic, then fry for 2 minutes more until the chorizo is starting to crisp. Tip in the passata, beans, cabbage and sugar, season, then simmer for 5 minutes.
2 Add the fish to the pan, leaving the tops of the fillets peeking out of the sauce, then cover with a lid and leave to cook for 3–5 minutes or until the flesh flakes easily. Delicious served with crusty bread.

PER SERVING 304 kcals, carbs 27g, fat 6g, sat fat 1g, salt 1.23g

One-pan salmon with roast asparagus

 For an easy side dish to complement a spring roast, just cook this recipe without the salmon.

SERVES 2 • PREP 20 MINS • COOK 1 HOUR

400g/14oz new potatoes, halved if large
2 tbsp olive oil
8 asparagus spears, trimmed and halved
2 handfuls cherry tomatoes
1 tbsp balsamic vinegar
2 salmon fillets, about 140g/5oz each
handful basil leaves

1 Heat oven to 220C/200C fan/gas 7. Tip the potatoes and 1 tbsp of the oil into an ovenproof dish, then roast the potatoes for 20 minutes until starting to brown. Toss the asparagus in with the potatoes, then return to the oven for 15 minutes.
2 Throw in the cherry tomatoes and vinegar and nestle the salmon amongst the vegetables. Drizzle with the remaining oil and return to the oven for a final 10–15 minutes until the salmon is cooked. Scatter over the basil leaves and serve everything scooped straight from the dish.

PER SERVING 483 kcals, carbs 34g, fat 25g, sat fat 4g, salt 0.24g

Almond-crusted fish with saffron sauce

A delicate, restaurant-style fish that's so easy to make at home. Try with buttered baby potatoes and green beans or a salad.

SERVES 2 EASILY DOUBLED OR MORE • PREP 5 MINS COOK 15 MINS

2 sea bass fillets, about 175g/6oz each
a little softened butter, plus extra for greasing and frying
2 rounded tbsp toasted flaked almonds
1 shallot, finely chopped
150ml/¼ pint fresh fish stock
small pinch saffron strands
3 tbsp crème fraîche

1 Heat oven to 190C/170C fan/gas 5. Season the fish and spread a little butter over the flesh side of each. Put in a shallow, buttered, ovenproof dish and sprinkle with the flaked almonds, lightly pressing them on. Bake for 12–15 minutes until the flesh flakes easily.
2 Meanwhile, make the sauce. Gently fry the shallot with a small knob of butter in a small pan. Add the stock and saffron, bring to the boil, then boil until reduced by about two-thirds. Stir in the crème fraîche and bubble for a minute or so until slightly thickened. Pour a little sauce around each portion of fish.

PER SERVING 375 kcals, carbs 2g, fat 24g, sat fat 8g, salt 0.61g

tip Sea bass can be quite pricey, so you can make this recipe softer on your wallet by using plaice or lemon sole fillets instead. Reduce the cooking time to 8–10 minutes as these fillets are thinner than sea bass.

Italian tuna balls

 Short on time? Reach for a couple of cans of tuna for this quick and healthy take on meatballs.

SERVES 4 EASILY HALVED OR DOUBLED • PREP 15 MINS COOK 5 MINS
❄ **UNCOOKED**

2 x 160g cans tuna in sunflower or olive oil, drained (reserve a little oil)
small handful pine nuts
zest 1 lemon
small handful parsley leaves, roughly chopped
50g/2oz fresh breadcrumbs
1 egg, beaten
400g/14oz spaghetti
500g jar tomato pasta sauce

1 Flake the tuna into a bowl, then tip in the pine nuts, lemon zest, parsley, breadcrumbs and egg. Season and mix together with your hands until completely combined. Roll the mix into 12 walnut-size balls. Cook the pasta according to the pack instructions.
2 Heat a little of the tuna oil in a large non-stick frying pan, then fry the tuna balls for 5 minutes, turning every minute or so until completely golden. Drain on kitchen paper. Heat the tomato sauce, then toss together with the pasta and tuna balls.

PER SERVING 594 kcals, carbs 92g, fat 12g, sat fat 2g, salt 1.42g

try this...

Spicy tuna burgers
Tip the drained tuna, breadcrumbs and egg into a bowl with a handful sweetcorn kernels, a sprinkling Tex-Mex or fajita seasoning and a small handful of chopped coriander. Mould the mix into 4 burgers, cook as above and serve in buns with your favourite burger toppings.

Classic prawn cocktail

This retro starter is so good it'll never go out of fashion. If using ready-peeled prawns, use 350g/12oz.

SERVES 4 EASILY HALVED • PREP 25 MINS • NO COOK

400g/14oz cooked Atlantic shell-on prawns
4 Little Gems, washed and trimmed
5 heaped tbsp mayonnaise
5 tbsp tomato chutney
2 tsp Worcestershire sauce
2 tsp creamed horseradish
tiny splash Tabasco
squeeze lemon juice
paprika, for dusting
4 tsp snipped chives

1 Peel all but 4 of the prawns (reserve these for decoration). Break the lettuces into individual leaves, then divide the leaves evenly between 4 small glass bowls.
2 Sprinkle the peeled prawns over the lettuce and season with black pepper. Combine the mayonnaise, tomato chutney, Worcestershire sauce, horseradish and Tabasco. Season to taste with lemon juice and salt and pepper, then spoon sparingly over the prawns. Dust the top with a little paprika and sprinkle with chives. Top with the remaining prawns and serve immediately. Delicious with brown bread.

PER SERVING 292 kcals, carbs 8g, fat 25g, sat fat 4g, salt 2.23g

Mussels steamed with cider and bacon

Mussels are a much easier dish to serve up than you might realise, and make a very economical meal for friends.

**SERVES 2 GENEROUSLY AS A MAIN, 4 AS A STARTER
PREP 40 MINS • COOK 20 MINS**

small knob of butter
6 rashers bacon, chopped, or 140g/5oz lardons
2 shallots, finely sliced
small bunch thyme, leaves stripped
1.5kg/3lb 5oz small mussels, scrubbed and bearded
150ml/¼ pint dry cider
2 tbsp crème fraîche (optional)

1 Heat the butter in a pan large enough to easily fit the mussels, then fry the bacon for 4 minutes, turning occasionally until it starts to crisp up. Throw in the shallots and thyme leaves, then cook for 1 minute until softened.
2 Turn up the heat to maximum and add the mussels to the pan, then pour over the cider. Place the lid on the pan, give it a good shake, then cook the mussels for 5–7 minutes, shaking the pan occasionally, until all the mussels have opened. Discard any mussels that haven't opened.
3 Use a slotted spoon to scoop the mussels into bowls and place the pan back on the heat. Bring the juices to the boil and stir in the crème fraîche, if using. Pour the sauce over the mussels. Serve with hunks of crusty bread for mopping up the sauce.

PER SERVING 367 kcals, carbs 8g, fat 18g, sat fat 6g, salt 4.45g

tip For a classic moules marinière, follow the recipe as above, leaving out the bacon. Add a couple of chopped garlic cloves when you soften the shallot, and use dry white wine instead of cider. Finish with a handful chopped flat-leaf parsley.

Step-by-step: Opening an oyster

A fishmonger will be able to open your oysters, but if you are buying ahead, you'll need to open them yourself – this is known as 'shucking', and is relatively easy if you have an oyster knife, which is a short, blunt knife with a finger guard.

1 Hold the oyster very firmly in a thick cloth to protect your hands, then insert the knife into the hinge, or pointed end, of the oyster. Twist the tip of the knife into the hinge to get a very firm foothold.

2 Once you feel the knife is securely in place, release the pressure from the knife and gently lever or twist the knife to break the muscle of the oyster – you can usually hear the 'shucking' noise as the two half shells part.

tips

- As shucking oysters can take a little practice, you can open them an hour before serving, but keep them chilled.
- The traditional way to enjoy both types of oysters is raw with a squeeze of lemon juice or shallot vinegar (finely chopped shallots mixed with red wine vinegar).
- Another classic way to eat them is with a splash of Tabasco.

3 Loosen the opened oyster from the shell to make it easy to eat.

4 Serve them freshly opened on a chilled platter, nestled into a pile of crushed ice.

For more information about oysters, turn to page 169.

Crispy squid

No tapas menu is complete without some of these crisp but tender bites.

**SERVES 8 AS TAPAS • PREP 10 MINS
COOK 10 MINS**

200g/7oz plain flour
300g/11oz squid, cleaned and cut into finger-width
    slices (see page 171 for instructions)
2 ice cubes
3 eggs, beaten
oil for frying
smoked paprika, to serve

1 Put the flour into a large plastic food bag and season generously. Add the squid and give the bag a good shake to coat in flour.
2 Mix the ice cubes into the beaten egg. Remove the squid rings from the flour, patting off the excess, then toss through the egg mixture. Remove from the bowl, letting any excess mixture drip away and return to the bag of flour for a final shake.
3 When ready to eat, heat a wok or wide deep pan about a third full with oil. Carefully slide 10 rings or so at a time into the oil (they should immediately start bubbling; if not, heat the oil for a couple more minutes). Fry for 2 minutes or until golden and crisp, then remove with a slotted spoon and drain on kitchen paper. Repeat and serve sprinkled with the paprika.

PER SERVING 229 kcals, carbs 20g, fat 12g, sat fat 2g, salt 0.44g

Easy garlic prawns

Save time by using ready-cooked prawns; just cook the garlic then heat through the prawns with the wine.

SERVES 8 AS TAPAS • PREP 5 MINS • COOK 5 MINS

2 tbsp olive oil
2 garlic cloves, chopped
450g/1lb large peeled raw prawns
splash white wine
1 tbsp olive oil
handful chopped coriander or flat-leaf parsley

1 Heat the oil in large frying pan, add the garlic and cook for 30 seconds. Stir in the prawns. As they start to turn pink and the edges golden, after about 3 minutes, add the wine. Let it bubble away for about 2 minutes until reduced a little, then pour the prawns into a serving dish, season and scatter over the coriander or parsley.

PER SERVING 83 kcals, carbs 1g, fat 5g, sat fat 1g, salt 0.27g

Smoked salmon with prawns, horseradish cream and lime vinaigrette

This stunning starter can be assembled ahead then topped with dressed leaves just before serving.

SERVES 2 • PREP 20 MINS • NO COOK

1 tbsp crème fraîche
1 tsp horseradish sauce
4 slices smoked salmon
10 large cooked prawns, peeled but tails left on
FOR THE SALAD
juice 1 lime, finely grated zest ½
1 tsp clear honey
½ tsp finely grated fresh root ginger
2 tbsp mild olive oil
2 handfuls small leaf salad

1 Mix the crème fraîche with the horseradish and a little salt and pepper. For the dressing, whisk the lime juice and zest with the honey, ginger and seasoning, then whisk in the oil.
2 Lay the smoked salmon and prawns on two plates, then top with a dollop of the horseradish cream. Toss the salad in most of the dressing and pile on top. Drizzle the remaining dressing around each plate and serve.

PER SERVING 266 kcals, carbs 4g, fat 17g, sat fat 4g, salt 3.34g

Step-by-step: Preparing a cooked crab

For more information about crab, including how to cook your own from live, turn to page 170. Depending on the recipe you are going to make using the crabmeat, a 1.25kg/2lb 12oz crab will feed 2–4 people and give about 250g/9oz white and 125g/4½oz brown meat.

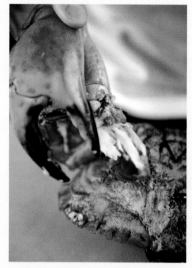

1 Lay the crab on its back and twist off the claws and legs.

2 Crack the claws and legs using a heavy object – but don't allow the shell to shatter into very small pieces as they will be difficult to find. Carefully remove the meat using a lobster pick or teaspoon and put it into a bowl (preferably metal). Check for stray shell by shaking the bowl from time to time – shell fragments 'ping' against the side and can be removed.

3 Put your thumbs on the base of the body, at the back of the crab, and push upwards to release it from the carapace.

4 Pull away and discard the lungs ('dead man's fingers') found around the main body and inside of the carapace. Press the mouth so that it snaps away from the main shell and pull away the stomach sac.

5 Cut the body in half and scoop out further white meat – it is worth taking time over this as there is a surprising amount in all the small cavities. Scoop out the brown meat. Some people like brown meat straight from the shell, others add seasoning, a little mustard and breadcrumbs, too. White meat is great just as it is.

Crab and corn cakes with chilli dipping sauce

 Kick-start a Thai supper with these spicy little fishcakes.

**MAKES 10 SMALL CAKES • PREP 10 MINS
COOK 15 MINS**

❄

1 egg
4 tbsp plain flour
1 small garlic clove, crushed
1 tbsp chopped coriander stalks and leaves
340g can sweetcorn, well drained
170g can white crabmeat, well drained and flaked
2 spring onions, finely sliced
sunflower or vegetable oil, for frying

FOR THE CHILLI DIPPING SAUCE

4 tbsp sweet chilli sauce
juice ½ lime
½ finger-length chunk cucumber, seeds scraped out,
    flesh finely chopped

1 Tip the egg, flour, garlic and coriander stalks into a food processor with a third of the corn. Whizz to a smooth paste. Mix with the remaining corn, crab, half the spring onions and some seasoning.

2 Stir together the sauce ingredients. Cover a large plate with kitchen paper. Heat 5cm depth oil in a large, heavy saucepan – it's hot enough when a cube of bread browns in 30–40 seconds. Drop in dessertspoons of the corn mixture, then fry for 2–3 minutes, turning, until golden and crisp. Lift onto the kitchen paper and keep warm. Repeat with the remaining mixture. Serve the hot cakes sprinkled with the last of the spring onion and the dipping sauce alongside.

PER CORN CAKE 149 kcals, carbs 16g, fat 8g, sat fat 1g, salt 0.64g

Maryland crabcakes

A famous way with crab from the USA, these crisp and slightly spicy cakes make an ideal starter or special lunch.

**MAKES 6 • PREP 35 MINS • COOK 15 MINS
❄ BEFORE FRYING IF CRAB IS FRESH**

FOR THE CRABCAKES

50g/2oz mayonnaise
1 egg
½ tbsp paprika (optional)
1 tbsp Dijon mustard
1 tsp Worcestershire sauce
juice 1½ lemons
handful chopped parsley
500g/1lb 2oz white crabmeat
50g/2oz breadcrumbs
5 tbsp olive oil

FOR THE BUTTER SAUCE

350ml/12fl oz white wine
3 shallots, diced
1 bay leaf and 1 sprig thyme
3 tbsp extra-thick double cream
300g/11oz butter, cut into small cubes
juice 1 lemon

1 To make the crabcakes: mix together the mayonnaise, egg, paprika (if using), Dijon mustard, Worcestershire sauce, lemon juice and parsley. Season well then fold the crabmeat and breadcrumbs into the mixture. Chill for 20 minutes before shaping into 6 equal-size cakes.

2 Heat oven to 190C/170C fan/gas 5. Heat the oil in a large ovenproof frying pan and brown the crabcakes on each side. Then transfer to the oven for 10 minutes or until cooked through.

3 To make the butter sauce: boil the white wine, shallots, bay leaf and thyme until reduced to about 3 tbsp. Add the cream and bring back to the boil. Remove from the heat and slowly add the butter, whisking all the time. Finish the sauce with lemon juice and seasoning to taste.

4 To serve, put the crabcakes onto plates, add a little pot of sauce and serve with dressed green salad leaves.

PER SERVING 693 kcals, carbs 11g, fat 63g, sat fat 31g, salt 2.18g

Golden beer-battered fish with chips

You don't need to be by the seaside to enjoy great British fish and chips.

**SERVES 2 • PREP 15 MINS, PLUS 30 MINS RESTING
COOK 40 MINS**

FOR THE FISH
50g/2oz plain flour
50g/2oz cornflour
1 tsp baking powder
¼ tsp turmeric
75ml/2½fl oz lager beer
75ml/2½fl oz sparkling water
about 1 litre/1¾ pints sunflower oil, for frying
400g/14oz fillet sustainable cod, hake or haddock, halved

FOR THE CHIPS
750g/1lb 9oz potatoes, Maris Piper or Desirée,
  peeled and cut into thick chips
2 tbsp plain flour
2 tbsp sunflower oil

1 For the batter, mix the dry ingredients in a large bowl and season. Set 1 tbsp aside for later. Gradually stir the beer and water into the bowl until you have a smooth batter. Set aside.
2 Heat oven to 200C/180C fan/gas 6. Boil a large pan of water, then add the chips and boil for 2–3 minutes. Drain well then tip onto a large baking sheet with the flour, oil and some salt. Toss until the chips are evenly coated and the flour is no longer dusty. Roast for 30 minutes, turning occasionally, until golden and crisp.
3 To cook the fish, heat the oil in a deep pan until a little batter dropped in sizzles and crisps up straight away. Pat the fish dry with kitchen paper, then toss in the reserved flour mix. Shake off any excess, then dip the fish into the batter. Carefully lower each fillet into the hot oil and fry for 6–8 minutes or until golden and crisp. Using a large slotted spoon, lift out the fish, drain on kitchen paper, then sprinkle with salt. Serve with the chips.

PER SERVING 1,040 kcals, carbs 120g, fat 43g, sat fat 6g, salt 1.16g

Cod with braised peas, lentils and bacon

The quick braise of lentils and peas works as a side dish with either fish or meat too.

SERVES 4 • PREP 15 MINS • COOK 20 MINS

25g/1oz butter
4 sustainable cod fillets, about 100g/4oz each, skin on
FOR THE PEAS
2 tbsp olive oil
4 thick slices smoked back bacon, cut into matchsticks
300g/11oz shelled peas (fresh or frozen)
410g can lentils, drained and washed
2 lemons, 1 juiced, 1 cut into wedges to serve
large handful mint leaves, roughly chopped

1 To make the pea braise, heat half the oil in a shallow saucepan, then sizzle the bacon for 5 minutes until crisp. Turn the heat down, add the peas to the pan, then cover and braise for 8–10 minutes until peas are tender (about 5 minutes if you're using frozen peas). Add the lentils to the peas and cook until heated, then remove from the heat and dress with the lemon juice, seasoning and a bit more oil, if necessary. Just before serving, stir through the mint.
2 Meanwhile, heat the butter in a frying pan until frothy, then add the fish, skin-side down, and cook for 4 minutes until the skin is crisp and the fish almost cooked. Flip the fillets over and cook for 1 minute. Divide the pea braise between four plates and top with fish. Drizzle with the remaining oil and serve with a wedge of lemon.

PER SERVING 372 kcals, carbs 18g, fat 18g, sat fat 7g, salt 2.70g

OPPOSITE *Golden beer-battered fish and chips*

Smoked fish and cherry tomato rarebit

Any kind of white-fleshed fish will do for this divine recipe - it's a great family dish to make at the weekend.

SERVES 4–6 • PREP 20 MINS • COOK ABOUT 50 MINS

FOR THE RAREBIT SAUCE
50g/2oz butter
50g/2oz plain flour
dash of Worcestershire sauce
600ml/1 pint milk
100g/4oz mature Cheddar, coarsely grated
2 tbsp wholegrain mustard

FOR THE FISH
50g/2oz unsalted butter
1 garlic clove, crushed
550g/1lb 4oz cherry tomatoes, halved
700g/1lb 9oz spinach, washed
pinch freshly grated nutmeg
550g/1lb 4oz undyed smoked haddock or cod fillets,
    skinned and checked for bones
50g/2oz Cheddar, coarsely grated

1 To make the rarebit sauce, melt the butter in a saucepan, stir in the flour and Worcestershire sauce. Cook, stirring, for 1 minute. Remove the pan from the heat and slowly whisk in the milk until combined. Bring to the boil, whisking, then simmer for 2 minutes. Mix in the grated cheese and mustard then season well.

2 Melt a knob of butter in a frying pan then sizzle the garlic for 1 minute. Add the tomatoes, cooking just enough to heat through. Spoon into a shallow baking dish in an even layer. Wilt the spinach in the remaining butter in a couple of batches, then squeeze the spinach to remove any excess liquid. Season with salt, pepper and nutmeg then spread over the tomatoes. Cover with the fish.

3 Heat oven to 190C/170C fan/gas 5. Spoon the sauce evenly over the fish, then sprinkle over the grated cheese. Bake for 30 minutes or until brown and bubbling and the fish is cooked through. You may like to finish off the rarebit under the grill to brown the top more.

PER SERVING 645 kcals, carbs 25g, fat 40g, sat fat 23g, salt 4.99g

Warm salad of scallops and bacon

Get the grill nice and hot before you start – that will make for crisp, golden bacon while allowing the scallops to stay succulent.

**SERVES 8 EASILY HALVED • PREP 40 MINS
COOK 6–8 MINS**

24 plump scallops
8 tbsp olive oil
4 tbsp lemon juice
12 thin slices streaky bacon
2 tsp Dijon mustard
1 tsp clear honey
2 tsp chopped capers
4 tbsp chopped parsley
1 head curly endive

1 Wash and dry the scallops and put them in a bowl. Mix 2 tbsp of the oil and 2 tbsp of the lemon juice in a bowl with a little salt and pepper, then immerse the scallops in the liquid. Leave for 15 minutes, until the scallops have turned white.

2 Cut each strip of bacon in half across and wrap around a scallop. Secure with cocktail sticks.

3 Whisk together the remaining lemon juice with the mustard, honey, salt and pepper. Whisk in the remaining oil until the dressing is thick, then stir in the capers and parsley. Divide the curly endive between 8 serving plates.

4 Heat the grill to High. Lay the scallops in one layer over a lined grill pan. Grill the scallops for 3–4 minutes each side, until the bacon is crisp and golden. Put 3 scallops on each plate and spoon over the dressing.

PER SERVING 231 kcals, carbs 1g, fat 14g, sat fat 3g, salt 1.79g

Pancetta-wrapped trout with almond beans

Sweet trout, salty bacon and nutty almonds were made for each other. Prep the fish up to a day ahead if you're entertaining.

SERVES 2 EASILY DOUBLED OR MORE • PREP 10 MINS COOK 20 MINS

1 lemon
2 small trout, rainbow or brown, cleaned
large handful thyme sprigs
1 garlic clove, chopped
4 slices pancetta, or rashers smoked streaky bacon
4 tbsp olive oil
100g/4oz fine green beans
2 tbsp toasted flaked almonds

1 Heat oven to 220C/200C fan/gas 7. Cut half the lemon into 4 thin slices and juice the other half. Score each fish 3 times on one side. Place the fish on a baking sheet, scored-side up, and season liberally inside and out with salt and pepper. Stuff each fish cavity with thyme, a sprinkling of garlic and a lemon slice. Lay the rest of the thyme on top of the fish and top with a lemon slice. Wrap the pancetta or bacon around the fish to hold the lemon and thyme in place. Drizzle with 1 tbsp oil and bake for 20 minutes until the pancetta is golden and the fish is cooked.

2 While the fish is cooking, boil the beans in a pan of salted water for 4–5 minutes until just cooked and still vibrant. Drain and toss with the lemon juice, remaining oil and almonds. Serve the fish with the beans on the side.

PER SERVING 554 kcals, carbs 4g, fat 40g, sat fat 7g, salt 1g

Skate with buttery parsley and capers

The butter sauce for this recipe is wonderful over any white fish. Stocks of some types of skate (also called ray) are under great pressure; see page 168 for more information on buying sustainably.

SERVES 2 • PREP 5 MINS • COOK 10 MINS

3 tbsp plain flour
450g/1lb skate wing, cut into 2 (ask your fishmonger)
50g/2oz butter
2 tbsp capers
small handful parsley leaves, chopped
1 lemon, ½ juiced and ½ cut into wedges

1 Tip the flour onto a large plate or dish and season with salt and pepper. Dredge the fish in the flour until completely coated. Place a large frying pan over a high heat and add half the butter. When the butter is sizzling, lay the fish into the pan and cook for 4–5 minutes on each side until golden, then transfer the fish to two plates and keep warm.

2 Working quickly, place the pan back on the heat with the remaining butter. When it's starting to foam and turn light brown, throw in the capers, then the parsley and sizzle for a moment. Add the lemon juice and simmer everything for a moment longer.

3 Season the buttery sauce in the pan with a touch of salt and pepper, then spoon half over each portion of fish. Serve with mashed potatoes and steamed spinach, and lemon wedges for squeezing over.

PER SERVING 415 kcals, carbs 19g, fat 22g, sat fat 13g, salt 1.83g

Bass with sizzled ginger, chilli and spring onions

 Bring the fish to the table still sizzling – the aroma will be almost too much to resist.

SERVES 6 • PREP 15 MINS • COOK 10 MINS

6 x sea bass fillets, about 140g/5oz each, skin on
   and scaled
about 3 tbsp sunflower oil
large piece ginger, peeled and cut into matchsticks
3 garlic cloves, thinly sliced
3 fat, fresh red chillies, deseeded and thinly shredded
bunch spring onions, shredded lengthways
1 tbsp soy sauce

1 Season the fish with salt and pepper then slash the skin 3 times. Heat a heavy-based frying pan and add 1 tbsp oil. Once hot, fry the fish, skin-side down, for 5 minutes or until the skin is very crisp and golden. The fish will be almost cooked through. Turn over, cook for another 30 seconds– 1 minute, then transfer to a serving plate and keep warm. You'll need to fry the fish in 2 batches.
2 Heat the remaining oil, then fry the ginger, garlic and chillies for about 2 minutes until golden. Take off the heat and toss in the spring onions. Splash the fish with a little soy sauce and spoon over the contents of the pan.

PER SERVING 202 kcals, carbs 2g, fat 9g, sat fat 1g, salt 0.26g

Foil-poached salmon with dill and avocado mayo

A whole baked salmon makes a centrepiece with wow factor. Cooking it in the oven is so much easier than bothering with a fish kettle.

**SERVES 10 • PREP 20 MINS PLUS COOLING
COOK 1 HOUR**

3.5kg/7lb 7oz whole salmon (ask your fishmonger
   to clean and gut it)
olive oil, for greasing
1 small onion, very thinly sliced
4 bay leaves
small bunch dill, half chopped, half kept in fronds
6 tbsp dry white wine
3 ripe avocados, preferably Hass
200ml/7fl oz mayonnaise
zest and juice 1 large lemon
½ cucumber, peeled, deseeded and diced
TO SERVE
bunch watercress, thick cucumber slices, lemon wedges,
   fresh dill

1 Heat oven to 150C/130C fan/gas 2. Put the salmon on a large sheet of oiled extra-wide foil. Stuff the cavity with the onion, bay leaves and dill fronds, sprinkle with wine, season, then seal the salmon in a loose parcel. Lift onto a baking sheet and bake for 1 hour. Cool for at least 10 minutes.
2 Meanwhile, whizz the avocado flesh in a food processor with the mayonnaise, lemon juice, zest and seasoning. Lift out the blade. Stir in the chopped dill and cucumber then transfer to a serving bowl. Chill for up to 3 hours.
3 Unwrap the salmon, then strip away the skin and fins from the uppermost side and remove the head. Carefully lift onto a platter, then dress with watercress, cucumber, lemon wedges and dill.
4 To serve, lift the fish from the bones in chunky fillets. When the top fillet has all gone, remove the stuffing, pull away the bones, then serve the bottom fillet, leaving the skin behind. Eat with the avocado mayo, warm buttery new potatoes, and salads or green beans.

PER SERVING 612 kcals, carbs 2g, fat 47g, sat fat 8g, salt 0.49g

Scallops with tomato sauce vierge

Sauce vierge is beautifully piquant, so it enhances the scallops' sweetness. A perfect summer starter.

SERVES 4 • PREP 30 MINS • COOK 5 MINS

FOR THE SAUCE
100ml/3½fl oz extra virgin olive oil
2 garlic cloves, very finely sliced
1 tsp coriander seeds
500g/1lb 2oz ripe tomatoes
3 tbsp red wine vinegar
small handful each basil, coriander and parsley leaves,
    finely chopped
FOR THE SCALLOPS
12 large scallops
drizzle olive oil

tip Any leftover sauce can be kept in the fridge and tossed through cooked pasta.

1 For the sauce, warm the oil, garlic and coriander seeds very gently in a pan, then set aside.
2 Nick a small cross in the bottom of each tomato and put them in a large bowl. Pour boiling water over the tomatoes and leave for about 10 seconds, then drain and cool under cold water. Peel and halve the tomatoes and squeeze out the seeds, then roughly chop the flesh. Tip the flesh into a bowl and season with salt and pepper. Stir in the vinegar, flavoured oil and herbs, then set aside for at least 20 minutes so all the flavours mingle.
3 For the scallops, heat a pan until very hot, toss the scallops with a drizzle of oil and sear for about 1 minute on each side until nicely caramelized. Spoon a nice pool of tomatoes onto plates and top each with 3 scallops.

PER SERVING 387 kcals, carbs 5g, fat 28g, sat fat 4g, salt 0.88g

Baked whole fish with romesco sauce

Cooking the fish on top of a layer of summer veg is a simple way to add heaps of flavour, and also stops the fish drying out as it roasts.

**SERVES 6 EASILY HALVED • PREP 20 MINS
COOK 45 MINS**

4 red peppers, deseeded and cut into large chunks
2 yellow peppers, deseeded and cut into large chunks
5 large tomatoes, halved (choose on the vine for
    best flavour)
1 large red onion, cut into wedges
4 large garlic cloves
4 tbsp olive oil, plus extra for drizzling
2 x 1kg/2lb 4oz whole line-caught sea bass or
    other large white fish, scaled and gutted
2 lemons, thinly sliced
2 large handfuls fresh mixed herbs (such as
    rosemary and thyme)
2 tsp balsamic vinegar
50g/2oz whole hazelnuts, toasted

1 Heat oven to 220C/200C fan/gas 7. Tip all the vegetables into a roasting tin with the unpeeled garlic cloves. Season, pour over the oil and toss together. Roast for 20 minutes until starting to soften.
2 Pat the fish dry with kitchen paper, then slash the skin on both sides with a sharp knife. Season the inside of the fish, then stuff with the lemon slices and half the herbs. Place on top of the veg, drizzle with more oil, scatter with the rest of the herbs, then roast for 20–25 minutes. When the fish is cooked, the flesh will feel firmer and the dorsal fin (the large one on the back) will pull away easily.
3 Lift the fish and half the vegetables onto a serving plate and cover with foil to keep them warm. Spoon the rest of the vegetables and most of the juice from the roasting tin into a food processor. Add the vinegar and hazelnuts, blend until smooth, then season. Serve the fish with the vegetables and sauce, lifting the fillets off the bone.

PER SERVING 457 kcals, carbs 15g, fat 24g, sat fat 3g, salt 0.43g

Summer fish stew with quick rouille

Conjure up thoughts of Mediterranean holidays with this light but indulgent meal for two.

SERVES 2 ● PREP ABOUT 30 MINS
COOK ABOUT 55 MINS

6 large, raw, shell-on prawns, heads removed and
    peeled, tails on
3 tbsp mild olive oil
150ml/¼ pint dry white wine
200ml/7fl oz fish stock
1 small fennel bulb, about 140g/5oz, halved and
    thinly sliced
1 small onion, thinly sliced
3 garlic cloves, thinly sliced
1 large potato, about 200g/7oz, cut into 2cm chunks
pared strip of orange zest
1 star anise
1 bay leaf
1½ tsp harissa paste
2 tbsp tomato purée
400g can chopped tomatoes
handful mussels or clams
200g/7oz skinless cod loin, in very chunky pieces
few thyme leaves
3 tbsp bought olive oil mayonnaise (or make your own,
    see page 206)

> *tip* Use the heads and shells from whole raw
> prawns to make a rich shellfish stock, and leave the
> prawn tails on so that they look special as you serve.

1 Devein each prawn. Fry the heads and shells in 1 tbsp oil for 5 minutes until dark pink and golden in patches. Add the wine, boil down by two-thirds, then pour in the stock. Strain into a jug, discarding the shells.

2 Heat the rest of the oil in a deep frying pan or casserole. Add the fennel, onion and garlic, season, then cover and gently cook for 10 minutes. Meanwhile, boil the potato for 5 minutes until almost tender. Drain in a colander.

3 Put the orange zest, star anise, bay leaf and ½ tsp harissa into the pan. Fry gently, uncovered, for 5–10 minutes until the vegetables are soft, sweet and golden.

4 Stir in the tomato purée, cook for 2 minutes, then add the tomatoes and reserved stock. Simmer for 10 minutes until slightly thickened. Season to taste.

5 Meanwhile, scrub the mussels or clams and pull away any stringy beards. Any that are open should be tapped sharply on the worktop – if they don't close after a few seconds, discard them.

6 Reheat the sauce, if necessary, then stir the potato, chunks of fish and prawns gently into the stew. Bring to the boil, then cover and gently simmer for 3 minutes. Scatter the mussels or clams over the stew, then cover and cook for 2 minutes more or until the shells have opened wide. Discard any that remain closed. The chunks of fish should flake easily and the prawns should be pink through. Scatter with the thyme leaves.

7 To make the quick rouille, stir the rest of the harissa through the mayonnaise. Serve the stew in bowls, topped with spoonfuls of rouille, which will melt into the sauce and enrich it. Have some good bread ready, as you'll want to mop up the juices.

PER SERVING 473 kcals, carbs 34g, fat 20g, sat fat 3g, salt 2.01g

OPPOSITE Clockwise from top left Smoked salmon with prawns, *horseradish cream and lime vinaigrette (page 187); Scallops with tomato sauce vierge (page 195); Skate with buttery parsley and capers (page 193); Lobster with Thermidore butter (page 198); Summer fish stew with quick rouille; Pancetta-wrapped trout with almond beans (page 193)*

Lobster salad with fennel and lime

A luxurious starter to share with someone special.

SERVES 2 AS A MAIN COURSE • PREP 45 MINS
NO COOK

meat from 1 cooked lobster weighing about 800g/1lb 12oz
1 small ripe avocado, sliced and tossed with a little
    lime juice
2 handfuls salad leaves
1 small head fennel, finely shredded, fronds reserved
seeds of 1 small pomegranate
FOR THE DRESSING
1 egg yolk
1 tbsp Dijon mustard
100ml/3½fl oz mild olive oil, plus 3 tbsp extra
juice 2 limes (about 4 tbsp)
small handful fresh coriander, roughly chopped

1 In a small bowl, whisk the egg yolk together with the mustard and using a small whisk, whisk the oil into the egg yolk, starting with a very little then gradually working in more and more. Continue until you have a thickish mayonnaise. Stir in half the lime juice and most of the chopped coriander. The sauce should be thick but slightly runny; whisk in a teaspoon of water if needed. Season to taste. Whisk the remaining lime juice with the 3 tbsp oil to make a dressing.
2 Divide all the meat except the tail meat between the two tail-shell halves then top with overlapping slices of tail meat and avocado. Put on to plates with the claws. Lightly dress the salad leaves and any remaining avocado in a little of the dressing, then pile them next to the lobster. Toss the fennel with the pomegranate seeds, remaining dressing and coriander. Pile on top of the leaves. Drizzle the lime mayonnaise over the lobster and serve what's left for dipping.

PER SERVING 890 kcals, carbs 9g, fat 79g, sat fat 11g, salt 1.82g

Lobster with Thermidor butter

We have taken a classic lobster dish and simplified it by putting all the same flavours in an easy-to-use, prepare-ahead butter.

SERVES 4 AS A STARTER, 2 AS A MAIN • PREP 15 MINS
COOK 15 MINS
❄ BUTTER ONLY

2 cooked lobsters
FOR THE BUTTER
150ml/¼ pint dry white wine
1 shallot, very finely chopped
handful tarragon leaves, chopped
handful parsley leaves, chopped
1 tsp Dijon mustard
juice ¼ lemon
pinch paprika
dash Tabasco sauce
5 tbsp Parmesan, finely grated
140g/5oz butter, softened

1 First make the butter. Put the wine and shallot into a pan, then bring to the boil and simmer until nearly dry. Tip into a bowl to cool, then mix in all the other ingredients, roll into a log (using cling film or foil), and chill to harden. (Can be frozen for up to 1 month.)
2 Snap away the claws from the lobster. Using a large chef's knife, cut the lobster in half and wash the head cavity under cold water, then dry with kitchen paper. Lay the lobsters, cut-side up, on a baking sheet. Crack the claws and remove the meat. Divide the claw meat between the head cavities. This can be done the day before and the lobster kept in the fridge ready for grilling.
3 Heat grill to High. Slice the butter into thin rounds and lay it along the lobsters so all the meat is covered. Grill for 5–8 minutes until the butter is bubbling and starting to brown. Put the lobsters on plates, pouring any butter from the baking sheet over them. Serve with new potatoes and some dressed salad leaves.

PER SERVING 419 kcals, carbs 3g, fat 34g, sat fat 20g, salt 1.62g

Step-by-step: Preparing a lobster

The meat from a lobster can be prepared up to a day ahead and kept in the fridge.
To dismantle a lobster, you will need a heavy kitchen knife, kitchen scissors, a bowl
for the shells and a plate for the meat.

1 Twist the head away from the tail. Do not throw any of the shell away, but put it into the shell bowl, including the head.

2 Snap off the eight lobster legs as close to the body as you can. Using a rolling pin, roll and squeeze the meat from the legs and set the meat aside on a small plate.

try this...

No chef worth their salt would ever throw away lobster shells. With very little effort you can make a great stock to use in soups, sauces and risottos. Simply heat a generous glug of olive oil in a large saucepan until hot, throw in the shells then fry until they crackle and blister. Add a sliced onion and a smashed garlic clove. Cover with cold water and add a glass of white wine, if you have a bottle open. Simmer for 1 hour then strain through a fine sieve. (Will keep in the fridge for up to 3 days or can be frozen for up to 1 month.)

3 Use scissors to cut along the underside of the tail. You should now be able to release the tail meat in one piece.

4 Once released, cut the tail meat into 10–12 neat slices and remove and discard the grey spot from the middle of each segment by poking it out with the point of a small knife or cocktail stick.

5 Use the blunt side of a heavy knife or a meat mallet to crack the claws and claw joints. If you want to serve the claws ready to pick at the table, leave them at this point.

6 To remove all the meat from the claws, use a skewer to prise out the meat.

8

Vegetables and side dishes

Where would a side of beef be without roast potatoes? Fish and chips without the peas? The barbecue without the salads and slaw? Often it's the sides that make the meal – offering complementary flavours but also contrasting textures, temperatures and the chance to inject some real seasonality into our cooking. With a little persuasion – a dash of dressing, a grilling with cheese – vegetables and salads are easily transformed into interesting, healthy dishes that can steal the show.

There is so much to say about vegetables, so we have focused on the ones that feature in this book, dividing the most common (and a few unusual) vegetables into types with useful tips on how to buy, prepare and enjoy them at their best.

LEAFY GREENS

Salad leaves can vary from mild and soft to crunchy and peppery or firm and bitter. To store lettuce and salad leaves, wrap them in damp kitchen paper then seal them in a food bag and chill. When dressing leafy salads, the golden rule is to add the dressing just before serving – do it too soon and the leaves will become soggy as they sit.

All **cabbages, kale** and **greens** should look bright, with crisp leaves. Remove the tough outer leaves, slice out any hard stalks then shred the remaining leaves. Tender **Asian greens** such as pak choi are best cooked quickly in a wok or steamed – cook all of it, as the stems are fleshy and edible. **Spinach** needs washing thoroughly and wilts dramatically on cooking. It usually must be squeezed dry before use.

FRUITING VEGETABLES

Choose **tomatoes** that are firm but not hard, with fresh green stems and an earthy smell. Don't chill them unless you absolutely have to – it dulls their flavour. **Round tomatoes** are good for general use. Other varieties include large **beefsteak** for slicing and stuffing; sweet, small **cherries** for salads; and **yellow, orange** and **green varieties**, which are pretty in salads and salsas. Some green tomatoes are simply unripe but perfect for chutneys or frying. **Heirloom tomatoes** come in all sorts of shapes, sizes and colours and are renowned for their flavour.

Squashes and **pumpkins** are perfect for sautéing, mashing or adding to soups and stews. Thin-skinned squash, such as **butternut**, can be roasted and eaten with the skin on, which saves prep time.

When choosing **courgettes** and **cucumbers**, pick the smaller ones on offer. Courgettes are best griddled, grilled, fried or roasted. Their flowers are

OPPOSITE Roasted red peppers with tomatoes, anchovies and olives (page 210).

also edible – classically dipped in batter or stuffed, then deep-fried. **Aubergines** should be firm and plump with a green stalk – they are perfect for griddling, using in ratatouille or moussaka, and also roasted for dips.

Creamy **avocados** should be unblemished, and yield slightly when gently squeezed. **Hass** have a dark, knobbly skin, and **Fuerte** are greener and smooth-skinned. Ripen at room temperature then keep them in the fridge.

ROOTS AND TUBERS

Roots and tubers such as **carrots, parsnips, turnips, swede** and **Jerusalem artichokes** are excellent roasted or mashed. Some are excellent raw in salads and slaws, too (don't forget radishes). Young root veg need nothing more than a quick scrub; larger veg will need to be peeled.

Put on a pair of rubber gloves before preparing earthy **beetroot**, as their blood-red juice will stain your skin. Tasty **celeriac** needs to be peeled with a knife and, as with the nutty **Jerusalem artichoke**, the flesh should be kept under acidulated water (water with a squeeze of lemon juice) or it will turn brown.

Look for firm, blemish-free **potatoes** without green tinges. There's a lot of goodness just under the skin, so leave it on, or peel very thinly, then rinse. New potatoes just need a scrub. **Waxy** potatoes are firm and moist. They are good for boiling, steaming and salads. Varieties include Nicola, Charlotte and Anya. **Floury** potatoes have a dry, fluffy texture. These are ideal for roasting, mashing and baking. Varieties include King Edward and Russet. '**All-rounders**' are good for mash, chips, bakers and roasties. Varieties include Desiree and Maris Piper. **Salad potatoes** are small and enjoyed skin-on. Varieties include Jersey Royals and Pink Fir Apple. **Sweet potatoes** are quicker to cook and have a sweetish, softer, white or orange flesh.

STALKS AND BULBS

Buy **asparagus** in springtime and snap away the tough bases before cooking. Some people peel the stems, too.

Fennel is delicious both raw or cooked – cooking will mellow its aniseed flavour. Look for tightly packed leaves and perky fronds when buying fennel bulbs.

Celery is an essential base flavouring to many soups, and stocks, adds crunch to salads and is wonderful braised. Choose firm, tightly formed heads.

Depending on how they're used, **onions** add depth of flavour, sweetness, bite and acidity, while **leeks** give their own, more mellow, 'greener' onion flavour. Onion varieties differ in size, strength and colour, from the all-purpose **yellow onion**, mild **Spanish onions** and sweeter **red onions** to **shallots** and **baby** and **pickling onions**. Shallots are a pain to peel in any great number, so to make this easier, cover shallots with boiling water, set aside for 5 minutes, then drain. Their skins should peel off more easily.

BEANS, PEAS AND SWEETCORN

All fresh pods should snap when you try to bend them and they should be cooked quickly to preserve their colour and flavour and in order to retain just a little crunch.

In the case of **fine** and **round** beans, trim the stalk ends away but leave the pretty curly ends alone. **Runner beans** should be topped and tailed and the stringy edges removed (use a peeler). Preparing **broad beans** takes time; each bean within the pod has a fine shell that needs removing. When buying, remember that you'll need to buy 1kg of pods to accrue 300g beans! **Frozen soya beans** make a good alternative to peas or broad beans – and don't need shelling.

If you do buy **fresh peas,** choose vibrant pods that don't rattle when they are shaken. **Frozen peas** are frozen very quickly after picking, so these are often 'fresher' than fresh; petits pois are sweet and small and cook in minutes. **Mange tout** and **sugar snaps** have edible pods – which are great for stir-fries. Fresh **sweetcorn** on the cob is best bought still in its husk, with tightly packed, plump and yellow kernels below.

FLOWERING VEGETABLES

Ordinary **broccoli** should be firm and bright vibrant green and should be cut into evenly sized 'florets' before cooking. Other varieties include **Tenderstem broccoli**, which has a long, edible stem, and **purple sprouting broccoli**, which blushes purple when raw but turns green when cooked. **Cauliflower** should be creamy-white in colour and is good eaten raw as well as cooked. **Globe artichokes** are members of the thistle family, and are no relation to Jerusalem artichokes. The tender ends of the leaves and the heart of the bud are both edible; the furry central choke isn't and should be removed.

Summer crunch salad

SERVES 4 • PREP 15 MINS • COOK 5 MINS
V

200g pack small button mushrooms, finely sliced
juice 1 lemon
200g/7oz green beans, trimmed
handful chopped soft green herbs, such as basil,
    chervil, parsley and tarragon
100g/4oz cherry tomatoes, quartered
3 tbsp olive oil
75g/2½oz Parmesan, shaved

1 In a bowl, toss the mushrooms with half the lemon juice and set aside – the lemon juice will soften the mushrooms. Boil the beans in salted water for 5–6 minutes until they still have a crunch but are not squeaky, then drain and cool in iced water.
2 Toss the beans and mushrooms together in a bowl with the herbs and season with salt and pepper. Toss through the tomatoes, remaining lemon juice and the oil and scatter with Parmesan just before serving.

PER SERVING 178 kcals, carbs 3g, fat 15g, sat fat 5g, salt 0.38g

try this...

Warm dressed green beans are ideal for serving with a summer roast chicken. Toss hot green beans with a finely chopped shallot, a dash of wine vinegar and walnut oil.

Indian summer salad

 SERVES 6 • PREP 20 MINS • NO COOK
V

3 carrots
bunch radishes
2 courgettes
½ small red onion
small handful mint leaves, roughly torn
FOR THE DRESSING
1 tbsp white wine vinegar
1 tsp Dijon mustard
1 tbsp mayonnaise
2 tbsp mild olive oil

1 Grate the carrots into a large bowl. Thinly slice the radishes and courgettes and finely chop the onion. Mix all the vegetables together in the bowl with the mint leaves.
2 Whisk together the vinegar, mustard and mayonnaise until smooth, then gradually whisk in the oil. Taste and add salt and pepper, then drizzle over the salad and mix well. Leftovers will keep in a covered container in the fridge for up to 24 hours.

PER SERVING 79 kcals, carbs 5g, fat 6g, sat fat 1g, salt 0.35g

Tomato, cucumber and coriander salad

 SERVES 6 • PREP 15 MINS • NO COOK
V

6 vine-ripened tomatoes
1 small cucumber, diced
1 onion, finely chopped
2 tbsp chopped coriander

1 Deseed and chop the tomatoes and mix with the diced cucumber, chopped onion and coriander. Season just before serving.

PER SERVING 34 kcals, carbs 6g, fat none, sat fat none, salt 0.03g

Crunchy celeriac, apple and pecan salad

**SERVES 8–10 • PREP 20 MINS, PLUS COOLING
COOK 15 MINS**
V

100g/4oz shelled pecans or walnuts
1 tbsp honey
pinch cayenne pepper
1 celeriac, about 800g/1lb 12oz
2 lemons, zested
2 red-skinned eating apples, cored and thinly sliced
2 medium fennel bulbs, thinly sliced
pinch paprika, to serve
FOR THE DRESSING
150g pot Greek yogurt
4 tbsp mayonnaise
1 tsp Dijon mustard
1 tbsp olive oil

1 Heat oven to 150C/130C fan/gas 2. Combine the nuts, honey, ½ tsp salt and the cayenne pepper and spread over a baking sheet. Bake for 15 minutes until toasted. Leave to cool then roughly chop most of the nuts.
2 Peel the celeriac and cut into slices the thickness of a £1 coin. Stacking a few slices together, cut across into matchsticks. Alternatively, coarsely grate the celeriac in a food processor. Drop the matchsticks into a bowl of water and add the juice of ½ lemon. Add the sliced apple to the bowl.
3 Mix the lemon zest with the rest of the dressing ingredients. Drain the celeriac and apple, add the fennel and chopped nuts, then stir in the yogurt mixture. Pile into a bowl and scatter over the whole nuts. Serve sprinkle with a little paprika.

PER SERVING 215 kcals, carbs 10g, fat 18g, sat fat 3g, salt 0.72g

Thai cucumber salad with sour chilli dressing

SERVES 4 • PREP 10 MINS • NO COOK

1 cucumber, cut into ribbons with a peeler
1 Little Gem lettuce, shredded
140g/5oz beansprouts
bunch coriander, leaves roughly chopped
bunch mint, leaves roughly chopped
FOR THE DRESSING
1 tsp rice wine vinegar
1 tbsp fish sauce
½ tsp light muscovado sugar
2 red chillies, deseeded and finely chopped

1 Mix the dressing ingredients together, stirring until the sugar is dissolved.
2 Place the salad ingredients in a bowl, then pour over the dressing, mixing well to combine. Serve immediately.

PER SERVING 27 kcals, carbs 4g, fat 1g, sat fat none, salt 0.75g

South western-style salad

SERVES 2 EASILY DOUBLED • PREP 20 MINS • COOK 10 MINS
V

2 sweetcorn cobs
400g can black beans, drained and rinsed
1 avocado, cut into chunks
200g/7oz cherry tomatoes, halved
4 spring onions, roughly chopped
1 tsp ground cumin
1 tbsp chipotle chilli sauce
juice and zest 2 limes
1 tbsp sherry vinegar
2 tbsp extra virgin olive oil
100g/4oz feta cheese, crumbled

1 Boil the corn for 10 minutes in salted water, cool under the cold tap, then cut the kernels away from the core. Tip the beans into a bowl with the cooked corn, avocado, tomatoes and spring onions.
2 Mix the cumin, chill sauce, lime zest and juice, vinegar and oil with some seasoning, then pour over the salad. Toss together well, scatter the feta over the top and serve.

PER SERVING 612 kcals, carbs 47g, fat 38g, sat fat 9g, salt 2.83g

Healthy coleslaw

SERVES 6 • PREP 10 MINS • NO COOK
V

6 tbsp plain yogurt
½ tsp Dijon mustard
2 tbsp mayonnaise
½ white cabbage
2 carrots
½ onion, very finely chopped

1 Mix the yogurt, mustard and mayonnaise together in a bowl.
2 Using a grater attachment on a food processor or a box grater, grate the cabbage and carrots. Either grate the onion or chop as finely as you can. Tip all the vegetables into the bowl and stir through the dressing. Will keep in the fridge for up to 3 days.

PER SERVING 76 kcals, carbs 8g, fat 4g, sat fat 1g, salt 0.15g

Spring salad with watercress dressing

SERVES 4 • PREP 20 MINS • COOK 50 MINS

550g/1lb 4oz new potatoes, scrubbed
800g/1lb 12oz young broad beans (to give 200g/7oz shelled beans)
200g/7oz fresh young asparagus
100g/4oz fresh podded peas or frozen petits pois
90g pack prosciutto, sliced into ribbons
50g/2oz fresh watercress, roughly chopped
6 tbsp extra virgin olive oil
2 tbsp cider vinegar
125g bag mixed salad leaves
100g/4oz Pecorino (or Parmesan), shaved

1 Boil the potatoes in salted water for 10–15 minutes until tender. Lift out of the water then blanch the shelled broad beans and the asparagus in the boiling water for 2–3 minutes. Scoop out with a slotted spoon, cool under running cold water. Pop the beans from their pods. Blanch the peas in the boiling water for 1 minute, cool and drain. Toss the asparagus, beans, peas, potatoes and prosciutto together.
2 For the dressing, put the watercress, oil and vinegar in a blender or food processor and blitz until really smooth. Season. Toss the salad leaves with a spoonful or two of dressing and arrange on plates. Pile the vegetable mixture on top, season, then drizzle over the remaining dressing and scatter with the cheese shavings.

PER SERVING 493 kcals, carbs 31g, fat 31g, sat fat 9g, salt 1.57g

try this...

Love asparagus? For a spring treat, cover the base of a large baking dish with asparagus. Mix a 142ml pot double cream, 1 tbsp grated Parmesan, salt, pepper and a pinch of nutmeg and pour over. Scatter with more grated Parmesan then bake at 200C/180C fan/gas 6 for 20 minutes until bubbling and the spears are tender. Great with roast chicken.

Homemade mayonnaise

MAKES 250ML • PREP 5 MINS • NO COOK

125ml/4fl oz sunflower oil
125ml extra virgin olive oil
2 large egg yolks
2tsp Dijon mustard

1 Mix the sunflower oil and extra virgin olive oil in a jug. Put the egg and Dijon mustard into a blender or food processor then, with the motor running, drizzle the oil through the funnel until thick. (Alternatively, whisk the oils into the beaten egg yolk and Dijon very slowly.) Season to taste with lemon juice, salt and pepper.

PER SERVING 127 kcals, carbs 0.1g, fat 13.8g, sat fat 1.9g, salt 0.06g

Classic French dressing

MAKES 120ML • PREP 5 MINS • NO COOK

2 tbsp white or red wine vinegar
6 tbsp mild olive or sunflower oil
2 tsp Dijon mustard

1 Put the white or red wine vinegar, oil and mustard into a jug or jar. Season with salt and pepper then whisk together or shake vigorously until the mix thickens.

PER SERVING 74 kcals, carbs none, fat 8.2g, sat fat 1.2g, salt none

Asian-style dressing

MAKES 60ML • PREP 5 MINS • NO COOK

juice 2 limes
1 tbsp fish sauce
1 tbsp golden caster sugar
1 crushed garlic clove
1 red chilli, deseeded and shredded
handful chopped coriander or mint leaves

1 Mix together the lime juice, fish sauce, sugar, garlic and red chilli. Just before serving, add a handful of chopped coriander or mint leaves. Season with more fish sauce if it needs it.

PER SERVING 21 kcals, carbs 4.7g, fat 0.1g, sat fat none, salt 0.74g

Real salad cream

MAKES 200ML • PREP 5 MINS • NO COOK

2 large eggs
1 tbsp Dijon mustard
1 tbsp golden caster sugar
2 tbsp lemon juice
2 tbsp extra virgin olive oil
6 tbsp double cream

1 Put the eggs into a pan of boiling water, then boil for 5 minutes. Cool quickly under running water, then peel. Cut the eggs carefully in half, then scoop the yolks into a bowl. Whisk in the Dijon mustard, sugar, lemon juice. Whisk in the extra virgin olive oil and double cream, then season to taste.

PER TBSP 55 kcals, carbs 1.5g, fat 4.8g, sat fat 2.4g, salt 0.12g

OPPOSITE Clockwise from top left Layered roast summer vegetables (page 208); Aubergine tomato and Parmesan bake (page 209); Buttered leeks (page 213); Melting cheese courgettes (page 210); Ultimate roast potatoes (page 219); Thai cucumber salad with sour chilli dressing (page 204)

Tofu, greens and cashew stir-fry

SERVES 4 • PREP 10 MINS • COOK 10 MINS
V

1 tbsp vegetable oil
1 head broccoli, cut into small florets
4 garlic cloves, sliced
1 red chilli, deseeded and finely sliced
1 bunch spring onions, sliced
140g/5oz soya beans
2 heads pak choi, quartered
300g/11oz marinated tofu pieces
1½ tbsp hoisin sauce
1 tbsp reduced-salt soy sauce (add extra to suit
    your own taste)
25g/1oz roasted cashews

1 Heat the oil in a non-stick wok. Add the broccoli, then fry on a high heat for 5 minutes or until just tender, adding a little water if it begins to catch. Add the garlic and chilli, fry for 1 minute, then toss through the spring onions, soya beans, pak choi and tofu. Stir-fry for 2–3 minutes. Add the hoisin, soy and nuts to warm through.

PER SERVING 358 kcals, carbs 13g, fat 23g, sat fat 3g, salt 3.49g

tip This recipe contains an amazing five of your 5-a-day in each serving!

Indian spiced greens

SERVES 4 • PREP 10 MINS • COOK 10 MINS
V ❄

1 tbsp vegetable oil
1 tsp each cumin and black mustard seeds
4 green chillies, finely chopped
large piece fresh root ginger, grated
½ tsp ground turmeric
500g/1lb 2oz shredded greens
100g/4oz frozen peas
juice 1 lemon
½ tsp ground coriander
small bunch coriander, roughly chopped
2 tbsp unsweetened desiccated coconut

1 Heat the oil in a large non-stick pan or wok, sizzle the cumin and mustard seeds for 1 minute, then add the chillies, ginger and turmeric. Fry until aromatic, then add the greens, a pinch of salt, a splash of water and the peas.
2 Cover the pan and cook for 4–5 minutes until the greens have wilted. Add the lemon juice, ground coriander, half the fresh coriander and half the desiccated coconut, then toss everything together. Pile into a serving dish and scatter with the rest of the coconut and coriander.

PER SERVING 117 kcals, carbs 9g, fat 7g, sat fat 3g, salt 0.03g

Layered roast summer vegetables

SERVES 4 • PREP 30 MINS • COOK 1 HOUR
V

6 tbsp good-quality olive oil
4 large courgettes, thickly sliced (yellow ones look pretty)
5 ripe plum tomatoes, sliced
2 aubergines, sliced
1 large garlic bulb, kept whole
small bunch rosemary, broken into sprigs

1 Heat oven to 220C/200C fan/gas 7. Drizzle a round ovenproof dish with a little oil; then, starting from the outside, tightly layer alternate slices of the vegetables in concentric circles until you get to the middle – sit the head of garlic here. Stick the sprigs of rosemary among the vegetables, drizzle everything generously with oil, then season with salt and pepper. Roast everything together, drizzling with more oil occasionally, for 50 minutes to 1 hour until the vegetables are soft and lightly charred.
2 Remove from the oven and leave to stand for a few minutes, then remove the garlic and separate it into cloves for squeezing over the vegetables.

PER SERVING 240 kcals, carbs 12g, fat 18g, sat fat 3g, salt 0.54g

Aubergine, tomato and Parmesan bake

 SERVES 6 • PREP 10 MINS • COOK 50 MINS
❄ Ⅴ **WITHOUT TOPPING**

2 garlic cloves, crushed
6 tbsp olive oil
2 x 400g cans chopped tomatoes
2 tbsp tomato purée
4 aubergines, cut into long 5mm-thick slices
85g/3oz Parmesan cheese, finely grated
small bunch pack basil, leaves torn
1 egg, beaten

1 Heat oven to 200C/180C fan/gas 6. Soften the garlic in 4 tbsp oil for 3 minutes then tip in the tomatoes. Simmer for 8 minutes then stir in the tomato purée.
2 Meanwhile, heat a griddle pan until very hot. Brush a few of the aubergines with a little oil, then add to the pan. Cook over a high heat until well browned and cooked through, about 5–7 minutes, turning them halfway through cooking. Remove and drain on kitchen paper.
3 Lay some aubergine slices in the bottom of an ovenproof dish, then spoon over some sauce. Sprinkle with Parmesan and basil. Season, then repeat. Pour the egg over the top, sprinkle over a little more Parmesan, then bake for 20 minutes or until golden.

PER SERVING 225 kcals, carbs 8g, fat 17g, sat fat 5g, salt 0.52g

Ratatouille

 SERVES 4 • PREP 25 MINS • COOK 25 MINS
Ⅴ ❄

5 tbsp olive oil
2 large aubergines, cut into chunks
4 small courgettes, cut into chunks
2 red or yellow peppers, peeled, deseeded and
    thickly sliced
1 medium onion, peeled and thinly sliced
3 garlic cloves, peeled and crushed
1 tbsp red wine vinegar
1 tsp sugar (any kind)
4 large ripe tomatoes, peeled, deseeded and roughly
    chopped (see below)
small bunch basil

1 Set a large frying pan or sauté pan over a medium heat and add 2 tbsp oil. Fry the aubergines until golden and softened. Set aside then fry the courgettes in another 1 tbsp oil until golden. Repeat with the peppers. Don't overcook the vegetables at this stage as they'll be cooked more later.
2 Fry the onion in the remaining oil for 5 minutes or until soft, then add the garlic and fry for a further minute. Stir in the vinegar and sugar, then tip in the tomatoes and half the basil. Return the vegetables to the pan, season, and cook for 5 minutes. Serve scattered with torn basil leaves.

PER SERVING 241 kcals, carbs 20g, fat 16g, sat fat 2g, salt 0.05g

try this...

Caponata is a Sicilian dish similar to ratatouille but with a more sweet/sour flavour and a few more ingredients. To make your own, follow the recipe above, and add a handful chopped green olives and drained capers. Serve at room temperature.

To remove the skin from a tomato, score a small cross at the rounded end. Put in a bowl and pour over boiling water, leaving it for a few seconds, then dunk it into cold water. The tomato skin will have started to peel where you cut the cross – so simply peel away with your fingers. Quarter the tomatoes, scrape away the seeds with a spoon, then roughly chop the flesh.

Roasted peppers with tomatoes, anchovies and olives

**SERVES 4 EASILY DOUBLED • PREP 10 MINS
COOK 1 HOUR 10 MINS**

4 red peppers, halved and deseeded
50g can anchovies in oil, drained and oil reserved
8 smallish tomatoes, halved
2 garlic cloves, thinly sliced
2 rosemary sprigs
2 tbsp olive oil
50g black olives
(recipe photo on page 200)

> *tip* The best roasted peppers are always those left
> to sit in their own juices for a good while – overnight
> even – until the flesh gives in completely and the
> flavours merge together.

1 Heat oven to 160C/140C fan/gas 3. Put the peppers into a large baking dish, toss with a little of the oil from the anchovy can, then turn cut-side up. Roast for 40 minutes until soft but not collapsed.

2 Put 2 halves of tomato, several garlic slices, a few little rosemary sprigs and two olives into the hollow of each pepper. Slice 8 anchovies along their length and add two slices to each pepper. Drizzle over the oil then roast again for 30 minutes until the tomatoes are soft and the peppers are filled with pools of tasty juice. Leave to cool and serve warm or at room temperature, scattered with the olives.

PER SERVING 162 kcals, carbs 13g, fat 11g, sat fat 1g, salt 1.44g

Melting cheese courgettes

**SERVES 2 EASILY DOUBLED • PREP 5 MINS
COOK 10 MINS**
V

1 tbsp olive oil, plus extra for drizzling (optional)
200g baby courgettes, halved lengthways (or 4 ordinary
    courgettes, sliced thickly)
handful Parmesan, finely grated
zest 1 lemon

1 Heat the oil in a large non-stick frying pan or, if griddling, rub the courgettes with the oil. Season, then fry or griddle for 3–5 minutes on each side until softened and golden. Transfer to a serving bowl and toss with the Parmesan, lemon zest and plenty of black pepper. Drizzle with a little oil, if liked. Try serving with grilled chicken or fish.

PER SERVING 100 kcals, carbs 2g, fat 8g, sat fat 2g, salt 0.16g

Wilted chicory with melted Taleggio cheese

**SERVES 2 EASILY DOUBLED • PREP 5 MINS
COOK 15 MINS**
V

2 heads white chicory
2 tbsp olive oil
1 small shallot, chopped
100g/4oz Taleggio
pinch dried oregano

1 Heat grill to High. Trim the chicory and cut lengthways into quarters. Heat the oil in a shallow pan over a medium heat and soften the shallot for 2 minutes. Add the chicory quarters, cut-side down, and cook for 3 minutes. Turn them over, cover the pan and cook for another 3 minutes, then season.

2 Slice the cheese, arrange the pieces over the chicory and sprinkle the oregano on top. Slide under the hot grill for a few minutes until the cheese is bubbling.

PER SERVING 268 kcals, carbs 3g, fat 24g, sat fat 9g, salt 1.16g

Artichokes with Parmesan butter sauce

SERVES 4 • PREP 5 MINS • COOK 50 MINS
V

2 lemons, 1 halved and 1 juiced
4 large globe artichokes
200g/7oz unsalted butter, chilled
1 glass (about 100ml/3½fl oz) dry white wine
25g/1oz Parmesan, finely grated

> *tip* This recipe lets you enjoy the delicacy that is globe artichokes without the need for any fiddly prep. The sauce is delicious drizzled over asparagus or sprouting broccoli too.

1 Bring a large pan of salted water to the boil with the lemon halves. Cut the stalks from the artichokes. Drop the artichokes into the water and boil for 40–45 minutes.
2 Dice the butter. Pour the wine into a pan, reduce by half, then reduce the heat and whisk in the butter one small piece at a time. Whisk in the Parmesan and lemon juice. Season to taste.
3 To eat, pull off the leaves one at a time. Dip the broken end of the leaf into the sauce, eat the fleshy base then discard the rest. When you reach the middle, lift out the central leaves, scrape away the hairy choke and eat the artichoke heart.

PER SERVING 502 kcals, carbs 10g, fat 44g, sat fat 27g, salt 1.10g

Quick braised cabbage with pancetta

SERVES 6 • PREP 10 MINS • COOK 15 MINS

1 tbsp sunflower oil
200g/7oz diced pancetta or smoked bacon
pinch golden caster sugar
splash white wine vinegar
1 large Savoy cabbage, shredded
200ml/7fl oz chicken stock

1 Heat the oil in a pan and sizzle the pancetta or bacon until crispy. Sprinkle over the sugar and splash in the vinegar. Stir the cabbage into the pan, then pour over the stock. Simmer it all for 10 minutes until the cabbage is tender but still slightly crunchy.

PER SERVING 174 kcals, carbs 7g, fat 12g, sat fat 4g, salt 1.88g

Lentil salad with soy beans, sugar snaps and broccoli

 SERVES 4 • PREP 5-10 MINS • COOK 15 MINS
V

200g/7oz Puy lentils
200g/7oz tenderstem broccoli
140g/5oz each defrosted soy beans and fresh
    sugar snap peas
1 red chilli, deseeded and sliced
FOR THE DRESSING
2 tbsp sesame oil
juice 1 lemon
1 garlic clove, chopped
2½ tbsp reduced-salt soy sauce
3cm piece fresh root ginger, finely grated
1 tbsp clear honey

1 Boil the lentils in water until just tender, about 15 minutes. Drain, then tip into a large bowl. Bring a saucepan of salted water to the boil, throw in the broccoli for 1 minute, add the beans and peas for 1 minute more. Drain, then cool under cold water. Pat dry, then add to the bowl with the lentils.
2 Mix together the dressing ingredients with some seasoning. Pour over the lentils and veg, then mix in well with the chopped chilli. Pile onto a serving platter or divide between 4 plates and serve.

PER SERVING 302 kcals, carbs 42g, fat 7g, sat fat 1g, salt 1.41g

Broccoli with garlic and chilli breadcrumbs

SERVES 4 • PREP 15 MINS • COOK 8 MINS
V

500g/1lb 2oz tenderstem or purple-sprouting broccoli
2 tbsp olive oil
knob of butter
2 small garlic cloves, finely chopped
1 small red chilli, deseeded and finely chopped
50g/2oz white breadcrumbs

1 Steam the broccoli for 5 minutes until tender. Meanwhile, heat the oil and butter in a pan, then fry the garlic and chilli for 1 minute. Add the breadcrumbs, then fry for 5 minutes until crisp. Season the broccoli, arrange in a dish, scatter over the breadcrumbs and serve.

PER SERVING 142 kcals, carbs 13g, fat 8g, sat fat 2g, salt 0.31g

Cauliflower cheese

SERVES 6 • PREP 10 MINS • COOK 35 MINS
V ❄

1 large cauliflower, trimmed and broken into florets
500ml/18fl oz milk
4 tbsp plain flour
50g/2oz butter
100g/4oz strong Cheddar, grated
2–3 tbsp breadcrumbs (optional)

tip This recipe is easily made with a mix of cauliflower and broccoli, or broccoli by itself. Cook the broccoli for about 3 minutes.

1 Bring a large saucepan of water to the boil, then add the cauliflower and cook for 5 minutes – lift out a piece to test, it should be just tender. Drain the cauliflower, then tip into an ovenproof dish.
2 Heat oven to 220C/200C fan/gas 7. Put the saucepan back on the heat and add the milk, flour and butter. Keep whisking fast as the mixture comes to the boil. Whisk for 2 minutes while the sauce bubbles and thickens. Turn off the heat, stir in most of the cheese and pour over the cauliflower. Scatter over the remaining cheese and breadcrumbs, if using. (Can now be frozen for up to a month.)
3 Pop the cauliflower cheese in the oven and bake for 20 minutes until bubbling.

PER SERVING 250 kcals, carbs 16g, fat 15g, sat fat 9g, salt 0.62g

Braised lettuce with peas

SERVES 4 • PREP 10 MINS • COOK 15 MINS

knob of butter
1 small onion, finely chopped
4 Little Gem lettuces, halved lengthways and any tough
    leaves discarded
200ml/7fl oz chicken stock
4 tbsp crème fraîche or single cream
500g/1lb 2oz frozen petits pois

1 Melt the butter in a large wide pan. Soften the onion for 5 minutes. Put the lettuce, cut-side up, on top of the onion and cook for 30 seconds, then turn over and cook for another 30 seconds. Pour over the stock and lightly season. Cover, reduce the heat to the minimum, then cook for 10 minutes.
2 With a slotted spoon, lift the lettuces out and into a sieve over a bowl. Boil the juices until reduced by half. Add the crème fraîche or cream and petits pois and boil for 1 minute until heated through. Arrange the lettuces in a serving dish and pour over the sauce and peas.

PER SERVING 114 kcals, carbs 9g, fat 5g, sat fat 3g, salt 0.20g

Fennel gratin

SERVES 4 • PREP 5 MINS • COOK 25 MINS
V

4 large fennel bulbs
pinch grated nutmeg
1 garlic clove, crushed
200ml/7fl oz double cream
50g/2oz Parmesan, finely grated

1 Heat oven to 200C/180C fan/gas 6 and put a pan of salted water on to boil. Trim the fennel tops, then cut the bulbs into wedges. Boil for 5–6 minutes, then drain well. Arrange in an ovenproof dish, season and sprinkle with nutmeg. Stir the garlic into the cream and pour over the fennel. Top with the Parmesan, then bake for 20 minutes until golden.

PER SERVING 320 kcals, carbs 4g, fat 31g, sat fat 17g, salt 0.56g

Garlic and shallot spinach

SERVES 2 • PREP 10 MINS • COOK 10 MINS
V

250g/9oz large leaf spinach, washed
2 tbsp mild olive oil
handful small shallots, peeled
1 garlic clove, peeled but left whole

1 Tip the spinach into a pan of boiling water. Leave until just wilted and bright green, then drain and cool under cold running water. Squeeze as much water as you can from the leaves.
2 To serve, heat the oil in a frying pan and sauté the shallots for 5 minutes or until tender. Add the garlic, fry for 30 seconds, then toss in the spinach. Season, then stir until reheated.

PER SERVING 135 kcals, carbs 3g, fat 12g, sat fat 2g, salt 0.45g

Buttered leeks

 super healthy **SERVES 8 • PREP 5 MINS • COOK 15 MINS**
V

1.8 kg/4lb leeks, trimmed
50g/2oz butter, plus extra for serving
thyme leaves, to serve

1 Cut a slit down the leeks from top to root and wash thoroughly under cold running water. Put a large pan over a medium heat, add the butter and let it melt over the base of the pan. Add the leeks and plenty of seasoning and stir to coat in the butter.
2 Turn the heat down to low, cover the pan and cook the leeks gently for about 15 minutes, stirring halfway through until they are tender. Serve with extra butter and a sprinkling of thyme leaves.

PER SERVING 81 kcals, carbs 5g, fat 6g, sat fat 3g, salt 0.13g

Chunky oven chips

SERVES 4 EASILY HALVED • PREP 2 MINS • COOK 50 MINS

4 baking potatoes, scrubbed
3 tbsp olive oil
good pinch chilli powder or paprika (optional)

> **Masala wedges**
> Toss the wedges with ½ tsp turmeric and 1 tsp roughly
> crushed cumin seeds then roast as before.

1 Heat oven to 200C/180C fan/gas 6. Cut each potato into 8 wedges. Transfer to a roasting tin and drizzle over the olive oil.
2 Season well, then sprinkle with a good pinch of chilli powder or paprika (optional) and bake for 40–50 minutes, turning occasionally.

PER SERVING 209 kcals, carbs 31g, fat 8.6g, sat fat 1.2g, salt 0.03g

The perfect mash

SERVES 6 • PREP 10 MINS • COOK 20 MINS
V ❄

1.3kg3lb floury potatoes (King Edwards, Maris Piper
   or Cara), peeled
150ml/¼ pint milk
50g/2oz butter
a little freshly grated nutmeg

1 Cut the potatoes into chunks. Boil in salted water for 15–20 minutes until tender right through. Drain well in a colander, then return the potatoes to the pan, cover with a lid and leave to steam and dry off for 5 minutes.
2 Meanwhile heat the milk in a small pan with the butter. Mash the potatoes until they are smooth, or put them through a potato ricer, then add the hot milk and butter gradually, mashing all the time. Season well with salt, freshly ground pepper and freshly grated nutmeg.

PER SERVING 233 kcals, carbs 37.7g, fat 7.8g, sat fat 4.6g, salt 0.17g

Mustard potato salad

 SERVES 8 • PREP 5 MINS • COOK 10–15 MINS
V

1.5kg/3lb 5oz new potatoes, halved if large
3 tbsp olive oil
1 tbsp wholegrain mustard
juice 1 lemon
3 spring onions, chopped

1 Boil the potatoes in a large pan of salted water until just tender, about 10–15 minutes. Meanwhile, whisk together the oil, mustard and lemon juice in a large bowl. Drain the potatoes and leave to cool for 5 minutes, then tip into the bowl along with the spring onions. Toss everything until the potatoes are well coated. Leave to cool. (Will keep in a covered container in the fridge for up to 2 days.)

PER SERVING 172 kcals, carbs 30g, fat 5g, sat fat 1g, salt 0.13g

> *tip* Pour over the dressing while the potatoes are
> still warm so they absorb the flavour.

Smashed celeriac

SERVES 4 • PREP 10 MINS • COOK 45 MINS

5 tbsp olive oil
4 garlic cloves, very finely sliced
2 red chillies, deseeded and finely chopped
few thyme sprigs
2 small or 1 large celeriac, peeled and cut into
    1cm cubes
splash of white wine (optional)

1 Heat the oil in a shallow pan and sizzle the garlic for 1 minute until fragrant. Add the chilli, thyme and celeriac. Toss everything to coat in the oil, then season with salt.
2 Turn the heat down to low, cover the pan and cook everything very gently for 40 mins or until soft enough to squash. Stir occasionally and add a splash of white wine or water if it starts to catch. When cooked, crush the celeriac lightly with a wooden spoon and serve. The celeriac may now be left to cool in the pan – reheat on the hob with a drizzle more oil.

PER SERVING 171 kcals, carbs 7g, fat 15g, sat fat 2g, salt 0.58g

Coconut rice and peas

SERVES 4 (EASILY DOUBLED) • PREP 5 MINS COOK 12 MINS
V

200g/7oz basmati rice
1 sprig thyme or pinch dried thyme
pinch chilli flakes or powder
4 spring onions, sliced
400g can coconut milk
400g can red kidney beans

1 Rinse the rice in a sieve and tip it into a pan. Add the thyme, chilli and 2 spring onions. Add the coconut milk, 200ml water and a little salt. Bring to the boil, cover, and simmer for 8 minutes.
2 Drain and rinse the beans and gently stir into the rice. Cook, covered, for 3–4 minutes until the rice is tender. Sprinkle with the remaining onions to serve.

PER SERVING 394 kcals, carbs 54g, fat 17g, sat fat 14g, salt 0.9g

Harissa couscous

SERVES 8–10 • PREP 10 MINS, PLUS STANDING TIME NO COOK

400g/14oz couscous
small bunch spring onions, finely sliced
3 tbsp roughly chopped mint
250g cherry tomatoes, halved
1 tsp harissa
400ml/14fl oz vegetable stock
3 tbsp olive oil
juice 1 lemon

1 Tip the couscous into a heatproof bowl. Add the sliced spring onions, roughly chopped mint and halved cherry tomatoes. Stir the harissa into the stock then pour over the couscous mixture. Stir and cover with a plate. Leave for 5 minutes, then pour over the olive oil and the lemon juice and stir through.

PER SERVING 163 kcals, carbs 27.6g, fat 5g, sat fat 0.7g, salt 0.14g

Potatoes dauphinoise

SERVES 6 • **PREP 20 MINS** • **COOK 1–1¼ HOURS**
V ❄

knob of butter, for greasing
1kg/2lb 4oz waxy potatoes, such as Desirée, sliced to
    £1 thickness
150ml/¼ pint full-fat milk
142ml carton double cream
1 garlic clove, peeled and halved
2 sprigs thyme
pinch freshly grated nutmeg
25g/1oz Parmesan, freshly grated

1 Heat oven to 160C/140C fan/gas 4. Line a small baking dish with greaseproof paper, making sure there are no holes for the liquid to seep through, then butter the paper. Pat the potatoes dry.
2 Pour the milk and cream into a pan, then add the garlic and thyme. Bring up to a boil then take off the heat and add the nutmeg. Set aside.
3 Layer the potatoes in the dish, overlapping the slices and seasoning each layer. Pour over the liquid and scatter over the cheese. Bake for 1–1¼ hours until the potatoes are tender and the top is golden. Leave to stand for 5 minutes, then cut into 6 portions and serve.

PER SERVING 289 kcals, carbs 30g, fat 17g, sat fat 9g, salt 0.2g

Leek, potato and bacon bake

SERVES 8 • **PREP 15 MINS** • **COOK 45 MINS**
❄

600ml/1 pint vegetable or chicken stock
1kg/2lb 4oz potatoes, thinly sliced
6 leeks, thinly sliced into rounds
25g/1oz butter
3–4 rashers streaky bacon, snipped
3 tbsp double cream (optional)

1 Heat oven to 200C/180C fan/gas 6. Put the stock in a large pan, bring to the boil, then add the potatoes and the leeks. Bring back to the boil for 5 minutes, then drain well, reserving the stock in a jug.
2 Meanwhile, butter a large baking dish. Layer up the potatoes and leeks higgledy-piggledy, seasoning as you go, then scatter the bacon over the top. Season well, pour over 200ml of the reserved stock, then spoon over the cream (if using) and cover with foil. (Can be made up to 1 day ahead and chilled.) Bake for 40 minutes, uncovering halfway through so that the bacon crisps.

PER SERVING 153 kcals, carbs 24g, fat 5g, sat fat 2g, salt 0.35g

Wild mushroom and potato cake

SERVES 8 • **PREP 35 MINS** • **COOK 1 HOUR 25 MINS**
V

100g/4oz dried porcini mushrooms
2 garlic cloves, finely chopped
140g/5oz butter
1kg/2lb 4oz large potatoes

1 Tip the mushrooms into a bowl and cover with boiling water. Leave to cool, then squeeze out any excess liquid.
2 Soften the garlic in 25g butter for 3–4 minutes then add the mushrooms and some seasoning and cook for 15–20 minutes until tender.
3 Heat oven to 200C/180C fan/gas 6. Peel and slice the potatoes. Butter a 20cm ovenproof frying pan, then overlap a layer of potatoes on the bottom. Layer up the cake with potato, scatterings of mushroom, dots of butter and seasoning, finishing with potatoes on top. Cover with foil and bake for 50–60 minutes, until a knife slides into the cake easily. Remove from the oven, loosen the edges, then leave to relax for at least 5 minutes.

OPPOSITE Leek, potato and bacon bake

PER SERVING 245 kcals, carbs 22g, fat 15g, sat fat 9g, salt 0.31g

Twice-baked potatoes with goat's cheese

SERVES 4 • PREP 10 MINS • COOK 1 HOUR 10 MINS
V

1kg/2lb 4oz floury potatoes
25g/1oz butter, melted
200g/7oz goat's cheese
50ml/2fl oz single cream

1 Heat oven to 190C/170C fan/gas 5. Prick each potato a few times with a fork. Bake for 1 hour. Remove from the oven and, using a tea towel to protect your hands, cut the potatoes in half lengthwise. Use a spoon and scoop out the flesh, leaving behind enough skin and flesh to form a shell.
2 Heat grill to High. Place the potato halves, cut-side up, onto a baking sheet. Brush with melted butter then grill for 3–5 minutes until starting to crisp. Meanwhile, mash the potato flesh with half the cheese, any leftover butter and the cream and seasoning. Spoon the mash back into each potato shell, then top with a slice of goat's cheese. Grill for 5 minutes until golden.

PER SERVING 369 kcals, carbs 44g, fat 17g, sat fat 11g, salt 0.75g

Goat's cheese and bacon rösti

SERVES 3-4 • READY IN 35–45 MINS • PREP 10 MINS COOK 50 MINS

1kg/2lb 4oz medium-sized floury potatoes
olive oil, for frying
1 onion, finely chopped
100g/4oz lardons
8 fresh sage leaves
100g/4oz firm goat's cheese, crumbled

1 Boil the potatoes in their skins for 20–25 minutes until just tender. Cool, peel, then coarsely grate into a bowl. Heat 1 tbsp oil in a medium non-stick frying pan. Fry the onion and lardons for 7–8 minutes until golden. Stir in the sage then stir into the grated potato. Season and mix well.
2 Heat 1 tbsp oil in the pan, add half the potato mix and pat out evenly. Scatter with cheese then top with the rest of the potato. Press down lightly to seal the cheese in. Cook over a medium heat for 8 minutes until browned, then turn out onto a plate. Add 1 tbsp oil to the pan then slide the rösti back into it, on the other side, and cook for 8 minutes more.

PER SERVING 438 kcals, carbs 55g, fat 17g, sat fat 9g, salt 1.72g

Roast sweet potato, squash and garlic mash

SERVES 4 • PREP 15 MINS • COOK 45 MINS
V

1kg/2lb 4oz squash
1kg/2lb 4oz sweet potatoes
2 garlic bulbs, halved
1 red chilli
3 tbsp olive oil

1 Heat oven to 200C/180C fan/gas 6. Peel and cut the squash and sweet potatoes into chunks. Divide between 2 roasting tins with the halved garlic bulbs and whole red chilli. Toss with the olive oil. Roast for 45 minutes. Halve and deseed the chilli, then chop. Squeeze out the garlic and mash everything together. Season and drizzle with oil to serve.

PER SERVING 335 kcals, carbs 62.1g, fat 9.1g, sat fat 1.4g, salt 0.23g

Roasted mixed roots

SERVES 6–8 • PREP 20 MINS • COOK 1 HOUR 20 MINS

1.5kg/3lb 5oz floury potatoes, peeled and chopped
    into large chunks
1 celeriac, chopped into large chunks
3 large carrots, peeled and chopped into very
    large chunks
3 parsnips, peeled and chopped into large chunks
2 tbsp plain flour
about 100g/4oz goose fat (or use vegetable oil)

1 Heat oven to 200C/180C fan/gas 6. Put all the vegetables into a pan of cold salted water, then bring to the boil. Boil for exactly 3 minutes, then drain well. Scatter the flour over the veg in the colander, then toss well to coat.
2 Put the goose fat or oil into a roasting tin and heat in the oven for 10 minutes. Carefully lay the vegetables in the hot fat, then use a fish slice to turn them until completely coated. Roast for 1 hour, turning halfway through cooking, until golden and crisp.

PER SERVING (6) 476 kcals, carbs 63g, fat 23g, sat fat 7g, salt 0.37g

The ultimate roast potatoes

 SERVES 4 EASILY DOUBLED • PREP 15–20 MINS COOK 40–50 MINS

1kg/2lb 4oz Maris Piper potatoes, peeled and cut into
    chunks about 5cm across
100g/4oz olive oil (or goose or duck fat for a more
    luxurious taste)
2 tsp plain flour
flaky sea salt, to serve

1 Heat oven to 200C/180C fan/gas 6 and put in a large roasting tin to warm. Put the potatoes in a large pan of cold water, add salt, then bring to the boil. When at a rolling boil, lower the heat, and simmer for 2 minutes. Meanwhile, carefully put the fat or oil into the hot roasting tin and return to the oven.
2 Drain the potatoes in a colander and give them a shake to fluff up the outsides. Sprinkle with the flour, then shake again. Carefully put the potatoes into the hot fat, then turn them to coat. Spread them in a single layer, making sure they have plenty of room.
3 Roast for 40–50 minutes, turning twice, or until really golden and crisp. Scatter with salt.

PER SERVING (using olive oil) 391 kcals, carbs 43g, fat 23g, sat fat 3g, salt 0.42g

Honey-roast beetroot

SERVES 6 • PREP 5 MINS • COOK 25 MINS
V

750g/1lb 10oz large cooked beetroots, unvinegared
2 tsp fresh thyme
2 tsp balsamic vinegar
2 tbsp olive oil
2 tbsp clear honey

1 Heat oven to 200C/180C fan/gas 6. Cut each beetroot into 4–6 wedges and arrange in a large roasting tin. Mix together the remaining ingredients and pour over the beetroot. Season well, and toss together so all the beetroot is thoroughly coated in the dressing. Roast for 25 minutes until the beetroot is sticky and glazed.

PER SERVING 106 kcals, carbs 16g, fat 4g, sat fat 1g, salt 0.35g

9

Cooking for children

Children are sophisticated consumers these days, influenced by advertising, their peers and, of course, their parents' attitude to food and what they see cooked in the home. There are family-friendly meals throughout this entire book, however sometimes kids will want, or need, that something just for them. Within this chapter you'll find lunchbox and snack ideas that will appeal to kids without being faddy, party food without artificial colours, cute bakes for special occasions, as well as child-friendly recipes that you can cook together.

Growing bodies have very different requirements to those of an adult, and so every parent worries about providing their little one with enough fruit and veg and avoiding processed foods with too much fat, salt or sugar. This challenge, combined with the influence of branded food aimed squarely at kids, can be overwhelming. Teens and older children can be left to reheat and assemble simple meals by themselves, so keeping the fridge and storecupboard stocked with healthy options will help them to stay away from junk food.

PACKED LUNCHES
Lunchtimes can be a particular battleground, so why not get clever and add goodness at every opportunity? Make a smoothie instead of packing fruit juice (there's so much more fibre in whole blended fruit), or put in a pot of pasta with sweet vegetables like sweetcorn and cherry tomatoes instead of a sandwich.

What makes a healthy lunchbox?
- A satisfying, starchy carbohydrate food such as bread or pasta.
- A protein food, such as cooked meat, fish, egg or chicken.
- A calcium-rich item, such as milk, cheese, yogurt or fromage frais.
- At least one portion of fruit and veg to count towards the 5-a-day recommendation.
- A small treat, such as crisps or a cake, if you like – but don't allow kids to fill up on these at the expense of more nourishing foods.
- Trying for variety is great, but kids do like to know what's coming – so always include something familiar.
- No one wants to eat a soggy sandwich or warm yogurt, so include a frozen drink, which can defrost throughout the day and chill at the same time. Natural fruit juices are high in natural sugars, so pop a straw in with the drink to help protect your child's teeth.

OPPOSITE Eyeball pasta (page 232)

FUSSY EATERS

Introducing new foods to children can be tricky. You could involve the kids and get them to help make their own packed lunches (though this is perhaps not the best idea if you're pressed for time). Or, if you're trying something new, why not eat it as a family first. Sometimes the hardest thing for kids is to stand up to their friends' comments about their lunchbox. If they already know they like the food, they are more likely to ignore this and tuck in.

PARTY TIME

The message about healthy food for kids sometimes goes straight out of the window at parties, where they are served lots of brightly coloured treats, full of hidden nasties guaranteed to make them hyper. There are plenty of healthy ideas for party food on page 228–238, but try to follow these tips, too, to ease the stress:

- Don't go overboard with quantities, as children will be far too excited to sit down and eat for any length of time.
- Children eat with their eyes just as much, if not more, than adults, so it is worth making an extra effort with little things. For example: sandwiches cut into fun shapes using biscuit cutters; chopped-up fruit arranged in shapes on the table (in the hope that they will eat some).
- Forget sugary sweets and serve up matchbox-size packets of raisins instead.
- Make the base sponge for the birthday cake well ahead and freeze it.

It's not just birthday parties that kids get excited about. That's why we've included ideas for Halloween, bonfire night and Easter – all of which they'll love to lend a hand with. For Christmassy ideas turn to pages 238 and 413.

COOKING WITH KIDS

Apart from being fantastic fun, enjoying time in the kitchen with children is sociable, creative, builds their confidence and gives them a great sense of pride and achievement – especially when baking something the rest of the family can't wait to eat.

A few golden rules

- Be strict with food hygiene. Get kids to wash their hands before cooking and during preparation, and only allow licking of bowls and fingers at the end of cooking.
- To prevent bowls slipping, put a damp folded tea towel under them.
- Never leave children unsupervised, particularly when working with sharp knives, electric gadgets and the oven.
- Help younger children to lift items in and out of the oven and always use oven gloves.
- If you're cooking with children you don't know well, check whether they have any food allergies.

What can they do?

- Between the ages of three and five, children love to measure with spoons and get mixing and stirring.
- By about six years old children can grate cheese and peel fruit and veg safely.
- At around seven to eight, they are ready to be shown how to use sharp knives. (A small, round-edged serrated knife is a great choice).
- By nine or ten kids should be able to carry out major tasks with supervision.

How cooking helps children learn

As well as familiarising kids with ingredients and new foods, other benefits that come out of a kitchen session include:

- **Maths** Younger children can count ingredients and older kids can add and subtract using scales. Read out the required measurements and count aloud as you go along.
- **Science** Talk children through exactly what is happening in the pan or in the oven, and why.
- **Reading and writing** Read labels and basic recipes and get them to write out their own recipes once they have finished. Children will enjoy keeping a kitchen diary.
- **Geography** Explain where ingredients or dishes originate from and show them on a map.
- **Articulacy** Cooking is full of unfamiliar words that will expand your child's vocabulary.

Keep them interested

Very young children have short attention spans, so choose recipes that they can taste as they go along and that will provide a result reasonably quickly – for instance, cookies or cupcakes, which are ready to be eaten as soon as they are made. While kneading the bread dough is fun, younger children will have forgotten about it by the time it's risen. A short burst of very messy cooking is your best bet.

Fruity smoothie

Fresh berries are packed full of vitamins and antioxidants, so make the most of them in this healthy smoothie.

SERVES 1 EASILY DOUBLED • PREP 2 MINS • NO COOK
❄

1 small, ripe banana
about 140g/5oz blackberries, blueberries, raspberries
 or strawberries (or use a mix)
apple juice or mineral water (optional)
runny honey, to taste

1 Slice the banana into your blender or food processor and add the berries of your choice. Whizz until smooth. With the blades whirring, pour in juice or water to achieve the consistency you like. Sweeten to taste with honey and serve or put into a bottle ready for their lunchbox.

PER SERVING 123 kcals, carbs 29g, fat none, sat fat none, salt 0.02g

try this...

Use melon or a slightly over-ripe mango instead of the banana. Or add a pot of low-fat natural yogurt to make an extra creamy smoothie.

Apricot yogurt granola pots

 Sustaining wholegrains, creamy yogurt and fruit make a balanced start to the day. The jam can be any flavour; just make sure it's the no-added-sugar fruit purée type.

**MAKES 8 SERVINGS • GRANOLA PREP 5 MINS
COOK 14 MINS**
Ⓥ

200g/7oz oats
2 tbsp honey
1 tbsp sunflower oil
150g/5½oz dried fruits, such as raisins or cranberries
TO SERVE (PER SERVING)
100ml/3½fl oz natural yogurt
1 tbsp sugar-free apricot jam

1 Heat oven to 200C/180C fan/gas 6. Mix the oats, honey and oil on a baking sheet, spread out and bake for 7 minutes until turning golden at the edges. Stir, then bake for 7 minutes more. Cool.
2 Mix with the dried fruit. To serve, mix the yogurt with the jam in a container ready for use. Store the granola in an airtight container and portion into a small bag when packing up a lunchbox.

PER SERVING 281 kcals, carbs 49g, fat 6g, sat fat 2g, salt 0.24g

Cheese stackers

Tasty little crackers to enjoy spread with soft cheese or topped with ham and pickle – or whatever takes their fancy.

MAKES 28 • PREP 15 MINS • COOK 15 MINS
V

100g/4oz olive oil spread (or use butter)
50g/2oz Emmental cheese, finely grated
75g/3oz mozzarella cheese, grated
200g/7oz malted grain flour
1 tsp baking powder
pinch English mustard powder (optional)
1 tbsp mixed seeds

1 Heat oven to 190C/170C fan/gas 5. Line two baking sheets with baking parchment. Put the olive oil spread into a bowl and mix in the cheeses. Add the flour, baking powder, mustard powder, if using, a pinch of salt and the mixed seeds, then stir to combine. Squeeze the mixture together with your hands. Roll the mixture into balls the size of cherry tomatoes. Arrange spaced out on the baking sheet, then flatten each one with the palm of your hand. (Or use a cookie cutter to make fun shapes.)
2 Prick each stacker several times with a fork, then bake for 12–15 minutes until golden. Cool, then store in an airtight container for up to 1 week.

PER SERVING 70 kcals, carbs 5g, fat 5g, sat fat 1g, salt 0.10g

Fruit, oat and seed bars

A tasty twist on flapjacks with a luscious layer of fruit inside.

MAKES 16 • PREP 5 MINS • COOK 40 MINS

140g/5oz light muscovado sugar
3 tbsp golden syrup
140g/5oz butter
250g/9oz rolled oats
85g/3oz raisins or sultanas
85g/3oz walnut pieces (or use your favourite nuts, roughly chopped)
50g/2oz sesame or mixed seeds
25g/1oz dried cranberries
50g/2oz ready-to-eat apricots, finely chopped

1 Heat oven to 160C/140C fan/gas 3. Gently heat the sugar, golden syrup and butter in a pan until the sugar and butter have both melted. Stir the oats, raisins, walnuts, seeds and cranberries into the pan until coated in the butter.
2 Spoon half the oaty mix into a traybake tin (23 x 23cm or thereabouts). Scatter the apricots over the top, then top with the remaining oat mix. Pack the mix down well and smooth with the back of a metal spoon. Bake for 35 minutes or until dark golden. Leave to cool completely before cutting into 16 bars with a sharp knife.

PER BAR 244 kcals, carbs 28g, fat 14g, sat fat 6g, salt 0.18g

10 Super sarnies and wraps

These ideas for the kids' sarnies are so tasty that you'll be taking them to work for your lunch, too. We've matched the fillings with their ideal bready partners, but use whatever you have in, if that's easier.

1 **Cheesy apple slaw** Mix your favourite grated hard cheese with grated apple, chopped spring onions, a squeeze of lemon and a little mayonnaise. Delicious with wholemeal bread or rolls.

2 **Salmon smash** Mash up a drained and boned can red salmon with a little tomato ketchup. Spread onto granary bread and sprinkle with lots of mustard and cress.

3 **Tandoori chicken** Roll chapattis around a filling of ready-cooked tandoori chicken pieces, shredded lettuce and chopped tomato. Serve with dollops of bought chunky cucumber raita.

4 **Marmite, cheese and cucumber** Try Marmite, grated Cheddar and sliced cucumber in a crusty baguette.

5 **Cream cheese and roasted red pepper** Fill onion or regular bagels with soft cheese and roasted peppers from a jar.

6 **Creamy smoked mackerel** Skin and flake smoked mackerel fillets, then mix with a little mayonnaise and Greek yogurt. Spread onto thick wholemeal bread and top with crisp lettuce leaves.

7 **Mexican cheese** Layer up spicy tomato salsa, fresh or from a jar, with a sprinkling of grated Cheddar and sliced spicy jalapeño peppers in a tortilla wrap, then roll up.

8 **Deli special** Spread green or red pesto into ciabatta rolls and pile in torn mozzarella and sliced ripe tomatoes.

9 **Egg and ham mayo** Mash hardboiled egg with mayonnaise and snipped ham or crisp bacon. Use to fill sub rolls, and top with a scrunched handful of soft leaves such as lamb's lettuce.

10 **Sticky mustard and sausage** Halve ready-cooked chipolata sausages (you can find them in the cooked meat aisle or use leftover cooked sausages) and roll in a tortilla with sliced red onion, a squeeze honey and a dollop of grainy mustard.

Bean dip with veggie sticks

 If your kids like houmous then give this speedy dip a try. Great served with the pitta crisps below.

SERVES 1 EASILY DOUBLED OR MORE • PREP 10 MINS NO COOK

V

215g can butterbeans, drained
squeeze lemon juice
1 small crushed garlic clove
1 tbsp each chopped parsley and mint
2 tsp olive oil
FOR DIPPING
1 celery stick
1 carrot
½ red pepper

1 Whizz all the dip ingredients together in a food processor with 1 tbsp water. Serve with the celery, carrot and red pepper cut into slices to dip.

PER SERVING 253 kcals, carbs 34g, fat 10g, sat fat 1g, salt 0.3g

---

tip Wrap veg sticks in a damp piece of kitchen paper to stop them from drying out and losing their appetising crunch.

Lime and chilli pitta crisps

 For younger children, simply season the bread with a sprinkling of grated Parmesan, and bake.

SERVES 2 EASILY DOUBLED • PREP 5 MINS COOK 10 MINS

V

2 pitta breads
1 tsp olive oil
zest 1 lime
½ tsp chilli flakes

1 Heat oven to 180C/160C fan/gas 4. Tear the pitta breads into crisp-size pieces and brush with the oil. Sprinkle with the lime zest and chilli flakes. Bake for 10 minutes until crisp. Sprinkle with salt, if you like.

PER SERVING 216 kcals, carbs 34g, fat 3g, sat fat none, salt 0.41g

OPPOSITE Clockwise from top left Bean dip with veggie sticks; Smoothie jellies with icecream (page 230); Cheese stackers (page 224); Crisp chicken bites (page 229); Really easy lemonade (page 231); Pizza rolls (page 229)

Mini chicken bagel burgers

A better-for-you burger, packed with hidden but healthy stuff. Serve in mini burger buns if the mini bagels are hard to find.

MAKES 12 BURGERS EASILY DOUBLED • PREP 15 MINS COOK 10 MINS
❄ UNCOOKED

½ x 400g can chickpeas, drained
1 small onion, finely chopped
1 garlic clove, crushed
500g/1lb 2oz chicken or turkey mince
1 small sweet potato (about 100g/4oz), grated
olive oil, for brushing
TO SERVE
12 mini bagels
2 tbsp low-fat mayonnaise
¼ iceberg lettuce, shredded
2 tomatoes, sliced
¼ cucumber, sliced

1 Heat grill to Medium. Whizz the chickpeas in a food processor or mash until well broken up. Put into a bowl with the onion, garlic, mince and sweet potato. Mix well and season. (Can be frozen for up to 1 month.)
2 Line a baking sheet with foil. Divide the mixture into 12 and shape into mini burgers. Put onto the baking sheet, brush with oil and grill for 10 minutes, turning once. (Can be chilled and reheated in the microwave on High for 2 minutes.)
3 Split the bagels and toast the cut sides under the grill, if you like. Spread the bases with mayonnaise, top with a chicken burger, some shredded lettuce, tomatoes, cucumber and the bagel tops.

PER SERVING 144 kcals, carbs 18g, fat 3g, sat fat 1g, salt 0.40g

Sausage roll twists with tomato dip

Perfect for any party – just make sure the mums and dads don't eat them all!

MAKES 24 EASILY DOUBLED • PREP 10 MINS COOK 20 MINS
❄ RAW, IF INGREDIENTS NOT PREVIOUSLY FROZEN

400g pack pork chipolatas (12 sausages)
½ x 500g block all-butter puff pastry, defrosted if frozen
FOR THE TOMATO DIP
6 tbsp reduced-sugar tomato ketchup
2 tsp malt vinegar
6 cherry tomatoes, finely chopped

1 Heat oven to 220C/200C fan/gas 7. Twist the chipolatas in half, then snip to create 24 small sausages. Roll out the pastry to £1 coin thickness (about 20 x 30cm) and cut into strips about 1cm wide, cutting from the shorter edge. Wind one pastry strip around each half-sausage, then place on a baking sheet, pastry ends down.
2 Bake for 20 minutes until the sausages and pastry are golden. Meanwhile, mix together the ketchup, vinegar and cherry tomatoes. Serve in little bowls alongside the sausage twists.

PER TWIST AND DIP 95 kcals, carbs 7g, fat 7g, sat fat 2g, salt 0.54g

Pizza rolls

 low fat

Quicker and easier to make than pizza from scratch, yet just as tasty.

**MAKES 6 EASILY DOUBLED • PREP 15 MINS
COOK 15 MINS**

6 crusty bread rolls
2 tbsp tomato purée
6 slices ham
3 tomatoes, sliced
125g/4½oz mozzarella, sliced
2 tsp dried oregano
6 black olives (optional)

1 Heat oven to 180C/160C fan/gas 4. Cut the tops off the rolls and scoop out the insides. Spread the rolls with tomato purée, then fill with ham, tomatoes and finally the mozzarella. Scatter with dried oregano and top each with an olive, if you like.
2 Place the rolls on a baking sheet and bake for 15 minutes until the rolls are crusty brown and the cheese is bubbling. Leave to rest for a minute, then serve hot with a side salad.

PER SERVING 275 kcals, carbs 30g, fat 11g, sat fat 6g, salt 1.99g

> *tip* Turn the roll tops and scooped-out insides into breadcrumbs by whizzing in a food processor. Or make crunchy croutons: cut the bread into chunks, toss with a little oil, then bake for 10 minutes.

Crisp chicken bites

 good for you

Healthy and easy to make at home, these little nuggets will go down brilliantly.

**SERVES 12 CHILDREN, EASILY HALVED
PREP 10 MINS • COOK 10-15 MINS**
❄

4 boneless skinless chicken breasts
6 tbsp red pesto (see below)
3 large handfuls dried or fresh breadcrumbs (about 300g/11oz)
olive oil

1 Heat oven to 220C/200C fan/gas 7. Cut the chicken breasts into small chunks, each about the size of a marble (you should get roughly 15 pieces per breast). Put the pesto in a bowl and mix together with the chicken until coated all over. Tip the breadcrumbs into a large freezer bag. Then add the chicken and shake well to coat.
2 Pour a little oil onto a shallow baking sheet, just enough to cover it. Put the sheet in the oven and let it heat up for 5 minutes. Tip the chicken onto the sheet and return to the oven for 10–15 minutes until crisp and cooked through.
3 To freeze ahead, lay a piece of greaseproof paper on a baking sheet, then add the raw chicken pieces to the sheet, making sure none of them are touching. When frozen solid, take off the baking sheet and store in a freezer bag.

> **Using pesto adds flavour and means there's no need to dip the chicken in flour and egg before coating with crumbs.**

PER SERVING 195 kcals, carbs 20g, fat 7g, sat fat 2g, salt 0.65g

Smoothie jellies with ice cream

Making your own jelly using a good-quality smoothie means a lot more flavour and a lot less sugar.

SERVES 12 EASILY DOUBLED (MAKES 12 SMALL OR 24 MINI POTS) • PREP 5 MINS, PLUS SETTING • COOK 2 MINS
❄

6 sheets leaf gelatine
1-litre bottle orange, mango and passion fruit smoothie
500ml tub good-quality vanilla ice cream (you might not need it all), to serve

1 Put the leaf gelatine into a bowl and cover with cold water. Leave for a few minutes until soft and floppy. Meanwhile, gently heat the smoothie in a saucepan without boiling. Take off the heat. Lift the gelatine out of the water, squeeze out the excess water, then add it to the smoothie pan. Stir well until smooth, then pour into 12 moulds, pots or glasses, or use 24 shot-glass-sized pots. Chill for at least 1 hour to set.
2 For perfect mini scoops of ice cream, dip a tablespoon measuring spoon into a cup of hot water, then shake off the excess. Scoop the ice cream, dipping the spoon in the hot water each time. Serve each smoothie jelly topped with ice cream.

PER SERVING (with 1 tbsp ice cream) 92 kcals, carbs 15g, fat 2g, sat fat 1g, salt 0.05g

Iced fairy cakes

These sweet little cakes make a fun activity for 8–14 year-olds, and younger kids can help out.

MAKES 12 • PREP 40 MINS • COOK 20 MINS, PLUS COOLING
❄ **BASES ONLY**

100g/4oz golden caster sugar
100g/4oz very soft butter
100g/4oz self-raising flour
2 eggs, beaten
1 tsp vanilla extract
FOR THE ICING
200g/7oz very soft butter
200g/7oz icing sugar
food colouring, sprinkles, marshmallows, etc (optional)

1 Heat oven to 180C/160C fan/gas 4. Line a 12-hole bun tin with paper cases. Put the sugar and butter in a bowl and beat together until creamy. Sift in the flour then add the eggs and vanilla and mix well.
2 Divide the mix between the cases then bake for 20 minutes or until golden and risen. Cool completely.
3 For the icing, mix the butter and icing sugar until creamy. Add colouring, if you like. Pipe icing onto each cake and decorate with marshmallows or sprinkles, or whatever you like.

PER CAKE 331 kcals, carbs 39g, fat 22g, sat fat 13g, salt 0.5g

try this...

For a summer party treat, make cookie and ice cream sandwiches.

Allow good-quality vanilla or chocolate ice cream to soften, and sandwich between choc-chip cookies along with blueberries and raspberries. Pop back into the freezer for later or eat straight away.

Really easy lemonade

A refreshingly simple way to make your own.

SERVES 4 ● PREP 10 MINS

3 unwaxed lemons, roughly chopped
140g/5oz caster sugar
1 litre/1¾ pints cold water (use fizzy water if you like)

1 Tip the lemons, sugar and half the water into a food processor and blend until the lemon is finely chopped.
2 Pour the mixture into a sieve over a bowl, then press through as much juice as you can. Top up with the remaining water and serve with plain ice or ice cubes with slices of lemon and lime frozen into them.

PER SERVING 140 kcals, carbs 37g, fat none, sat fat none, salt 0.1g

Chocolate krispie chick

Have fun with the children making this egg using chocolate egg moulds. This recipe is based on an old favourite, chocolate krispie cakes.

PREP 30 MINS, PLUS COOLING AND SETTING COOK 10 MINS

FOR THE EGG
50g/2oz Rice Krispies
175g/6oz milk chocolate, melted
TO DECORATE
2 x 50g bags chocolate mini eggs
25g/1oz white chocolate, broken into pieces, melted and cooled a little
a little melted milk chocolate
2 white chocolate buttons
50g/2oz golden marzipan

> To melt chocolate, break it into chunks and put it into a large heatproof bowl. Put the bowl over a pan of just-simmering water, making sure that the bowl does not touch the water. Leave for 5 minutes or so, stirring now and again, until the chocolate is smooth and silky. Alternatively, put the bowl in the microwave and cook on High for 1½ minutes, stirring halfway. Be very careful whichever way you melt chocolate; if it gets too hot it will become grainy and unusable.

1 Stir together the Rice Krispies and melted chocolate, mixing well to coat. Spoon half the mix into one of the plastic chocolate egg moulds, then use the back of your spoon to press it into a thick, even layer. Be sure to cover the whole of the inside, leaving a thick edge. Repeat with the other mould and leave in a cool place to set. Put the moulds in the fridge for 5 minutes.
2 Carefully unmould the eggs. Fill one half with a few mini eggs, then fix the halves together with melted white chocolate. Patch any holes with a few extra Rice Krispies and melted chocolate. Leave in a cool place to set.
3 Meanwhile, make the eyes by painting blobs of milk chocolate onto the white buttons. Fix onto the egg with more chocolate. Spoon the white chocolate into a small piping bag, then pipe a beak and wings onto the egg. Leave to set.
4 For the feet, roll the marzipan on a sheet of greaseproof paper to about ½cm thick. Cut out feet, making them large enough for the egg to sit on. Once completely set, place the chick on its feet, pressing down so that it stays upright.

PER ¼ EGG SERVING 241 kcals, carbs 33g, fat 12g, sat fat 5g, salt 0.2g

Witches' brew (pea and bacon chowder)

You'll love this soup all through the year, but it really comes into its own at Halloween – for obvious reasons!

**MAKES 6 KIDS' SIZE SERVINGS • PREP 20 MINS
COOK 12 MINS**
❄

1 tbsp olive oil
1 onion, finely chopped
1 garlic clove, crushed
650g/1lb 7oz frozen petit pois
700ml/1¼ pints vegetable stock
6 rashers streaky bacon
1 tbsp butter (optional)

1 Heat the oil in a saucepan. Add the onion and gently cook over a medium heat for 5–6 minutes until softened but not coloured. Add the garlic and cook for a further minute. Stir in three-quarters of the petit pois, then pour in the stock. Bring to the boil and simmer for 10–12 minutes.
2 Meanwhile, heat the grill to High and grill the bacon until crisp. Allow the soup to cool for a few minutes, then carefully transfer to a food processor and whizz until smooth. You might need to do this in two batches, depending on the size of your processor.
3 Return the soup to the pan and add the remaining petit pois. Bring to the boil and simmer for 2 minutes or until the whole peas are tender. Season to taste, then stir in the butter, if using. Break the bacon into pieces and scatter over bowls or mugs of soup. The soup can be made up to a day ahead or frozen; just grill the bacon on the day.

PER SERVING 131 kcals, carbs 12g, fat 5g, sat fat 1g, salt 1.11g

Eyeball pasta

Get everyone in the Halloween mood with this gory but tasty pasta. Children will love it. (See recipe photo on page 220.)

SERVES 4–6 CHILDREN • PREP 15 MINS • COOK 10 MINS
V

100g/4oz cherry tomatoes
150g pack mini mozzarella balls, drained
handful basil
400g/14oz green tagliatelle
350g jar tomato sauce
4 tbsp fresh pesto

1 Halve the cherry tomatoes and use a small, sharp knife or a teaspoon to remove the seeds. Cut the mozzarella balls in half. Place one half inside each tomato, trimming the edges if necessary to fit it in. Cut small circles from the basil leaves and place one at the centre of each mozzarella ball to make a pupil.
2 Cook the pasta according to the packet instructions. Meanwhile, heat through the tomato sauce. When the tagliatelle is cooked, drain and stir through the pesto and any remaining basil, chopped finely. Divide between 4–6 serving bowls. Spoon over some tomato sauce, then arrange the stuffed tomato eyeballs on top.

PER SERVING (4) 568 kcals, carbs 85g, fat 17g, sat fat 7g, salt 1.69g

OPPOSITE Clockwise from top left Chocolate krispie chick (page 231); Campfire cupcakes (page 237); Witches' brew (page 232); Blueberry butterfly cakes (page 243); Tomato soup with cheese and Marmite twists (page 240); Chocolate birthday cake (page 238)

Hooting Halloween owls

Delicious and simple chocolate cupcakes with a whole lot of character!

**MAKES 12 ● PREP 15 MINS, PLUS COOLING AND
DECORATING ● COOK 20–25 MINS**
❄ (CAKE BASES ONLY)

280g/10oz butter, softened
280g/10oz golden caster sugar
200g/7oz self-raising flour, minus 1 rounded tbsp
1 rounded tbsp cocoa powder
6 medium eggs
FOR ICING AND DECORATION
200g/7oz butter, softened
280g/10oz icing sugar, sifted
1 tube orange ready-to-use icing
1 small bag Maltesers
1 tube mini chocolate buttons
1 tub jelly diamonds (just the orange ones)

1 Heat oven to 190C/170C fan/gas 5. Line a 12-cup muffin tin with brown muffin cases. Beat the first 5 ingredients to a smooth batter and spoon between the cases, almost filling them to the top. You may have a little left over. Bake for 20–25 minutes until risen and spongy. Cool on a rack.
2 Beat the butter and icing sugar until smooth. Slice off the very tops of the cakes and cut each piece in half. Spread a generous layer of icing over each cake.
3 To make an owl, squirt a pea-sized blob of orange icing onto two Maltesers and use to fix a chocolate button on each. Sit the eyes, two pieces of cake top (curved edge up) and a jelly diamond 'beak' on the icing.

PER CAKE 615 kcals, carbs 68g, fat 38g, sat fat 23g, salt 1.06g

try this...

For a simple party activity, make the cupcakes and icing as above. Buy lots of differently shaped and coloured sweets, then let the kids make up their own monster faces as decoration. Give a prize for the most ghoulish or inventive.

Freaky fingers

*Gnarly shortbread fingers that look creepy but taste divine. If you don't want to use nuts
for the fingernails, you can use pieces of glacé cherry instead.*

PREP 15 MINS, PLUS CHILLING ● COOK 12–15 MINS

100g/4oz caster sugar
100g/4oz butter
1 egg yolk
200g/7oz plain flour
½ tsp vanilla extract
20 blanched almonds
red food colouring, paste is best (optional)

1 Line a baking sheet with parchment and heat oven to 180C/160C fan/gas 4. Place the first five ingredients and a pinch of salt in a food processor and whizz to form a dough.
2 Tear off golfball-size pieces of dough and use your hands to roll into finger shapes. You should get about 20. Put onto the baking sheet, well spaced apart.
3 Use a knife to make a few cuts, close together, for the knuckles. Place an almond at the end of each finger and trim away excess pastry around the edge to neaten. Chill for 30 minutes, then bake for 10–12 minutes just until firm. Leave to cool a little, then paint the almond with food colouring, if you like. (Can be made up to 3 days ahead and stored in an airtight container.)

PER SERVING 102 kcals, carbs 13g, fat 5g, sat fat 3g, salt 0.08g

Bonfire bangers and beans

Proper baked beans are easy to make and great for feeding a crowd. Make them earlier in the day, then simply warm up in the oven when you're ready to eat.

SERVES 8 • PREP 10 MINS • COOK 1 HOUR

3 tbsp vegetable oil
1 onion, finely chopped
2 celery sticks, finely chopped
4 rashers streaky bacon, chopped
1 tbsp tomato purée
2 x 400g cans chopped tomatoes
2 tbsp dark brown sugar
2 tsp Dijon mustard
2 thyme sprigs
2 tsp Worcestershire sauce
2 x 400g cans cannellini beans, rinsed and drained
2 red peppers, deseeded and chopped
2 x 450g packs herby sausages
handful parsley leaves, chopped, to serve (optional)

1 Heat 2 tbsp oil in a large flameproof casserole. Add the onion, celery and bacon, then cook for 5–10 minutes until softened. Turn up the heat and add the tomato purée. Cook for 2 minutes, then add the chopped tomatoes, sugar, mustard, thyme, Worcestershire sauce and 200ml water, then bring to the boil. Cook, uncovered, over a low heat for 15 minutes. Add the beans and peppers, then simmer for 15 minutes more, topping up with a little boiling water if needed.
2 Meanwhile, heat oven to 190C/170C fan/gas 5. Toss the sausages with the remaining 1 tbsp oil and spread out on a baking sheet. Cook for 30 minutes until browned all over, turning occasionally. Nestle the sausages among the beans, then cover and place the pan in the oven. Cook for 30 minutes more. Remove from the oven, sprinkle over the parsley, if using, and serve. (Can be made up to 2 days in advance and reheated in a low oven or on the hob.) Great with baked potatoes.

PER SERVING 454 kcals, carbs 28g, fat 28g, sat fat 8g, salt 2.66g

Chilli con carne soup

 This is a soupy version of a classic chilli. It's mellow enough for children to enjoy, but feel free to pep up adults' portions with cayenne or chilli powder.

SERVES 6 • PREP 10 MINS • COOK 1 HOUR 10 MINS

1 small onion, finely chopped
2 garlic cloves, finely chopped
1 tbsp vegetable oil
500g/1lb 2oz lean minced beef
410g can pinto or red kidney beans, drained
2 x 400g cans chopped plum tomatoes
700ml/1¼ pints hot chicken stock
large pinch crushed dried chillies
2 squares dark chocolate (at least 70% cocoa solids)
fresh coriander or parsley leaves and some grated
    Gruyère, to serve

1 Gently fry the onion and garlic in the oil for a couple of minutes until beginning to soften, then add the mince. Raise the heat and cook for 5 minutes, stirring from time to time, until the meat is no longer pink.
2 Stir in the beans, tomatoes, stock, chillies, chocolate and plenty of salt and pepper. Bring to the boil, cover and simmer very gently for 1 hour, or longer if you have the time. (You can make it up to a day ahead to this point, then cool and chill.)
3 Ladle into mugs or large cups and scatter with herbs, cheese and black pepper. You'll need spoons to eat it.

PER SERVING 252 kcals, carbs 14g, fat 12g, sat fat 5g, salt 1.29g

Homemade toffee apples

Bonfire night wouldn't be the same without a crisp toffee apple – so much better than shop-bought.

MAKES 8 • PREP 10 MINS • COOK 10 MINS

8 Granny Smith apples
400g/14oz golden caster sugar
1 tsp vinegar
4 tbsp golden syrup

If you don't have a thermometer, you can test the toffee by pouring a little into a bowl of cold water. When ready, it should harden instantly and, when removed, be brittle and easy to break. If you can still squish the cooled toffee, continue to boil it and test again. Take great care if children are around.

1 Place the apples in a large bowl, then cover with boiling water. This will remove their waxy coating and help the caramel to stick. Dry thoroughly and twist off any stalks. Push a wooden skewer or lolly stick into the stalk end of each apple.

2 Lay out a sheet of baking parchment and place the apples on this, close to your stovetop. Tip the sugar and 100ml water into a pan and heat very gently until the sugar dissolves. Stir in the vinegar and syrup. Set a sugar thermometer in the pan and boil to 140C or 'hard crack' stage (or, see left).

3 Working quickly and carefully, dip and twist each apple in the hot toffee until covered, let any excess drip away, then place on the baking parchment. You may have to heat the toffee a little if the temperature drops and it starts to feel thick and viscous. Leave the toffee to cool and harden. (Can be made up to 2 days in advance, stored in a dry place.)

PER SERVING 278 kcals, carbs 73g, fat none, sat fat none, salt 0.06g

Chocolate fondue and toasted marshmallows

There's no getting away from the fact that toasted marshmallows can be a bit messy – but they're all the better for it!

SERVES 8 • PREP 5 MINS • COOK 5 MINS

400g/14oz dark chocolate
85g/3oz unsalted butter
284ml carton double cream
300ml/½ pint milk
bag marshmallows, for dipping

1 Put the chocolate, butter, cream and milk into a saucepan, then heat gently, stirring occasionally, until the chocolate is melted and the sauce is smooth. Thread marshmallows onto skewers, then carefully toast on the fire, or leave cold. Dip into the fondue and eat straight away. (Fondue can be made up to a day ahead and reheated in the microwave for 1 minute on Medium, stirring halfway through.)

PER SERVING 609 kcals, carbs 55g, fat 42g, sat fat 25g, salt 0.09g

Campfire cupcakes

These look really impressive, but are simple to make – and will take you back to toasting marshmallows around an open fire.

MAKES 12 • PREP 10 MINS • COOK 20 MINS
▣ BASES ONLY

140g/5oz light muscovado sugar
100g/4oz self-raising flour
50g/2oz cocoa powder
1 tsp baking powder
3 eggs
125ml/4fl oz vegetable oil
3 tbsp milk
50g/2oz milk chocolate chips
30g pack mini marshmallows

1 Heat oven to 180C/160C fan/gas 4. Place cupcake cases into a 12-hole bun tin. Tip the sugar, flour, cocoa and baking powder into a large bowl. Whisk together the eggs, vegetable oil and milk, then stir together with the dry ingredients until well combined. Add the milk chocolate chips. Divide the mixture between the cases, then bake for 20 minutes until risen and cooked through. (You can now leave to cool and store for up to 2 days in an airtight container.)
2 Just before serving (either warm from the oven or cold), arrange marshmallows over the tops of the cakes. Heat grill to Medium and pop the cakes under it for 30 seconds, watching all the time, just until the marshmallows are lightly browned. Remove and eat straight away.

PER SERVING 233 kcals, carbs 25g, fat 14g, sat fat 3g, salt 0.27g

Chocolate crunch bars

If you like rocky road, you'll really enjoy this endlessly versatile recipe. Use honeycomb or any other sweets instead of Turkish Delight, and try digestive or ginger biscuits, if you like.

MAKES 12 • PREP 20 MINS, PLUS CHILLING
COOK 5 MINS

100g/4oz butter, roughly chopped
300g/11oz dark chocolate, broken into squares
3 tbsp golden syrup
140g/5oz rich tea biscuits, roughly crushed
12 pink marshmallows, quartered (use scissors)
2 x 55g bars Turkish Delight, halved and sliced

1 Line a 17cm square tin with foil. Gently melt the butter, chocolate and syrup in a pan over a low heat, stirring frequently until smooth, then cool for about 10 minutes.
2 Stir the biscuits and sweets into the pan until well mixed, then pour into the tin and spread the mixture to roughly level it. Chill until hard, then cut into fingers.

PER BAR 294 kcals, carbs 39g, fat 15g, sat fat 9g, salt 0.29g

Double ginger gingerbread men

Even the smallest hands can help to make these friendly little fellows.

**MAKES 12 BIG GINGERBREAD MEN • PREP 45 MINS
COOK 15 MINS**

140g/5oz unsalted butter
100g/4oz dark muscovado sugar
3 tbsp golden syrup
350g/12oz plain flour
1 tsp bicarbonate of soda
2 tsp ground ginger
1 tsp ground cinnamon
pinch cayenne pepper (optional)
2 balls stem ginger from a jar, finely chopped
TO DECORATE
50g/2oz icing sugar
a few glacé cherries (we used undyed)
2 balls stem ginger from a jar

1 Heat oven to 200C/180C fan/gas 6. Line 2 baking sheets with baking parchment. Melt the butter, sugar and syrup in a pan. Mix the flour, bicarb, spices and a pinch of salt in a bowl. Stir in the butter mix and ginger to make a stiff-ish dough.
2 Wait until cool enough to handle, then roll out the dough to about 5mm thick. Stamp out gingerbread men, re-rolling and pressing the trimmings back together and rolling again. Lift onto baking sheets. Bake for 12 minutes until golden. Cool for 10 minutes on the sheets, then lift onto cooling racks.
3 To decorate, mix icing sugar with a few drops of water until thick and smooth. Halve then slice the cherries thinly to make smiles, and cut the ginger into small squares. Spoon the icing into a food bag, snip off the tiniest bit from one corner, then squeeze eyes and buttons, and a tiny smile onto 1 man at a time. Stick on a cherry smile and ginger buttons. Repeat; leave to set. (Will keep up to 1 week in an airtight tin.)

PER SERVING 264 kcals, carbs 43g, fat 10g, sat fat 6g, salt 0.33g

Chocolate birthday cake

Wish you could find a nastie-free cake for the kids' party? This is the recipe for you.
Add colour with candles and flags rather than the usual coloured sweeties and icing.

**SERVES 12 • PREP 20 MINS • COOK 20–25 MINS
❄ UN-ICED**

140g/5oz butter, plus extra for the tin
175g/6oz golden caster sugar
2 large eggs
225g/8oz self-raising wholemeal flour
50g/2oz cocoa powder
½ tsp bicarbonate of soda
250ml/9fl oz natural yogurt
TO DECORATE
300g/11oz golden icing sugar, sieved
2 tbsp cocoa powder, sieved
1 tbsp butter, melted
3–4 tbsp boiling water
50g/2oz each milk, plain and white chocolate, broken
    into squares and melted separately

1 Heat oven to 180C/160C fan/gas 4. Butter and line the base of a 18 x 28cm cake tin. Beat the butter and sugar together until creamy, then add the eggs gradually until fluffy.
2 Sieve the flour, cocoa and bicarbonate of soda into the bowl, then tip in any bran that's collected in the sieve. Stir in the yogurt to a smooth mixture then spoon into the tin. Bake for 20–25 minutes until risen and springy. Cool for 5 minutes, then turn onto a wire rack.
3 For the icing, sieve the icing sugar and cocoa into a bowl, then pour in the butter and 2 tbsp hot water. Stir together until smooth. Spread over the cold cake, using a palette knife dipped in hot water.
4 Spoon the melted chocolates into freezer bags. Snip the ends off then pipe shapes on top of the cake. Once set, cut into squares and push in the candles.

PER SLICE 432 kcals, carbs 65g, fat 18g, sat fat 10g, salt 0.41g

OPPOSITE Double ginger gingerbread men

Tomato soup with cheese and Marmite twists

Kids all love tomato soup and, if you have more homegrown tomatoes in the garden than you know what to do with, it's a great way of using them up.

SERVES 4 • PREP 25 MINS • COOK 25 MINS
❄ **SOUP ONLY, WITHOUT CREAM**

FOR THE CHEESE AND MARMITE TWISTS
50g/2oz Red Leicester or Cheddar
1 ready-to-use sheet puff pastry
2 tsp Marmite (if you don't like Marmite, use a little mustard instead)

FOR THE SOUP
1 large onion
2 tbsp olive oil
8 large tomatoes
400ml/14fl oz vegetable stock
4 tbsp tomato ketchup
½ tsp dried oregano
300ml pot double cream

1 Heat oven to 200C/180C fan/gas 6. Finely grate the cheese. Unravel the pastry, spread evenly with the Marmite, then sprinkle the cheese on top. Now fold the pastry in half to make a sandwich and press down well.

2 Cut the pastry into 12 equal strips. Carefully twist each strip and place on a lightly greased baking sheet. Bake for 15 minutes until golden. Leave for 5 minutes to firm up a little, then lift onto a cooling rack with a fish slice.

3 Peel and chop the onion. Fry in the oil for about 5 minutes, stirring with a wooden spoon until soft but not coloured.

4 Chop the tomatoes, then add to the pan with the stock, ketchup and oregano. Season. Bring to the boil, then turn down the heat. Cover the pan, then simmer for 15 minutes until the veg are soft.

5 Using a hand blender, blend the soup in the pan until smooth, or purée the soup in batches in a food processor, then tip back into the pan. Take care not to over-fill your food processor as the hot soup could splash you.

6 Tip the cream into the soup, then gently heat, stirring with the wooden spoon until it just starts to bubble. Don't boil vigorously as the cream could curdle. Ladle into bowls and serve with the cheese and Marmite straws.

PER SERVING 912 kcals, carbs 54g, fat 73g, sat fat 35g, salt 2.06g

Blueberry and pecan oaties

These are easy to make and the unbaked roll is really useful to keep in the freezer, so delicious homemade biscuits are always close at hand. Leave out the nuts if you need to.

MAKES 12 • PREP 20 MINS, PLUS CHILLING COOK 15 MINS

175g/6oz plain flour, plus extra for dusting
½ tsp baking powder
85g/3oz porridge oats
175g/8oz golden caster sugar
1 tsp ground cinnamon
140g/5oz butter, chopped
70g pack dried blueberries
50g/2oz pecan nuts, roughly broken
1 egg, beaten

1 Tip the flour, baking powder, oats, sugar and cinnamon into a bowl, then mix well with your hands. Add the butter, then rub it into the mixture until it has disappeared.

2 Stir in the blueberries and pecans, add the egg, then mix well with a cutlery knife or wooden spoon until it all comes together in a big ball. Lightly flour the work surface, then roll the dough into a fat sausage about 6cm across. Wrap in cling film, then chill in the fridge until solid.

3 To bake, heat oven to 180C/160C fan/gas 4. Unwrap the cookie log, thickly slice into discs, then arrange on baking sheets. Bake for 15 minutes (or a few minutes more if from frozen) until golden, leave on the sheets to harden, then cool completely on a wire rack before tucking in.

PER BISCUIT 274 kcals, carbs 36g, fat 14g, sat fat 7g, salt 0.27g

Squished tomato pasta sauce

A superhealthy fresh tomato sauce that doesn't need any cooking; perfect for very young children.

SERVES 2 • PREP 10 MINS • NO COOK

V

12 cherry tomatoes
2 ordinary tomatoes, halved
4 basil leaves
8 black or green olives, stoned (optional)
olive oil, for drizzling
200g/7oz pasta, cooked and kept warm
Cheddar or Parmesan, grated

1 Put the cherry tomatoes into a large bowl, reach down into the bowl and squeeze each one hard until it bursts (mind out, they'll squirt!). Pull the tomatoes into pieces.
2 Squeeze the halved big tomatoes on a lemon squeezer to make as much juice as you can. Pour this into the bowl. (You can use the squeezed skins in a stew or soup.)
3 Rip up the basil leaves with your fingers and put them into the bowl with the tomatoes. Then, if you are using them, snip or pull the olives in half and throw them in, too.
4 Add a dribble of olive oil, divide the cooked pasta among two bowls, spoon your sauce on top and sprinkle with the cheese.

PER SERVING 472 kcals, carbs 80g, fat 12g, sat fat 4g, salt 0.34g

> *tip* If your child is able, they can do all their own chopping and slicing; very little ones will enjoy the squishing. If herbs are a step too far, stick to the tomatoes and add vegetables your child enjoys, such as red pepper or cooked peas. If you'd like some more protein in the dish, try adding chopped cooked chicken or bacon.

Sweet and sticky chicken noodles

Turn teatime into playtime and make these yummy noodles with kids aged 5–9.

SERVES 2 • PREP 15 MINS • COOK 5 MINS

1 skinless cooked chicken breast
3 spring onions
½ red pepper, stalk and seeds removed
1 tbsp soy sauce
1 tbsp sesame oil and/or 1 tbsp sesame seeds
2 tbsp runny honey
150g/5½oz egg noodles
handful coriander (optional)

1 Pull the chicken into strips, then cut it into chunks small enough to pick up on a fork. Put in a large bowl. Use your scissors to snip the hairy root ends off the spring onions and throw away. Snip the rest of the spring onion into pieces. Add to the chicken.
2 Use scissors or a small knife to cut the pepper into strips and then pieces. Like the chicken, you want the pieces to be small enough to pick up. Measure the soy sauce, sesame oil (and/or seeds) and honey into the bowl and mix together. Cook the noodles according to the pack instructions.
3 Tip the hot noodles into the bowl and toss everything together with a large spoon or pair of tongs. Divide the noodles between 2 bowls and add some fresh coriander to each one, if you like it.

PER SERVING 500 kcals, carbs 69g, fat 14g, sat fat 2g, salt 1.81g

Chicken and sweetcorn pies

A creamy pie, perfect for getting kids aged between 8 and 14 busy in the kitchen.

SERVES 6 • PREP 25 MINS • COOK 35 MINS

500g pack puff pastry, defrosted if frozen, plus flour
    for dusting
oil, for brushing
2 skinless cooked chicken breasts
3 tbsp canned or frozen and defrosted sweetcorn
3 tbsp frozen peas, defrosted
6 tbsp double cream
1 tsp Dijon mustard
1 egg, beaten

1 Heat oven to 180C/160C fan/gas 4. Roll out the pastry on a floured surface and trim to make a rectangle about 24 x 36cm. Cut the pastry in half, lengthways, then cut each half into 3 equal squares, about 12cm along each side, using a small knife or scissors. Brush oil inside the wells of a 12-hole muffin tin.

2 Push each square into the oiled tin, making sure it is pushed right into the edges. Use scissors or a small knife to cut the chicken into strips, then cut into chunks. Put the chicken in a bowl. Add the sweetcorn, peas, cream and mustard. Mix together.

3 Divide the mixture between the pies. Fold the tops of the pies over roughly and press together. Don't worry if they don't cover all the filling. Brush the pastry with the beaten egg and bake in the oven for 35 minutes or until they brown and the filling bubbles.

PER PIE 488 kcals, carbs 33g, fat 32g, sat fat 13g, salt 0.83g

Courgette muffins

These scrummy courgette muffins are perfect for cooks aged between 8 and 14.

**MAKES 12 • PREP 20 MINS, PLUS COOLING
COOK 20–25 MINS**
🔲 **BASES ONLY**

oil, for greasing
50g/2oz courgettes, cut into chunks
1 apple, peeled and quartered
1 orange, halved
1 egg
75g/2½oz butter, melted
300g/11oz self-raising flour
½ tsp baking powder
½ tsp cinnamon
100g/4oz golden caster sugar
handful sultanas
1 tub soft cheese mixed with 3 tbsp icing sugar,
    to make icing

1 Brush oil inside the wells of a 12-hole muffin tin. Heat oven to 190C/170C fan/gas 5. Grate the courgettes and put them in a large bowl. Grate the apple and add to the bowl. Squeeze the orange and add the juice to the bowl.

2 Break the egg into a bowl; if any bits of shell get in, scoop them out with a spoon. Stir the butter and egg into the courgette and apple mix. Sieve the flour, baking powder and cinnamon into the bowl. Add the sugar and sultanas.

3 Mix with a spoon until everything is combined, but don't worry if it is lumpy. Spoon the mixture into the tin. Ask a grown up to put it in the oven and cook for 20–25 minutes. Cool the muffins in the tin and use the cutlery knife to spread some icing on each.

PER SERVING 272 kcals, carbs 35g, fat 14 g, sat fat 9g, salt 0.5 g

Blueberry butterfly cakes

Berry-baking fun for all the family, or great for your teacher as a last-day-of-term treat.

**MAKES 12 • PREP 30 MINS, PLUS COOLING
COOK 15 MINS**
❄ **BASES ONLY**

FOR THE CAKES
140g/5oz self-raising flour
½ tsp baking powder
85g/3oz butter, at room temperature
85g/3oz golden caster sugar
50g/2oz lemon curd
2 large eggs
100g/4oz blueberries
FOR THE TOPPING
175g/6oz reduced-fat mascarpone
50g/2oz lemon curd
100g/4oz blueberries
icing sugar, for dusting

1 Heat oven to 180C/160C fan/gas 4. Line a 12-hole bun tin with paper cases. Next, take a large mixing bowl and add the flour, baking powder, butter, sugar and lemon curd. Break the eggs into a small bowl, then add them to the other ingredients.
2 Whisk everything together really well until creamy with an electric hand whisk. Then carefully stir in the blueberries with a metal spoon or spatula. Use an ice-cream scoop or spoon to drop the mixture evenly into the paper cases. Bake the cakes for 15 minutes until golden. Cool for a few minutes, then lift the cakes onto a cooling rack.
3 Clean and dry the mixing bowl. Put the mascarpone and lemon curd into the bowl and beat together with a wooden spoon until well mixed. Carefully cut a circle out of the top of each cake. Lift off the circle and fill the space with the lemon filling followed by some blueberries. Halve the circle of the cake that you have cut out and place on top to create butterfly wings. Put some icing sugar in a tea strainer and dust over the cakes.

PER CAKE 206 kcals, carbs 23g, fat 12g, sat fat 7g, salt 0.37g

Kids' crumble

Kids love to help make dessert for the Sunday roast – and you'll enjoy the spoils.

SERVES 6 • TAKES 1 HOUR 10 MINS

8 eating apples
1 tsp cinnamon
3 tbsp sugar, any kind
½ orange
1 punnet raspberries or blackberries
75g/2½oz cold butter
50g/2oz plain flour
50g/2oz rolled oats

1 Heat oven to 200C/180C fan/gas 6. Peel the apples with a potato peeler, quarter them, cut out the cores, then chop up. Tip the apple into a bowl with the cinnamon and 1 tbsp sugar. Squeeze the juice from the halved orange and add to the bowl too.
2 Add the berries to the bowl and mix everything together. Tip the fruit mixture into a baking dish and pat it down. Chop three quarters of the butter into small pieces. Put it in a bowl with the flour. Use your fingers to pinch and rub the butter into the flour.
3 Stir the oats and the rest of the sugar into the flour mixture, then sprinkle it on top of the apple and berries in the baking dish. Dot the rest of the butter over the crumble. Ask a grown-up to put it in the oven for 40 minutes or until the apple is cooked. Eat with ice cream or custard.

PER SERVING 260 kcals, carbs 39g, fat 11g, sat fat 7g, salt 0.17g

10

Breads and doughs

Many people bake bread simply for the joy of the process – the nurturing and hand-crafting of something uniquely delicious. Some make it as an alternative to shop-bought bread, for reasons of quality and cost, and some breads are total storecupboard saviours; quick enough to make when the last slice is gone and the shops are shut. At its most basic level, bread is a mix of flour, yeast, liquid, salt and a little fat. Once you understand how these simple ingredients work together, you'll discover that making your own bread is simple and enjoyable.

BREAD FLOURS

Most bread recipes will call for bread, or 'strong', flour made from wheat:
Strong white flour contains a higher proportion of gluten than plain flour; this gives elasticity to dough, which in turn makes a lighter loaf.
Strong wholemeal bread flour retains the germ from the outside of the wheat grain. It makes a dense loaf if used on its own, so bakers often lighten it by mixing it with white bread flour.
Granary flour includes whole grains and has a malty taste.
Rye flour is made from the rye grain, which gives a heavier texture and nutty flavour. It is often mixed with wheat flour to lighten it.
Gluten-free flour is usually a blend of rice, potato and other non-wheat flours, with an added agent called xanthan gum, which improves the structure of gluten-free breads and makes them less crumbly.

YEAST

Yeast is a living organism that needs food (from sugars in flour or added sugar) and warm conditions to grow. As yeast grows, it produces carbon dioxide, which creates the bubbles within the dough. As the bread goes into a hot oven these bubbles expand, and the bread rises. A bread that has yeast added is known as 'leavened'. Some breads are leavened with wild yeasts from the natural environment (see sourdoughs, page 246), but these days most of us cook with fast-action, dried or fresh yeast.

Low temperatures and lots of sugar or salt will suppress the growth of yeast, and slow the rising of bread. Extreme heat will kill yeast, so always be careful to make sure that any liquid added to a dough is just tepid, not hot, and that you leave the dough to rise somewhere warm, rather than hot.

Types of yeast

Fast-action yeast (sometimes called easy blend) usually comes in 7g sachets, or it can be bought in a tub, in which case, use 1 teaspoon instead of a 7g sachet. The yeast looks like very fine, elongated grains. This yeast can be added straight to the flour and other dry ingredients and does not

OPPOSITE *Pizza magherita (page 256)*

need to be activated in any way beforehand. Fast-action yeast generally has added ascorbic acid (Vitamin C) – an additive than helps the yeast to work even more quickly. Because of this, 7g fast-action yeast is equal to 15g ordinary dried yeast.

Dried yeast comes shaped into small balls which need to be dissolved in a little warm water before they can be added to the bread with the rest of the liquid ingredients. Follow the pack instructions for the best result.

Fresh yeast is available from the bakery counter in supermarkets where bread is baked on the premises; dried yeast is more readily available. Fresh yeast should be putty-coloured, smooth and softly crumbly. It can be frozen; wrap 30g portions tightly in cling film and freeze for up to a month. Fresh yeast needs to be 'sponged' before it's used; that is, stirred together with a splash of warm water and 1 teaspoon sugar then left to sit for 5 minutes or until frothy. Using 30g fresh yeast will have the same effect as 15g dried or 7g fast-action.

SALT

Most bread recipes will call for 1 teaspoon salt per 250g flour or thereabouts. Use sea salt for flavour, but make sure that you grind it finely first – large flakes won't distribute properly through the dough.

LIQUID

Most recipes call for liquid to be tepid to help speed the yeast's activity. Too hot and it will kill the yeast. Cold liquid gives good results as it slows down the yeast's activity, giving the bread a better flavour. Each batch of flour will absorb liquid differently, rather like risotto rice, so you may find that you sometimes need to add more or less. Some breads are made with milk, which gives a softer crust. Beer is used too – and gives the bread a malty flavour.

FATS

Fats are added to dough to make a softer bread, and in some cases, such as for brioche, to give it a cakey texture. Both melted butter and oil can be added with the rest of the liquid ingredients; hard butter can be rubbed into the dry ingredients; and soft butter can be worked into a dough during the kneading.

SOURDOUGH BREADS

These are chewy and crusty, with a characteristically sour (but delicious) flavour. They are made with a starter (sometimes called a 'biga'), which is a sloppy, fermented dough. The most authentic, but the most unpredictable, way to make a starter is to let a paste of flour and water slowly ferment over several days as wild yeasts find their way into the mixture. The quickest way is to add yeast and let it ferment. This starter dough is then 'sponged' with more flour and liquid to make a bread dough.

ENRICHED BREADS

These are generally softer and more cake-like in texture and have dried fruit, chocolate or other chunks worked into the dough or wrapped around them – festive panettone, stollen and hot cross buns, for example. It's worth being gentle with the dough when it comes to shaping it; knock it back too firmly and it will become springy and difficult to shape. Let the action of shaping the bread and adding flavourings do the knocking back for you.

DON'T HAVE TIME TO MAKE BREAD?

You might be surprised. Modern bread-makers give great results and can either be used just to mix and rise your dough, before you bake it in the oven, or to cook a loaf from start to finish. Another way clever cooks fit bread-making into their day is to start off a dough the day before, then leave it to rise slowly overnight in the fridge. The dough can then be shaped, proved and baked. And the slower you rise your bread, the better the flavour.

Soda breads are quick to make because they rely on bicarbonate of soda or flours containing raising agents to rise the bread instead of yeast. The resulting bread is softer and won't be chewy like yeasted bread, but has a rustic charm of its own. These doughs don't require kneading – in fact, the less you work a soda bread dough, the better the result. **Cornbread** made with cornmeal or fine polenta is an ideal gluten-free choice. **Flatbreads**, such as tortillas, pitta, chappatis, naan and lavash are the most ancient and simplest kind of bread there is, and often won't include yeast. These breads are rolled then cooked in a frying pan, or a griddle, or slapped onto the inside of a hot tandoor oven. Once cooked, they are used to pick up food or to wrap around an unending array of fillings.

Step-by-step: Making a basic loaf

The basic stages of baking yeasted bread are mixing, kneading, rising, knocking back, shaping, proving and then baking. If you're a beginner, make your first few loaves freeform on a baking sheet rather than by using a loaf tin – it's far easier to get right.

1 Mix the dry ingredients together. This will include the yeast if you are using fast-action yeast. Pour in the wet ingredients. Mix to a soft dough using a wooden spoon or a cutlery knife. Work quickly so that you don't end up with some very wet and some very dry patches. A wetter dough will give you a better bread, so if the dough feels solid or tight, add more liquid and work it in.

2 Knead the dough (photo 1). Kneading continues the mixing process, distributing the yeast through the dough and working the gluten into the flour. Start with the ball of dough and lightly make an indent in the middle of it with the heel of your palm. Bring the top of the ball into that dent, now turn the dough through 90 degrees and make another indentation.

3 Repeat the process, turning each time, for at least 10 minutes. Slowly the dough will start to soften and take on a satin-smooth appearance (photo 2). This can also be done using a mixer fitted with the dough hook attachment.

4 Leave the dough to rise. Rising allows the dough to rest and expand until it has doubled in size. For the best result, shape the dough into a ball, then put it into large bowl that has been greased with oil. Turn the ball in the oil until it is covered with a thin film, then cover the bowl with cling film or a tea towel and set aside until doubled in size (photo 3). The oil will prevent a dry crust forming.

5 Shaping and knocking back. Before shaping bread the bubbles need to knocked out of the dough. Knocking back is easy: just hammer the dough flat with your knuckles, then knead until the dough feels tight. The dough is now ready to be shaped into a loaf or rolls in a tin or on a baking sheet.

6 Proving. This is the second rise for the dough. Cover the dough loosely with the oiled cling film or a tea towel. Once it has doubled in size, feels pillowy to the touch and fingertip marks bounce back slowly, it is ready for the oven.

7 Decorating. Slashing the top of a loaf controls the way that the dough expands in the oven and looks great, too. Glazes add a sheen, so brush them on before baking. Egg wash or milk gives a shiny golden crust, olive oil adds extra shine and a subtle olive oil flavour. For a sweeter finish, brush with honey after baking.

8 Baking – is it ready? Whatever the cooking temperature and timing, the universal way to check if bread is ready is to tap the bottom. If the bread is a golden brown colour and sounds hollow like a drum when you tap the bottom, it is ready. If not, give it another 10 minutes in the oven and test again.

For a soft crust, cover the bread with a tea towel. For a crusty crust, leave to cool uncovered and on a rack.

Easy white bread

This loaf is so easy it doesn't even need a special tin. The recipe also works well in a breadmaker.
Just add all the ingredients to the machine and follow the manufacturer's instructions.

MAKES 1 LOAF • PREP 20 MINS, PLUS 2 HOURS PROVING COOK 25–30 MINS

500g/1lb 2oz strong white flour, plus extra for dusting
2 tsp salt
7g sachet fast-action yeast
3 tbsp olive oil, plus extra for greasing

 To make your dough into rolls, divide it into 12 equal balls, then roll each one on the worktop, pinching the top of the ball with your fingers to stretch the underside of the dough into a smooth surface. Turn the roll over then put it on a baking sheet and press down lightly.

1 Mix the flour, salt and yeast in a large bowl. Make a well in the centre, then add the oil and 300ml/½ pint warm water and mix well. If the dough seems a little stiff, add 1–2 tbsp water, mix well then tip onto a lightly floured work surface and knead until it is satin-smooth (see page 247 for full kneading instructions). Place it in a lightly oiled bowl, covered with cling film or a tea towel. Leave to rise for 1 hour until doubled in size, or place in the fridge overnight.
2 Line a baking sheet with baking parchment. Knock back the dough, then gently mould it into a ball. Place it on the baking parchment to prove for a further hour until it has doubled in size.
3 Heat oven to 220C/200C fan/gas 7. Dust the loaf with flour then cut a cross about 6cm long into the top of the loaf with a sharp knife. Bake for 25–30 minutes until golden brown and the loaf sounds hollow when tapped underneath. Cool on a wire rack.

PER SERVING 204 kcals, carbs 38g, fat 4g, sat fat 1g, salt 1g

Granary bread

 A nutty and sustaining loaf that's good for slicing. If you like the lightness of white bread but the goodness of granary, replace half the flour with strong white.

MAKES 1 LOAF • PREP 15 MINS, PLUS RISING COOK 35 MINS

500g/1lb 2 oz granary bread flour
7g sachet fast-action yeast
1 tsp salt
2 tbsp olive oil
1 tbsp clear honey

1 Tip the flour, yeast and salt into a large bowl and mix together with your hands. Stir 300ml warm water with the oil and honey, then stir into the dry ingredients to make a soft dough.
2 Turn the dough out onto a lightly floured surface and knead for 5 minutes until the dough no longer feels sticky, sprinkling with a little more flour if you need it.
3 Oil a 900g loaf tin and put the dough in the tin, pressing it in evenly. Put in a large plastic food bag and leave to rise for 1 hour, until the dough has risen to fill the tin and it no longer springs back when you press it with your finger.
4 Heat oven to 200C/180C fan/gas 6. Make several slashes across the top of the loaf with a sharp knife, then bake for 30–35 minutes until the loaf is risen and golden. Tip it out onto a cooling rack and tap the base of the bread to check it is cooked. It should sound hollow. Leave to cool.

PER SLICE 231 kcals, carbs 42g, fat 4g, sat fat 1g, salt 0.63g

Homemade sourdough

This recipe has all the authentic tang of a proper sourdough, without the hassle.

MAKES 1 VERY LARGE LOAF • PREP 20 MINS, PLUS OVERNIGHT RESTING, PLUS RISING • COOK 45 MINS
❄

FOR THE STARTER
225g/8oz strong white bread flour
7g sachet fast-action yeast
oil, for greasing

FOR THE BREAD
500g/1lb 2oz strong white bread flour, plus extra for
    kneading and dusting
2 x 7g sachet fast-action yeast
2 tsp salt
75ml/2½fl oz plain yogurt

1 First, make the starter. Tip the flour and yeast into a bowl. Pour over 200ml warm water, use a wooden spoon to mix together, then cover the bowl with a piece of oiled cling film. Leave in the fridge overnight, after which the dough should look fairly frothy and bubbly, with a sweet yeasty smell.

2 Now make the bread. Tip the flour into a bowl along with the yeast and salt. Pour 150ml warm water and the yogurt into the starter mixture, stir until well combined, then pour this into the bowl with the flour. Use a spoon to bring the mixture together into a ball – this will take a couple of minutes as the flour needs to absorb the water. Add another 50ml water if the dough feels tight.

3 Tip out the dough onto a surface lightly dusted with flour. Push down and away, using the heel of your hand to stretch out the dough, then fold the outside edge back over itself to make a ball again. Twist the dough round and start again. Keep kneading like this for about 10 minutes, depending on how vigorous you are. When it's ready the dough should feel slightly springy when touched and have a smooth surface when shaped into a ball. Alternatively, you can knead the dough for about 5 minutes in a table-top mixer or food processor with a dough attachment.

4 Lightly oil a large bowl and place the dough inside. Oil a piece of cling film, lay this loosely over the top, then leave in a warm, draught-free place until nearly trebled in size – this can take from 45 minutes to about 1½ hours. Remove the cling film and punch down the airy dough with your hand. Tip out onto your floured surface, knead a couple of times until smooth and the air has been knocked out, then lightly oil a large baking sheet. Shape the dough into a round ball and place on the sheet. Re-cover with the oiled piece of cling film and leave until doubled in size, about 1 hour.

5 Heat oven to 230C/210C fan/gas 8. Place a roasting tin on the bottom shelf of the oven and carefully half-fill it with boiling water from the kettle. Leave in the oven for 10 minutes so it gets steamy. If your dough has spread, gently tuck the ends under to make a neat ball, then use a sharp knife to make a few slashes across the bread before lightly dusting with flour. Place the baking sheet on the top shelf of the oven and bake for 20 minutes.

6 Turn the heat down to 220C/200C fan/gas 7, bake for 25 minutes more. Tap the bottom of the loaf – it should sound hollow. Return to the oven for another 10 minutes if not. Leave to cool on a wire rack.

PER SLICE 265 kcals, carbs 56g, fat 2g, sat fat none, salt 1.02g

The best breads are all made with wetter doughs – but of course this makes for trickier kneading. To knead a sticky dough, make sure that your surface is clean and, as you knead, scrape up any dough that has stuck to the worktop. Flour your hands and worktop before you start and add more flour as you go if you need to, but try to avoid adding too much as it will affect your end result. Persevere – a wet dough will eventually become springy and hold together in a ball, as the gluten in the flour starts to form long strands.

Dark mixed seed bread

If you like your bread with plenty of character, try this dark treacly loaf.
Excellent with smoked salmon and other Scandinavian flavours.

**MAKES 1 LARGE LOAF • PREP 25 MINS, PLUS RISING
COOK 30 MINS**

350g/12oz wholemeal flour
100g/4oz rye flour
50g/2oz quinoa flour or extra rye flour
2 tsp salt
7g sachet fast-action yeast
125g pack sunflower seeds
25g/1oz caraway seeds
50g/2oz poppy seeds
75ml/2½fl oz black treacle
50g/2oz sesame seeds

1 Mix the flours, salt, yeast and sunflower, caraway and poppy seeds in a large bowl. Add the black treacle and 300ml warm water, then mix well. If the dough seems a little stiff, add 1 tbsp or more extra water. Mix well, then put on a lightly floured work surface and gently knead the dough for 7 minutes. Put it back into a lightly oiled bowl for about 2 hours until doubled in size.
2 Line a baking sheet with baking parchment. Tip the dough onto a lightly floured work surface and knock back, then gently mould the dough into a ball. Roll the dough in the sesame seeds and place on the baking sheet to prove for a further hour until doubled in size.
3 Heat oven to 220C/200C fan/gas 7. Cut the top into criss-cross slashes with a sharp knife and bake for 30 minutes until golden brown and the loaf sounds hollow when tapped underneath. Cool on a wire rack.

PER SERVING 315 kcals, carbs 42g, fat 13g, sat fat 1g, salt 1g

Easy Irish soda bread

A life-saver loaf when the shops are shut, and completely delicious too. The less you handle
the dough the better. The bread is at its very best when eaten while still faintly warm.

MAKES 1 LOAF • PREP 15 MINS • COOK 30–35 MINS

250g/9oz plain white flour (not strong flour), plus extra
    for dusting
250g/9oz plain wholemeal flour
100g/4oz rolled oats
1 tsp bicarbonate of soda
1 tsp salt
25g/1oz butter, cut into pieces
500ml/18fl oz buttermilk (or see below)

Depending on where you shop, buttermilk can be tricky to find. As a substitute, mix 500ml whole or semi-skimmed milk with a good squeeze of lemon juice. Wait until the milk looks thickened and a bit lumpy, then use as before. Natural yogurt is also a good option.

1 Heat oven to 200C/180C fan/gas 6 and dust a baking sheet with flour. Mix the dry ingredients in a large bowl, then rub in the butter until the mixture resembles fine crumbs. Pour in the buttermilk and mix it in quickly with a table knife, then bring the dough together very lightly with your fingertips (handle it very, very gently). Now shape it into a flat, round loaf measuring 20cm/8in in diameter.
2 Put the loaf on the baking sheet and score a deep cross in the top. (Traditionally, this lets the fairies out, but it also helps the bread to cook through.) Bake for 30–35 minutes until the bottom of the loaf sounds hollow when tapped. If it isn't ready after this time, turn it upside down on the baking sheet and bake for a few minutes more.
3 Transfer to a wire rack, cover with a clean tea towel (this keeps the crust nice and soft) and leave to cool. To serve, break into quarters, then break or cut each quarter in half to make 8 wedges or slices – or simply slice across. Eat very fresh, or toast it the next day.

PER SLICE 296 kcals, carbs 56g, fat 5g, sat fat 3g, salt 1.21g

Gluten-free sun-dried tomato bread

*Another quick loaf, this time made with gluten-free flour. The sun-dried tomatoes can
easily be swapped for olives, if you prefer.*

MAKES 1 LOAF • PREP 15 MINS • COOK 50–60 MINS

V ❄

200g/7oz gluten-free white flour
1 tsp salt
3 tsp gluten-free baking powder
284ml pot buttermilk
3 eggs
1 tsp tomato purée
2 tbsp olive oil
50g/2oz sun-dried tomatoes in oil (about 6–8),
    coarsely chopped
25g/1oz Parmesan, finely grated

1 Heat oven to 180C/160C fan/gas 4 and grease a 900g loaf
tin. Mix the flour, salt and baking powder in a large bowl. In
a separate bowl, whisk together the buttermilk, eggs, tomato
purée and oil.
2 Fold the wet ingredients into the dry, then add the
sun-dried tomatoes and half the Parmesan. Pour the mixture
into the tin and sprinkle the remaining Parmesan on top.
Bake for 50–60 minutes until a skewer inserted in the middle
comes out clean. Turn out onto a wire rack to cool.

PER SERVING 74 kcals, carbs 10g, fat 3g, sat fat 1g, salt 0.7g

Cheesy garlic bread

*A really useful bread that goes with so many family dishes, such as chilli con carne, soups,
salads and barbecues.*

**CUTS INTO 12 SQUARES • PREP 20 MINS, PLUS RISING
COOK 30 MINS**

V ❄

500g/1lb 2oz strong white bread flour, plus extra
    for dusting
7g sachet fast-action yeast
1 tsp salt
2 tbsp olive oil, plus extra for greasing
1 tbsp clear honey
2 garlic cloves, crushed
25g/1oz soft butter
100g/4oz mature Cheddar, grated
handful thyme leaves

1 Measure the flour, yeast and salt into a large bowl.
Mix 300ml warm water with the oil and honey in a jug,
then pour it into the dry mixture, stirring all the time to
make a soft dough.
2 Turn the dough out onto a lightly floured surface, then
knead for 5 minutes until the dough no longer feels sticky,
sprinkling with a little more flour as you need it. Now stretch
it to fit the Swiss roll tin.
3 Mix the garlic with the butter, then dot over the dough.
Sprinkle over the cheese and snip over the thyme. Cover the
bread with lightly oiled cling film, then leave in a warm place
to rise for 40 minutes.
4 Heat oven to 200C/180C fan/gas 6. Remove the cling film,
then bake the bread for 30 minutes until golden and risen.
Leave to cool for 10 minutes, then cut into 12 pieces and
serve.

PER SQUARE 215 kcals, carbs 33g, fat 7g, sat fat 3g, salt 0.61g

Bagels for brunch

 These bagels are just as they should be – chewy and dense.

**MAKES 10 ● PREP 30 MINS, PLUS RISING
COOK 30 MINS**
V ❄

7g sachet fast-action yeast
4 tbsp golden caster sugar
2 tsp salt
450g/1lb strong white flour
oil, for greasing
poppy, fennel and/or sesame seeds to sprinkle on top
    (optional)

1 Tip the yeast and 1 tbsp sugar into a large bowl, and pour over 100ml warm water. Leave for 10 minutes until the mixture becomes frothy.

2 Pour 200ml warm water into the bowl, then stir in the salt and half the flour. Keep adding the remaining flour (you may not have to use it all) and mixing with your hands until you have a soft, but not sticky, dough. Knead for 10 minutes until the dough feels smooth and elastic. Shape into a ball and put in a clean, lightly oiled bowl. Cover loosely with cling film and leave in a warm place until doubled in size, about 1 hour.

3 Heat oven to 220C/200C fan/gas 7. On a lightly floured surface, divide the dough into 10 pieces, each about 85g. Shape each piece into a flattish ball, then take a wooden spoon and use the handle to make a hole in the middle of each ball. Slip the spoon into the hole, then twirl the bagel around the spoon to make a hole about 3cm wide. Cover loosely with cling film while you shape the remaining dough.

4 Meanwhile, bring a large pan of water to the boil and tip in the remaining sugar. Slip the bagels into the boiling water – no more than four at a time. Cook for 1–2 minutes, turning them over in the water until the bagels have puffed up slightly and a skin has formed. Remove with a slotted spoon and drain away any excess water. Sprinkle over your choice of topping and place on a baking sheet lined with parchment. Bake in the oven for 25 minutes until browned and crisp – the bases should sound hollow when tapped. Leave to cool on a wire rack, then serve with your favourite filling.

PER BAGEL 178 kcals, carbs 40g, fat 1g, sat fat 1g, salt 1g

OPPOSITE Clockwise from top left Bagels for brunch; Gluten-free
sundried tomato bread (page 251); Cinnamon pecan sticky buns
(page 259); Easy Irish soda bread (page 250); Onion and bacon
fougasse (page 255); Easy Easter brioche (page 257).

Naan bread

Authentic Indian flatbreads, or naan, are baked in a special brick oven, but you can shallow-fry the dough instead, which gives a pale golden finish. Here, they are cooked in a dry pan for a lighter, but equally tasty result.

**MAKES 8 BREADS • PREP 20–30 MINS, PLUS PROVING
COOK 15 MINS (IN BATCHES)**
V ❄

500g/1lb 2oz strong white flour
2 tsp salt
7g sachet fast-action yeast
3 tbsp olive oil

1 Mix the flour, salt, yeast and oil in a large bowl and 300ml/½ pint of water to make a soft, but not sloppy, dough. Knead well. Put into a lightly oiled bowl to rise for 1 hour until doubled in size.

2 Divide the dough into 8 pieces and use a rolling pin to flatten each one into a circle, 15cm in diameter and about 1cm thick. Then leave the pieces on a lightly floured baking sheet to prove for 5 minutes. Heat a large frying pan to a medium heat and dry-fry each piece until browned on both sides, about 5 minutes in total. Set aside to cool slightly before serving.

PER SERVING 255 kcals, carbs 48g, fat 5g, sat fat 1g, salt 1.3g

Artichoke focaccia

 Oozing with olive oil and scented with rosemary, this focaccia is an irresistible summer treat, great for a big gathering.

**SERVES 10 • PREP 40 MINS, PLUS RISING TIME
COOK 15 MINS**
V ❄

FOR THE DOUGH
500g/1lb 2oz strong white flour
7g sachet fast-action yeast
1 heaped tsp salt
oil, for greasing
FOR THE FILLING
large bunch rosemary
285g jar chargrilled artichoke antipasti in extra
    virgin olive oil
50g/2oz freshly grated Parmesan, plus extra
    to finish

1 Tip the flour into a large bowl and make a well in the centre. Add the yeast and salt, then gradually pour in 350ml warm water, stirring as you go. Bring the dough together with a spoon, then with your hands. It should be soft, but not too sticky or wet. Add extra flour or water as needed. Tip onto a floured work surface and knead for about 10 minutes, or until it's smooth, soft and springs back when pushed with a finger. Leave to rise in an oiled bowl covered with cling film in a warm place for 1 hour or until the dough has doubled in size.

2 Strip leaves from half the rosemary and finely chop. Break the rest into small pieces. Drain the artichokes, reserving the oil, and chop into chunks.

3 When risen, tip the dough onto an oiled work surface and roll out into a 35 x 45cm rectangle. Slip an oiled baking sheet under half of the dough. Top the half with artichokes, all the Parmesan and rosemary. Grind over black pepper and drizzle with a little of the reserved oil. Fold over the other dough half, pressing the edges together and under to seal. Leave to prove in a warm place, covered with the oiled cling film, for 30 minutes. Heat oven to 240C/220C fan/gas 9.

4 Drizzle with a little more of the oil and make dimples in the top with your fingers. Poke the rosemary sprigs into the dimples and grate over a little more cheese. Bake for 15 minutes, until golden and risen. Cool on a rack for 30 minutes, cut into squares and serve.

PER SERVING 269 kcals, carbs 39g, fat 10g sat fat 2g, salt 1.38g

Onion and bacon fougasse

A traditional French bread is really beautiful to look at and, with our recipe, easy to achieve.

**MAKES 3 LOAVES • PREP 45 MINS, PLUS RISING TIME
COOK 15 MINS**
Ⓥ ❄

400g/14oz strong white flour
7g sachet fast-action yeast
1 tsp salt
4 tbsp olive oil, plus extra for brushing
1 onion, finely chopped and fried
2 rashers back bacon, finely chopped and fried
sea salt, for sprinkling (optional)

1 Mix half the flour with all the yeast and 150ml warm water in a bowl, then beat together into a thick batter for 3 minutes. Leave the mix to rise and then fall; this should happen in 3–4 hours. Then add the rest of the flour, salt, 150ml warm water and the oil, and mix well. Turn out onto a lightly floured work surface and knead to a smooth dough. Put back in the bowl to rise for a further 1 hour until doubled in size.
2 Line 3 baking sheets with baking parchment. Knock back the dough, then knead to incorporate the onion and bacon. Divide the dough into 3 pieces, about 225g each. Use a rolling pin to flatten out each piece to about 2.5cm high, then shape roughly into a circle. Put on the baking sheets. Using a sharp knife, cut three diagonal slashes right through the dough down each side and two down the middle to form the shape of a leaf. Brush with olive oil, sprinkle with sea salt, if you like, and leave for a further hour to prove until doubled in size.
3 Heat oven to 230C/210C fan/gas 8 and bake the loaves for 15 minutes until golden brown, then cool on a wire rack.

PER SERVING 179 kcals, carbs 26g, fat 7g, sat fat 1g, salt 0.6g

Cracked black pepper and figgy bread

You'll be hard pressed to find a better bread to serve with cheese, or simply to pass around before a meal.

**MAKES 1 LARGE LOAF • PREP 15 MINS, PLUS RISING
COOK 40–45 MINS**
Ⓥ ❄

650g/1lb 7oz strong white flour, plus extra for dusting
2 tsp cracked black pepper
2 tsp salt
7g sachet fast action yeast
2 tbsp olive oil
425–450ml/¾ pint-16fl oz warm water
350g/12oz dried, ready-to-eat figs, roughly chopped

1 In a large bowl, stir together the flour, pepper, salt and yeast. Stir in the oil and enough warm water to form a soft dough. Turn out onto a lightly floured surface and knead for 10 minutes until smooth and elastic.
2 Put the dough in a lightly oiled large bowl. Cover with oiled cling film and leave in a warm place for about 1 hour or until doubled in size.
3 Heat oven to 200C/180C fan/gas 6. When the dough has risen, knead it again to incorporate the figs, by pushing the dough and lightly kneading them in. Don't overwork the dough; it can look quite rough.
4 Shape the dough into a rough oval and put on a lightly floured baking sheet. Using scissors, slash the top of the loaf and sprinkle over a little flour. Leave it to prove, uncovered, until slightly swollen, about 10–15 minutes (if the kitchen is warm). Bake for 40–45 minutes until it sounds hollow when you tap it underneath, then cool on a wire rack.

PER SLICE 266 kcals, carbs 56g, fat 3g, sat fat 1g, salt 0.88g

Pizza margherita

Our thin-crust cheese and tomato pizza is loads of fun to make from scratch, and tastes so much better than shop-bought versions. (See recipe photo on page 244.)

**SERVES 4 (MAKES 2 PIZZAS) ● PREP 25 MINS
COOK 10 MINS
V ❄ UNCOOKED**

FOR THE BASE
300g/11oz strong bread flour
7g sachet fast action yeast
1 tsp salt
1 tbsp olive oil, plus extra for drizzling

FOR THE TOMATO SAUCE
100ml/3½fl oz passata
handful fresh basil or 1 tsp dried
1 garlic clove, crushed

FOR THE TOPPING
125g ball mozzarella, sliced
handful grated or shaved Parmesan
handful cherry tomatoes, halved

TO FINISH
handful basil leaves (optional)

try this...

> **Calzone** – try a folded pizza. Pile sauce and toppings onto one half of the dough circle, brush the edge with a little water, then fold and pinch to make a pasty shape. Bake until golden as before.
>
> **Stromboli** – a rolled pizza. Roll dough into a rectangle, top as before, then roll up into a sausage shape. Brush with a little oil. Bake for 20 minutes or until cooked through. Serve cut into rounds.

1 Put the flour into a large bowl, then stir in the yeast and salt. Make a well, pour in 200ml warm water and the oil and bring together with a wooden spoon until you have a soft, fairly wet dough. Turn onto a lightly floured surface and knead for 5 minutes until smooth (photo 1). Cover with a tea towel and set aside. (You can leave the dough to rise if you like, but it's not essential for a thin crust.)

2 Mix the passata, basil and garlic together, then season to taste (photo 2). Leave to stand at room temperature while you get on with shaping the base.

3 If you've let the dough rise, give it a quick knead, then split into two balls. On a floured surface, roll out the dough into two large rounds, about 25cm across, using a rolling pin (photo 3). The dough needs to be very thin as it will rise in the oven. Lift the rounds onto two floured baking sheets.

4 Heat oven to 240C/220C fan/gas 8. Put another baking sheet or an upturned baking sheet in the oven on the top shelf. Smooth sauce over the bases with the back of a spoon. Scatter with the cheese and tomatoes, drizzle with oil and season (photo 4). Put one pizza, still on its baking sheet, on top of the preheated sheet. Bake for 8–10 minutes until crisp. Serve with a little more oil and basil leaves, if using. Repeat step for remaining pizza.

PER SERVING 431 kcals, carbs 59g, fat 15g, sat fat 7g, salt 1.87g

1   2   3   4

Quick chilli cornbread

This spicy dense bread is an ideal accompaniment for soup or a chowder – and it's ready in less than an hour.

SERVES 8 • PREP 15 MINS • COOK 35–40 MINS
V ❄

butter, for greasing
280g/10oz fine semolina or polenta
85g/3oz plain flour
2 tsp bicarbonate of soda
1 large egg
150ml/¼ pint milk
425ml/¾ pint buttermilk or natural yogurt
2 large red chillies, deseeded and finely chopped

1 Heat oven to 190C/170C fan/gas 5. Generously butter a 25 x 16cm baking tin or shallow roasting tin. Combine the semolina or polenta, flour and bicarbonate of soda in a large bowl and season generously with salt and pepper. In a jug, combine the egg, milk, buttermilk or yogurt and chillies.
2 Pour the contents of the jug into the bowl of dry ingredients and stir lightly to combine. Do not over-stir as this will cause the bread to be tough. Pour the batter into the tin and bake in the oven for 35–40 minutes until firm and golden on top. Cut the warm cornbread into pieces to serve. Serve immediately or leave to cool and re-heat, wrapped in foil. (Can be frozen for up to 1 month.)

PER SERVING 198 kcals, carbs 39g, fat 2g, sat fat 0.7g, salt 1g

Easy Easter brioche

Mixing and kneading this buttery dough in the food processor makes brioche-making a doddle. It will keep for two days – delicious with apricot jam.

SERVES 6 • PREP 2¼ HOURS • COOK 20–25 MINS
V ❄

250g/9oz plain (not strong) flour, plus extra for dusting
100g/4oz butter, cut into small pieces, plus extra
     for greasing
2 rounded tbsp caster sugar
7g sachet fast-action yeast
3 eggs, beaten
egg yolk, to glaze
2–3 sugar cubes, lightly crushed

1 Tip the flour into a food processor fitted with a plastic kneading blade and add the butter. Process until the mixture looks like breadcrumbs. Stir in the caster sugar, a good pinch of salt and the yeast.
2 Add the eggs and mix to a soft dough, then knead in the machine for 2 minutes. Butter a brioche mould or 900g loaf tin. Sprinkle a layer of flour onto a work surface and tip the dough onto it. With floured hands, knead very briefly to form a ball, then drop the dough into the tin, smooth-side up. Cover with cling film and leave in a warm place to rise until doubled in size, about 2 hours.
3 Heat oven to 200C/180C fan/gas 6. Brush the top of the brioche with egg yolk, then sprinkle over crushed sugar and bake for 20–25 minutes until golden brown and the loaf sounds hollow when tapped. Tip out onto a wire rack and leave to cool.

PER SERVING 365 kcals, carbs 43g, fat 19g, sat fat 10g, salt 0.71g

tip If you don't have a processor, simply rub the butter into the flour by hand, stir in the sugar, salt and yeast, then add the eggs and mix to a soft dough. Cover and chill for 20 minutes (this makes it easier to handle), then knead on a floured surface for 5 minutes. Drop into the tin and carry on as recipe.

Richly fruited hot cross buns

The ultimate sticky spicy bun for teatime. Simply split and butter or toast until golden.

**MAKES 12 BUNS • PREP 30 MINS, PLUS RISING TIME
COOK 15-20 MINS**

V ❄

500g pack white bread mix (or see below)
50g/2oz golden caster sugar
1 tbsp mixed spice
85g/3oz butter
250ml/9fl oz milk
1 egg, beaten
250g bag mixed fruit (including peel)

TO DECORATE
100g/4oz plain flour, plus extra for dusting
2 tbsp golden syrup or honey, to glaze

1 Tip the bread mix into a large bowl, stir in the sugar and mixed spice and make a well. Melt the butter in a pan, stir in the milk and take off the heat. Pour into the well along with the egg. With a knife or wooden spoon, draw the dry ingredients into the wet and stir to form a soft dough. Tip onto a work surface and knead for about 5 minutes until smooth (photo 1). Transfer to a lightly oiled bowl, cover with oiled cling film and leave to rise in a warm place for about 30 minutes or until the dough has risen to twice its size.
2 Turn out the dough onto a lightly floured surface and punch the air out. Press the dough out into a large rectangle (about A3 size) and sprinkle the fruit over (photo 2). Roll the dough up around the fruit and knead until the fruit is evenly dispersed through the dough. Split into 12 even pieces and shape into smooth balls, pinching the bottoms of each ball to create a smooth top (photo 3).
3 Grease a large baking sheet and sit the shaped buns on it, 2–3cm apart so they have room to rise. Re-cover with the oiled cling film and set aside again in a warm place until risen and the dough feels pillowy when prodded gently.
4 Heat oven to 200C/180C fan/gas 6. To make the crosses, make a well in the flour and gradually stir in 6 tbsp water to make a smooth, pipeable paste. Spoon the paste into a piping bag (or use a freezer bag – just snip off the end) and pipe across the buns (photo 4). Bake for 15–20 minutes until well risen and golden brown. Leave to cool for a few minutes then lift onto a cooling rack.
5 Heat the syrup or honey in a small pan or microwave in a bowl for a few seconds until melted. Brush over the warm buns and leave them to cool completely.

PER HOT CROSS BUN 300 kcals, carbs 52g, fat 9g, sat fat 4g, salt 1.16g

tip If you'd rather make your own bread mix, simply combine 500g strong white flour with a 7g sachet fast-action yeast plus 1 tsp salt then continue as in Step 1.

Cinnamon pecan sticky buns

Enjoy a lazy Sunday morning with this indulgent brunch recipe.

MAKES 16 • PREP 30 MINS, PLUS RISING • COOK 30 MINS
V ❄

450g/1lb strong white flour
50g/2oz caster sugar
85g/3oz butter, cut into small pieces
7g sachet fast action yeast
2 large eggs, beaten
150ml/¼ pint full-fat milk
vegetable oil, for greasing
FOR THE FILLING
2 tsp ground cinnamon
85g/3oz light brown sugar
100g/4oz pecan nuts
FOR THE TOPPING
125g/4½oz melted butter, plus extra
125ml/4fl oz maple syrup
50g/2oz light brown sugar
100g/4oz pecan nuts, roughly chopped

1 Mix the flour, sugar and 1 tsp salt, then rub in the butter to make fine crumbs. Tip in the yeast, eggs and milk then mix to a soft dough. Knead for 10 minutes until elastic then tip into an oiled bowl. Cover and leave to rise for 1 hour or until doubled in size. For the filling, whizz everything in a processor until fine.
2 Knead the dough and split in two. Roll each to a 25 x 35cm rectangle. Brush with half the melted butter, then sprinkle the filling over and press in. Roll up tightly from the long edge, then pinch to seal. Slice each piece into 8.
3 Grease two 20 x 30cm baking sheets. Mix the remaining butter and topping ingredients and spread over the sheets. Sit the buns on top, spacing well apart. Cover with lightly oiled cling film and leave to prove for 30 minutes.
4 Heat oven to 180C/160C fan/gas 4. Bake buns for 30 minutes until golden and firm. Serve warm, sticky-side up.

PER BUN 731 kcals, carbs 80g, fat 43g, sat fat 16g, salt 1.13g

Baked doughnuts

Rolling the freshly baked doughnuts in a light sugar glaze before tossing them in caster sugar gives them the authentic crunchy coating without deep frying.

MAKES 12 • PREP 2¼ HOURS, INCLUDING 1½ HOURS RISING • COOK 10–12 MINS
V ❄

200g/7oz strong white bread flour
1 rounded tbsp caster sugar
25g/1oz butter, cut into small pieces
7g sachet fast action yeast
5 tbsp milk
1 egg, beaten
4 tbsp raspberry jam (or use mincemeat)
TO COAT
3 tbsp icing sugar
85g/3oz caster sugar
1 tsp cinnamon

1 Tip the flour, sugar and a good pinch of salt into a large bowl. Add the butter and rub into the flour with your fingertips. Stir in the yeast.
2 Warm the milk to hand hot. Make a well in the centre of the flour and add the milk and egg. Mix everything together to make a soft dough. Tip onto a lightly floured surface and knead for 5 minutes until the dough is smooth, elastic and no longer sticky. Put the dough back in the bowl, cover with a tea towel and leave to rise for about 1 hour or until doubled in size.
3 Knead the dough again briefly, then divide into 12 equal pieces. Roll out each piece to a 9cm round and put 1 tsp jam in the centre of each. Gather up the edges of the dough to enclose the filling, pinching it well to seal. Shape into a ball between your hands and put on a baking sheet lined with baking parchment, sealed-side down, allowing space for the dough to rise. Cover with a tea towel and leave for 30 minutes.
4 Heat the oven to 190C/170C fan/gas 5. Bake the doughnuts for 10–12 minutes until risen and golden. Mix the icing sugar with 2 tbsp cold water in a bowl. Mix the sugar and cinnamon in another bowl. Roll each doughnut first in the sugar syrup, then into the caster sugar to coat all over. Leave to cool.

PER DOUGHNUT 149 kcals, carbs 30g, fat 3g, sat fat 2g, salt 0.06g

11

Pastry, pancakes and batters

One thing's for sure – no matter what the filling in your pie or tart, the quality of the pastry can make or break it. Whether you want to make your own or pick up some ready-made, this chapter will provide all you need to know; from how to make a basic shortcrust to creating the perfect puffy choux buns. If the only batter you ever whip up is for pancakes on Shrove Tuesday, there's a little more year-round inspiration in here too.

PASTRY

Many people feel daunted at the idea of pastry-making. It's true that you may need a few goes to get your technique perfect, but as long as you follow some basic rules you'll discover it's simple and easy to do. If you have a food processor, you're in luck – a processor can take away most of the (human) variables within pastry-making. This machine will work the fat into the flour quickly, without warming it, and bind the pastry together swiftly when the liquid is added, preventing you adding too much.

Fresh, raw pastry can be chilled for up to 3 days or frozen for 1 month, with the exceptions of choux and suet pastries. Be careful not to use frozen and then defrosted pastry in a recipe if you intend to freeze the finished dish. Don't be caught out by how long pastry can take to defrost either – defrost overnight in the fridge.

Shortcrust pastry

Out of all the pastries, shortcrust is the most useful, everyday pastry you can make. Made with approximately half the quantity of fat to flour, with just a little water to bring it together, it has a crisp, 'short' texture. It's useful for savoury pies and tarts, and also some sweet recipes, where the filling adds plenty of sweetness in itself. Ready-made shortcrust comes in fresh or frozen rolled sheets (often already cut into rounds, ready for lining a tart tin), or in blocks. Block pastry gives the best result, as rolled sheets can sometimes crack, but the choice is yours.

Rich shortcrust has added egg yolk, which makes the pastry a little more luxurious. A common use for rich shortcrust pastry is in mince pies. Sweet shortcrust is enriched with egg yolks and sugar and is used solely for desserts and sweet baking. The high sugar content gives it lovely biscuity quality. Sweet shortcrust is a little harder to handle, as it can be quite soft.

When making and handling shortcrust pastry remember:
• A cool kitchen, worktop, and, ideally, cool hands and cold butter are key to the success of your pastry. Cut the butter into small cubes before you begin. Even if you're going to be using a food processor, this is important.

OPPOSITE *Danish pastries (page 286)*

- **Sift the flour first**. It will lighten the finished result.
- **Rub it in**. The fat and flour need to be rubbed together very well so that no lumps of butter remain (this could lead to holes later). As you rub in, give the bowl a shake now and again. Any bigger lumps remaining will rise to the top.
- **Go easy on the liquid**. Shortcrust pastry needs only a little liquid to bring it together. Add too much and the pastry will shrink a lot as it cooks and be tough.
- **Don't overwork it**. Overhandled pastry can become tough as the gluten within it becomes more elastic. Mix the liquid into the pastry with a cutlery knife and avoid kneading the dough beyond the first few necessary times.
- **Relax it**. Chilling your pastry is essential – it will make it easier to roll and prevents shrinkage.
- **Rolling out**. If your pastry is very hard after chilling, let it sit out for 15 minutes or so – too hard and it will crack. To minimise stretching the pastry (and avoid shrinkage later), press ridges into the pastry with the rolling pin, turning a quarter turn a few times, until the pastry is about 1cm thick. Then start to roll. Roll in one direction only, and make sure that the work surface and pin are both well floured.

To make 400g (14oz) of **basic shortcrust pastry**, sift 250g (9oz) plain flour into a large bowl, add ½ tsp salt and 125g (4½ oz) cold cubed butter. Using your fingertips, rub the butter and flour together until the mix resembles fine breadcrumbs. If the butter becomes warm, put the bowl in the fridge for a few minutes then continue. If making pastry with a food processor, simply pulse the flour, salt and butter together until fine. Splash 4 tbsp water evenly over the crumbly mix, then use a cutlery knife to bring everything together. Try to resist adding more water. When the mix has come together in clumps, go in with your hands and press the dough into a ball. You may need to give it a quick knead to smooth the surface, but take care not to overwork it. If using a processor, add the liquid and pulse again until large clumps of dough come together. Shape the pastry into a flat disc, cover in cling film, then chill it for 30 minutes (or for up to 3 days), or freeze it. This chilling time relaxes the dough, which will make it more tender and also easier to roll.

To make 400g (14oz) **sweet shortcrust pastry**, sift 200g (7oz) plain flour and 85g (3oz) icing sugar together, then add 100g (4oz) cold, cubed unsalted butter. Follow the method as for basic shortcrust pastry. Beat 1 egg yolk with 1 tablespoon water and work it into the dry ingredients. Shape the pastry into a disc, wrap in cling film and chill. If making in a processor, put the flour, icing sugar and butter into the bowl then pulse together until fine, then follow the method as above.

OTHER PASTRIES
Puff pastry is tricky for even the most experienced cook to make, and it takes a lot of time, too. It's made by layering a simple flour and water dough with butter, then rolling and folding it many times until the layers of butter and dough are incredibly thin. We recommend that you buy a good all-butter brand, either frozen or fresh. Blocks give the best result, but ready-rolled pastry is a good, quick option for tarts and pies. Puff pastry needs to be kept chilled, or else the layers of butter will melt and make the pastry greasy and heavy rather than light and crisp.

Choux pastry defies all the usual rules of pastry-making. More of a batter than a pastry, it is made by adding flour and salt to boiling water and butter, beating it to a smooth paste, then beating in the eggs. This is usually piped into balls or finger shapes, then baked. The pastry puffs up dramatically as it cooks, creating a hollow middle ready to be filled. For the best choux pastry, remember these points:

- Don't leave the dough hanging around once it's made; have lined baking sheets ready, the oven preheated and piping bag ready (if necessary) before you begin.
- Don't allow the water to boil for too long before adding the flour. If too much water evaporates, it will skew the quantities.
- Beat the flour into the water as quickly as you can to avoid any lumps.
- Let the mix cool for a few minutes before adding the eggs, as they can start to cook in the heat.
- Beat in the eggs gradually until the mix is smooth and glossy. You may not need all of the egg in the recipe – once the pastry is of a dropping consistency, stop.

Choux normally needs to be dried out once baked, or it quickly becomes soggy. Pierce a hole in the base of choux buns (or cut a slit), put them back on their tray upside-

Step-by-step: Lining a tart tin

A metal, loose-bottomed tin is the best option for making tarts and quiches. Glass and ceramic dishes won't conduct the heat as well as metal, giving a soggy crust.

1 Roll the pastry until it's large enough to cover your tin, allowing for a few centimetres extra. Fold the pastry in half and then unfold it so that the centre of the pastry is in the centre of the tin.

2 Gently ease the pastry into the bottom edge so that there's no air trapped underneath it.

3 Either trim the pastry by rolling a rolling pin across the top or leave the pastry overhanging - the latter is safest if you are worried about your pastry shrinking.

4 Push the pastry into the fluted edge around the edge of the tin, pushing it slightly above the rim of the tin. Lightly prick the base with a fork.

5 Put the tin onto a baking sheet. Line the case with a large, crumpled piece of baking parchment or foil, big enough to cover the edges and any overhang. Fill with baking beans, making sure they go right up to the edges. Bake blind according to your recipe, then remove the beans and paper. Cook the pastry until it looks dry and is starting to turn golden.

6 If you left the pastry overhanging when it was lined, now is the time to trim it. Let the pastry cool for a few minutes then saw away the excess pastry using a small serrated knife, to leave a neat edge that's flush with the top of the tin. The pastry case is now ready to be filled.

Step-by-step: Lining and covering a pie

This technique will be the same whether you are using sweet or savoury shortcrust pastry and gives a brilliantly rustic finish.

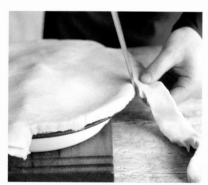

1 Grease your pie dish with butter or oil, then dust with flour – this will create a non-stick layer. Roll out two-thirds of the pastry to a round that will easily line the pie dish with an overhang.

2 Spoon in the cooled filling. Roll out the remaining pastry until large enough to cover the dish. Brush the edges of the pastry in the dish with water (or glaze, depending on the recipe), then cover with the pastry lid.

3 Trim the edges with a sharp knife using the side of the dish as your guide.

4 Press together the edges then seal the edges by crimping them with your fingers and thumb. Re-roll your trimmings to make a decoration, if you like. Glaze the pie and chill.

tips

• If you are making a pie with pastry just on the top, you'll need a pie dish with a lip, so that the pastry has something to stick to. Roll out the pastry to about £1-coin thickness, then cut a strip of pastry the same width as the lip of the dish, and long enough to go all the way around it (you may need to cut two pieces). Brush the lip of the dish with water, then stick the strip around it. Brush this with water, then cover with the pastry.

• For any lidded pie, make sure that your filling is cold, and that you cut a few ventilation holes in the pastry lid, to let steam escape and prevent a sogginess. Just as with a lined tart tin, a pie will need chilling before it is baked. This will allow the pastry to rest, and prevent any shrinking.

down, then return to the oven to crisp up. See the recipe for profiteroles on page 285 for the full method.

Filo is a paper-thin pastry sold in sheets that is great for sweet and savoury recipes. Unlike most pastry, it's low in fat, although the classic way to cook with it is in layers brushed with melted butter or oil. Filo pastry dries out very quickly, so be sure to cover the sheets with a slightly damp clean tea towel while you're assembling your recipe.

Suet pastry is made with self-raising flour (or plain flour mixed with baking powder), suet (or grated frozen butter), and hot water. It's very easy to make and is a must for classic, comforting steamed puddings. Suet pastry needs to be used as soon as it's made.

Danish pastry is a cross between pastry and bread. Layers of yeasted dough and butter are rolled and folded together to produce a flaky and deliciously light pastry.

BATTERS

At their simplest, batters are a mix of egg, milk and flour – but it's the proportions of each that make all the difference. Liquidy batters make delicate pancakes and puffy Yorkshire puds, whereas thicker batters with added baking powder, whisked egg whites, or even yeast, will give thick, fluffy pancakes, light-as-air fritters and blinis.

With the exception of tempura batter, which is made very quickly and best left a bit lumpy, most batters need to be smooth and even in order to give a good end result. The best way to ensure this is to make a well in the dry ingredients, then add some of the liquid ingredients (usually one or more eggs). Whisk tentatively at first, gradually drawing the dry ingredients into the middle of the bowl, until you have a smooth, thick paste. This is the point at which you will be able to beat out any lumps. Once smooth, you can whisk in the rest of the liquid.

Some batter recipes incorporate resting time, during which the flour particles swell and the gluten relaxes, giving a more tender and lighter pancake. If you don't have time, though, get straight on with the cooking. Batters made with self-raising flour or added baking powder or bicarbonate of soda need to be cooked straight away as the raising agents become active as soon as they mix with liquid ingredients.

Pancakes and crepes

Although traditionally cooked on Shrove Tuesday (in February), pancakes are a great idea whenever the cupboard is looking a little bare. For a really good stack of pancakes, remember:

- A good pancake batter will be the consistency of double cream. Loosen the mixture if you need to, but don't add flour to the bowl as it will turn lumpy. In a separate bowl, mix a little extra flour with some of the batter until smooth, then beat it into the rest of the batter.
- Use a heavy-based, medium pan (ideally 20cm across).
- Don't use butter to fry pancakes, unless it is clarified. A little flavourless oil is best.
- Add the batter to the pan with a ladle or use a jug. Leave it alone until you can see gold appearing at the edges and the top of the pancake looks set, then flip.
- The first pancake made is normally a disaster – it happens to everyone!
- If you're not eating the pancakes straightaway, keep them warm by interleaving them with greaseproof paper and covering them with a tea towel. They can be reheated wrapped in foil at 180C/160C fan/gas 4 for 10 minutes or microwaved (no foil) for 30 seconds. Pancakes also freeze well.

Thick pancakes

American-style thick pancakes, made with self-raising flour (or plain flour mixed with baking powder or bicarbonate of soda), need to be cooked as soon as the batter is made, otherwise your pancakes will be heavy. **Blinis** are (like crumpets and pikelets) leavened with yeast.

Deep-frying

Batter acts as a protective casing for deep-fried food – as it hardens it provides a little jacket within which the food steams. A batter for frying must be thick enough to cling to the food without dripping away, but not so thick that it becomes claggy.

Baking

Yorkshire puddings, popovers, toad-in-the-hole and clafoutis are all oven-baked batters. In any recipe where you expect the batter to puff up dramatically, make sure that the tin is hot, the oil inside it is hot, and that you avoid opening the oven door for the first 15 minutes – a blast of cold air will cause instant deflation.

Easiest-ever pancakes

*This recipe couldn't be simpler. Make up the batter, add melted butter and your mix will
make delicious thick pancakes ready to serve with your favourite filling.*

MAKES 12 • PREP 5 MINS • COOK A STAGGERED 20 MINS
V ❄

FOR THE BASIC BATTER
140g/5oz plain flour
4 eggs
200ml/7fl oz milk
FOR THE PANCAKES
50g/2oz butter, melted
sunflower oil, for cooking

1 To make the batter, tip the flour into a bowl and beat in the
eggs until smooth. Gradually add the milk and carry on
beating until the mix is completely lump-free.
2 Now whisk in the melted butter. Place a pancake pan over
a medium heat and wipe with oiled kitchen paper. Ladle some
batter into the pan, tilting the pan to move the mix around
the pan then pour off any excess. Cook for about 30 seconds
until golden, then flip over and cook on the other side. Pile
the pancakes up and serve with your favourite filling.

PER PANCAKE 209 kcals, carbs 10g, fat 17g, sat fat 4g, salt 0.14g

> Spoon good-quality lemon curd over the pancake,
> then top with crushed meringue pieces and a little
> crème fraîche.

American blueberry pancakes

*Light, fluffy and fruity, these pancakes make a deliciously different way to celebrate Pancake Day.
Stack them high with extra blueberries and drizzled generously with golden or maple syrup.*

MAKES 10 PANCAKES • PREP 25 MINS • COOK 10 MINS
V

200g/7oz self-raising flour
1 tsp baking powder
1 egg
300ml/½ pint milk
knob of butter, melted
150g pack blueberries
sunflower oil, for cooking
golden or maple syrup, to serve

1 Mix together the flour, baking powder and a pinch of salt
in a large bowl. Beat the egg with the milk, make a well in the
centre of the dry ingredients and whisk in the liquid to make
a thick smooth batter. Beat in the melted butter, then stir in
half the blueberries.
2 Heat 1 tsp oil in a large non-stick frying pan. Drop 3 or 4
large tbsp of batter into the pan to make pancakes about
7.5cm across. Cook for about 3 minutes over a medium heat
until small bubbles appear on the surface of each pancake.
Turn and cook for another 2–3 minutes until golden. Keep
warm while you use up the rest of the batter. Serve with
golden or maple syrup and the rest of the blueberries.

PER PANCAKE (without syrup) 108 kcals, carbs 18g, fat 3g, sat fat 1g,
salt 0.41g

Cheesy leek and potato pie

This pie is made like an extra-large pasty, so you don't need a special dish or tart case. It uses ready-made pastry for speed, but if you want to make your own, try the recipe on page 262.

SERVES 6 • PREP 10 MINS • COOK 1 HOUR
V ❄ UNCOOKED

3 leeks, cut into chunks
small knob of butter
pinch dried rosemary or thyme
450g/1lb floury potatoes
140g/5oz melting cheese, such as mature Cheddar, cut into small chunks
500g pack shortcrust pastry, defrosted if frozen
plain flour, for rolling out
1 egg, beaten

1 Put the leeks, butter and herbs in a pan, cover and cook over a low heat for about 20 minutes until very soft, stirring occasionally. Meanwhile, boil the potatoes for 4–5 minutes from cold, until just cooked. Drain and stir into the leeks. Cool, stir in the cheese, then season. (Can be chilled for use the following day, if you like.)

2 Heat oven to 200C/180C fan/gas 6. Divide the pastry in two and roll one piece to the size of a dinner plate. Transfer to a baking sheet. Roll the remaining pastry and any trimmings to a round about 5cm bigger than the first. Pile the filling in the middle of the round on the baking sheet, leaving a 4cm border. Brush border with the beaten egg, then drape over the larger piece of pastry. Trim the edges to neaten, then press the sides together with your thumb. Brush the tart all over with egg. Bake for 35–40 minutes until golden. Leave to rest for 10 minutes before cutting into wedges and serving with beans or greens.

PER SERVING 555 kcals, carbs 52g, fat 34g, sat fat 17g, salt 0.83g

Cornish pasties

The black pepper is essential in this recipe, giving the pasties their spicy kick.

MAKES 4 • PREP 25 MINS, PLUS CHILLING
COOK 55 MINS
❄ UNCOOKED

FOR THE PASTRY
125g/4½oz butter, chilled and diced
125g/4½oz lard, diced
500g/1lb 2oz plain flour, plus extra for rolling out
1 egg, beaten, to seal and glaze
FOR THE FILLING
350g/12oz beef skirt or chuck steak, finely chopped
1 large onion, finely chopped
2 medium potatoes, peeled, thinly sliced
175g/6oz swede, peeled, finely diced
1 tbsp freshly ground black pepper

1 Rub the butter and lard into the flour with a pinch of salt using your fingertips or a food processor, then blend in 6 tbsp cold water to make a firm dough. Cut equally into 4, then chill for 20 minutes.

2 Heat oven to 220C/200C fan/gas 7. Mix together the filling ingredients with 1 tsp salt. Roll out each piece of dough on to a lightly floured surface until large enough to make a round about 23cm across – use a plate to trim it to shape. Firmly pack a quarter of the filling along the centre of each round, leaving a margin at each end. Brush the pastry all the way round the edge with beaten egg, carefully draw up both sides so that they meet at the top, then pinch them together to seal. Lift onto a non-stick baking sheet and brush with the remaining egg to glaze.

3 Bake for 10 minutes, then lower oven to 180C/160C fan/gas 4 and cook for 45 minutes more until golden. Great served warm.

PER PASTY 1,174 kcals, carbs 114g, fat 68g, sat fat 35g, salt 1.96g

Bacon and blue cheese tart

Filo makes this tart light to eat and easy to make. Any leftovers are great for packed lunches too.

SERVES 4 • PREP 10 MINS • COOK 30 MINS

6 large sheets filo pastry or 10 sheets if small
1 tbsp olive oil
100g/4oz sliced ham, chopped
1 bunch spring onions, sliced
2 eggs, lightly beaten
300g tub full-fat soft cheese, at room temperature
2 large handfuls rocket leaves
50g/2oz blue cheese, crumbled
2 tbsp pine nuts

1 Heat oven to 180C/160C fan/gas 4. Brush each filo sheet with a little oil and layer into a 20cm springform or loose-bottomed tin, overlapping each sheet at a different angle.
2 Mix together the ham, spring onions, eggs, soft cheese and rocket, then pour into the filo case. Sprinkle with blue cheese and pine nuts, then bake for 30 minutes until just set. Cool slightly, slice and serve with a salad.

PER SERVING 626 kcals, carbs 24g, fat 52g, sat fat 28g, salt 2.56g

Rustic courgette, pine nut and ricotta tart

This big, rustic tart has been simplified by making it straight on the baking sheet. If you'd like to make a smaller version, the recipe can be easily halved to make a tart about 25cm wide.

SERVES 6 • PREP 30 MINS • COOK 30 MINS
V

2 tbsp olive oil
4 courgettes, thinly sliced (try to use a mixture of different varieties if you can find them)
2 x 250g tubs ricotta
4 eggs
large handful basil leaves, shredded
grated nutmeg
50g/2oz Parmesan, grated
1 large garlic clove, crushed
500g block puff pastry, defrosted if frozen
flour, for dusting
large handful pine nuts

1 Heat oven to 200C/180C fan/gas 6. Heat half the oil in a frying pan. Sizzle the courgettes for 5 minutes until golden around the edges, then set aside. In a bowl, beat the ricotta with the eggs, basil, nutmeg, half the Parmesan and the garlic. Set aside.
2 Roll out the pastry on a lightly floured surface to a rough round about 40cm wide, then transfer to a baking sheet. Spread the pastry with the ricotta mix, leaving a 4cm border. Press the courgette slices into the ricotta, then scatter over the pine nuts and remaining Parmesan. Bring the sides up over the edge of the ricotta, pinch to encase the filling, then bake for 30 minutes until the filling is puffed up and golden. Leave to cool slightly and enjoy warm or cold with a crisp green salad.

PER SERVING 620 kcals, carbs 36g, fat 43g, sat fat 17g, salt 1.17g

The ultimate apple pie

Everyone loves apple pie. This one is pure perfection; tart apples, crisp pastry and a hint of spice.

SERVES 8 • PREP 40 MINS, PLUS CHILLING COOK 40–45 MINS
V ❄ UNCOOKED

FOR THE FILLING
1kg/2lb 4oz Bramley apples, peeled, cored and
    sliced 5mm thick
140g/5oz golden caster sugar
½ tsp cinnamon
3 tbsp flour
FOR THE PASTRY
225g/8oz butter, at room temperature
50g/2oz golden caster sugar, plus extra
2 eggs, one separated
350g/12oz plain flour
softly whipped cream, to serve

1 Put a layer of kitchen paper on a large baking sheet and spread the apples over it. Cover with more paper then set aside. For the pastry, beat the butter and sugar in a large bowl until just mixed. Beat in an egg plus an extra yolk, then stir in the flour until clumpy. Gently work into a ball, wrap, then chill for 45 minutes.

2 Heat the oven to 190C/170C fan/gas 5. Meanwhile, make the filling by mixing the sugar, cinnamon and flour in a large bowl. Use two-thirds of the pastry to line a deep, 20cm/8in pie tin, leaving an overhang. Roll the remaining pastry to a 28cm circle. Pat the apples dry, mix with the cinnamon sugar then pile high in the tin.

3 Dampen the rim, put the pastry lid on and press the edges together to seal. Trim, then make 5 little slashes on top. (Can be frozen at this stage.) Brush with the lightly beaten egg white, sprinkle with sugar then bake for 40–45 minutes, until golden. Let it sit for 5–10 minutes before serving.

PER SERVING 695 kcals, carbs 95g, fat 33g, sat fat 20g, salt 0.79g

Custard tart with nutmeg pastry

In a twist on the old-fashioned favourite, this creamy set custard has a little extra nutmeg built into its crisp pastry case.

SERVES 12 • PREP 15 MINS, PLUS CHILLING COOK 1 HOUR 35 MINS
V

500g pack shortcrust pastry
½ tsp freshly grated nutmeg, plus extra
4 large eggs
140g/5oz golden caster sugar
300ml/½ pint double cream
300ml/½ pint whole milk
1 vanilla pod, seeds scraped out

1 Heat oven to 200C/180C fan/gas 6. Roll the pastry out to about 1cm thick, sprinkle with nutmeg, then fold the dough in half. Roll out again, to the thickness of 2 x £1 coins and large enough to line a 20cm loose-bottomed sandwich tin with some overhang. Put onto a baking sheet and chill for 10 minutes. Bake blind for 20 minutes (see page 263), then remove the beans and baking parchment. Bake for another 15 minutes until golden and sandy all over. Trim the edges of the tart with a sharp serrated knife.

2 Turn oven down to 150C/130C fan/gas 2. Whisk the eggs and sugar in a large bowl. Put the cream, milk, vanilla pod and seeds into a saucepan and bring to the boil. Pour onto the eggs, whisking as you go. Sieve into a jug. Put the baking sheet onto the pulled-out oven shelf, then pour in the custard, right to the top. Sprinkle with nutmeg, slide into the oven and bake for 1 hour until set and pale golden on the top, with the merest tremor in the centre when jiggled. Cool completely.

PER SERVING 405 kcals, carbs 33g, fat 28g, sat fat 13g, salt 0.54g

Baked fruity autumn pudding

This classic steamed pud is bursting with autumn flavours and can be made up to a day ahead – just reheat in the microwave.

SERVES 4–6 • PREP 20–25 MINS • COOK 2 HOURS
V IF USING VEGETABLE SUET

450g/1lb mixed autumn fruit – we used ripe plums, pears and peeled apples, cut into 1cm cubes, and whole blackberries
2 tbsp butter, cut into small chunks, plus extra for greasing
200g/7oz caster sugar
1½ tsp cinnamon
300g/11oz self-raising flour, sifted
140g/5oz shredded suet
zest 1 lemon

1 Butter a 1.2-litre pudding basin. Cut 2 x long 5cm-wide strips of parchment, grease and cross them in the base. To make the filling, mix the fruit, butter, 125g of the sugar and cinnamon.
2 Mix the remaining ingredients together with the rest of the sugar to make the pastry. Add a few drops of water, working it through with a cutlery knife, then keep adding water until you have soft dough. Bring together into a smooth ball. Roll three-quarters of the dough to a 20cm circle. Use to line the bowl with a slight overhang. Fill with fruit. Roll the remaining pastry to make a lid, then press the edges to firmly seal.
3 Heat oven to 180C/160C fan/gas 4. Cover the pudding with a pleated square of parchment and foil, foil-side up, scrunching it around the bowl to make a tight-fitting tid. Secure with string. Put in a deep roasting tin, then pour boiling water to 1–2cm below foil line. Cook for 2 hours, topping up the water level if it gets too low. Unwrap, release the edges using the parchment tabs and invert onto a plate.

PER SERVING (4) 841 kcals, carbs 124g, fat 39g, sat fat 19g, salt 0.83g

Pumpkin pie with pecan and maple cream

A great way to use up pumpkin flesh from your lantern carving.

SERVES 8 • PREP 20 MINS • COOK 1 HOUR 15 MINS
V ❄

550g/1lb 4oz piece pumpkin, peeled and cut into chunks
500g pack shortcrust pastry
175g/6oz light muscovado sugar
2 eggs
142ml pot double cream
1 tsp cinnamon
1 tsp allspice
1 tsp ground ginger
small grating nutmeg
FOR THE PECAN AND MAPLE CREAM
142ml pot double cream
5 tbsp maple syrup
25g/1oz pecans, finely chopped

1 Place the pumpkin pieces in a large microwaveable bowl. Cover, then cook on High (850W) for 15 minutes or until soft. Drain and cool in a colander.
2 On a lightly floured surface, roll out the pastry until wide enough to line a 25cm tart tin with some overhang. Chill for 30 minutes. Heat oven to 200C/180C fan/gas 6. Bake the pastry blind for 15–20 minutes, then cook for a further 10 minutes until sandy and golden. Turn oven down to 160C/140C fan/gas 3.
3 Meanwhile, place the pumpkin, sugar, eggs, cream and spices in a food processor, then blend until smooth. Pour into the baked pastry case and bake for 1 hour until the filling has puffed up in the centre (it will sink as it cools). Cool. Whip the cream with the maple syrup until thickened, then fold in the pecans and serve with the pie.

PER SERVING 624 kcals, carbs 61g, fat 41g, sat fat 18g, salt 0.73g

*OPPOSITE **Clockwise from top left** Cornish pasties (page 267); American blueberry pancakes (page 266); Apricot and almond Bakewell (page 274),; The ultimate apple pie (page 269); Chocolate and pecan tart (page 273); Onion, walnut and mushroom tart Tatin (page 276)*

Flip-over damson pie

If you can't find damsons, use sliced plums instead and reduce the amount of sugar,
as plums are a lot sweeter.

SERVES 4 • PREP 10 MINS • COOK 30 MINS
V ❄

500g/1lb 2oz damsons, halved and stoned
140g/5oz golden caster sugar
pinch ground cinnamon
425g pack (2 sheets) ready-rolled puff pastry
1 egg, beaten
icing sugar, to serve

1 Heat oven to 220C/200C fan/gas 7. Mix the damsons, sugar and cinnamon together in a bowl. Lay one of the pastry sheets on a baking sheet and pile the damsons down the middle, leaving space around the edge. Brush the edges with egg and drape the other sheet of pastry over. Trim the edge of the pie and press down to seal. (Can be prepared up to 2 hours in advance and chilled.)

2 Brush the pie with egg and make a series of parallel slits across it, like a ladder, avoiding the edges. Bake for 30 minutes until puffed up and golden. Leave to stand for a few minutes, dust with icing sugar, slice, and serve with custard.

PER SERVING 605 kcals, carbs 88g, fat 27g, sat fat 10g, salt 0.9g

Rhubarb, ginger and apple scrunch pie

A cheat's dessert that tastes every bit as gorgeous as a full-blown fruit pie, without all
the work and washing up.

SERVES 6 • PREP 15 MINS • COOK 35 MINS
V

375g pack ready-rolled shortcrust pastry
400g/14oz Bramley apples, sliced
400g pack trimmed rhubarb, cut into lengths
100g/4oz demerara sugar, plus extra for sprinkling
2 balls stem ginger, chopped
2 tbsp cornflour
milk, for brushing

1 Heat oven to 180C/160C fan/gas 4 and grease a large baking sheet. Unravel the pastry and place on the baking sheet. Mix the sliced apple and rhubarb with the sugar, ginger and cornflour then pile into the centre of the pastry. Gather up the sides of the pastry to enclose the fruit so that the pie looks like a rough tart – you need to work with the size of the pastry so it will be more of an oblong shape than round.

2 Brush the pastry with milk and scatter with demerara. Bake for 35 minutes until the pastry is golden and the fruit is tender. Cut into slices and serve with custard.

PER SERVING 397 kcals, carbs 59g, fat 18g, sat fat 9g, salt 0.27g

Apple pie turnovers

 Tasty little triangles that make a great low-fat alternative to proper apple pie.

**SERVES 4 EASILY DOUBLED • PREP 20 MINS
COOK 20–25 MINS**
V ❄

2 cooking apples, peeled, cored and chopped
50g/2oz caster sugar
1 tsp ground mixed spice
50g/2oz sultanas
4 sheets filo pastry
25g/1oz low-fat spread, melted

1 Heat oven to 200C/180C fan/gas 6. Place the apples, sugar, mixed spice and sultanas in a saucepan with 2 tbsp water and cook, covered, for 6 minutes or until the apples are soft, stirring once or twice. Tip into a shallow dish and spread out to cool slightly.
2 Cut the sheets of filo in thirds lengthways, then brush lightly with the melted spread. Place a spoonful of the apple filling at the top of each strip, then fold over and over to form triangular parcels. Place on a baking sheet and bake for 15–20 minutes until crisp and golden. Serve with low-fat yogurt, if you like.

PER SERVING 196 kcals, carbs 42g, fat 3g, sat fat 1g, salt 0.58g

Chocolate and pecan tart

This make-ahead pud is a real family favourite – especially with the younger members of the family. A cross between pecan pie and chocolate tart, what's not to love?

SERVES 6–8 • PREP 30 MINS • COOK 1 HOUR 15 MINS
V

375g pack sweet shortcrust pastry
a little plain flour, for dusting
185g/6½oz dark chocolate
50g/2oz salted butter
4 eggs, beaten
200ml/7fl oz maple syrup
200g/7oz whole pecan nuts

1 Heat oven to 180C/160C fan/gas 4. Roll the pastry out on a lightly floured surface and use to line a 20cm loose-bottomed tart tin. Fill the tart with baking parchment and baking beans, bake blind for 25 minutes, then remove the parchment and beans. Continue to cook for 10 minutes more until golden. Remove from the oven and cool.
2 Melt the chocolate and butter together in a large bowl over a pan of simmering water. Whisk the eggs and maple syrup together, then stir into the chocolate with most of the nuts. Pour into the tart shell, top with the remaining nuts and bake for 30–40 minutes until set. Cool and serve with vanilla ice cream or double cream.

PER SERVING (6) 898 kcals, carbs 75g, fat 63g, sat fat 19g, salt 0.6g

Apricot and almond bakewell

A winning combination of sweet pastry, moist almonds and sharp compote. Use raspberry compote, if you prefer.

**CUTS INTO 8 SLICES • PREP 20 MINS, PLUS CHILLING
COOK 1 HOUR 25 MINS**

400g/14oz sweet shortcrust pastry
140g/5oz self-raising flour, plus a little extra for dusting
140g/5oz Madeira cake
200g/7oz butter, softened
140g/5oz ground almonds
140g/5oz golden caster sugar
3 eggs, beaten
600ml jar apricot compote
1 tbsp flaked almonds
icing sugar, Greek yogurt and clear honey, to serve

1 Roll out the pastry with a little flour until big enough to line a deep 20–23cm loose-bottomed tart tin. Line the tin with the pastry, leaving any excess overhanging. Chill or freeze for 30 minutes.
2 Heat oven to 180C/160C fan/gas 4. Line the pastry with baking parchment, fill with baking beans, then bake blind for 20 minutes. Remove the parchment and beans, then bake for 5 minutes more until the pastry is pale biscuit coloured.
3 Meanwhile, make the filling. Whizz the Madeira cake in a food processor, then tip into a large bowl with the flour, butter, ground almonds, caster sugar and eggs. Briefly beat together until smooth.
4 Reduce oven to 160C/140C fan/gas 3. Tip the compote into the pastry case and spread to cover the base. Spoon over the almond mixture and gently spread to cover the compote. Scatter with the flaked almonds, then bake for 1 hour until golden and firm to the touch. Cool. Remove to a serving plate and serve slightly warm, dusted with icing sugar with Greek yogurt and a drizzle of honey alongside.

PER SERVING 814 kcals, carbs 79.4g, fat 51.8g, sat fat 21.1g, salt 1.13g

Treacle tart hearts

Make a sweet heart for your sweetheart. If you'd rather make one large tart to slice, see below.

MAKES 8 • PREP 20 MINS, PLUS CHILLING • COOK 25 MINS
V

200g/7oz cold, unsalted butter, cubed
350g/12oz plain flour, plus extra for rolling out
½ tsp ground ginger (optional)
100g/4oz golden caster sugar
1 egg yolk
FOR THE FILLING
400g/14oz golden syrup
zest 1 lemon and juice of ½
100g/4oz white breadcrumbs

1 Blitz the butter, flour and ginger, if using, to fine crumbs in a food processor. Stir in the sugar, then add the egg yolk and 2 tsp cold water. Pulse until the dough clumps together, adding more water if needed. Turn out onto a lightly floured surface, press into a smooth round then chill for 30 minutes.
2 Roll the pastry to the thickness of 2 x £1 coins and stamp out 8 x 11cm circles. Line 8 x 10cm width heart-shaped tins with the pastry. Re-roll the trimmings. Stamp out 8 small hearts to decorate. Chill tins and hearts for 15 minutes or until firm. Heat oven to 170C/150C fan/gas 5 and put a baking sheet inside to warm.
3 Stir the syrup, lemon juice and zest together. Divide the breadcrumbs between the tins then spoon the syrup over slowly. Top with the small hearts. Put the tins onto the hot sheet and bake for 25 minutes or until the pastry is golden and the filling is orangey-gold. Cool for 15 minutes, then turn onto a wire rack. Serve just warm.

PER SERVING 452 kcals, carbs 78g, fat 16g, sat fat 10g, salt 0.59g

> To make this recipe as a large tart, use the pastry to line a 23cm tart tin, leaving the pastry. Fill with the filling, then bake for 45–50 minutes until the filling and pastry are golden.

Vegetable tempura with soy and dipping sauce

These crisp Japanese-style treats are great for nibbles or a veggie main course.

SERVES 4 • PREP 10 MINS • COOK 10–15 MINS
V

100g/4oz (approx) each of a mix of firm veg, cut into
    bite-size pieces, such as aubergine, broccoli, courgettes,
    mushrooms, red pepper and sweet potatoes
groundnut or sunflower oil, for deep frying

FOR THE SAUCE
3 tbsp soy sauce
3 tbsp dry sherry
1 tbsp sugar
zest 1 lemon

FOR THE BATTER
85g/3oz plain flour
1 tbsp cornflour
200ml/7fl oz ice-cold sparkling mineral water
ice cubes

try this...

Use peeled but tail-on raw prawns instead of the
vegetables.

1 Heat oven to 150C/130C fan/gas 2. Mix together the sauce ingredients in a small bowl. Cover a baking sheet with kitchen paper. Start heating a deep, wide pan or large wok a third full of oil and have a frying basket or a slotted spoon to hand.
2 To make the batter, sift the flours and ½ tsp fine sea salt into a large mixing bowl. Whisk in the cold water along with a few ice cubes using a whisk, but don't over beat – it doesn't matter about a few lumps. Use immediately.
3 When the oil reaches 190C dip some of the prepared veg briefly into the batter, shake off any excess, then lower straight into the hot oil. Don't crowd the pan. Fry for about 2 minutes until light golden and crisp, then carefully lift out and drain on kitchen paper.
4 Repeat with the remaining veg in batches, dipping them into the batter just before you fry them. Remember to let the oil heat back up to 190C between each batch. Keep the tempura warm in the oven, leaving the door slightly ajar so they stay crisp. Best served immediately on a warm plate with the sauce alongside for dipping.

PER SERVING 471 kcals, carbs 33g, fat 35g, sat fat 6g, salt 2.08g

Blinis

Top with soured cream flavoured with horseradish or dill and smoked salmon.

**MAKES ABOUT 20 BLINIS • PREP 10 MINS, PLUS RISING
COOK 20 MINS**
V ❄

140g/5oz buckwheat flour
150ml/¼ pint milk, warmed
1 tsp sugar
1 tsp salt
2 eggs, separated
7g sachet fast-action yeast
1 tbsp sour cream, plus extra to serve
small knob of butter
1 tbsp vegetable oil

tip To freeze, separate blinis with greaseproof
paper, wrap in cling film and freeze for up to a month.
Defrost overnight and reheat at 190C/170C fan/gas 5
for 5 minutes.

1 To make the blinis, tip the flour into a large bowl and make a well in the centre. Mix together the milk, sugar, salt, egg yolks and yeast, then pour into the well and carefully start mixing with the flour until you have a smooth batter. Cover the bowl with cling film and leave in a warm place for about 1 hour, until the mixture has doubled in size.
2 Whisk the egg whites in a clean bowl until they form soft peaks. Stir the sour cream into the blini mixture, then carefully fold in the egg whites.
3 Heat a heavy non-stick frying pan on a medium-high heat. When really hot, add the butter and a little oil and swirl around the pan. Drop in dessertspoonfuls of batter to make 3 pancakes roughly 5cm across. Cook for about 30 seconds, then flip over and cook for another 30 seconds until golden brown all over. Set aside and repeat with the remaining mixture.

PER SERVING 49 kcals, carbs 6.5g, fat 1.9g, sat fat 0.6g, salt 0.29g

Leek and goat's cheese tartlets

Topped with a few rocket leaves and drizzled with a flavoured oil, such as walnut or truffle, these tarts make a smart vegetarian main course.

SERVES 4 • PREP 15 MINS • COOK 45–50 MINS
V ❄

4 leeks, trimmed, halved and finely sliced
large knob of butter
2 tbsp thyme leaves and 4 nice sprigs
375g block puff pastry
4 slices goat's cheese (with a rind)
truffle oil or walnut oil (optional)

1 Wash the leeks in a colander but don't worry about drying them as you want a bit of water clinging on. Heat the butter in a wide saucepan until sizzling, then add the wet leeks and thyme leaves plus some salt and pepper. Sweat the leeks really gently for 20–25 minutes until they have practically melted but not coloured, adding a little more butter if needed. Set aside and allow to cool.
2 Heat oven to 220C/200C fan/gas 7. Roll the pastry out to the thickness of a £1 coin. Cut out 4 saucer-size circles and place on a baking sheet. Spread the leeks over the circles, leaving a slight border around the edge. Put a slice of goat's cheese in the middle of each tart and top with a thyme sprig. Pinch the pastry edge together to slightly encase the leeks. (Can be chilled for up to 1 day or frozen for 1 month.) Bake the tarts for 25 minutes until puffed up and golden. Serve hot and drizzled with flavoured oil, if you have it.

PER SERVING 606 kcals, carbs 32g, fat 46g, sat fat 24g, salt 1.82g

Onion, walnut and mushroom tarte tatin

This makes a substantial main course that's full of flavour and which can be prepared a day in advance. If you want to serve this as a glamorous starter, make individual tarts in Yorkshire pudding tins.

SERVES 4 • PREP 20 MINS • COOK 50 MINS
V

4 onions
3 tbsp olive oil
200g/7oz chestnut mushrooms, halved if large
2 tsp light muscovado sugar
50g/2oz walnuts
100g/4oz blue cheese, such as Stilton
250g/9oz puff pastry
flour, for dusting

1 Heat oven to 200C/180C fan/gas 6. Peel the onions and cut each into 6 wedges through the root. Heat the oil in a large pan, add the onions, then gently fry for 20 minutes until softened and lightly coloured.
2 Add the mushrooms, sugar, salt and pepper and give it a good stir. Gently cook, stirring now and then for a further 5 minutes. Stir in the walnuts. Line the base of a 20–23cm sandwich cake tin (not loose-bottomed) or ovenproof frying pan with baking parchment. Spoon over the onion mixture and press it down lightly. Crumble the cheese over.
3 Roll out the pastry on a lightly floured surface and trim to a round, about 5cm larger than the tin. Put the pastry over the filling and tuck in the ends. Bake for 35–40 minutes until the pastry is crisp and golden. Cool for 5 minutes in the tin, then turn out onto a flat plate and cut into wedges. Serve with a green salad.

PER SERVING 546 kcals, carbs 30g, fat 43g, sat fat 16g, salt 1.43g

OPPOSITE *Leek and goat's cheese tartlets.*

Spinach and artichoke filo pie

A special vegetarian main course for friends and family, and a great alternative to quiche.

SERVES 8 • PREP 30 MINS • COOK 1½ HOURS
V

2 small leeks, very thinly sliced
50g/2oz butter, plus a knob
400g/14oz frozen leaf spinach, thawed, well drained
    and chopped
250g tub ricotta cheese
4 large eggs, beaten
140g/5oz grated Parmesan cheese
½ nutmeg, finely grated
400g can artichoke hearts, drained and halved
85g/3oz sunblushed (semi-dried) tomatoes
270g pack filo pastry
2 tbsp olive oil

1 Soften the leeks in a pan with the butter for a couple of minutes. Add the spinach to the pan, and cook for a couple of minutes more. In a separate bowl, beat the ricotta and eggs with the Parmesan, spinach mix, nutmeg and plenty of seasoning. Stir in the artichokes and tomatoes.
2 Heat oven to 180C/160C fan/gas 4. Line the base and sides of a greased 23cm springform or loose-bottomed tin with the filo pastry. Brush each sheet lightly with the oil and place in the tin, oil-side down, leaving the excess to hang over the edge. Turn the tin a quarter turn after each sheet.
3 Tip the filling into the tin, fold the excess pastry onto the top of the pie, a sheet at a time, crumpling to give a ruffled effect. Bake for 1½ hours until golden and firm.

PER SERVING 371 kcals, carbs 25g, fat 23g, sat fat 11g, salt 2.06g

Asparagus, mascarpone and Parmesan pastries

Celebrate the British asparagus season with these pretty tarts. They're ideal for a springtime lunch or starter and take no time at all to prepare.

SERVES 4 • PREP 10 MINS • COOK 20–25 MINS
V

6 tbsp mascarpone
40g/1½oz Parmesan, finely grated, plus extra shavings
    to serve
3 tbsp finely chopped basil
zest ½ lemon
375g pack ready-rolled puff pastry, quartered then cut
    to the length of the asparagus
350g pack asparagus spears
1 tbsp olive oil
TO SERVE
good handful pretty salad leaves, such as rocket,
    basil, frisée and little red chard leaves, tossed in
    vinaigrette

1 Heat oven to 200C/180C fan/gas 6. Mix the mascarpone with the Parmesan, basil and lemon zest, then season.
2 Lift the pastry onto 2 baking sheets, then score around the edges of each piece to make a thin border. Spread the cheese mixture within the borders.
3 Toss the asparagus in the oil then arrange the bundles on top of the pastry (these can be stacked a bit for height). Bake the pastries for 20–25 minutes until golden, then serve warm, topped with the dressed salad leaves and a few shavings of Parmesan.

PER SERVING 535 kcals, carbs 37g, fat 39g, sat fat 18g, salt 0.99g

Lemon meringue pie

Easy to make and stunning to look at.

**SERVES 6–8 ● PREP 30 MINS, PLUS CHILLING
COOK 50 MINS**
V

FOR THE PASTRY
175g/6oz plain flour, plus extra for dusting
100g/4oz cold butter, cut in small pieces
1 tbsp icing sugar
1 egg yolk

FOR THE FILLING
2 level tbsp cornflour
100g/4oz golden caster sugar
finely grated zest 2 large lemons
125ml/4fl oz fresh lemon juice (from 2–3 lemons)
juice 1 small orange, made up to 200ml/7fl oz with water
85g/3oz butter, cut in pieces
3 egg yolks and 1 whole egg, beaten together

FOR THE MERINGUE
4 egg whites, room temperature
200g/7oz golden caster sugar
2 level tsp cornflour

1 Put the pastry ingredients and 1 tbsp cold water into a food processor. Pulse to a clumpy dough then press into a smooth round. Flour the surface then roll out and use to line a 23 x 2.5cm fluted tart tin. Trim then prick the base with a fork, line with foil, and chill for 30 minutes to 1 hour until firm.

2 Put a baking sheet in the oven and heat oven to 200C/180C fan/gas 6. Bake pastry blind (see page 263), then bake 5–8 minutes more until sandy and golden. Reduce oven to 180C/160C fan/gas 4.

3 For the filling, mix the cornflour, sugar and zest in a saucepan. Gradually stir in the lemon and diluted orange juice. Bring to the boil over a medium heat, stirring constantly, until thickened and smooth. Off the heat, beat in the butter. Stir the egg and yolks into the pan and return to medium heat, stirring, until the mixture thickens and plops from the spoon. Set aside.

4 In a large bowl, whisk the egg whites to soft peaks, then add half the sugar a spoonful at a time, whisking between each addition. Whisk in the cornflour, then the rest of the sugar until smooth and thick. Quickly reheat the filling and pour it into the pastry case. Spoon some of the meringue around the edge of the filling then spread so it just touches the pastry. Pile the rest into the centre, swirl, then bake for 18-20 minutes until the meringue is crisp and slightly coloured. Cool in the tin for 30 minutes, then remove and leave for 30 minutes to 1 hour before slicing. Eat on the day.

PER SERVING (8) 480 kcals, carbs 64g, fat 24g, sat fat 13g, salt 0.53g

try this...

Gooseberry meringue pie
Gooseberries are also particularly good under a fluffy crown of meringue. Bake the pastry blind as before. While the case is cooking, heat 50g/2oz butter and 100g/4oz light muscovado sugar in a shallow pan. When the sugar has completely dissolved, throw in 500g gooseberries and toss in the caramel. Cook for a few minutes until they start to split, but before they have burst completely. Remove from the heat. Make the meringue as before. Tip the gooseberries into the case, then top with the meringue and bake.

Raspberry tart with almond pastry

The perfect summer dessert for a crowd.

CUTS INTO 10 SLICES • PREP 40 MINS, PLUS COOLING COOK 30 MINS

V

FOR THE PASTRY
200g/7oz plain flour
175g/6oz ground almonds
175g/6oz golden caster sugar
200g/7oz cold butter, diced, plus extra for greasing
1 egg yolk

FOR THE FILLING
200ml tub crème fraîche
85g/3oz golden caster sugar
½ tsp vanilla essence
juice and zest ½ lemon
about 700g/1lb 9oz raspberries

FOR THE GLAZE
5 tbsp raspberry jam

1 Put the pastry ingredients, except the yolk, into a food processor and pulse to the texture of breadcrumbs. Add the yolk, then pulse to a soft pastry. Press it evenly into a greased, loose-bottomed 25cm tart tin until the pastry comes up above the edges of the tin. Chill in the freezer for at least 20 minutes.

2 Heat oven to 190C/170C fan/gas 5. Line the tart case then bake blind for 20 minutes (see page 263) Remove the beans and parchment, then continue to cook for 10 minutes until biscuity. Leave to cool, trim the edges with a knife, then carefully remove from the tart tin.

3 To make the filling, whisk the crème fraîche with the sugar, vanilla, lemon juice and zest until thick. Spread over the bottom of the tart case, then meticulously place the raspberries on top in concentric circles. Meanwhile, heat the jam in the microwave or in a pan with 2 tbsp water until bubbling. Push the glaze through a sieve into a bowl, then paint it over the raspberries with a pastry brush. Bring the whole tart to the table and serve in slices.

PER SERVING 659 kcals, carbs 63g, fat 43g, sat fat 22g, salt 0.36g

Millionaire's chocolate tart

This gorgeous tart will wow dinner guests, but isn't too bitter to put off kids.

SERVES 10 • PREP 30 MINS, PLUS CHILLING COOK 55 MINS

V

375g pack sweet shortcrust pastry
plain flour, for dusting
250g/9oz caramel (the type available in a can)
100g/4oz plain chocolate, 70% cocoa solids, broken into pieces
100g/4oz white chocolate, broken into pieces
6 tbsp melted butter
2 eggs, plus 3 egg yolks
4 tbsp golden caster sugar
icing sugar, to serve

1 On a floured surface, roll the pastry to line a 23cm tart tin, leaving an overhang. Chill for 30 minutes.

2 Heat oven to 200C/180C fan/gas 6. Bake the pastry blind (see page 263), then remove the parchment and beans and bake for 5–10 minutes more until sandy and golden. Carefully spread the caramel over the base and set aside while you make the filling. Lower oven to 180C/160C fan/gas 4.

3 Melt the chocolates in a bowl over a pan of barely simmering water, then stir in the melted butter. Whisk the eggs, yolks and sugar together with an electric whisk in a large mixing bowl for 10 minutes, until pale and thick enough to leave a trail when the beaters are lifted up. Fold in the melted chocolate with a large metal spoon, then scrape into the tin. Bake for 20–25 minutes – the surface should be set and puffed but still with a slight wobble. Cool, then chill for at least 3 hours or overnight, before dusting with icing sugar.

PER SERVING 618 kcals, carbs 62g, fat 39g, sat fat 18g, salt 0.59g

Tangy lemon tart

A classic tarte au citron with a creamy citrus filling and crisp, sweet pastry. The quantity of pastry given is double what you'll need – put what's left in the freezer for next time.

SERVES 8 • PREP 25 MINS, PLUS CHILLING COOK 1 HOUR
V

FOR THE PASTRY
500g/1lb 2oz plain flour, plus extra for dusting
140g/5oz icing sugar
250g pack butter, cubed
4 egg yolks
FOR THE FILLING
5 eggs
140g/5oz caster sugar
150ml/¼ pint double cream
juice 2–3 lemons (about 100ml/3½ fl oz) and 2 tbsp
    lemon zest

1 To make the pastry, mix the flour and icing sugar in a bowl. Rub the butter into the flour until crumbly. Mix in the egg yolks to make a dough. Add 1–2 tbsp water if needed. Roll into a ball and divide in half (freeze one half for another time). Flatten into a disc, wrap in cling film, then chill for at least 30 minutes.
2 Meanwhile, beat together all the filling ingredients, except the zest. Sieve, then stir in the zest.
3 Roll out the pastry on a lightly floured surface to £1 coin thickness, then lift into a 23cm tart tin. Prick the base with a fork, trim the edges then chill for 30 minutes.
4 Heat oven to 160C/140C fan/gas 3. Bake the pastry blind for 10 minutes (see page 263), then for another 20 minutes until biscuity. When ready, remove the pastry from the oven, pour in the lemon mixture and bake again for 30–35 minutes until just set. Leave to cool, then remove the tart from the tin and serve at room temperature or chilled.

PER SERVING 770 kcals, carbs 86g, fat 44g, sat fat 24g, salt 0.18g

Strawberries and cream layer

Turn strawberries and cream into a pudding to remember with the simple addition of crisp, caramelised puff pastry sheets.

SERVES 4 • PREP 20 MINS • COOK 20 MINS
V

375g pack all-butter puff pastry
4 tbsp icing sugar
450g/1lb ripe small strawberries, or a mix of normal
    and wild
1 vanilla pod, or 1 tsp vanilla extract
300ml pot double cream
140g/5oz golden caster sugar

1 Heat oven to 220C/200C fan/gas 7. Roll the pastry out to a square about 30 x 30cm. Lay on a large baking sheet, place another baking sheet on top and bake for about 20 minutes until golden. Heat the grill to High, dust the pastry liberally with icing sugar and carefully caramelise under the grill. Dust with another layer of icing sugar and return to the grill to caramelise again. While warm, cut the pastry into 12 neat rectangles, trimming the edges as you go. These can now be kept in an airtight container for a day.
2 Halve or quarter the strawberries, depending on their size, then dust with a little icing sugar and set aside. Split the vanilla pod and scrape the seeds into the cream, then whip lightly with the caster sugar until it just holds its shape.
3 To assemble, place a blob of cream on each plate and, at jaunty angles, stack the biscuits, cream and strawberries.

PER SERVING 931 kcals, carbs 96g, fat 60g, sat fat 30g, salt 0.81g

Apricot gâteau pithiviers

Adding apricots makes this traditional French tart lighter.

**SERVES 10 ● PREP 30 MINS, PLUS CHILLING
COOK 30–35 MINS**
Ⅴ ❄ **UNCOOKED, IF PASTRY NOT PREVIOUSLY FROZEN**

FOR THE FILLING
100g/4oz butter, softened
140g/5oz golden caster sugar
1 egg, plus 1 egg yolk
100g/4oz ground almonds
1 tbsp plain flour, plus extra for dusting
1 tbsp Grand Marnier or Disaronno
500g pack ready-made puff pastry
200g/7oz ripe apricots, stoned and thickly sliced
1 egg, beaten to seal and glaze
3 tbsp apricot jam, melted and sieved

1 Beat the butter, sugar, egg and yolk, almonds, flour and liqueur until smooth. Roll out half the pastry to 2 x £1 coin thickness on a lightly floured surface, then cut a circle about 25cm in diameter. Roll out the remaining pastry and cut a second circle, slightly larger than the first.
2 Place the smaller circle on a baking sheet and top with half the almond filling, then the apricots, then the rest of the filling, leaving a 2.5cm border. Brush the border with egg and set the remaining pastry on top, pressing edges firmly together.
3 With a sharp knife, score lines around the outer edge of the pastry. Press the back of the knife 1cm into the edge at regular intervals to give a scalloped appearance. Brush the top with more beaten egg then score radiating curved line (see picture on page 284). Chill for 20 minutes.
4 Heat oven to 200C/180C fan/gas 6. Bake for 30–35 minutes until puffed up and golden. Leave to cool then glaze with the jam.

PER SERVING 429 kcals, carbs 40g, fat 28g, sat fat 11g, salt 0.60g

Walnut and rosewater baklava

These little Turkish-inspired pastries are particularly good with a strong cup of coffee at the end of a meal.

**MAKES 16 SMALL PIECES ● PREP 15 MINS
COOK 20 MINS**
Ⅴ

FOR THE SYRUP
140g/5oz caster sugar
2 tbsp rosewater
FOR THE LAYERS
200g/7oz walnuts, finely chopped
50g/2oz golden caster sugar
1 heaped tsp cinnamon
½ tsp ground cloves
400g pack filo pastry (you will need 12 sheets)
100g/4oz butter, melted

1 For the syrup, dissolve the sugar into 250ml/9fl oz just-boiled water over a low heat, then boil for 15 minutes or until thickened but not coloured. Stir in the rosewater and leave to cool.
2 Meanwhile, lightly butter a 15 x 25cm baking tray. Mix together the walnuts, sugar and spices in a bowl. Unroll the pastry, peel off 12 sheets and, keeping the layers together, cut a rectangle just big enough to fit on the baking tray. Re-wrap any leftover pastry for another time.
3 Heat oven to 180C/160C fan/gas 4. Brush 4 pastry sheets with the melted butter and use to cover the bottom of the tray. Top with half of the nut mix then repeat, using 4 sheets of buttered pastry for each layer and finishing with pastry. Using a sharp knife, cut diagonal lines all the way through to create small diamonds. Bake for 15–20 minutes until golden. Pour the syrup over, then cool.

PER SERVING 169 kcals, carbs 16g, fat 11g, sat fat 3g, salt 0.29g

Strawberry gâteau St Honoré

All the main elements of this spectacular, light summer dessert can be prepared in stages. For helpful information on choux pastry, see page 262.

SERVES 12 • PREP 1½ HOURS • COOK 1 HOUR
Ⓥ

FOR THE PASTRY BASE
100g/4oz plain flour
50g/2oz ground almonds
85g/3oz butter
50g/2oz caster sugar
1 egg, separated

FOR THE CHOUX PASTRY
50g/2oz butter
75g/2½oz plain flour, sifted into a bowl
2 eggs, lightly beaten
3 tbsp flaked almonds

FOR THE FILLING AND TO FINISH
2 tbsp custard powder
2–3 tbsp caster sugar
300ml/½ pint milk
1 tsp vanilla extract
284ml pot double cream
750g/1lb 10oz strawberries, hulled and halved if large
100g/4oz caster sugar
icing sugar, for dusting

1 Whizz the flour, almonds, butter and sugar together in a food processor to fine crumbs. Add the egg yolk (reserve the white for later) and pulse until the dough comes together. Wrap in cling film and chill for 1 hour.

2 Heat oven to 200C/180C fan/gas 6. Roll out the pastry on a large square of baking parchment, then trim to a 26cm round using a cake tin or plate as a guide. Carefully transfer the pastry, still on the parchment, to a large baking sheet. Bake for 12–15 minutes until golden. Cool on the parchment, then transfer to a large, flat serving plate.

3 To make the choux pastry, line a baking sheet with baking parchment. Heat the butter in a pan with 125ml water until melted, then increase the heat until boiling. Remove from the heat, then add the flour in one go, quickly stirring until everything comes together as a thick paste. Leave to cool for 10 minutes. Beat the eggs into the paste using a wooden spoon, a little at a time, until you have a thick, glossy mixture. Spoon 12 equal-size blobs of choux, a little apart, over the baking sheet. Lightly whisk the reserved egg white, then brush over each blob of pastry. Sprinkle with flaked almonds.

4 Bake the buns for 25–30 minutes until crisp and golden. Remove from the oven, carefully split each bun, then return to the oven for 5 minutes more to dry out the insides. Cool on a rack, then scoop out any soft insides.

5 To make the filling, mix the custard powder and sugar in a pan. Blend in a little milk to a smooth paste. Add the rest of the milk, then gently bring to the boil, stirring, until you have a thick custard. Remove from the heat, then stir in the vanilla. Transfer to a bowl, cover the surface with cling film and cool.

6 Stir the custard to loosen a little. Whip the cream to soft peaks, then fold into the custard. Slice a third of the strawberries. Spread a thin layer of custard over the pastry base. Add the sliced strawberries to the remaining custard, then use to fill the choux buns. Arrange the buns around the edge of the pastry base. Spoon any remaining custard into the centre, then top with the remaining strawberries.

7 To make the caramel, tip the caster sugar into a heavy based pan with 2 tbsp cold water. Heat, without stirring, to dissolve the sugar, then boil hard until it becomes a light caramel. Remove from the heat and, when the bubbles subside, drizzle carefully over the choux buns. Dust with icing sugar and serve.

PER SERVING 419 kcals, carbs 38g, fat 28g, sat fat 14g, salt 0.3g

Fruity clafoutis

This French pud takes next to no time to make. It's good on its own, but extra yummy with coulis or cream.

**SERVES 6 • PREP 15 MINS, PLUS RESTING
COOK 25 MINS**
Ⓥ

a little oil or softened butter, for greasing
400g/14oz mixed blackberries, blueberries and raspberries
FOR THE BATTER
50g/2oz ground almonds
2 tbsp plain flour
100g/4oz golden caster sugar
2 eggs, plus 2 egg yolks
250ml/9fl oz double cream

1 Heat oven to 190C/170C fan/gas 5. Oil or butter a shallow baking dish and scatter the berries over the base.
2 Whizz all the batter ingredients in a blender until smooth, pour it over the fruits and bake for 20–25 minutes until risen and golden brown. Serve warm.

PER SERVING 393 kcals, carbs 27g, fat 29g, sat fat 14g, salt 0.55g

Moreish mocha profiteroles

A classic profiterole recipe that's crisp and creamy, and has an added kick for coffee lovers.

SERVES 6 • PREP 45 MINS • COOK 30 MINS
Ⓥ ❄ **UNFILLED BUNS**

100g/4oz plain flour
85g/3oz unsalted butter
3 eggs, beaten
FOR THE FILLING
4 tbsp custard powder
6 tbsp golden caster sugar
600ml/1 pint milk
2 tbsp coffee essence (dissolve 2 tbsp instant coffee
    granules in 2 tbsp hot water)
284ml pot double cream
100g/4oz icing sugar
FOR THE SAUCE
100g/4oz dark chocolate, in pieces
50g/2oz butter
50ml/2fl oz strong coffee
1–2 tbsp coffee liqueur

1 Sift the flour into a bowl and stir in a pinch of salt. Put the butter and 200ml cold water into a pan, bring to a rolling boil, then take off the heat. Tip in the flour and beat to a smooth paste. Beat until the mix comes away from the sides of the pan. Cool for 10 minutes.
2 Heat oven to 200C/180C fan/gas 6. Beat the eggs into the pan. Spoon walnut-sized balls onto a baking sheet and bake for 20–25 minutes until golden. Poke a hole in the bottom of each roll with a teaspoon handle, turn upside-down, then bake for 5 minutes to dry out. Cool on a rack before filling.
3 Mix the custard powder, sugar and a splash of milk to a smooth paste. Bring the remaining milk to boil, then stir into the paste. Pour into a clean pan and bring to the boil, stirring, until thick and smooth. Stir in the coffee and leave to cool. Whip the cream with the icing sugar then fold into the custard. Pipe into each choux bun.
4 Melt the chocolate and butter with the coffee then stir in the liqueur. Serve the sauce with the buns.

PER SERVING 807 kcals, carbs 73g, fat 54g, sat fat 31g, salt 0.63g

try this...

To make Chocolate éclairs, make the choux pastry as before and pipe it in long fingers onto the baking sheet. Bake as before, then split and fill with the custard cream, leaving out the coffee and alcohol. Finish with a quick icing by melting together the chocolate, butter, 75ml double cream and 1 tbsp icing sugar. Cool, then spread over the top of the éclairs.

OPPOSITE Clockwise from top left *Millionaire's chocolate tart (page 280); Strawberry gâteau St Honoré (page 283); Moreish mocha profiteroles; Fruity clafoutis; Apricot gâteau Pithiviers (page 282); Spinach and artichoke filo pie (page 278).*

Danish pastries

Danish pastries need love and patience, and if you're really into baking there's no better way to test your skills and escape to the kitchen at the weekend. Always use the best-quality butter and flour.

MAKES 18 PASTRIES • PREP ABOUT 1 HOUR, PLUS RISING AND CHILLING • COOK 20 MINS
V ❄

250g/9oz strong white flour, plus extra for dusting
250g/9oz plain flour
7g sachet fast-action yeast
50g/2oz golden caster sugar
150ml/¼ pint whole or semi-skimmed milk
1 large egg, beaten, plus extra beaten egg to glaze
oil, for greasing
250g pack lightly salted butter, not fridge cold but
    not soft, cut into 8 even slices

try this...

To make 18 pecan pinwheels

Whizz 85g pecans until fine, then stir in 50g light muscovado sugar, 1 tbsp maple syrup and 25g butter. Cut each square of pastry almost to the middle from each corner, spoon on 1 tsp filling, then fold each point over and press into the middle (photo 2). Scatter more chopped pecans and a little sugar over before baking. Drizzle with maple syrup to serve.

For 18 apricot custard turnovers

You will need 150g tub custard, 2 x 320g cans apricots and a few tsps apricot jam. Put 2 tsp custard in the middle, sit 2 apricot halves on top, dot with jam, then pull 2 corners over and pinch to seal (photo 3).

To make 18 raisin swirls

Mix 50g raisins, 25g caster sugar, 1 tsp mixed spice and 50g soft butter. Instead of cutting the dough into 9, leave it whole and spread the filling over. Roll up, slice into 9 rounds, then squash each one (photo 4). Blend 50g icing sugar and a few drops of water to drizzle over once baked.

1 Pulse together the dry ingredients plus 2 tsp salt in a processor, then pulse in the milk and egg until you have a smooth, slightly sticky dough. Knead for 1 minute, using a little flour, until just smooth. Put into an oiled bowl, cover with oiled cling film and leave to rise in a warm place for 1 hour until doubled in size (overnight in the fridge if you like).

2 Flour your surface, then pat the dough out to a rectangle, 1cm thick. Lay the butter slices over the middle of the dough, in a rectangle. Fold the pastry over the top, bottom and sides until the butter is completely hidden. Press the edges down.

3 Roll the dough out to a 50 x 30cm rectangle, first tapping the dough with the rolling pin in gentle ridges, so that you can tell the butter is being squashed out evenly inside the pastry, before rolling properly. Turn the dough 90 degrees, then fold the right third over and the left third over that. Do this three times, chilling for 15 minutes after each roll (photo 1).

4 Cut the dough in half into 2 squares. Roll one piece of dough to 35 x 35cm. Cut into 9 squares, then follow the instructions for each filling and shape.

5 Once shaped and filled, let the pastries rise on baking sheets for 30 minutes until puffed and doubled in size. Heat oven to 180C/160C fan/gas 4. Brush with beaten egg, make sure you pinch any edges together again, then bake for about 20 minutes until golden and risen.

PER PASTRY 218 kcals, carbs 25g, fat 12g, sat fat 8g, salt 0.26g

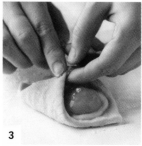

1

2

3

4

Rhubarb and almond crumble tart

For a simpler dessert, the roasted rhubarb is delicious served warm with vanilla ice cream and shop-bought shortbread.

CUTS INTO 10 SLICES • PREP 30 MINS • COOK 1½ HOURS
V ❄

375g pack dessert pastry
plain flour, for dusting
750g/1lb 10oz rhubarb, sliced into thumb-size chunks
140g/5oz golden caster sugar
juice 1 large orange
FOR THE STREUSEL TOPPPING
¼ tsp ground cinnamon
140g/5oz cold butter, diced
100g/4oz ground almonds
140g/5oz plain flour
175g/6oz light muscovado sugar
handful flaked almonds

1 Heat oven to 200C/180C fan/gas 6. Roll out the pastry on a lightly floured surface, then line a 23cm tart tin with it. Chill in the fridge.
2 Tip the rhubarb into a roasting tin with the sugar and orange juice, then toss together. Cover with foil, then bake for 30–40 minutes. Tip into a sieve over a bowl, then reserve the syrup. While the rhubarb is cooking, press a sheet of baking parchment into the tart case, tip in baking beans, then bake blind for 20 minutes. Remove beans and parchment, then bake for 10 minutes more.
3 Rub the topping ingredients, except the flaked almonds, together until crumbly. When the case is cooked, lower oven to 180C/160C fan/gas 4. Spoon the rhubarb evenly over the case and crumble over the topping. Scatter with the flaked almonds, then bake for 20 minutes. Leave the tart until just warm, then turn out and serve with the rhubarb syrup and some crème fraîche.

PER SERVING 545 kcals, carbs 65g, fat 30g, sat fat 12g, salt 0.42g

Tarte tatin with brandy cream

An updated version of the original apple tart using ready-rolled pastry – so you don't even need a rolling pin.

SERVES 4 • PREP 30 MINS • COOK 20-25 MINS
V

50g/2oz butter
50g/2oz golden caster sugar
½ tsp ground cinnamon
6 medium Cox's or similar apples, peeled, quartered and cored
375g pack ready-rolled puff pastry
FOR THE BRANDY CREAM
200ml pot crème fraîche
2 tbsp icing sugar
1 tbsp brandy or Calvados

1 Heat oven to 220C/200C fan/gas 7. Melt the butter in a 20cm tarte tatin tin or ovenproof frying pan over a medium heat, then stir in the sugar and cook until starting to caramelise. Stir in the cinnamon. Add the apples then cook for 10 minutes, stirring every so often. The apple juices will ooze out at first but will soon thicken and make a sauce. Remove from the heat.
2 Prick the pastry all over with a fork. Lay it over the apples. Trim away to fit the top of the pan, then tuck the pastry snugly around the apples, down around the inside of the tin.
3 Bake for 20–30 minutes until golden. Leave to settle for 5 minutes, then run a knife round the edge to loosen. Turn onto a plate to serve. For the brandy cream, mix the crème fraîche with the sugar and brandy or Calvados.

PER SERVING 761kcals, carbs 77g, fat 48g, sat fat 15g, salt 1.12g

tip To get ahead, cool the apples before topping with the pastry. Chill for up to 24 hours, then continue with Step 3.

12

Cakes, bakes and biscuits

Baking a cake, traybake or a batch of biscuits has to be one of the most satisfying kinds of cooking. As well as being fun, you can be pretty sure that the end result is going to be devoured by very happy recipients. There are recipes here suitable for the family cake tin, chocolate treats, cute cupcakes, crumbly biscuits and cut-and-come-again traybakes, all straightforwardly explained. If you're new to baking, make sure you follow the 'baking basics' before you begin.

BASICS OF BAKING

Baking recipes are a careful balance of ingredients, so there are a few basic rules you need to follow to get the best results.

- Always use measuring spoons and scales, and try not to substitute ingredients unless you have to. If you do, always choose like for like – one sugar for another and not honey for sugar, for instance.
- Preheat your oven and check shelf positions before you start. Most cakes will cook best on the middle shelf, though if you have a fan oven (with even heat), this is less important.
- Line tins before you begin mixing ingredients.
- If your recipe involves self-raising flour, baking powder or bicarbonate of soda, don't hang about – the sooner you get it in the oven the better.
- Don't open the oven door too soon or keep peeking; the cold air will cause the cake to sink.

CAKES

Cakes can be made by using four main methods: creaming, whisking, melting and rubbing in.

Creaming

This involves beating sugar and butter together until light and fluffy, gradually incorporating eggs, and then folding in flour and other dry ingredients. A Victoria sponge is a good example. All-in-one cakes are a quick alternative to creaming when you're short of time. They often have extra raising agent added, to make up for the absence of the creaming process.

Tips for success:
- Always use softened butter and room-temperature eggs.
- Don't stop creaming the sugar and butter until it is pale and fluffy.
- Add the eggs gradually, in small drips, to prevent curdling.
- If the mix does start to curdle, add a spoonful of flour and carry on.
- Use a large metal spoon to fold the flour into the batter. Cut and fold the

OPPOSITE *Lemon and poppyseed cupcakes* (page 312)

flour in, rather than stirring, and stop as soon as the mix is evenly blended.

• Creamed cakes are best eaten within a few days of making, kept in an airtight tin. They also freeze well, unfilled, for up to 1 month.

Whisking

Light-as-air sponges and roulades rely on this method, where eggs and sugar are whisked together until billowy and thick. Flour is then folded in, sometimes preceded by melted butter for richness.

Tips for success:

• If the bowl is whisked over hot water, be sure that the bottom of the bowl doesn't touch its surface.

• Whisk the eggs and sugar until it 'holds a trail' – in other words, when you let the mix fall from the beaters, it holds a shape on the surface for a few seconds, rather than disappearing instantly.

• Fold flour in carefully, again with a large metal spoon.

• Tip the mix around the cake tin until even – don't spread it or you'll burst all those bubbles.

• Whisked cakes go stale quickly, but they do freeze well, unfilled, for up to 1 month.

Melting

Dense cakes such as gingerbread are made by the melting method, where the fat and sugar are melted together before adding the eggs and flour. It's a very easy method, and often a whole cake can be mixed up in a saucepan.

Tips for success:

• Let the melted mix cool before the eggs are added, or they'll cook.

• Work fast once you add the dry ingredients to the wet, and don't hesitate to get it into the oven.

• Heavy, moist cakes will keep, well wrapped, in an airtight tin for a week or longer, and will improve in flavour as they mature.

Rubbing in

These cakes start life much like pastry – the fat is kept cold and hard for rubbing into the dry ingredients, then the whole lot is brought together with liquid. Scones are a good example of this method.

Tips for success:

• Always make sure the fat is cold before use.

• Work the wet ingredients into the dry quickly and evenly, to avoid any overly wet or dry patches.

• Don't overwork the mix, as it will become tough…

•…and don't roll it too thin.

• When stamping out scones, flour the cutter first to prevent it sticking.

MUFFINS

Muffins are quick to make and should be light and moist – but there are few golden rules to follow for success:

• Mix all the wet ingredients together first, then stir them into the dry.

• Fold in any chunky ingredients at the end.

• Don't over-mix.

The best muffins are naturally quite squidgy in texture, so don't be fooled into overcooking them. They're done when risen and just golden. If you can resist eating them as soon as they've cooled, keep them in an airtight container for up to two days, or frozen for up to 1 month.

   More and more sponge-type cakes are made by a muffin method these days. Melted butter (or oil) is beaten with eggs and buttermilk or yogurt. This mix is then stirred into the flour and sugar. The resulting cake is tender and moist.

BISCUITS

Chewy, crisp, crumbly, spicy or plain – there's a biscuit for everyone. Kids especially love cooking biscuits and cookies, as they are almost instant – mixed in minutes, baked in minutes and ready to eat not long after.

Tips for success:

• Depending on your oven, you may need to swap sheets of biscuits around as they cook. Biscuits nearer the top of a conventional oven will brown more quickly than those on the sheet below.

• Much like good pastry, a good biscuit dough is not overworked. Over-kneading, mixing or processing the dough will lead to a tough crumb, so work quickly and deftly. Try not to re-roll off-cuts more than once.

• Many biscuits spread significantly as they cook – so be sure to allow plenty of room around each blob of dough.

• Always let biscuits cool before you lift them from the

baking sheet, as they need this time to firm up. Then cool them on a rack.

- Always err on the side of caution with baking times. Biscuits have a high sugar content so when they burn, they burn fast!
- Biscuit dough can be chilled and used later, or frozen. To do this, wrap the dough in cling film or greaseproof paper in a sausage-shape, then wrap well and freeze for up to a month. When the biscuit urge hits, the dough can be sliced off and baked. Most homemade biscuits will last for a few days in an airtight container.

BAKING INGREDIENTS

Flour

Most cakes are made with self-raising flour, which is finely ground wheat flour that has had baking powder added to help the cake to rise. Wholemeal flour can add a nice nuttiness to cakes and bakes, but don't substitute brown for white completely – the result will be heavy and dry. Sifting flour isn't always essential these days, but doing so can help to aerate your mix and, of course, remove lumps.

If you find that you have run out of self-raising flour, use 4 teaspoons of baking powder to every 250g/9oz plain flour.

Special gluten-free flours, polenta and ground almonds can all be used in place of flour for gluten-free baking. Polenta and ground almonds in particular make deliciously moist cakes – such as the Orange and almond cake on page 321.

Bicarbonate of soda

This is a raising agent used mainly in fluffy pancakes, biscuits and some cakes. It is an alkali, which, when it meets an acidic ingredient such as buttermilk or lemon juice (or perhaps, surprisingly, honey and golden syrup) froths to produce bubbles of carbon dioxide, which in turn rise the cake. Too much bicarb can give a cake a slightly soapy flavour, though.

Baking powder

This powder is a mix of cream of tartar and bicarbonate of soda. The cream of tartar provides the acidic element here. There's normally some kind of filler, too, such as cornflour to keep the active ingredients dry.

Eggs

Use large eggs in all of the recipes in this chapter, unless specified. (There's more information about eggs on page 31.) Even when baking, it's worth buying the best eggs you can, for flavour as well as for ethical reasons.

It's very important that your eggs are not cold when making cakes; cold eggs can cause the fat in the recipe to solidify and make the mix curdle. If you're in a rush and the eggs are cold, pop them into a bowl of warm water for a few minutes.

Butter and oils

Choose unsalted or slightly salted butter when you bake, and add a pinch of salt to the ingredients. Salted butter can be too salty and skew the flavour of the recipe. We tend not to use margarines at *Good Food*, however, you can easily substitute butter for full-fat baking margarine (not low-fat spreads), if you like.

Most cakes are better made with butter that's soft. If you soften the butter in a microwave, set the oven to defrost and check it every few seconds, but be careful, as melted butter will not cream properly.

Some cakes are made with flavourless sunflower oil, vegetable or corn oil, or, in the case of some Italian cakes, olive oil. This gives a very moist and tender result, with a lower saturated fat content, of course.

Sugars for baking

Choose unrefined sugars whenever possible, or suitable. The name unrefined is a little misleading, as all sugar undergoes a certain amount of processing to extract the sucrose from the raw cane or beet, to remove impurities, and to form crystals. The difference lies in the extent of processing. Refined sugar undergoes further processing until it is pure sucrose; in many cases cane molasses is added back to white sugar, turning it brown. Unrefined sugars contain their own molasses, have much more depth of flavour, and are identical to refined sugars in lightness and texture when used in baking.

Golden caster This sugar has a delicate buttery taste and is ideal for all cakes (particularly sponges), meringues, biscuits and shortbreads.

Golden icing With its light, fudgy flavour and honey colour, this is perfect for all buttercreams and frostings, for sweet pastries, and for dusting over bakes and desserts. There are, of course, times when white sugar is what you need, for example, pure white meringues or white royal icing. Golden icing sugar can sometimes be a more granular than the white version.

Light muscovado A useful sugar, packed full of natural butterscotch flavour, which makes it ideal for making toffee and caramel sauces, cakes (particularly light fruit or carrot cakes), cookies and cinnamon rolls.

Dark muscovado With its sticky texture and deep toffee flavour, this is the one for gingerbreads, rich fruit cakes, parkins and truly squidgy brownies.

Demerara With its lovely crunchy texture, unrefined demerara is ideal in crumbles and streusel cake toppings.

Molasses sugar The richest and darkest of all. The glorious treacly taste of molasses sugar is perfect for mincemeat, wedding and Christmas cakes, dark gingerbreads and parkin.

BAKING TINS

Loose-bottomed tins are the most useful for all-round baking, as they allow you to remove your bakes more easily. The easiest way to remove a cake from a loose-bottomed round tin (or a tart from a loose-bottomed tart tin) is to stand the cake on a straight-sided object that's narrower than the base of the tin and taller than the sides (a can is ideal). Gently push the tin downwards, leaving the cake on its base. Runny cake mixtures will find their way out of loose-bottomed tins unless you've lined properly, so do be careful.

Springform tins have a spring-clip that holds the sides and the base tightly together. A 23cm round springform tin is very handy for very delicate cakes that might be served as desserts and is really useful for cheesecakes too.

Lining tins

We like to use baking parchment, which has a non-stick silicone coating. If you choose to use greaseproof paper, make sure that it is well buttered.

To line the base of a **round tin**, first rub a little butter around the inside of the tin. To line the base, draw an outline around the outside of the tin, then cut just within the line. Sit the disc of paper in the tin and you're done.

To line the side and the base of a round tin, cut a strip of baking parchment or greaseproof paper 5cm/2in deeper than your tin and long enough to wrap around it with a slight overlap. Make a 3cm/1in crease along one edge, then snip up to the crease at regular intervals to make a fringe (photo 1). Now cut a circle of paper to fit the base of the tin, as above, and grease it. Grease the tin, fit the strip of paper round the sides of the tin with the fringed edge flat on the base (photo 2). Top with the circle of paper, buttered-side down. If the recipe states to double-line the tin, then follow the above instructions, using a double thickness of parchment.

For a **square tin**, either simply butter then line the base with a square of parchment, or cut four strips about 5cm/2in deeper than the tin. As with the round tin, make a 3cm/1in crease along one edge, then snip at regular intervals to make a fringe. Grease the tin, fit the strip of parchment around the sides of the tin with the fringed edge flat on the base. Top with a square of paper.

For a **loaf tin**, butter all around the inside then cut a strip of paper that is long enough to line the tin along the base and up the two smaller sides (photo 3). To line the complete tin, cut another sheet – this time wide enough to cover the longer sides and base – and lay it over the top of the first piece of paper (photo 4).

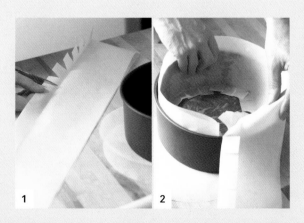

For a **baking sheet**, **Swiss roll or roasting tin**, lightly butter the inside of the tin. Cut a rectangle of parchment that is about 7cm/3in wider and longer than the tin. Press the paper into the tin, cut a slit at each corner, then fold the paper over neatly.

If you find yourself in an emergency no baking parchment situation, then it is possible to make your own 'non-stick' lining. Brush all around the inside of the tin with melted butter, then spoon in 1 tbsp flour (not from the recipe quantities), or cocoa if it is a chocolate cake. Tip the flour or cocoa around the pan until all of the butter is coated, then tap out the excess.

Tin sizes

A 20cm/8in square tin will have a bigger volume than a 20cm/8in round tin, and vice versa. If you want to use a round tin instead of a square, choose one that is 2.5cm/1in bigger in diameter. If choosing a square tin in place of a round one, choose one that is 2.5cm/1in smaller in diameter. We don't recommend that cake recipes are scaled up and down.

Loaf tin sizes can be confusing. We refer to most larger tins as 900g loaf tins, which in old money is 2lb (this originates from the amount of raw bread dough that would fit into this size tin). These tins measure about 20cm by 10cm when measured across the top. We like loaf tins with slightly-sloping sides which are wider at the top than the bottom. Straight-sided tins can be just too big in volume for some recipes, giving thinner, flatter loaf cakes.

IS IT READY?

A cake is ready when it has turned golden all over, shrunk away from the sides, and feels firm but springy in the middle. If it looks at all wobbly as you start to pull it from the oven, then stop and slide it back; it isn't ready.

Test the middle by poking in a skewer or cocktail stick. If it comes out coated with wet cake mix, return to the oven for 5 minutes then test again. If there are a few damp crumbs or if it comes out clean, then it's done.

Traybakes should be golden and set or risen in the middle, biscuits should be dry-looking, golden and smelling biscuity, and scones should be puffed up and a good golden colour on the top and the base.

Once your cake or bake is ready, allow it to settle in the tin or on the baking sheet for a few minutes before removing to a cooling rack (or let it cool completely in the case of some traybakes). Cakes that are to be iced need to be completely cold first.

FREQUENTLY ASKED QUESTIONS

Q My sponge cakes are dry

A When making a sponge, the mix should always be 'soft dropping consistency', which means that it will drop from a spoon rather than stick to it stubbornly. A dry cake mix will make a dry cake that won't rise well – add 1 tbsp milk if the mix is not quite soft enough.

Q My cakes always seem to sink in the middle

A Sinking cakes are normally down to the temperature in the oven being too low, or the oven door being opened too early. Although it's tempting, try not to peep at your cake for at least three-quarters of the cooking time. By this point the mix should be set just enough to cope with the change in air temperature. Melting method cakes, such as ginger cake, are particularly vulnerable.

Q Why has my cake domed up and cracked?

A Your tin is too small, or the oven too hot. Check it with a thermometer and make sure that you're not cooking on too high a shelf.

Q Whenever I cream butter and sugar then add beaten egg, it curdles

A Always use room temperature eggs. Add the egg little by little (about a tbsp at a time), and beat it in completely before adding the next amount. If you see that the mix is starting to look slippery or lumpy rather than creamy and light, add 1 tsp of the flour to stabilize things.

Q My cakes brown on top before the middle is cooked

A Have you checked your oven temperature and shelf position? Cover the browned cake loosely with a sheet of parchment or foil and carry on cooking. But don't open the oven too soon (see point 2). Be sure to level the top of the mix, either by tipping the tin from side to side (in the case of very delicate whisked sponges), or with the back of a spoon. Shaping a dimple in the top of a heavy fruit cake mix will prevent the top from peaking.

Classic Victoria sandwich

Sandwiched with a simple buttercream and jam, this is the perfect party cake, afternoon-tea cake or any-excuse cake. It takes only 5 minutes to mix and it will rise every time.

**CUTS INTO 10 • PREP 15 MINS, PLUS COOLING
COOK 20 MINS**
V ❄ **BASES ONLY**

FOR THE CAKE
200g/7oz softened butter, plus extra for greasing
200g/7oz caster sugar
4 eggs, beaten
200g/7oz self-raising flour
1 tsp baking powder
2 tbsp milk
FOR THE FILLING
100g/4oz butter, softened
140g/5oz icing sugar, sifted
drop vanilla extract (optional)
340g jar good-quality strawberry jam
icing sugar, to decorate

1 Heat oven to 190C/170C fan/gas 5. Butter 2 x 20cm sandwich tins and line with non-stick baking parchment. In a large bowl, beat all the cake ingredients together until you have a smooth, soft batter.
2 Divide the mixture between the tins, smooth the surface with a spatula or the back of a spoon, then bake for about 20 minutes until golden and the cake springs back when pressed. Turn out onto a cooling rack and leave to cool completely.
3 To make the filling, beat the butter until smooth and creamy, then gradually beat in the icing sugar. Beat in the vanilla extract, if you're using it. Spread the buttercream over the bottom of one of the sponges, top it with jam and sandwich the second sponge on top. Dust with a little icing sugar before serving. Keep in an airtight container and eat within 2 days.

PER SERVING 558 kcals, carbs 76g, fat 28g, sat fat 17g, salt 0.9g

try this...

Simply use the classic Victoria sandwich recipe as a base to make all these delicious cakes. All cake bases freeze well for 3 months.

Sticky toffee banoffee
Add 1 tsp vanilla extract to the mix along with 2 mashed ripe bananas. Whip 300ml/11fl oz double cream and fold through 4 tbsp banoffee toffee from a jar (or thick toffee sauce). To serve, spread half of the cream over one of the cakes, then top with another sliced banana. Sandwich together, cover with more cream, then decorate the cake with an elegant drizzle of toffee.

Pistachio praline and vanilla
Replace 50g/2oz flour with 100g/4oz pistachios blitzed in a food processor until very fine. Add 150g/5oz self-raising flour and 200g/7oz golden caster sugar to the nuts and blitz until completely combined. Add eggs, baking powder and milk as before and mix together. Instead of buttercream icing, simply mix 200g/7oz pot full-fat soft cheese with 100g/4oz caster sugar and a few drops of vanilla essence. Sandwich the sponges with the filling. For the topping, stir 2 tbsp water with 100g/4oz caster

sugar in a microwaveable bowl and microwave on High for 3–4 minutes, until bubbling and starting to caramelise. Stir in a handful roughly chopped pistachios then quickly spoon onto the cake.

Spotty blueberry and clotted cream
Make the basic sponge and fold 150g/5oz blueberries through the batter before baking. Instead of buttercream, stir 50g/2oz caster sugar into a 227g pot clotted cream for a simple filling. Sandwich the sponges with 4 tbsp blueberry conserve and a third of the clotted cream filling. Top with remaining cream and some blueberries.

Boozy coffee and walnut
Toast 15 walnut halves in the oven for 10 minutes. Reserve 10 and chop the rest. Dissolve 2 heaped tbsp instant coffee in 1 tbsp boiling water, cool, and add to the basic cake mix instead of the milk. For the filling, beat 500g tub mascarpone with 85g/3½oz light muscovado sugar and 4 tbsp Tia Maria until smooth. Sandwich the cooled cakes with a third of the filling and the chopped nuts. Decorate the top and sides of the cake with the rest of the icing and the remaining toasted walnut halves.

Chocolate marble cake

Making a marble cake is sure to bring the memories flooding back. To add a few pink swirls, split the mix into three and add a little pink colouring to one batch.

SERVES 8 • PREP 15 MINS, PLUS COOLING
COOK 45 MINS
V ❄

225g/8oz butter, softened, plus extra for greasing
225g/8oz caster sugar
4 eggs
225g/8oz self-raising flour
3 tbsp milk
1 tsp vanilla extract
2 tbsp cocoa powder

1 Heat oven to 180C/160C fan/gas 4. Grease and line a deep round 20cm tin. Beat the butter and sugar together, then gradually beat in the eggs, mixing well after each addition. Fold through the flour, milk and vanilla extract until the mixture is smooth.
2 Divide the mixture between 2 bowls. Stir the cocoa powder into the mixture in one of the bowls. Dollop the chocolate and vanilla cake mixes into the tin alternately. When all the mixture has been used up, gently tap the bottom to remove any air bubbles. Take a skewer and swirl it around the mixture in the tin a few times to create a marbled effect.
3 Bake the cake for 45–55 minutes until a skewer inserted into the centre comes out clean. Turn out onto a cooling rack and leave to cool.

PER SERVING 468 kcals, carbs 52g, fat 27g, sat fat 16g, salt 0.81g

Date, banana and rum loaf

 This fruity, crumbly loaf has loads of flavour but no added fat or sugar – ideal if you're watching your waistline.

CUTS INTO 10 SLICES • PREP 15 MINS, PLUS COOLING
COOK 1 HOUR
V ❄

oil, for greasing
250g pack stoned, ready-to-eat dates
2 small or 1 large banana (140g/5oz weight in total)
100g/4oz pecans, 85g roughly chopped, rest left whole
200g/7oz raisins
200g/7oz sultanas
100g/4oz fine polenta
2 tsp mixed spice
2 tsp baking powder
3 tbsp dark rum
2 egg whites
a few banana chips and 1 tsp sugar (optional),
    to decorate

1 Heat oven to 180C/160C fan/gas 4. Line a 900g loaf tin with non-stick baking parchment, using a little oil to make it stick. Put the dates into a small pan with 200ml boiling water and simmer for 5 minutes. Drain the liquid into a jug, then put the dates into a food processor. Add the bananas and 100ml of the date liquid and whizz until smooth. Mix the nuts, dried fruit, polenta, spice and baking powder in a bowl, then add the date purée and rum, and stir until combined.
2 Whisk the egg whites to soft peaks and fold into the cake mix. Tip into the tin (it will be quite full), then top with the remaining pecans and the banana chips and sugar, if using. Bake for 1 hour until golden and crusty and a skewer inserted in the centre comes out clean. Cool completely before cutting into slices.

PER SERVING 310 kcals, carbs 57g, fat 8g, sat fat 1g, salt 0.39g

Cherry Bakewell cake

If you know someone who likes Bakewell tart or Bakewell slices, then they will just love this cake – it's full of almond flavour and sandwiched with cherry jam.

**SERVES 8 • PREP 15 MINS, PLUS COOLING
COOK 30 MINS**
V ❄ **BASES ONLY**

FOR THE CAKE
200g/7oz butter, well softened, plus extra for greasing
200g/7oz golden caster sugar
100g/4oz ground almonds
100g/4oz self-raising flour
1 tsp baking powder
½ tsp almond extract or essence
4 large eggs

FOR THE FILLING AND TOP
½ x 340g jar morello cherry conserve
175g/6oz icing sugar
5–6 tsp water or lemon juice
1 tbsp ready-toasted, flaked almonds

1 Heat oven to 180C/160C fan/gas 4 and make sure there's a shelf ready in the middle. Butter and line the bases of 2 x 20cm round sandwich tins with baking parchment.
2 Beat together all the cake ingredients with a pinch of salt until smooth, then spoon into the tins and level the tops. Bake for 30 minutes or until golden and springy.
3 Cool the sponges in their tins for 10 minutes, then turn out onto a wire rack to cool completely. Make sure the top of one of the cakes is facing up as you'll want a smooth surface for the icing later on.
4 When cool, put one sponge on a serving plate, then spread with jam. Sandwich the second sponge on top. Sieve the icing sugar into a large bowl. Add the water or lemon juice, then stir until smooth and thick. Spread evenly over the top and let it dribble over the sides. Scatter with the nuts and leave to set for a few minutes before cutting.

PER SERVING 600 kcals, carbs 75g, fat 32g, sat fat 15g, salt 0.83g

Porter cake

A lovely old-fashioned fruit cake that gets even better if left undisturbed in the cake tin for a couple of days.

**CUTS INTO 12 SLICES • PREP 30 MINS PLUS COOLING
COOK 1¼ TO 1½ HRS**
V ❄

175g/6oz butter, plus extra for greasing
450g/1lb mixed dried fruit
zest and juice 1 orange
175g/6oz light muscovado sugar
200ml/7fl oz porter
1 tsp bicarbonate of soda
3 eggs, beaten
300g/11oz plain flour
2 tsp mixed spice

FOR THE TOPPING
2 tbsp flaked almonds
2 tbsp demerara sugar

1 Heat oven to 150C/130C fan/gas 2. Butter and line the base of a deep 20cm round cake tin. Put the butter, dried fruit, orange zest and juice, sugar and porter in a large pan. Bring slowly to the boil, stirring until the butter has dissolved, then simmer for 15 minutes.
2 Cool for 10 minutes, then stir in the bicarbonate of soda. The mixture will foam up, but don't worry, this is normal.
3 Stir the eggs into the pan, then sift in the flour and spice, then mix well. Pour into the prepared tin, smooth the top with the back of a spoon and sprinkle with the flaked almonds and demerara sugar. Bake for 1¼–1½ hours. Cool in the tin for 15 minutes, then turn out and cool on a wire rack.

PER SERVING 404 kcals, carbs 63.5g, fat 15.5g, sat fat 8.4g, salt 0.54g

Cappuccino cake

If you've offered to bake a treat for a stall or your local coffee morning, this version of a cake-stall classic will be just the thing.

**CUTS INTO 12 SLICES • PREP 15 MINS, PLUS COOLING
COOK 25–30 MINS**
V ❄ **BASES ONLY**

250g pack butter, softened, plus extra for greasing
250g/9oz light soft brown sugar, plus 2–3 tbsp
300g/11oz self-raising flour
4 eggs, beaten
50g/2oz walnuts, toasted and finely chopped (optional)
200ml/7fl oz very strong coffee (made fresh or with
    instant), cooled
FOR THE FROSTING
500g tub mascarpone
2 tbsp light soft brown sugar
cocoa powder or drinking chocolate, to decorate

1 Heat oven to 180C/160C fan/gas 4. Butter 2 x 20cm sandwich tins and line the bottoms with greaseproof paper. Beat the butter and sugar together until pale. Add the flour and eggs and keep beating until evenly mixed. Fold in the walnuts (if using) and half of the coffee. Spoon into the prepared tins and bake for 25–30 minutes or until golden and well risen.
2 Leave in the tins for 5 minutes before turning out onto a cooling rack. Sweeten the remaining coffee with the extra sugar and sprinkle 4 tbsp over the sponges. Leave to cool completely.
3 For the frosting, beat the mascarpone, sugar and remaining coffee until smooth and creamy. Use about half of the frosting to sandwich the sponges together then spread the rest over the top of the cake. Decorate with a dusting of cocoa powder or drinking chocolate.

PER SERVING 559 kcals, carbs 48g, fat 39g, sat fat 23g, salt 0.72g

Cinnamon and hazelnut cake

So simple – just chuck the ingredients into a bowl, give it a quick beat and it's ready to bake.

**SERVES 12 • PREP 20 MINS, PLUS COOLING
COOK ABOUT 1 HOUR**
V ❄

175g/6oz butter, softened, plus extra for greasing
175g/6oz golden caster sugar
3 eggs
200g/7oz self-raising flour
1 tsp baking powder
2 tsp ground cinnamon
4 tbsp milk
4 rounded tbsp chocolate hazelnut spread
50g/2oz hazelnuts, roughly chopped

1 Heat oven to 180C/160C fan/gas 4. Butter and line the base of a deep 20cm round cake tin. Put the butter, sugar, eggs, flour, baking powder, cinnamon and milk into a bowl. Beat until light and fluffy.
2 Tip three-quarters of the mixture into the tin, spread it level, then spoon the hazelnut spread on in four blobs. Top with the remaining mixture, swirl a few times with a skewer, then smooth.
3 Sprinkle with the nuts. Bake for 1 hour to 1 hour 10 minutes until risen, nicely browned, feels firm to the touch and springs back when lightly pressed (cover with foil if it starts to brown too quickly). Cool in the tin for 10 minutes, then turn out, peel off the paper and cool on a wire rack.

PER SERVING 320 kcals, carbs 34g, fat 19g, sat fat 8g, salt 0.63g

Gluten-free lemon drizzle cake

It can be hard to find special gluten-free ingredients, so this cake uses a cheap and starchy staple that almost everyone has knocking about in the kitchen... potatoes.

**SERVES 8–10 • PREP 30 MINS, PLUS COOLING
COOK 40 MINS**
V

200g/7oz butter, softened, plus extra for greasing
200g/7oz golden caster sugar
4 eggs
175g/6oz ground almonds
250g/9oz mashed potatoes
zest 3 lemons
2 tsp gluten-free baking powder
FOR THE DRIZZLE
4 tbsp granulated sugar
juice 1 lemon

1 Heat oven to 180C/160C fan/gas 4. Butter and line a deep, 20cm round cake tin. Beat the sugar and butter together until light and fluffy, then gradually add the eggs, beating after each addition. Fold in the almonds, cold mashed potato, lemon zest and baking powder.
2 Tip the mixture into the tin, level the top, then bake for 40–45 minutes or until golden and a skewer inserted into the middle of the cake comes out clean. Turn out onto a wire rack after 10 minutes cooling. Mix the granulated sugar and the lemon juice together, then spoon over the top of the cake, letting it drip down the sides. Let the cake cool completely before slicing.

PER SERVING 514 kcals, carbs 41g, fat 36g, sat fat 2g, salt 0.88g

Rhubarb and custard cake

That great British combo come together in a moist, tasty cake that's perfect for tea, or served warm for dessert.

**SERVES 16 • PREP 20 MINS, PLUS RHUBARB COOKING
AND COOLING • COOK 55 MINS-1 HOUR**
V

400g/14oz rhubarb
50g/2oz golden caster sugar
250g pack butter, softened, plus extra for greasing
150g pot ready-made custard (not the chilled kind)
250g/9oz self-raising flour
½ tsp baking powder
4 large eggs
1 tsp vanilla extract
250g/9oz golden caster sugar
icing sugar, for dusting

1 Heat oven to 200C/180C fan/gas 6. Rinse the rhubarb and shake off excess water. Trim then cut the rhubarb into little-finger-size pieces. Put in a shallow dish or a baking sheet, tip over the sugar, toss together, then arrange in a single layer. Cover with foil, roast for 15 minutes then uncover and roast for 5 minutes more or until tender and syrupy. Drain off the juices and leave to cool.
2 Butter and line a 23cm loose-bottomed or springform cake tin. Heat oven to 180C/160C fan/gas 4. Reserve 3 tbsp custard in a bowl. Beat the rest with the butter, flour, baking powder, eggs, vanilla and caster sugar until creamy and smooth.
3 Spoon one-third of the mix into the tin, add some of the rhubarb, dot with one-third more cake mix and spread it out. Top with more rhubarb, then spoon over the remaining cake mix. Scatter over the last of the rhubarb then dot with the 3 tbsp custard. Bake for 40 minutes until risen and golden, then cover with foil and bake for 15–20 minutes more or until a skewer inserted into the middle comes out clean. Cool in the tin, then dredge with icing sugar when cool.

PER SERVING 278 kcals, carbs 34g, fat 15g, sat fat 9g, salt 0.50g

OPPOSITE Clockwise from top left Cappuccino cake (page 297); Cherry Bakewell cake (page 296); Classic Victoria sandwich (page 294); Chocolate marble cake (page 295); Rhubarb and custard cake; Caramel apple loaf cake (page 300).

Bitter orange and poppy seed cake

An easy Middle Eastern-style cake that uses a very British ingredient.

CUTS INTO 8 SLICES • PREP 15 MINS • COOK 1 HOUR
V ❄ WITHOUT TOPPING

175g/6oz butter, softened, plus extra for greasing

3 tbsp good-quality thick-cut marmalade

150g pot natural bio-yogurt

3 eggs

175g/6oz golden caster sugar

200g/7oz self-raising flour

½ tsp baking powder

zest 1 orange

2 tsp poppy seeds, toasted

FOR THE STICKY TOPPING

juice ½ orange

5 tbsp good-quality thick-cut marmalade

1 Heat oven to 160C/140C fan/gas 3. Butter a 900g loaf tin then line the base with baking parchment. Melt the marmalade gently in a pan over a medium heat, remove from the heat, beat in the yogurt and let it cool.

2 Beat together the remaining cake ingredients until smooth. Quickly beat in the yogurt mix, then pour the batter into the tin. Leave it mounded in the middle to help it rise in the middle.

3 Bake for 1 hour to 1 hour 10 minutes until golden and a skewer inserted comes out clean. If the cake has taken on a lot of colour after 45 minutes, loosely cover with baking parchment. Meanwhile, melt the orange juice and marmalade together. When the cake is ready, cool in the tin for 10 minutes, then turn out onto a wire rack. Once the cake is just warm, spoon the glaze over.

PER SERVING 422 kcals, carbs 54g, fat 21g, sat fat 12g, salt 0.80g

Caramel apple loaf cake

A moist cake topped with a sticky, crunchy topping that will keep you coming back for more.

CUTS INTO 8–10 SLICES • PREP 20 MINS, PLUS COOLING
COOK 1½ HOURS
V ❄ BEFORE DECORATING

175g/6oz soft butter, plus extra for greasing

175g/6oz golden caster sugar

1 tsp vanilla extract

2 eggs

225g/8oz self-raising flour

½ tsp cinnamon

4 rounded tbsp Greek yogurt

2 eating apples, peeled, cored and chopped small

50g/2oz walnuts, very roughly chopped, plus 1 tbsp extra, chopped

50g/2oz soft toffees

2 tbsp double cream

1 Heat oven to 160C/140C fan/gas 3. Grease a 900g loaf tin and line the base and ends with a long strip of baking parchment. Beat together the butter, sugar and vanilla until pale, then gradually beat in the eggs. Tip in the flour, cinnamon and yogurt. Add the apples then mix everything together with a wooden spoon.

2 Scrape into the tin, smooth the top and scatter the 50g walnuts down the middle. Bake on a middle shelf for 1 hour 20–30 minutes until a skewer poked in comes out clean. Cool in the tin.

3 To decorate, put the toffees in a small saucepan with the double cream. Gently heat, stirring, until the toffees have melted into a smooth caramel sauce. Cool for about 1 minute while you gently turn out the cake. Slowly drizzle the toffee sauce over the top of the cake. Scatter immediately with the extra walnuts – they should stick where they hit toffee. Leave for 10 minutes before serving. (Best fresh but will keep in an airtight tin for 3–4 days.)

PER SERVING 490 kcals, carbs 53g, fat 29g, sat fat 15g, salt 0.64g

Orange and white chocolate sponge

This cake is a total crowd-pleaser – moist, chocolatey and totally indulgent.

**CUTS INTO 10 SLICES • PREP 30 MINS, PLUS COOLING
COOK 40 MINS**
V ❄ **BASES ONLY**

175g/6oz butter, softened, plus extra for greasing
175g/6oz golden caster sugar
zest 4 oranges and juice of 1
4 eggs, separated
100g/4oz self-raising flour
1 tsp baking powder
100g/4oz ground almonds
FOR THE ICING
200g/7oz white chocolate
200ml tub crème fraîche
chocolate curls, to serve (optional)

1 Heat oven to 180C/160C fan/gas 4. Butter and line two 20cm sandwich tins. Beat the sugar, butter and orange zest until pale and fluffy, then beat in the egg yolks. Sift in the flour and baking powder then fold in lightly. Finally, fold in the almonds and orange juice.
2 In a separate bowl, whisk the egg whites until they just hold their shape. Fold into the batter in three lots, taking care not to over-mix.
3 Divide the mix between the tins and bake for 30–35 minutes. Cool in the tin for 5 minutes, then cool completely on a rack.
4 For the icing, melt the chocolate over a pan of barely simmering water, then leave to cool. Whip the crème fraîche until thick, then fold in the white chocolate. Sandwich and top the cake with the icing then set in the fridge for at least 1 hour. Top with chocolate curls, if using.

PER SERVING 567 kcals, carbs 45g, fat 40g, sat fat 21g, salt 0.7g

Banana cake with nutty crumble crunch

Don't waste overripe bananas – make a delicious banana cake instead, perfect with a cup of tea.

**SERVES 10 • PREP 20 MINS, PLUS COOLING
COOK 1 HOUR**
V

250g/9oz golden caster sugar
250g/9oz self-raising flour
140g/5oz pecans, walnuts or hazelnuts, roughly chopped
1 tbsp butter, chopped
2 eggs, beaten, plus 2 egg whites
3 large ripe bananas, or 4 small, mashed
150ml/¼ pint sunflower oil
100ml/3½fl oz milk
1 tsp cinnamon
1 tsp baking powder

1 Heat oven to 180C/160C fan/gas 4, and line the base and sides of a deep round 20cm cake tin with baking parchment. Stir together 2 tbsp each of the sugar, flour and nuts, then add the butter and rub into sticky crumbs.
2 Whisk the egg whites until just stiff. In a separate bowl, mix the whole eggs with the bananas, oil and milk. In a large bowl, mix the remaining sugar, flour, pecans, cinnamon and baking powder. Tip the banana mix into the dry ingredients and quickly stir. Fold in the egg whites then pour the mixture into the tin.
3 Scatter over the crumb topping and bake for 1 hour, until a skewer inserted in the middle comes out clean. Check with 15 minutes to go; if the surface is browning too quickly, cover with another piece of paper.
4 Leave in the tin for 5 minutes, then turn out to cool on a wire rack.

PER SLICE 476 kcals, carbs 56.2g, fat 26.6g, sat fat 3.9g, salt 0.5g

Triple ginger and spice cake

If you're looking for a slice with spice, try this deliciously moist ginger cake. If you can resist cutting it, the cake is best eaten a day or two after baking, when it gets even stickier.

MAKES 16 SQUARES • PREP 15 MINS, PLUS COOLING COOK 1 HOUR
V ❄ UNICED

250g pack unsalted butter, plus extra for greasing
250g/9oz dark brown muscovado sugar
250g/9oz black treacle
300ml/½ pint milk
2 eggs
100g/4oz glacé ginger from a jar, finely chopped
375g/13oz plain flour
2 tsp bicarbonate of soda
1 tsp allspice
2 tsp ground ginger
FOR THE ICING
3 tbsp ginger syrup from the jar
5 tbsp icing sugar, sifted

1 Butter and line a 23cm square baking tin (or use a shallow roasting tin, approx 30 x 20cm). Heat oven to 160C/140C fan/gas 3. Gently melt together the butter, sugar and treacle in a pan. Take off the heat then stir in the milk. Beat in the eggs.
2 Mix the chopped ginger and dry ingredients in a large bowl and make a well in the centre. Pour in the melted mix then stir to a smooth batter. Pour into the tin, then bake for 1 hour until risen and firm and a skewer inserted in the centre comes out clean. Resist taking a peek beforehand as this cake can easily sink. Cool in the tin, then ice, or wrap well and keep in a cool, dry place for up to a week.
3 Stir together the syrup and icing sugar to make the icing and drizzle it over. Cut into squares.

PER SLICE 360 kcals, carbs 57g, fat 14g, sat fat 9g, salt 0.81g

Frosted courgette and lemon cake

Courgettes, much like carrots, make fantastically moist cakes. This is a great way to use up a glut from the garden.

CUTS INTO 12 SLICES • PREP 20 MINS, PLUS COOLING COOK 25 MINS
V ❄ DRIZZLED BASES ONLY

3 unwaxed lemons
250g pack unsalted butter, very soft, plus extra for greasing
200g/7oz golden caster sugar
3 eggs
2 medium courgettes, coarsely grated (you'll need 300g/11oz flesh)
1 tsp poppy seeds, plus extra to decorate
1 tsp vanilla extract
100g/4oz self-raising flour
100g/4oz plain wholemeal flour
1 tsp baking powder
85g/3oz icing sugar
200g pack full-fat soft cheese
4 tbsp lemon curd (optional)

1 Heat oven to 180C/160C fan/gas 4. Butter 2 x 20cm sandwich tins and line the bases with baking parchment. Zest 2 lemons, then squeeze their juice into a separate bowl. Put 200g butter, the caster sugar, eggs, courgettes, poppy seeds, vanilla and lemon zest into a mixing bowl. Beat to a creamy batter. Stir in 1 tbsp lemon juice, the flours, baking powder and ¼ tsp salt. Spoon into the tins, then bake for 25 minutes or until golden and springy in the middle.
2 Make a drizzle by mixing 1 tbsp lemon juice with 25g of the icing sugar. Put the remaining icing sugar and butter into a bowl, add the cheese, remaining lemon juice (about 2 tbsp) and the final lemon's zest. Beat to make a creamy, smooth frosting.
3 Cool the cakes in their tins for 15 minutes then turn out onto a wire rack. Prick several times with a cocktail stick, spoon over the drizzle then cool completely. (Can be frozen at this stage for up to 1 month.) Sandwich the cakes together with the frosting and lemon curd, if using, then top with more frosting and sprinkle with poppy seeds.

PER SLICE 375 kcals, carbs 38g, fat 23g, sat fat 14g, salt 0.68g

OPPOSITE *Frosted courgette and lemon cake.*

Whoopie pies

Rivalled to be the new cupcakes, whoopie pies are a cross between a cake and a soft cookie, sandwiched with buttercream.

MAKES 10 • PREP 30 MINS • COOK 10–15 MINS
V

300g/11oz self-raising flour
50g/2oz cocoa powder
2 tsp bicarbonate of soda
175g/6oz soft light brown sugar
1 egg
75ml/2½ fl oz sunflower oil
150ml/¼ pint buttermilk
75ml/2½ fl oz boiling water
hundreds and thousands sprinkles, to decorate
FOR THE FILLING
175g/6oz softened butter
300g/11oz icing sugar
1 tsp vanilla extract
FOR THE GLAZE
100g/4oz icing sugar, sifted
100ml/3½fl oz boiling water
100ml/3½fl oz double cream
50g/2oz cocoa, sifted

1 Heat oven to 180C/160C fan/gas 4 and line two baking sheets with baking parchment. Mix the flour, cocoa, bicarbonate of soda and sugar in a bowl with a pinch of salt. Whisk the egg, oil and buttermilk together, then mix into the dry ingredients until smooth. Stir in the boiling water until completely incorporated, then transfer to a piping bag. Pipe dollops of the mixture, about 5cm in diameter, onto the sheets. Bake for 10–15 minutes. Cool.
2 Beat the filling ingredients together until smooth. Put the glaze ingredients into a small pan and heat gently until melted and syrupy.
3 Put half of the cakes on a wire rack set over baking parchment, then spoon a little glaze over each one to cover. Scatter with some sprinkles, then leave to set.
4 To assemble, pipe or spread a little of the filling onto the bottom of the unglazed whoopie halves, then stick a decorated one on top.

PER SERVING 647 kcals, carbs 91g, fat 32g, sat fat 15g, salt 1.17g

Sticky chocolate drop cakes

A simple crowd-pleasing cake that will keep well. The fudgy topping is a great recipe to have up your sleeve for children's birthday cakes, too.

MAKES 15 SQUARES • PREP 10 MINS, PLUS COOLING
COOK 30 MINS
V 🞶 WITHOUT ICING

250g/9oz unsalted butter
300g/11oz golden caster sugar
1 tsp vanilla extract
3 large eggs
200g/7oz self-raising flour
50g/2oz cocoa powder
100g/4oz milk chocolate drops
FOR THE TOPPING
85g/3oz butter
85g/3oz golden caster sugar
200g/7oz light condensed milk
50g/2oz milk chocolate drops, plus extra to decorate

1 Butter and line a traybake or small roasting tin, about 20 x 30cm. Heat oven to 180C/160C fan/gas 4. Gently melt the butter in a large saucepan, cool for 5 minutes, then add the sugar, vanilla and eggs, then beat until smooth with a wooden spoon. Stir in the flour, cocoa and ¼ tsp salt. Stir in the chocolate drops then bake for 35 minutes until risen all over and a skewer comes out of the centre with a few damp crumbs.
2 For the topping, gently heat the butter and sugar together until both are melted. Stir in the condensed milk and bring to a boil. Cool for 5 minutes then stir in the chocolate drops to melt. Spread the topping over the cold cake, scatter with more chocolate drops and cut into squares.

PER SERVING 433 kcals, carbs 54g, fat 24g, sat fat 14g, salt 0.31g

Best-ever brownies

A fudgy and decadent brownie studded with extra chunks of chocolate. This recipe promises perfection with every batch.

CUTS INTO 32 TRIANGLES • **PREP 20 MINS, PLUS COOLING COOK 25 MINS**
Ⓥ ❄

185g/6½oz unsalted butter, cubed
185g/6½oz dark chocolate, broken into cubes
3 eggs
275g/9½ oz golden caster sugar
40g/1½oz cocoa powder
85g/3oz plain flour
50g/2oz white chocolate, chopped into pieces
50g/2oz milk chocolate, chopped into pieces

1 Heat oven to 180C/160C fan/gas 4, and butter and line a 20cm square cake tin with baking parchment. Put the butter and chocolate into a non-metallic bowl, cover loosely with cling film and melt in the microwave for 2 minutes on High. Stir gently, then leave to cool a little.
2 Whisk the eggs and sugar until pale and about doubled in volume. Pour the cooled chocolate mixture into the egg then very gently fold together with a spatula. Sift the cocoa and flour over, then gently fold in. Stir in the white and milk chocolate chunks. Pour into the lined cake tin and level the top.
3 Bake for 25 minutes until the top has a shiny, papery crust all over the top and the sides of the cake are just beginning to come away from the tin. Cool completely in the tin. Cut the traybake into quarters, cut each quarter into four squares, then cut across again into small triangles.

PER TRIANGLE 144 kcals, carbs 17g, fat 8g, sat fat 5g, salt 0.06g

Peach melba squares

With juicy peach and raspberry in every bite, these squares are special enough for summer afternoon tea, or served warm as dessert with a scoop of ice cream.

MAKES 12 SQUARES • **PREP 10 MINS, PLUS COOLING COOK 1 HOUR**
Ⓥ

250g pack unsalted butter, plus extra for greasing
300g/11oz golden caster sugar
1 tsp vanilla extract
3 large eggs
200g/7oz self-raising flour
50g/2oz ground almonds
2 just ripe peaches, stoned, halved, then each half cut into 3
100g/4oz raspberries
handful flaked almonds
1 tbsp icing sugar, to serve

1 Butter and line a traybake or small roasting tin, about 20 x 30cm. Heat oven to 180C/160C fan/gas 4. Gently melt the butter in a large saucepan, cool for 5 minutes, add the sugar, vanilla and eggs, then beat until smooth with a wooden spoon. Stir in the flour, almonds and ¼ tsp salt.
2 Tip the mix into the tin, then lay the peach pieces evenly on top – that way each square of cake will have a bite of fruit. Scatter the raspberries and almonds over, then bake for 1 hour to 1 hour 10 minutes, covering with foil after 40 minutes. Test with a skewer; the middle should have just a tiny hint of squidginess which will firm up once the cake cools. Cool in the tin for 20 minutes, then lift out onto a cooling rack. Once cold, dredge with icing sugar, then cut into squares.

PER SERVING 385 kcals, carbs 43g, fat 23g, sat fat 12g, salt 0.22g

Sticky lime and coconut drizzle loaf

If you like lemon drizzle, you'll love this moist, slightly tropical-tasting loaf.

CUTS INTO 10 SLICES • PREP 20 MINS • COOK 40 MINS
V ❄ WITHOUT DRIZZLE

100g/4oz butter, softened, plus extra for greasing
175g/6oz self-raising flour
1 tsp baking powder
175g/6oz golden caster sugar
2 eggs
½ x 400g can coconut milk (use the other half for the icing)
finely grated zest 2 limes (use the juice for the icing)

FOR THE ICING AND DECORATION
remaining coconut milk
200g/7oz golden caster sugar
juice and finely grated zest 1 lime

1 Heat oven to 180C/160C fan/gas 4. Butter and line a 900g loaf tin with baking parchment. Beat all of the cake ingredients together until completely combined and the mixture drops off a spoon. Tip into the loaf tin, then smooth the top. Bake for 40 minutes until golden and firm to the touch. While the loaf is cooking, make the topping.
2 For the icing, tip the remaining coconut milk and 150g of the sugar into a saucepan. Boil for 5 minutes until syrupy and you can see the bottom of the pan when you stir. Stir in the lime juice and set aside. Crush the remaining sugar with the lime zest to a damp green paste, then set aside.
3 When the loaf is cooked, leave it in the tin and pour over the icing a little at a time, waiting for the cake to absorb it before adding more. By the time all the icing is used, it will be coming up the sides of the tin. Let cool. To serve, carefully remove the loaf from the tin, sprinkle with the lime sugar and cut into slices.

PER SERVING 364 kcals, carbs 54g, fat 16g, sat fat 11g, salt 0.62g

Yummy scrummy carrot cake

One of Good Food's most popular recipes ever, this carrot cake is moist, tasty, and simplicity itself to make.

CUTS INTO 15 SLICES • PREP 15 MINS, PLUS COOLING
COOK 40–45 MINS
❄ V

175ml/6fl oz sunflower oil, plus extra for greasing
175g/6oz light muscovado sugar
3 large eggs, lightly beaten
140g/5oz grated carrot (about 3 medium)
100g/4oz raisins
grated zest 1 large orange
175g/6oz self-raising flour
1 tsp bicarbonate of soda
1 tsp ground cinnamon
½ tsp grated nutmeg (freshly grated is best)

FOR THE FROSTING
175g/6oz icing sugar
1½–2 tbsp orange juice

1 Heat oven to 180C/160C fan/gas 4. Oil and line the base and sides of an 18cm square tin with baking parchment. Tip the sugar into a large mixing bowl, pour in the oil and add the eggs. Lightly mix with a wooden spoon. Stir in the grated carrots, raisins and orange zest.
2 Mix the flour, bicarbonate of soda and spices together in a separate bowl, then sift into the carrot mixture and lightly mix all the ingredients. Pour the mixture into the prepared tin and bake for 40–45 minutes, until it feels firm and springy when you press it. Cool in the tin for 5 minutes, then turn it out, peel off the paper and cool on a wire rack. (Can be frozen at this point.)
3 Beat together the frosting ingredients in a bowl until smooth and as runny as single cream. Drizzle the icing over the cake. Leave to set, then cut into slices.

PER SERVING 265 kcals, carbs 39g, fat 12g, sat fat 2g, salt 0.41g

tip If you prefer a cream cheese frosting, use the recipe from the Courgette cake on page 302, flavouring it with orange juice and zest instead of lemon.

Moccachino slices

These luscious bites are great for coffee lovers and the all-in-one pan method means they're simple to make.

**MAKES 12 • PREP 10 MINS, PLUS COOLING
COOK 20 MINS**
❄ **UNICED**

100g/4oz butter, plus extra for greasing
225g/8oz dark muscovado sugar
2 large eggs
3 tbsp espresso coffee (or try mixing 3 tbsp boiling
    water with 1 tbsp instant coffee)
2 tsp baking powder
125g/4½oz plain flour
FOR THE TOPPING
300ml pot soured cream
280g/11oz white chocolate, broken into chunks
4 tsp caster sugar
cocoa powder, to dust

1 Heat oven to 180C/160C fan/gas 4 and butter and line the base and sides of a traybake tin (approx 30 x 23cm) with baking parchment. Melt the butter in a large pan, stir in the sugar and mix well. Take off the heat and stir in the eggs and coffee. Tip in the baking powder and flour, then mix well. Pour into the baking tin and bake for 20 minutes. Cool then turn onto a board.
2 Meanwhile, melt together the soured cream, white chocolate and sugar in a small bowl set over a pan of simmering water. Stir well, then leave to cool for 15 minutes. Spread all over the top of the cake. Shake over the cocoa powder to lightly dust, then leave to set. Cut into 12 squares and serve.

PER SERVING 372 kcals, carbs 45g, fat 20g, sat fat 12g, salt 0.51g

Plum and almond crumble slice

A cross between crumble and plum pie, these slices make an irresistible addition to the cake tin, or served warm with custard.

**CUTS INTO 16 SLICES • PREP 15 MINS, PLUS COOLING
COOK 1 HOUR 5 MINS**
Ⓥ

250g pack butter (this must be very cold), plus extra
    for greasing
225g/8oz caster sugar, plus extra to finish
300g/11oz ground almonds
140g/5oz plain flour, plus 25g/1oz for the filling
2 eggs
1 tsp cinnamon, plus extra to finish
1 tsp baking powder
about 6 plums, stoned and each cut into 6
50g/2oz flaked almonds

1 Heat oven to 180C/160C fan/gas 4. Butter and line a 20 x 30cm traybake tin. Put the butter, sugar and ground almonds into a food processor, then pulse to a very rough crumble. Spoon half into a bowl and set aside.
2 Add 140g flour to the mix in the processor and whizz until it just forms a dough. Tip into the tin, press down well and bake for 15–20 minutes until golden. Cool for 10 minutes.
3 To make the filling, tip all but a few tbsp of the crumble mix back into the mixer. Add the eggs, the 25g flour, cinnamon and baking powder and whizz to a soft batter. Spread over the base of the cake.
4 Top with plums, a little extra caster sugar and cinnamon. Bake for 20 minutes, then sprinkle with the remaining crumble and flaked almonds. Cook for another 20 minutes or until golden. Cool completely before slicing.

PER SERVING 360 kcals, carbs 26g, fat 26g, sat fat 9g, salt 0.37g

Chocolate chunk pecan cookies

You can't beat American-style cookies with big chunks of chocolate and nuts.
The perfect grown-up biscuit.

MAKES 12 • PREP 10 MINS, PLUS COOLING
COOK 12 MINS
V ❄ RAW DOUGH

200g/7oz dark chocolate, 70% cocoa solids, broken
    into squares
100g/4oz butter, chopped
50g/2oz light muscovado sugar
85g/3oz golden caster sugar
1 tsp vanilla extract
1 egg, beaten
100g/4oz whole pecans
100g/4oz plain flour
1 tsp bicarbonate of soda

1 Heat oven to 180C/160C fan/gas 4. Melt 85g chocolate in the microwave on High for 1 minute or over a pan of simmering water. Beat in the butter, sugars, vanilla and egg until smooth, then stir in three-quarters of both the nuts and remaining chocolate, then add the flour and bicarbonate of soda.

2 Heap 12 spoonfuls, spaced apart, on 2 baking sheets (don't spread the mixture), then poke in the reserved nuts and chocolate. Bake for 12 minutes until firm, then leave to cool on the sheets. (Can be stored in a tin for up to 3 days.)

PER SERVING 294 kcals, carbs 27g, fat 20 g, sat fat 8g, salt 0.44 g

Anzac biscuits

These delicious oaty biscuits were made to send to the ANZACs (Australian and New Zealand
Army Corps) serving in Gallipoli.

MAKES 20 • PREP 15 MINS • COOK 8–10 MINS
V

85g/3oz porridge oats
85g/3oz desiccated coconut
100g/4oz plain flour
100g/4oz caster sugar
100g/4oz butter, plus extra for greasing
1 tbsp golden syrup
1 tsp bicarbonate of soda

1 Heat oven to 180C/160C fan/gas 4. Put the oats, coconut, flour and sugar in a bowl. Melt the butter in a small pan and stir in the golden syrup. In a small bowl, blend the bicarbonate of soda with 2 tbsp boiling water, then stir into the golden syrup and butter mixture.

2 Make a well in the middle of the dry ingredients and pour in the butter and golden syrup mixture. Stir gently to incorporate the dry ingredients.

3 Put dessertspoonfuls of the mixture onto buttered baking sheets, about 2.5cm apart to allow room for spreading. Bake in batches for 8–10 minutes until golden. Transfer to a wire rack to cool.

PER BISCUIT 118 kcals, carbs 13g, fat 7g, sat fat 5g, salt 0.28g

Simple jammy biscuits

Kids will love to help you make these simple biscuits; you only need five storecupboard ingredients.

**MAKES 12 • PREP 15 MINS, PLUS COOLING
COOK 10–15 MINS**
V

200g/7oz self-raising flour, plus extra for dusting
100g/4oz caster sugar
100g/4oz butter
1 large egg, lightly beaten
4 tbsp strawberry jam

1 Heat oven to 190C/170C fan/gas 5. Rub the flour, sugar and butter together until the mixture resembles breadcrumbs. Alternatively, you can do this in the food processor. Add enough egg to bring the mixture together to form a stiff dough.
2 Flour your hands and shape the dough into a cylinder, about 5cm across. Cut into finger-width slices and place on a large baking sheet. Space them out as the mixture will spread while baking.
3 Make a small indentation in the middle of each biscuit with the end of a wooden spoon, then drop 1 tsp of jam in the centre. Bake for 10-15 minutes until slightly risen and just golden. Cool on a wire rack.

PER BISCUIT 170 kcals, carbs 25g, fat 8g, sat fat 5g, salt 0.3g

All-butter shortbread

Melt-in-the-mouth shortbread fingers are so simple to make – and contain just four ingredients.

**MAKES 24 SLICES • PREP 10 MINS, PLUS COOLING
COOK 20–25 MINS**
V

300g/11oz butter, softened
140g/5oz golden caster sugar, plus 4 tbsp
300g/11oz plain flour
140g/5oz rice flour

1 Place the butter and 140g sugar in a food processor and whizz until smooth. Tip in both the flours and a pinch of salt, then pulse until the mixture comes together.
2 Using your hands, roughly spread the mixture out on a 20 x 30 x 4cm baking sheet. Cover with cling film and smooth over until there are no wrinkles. Place in the fridge for at least 30 minutes.
3 Heat oven to 180C/160C fan/gas 4. Remove cling film, then lightly mark the shortbread all over with a fork. Sprinkle with the remaining sugar, then bake for 20–25 minutes. Leave to cool in the tin, then cut into 24 thin slices. (Will keep in an airtight container for up to 1 week.)

PER SLICE 188 kcals, carbs 23g, fat 11g, sat fat 7g, salt 0.2g

Basic vanilla biscuit dough

This dough makes a lightly flavoured vanilla biscuit with a lovely crumbly texture.
It's delicious as it is, but can also be transformed by adding other flavours.

**MAKES ABOUT 30 COOKIES • PREP 15 MINS, PLUS
COOLING • COOK 10–12 MINS**

V

250g/9oz unsalted butter, softened
140g/5oz caster sugar
1 egg yolk
2 tsp vanilla extract
300g/11oz plain flour

1 Heat oven to 180C/160C fan/gas 4. Mix the butter and sugar in a large bowl with a wooden spoon, then add the egg yolk and vanilla and briefly beat to combine. Sift over the flour, add a pinch salt, then stir until the mixture is well combined – you might need to get your hands in at the end to give everything a really good mix and press the dough together.

2 On a well-floured surface, or between two sheets of baking parchment, roll the dough to the thickness of a £1 coin then stamp out 7-cm rounds with a cutter. Put onto baking sheets lined with parchment then bake for 10–12 minutes until pale gold. Cool for a few minutes on the sheets then lift onto a cooling rack and cool completely.

PER COOKIE 118 kcals, carbs 13g, fat 7g, sat fat 4g, salt 0.13g

try this...

Peanut butter cookies
Makes 20 Make the Basic biscuit dough, stirring in 100g crunchy peanut butter with the egg yolk and vanilla extract. Spoon heaped tablespoons of the dough onto a baking sheet, flatten slightly and top each with a whole roasted peanut. Bake for 12–15 minutes, until the cookies are golden. Let them firm up before transferring to a cooling rack.

Cranberry and orange polka dots
Makes 30 Add 100g dried cranberries and zest 2 of oranges to the Basic biscuit dough when mixing in the flour. Roll into a thin log, wrap in cling film, then chill or freeze. To make the biscuits, slice the log into 5mm slices and bake for just 8–10 minutes.

Chocolate fudge cupcakes

These bright and fun cupcakes are perfect for kids' parties.

**MAKES 12 • PREP 30 MINS, PLUS COOLING
COOK 25–30 MINS**
V ❄ UN-ICED

200g/7oz butter
200g/7oz plain chocolate, under 70% cocoa solids is fine
200g/7oz light, muscovado sugar
2 eggs, beaten
1 tsp vanilla extract
250g/9oz self-raising flour
sweets and sprinkles, to decorate

FOR THE ICING
200g/7oz plain chocolate (as above)
100ml/3½fl oz double cream, not fridge-cold
50g/2oz icing sugar

1 Heat oven to 160C/140C fan/gas 3 and line a 12-hole muffin tin with paper cases. Gently melt the butter, chocolate, sugar and 100ml hot water together in a large saucepan, stirring occasionally, then set aside to cool a little.
2 Stir the eggs and vanilla into the chocolate mixture. Put the flour into a large mixing bowl, then stir in the chocolate mixture until smooth. Spoon or pour into cases until just over three-quarters full (you may have a little mixture leftover), then set aside for 5 minutes before putting on a low shelf in the oven and baking for 20–22 minutes. Leave to cool.
3 For the icing, melt the chocolate in a heatproof bowl over a pan of barely simmering water. Once melted, turn off the heat, stir in the double cream and sift in the icing sugar. When spreadable, top each cake with some icing and decorate with your favourite sprinkles and sweets.

PER SERVING 505 kcals, carbs 59g, fat 29g, sat fat 17g, salt 0.51g

Doughnut cupcakes

A great marriage of two sweet classics, these will disappear in no time.

**MAKES 12 • PREP 15 MINS, PLUS COOLING
COOK 25 MINS**
V

200g/7oz softened butter, plus 3 tbsp melted
200g/7oz sugar
2 eggs, plus 1 yolk
300g/11oz self-raising flour
100ml/3½fl oz milk
½ tsp baking powder
4 tbsp strawberry jam
3–4 sugar cubes, roughly crushed

1 Heat oven to 180C/160C fan/gas 4. Tip the softened butter, sugar, eggs, flour, milk and baking powder into a large bowl. Beat together just until you have a smooth soft batter.
2 Line a 12-hole muffin tin with paper cake cases. Fill the cases two-thirds full with the batter then make a small dip in the batter and spoon in 1 tsp jam. Cover with another tablespoon cake batter and repeat for remaining cupcakes. Bake in oven for 25 minutes until risen and cooked through.
3 Brush some melted butter over each cake, then sprinkle with the crushed sugar and serve. (Will keep for up to 2 days in an airtight container.)

PER SERVING 363 kcals, carbs 47g, fat 19g, sat fat 11g, salt 0.66g

Pistachio cupcakes

Chic little cupcakes, perfect for a special afternoon tea.

MAKES 12 • PREP 25 MINS, PLUS COOLING
COOK 22–25 MINS
V ❄ **UNICED**

100g/4oz pistachios
140g/5oz golden caster sugar
140g/5oz butter, very soft
2 eggs
140g/5oz self-raising flour
5 tbsp milk
edible glitter, to decorate
FOR THE ICING
250g/9oz icing sugar, sifted
mint green food colouring

1 Heat oven to 160C/140C fan/gas 3 and line a 12-hole muffin tin with paper cases. Put 85g pistachios into a food processor with about half the sugar, then whizz until very finely chopped. Tip into a large mixing bowl with the remaining sugar, butter, eggs, flour and milk and beat until smooth. Divide between the cases, then bake for 22–25 minutes until a skewer inserted in the centre comes out clean. Cool on a wire rack.
2 For the icing, stir some water, teaspoon by teaspoon, into the icing sugar to get a very thick but still runny icing. Stir in enough food colouring to give a pretty pale green colour. If any cakes poke above the top of the cases, trim with a small knife, or scoop out with a teaspoon – being very careful not to release any of the case from the sides of the cake. Put a generous spoonful of icing on each cake and let it gently spread to cover. Chop the remaining pistachios and scatter these over with a pinch of edible glitter. Leave to set, then serve.

PER SERVING 326 kcals, carbs 45g, fat 16g, sat fat 7g, salt 0.34g

Lemon and poppyseed cupcakes

Birthdays, baby showers, weddings… these cupcakes are pretty enough for any occasion, and totally scrumptious too. (See recipe photo on page 288.)

MAKES 12 EASILY DOUBLED • PREP 40 MINS, PLUS
COOLING • COOK 20–22 MINS
V ❄ **UNICED**

225g/8oz self-raising flour
175g/6oz golden caster sugar
zest 2 lemons
1 tbsp poppy seeds, toasted
3 eggs
100g/4oz natural yogurt
175g/6oz butter, melted and cooled a little
FOR THE ICING
225g/8oz butter, softened
400g/14oz icing sugar, sifted
juice 1 lemon
few drops yellow food colouring
icing flowers or yellow sprinkles, to decorate

1 Heat oven to 180C/160C fan/gas 4 and line a 12-hole muffin tin with paper cake or muffin cases. Mix the flour, sugar, lemon zest and poppy seeds together in a large mixing bowl. Beat the eggs into the yogurt, then tip this into the dry ingredients with the melted butter. Beat together until smooth, then divide between the cases. Bake for 20–22 minutes until a skewer inserted in the centre comes out clean. Cool for 5 minutes in the tin, then lift onto a cooling rack.
2 To ice, beat the softened butter until really soft in a large bowl, then gradually beat in the icing sugar and lemon juice. Add a little colouring then spoon into a piping bag with a large star nozzle. Pipe a swirl of icing onto each cake, then top with sugar decorations or scatter with sprinkles.

PER SERVING 529 kcals, carbs 66g, fat 30g, sat fat 18g, salt 0.75g

Strawberry and polenta cupcakes

Using polenta and fresh strawberries makes these little cakes especially light and fragrant.

**MAKES 12 • PREP 15 MINS, PLUS COOLING
COOK 20 MINS**
V ❄ **UNICED**

140g/5oz unsalted butter, softened
140g/5oz golden caster sugar
zest ½ lemon
85g/3oz polenta
3 eggs, beaten
140g/5oz plain flour
1 tsp baking powder
1 tbsp milk
140g/5oz strawberries, hulled and chopped

TO DECORATE
3 strawberries, hulled and roughly chopped, plus
    6 halved, for decoration
juice 1 lemon
140g/5oz icing sugar, sifted

1 Line a 12-hole muffin tin with paper cases and heat oven to 180C/160C fan/gas 4. Beat together the butter, sugar and lemon zest until pale. Beat in the polenta followed by the eggs, a little at a time.
2 Sift in the flour and baking powder, then fold in quickly with a large metal spoon. Stir in the milk, then fold in the chopped strawberries. Spoon into the cases and bake for 20 minutes or until golden and risen. Cool on a wire rack.
3 Peel the cases from the cakes. For the icing, place the chopped strawberries in a bowl with 1 tsp lemon juice and mash to a pulp. Sieve, then add the juice to the sugar to turn it pink. Stir in more lemon juice drop by drop to make a thick, but flowing icing. Dip each cake into the icing, then top with a strawberry half. Leave to set, then serve.

PER CAKE 271 kcals, carbs 40g, fat 12g, sat fat 7g, salt 0.19g

Feel-good muffins

 These muffins have the bonus of lots of health-giving ingredients, which not only give you slow-release energy but also help to lower cholesterol levels.

**MAKES 8 • PREP 10 MINS, PLUS COOLING
COOK 25 MINS**
V

175g/6oz self-raising flour
50g/2oz porridge oats
140g/5oz light muscovado sugar
2 tsp ground cinnamon
½ tsp bicarbonate of soda
1 egg, beaten
150ml/¼ pint buttermilk
1 tsp vanilla extract
6 tbsp sunflower oil
175g/6oz stoned prunes, chopped
85g/3oz pecans

1 Heat oven to 200C/180C fan/gas 6. Line 8 wells of a muffin tin with muffin cases. Put the flour, oats, sugar, cinnamon and bicarbonate of soda in a large bowl, then rub everything through your fingers, as if making pastry, to ensure the ingredients are evenly blended.
2 Beat the egg, then stir in the buttermilk, vanilla and oil. Lightly stir the egg mix into the flour. Fold the prunes and nuts into the mixture.
3 Divide between the tins, filling the cases to the brim, then bake for 20–25 minutes until risen and golden. Serve warm or cold.

PER MUFFIN 478 kcals, carbs 66g, fat 22g, sat fat 2g, salt 0.66g

Classic blueberry muffins

An easy recipe for light, fluffy blueberry muffins every time.

**MAKES 12 • PREP 10 MINS, PLUS COOLING
COOK 15–18 MINS**
❄ Ⓥ

140g/5oz caster sugar
250g/9oz self-raising flour
1 tsp bicarbonate of soda
85g/3oz butter, melted and cooled
2 large eggs, beaten
200ml/7fl oz milk
1 tsp vanilla extract
150g punnet blueberries

1 Heat oven to 200C/180C fan/gas 6. Line a 12-hole muffin tin with muffin cases. In a bowl, combine the dry ingredients. Mix the butter, eggs, milk and vanilla in a jug, pour into the flour mix then stir until just combined. Don't over-mix or the muffins will be tough. Fold in the blueberries.
2 Spoon the mix into the cases and bake for 15–18 minutes until golden and firm. Cool on a wire rack.

PER MUFFIN 194 kcals, carbs 30g, fat 7g, sat fat 4g, salt 0.68g

Triple chocolate chunk muffins

Dark, milk and white chocolate melt together to make these muffins completely irresistible.

**MAKES 11 • PREP 10 MINS, PLUS COOLING
COOK 20 MINS**
Ⓥ

85g/3oz butter, melted, plus extra for greasing
250g/9oz plain flour
25g/1oz cocoa powder
2 tsp baking powder
½ tsp bicarbonate of soda
85g/3oz each plain and white chocolate, broken
    into chunks
100g/4oz milk chocolate, broken into chunks
2 large eggs, beaten
284ml pot soured cream
85g/3oz light muscovado sugar

1 Heat oven to 200C/180C fan/gas 6. Butter 11 holes of a muffin tin. In a large bowl, combine the flour, cocoa, baking powder, bicarbonate of soda and all the chocolate. In a separate bowl, mix together the eggs, soured cream, sugar and butter.
2 Add the soured cream mixture to the flour mixture and stir until just combined and fairly stiff; don't overmix – the mixture should look quite lumpy. Spoon the mixture into the muffin tin to fill the holes generously.
3 Bake for 20 minutes until well risen. Leave in the tin for about 15 minutes as the mixture is quite soft. Remove from the tin and cool on a wire rack. Eat while still warm and the chocolate is gooey.

PER MUFFIN 325 kcals, carbs 37g, fat 18g, sat fat 11g, salt 0.72g

*OPPOSITE Clockwise from top left Chocolate fudge cupcakes
(page 311); Ultimate chocolate cake (page 318); Lemon mascarpone
roulade (page 318); Plum, hazelnut and chocolate cake (page 323);
All-butter shortbread (page 309); Classic scones (page 316)*

Classic scones

You can have a batch of scones on the table in 20 minutes with this storecupboard recipe.
Eat just warm or cold on the day of baking, generously topped with jam and clotted cream.

MAKES 8 • PREP 10 MINS, PLUS COOLING • COOK 10 MINS
V

350g/12oz self-raising flour, plus extra for dusting
1 tsp baking powder
85g/3oz butter, cut into cubes
3 tbsp golden caster sugar
175ml/6fl oz milk, warmed
1 tsp vanilla extract
squeeze lemon juice
beaten egg, to glaze

try this...

If you like your scones fruited, stir 85g plum sultanas
or chopped glacé cherries into the mix at the same
time as the sugar.

1 Heat oven to 220C/200C fan/gas 7 and put a baking sheet in the oven. Tip the flour into a large bowl with ¼ tsp salt and the baking powder, then mix. Rub in the butter until the mix looks like fine crumbs. Stir in the sugar, then make a well in the centre.
2 Mix together the milk, vanilla and lemon juice then tip into the bowl and combine quickly with a cutlery knife – it will seem quite wet. Tip the dough out onto a lightly floured surface. Dredge the dough and your hands with flour, then fold the dough over 2–3 times until it's a little smoother. Pat into a round about 4cm deep.
3 Take a plain 5cm cutter and dip it into some flour. Plunge into the dough, then repeat, cutting out four scones. Press what's left back into a round and repeat. Brush the tops with egg, then place onto the hot baking sheet. Bake for 10 minutes until risen and golden on the top.

PER SERVING 268 kcals, carbs 41g, fat 10g, sat fat 6g, salt 0.95 g

Crusted citrus scones

This is a clever twist on a traditional scone recipe. Ricotta makes them lovely and moist and
the orange zest gives a nice citrus tang.

MAKES 6 • PREP 10 MINS, PLUS COOLING
COOK 20–25 MINS
V

175g/6oz ricotta
finely grated zest 1 orange
100g/4oz golden caster sugar
200g/7oz self-raising flour, plus extra for dusting and
    sprinkling
50g/2oz butter, cubed, plus extra for greasing
1–2 tbsp milk, plus extra for brushing
1 tbsp demerara sugar
cream or butter and lemon or orange curd, to serve

1 Heat oven to 200C/180C fan/gas 6 and grease a baking sheet. Mix the ricotta, orange zest and half the sugar until combined. Sift the flour and remaining sugar into another bowl. Rub the butter into the flour mix so it looks like fine crumbs.
2 Stir the ricotta mix into the flour mix, adding a tablespoon or two of milk to get a soft, but not sticky, dough. Tip onto a floured work surface and knead very lightly a few times only – if you over-knead the scones will be tough. Roll or press the dough to a neat round about 4cm thick. Put onto the baking sheet and mark into 6 wedges.
3 Brush with milk, sprinkle with a little flour and the demerara. Bake for 20–25 minutes until well risen and brown. Transfer to a rack to cool slightly. Serve warm, with cream or butter and lemon or orange curd.

PER SCONE 299 kcals, carbs 48g, fat 11g, sat fat 6g, salt 0.39g

Cheddar and sweetcorn scones

*Savoury scones make a great meal with a bowl of soup, or a tasty addition to afternoon
tea. Simply spread with butter, or maybe top with ham or cheese and pickle.*

**MAKES 10 • PREP 15 MINS, PLUS COOLING
COOK 10–12 MINS EASY**
V

350g/12oz self-raising flour, plus extra for dusting
1 tsp baking powder
2 tsp English mustard powder
¼ tsp ground cayenne or paprika, plus extra for sprinkling
few thyme sprigs, leaves picked
50g/2oz cold unsalted butter, cut into cubes
175g/6oz mature Cheddar, grated
kernels from 2 large fresh sweetcorn cobs (or 250g
    sweetcorn kernels from a can, drained weight)
175ml/6fl oz semi-skimmed milk, plus extra for brushing
juice ½ lemon

1 Heat oven to 220C/200C fan/gas 7. Mix the flour, baking powder, mustard, cayenne or paprika, 1 tsp salt and 1 tsp thyme leaves in a large bowl, then rub in the butter until the mix looks like fine crumbs. Tip in most of the cheese and all of the corn. Mix the milk with the lemon juice, then stir into the bowl to make a slightly sticky dough. Don't over-work the dough.

2 Tip the dough onto the floured work surface, knead 2–3 times to smooth a little, then divide into 10 balls. Shape each roughly with your hands and put onto a floured baking sheet. Brush each with a little milk, then scatter with a little cheese, cayenne and a few thyme leaves. Bake for 10–12 minutes or until the scones are risen, golden and sound hollow when tapped on the bottom. Cool on a wire rack.

PER SCONE 261 kcals, carbs 32g, fat 12g, sat fat 7g, salt 0.9g

Welsh cakes

*Pice ar y maen are a Welsh teatime treat passed on through generations and still as
popular as ever. Serve buttered and hot straight from the griddle.*

MAKES 16 • PREP 10 MINS • COOK 15 MINS
❄ **V**

225g/8oz plain flour, plus extra for dusting
85g/3oz caster sugar
½ tsp mixed spice
½ tsp baking powder
50g/2oz butter, cut into small pieces
50g/2oz lard, cut into small pieces, plus extra for frying
50g/2oz currants
1 egg, beaten
splash of milk

1 Tip the flour, sugar, mixed spice, baking powder and a pinch of salt into a bowl. Then, with your fingers, rub in the butter and lard until crumbly. Mix in the currants. Work the egg into the mixture until you have soft dough, adding a splash of milk if it seems a little dry – it should be the same consistency as pastry.

2 Roll out the dough on a lightly floured work surface to the thickness of your little finger. Cut out rounds using a 6cm cutter, re-rolling any trimmings. Grease a flat griddle pan or heavy frying pan with lard, and place over a medium heat. Cook the Welsh cakes in batches, for about 3 minutes each side, until golden brown, crisp and cooked through. Delicious served warm with butter and jam, or simply sprinkled with caster sugar.

PER CAKE 138 kcals, carbs 20g, fat 6g, sat fat 1g, salt 0.13g

Ultimate chocolate cake

Quite simply the best chocolate cake you'll ever make!

**CUTS INTO 14 SLICES • PREP 40 MINS
COOK 1 HOUR 25–30 MINS
V ❄ WITHOUT ICING**

200g/7oz good-quality dark chocolate, about 60% cocoa
    solids, broken into chunks
200g/7oz butter, cut in pieces, plus extra for greasing
1 tbsp instant coffee granules, dissolved in 125ml
    cold water
85g/3oz self-raising flour
85g/3oz plain flour
¼ tsp bicarbonate of soda
200g/7oz light muscovado sugar
200g/7oz golden caster sugar
25g/1oz cocoa powder
3 medium eggs, beaten
5 tbsp buttermilk
grated chocolate or curls, to decorate

FOR THE GANACHE
200g/7oz good-quality dark chocolate, chopped
284ml pot double cream
2 tbsp golden caster sugar

1 Butter a 20cm round cake tin (7.5cm deep) and line the
base. Heat oven to 160C/140C fan/gas 3. Put the chocolate
into a heavy-based pan. Add the butter and coffee. Melt over
a very low heat until smooth.
2 Mix the flours, bicarbonate of soda, sugars and cocoa in a
big bowl, mixing with your hands to get rid of any lumps.
3 Pour the chocolate mixture, eggs and buttermilk into the
dry ingredients, stirring until smooth. Pour into the tin and
bake for about 1 hour 25 minutes – a skewer pushed in the
centre should come out clean and the top should feel firm
(don't worry if it cracks a bit). Cool in the tin then turn out
onto a wire rack to cool completely.
4 When cold, cut horizontally into three. To make the
ganache, put the chocolate into a bowl. Put the cream and
sugar into a pan and heat until about to boil. Pour over the
chocolate, then stir until melted.
5 Sandwich the cake layers with a little of the ganache. Pour
the remainder over the cake, then use a palette knife to
smooth and cover. Decorate with a pile of chocolate curls.

PER SERVING 541 kcals, carbs 55g, fat 35g, sat fat 20g, salt 0.51g

Lemon mascarpone roulade

*Swiss roll gets a makeover with this delicious lemony filling. If not using homemade lemon
curd, add a little more lemon juice to shop-bought for extra tang.*

**SERVES 6 • PREP 15 MINS, PLUS COOLING
COOK 12–15 MINS
V**

FOR THE SPONGE
6 eggs
175g/6oz golden caster sugar, plus extra for dusting
175g/6oz self-raising flour
1 heaped tsp caraway seeds (optional)
grated zest 1 lemon (save the juice for the filling)
50g/2oz butter, melted

FOR THE FILLING
juice 1 lemon
300g/11oz lemon curd
250g tub mascarpone
icing sugar, to serve

1 Heat oven to 200C/180C fan/gas 6. Line a 27 x 40cm Swiss
roll tin with non-stick baking parchment. Whisk the eggs
and sugar together until light and fluffy – this can take about
5 minutes. Fold in the flour, caraway (if using) and lemon
zest, then gradually fold in the butter. Tip the mix into the tin
and bake for 12-15 minutes until pale, but springy in the
middle. Cool a little, then turn out onto a sheet of non-stick
baking parchment dusted with sugar, roll up with the lining
paper inside and cool.
2 While the sponge is cooling, mix the lemon juice and half
the lemon curd with the mascarpone and set aside. When
the sponge is completely cool, unravel, remove lining and
spread with the mascarpone mix. Spread the remaining curd
over the top, then roll up again. Dust heavily with icing sugar
and serve in slices.

PER SERVING 708 kcals, carbs 90g, fat 36g, sat fat 18g, salt 0.8g

Toffee pecan cake

*This special cake will go perfectly with coffee or makes a dessert to die for when served warm
with ice cream. If maple syrup seems a little extravagant, use a little squeezy toffee sauce instead.*

**SERVES 8 ● PREP 15 MINS, PLUS COOLING
COOK 40 MINS**
V ❄

300g/11oz pecan halves
140g/5oz stoned dates
200g/7oz butter, softened, plus extra for greasing
200g/7oz light soft muscovado sugar
1 tsp mixed spice
4 eggs, beaten
140g/5oz self-raising flour
maple syrup, to serve

1 Tip 100g pecans into a processor and whizz until fine –
then tip into a bowl. Put the dates into a small pan with
enough water to cover, boil for 5 minutes until very soft,
then drain, discarding the liquid, and whizz in the processor
until smooth.
2 Heat oven to 180C/160C fan/gas 4. Butter and line the
base of a 23cm cake tin. Beat the butter, sugar and spice
together until light and creamy, then tip in the dates, ground
pecans, eggs and a pinch salt and beat briefly until smooth.
3 Fold in the flour with a metal spoon, then spoon into the
tin and level the top. Sprinkle the remaining nuts over the top
(don't press them in) then bake for 40 minutes, or until risen
and golden and a skewer inserted in the centre comes out
clean. Serve warm, with generous drizzles of maple syrup.

PER SERVING 692 kcals, carbs 53g, fat 51g, sat fat 16g, salt 0.68g

Raspberry layer cake

A decadent, creamy cake that transports excellently – try it for a posh picnic treat.

**SERVES 8 ● PREP 25 MINS, PLUS CHILLING OVERNIGHT
COOK 25-30 MINS**
V

FOR THE CAKE
200g/7oz caster sugar
200g/7oz softened butter, plus extra for greasing
4 eggs, beaten
200g/7oz self-raising flour
1 tsp baking powder
icing sugar, to decorate
FOR THE SYRUP
85g/3oz caster sugar
50ml/2fl oz almond liqueur
FOR THE FILLING
300ml pot double cream
250g pot mascarpone
3 tbsp caster sugar
150g punnet raspberries

1 Heat oven to 190C/170C fan/gas 5. Butter and line 2 x
20cm sandwich tins. In a large bowl, beat together all the
cake ingredients (except the icing sugar) to a smooth, soft
mixture. Spoon equally into the two tins, smoothing the tops,
then bake for 25–30 minutes or until golden and the cake
springs back when gently pressed. Turn the cakes out onto
a cooling rack.
2 Heat the sugar, 2 tbsp water and the liqueur together until
the sugar has dissolved. Cool a little. Use a large serrated
knife to cut each cake in half. Brush the syrup all over all four
pieces of cake with a pastry brush.
3 For the filling, whip the cream until it forms soft peaks.
Beat the mascarpone and caster sugar in a large bowl to
loosen, then fold in the cream. Layer the fruit, cream and
sponges, finishing with a layer of sponge. Press lightly then
wrap tightly in cling film and chill overnight.

PER SERVING 819 kcals, carbs 68g, fat 58g, sat fat 33g, salt 1.02g

Raspberry bakewell cake

Homely and easy to make, this cake is a great way of using up pick-your-own raspberries.

**SERVES 8 • PREP 10 MINS, PLUS COOLING
COOK 50 MINS**
V ❄

140g/5oz butter, softened, plus extra for greasing
140g/5oz ground almonds
140g/5oz golden caster sugar
140g/5oz self-raising flour
2 eggs
1 tsp vanilla extract
250g/9oz raspberries
2 tbsp flaked almonds
icing sugar, to serve

1 Heat oven to 180C/160C fan/gas 4 and base-line and grease a deep, 20cm, loose-bottomed cake tin. Blitz the ground almonds, butter, sugar, flour, eggs and vanilla extract in a food processor until well combined.

2 Spread half the mix over the cake tin and smooth over the top. Scatter the raspberries over, then dollop the remaining cake mixture on top and roughly spread. Top with flaked almonds and bake for 50 minutes until golden. Cool, remove from the tin and dust with icing sugar to serve.

PER SERVING 411 kcals, carbs 35g, fat 28g, sat fat 10g, salt 0.5g

Orange and almond cake with citrus mascarpone

Give your dessert an Italian flavour with this moist and fruity polenta cake.

**SERVES 8 • PREP 1 HOUR 30 MINS (INCLUDES COOKING
THE ORANGES) • COOK 1 HOUR 10 MINS**
V ❄ **CAKE ONLY**

3 large oranges, 1 zested
knob unsalted butter, for greasing
140g/5oz polenta, plus 2 tbsp
200g/7oz ground almonds
1 scant tbsp baking powder
7 eggs, plus 2 egg yolks
350g/12oz golden caster sugar
FOR THE MARSCAPONE
3–4 tbsp Cointreau or other orange liqueur, to taste
3–4 heaped tbsp good quality lime marmalade, to taste
500g tub mascarpone

1 Boil two of the oranges (whole) in water, covered, for 1 hour or until squidgy. Drain and cool. Butter a 23cm springform tin. Add 2 tbsp polenta, tip it around until the tin is coated, then knock out the excess. Mix the almonds, polenta and baking powder in a large bowl.

2 Heat oven to 180C/160C fan/gas 4. Halve the cooked oranges, remove any pips. Put into a food processor, skin and all, with the zest. Whizz to a smooth purée. Beat the eggs, yolks and sugar for a good 5–7 minutes until very thick.

3 Quickly beat in the almond mixture, then the orange purée. Pour into the tin, bake for 10 minutes, reduce oven to 150C/130C fan/gas 2 and bake for 30 minutes, then reduce again to 140C/120C fan/gas 1 for a further 30 minutes until risen, golden brown and just firm in the middle.

4 Cool the cake in the tin, loosen around the edge with a knife, then unclip the tin. Whisk the liqueur and marmalade into the mascarpone and serve alongside slices of cake.

PER SERVING 839 kcals, carbs 79g, fat 51g, sat fat 22g, salt 0.84g

OPPOSITE Raspberry Bakewell cake

Berry cheesecake gateau

For this taller cake, an all-in-one cake mix is baked, split and sandwiched with a tempting cheesecakey filling. How can you resist?

SERVES 12 ● **PREP 15 MINS** ● **COOK 50 MINS**
Ⓥ ❄ **BASE ONLY**

225g/8oz self-raising flour
1 tsp baking powder
200g/7oz caster sugar
200g/7oz butter, very soft, plus extra for greasing
4 eggs
1 tbsp milk
FOR THE ICING AND DECORATION
400g/14oz half-fat soft cheese
zest 2 limes, juice 1
100g/4oz icing sugar
200g/7oz blueberries (or use raspberries or
    strawberries)

1 Heat oven to 180C/160C fan/gas 4. Butter a deep, 18cm round cake tin and line the base with parchment. Put the flour, baking powder, sugar, butter and eggs into a large bowl and beat with an electric mixer on low speed until everything is mixed together. Increase the speed and whisk for 2 minutes. Stir in the milk.
2 Spoon into the tin and level the top. Bake for 50 minutes or until risen and a skewer inserted into the middle comes out clean. Cool in the tin for 5 minutes, then turn out onto a wire rack and cool completely. (Can be made a day ahead, or frozen for 1 month.) Split into three layers.
3 Beat the cheese until soft, then beat in the lime zest and juice and the icing sugar. Sandwich the cake back together with two-thirds of the cheese mixture, and spread the rest on the top. Arrange the blueberries in tight circles around the top of the cake, starting in the centre. (Keeps for 1 day in the fridge.)

PER SERVING 375 kcals, carbs 43.2g, fat 20.4g, sat fat 11.8g, salt 0.90g

Pineapple upside-down cake

This scrumptious cake gives a serious nod to nostalgia but tastes better than you remember.

SERVES 8 ● **PREP 15 MINS** ● **COOK 50 MINS–1 HOUR**
Ⓥ ❄

FOR THE BASE
85g/3oz butter
85g/3oz dark muscovado sugar
85g/3oz toasted flaked almonds
1 pineapple, peeled, cored and sliced, any juices reserved
    (or use canned pineapple in juice, drained)
100g/4oz natural glacé cherries
FOR THE BATTER
250g/9oz softened butter
250g/9oz light muscovado sugar
4 eggs
200g/7oz plain flour
2 tsp baking powder
50g/2oz ground almonds
2 tbsp pineapple juice or rum

1 Heat oven to 190C/170C fan/gas 5. Cream the butter and sugar and liberally brush over the bottom and sides of a 22cm square (or 20cm round) tin. Scatter over the toasted almonds so some stick to the sides, then line the base with overlapping pineapple slices. Decorate with the cherries.
2 Tip all of the batter ingredients into a food processor and blitz until smooth. Pour the batter over the pineapple and bake for 50 minutes to 1 hour until puffed up and golden. Leave the cake to relax for just a few minutes, then turn out and eat straightaway with lashings of custard.

PER SERVING 781 kcals, carbs 82g, fat 48g, sat fat 24g, salt 1.17g

Plum, hazelnut and chocolate cake

Plums, chocolate and hazelnuts – this is a perfect cake for an autumn celebration.
Enjoy a slice with your mid-morning coffee or serve it warm for dessert.

SERVES 8 • PREP 25 MINS • COOK 40–50 MINS
V

175g/6oz butter, softened, plus extra for greasing
500g/1lb 2oz plums
175g/6oz light muscovado sugar
175g/6oz self-raising flour
175g/6oz ground hazelnuts
3 eggs
1 tsp baking powder
50g/2oz dark chocolate (70% cocoa solids), chopped
2 tbsp hazelnuts
2 tbsp redcurrant, damson or plum jelly

1 Heat oven to 180C/160C fan/gas 4. Butter and line the base of a deep round 20cm cake tin. Halve and stone 4 plums and set them aside for later, then roughly chop the remainder.
2 Put the sugar, butter, flour, ground hazelnuts, eggs and baking powder into a large bowl and beat together for 1–2 minutes, until smooth and light. Stir in the chopped plums and chocolate, then tip into the prepared cake tin and smooth the top.
3 Arrange the halved plums over the top of the mixture, pressing them down lightly, then scatter over the hazelnuts. Bake for 40–50 minutes until the top is golden and the cake feels firm to the touch. Cool in the tin for 10 minutes, then turn out, remove the paper and cool on a wire rack. Heat the jelly, then brush over the top of the cake before serving.

PER SERVING 581 kcals, carbs 51g, fat 39g, sat fat 15g, salt 0.83g

Apple and blackberry traycake

A kind of right-way-up, upside-down cake – great with custard or cream.

SERVES 8 • PREP 20 MINS • COOK 50 MINS TO 1 HOUR
V ✳

175g/6oz butter, plus extra for greasing
300g/11oz plain flour, plus extra for dusting
4 Bramley apples (approx 800g/1lb 12oz)
squeeze lemon juice
284ml pot whipping cream
225g/8oz golden caster sugar, plus 1 tbsp for sprinkling
3 eggs
300g/11oz blackberries

1 Heat oven to 200C/180C fan/gas 6. Grease a small roasting tin (about 30 x 20cm) with butter, dust with a little flour, then set aside. Peel, core and slice the apples into rings, then toss in a little lemon juice to stop them going brown.
2 Tip the cream and butter into a pan, bring to the boil, then set aside. Whisk the sugar with the eggs until they thicken and turn pale, about 3 minutes. Whisk the buttery cream into the eggs, then fold in the flour until completely smooth.
3 Pour the batter into the tin and arrange the apple slices over the top. Scatter over the blackberries, then sprinkle with the remaining sugar. Bake for 50 minutes to 1 hour until golden and beginning to pull away from the sides of the tin. Leave to cool in the tin and serve cut into squares.

PER SERVING 587 kcals, carbs 64g, fat 35 g, sat fat 21g, salt 1.01g

13

Celebration cakes

Nothing says party like a cake; be it for a birthday, wedding, passing exams or purely a celebration of the season. Marking an occasion with a homemade cake says so much more than buying one in. You don't have to go to great lengths to create a stunner, although simple is often best – be it a traditional cake to slice, or a squidgy creation that doubles as dessert.

FESTIVE FRUIT CAKES

Forget all thoughts of dry, boring fruit cake, ours are full of plump fruit and can be made well ahead of time and fed with alcohol or fruit juice.

When cooking fruit cakes, always cover the outside of the tin with a double thickness of newspaper or brown paper – this will help protect the sides from overcooking before the middle of the cake is ready. You may also need to cover the top with a disc of parchment or foil if the top of the cake starts to colour up too much. If you are cooking a fruit cake in a gas oven, you will probably need to give it a little more time, as it is hard to regulate gas ovens at very low temperatures. Test the cake by inserting a skewer in the middle to be sure – if it comes out clean, the cake is ready.

Marzipan and icing

Easter and Christmas cakes are traditionally covered in marzipan and either royal or sugarpaste icing. You can buy very good ready-made marzipan and icings, but if you fancy making your own we've included simple recipes on pages 345, 346 and 350. You can make marzipan up to one week ahead. Wrap it tightly in cling film and store in the fridge. Although homemade marzipan contains raw eggs, the amount of sugar and lack of moisture prevents bacteria growing when left at room temperature, so your cake should last 1–2 months when iced. Don't scrimp on drying time when covering your cakes – once you've covered your cake leave it to dry out completely (up to 3 days) before you cover it with icing. Shop-bought marzipan is a good substitute for anyone in an at-risk group from raw eggs or short of time. Royal icing is a pourable consistency when first made and can be shaped into decorative swirls over the cake. As it dries it sets hard. Sugarpaste icing is pliable and smooth and sets to be firm and dry. It is rolled flat and smoothed over the cake in a similar way to marzipan. Sugarpaste icing can be used straight away, or kept very well-wrapped in an airtight food bag for up to 2 days. (See recipe on page 345 for more information on sugarpaste icing.)

For most of us, festive occasions are probably the only times in the year when we get to grips with marzipan and icing and cooking a proper fruit

OPPOSITE *Chocolate curl cake (page 327)*

cake. (On page 350 there are clear instructions on how to cover a cake.) Traditional fruity Christmas cakes taste best if made ahead, and fed with either alcohol such as brandy or rum, fruit juice or even a hot toddy made with tea and whisky (see the Hot toddy cake on page 345). As the cake matures, the flavours within it mellow and round-out, and the regular feeding keeps the inside moist. Cakes like this can be made up to 3 months ahead, wrapped in parchment and then in foil and kept in a cool, dry place. If you prefer your fruitcake lighter, then make it just before Christmas and just feed it a couple of times. If perhaps you'd like to give an iced Christmas fruit cake as a gift, you can ice the cake several weeks before Christmas and keep it cool and dry.

Of course, not everyone likes a traditional fruit cake, so there's a brilliant (and coincidentally gluten-free) recipe for a quick and very special-looking Clementine cake on page 347, and, for the more cocoa-minded among you, a Chocolate yule log. The beauty of cakes like this is that they take less time to bake than a fruit cake, and some of them can be made and frozen in advance, if you really want to get on top of things. (For more on Christmas preparation and cooking turn to page 389.)

WEDDINGS

Good Food magazine has become well known for its wedding cakes. All the recipes are carefully explained and do not assume any technical knowledge – they are essential guides for whoever is making the cake, particularly if they are a first-time baker. Cake decorating is seen as a bit of a dark art, but we have simplified the process of making a cake from start to finish – be it a stack of cupcakes, a formal tiered cake complete with flowers, or a croquembouche – the classic French pile of crisp choux buns.

Before you decide on the kind of cake you might want to make, think about the style of the event and who will be there to enjoy it. The days of three tiers of fruit cake have long gone – a stack of rich chocolate truffle or flavoured sponges is far more common, and often doubles up as part of the wedding breakfast dessert. Or perhaps vintage-style cupcakes are the order of the day, to be given away as favours at the end of the evening. The happy couple will have a good idea of what they want –

but remember that unless you are a professional cake maker (and we have to assume that you're probably not), you do need to be realistic about what you can achieve.

Luckily for most of us, fancy icing techniques can now seem a little old fashioned – and unnecessary – as so much can be done with fresh flowers or frosted petals. It's likely that the cake flowers will need to tie in with the bride's bouquet, so speak to the florist; they will be able to advise you as to whether the blooms can withstand being out of water, and the best way to use them.

To help you prepare ahead, we've included a plan of what can be done in advance of the big day alongside each wedding cake recipe. Some steps can be done up to one month before, although there are some jobs, such as stacking tiered cakes, that have to be done on the day.

Tips for success

- Remember that most cakes can be frozen, so much of the work can be done ahead. Even so, allow yourself plenty of time – and follow the suggested time plan on each recipe.
- When icing, make sure that the kitchen is spotless – the slightest speck of dirt can spoil the finish of your cake. Ban pets from your work area and, if possible, have a designated, cool and safe place (a room with the radiator turned off or the garage) in which the cakes can sit and dry.
- Cutting a cake into three? It is much easier to do this if the cake has been chilled first, as this firms up the crumb.
- Before icing a cake, sit it on a big sheet of baking parchment. This lets you lift and move the cakes about as you ice, without disturbing the icing around the bottom.
- Start by icing the smallest cake; that way once you know what you're doing, you'll feel more confident to do it on a larger scale.
- If possible, get someone to drive you and the cake to the venue. Some venues may have awkward parking and you may need to hop out. If you don't have a large car boot, level the back seats with blankets.
- Pack an emergency kit for when you arrive at the venue; bring tape, spare royal icing, frosting and sugar flowers if relevant, tweezers, scissors and a paint brush.
- If the cake has different-flavoured layers, make sure the caterers know which is which and if the wedding party have a preference over which flavour is served to whom.

Chocolate curl cake

This impressive cake requires a little care and patience to decorate, but is well worth the effort.

CUTS INTO 12 SLICES • **PREP 15–25 MINS, PLUS COOLING** • **COOK 45–50 MINS**
❄ **CAKE ONLY**

200g/7oz self-raising flour
25g/1oz cocoa powder
1 tsp baking powder
200g/7oz caster sugar
200g/7oz butter, softened, plus extra for greasing
4 eggs
1 tbsp milk
6 tbsp apricot jam, warmed and sieved
FOR THE TRIMMING
100g/4oz dark chocolate
100g/4oz white chocolate
FOR THE CHOCOLATE CREAM
150g bar dark chocolate
142ml tub double cream
FOR THE CURLS
100g/4oz dark chocolate
100g/4oz white chocolate

1 Heat oven to 180C/160C fan/gas 4. Grease and line a deep, round 20cm cake tin. Beat the flour, cocoa, baking powder, sugar, butter and eggs together until everything is mixed, then stir in the milk.

2 Spoon into the tin, level the top, then bake for 45–50 minutes. Leave in the tin for 5 minutes, then turn out and cool on a wire rack.

3 To make the trimming, cut two strips of greaseproof paper about 35 x 6cm and put on a lightly buttered baking sheet. Melt the dark chocolate and white chocolate in separate bowls over a pan of water, or in the microwave for 2–3 minutes, and use to fill two piping bags. Drizzle dark chocolate back and forth across the paper, working in thin lines to within 1cm of the short ends, then repeat with the white chocolate. Repeat lines of dark and white chocolate on top. Chill for 1–2 hours until firm. Refrigerate to speed this up – if it gets too cold, bring to room temperature to soften.

4 Split the cake in half and sandwich back together with half the jam. Brush the tops and sides with the remaining jam.

5 For the chocolate cream, break up the chocolate. Bring the cream almost to the boil, then, off the heat, stir in the chocolate until smooth. Cool until spreadable, then spread over the top and sides of the cake.

6 While the cream is still soft, carefully lift each piece of the trimming from the baking sheet, with the paper still attached. Wrap around the side of the cake and chill for at least 10 minutes. Peel off the paper.

7 Make white and dark chocolate curls using a potato peeler and scatter over the top of the cake. Tie a ribbon around the sides to finish.

PER SERVING 602 kcals, carbs 66g, fat 37g, sat fat 21g, salt 0.66g

Birthday bug cake

Children will love this birthday cake – and you'll love its simplicity.

**SERVES AT LEAST 16 CHILDREN • PREP 20 MINS,
PLUS 30 MINS FOR THE DECORATION, PLUS COOLING
• COOK 1 HOUR 20 MINS**
■ UN-ICED CAKE ONLY

FOR THE VANILLA CAKE
250g/9oz unsalted butter, softened, plus extra for greasing
250g/9oz golden caster sugar
seeds scraped from 1 vanilla pod or 1 tsp vanilla paste
5 eggs, cracked into a jug
85g/3oz plain flour
100g/4oz full-fat Greek yogurt
250g/9oz self-raising flour
3 tbsp semi-skimmed milk

FOR THE SYRUP
50g/2oz golden caster sugar
seeds ½ vanilla pod or ½ tsp vanilla paste

FOR THE TOPPING
100g/4oz white chocolate
basic vanilla buttercream (see below)
12 giant chocolate buttons, 6 cut in half
hundreds and thousands
2 chocolate sticks
treat-size pack chocolate buttons

---

tips The decorated cake can be left, loosely covered, in a cool, dry place (not the fridge) for up to 24 hours. If you're making the cake for a boy, then it's easy to turn the ladybirds into spiders – simply add a few liquorice legs.

---

try this...

A good, basic vanilla buttercream

Put 175g soft unsalted butter into a large bowl and beat with electric beaters for a few seconds until pale. Gradually add 300g sifted icing sugar, a spoonful at a time, beating well after each addition. The mixture will seem stiff by the time all the sugar has been added, but keep beating and it will become pale and creamy. Finally, beat in seeds from 1 vanilla pod or 1 tsp vanilla paste. Bring to room temperature and beat well before using.

---

1 Heat oven to 160C/140C fan/gas 3. Grease a round, deep 20cm tin, then line the base and sides with non-stick baking parchment. Beat the butter, sugar, vanilla and ¼ tsp salt together until pale and fluffy, then pour in the eggs, one at a time, giving the mix a really good beating before adding the next. Add 1 tbsp of the plain flour if the mix starts to look slimy rather than fluffy. Beat in the yogurt.

2 Mix the flours; then, using a large metal spoon, fold them into the batter, followed by the milk. Spoon the mix into the tin and bake for 1 hour 20 minutes or until well risen and golden – a skewer inserted into the middle should come out clean.

3 Meanwhile, make the syrup by gently heating 50ml water with the sugar and vanilla in a pan until the sugar dissolves. Set aside. Once the cake is out of the oven (leave the oven on), cool for 30 minutes in the tin, then use a skewer to poke holes all over the cake, going right to the bottom. Pour the syrup over, letting it completely soak in after each addition. Leave to cool completely, then either wrap the cake well or fill and ice it.

4 Break the white chocolate into a microwaveable bowl, and heat on High for 1 minute (or melt over a pan of simmering water). Stir, then leave any remaining lumps to melt in the warm liquid chocolate. Once just warm, beat the chocolate into the buttercream.

5 Start the butterflies. Put the whole giant buttons on a flat baking sheet on non-stick baking paper, then put into the oven for 20–30 seconds or until the chocolate looks shiny. Take out, scatter with hundreds and thousands, then leave to set completely before cutting in half with a large, non-serrated knife. For the ladybirds, pipe dots of icing all over the already cut giant button halves, then leave aside to dry.

6 Spread the buttercream over the cake, then start to arrange the butterflies. Cut each chocolate stick into 3 to make bodies. Press onto the cake, then stick four giant button halves around each body to make 'wings'. For the ladybirds, place two spotty button halves together, then use a small button for the head. Scatter more hundreds and thousands all over the cake, then poke in candles.

PER SERVING 536 kcals, carbs 64g, fat 30g, sat fat 18g, salt 0.28g

OPPOSITE Clockwise from top left Birthday bug cake; Lemon curd and blueberry loaf cake (page 330); Summer celebration cake (page 330); Ginger simnel cake (page 331)

Lemon curd and blueberry loaf cake

Lemon zest makes a simple, stylish topping – or let the kids loose with sprinkles and edible glitter! A great option for Mother's Day too.

CUTS INTO 8–10 SLICES • PREP 20 MINS, PLUS COOLING COOK ABOUT 1 HOUR 15 MINS
❄ UN-ICED

500ml tub Greek yogurt
300g jar good lemon curd
175g/6oz softened butter, plus extra for greasing
3 eggs
zest and juice 1 lemon, plus extra zest to serve (optional)
200g/7oz self-raising flour
175g/6oz golden caster sugar
200g punnet blueberries
140g/5oz icing sugar
edible flowers, such as purple or yellow primroses,
    to serve (optional)

1 Heat oven to 160C/140C fan/gas 3. Grease a 900g loaf tin and line with a long strip of baking parchment. Put 100g yogurt, 2 tbsp lemon curd, the softened butter, eggs, lemon zest, flour and caster sugar into a large mixing bowl. Quickly mix until the batter just comes together. Scrape half into the prepared tin. Weigh 85g blueberries and sprinkle half into the tin, scrape the rest of the batter on top, then scatter the other half of the 85g berries on top. Bake for about 1 hour 15 minutes until golden, and a skewer inserted into the centre comes out clean.
2 Cool in the tin, then carefully lift onto a serving plate to ice. Sift the icing sugar into a bowl and stir in enough lemon juice to make a thick, smooth icing. Spread over the top of the cake, then decorate with lemon zest and edible flowers, if you like, and serve with the remaining berries.

PER SERVING (8) 663 kcals, carbs 96g, fat 30g, sat fat 16g, salt 0.86g

Summer celebration cake

Transform a simple vanilla cake into something special, with lashings of crème fraîche and fresh berries.

SERVES 16 • PREP 20 MINS • COOK 1 HOUR 30 MINS

250g pack unsalted butter, softened, plus extra
    for greasing
250g/9oz golden caster sugar
seeds scraped from 1 vanilla pod or 1 tsp vanilla paste
5 large eggs
85g/3oz plain flour
100g/4oz full-fat Greek yogurt
250g/9oz self-raising flour
3 tbsp semi-skimmed milk
FOR THE TOPPING
350g punnet raspberries
225g punnet blueberries
225g pot crème fraîche
icing sugar (optional)

1 Butter and line a round, loose-bottomed 23cm cake tin. Heat oven to 160C/140C fan/gas 3.
2 Beat the butter, sugar, vanilla and ¼ tsp salt together until pale and fluffy, then pour in the eggs, one at a time, giving the mix a really good beating before adding the next. Add 1 tbsp plain flour if the mix starts to look slimy rather than fluffy. Beat in the yogurt.
3 Mix the flours then, using a large metal spoon, fold into the batter, followed by the milk. Spread half the mix in the tin. Stir half the berries into what is left. Spoon over the first layer and smooth the top. Bake for 1 hour 30 minutes until risen, golden and a skewer inserted in the centre comes out clean.
4 Cool in the tin for 30 minutes, then cool on a wire rack. Once cold, put onto a plate, smooth the crème fraîche over the top and finish with the remaining berries and a dusting of icing sugar, if using.

PER SERVING 349 kcals, carbs 35g, fat 22g, sat fat 13g, salt 0.24g

Ginger simnel cake

A hidden layer of gingery marzipan and clever decoration turns this from just fruit cake to a spectacular Easter centerpiece.

CUTS INTO 12 SLICES • **PREP 1½ HOURS, PLUS 2 HOURS DRYING FLOWERS** • **COOK 1 HOUR 35–50 MINS 1 HOUR 50 MINUTES**
❄ **WITHOUT FLOWERS**

FOR THE ALMOND PASTE
200g pack ground almonds
100g/4oz golden caster sugar
50g/2oz stem ginger, finely chopped
1 tbsp cornflour, plus extra for rolling the almond paste
1 egg white

FOR THE CAKE
100g/4oz sultanas
100g/4oz currants
100g/4oz raisins
50g/2oz stem ginger, finely chopped
2 tsp tea leaves or 1 tea bag
2 tbsp golden syrup
2 tsp ground ginger
100g/4oz plain flour
50g/2oz self-raising flour
100g/4oz butter, softened
100g/4oz golden caster sugar
2 eggs, beaten

FOR THE DECORATION
2 tbsp apricot jam, warmed in a microwave or small pan
icing sugar, for dusting
sugar-frosted edible flowers such as pansies (see page 338)
ribbon, to tie round the cake

1 Make the almond paste. Tip the ground almonds into a bowl and stir in the caster sugar, ginger and cornflour. Pour in the egg white and work together until you have a smooth paste. Roll into a ball, wrap in cling film and put in the fridge for at least half an hour, to firm up.

2 Heat oven to 180C/160C fan/gas 4. Double-line the base and sides of a deep, 18cm round cake tin with baking parchment.

3 Make the cake. Mix the dried fruits and stem ginger in a bowl. Put the tea in another bowl, pour over 125ml boiling water and infuse for 5 minutes. Strain the liquid over the fruit, then stir in the golden syrup and ground ginger.

4 Sift together the plain and self-raising flours. Beat the butter and sugar in a large bowl until the mixture is light in colour and drops softly from the beaters. Beat in the eggs a little at a time, then gently stir in the sifted flours until smooth. Finally, stir in the dried fruits and their liquid.

5 Spoon half the cake mixture into the tin and smooth the surface. Unwrap the almond paste on a surface lightly dusted with cornflour, and roll a third of it into a round to barely cover the surface of the mixture. Lift and place the paste inside the tin, then press down to remove any trapped air. Spoon the rest of the cake mixture on top and smooth the surface.

6 Cover the top of the tin with foil, scrunching it lightly at the sides to hold it in place. Bake for 50 minutes, remove the foil and bake for a further 45 minutes to 1 hour until a skewer inserted into the cake comes out clean (replace the foil if the cake shows signs of overbrowning during this time). Leave in the tin until completely cold, then remove and strip away the lining paper.

7 For the decoration, put the remaining almond paste on a surface lightly dusted with cornflour and roll into an 18cm round, using the base of the tin as a guide. Brush the jam over the surface of the cake, then press the paste firmly on top, making sure it is centred and even.

8 Preheat the grill until hot. Place the cake on a baking sheet and grill until light brown on top, rotating it to make sure it browns evenly. Remove and leave to cool.

9 To finish, put the cake on your prettiest serving plate and sift icing sugar over the almond paste. Decorate with a few sugar-frosted flowers (see page 338), dust lightly with a little extra icing sugar and tie a ribbon around the cake.

PER SLICE 405 kcals, carbs 59g, fat 18g, sat fat 5g, salt 0.15g

tip Homemade almond paste tastes nuttier than bought, but if you are in a hurry knead the ginger into 350g bought white or golden marzipan.

tip If the bridal party likes the idea of cupcakes, but still wants a cake to cut, make a batch of batter and bake in a lined, deep 20cm round cake tin at 190C/170C fan/gas 5 for 40–45 minutes. Serve on a pretty cake plate, with frosting and roses.

Romantic rose cupcakes

Cupcakes require less skill than making a tiered wedding cake, but look as impressive stacked on pretty plates.

MAKES 12 DEEP CUPCAKES • PREP 10 MINS, PLUS COOLING • COOK 18–20 MINS
❄ WITHOUT FROSTING

150ml pot natural yogurt
3 eggs, beaten
1 tsp vanilla extract
175g/6oz golden caster sugar
140g/5oz self-raising flour
1 tsp baking powder
100g/4oz ground almonds
175g/6oz unsalted butter, melted

TO DECORATE
100g/4oz white chocolate
140g/5oz unsalted butter
140g/5oz icing sugar
2.5m thin ribbon (optional)
36 simple sugar roses and leaves (see recipe below)

1 Line a 12-hole muffin tin with paper cases and heat oven to 190C/170C fan/gas 5. In a jug, mix the yogurt, eggs and vanilla extract. Put the dry ingredients, plus a pinch of salt, into a large bowl and make a well in the middle.
2 Add the yogurty mix and melted butter, and quickly fold in with a spatula or metal spoon – don't overwork it. Spoon into the cases (they will be quite full) and bake for 18–20 minutes or until golden, risen and springy to the touch. Cool for a few minutes, then lift the cakes onto a wire rack. (Keep in an airtight container for up to 3 days or freeze).
3 To make the white chocolate frosting, melt the white chocolate in the microwave on High for 1½ minutes, stirring halfway through. Beat the butter and icing sugar in a bowl until creamy. Beat in the cooled chocolate. Cover and chill for up to one month. Up to 48 hours before serving (or the day before if it's really hot), bring back to room temperature, then spread over the cakes. Put the ribbon around the cakes, tying or glueing in place. Keep cool, out of direct sunlight.

PER CUPCAKE 525 kcals, carbs 57g, fat 32g, sat fat 16g, salt 0.36g

Simple sugar roses

The roses can be made up to a month ahead and coloured to match the wedding theme. Keep in a cool place away from moisture and light.

MAKES ABOUT 40 ROSES AND LEAVES • PREP 1 HOUR PER BATCH • NO COOK
(YOU'LL NEED 36 LEAVES AND ROSES FOR 12 CAKES)

edible food colouring paste (we used Claret and Party Green)
200g/7oz white ready-to-roll icing
a little solid vegetable fat, for rolling
edible lustre, we used a shimmery pink
edible sparkles, we used bright pink (optional)

1 Start with the roses. Knead a little colouring paste into 150g icing until pale and even. Break into three balls, then add a little more colouring to two, giving three varying depths of colour. Keep under cling film. Rub a very thin layer of fat over a smooth work surface. Roll out one of the balls of icing thinly, about 1–2mm, then trim into a rectangle about 8 x 20cm. Cut off a 1cm strip of icing widthways, keeping the rest covered.
2 Carefully roll the strip up and around itself (photo 1). For a more realistic rose look, start rolling slightly skew-whiff so that the outside edge of the finished rose sticks out further than the middle. With about 2cm to go, start to guide the end of the icing down and under to make a neat rosebud. Pinch to shape, then cut or pinch off the bottom. Set aside for at least 1 hour until firm. Repeat with the rest of the icing.
3 For the leaves, colour the remaining icing green. Pinch off small pea-size pieces, roll into balls, then flatten a little. Pinch one end to make a leaf shape. Leave to dry.
4 Once the roses are dry and firm, dust a little lustre onto each rose using a paintbrush or your fingertip. Sprinkle with sparkles, if using. Position the roses onto the cupcakes in clusters of three, following with three leaves (photo 2).

Rose petal wedding cake

With three different tiers of fruit, lemon and chocolate cakes, this wedding cake has something for everyone.

For dessert, the cake will feed approx 100 people with a few slices left over (50 x 2.5cm pieces of chocolate cake, 30 x 2.5cm of lemon cake and 24 x 2.5cm of fruit cake)

You will need:

- 15cm, 23cm and 30cm deep round cake tins
- plenty of greaseproof paper
- thick 35cm silver cake drum (base)
- thin 15cm, 23cm and 30cm silver cake boards
- long serrated knife
- palette knife
- cream, ivory and dusky pink food colouring pastes
- long rolling pin
- 6 standard plastic dowelling rods
- strong kitchen scissors
- 1m ivory ribbon, 15mm wide
- medium artist's paintbrush
- cooling rack
- string for measuring
- 20cm, 25cm and 33cm cardboard cake, boxes with lids (if transporting the cake)

Getting ahead

1 MONTH BEFORE
- Make the fruit cake and cover with marzipan
- Make the chocolate and lemon cakes if freezing – they will freeze for up to 1 month but are best made fresh

4 DAYS BEFORE
- Make the chocolate and lemon cakes and keep well-wrapped in baking parchment and cling film in a cool place
- Make the chocolate and lemon buttercream and keep in the fridge

3 DAYS BEFORE
- Fill and cover the chocolate and lemon cakes with buttercream and cover all of the cakes and the 35cm drum with icing
- Insert the dowelling rods, then leave to dry

2 DAYS BEFORE
- Frost the rose petals

ON THE DAY
- Stack the cakes and decorate with petals once the cakes are in place

The top tier: Light fruit cake

This is totally different to a traditional dark fruit cake, so if you have a special family recipe that you'd rather use instead, bake that in a 15cm tin and feed with alcohol or fruit juice in the month leading up to the wedding.

SERVES 24 ● PREP 30 MINS, PLUS COOLING COOK 2 HRS 15 MINS

140g/5oz unsalted butter, softened
140g/5oz golden caster sugar
2 eggs, beaten
2 tbsp orange flower water
zest and juice 1 orange
zest and juice 1 lemon
175g/6oz plain flour
100g/4oz undyed glacé cherries, halved
100g/4oz dried apricots, roughly chopped
100g/4oz mixed peel, chopped (we used Sundora)
100g/4oz golden sultanas
50g/2oz shelled pistachios, left whole
50g/2oz (3 balls) stem ginger from a jar

1 Heat oven to 160C/fan 140C/gas 3. Grease and double-line the base and sides of a deep, 15cm round cake tin. Wrap a double layer of greaseproof or brown paper around the outside of the tin, too, then secure with string.
2 Cream the butter and sugar together until fluffy and light. Beat in the eggs gradually. In a small bowl, mix the orange flower water with the zest and juice of the orange and lemon. Fold the flour, then dried fruit, pistachios and ginger into the creamed mix, followed by the juice and zest mix.
3 Spoon the mix into the prepared tin and bake for 30 minutes, then turn the oven down to 150C/130C fan/gas 2 and bake for another 1 hour 45 minutes until risen, golden and an inserted skewer comes out clean. Leave to cool for 15 minutes before transferring to a wire rack to cool completely. The cake will keep well wrapped in a cool place for up to 1 month.

PER SERVING 157 kcals, carbs 24g, fat 7g, sat fat 3g, salt 0.06g

The middle tier: Zingy lemon syrup cake

This cake has a real citrus hit and the drenching of lemon syrup keeps it beautifully moist.

SERVES 30 ● PREP 30 MINS, PLUS COOLING ● COOK 2 HRS

350g/12oz unsalted butter, softened
350g/12oz golden caster sugar
6 eggs, beaten
140g/5oz plain flour
280g/10oz self-raising flour
zest of 4 lemons, juice of 3 (about 100ml/3½fl oz)
FOR THE SYRUP
zest and juice 2 lemons
100g/4oz golden caster sugar

1 Heat oven to 160C/140C fan/gas 3. Prepare the inside and outside of a 23cm round tin, as before. Cream the butter and sugar together until light and fluffy, then gradually beat in the eggs a little at a time. Add a tbsp of the plain flour if it starts to split. Fold in the flours and a pinch of salt, followed by the lemon zest and juice.
2 Spoon the mix into the tin and bake for 1 hour 15 minutes until well risen and golden and a skewer inserted comes out clean. Meanwhile, make the syrup by heating the sugar, lemon zest and juice in a small pan until the sugar dissolves. Set aside.
3 Once the cake is out of the oven, leave to cool until it's just warm, then use a skewer to poke holes down to the bottom all over the cake. Pour the syrup over, letting it completely soak in after each addition. Leave to cool completely, then either wrap or fill and ice the cake. The unfilled cake will keep for up to 4 days, if you wrap it with baking parchment and cling film, or in the freezer for up to a month.

PER SERVING 269 kcals, carbs 33g, fat 14g, sat fat 8g, salt 0.17g

▶

The bottom tier: Rich dark chocolate cake

Simply melting ingredients together makes for a decadently rich chocolate cake that's perfect for dessert with a splash of cream. It's also far easier than beating all that butter, sugar and 10 eggs.

SERVES 50 ● PREP 40 MINS, PLUS COOLING ● COOK 2 HRS 30 MINS

650g/1lb 7oz unsalted butter
650g/1lb 7oz plain chocolate (70% cocoa solids), broken into pieces
100ml/3½ fl oz very strong coffee – espresso is ideal
3 tsp vanilla essence
650g/1lb 7oz plain flour
2 tsp baking powder
2 tsp bicarbonate of soda
950g/2lb 2oz light soft brown sugar
10 eggs
2 x 284ml pots soured cream

1 Heat oven to 160C/140C fan/gas 4. Butter, double-line and wrap the sides of the 30cm round cake tin as before. Put the butter and chocolate into a medium saucepan, then stir over a low heat until melted and smooth. Stir in the coffee and vanilla.
2 Sift the flour, baking powder and bicarbonate of soda into the biggest bowl you have. Add the sugar, breaking down any lumps with your fingertips if necessary. Beat the eggs and soured cream together and pour into the flour mix. Pour in the melted chocolate mix as well, then stir with a wooden spoon until you have a thick, even chocolaty batter.
3 Pour into the prepared tin and bake for 2½ hours – don't open the oven door before 2 hours is up, as this will cause the cake to sink. Test with a skewer. Once cooked, leave in the tin to cool completely. The unfilled cake will keep for up to four days, wrapped as before, or frozen for a month.

PER SERVING 274 kcals, carbs 30g, fat 16g, sat fat 9g, salt 0.23g

Fill and cover the chocolate and lemon cakes with buttercream

500g/1lb 2oz unsalted butter, softened
1kg/2lb 4oz icing sugar, sifted
jar good-quality lemon curd
142ml pot double cream
200g/7oz plain (70% cocoa solids) chocolate, broken into pieces

1 Beat the butter until creamy, then gradually beat in the sifted icing sugar. Weigh 600g/1lb 5oz of the mix and stir 5 tbsp of the lemon curd into it.
2 In a small pan, bring the cream just to the boil, then pour over the chocolate. Leave to stand for 2 minutes, then stir until smooth. Once cool but still liquid, fold into the remaining basic buttercream.
3 Once each cake is completely cool, level off the top using a long serrated knife. Spread a little of the corresponding buttercream over the matching thin cake board. Turn the cake upside down onto the board and brush all over with a thin layer of the sieved apricot jam – this helps to prevent stray crumbs getting into the buttercream.
4 Cut the cake into three layers horizontally – don't worry if you cut the layers unevenly as it won't affect the finished cake. If it's a hot day or warm in your kitchen, refrigerate the cakes for a while – it will firm them up and make cutting and lifting much easier. Lift off each layer as you cut it, and set it aside so that when you re-stack the layers they are in the right order.
5 Using a palette knife, spread about ¼ of the buttercream over the first layer of the cake. For the lemon cake, swirl another tbsp or so of lemon curd over the icing. Stack the remaining layers, spreading the remaining icing over the top and sides of the cake, smoothing it down to meet the cardboard cake base (photo 1).

1

Cover the fruit cake with marzipan

half a 454g jar apricot jam (you'll use the rest later)
500g pack natural marzipan

1 Boil the apricot jam with 2 tbsp water and sieve into a bowl. Brush the 15cm cake board with a little of the apricot jam. Cut off the rounded top of the cake and turn upside-down onto the board. Measure across the top and sides of the cake with string, cut to length and set the string aside. Brush the cake all over with a thin layer of apricot jam.
2 Dust the work surface with icing sugar and roll the marzipan into a circle big enough to cover the cake top and sides, using the cut string as a guide. Lift over the cake and smooth with your hands. Trim the marzipan to the base of the cake (so you can't see the board) and leave to dry for one day, if there's time. If not, the cake can be iced straight away.

Cover all the cakes with ready-to-roll icing

FRUIT CAKE
500g/1lb 2oz white ready-to-roll icing
cream food-colouring paste
LEMON CAKE
1 kg/2lb 4oz white ready-to-roll icing
dusky pink food-colouring paste
CHOCOLATE CAKE
1.7kg/3lb 10oz white ready-to-roll icing
ivory food-colouring paste
FOR THE BOARD
800g/1lb 12oz white ready-to-roll icing
ivory food-colouring paste

1 For the marzipanned fruit cake only, first lightly brush with cooled, boiled water to help the icing stick. For all the cakes, dust the work surface with icing sugar and knead the icing until pliable. Add a few specks of the food colouring with a toothpick or the end of a skewer – be very sparing as a little goes a long way. Work the colour in until you have an evenly coloured, smooth paste. Add more and knead again if you want the colour to be more intense (photo 2).
2 Lightly dust the work surface again and roll the icing into a circle large enough to cover the sides and top of the cake, with a little excess. Use string to measure as before. Lift the icing over the cake, using your rolling pin to help you (photo 3).
3 Smooth the icing around the cake with your hands, then trim off the excess with a sharp knife (photo 4). Leave overnight to dry. Once iced, keep for 3 days.
4 Once you've iced the cakes, cover the 35cm base. Lightly brush with cooled, boiled water and cover with ivory-coloured icing. Trim and leave overnight to dry.

▶

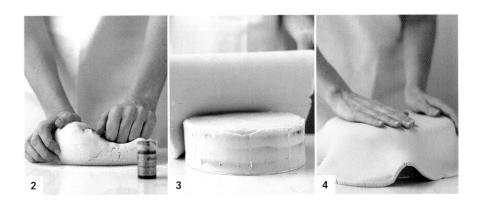

2   3   4

Stack the cakes

200g/8oz icing sugar
1 egg white

5

1 In a large bowl, gradually beat icing sugar into the egg white to make thick and smooth royal icing. Cover with cling film until ready to use.

2 Starting with the chocolate cake, insert three dowelling rods in a triangle, slightly offset to one side and no wider than the base of the lemon cake that's going to sit on top (photo 5). With a permanent pen, lightly mark where the top of the icing comes to on the dowel.

3 Carefully pull out the dowels and line up on the work surface. Using a ruler, re-mark each rod to the highest point. Score the dowels with scissors around the new marks and snap the plastic cleanly.

4 Re-insert the rods in their original holes, rounded end down. Cut the thin ivory ribbon to fit around the thick base board, securing at the back with glue or double-sided tape. To stack the cakes, spoon a little royal icing over each of the dowel holes. Carefully lift the chocolate cake onto the covered board, then stack cakes on top of one another, positioning each cake and gently lowering one side of it onto the base or cake below. Slide your palette knife under it at this point and gently lower the cake down. Slide the knife out at the last minute. (If you're moving the cake to the venue, put the cakes into their boxes and take the icing with you.)

Frosting the rose petals

6 roses in cream or pink, or a
   mixture of both
1 egg white
100g/4oz white caster sugar

1 Gently pull the petals from the roses. Lightly beat the egg white with a fork then, one by one, lightly brush the petals with egg white all over on both sides.

2 Sprinkle with caster sugar and set on a cooling rack to dry (photo 6). They will dry and harden within 2 hours. Keep the dried petals safely in one layer in a cool place (not the fridge). A large tray is ideal for this. Frosted petals can be made up to 2 days ahead.

6

 It's easiest to frost rose petals that are thicker and more waxy, so go for tight roses rather than old-fashioned, more delicate tea roses.

Make sure there's a safe, cool place for the cake to sit out of direct sunlight during the day.

Due to popular request, we have calculated quantities for smaller versions of the chocolate tier of the cake on page 336 (a 30cm/12in round cake). To make a 23cm/9in cake, use half the quantity of ingredients and bake it for 2 hours. Quarter the quantity for a 15cm/6in tin, and bake it for 1¾–2 hours. For all sizes, use deep cake tins and grease and line them fully, according to the recipe.

Orange berry wedding cake

A beautiful patisserie-style cake to enjoy at the end of the meal.

**SERVES 30–40 • PREP AND COOK 2–3 HRS FOR THE CAKES,
PLUS ANOTHER 3-4 HRS FOR THE OTHER ELEMENTS**
❄ **SPONGE CAKES ONLY**

FOR THE 30CM CAKE

8 eggs
200g/7oz golden caster sugar
50g/2oz unsalted butter, melted and cooled, plus extra
    for greasing
100g/4oz ground almonds
zest 2 oranges
200g/7oz plain flour
1 tsp baking powder

FOR THE 20CM CAKE

25g/1oz unsalted butter, melted and cooled,
    plus extra for greasing
4 eggs
100g/4oz caster sugar
50g/2oz ground almonds
zest 1 orange
100g/4oz plain flour
½ tsp baking powder

1 Heat oven to 160C/140C fan/gas 3. Butter and line the base of a deep, 30cm, round cake tin with baking parchment. Whisk the eggs and sugar together until the mixture leaves a trail when the whisk blades are lifted. This could take 8–10 minutes, but don't skimp this step as it is crucial to the success of the cake.

2 Fold in the butter, almonds and orange zest using a large metal spoon, then sift in the flour and baking powder. Fold everything together lightly, then pour into the tin. Bake for 50–60 minutes (30–40 minutes for the smaller cake) until firm to the touch. Cool in the tin for 5 minutes, then turn out, peel off the paper and leave to cool completely.

▶

> ## You will need:
>
> - 20cm and 30cm deep, round cake tins
> - plenty of baking parchment
> - cooling rack
> - 22cm and 32cm silver cake boards
> - long serrated knife
> - palette knife
> - rolling pin
> - 6 plastic dowelling rods

Make the orange sugar syrup

4 tbsp caster sugar
6 tbsp water
2 strips orange peel
4 tbsp orange liqueur

1 Put the caster sugar in a small pan with the water and orange peel. Heat gently, stirring until the sugar has melted, then boil hard for 2–3 minutes until slightly syrupy. Cool, then stir in the orange liqueur.

Make the crème patissière

6 egg yolks
3 tsp vanilla extract
140g/5oz golden caster sugar
50g/2oz plain flour
600ml/1 pint milk
25g/1oz unsalted butter
150ml pot double cream
500g pot crème fraîche

1 Whisk together the yolks, vanilla and caster sugar until the mixture is pale and thick. Whisk in the flour. Boil the milk, then gradually whisk into the egg mix. Return to the pan and cook over a gentle heat, whisking until the custard is thick and glossy. Cook gently, stirring for 2 minutes more to cook out the raw flour taste.
2 Remove from the heat and beat in the butter. Spoon into a clean bowl, then cover closely with cling film (so it's in contact with the custard) and leave to cool. Whip the cream, then fold into the cool custard. (This can be made up to 2 days ahead and stored in the fridge.) Just before using, stir in the crème fraîche.

Cover the cakes and make the decoration

1 quantity orange sugar syrup (see above)
400g/14oz fresh raspberries
200ml/7fl oz raspberry coulis
1 quantity crème patissière (see above)
400g/14oz redcurrants
1 egg white
4 tbsp white caster sugar
ingredients for chocolate modelling paste (see opposite)

1 The day before the party, split each cake in half. Brush the cut edges with syrup. Lightly crush the raspberries. Put the base of each cake on 22cm and 32cm round cake boards, then spread each with a layer of raspberry coulis. Scatter over the crushed raspberries, followed by a thin layer of crème patissière (about one-third of the total amount). Cover with the other halves of the cakes. Using a palette knife, spread crème patissière thinly over the tops and sides of the cakes, then chill for several hours.

2 Meanwhile, select about 6–8 long strands of redcurrants. Lightly beat the egg white and put the sugar in a shallow bowl. Brush the redcurrants lightly with egg white, then coat lightly with sugar and arrange over a flat tray lined with baking parchment. Leave overnight to dry out.
3 Make the modelling paste and leave to cool. Measure the depth and circumference of the small cake, then roll one-third of the modelling paste into a sausage. Put this shape between two large sheets of baking parchment, then roll to the circumference of the cake and about 3–4cm more than the depth. Once rolled sufficiently, flip the whole lot over and peel away the uppermost sheet of paper. Trim the base of the paste in a straight line, leaving the top wavy. Carefully wrap the modelling paste around the cake with the straight edge to the base, pressing in the sides, then peel off the parchment. Repeat with remainder of paste for the larger cake. Chill overnight.

Chocolate modelling paste

1.25kg/2lb 12oz plain chocolate, broken into pieces
700g/1lb 9oz liquid glucose (available from some supermarkets and most chemists)

1 Melt the chocolate in a bowl set over a pan of barely simmering water, then leave to cool for a few minutes. Heat the glucose gently in a pan, then tip into a large bowl. Gradually beat the chocolate into the glucose, beating to a thick paste that leaves the sides of the bowl clean. Place in a polythene bag and leave for about an hour until set firm. To use, knead lightly until slightly softened. Microwave on Defrost for 10–15 seconds if really firm. If the paste splits at any point, put it in a food processor with 1 tbsp oil and whizz it up, then re-knead and it should come back again to a smooth paste.

Stack cakes and finish the decoration

400g/14oz raspberries
800g/1lb 2oz small strawberries
200g/7oz blueberries
frosted, and remaining unfrosted redcurrants
icing sugar, for dusting

1 Cut 6 plastic dowels into equal lengths, about 2cm longer than the depth of the larger cake. Insert 4 into the centre of the larger cake in a square formation, just smaller than the size of the smaller cake, then put two in the middle. On the day, place the smaller cake on top of the larger one, then fill around the edge of the large cake and the top of the small cake with the berries, finishing with the frosted redcurrants. Dust with icing sugar.

PER SERVING (30) 639 kcals, carbs 84g, fat 31g, sat fat 16g, salt 0.37g

---

Getting ahead

UP TO 2 DAYS BEFORE, OR 1 MONTH IF FREEZING
• Make the two sponge cakes one at a time.
• Make the crème patissière and the orange syrup
1 DAY BEFORE
• Fill the cakes with crème patissière and chill well. Frost the redcurrants and insert the dowels. Make the chocolate modelling paste, then cover the cakes and chill overnight.
ON THE DAY
• Stack the cakes then finish with the remaining fruit and frosted redcurrants. Don't do this any earlier as they're not as sturdy as fruit cake.

Croquembouche

A towering cone of filled choux buns is a French wedding classic, best served as a dessert while the pastry is still crisp and fresh.

SERVES 20 • PREP 2–2¼ HRS • COOK 25 MINS
❄ **UNFILLED BUNS ONLY**

175g/6oz unsalted butter, cut in pieces, plus extra
    for greasing
185g/6½oz plain flour, sifted
6 eggs, beaten

1 Heat oven to 200C/180C fan/gas 6. Lightly butter 3 large baking sheets. Put the butter in a large, heavy-based saucepan with 450ml water and gently heat until the butter has melted. Bring to the boil then immediately tip in the flour, all in one go. Beat with a wooden spoon until the mixture forms a ball that comes away from the sides of the pan. Leave to cool for 5 minutes.

2 Beat in the eggs, a little at a time, beating well between each addition, until the mixture is glossy and only just holding its shape. You may not need to add all the beaten egg. Spoon half the mixture into a piping bag fitted with a 1cm plain nozzle or a large polythene freezer bag with the corner snipped off.

3 Pipe small rounds, about 2cm in diameter, onto the baking sheets, trimming the paste from the bag with a knife. Leave room between them to allow for spreading. You should end up with about 75 rounds. Bake for 25 minutes, in batches if necessary, depending on how many baking sheets you have, until well risen and golden, rotating the baking sheets halfway through cooking. As soon as the pastry is cooked, make a 1cm slit on the side of each bun to let the steam escape (this stops them drying out), then transfer to a wire rack to cool. (Store in an airtight container for up to three days or freeze for up to 1 month.)

> ### Getting ahead
>
> **3 DAYS BEFORE (OR FREEZE AHEAD)**
> • Make the choux buns and the cardboard cone
> **2 DAYS BEFORE**
> • Make the limoncello cream and chill.
> **1 DAY BEFORE**
> • Recrisp the buns if needed. Fill with limoncello cream, then assemble the croquembouche.
> **ON THE DAY**
> • Decorate the croquembouche

4 Make the cone. Make a pencil mark halfway along a long edge of the A1 card. Mark the halfway position along both short edges and draw a line from each point to the mark on the long edge. Attach one end of the string to the pencil, and holding the other end at the point on the long edge, draw a curve from the point on one short side to the point on the opposite side. Cut out the card shape and use as a template to cut out the same shape in foil. Tape the foil over the card and roll up (foil inside), overlapping the straight edges to make a cone shape with a 20cm diameter opening. Secure with tape and snip 10cm off the point of the cone.

Make the limoncello cream

9 egg yolks
150g/5oz golden caster sugar
50g/2oz plain flour, plus 1 tbsp
zest 2 lemons, plus 4 tbsp juice
500ml/18fl oz full-fat milk
7 tbsp limoncello (Italian lemon liqueur) or an orange-
    flavoured liqueur

1 Beat the egg yolks, sugar, flour, lemon zest and juice in a bowl to make a smooth paste. Bring the milk to the boil in a large, heavy-based saucepan. As soon as it reaches the boil, pour it over the egg mixture, stirring well. Return to the saucepan and cook over a low heat, stirring constantly until the sauce is very thick and bubbling. Stir in the liqueur and transfer to a bowl. Cover the surface with a circle of baking parchment to prevent a skin forming and leave to cool completely. Refrigerate until ready to use.

▶

Assemble the croquembouche

400g/14oz white chocolate
prepared cardboard cone

1 Take the buns out of their container. If they are a little soft, lay them in a single layer on baking sheets and re-crisp in a moderate oven for 5 minutes. Fill them sparingly with the limoncello cream by piping as before. You can always pipe in a little extra if you have any leftover mix.

2 Break the chocolate into a heatproof bowl and melt over a bowl of gently simmering water (or melt in the microwave on Medium for 2–3 minutes). Give the chocolate an occasional stir until it has just melted. Turn off the heat.

3 Rest the cone inside a vase or jug for support. Put a small bun into the point of the cone with the bun's base face up. Spoon 1 tsp of melted chocolate onto the base and secure two small buns over the first, again with base up. Spoon over another teaspoon of chocolate. It's a little difficult working at the tip of the cone but it gets much easier as the cone widens.

4 Work up the cone, packing in the buns quite firmly, drizzling the chocolate and working in horizontal layers until the cone is filled (photo 1). Make sure that each bun is firmly secured in place with chocolate before proceeding to the next layer and make sure the last layer forms a flat base for the cake. Keep the filled cone in a cool place overnight.

Decorate the croquembouche

200g/7oz white caster sugar
175g/6oz each cream and pink sugared almonds
2 x 100g tubs crystallized whole roses
icing sugar, for dusting

1 Carefully invert the cone on to a flat serving plate and lift away the cone. Gently peel away the foil if it hasn't come away already. Put the sugar in a small heavy-based saucepan with 5 tbsp water. Heat very gently, stirring slowly until it has dissolved to make a smooth syrup. Take care not to splash the syrup up the sides of the pan or it may crystallize and solidify.

2 Bring the syrup to the boil and cook for 4–6 minutes, watching closely until it turns a rich golden colour. Take off the heat and dip the base of the pan in cold water to prevent further cooking (stand back as the pan will splutter noisily). Carefully dip the ends of the sugared almonds and roses in the caramel and secure around the cake, scattering a few on the plate.

3 Using a teaspoon, drizzle more caramel around the buns so that it falls in fine threads. If the caramel hardens in the pan before you've finished decorating, gently reheat it, taking care not to burn it. Finish with a dusting of icing sugar. To serve the cake, it is easiest if you have someone to break pieces off for the guests, starting from the top and working down.

PER SERVING 438 kcals, carbs 55g, fat 22g, sat fat 11g, salt 0.20g

Hot toddy fruitcake

Soaking in whisky, tea and marmalade makes for juicy fruit and a rich, but not overpowering cake. If you use orange juice instead of whisky, the result will still be good. See pages for 348 and 351 decoration ideas.

CUTS INTO 12 SLICES • PREP 20 MINS, PLUS OVERNIGHT SOAKING • COOK 3 HOURS

❄

FOR THE CAKE

200ml/7fl oz hot, strong, black English Breakfast tea

3 tbsp whisky

3 tbsp good-quality orange marmalade, thin or medium shred

700g/1lb 9oz mixed dried fruit

100g/4oz mixed peel

100g/4oz glacé cherries (natural colour)

225g/8oz butter

225g/8oz golden caster sugar

4 eggs, beaten

225g/8oz plain flour

1 tsp ground mixed spice

1 tsp ground cinnamon

finely grated zest 1 lemon

TO FEED THE CAKE

2 tsp caster sugar

50ml/2fl oz hot black tea

1 tbsp whisky (or use orange juice, if you prefer)

1 Mix the hot tea, whisky and marmalade in a large bowl until the marmalade melts. Stir in all of the dried fruit, peel and cherries, then cover and leave to soak overnight.

2 Next day, heat oven to 160C/140C fan/gas 3 and grease and double-line a 20cm, round, deep cake tin with non-stick baking parchment. Cream together the butter and sugar until fluffy. Add the eggs a little at a time, beating well after each addition, then fold in the flour and spices, followed by the lemon zest and soaked fruit. Add any liquid that hasn't been absorbed by the fruit, too. Spoon into the prepared tin, level the top, then bake for 1½ hours. Turn the oven down to 140C/120C fan/gas 1 and bake for another 1½ hours or until a skewer inserted into the centre of the cake comes out clean. Cool on a wire rack in the tin.

3 While the cake is still warm, use the skewer to pepper the cake with holes, poking it all the way down. Dissolve the sugar in the tea, add the whisky or orange juice, then spoon over the surface. If you're making the cake ahead of time, feed it with a fresh swig of hot toddy every week, but take care not to make the cake soggy. (Can be kept for a month well-wrapped in an airtight container in a cool, dry place.) If short on time, the cake can be made the same day that you decorate it.

PER SERVING (UN-ICED) 531 kcals, carbs 88g, fat 18g, sat fat 10g, salt 0.51g

Sugarpaste icing

Sugarpaste icing, sometimes called ready-to-roll icing, is a play-dough like mix that is rolled out and used to cover all sorts of cakes. It can easily be bought, but if you'd like to make your own, here's a recipe to try.

MAKES 500G/1LB 2OZ • PREP 10 MINS • NO COOK

500g/1lb 2oz white icing sugar, plus extra for kneading

1 egg white

2 tbsp liquid glucose

cooled boiled water, to moisten, if needed

1 Sift the icing sugar into a very large bowl, then tip in the egg white and glucose. Use a wooden spoon to gradually work the sugar into the egg and glucose, until you have a rough dough. Dust (a scrupulously clean) worksurface with more sifted sugar, then knead to a smooth, pliable dough. Add a few drops of the water if it seems too dry, but take care not to make it too wet. Sugarpaste dries out quickly, so transfer to a food bag immediately, with the air squeezed out, until ready to use. Use within a few days of making.

Simmer-and-stir Christmas cake

For a really moist cake, the fruit in this recipe is simmered in butter, citrus zest and juice,
sugar and brandy until everything is plumped to bursting.

MAKES A 20CM ROUND CAKE • PREP 1¼ HOURS
COOK 1¾–2 HOURS (OR 2½ HOURS IN A GAS OVEN)
❄

175g/6oz butter, chopped
200g/7oz dark muscovado sugar
750g/1lb 10oz luxury mixed dried fruit (one that
    includes mixed peel and glacé cherries)
zest and juice 1 orange
zest 1 lemon
100ml/3½fl oz cherry brandy or brandy, plus 4 tbsp more
85g/3oz macadamia nuts or whole blanched (skinless)
    almonds
3 large eggs, lightly beaten
85g/3oz ground almonds
200g/7oz plain flour
½ tsp baking powder
1 tsp ground mixed spice
1 tsp ground cinnamon
¼ tsp ground allspice

1 Put the butter, sugar, fruit, zests, juice and 100ml/3½fl oz brandy in a large pan. Bring slowly to the boil, stirring until the butter has melted. Reduce the heat and bubble for 10 minutes, stirring occasionally. Cool for 30 minutes.

2 Meanwhile, heat oven to 150C/130C fan/gas 2 and line a 20cm, deep, round cake tin with a double layer or parchment. Toast the nuts in a dry frying pan, tossing them until evenly browned, or in the oven for 8–10 minutes – keep an eye on them as they burn easily. When they are cool, chop roughly. Stir the eggs, nuts and ground almonds into the fruit mixture and mix well. Sift the flour, baking powder and spices into the pan. Stir in gently, until there are no traces of flour left.

3 Spoon the mixture into the tin and smooth it down evenly – you will find this is easiest with the back of a metal spoon that has been dipped into boiling water.

4 Bake for 45 minutes, then turn down the heat to 140C/120C fan/gas 1 and cook for a further 1–1¼ hours (about a further 1¾ hours if you have a gas oven) until the cake is dark golden in appearance and firm to the touch. Cover the top of the cake with foil if it starts to darken too much. To check the cake is done, insert a fine skewer into the centre – if it comes out clean, the cake is cooked.

5 Make holes all over the warm cake with a fine skewer and spoon the extra 4 tbsp brandy over the holes until it has all soaked in. Leave the cake to cool in the tin. When it's cold, remove it from the tin, peel off the lining paper, then wrap first in baking parchment and then in foil. (The cake will keep in a cupboard for up to three months or you can freeze it for six months.)

Royal icing

If rolling out icing sounds too tricky, try topping your cake with traditional royal icing to
make a snowy scene, then add your favourite decorations.

MAKES ENOUGH TO THICKLY COVER A 20CM ROUND,
MARZIPANNED CAKE

4 egg whites
1kg/2lb 4oz icing sugar

1 Lightly beat the egg whites in a large grease-free bowl, then gradually beat in the icing sugar with a wooden spoon. If not using it straight away, put it into an airtight plastic container. Lay a piece of cling film on top of the icing, then fit the lid on top. Keep covered when not in use.

2 To cover a cake in royal icing, spread the icing over the cake in swirls and peaks, add whatever decorations you like (silver dragees are always easy to come by and look festive), then leave overnight to set.

Dark chocolate and cranberry roulade

This is a fantastic cake to serve as a dessert over the festive season and can be made up to a day in advance.

SERVES 10 • PREP 50 MINS, PLUS COOLING COOK 12-15 MINS

FOR THE SPONGE
butter, for greasing
1 tbsp plain flour, for dusting
50g/2oz self-raising flour
1 tsp baking powder
25g/1oz good-quality cocoa powder, sifted
50g/2oz ground almonds
5 eggs
100g/4oz caster sugar, plus extra for turning the cake out

FOR THE FILLING
2 x 250g tubs mascarpone
zest 1 orange
300g jar good-quality cranberry sauce

FOR THE FROSTING
175g/6oz unsalted butter, softened
50g/2oz icing sugar, sifted
200g/7oz good-quality dark chocolate, melted and cooled

TO DECORATE
cranberries and bay leaves (optional)
icing sugar, to dust

1 Heat oven to 190C/170C fan/gas 5. Butter and line a 30cm x 40cm Swiss roll tin then butter the parchment, dust with the plain flour and tip out any excess. Mix the flour, baking powder, cocoa and almonds. Beat the eggs and sugar for 7-10 minutes until pale and thick. Fold in the dry ingredients, pour into the tin, level, then bake for 12–15 minutes until firm.

2 Cool for 1 minute, then turn the cake out onto a sheet of sugared baking parchment. Remove lining paper. Roll the sponge up, short edge facing you, rolling the parchment inside, then leave it to cool. Beat the mascarpone and orange zest together. Unroll the sponge then spread with the mascarpone, leaving a border. Cover with cranberry sauce then roll back up tightly.

3 For the frosting, beat the butter and icing sugar until pale then stir in the chocolate. Leave the mix to firm up for 20 minutes, then spread over the roulade. Finish with cranberries and bay leaves (if using) and a dusting of icing sugar. Keep chilled.

PER SERVING 691 kcals, carbs 48g, fat 52g, sat fat 29g, salt 0.45g

Fruit-filled clementine cake

A beautiful, moist (and gluten-free) cake, packed with citrus flavours and ideal for making last minute.

SERVES 8–10 • PREP 30 MINS • COOK 2 HOURS 10 MINS ❄ CAKE ONLY

4 clementines
200g/7oz unsalted butter, softened, plus extra for greasing
200g/7oz dark muscovado
3 eggs, beaten
ground cinnamon
1 tsp mixed spice
pinch ground cloves
100g/4oz ground almonds
140g/5oz polenta
1 tsp baking powder (gluten-free)
140g/5oz raisins
140g/5oz sultanas
140g/5oz currants
100g/4oz glacé cherries, quartered
2 tbsp brandy
icing sugar, to decorate (gluten-free)

FOR THE TOPPING
140g/5oz caster sugar
4 clementines, cut into 5mm slices

1 For the cake, place the clementines in a small pan, cover with water and simmer for 1 hour or until tender. Drain, cool, then finely chop.

2 Heat oven to 180C/160C fan/gas 4. Butter and line a 20cm round cake tin. Cream the butter and sugar until pale, then add the eggs, spices, ground almonds, polenta and baking powder and beat together. Fold in the dried fruit, clementines and brandy.

3 Spoon into the tin, smooth the top then bake for 1 hour 10 minutes, turning down to 160C/140C fan/gas 3 after 30 minutes. Loosely cover with baking parchment for the final 20 minutes to prevent it over-browning. Cool.

4 For the topping, heat the sugar in 140ml water until dissolved. Simmer the clementines in the syrup (keep the slices submerged with a circle of greaseproof paper) for 45 minutes or until shiny and translucent. Dust the cake with icing sugar, then arrange the clementine slices, overlapping, on top.

PER SERVING 695 kcals, carbs 93g, fat 34 g, sat fat 15g, salt 0.36g

Jewelled fruit, nut and seed cake

If you're not keen on icing and/or marzipan, bake a crown of toasted nuts, seeds and juicy
cherries onto your cake instead. It's easy, full of crunch and needs no decoration.

SERVES 12 • PREP 30 MINS • COOK 3 HOURS

FOR THE CAKE
1 batch uncooked Hot toddy fruitcake mix (see page 345)
20cm thin cake board (optional)
approx 65cm length wide ribbon

FOR THE TOPPING
50g/2oz butter
50g/2oz golden syrup
2 tbsp large unsalted cashew nuts
3 tbsp whole blanched almonds
5 tbsp shelled pistachios
25g/1oz Brazil nuts
85g/3oz glacé cherries
50g/2oz dried cranberries
2 tbsp pumpkin seeds

1 Put the cake batter into a 20cm loose-bottomed round tin, but reserve 2 tbsp of the mix for later, and bake as per the instructions on page 345. Meanwhile, make the fruit and nut topping. Melt the butter and golden syrup together in a small pan, then toss with the nuts, dried fruit and seeds. Set aside; the mixture will thicken as it cools.

2 Take the cake out of the oven 30 minutes before the end of cooking, then gently spread over the remaining cake mix with the back of a spoon. The cake will take the weight, don't worry. Scatter the fruit and nut mix over the top evenly. Bake for the remaining 30 minutes until the cake is cooked and the nuts golden. Test it's ready by poking a skewer through the topping and into the cake. If it's underdone, but the nuts are golden, just cover with foil and cook for 10 minutes more then test again.

3 Cool completely in the tin. Loosen any obviously sticky edges, then push the cake out of the tin from the bottom. Transfer to the cake board and fix the ribbon around the base before serving. (Can be kept in an airtight tin for up to a week.)

PER SERVING 681 kcals, carbs 101g, fat 29g, sat fat 14g, salt 0.61g

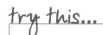

Snow-capped fairy cakes

Make the bases to Romantic rose cupcakes on page 333, then top with irresistible meringue frosting: Put 1 egg white and 4 tbsp orange juice into a heatproof bowl, sift in 175g icing sugar, then set over a pan of simmering water. Using an electric hand whisk, whisk the icing for 7 minutes until it is glossy and stands in soft peaks. Remove from the heat, then whisk for a further 2 minutes until it is slightly cooled. Thinly slice some fruit jelly diamonds. Spoon the icing onto the cakes, swirling it with a knife, then decorate with slices of jelly fruits and a few silver balls. Leave to set. (The cakes will keep for up to 3 days in the cake tin.)

OPPOSITE Clockwise from top left Fruit-filled clementine cake (page 347);
Dark chocolate and cranberry roulade (page 347); Star sparkle cake
(page 351); Hot toddy fruitcake (page 345); Snowman in the garden cake
(page 351); Jewelled fruit, nut and seed cake

Step-by-step: Covering a cake

After making, baking and feeding your fruit cake, there is nothing more satisfying than putting the finishing touches to your creation.

YOU WILL NEED

20cm round fruit cake
round cake board
1 x quantity vanilla marzipan, or 500g shop-bought marzipan
3 tbsp apricot jam or orange marmalade, warmed then sieved icing sugar, to dust
750g/1lb 10oz white, ready-to-roll or homemade sugarpaste icing
cooled boiled water, or clear alcohol such as vodka, for brushing

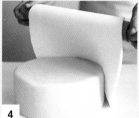

1 Place the cake on a cake board or plate and use small balls of marzipan to plug any holes in the cake. This will help to give a smooth result later (photo 1).

2 Brush a thin layer of jam or marmalade all over the top and sides of the cake. Dust your work surface with a little icing sugar, then roll out the marzipan, keeping the pressure even and turning a quarter turn every few rolls.

3 When large enough (about 40cm in diameter for a 20cm cake), flip the top of the circle back over your rolling pin so you can see the underside of the marzipan, then lift the pin up and lift the marzipan over the cake. Stop once you can see that the edge of the marzipan nearest you is about level with the bottom of the cake. Flop the front of the marzipan down (photo 2).

4 Smooth the top with your palms and continue down over the sides of the cake, smoothing out any folds. Trim with a knife where the marzipan meets the board. Leave to dry for at least 24 hours, or up to 3 days, in a cool dry place (photo 3).

5 Now cover the cake with sugarpaste. Using a pastry brush, lightly brush the marzipan with the water or alcohol, then cover with icing, using the same method as for the marzipan (photo 4). If necessary, roll the icing large enough to cover the board as well. Smooth with your hands, polishing the surface with the flat of your palm, then trim around the base with a sharp knife. Let the icing dry for at least a few hours before adding any extra decoration, if time allows.

Zesty orange marzipan

The orange zest really complements any Christmas cake. Or leave out the zest and replace it with the seeds from a vanilla pod, if you like.

COVERS A 20CM/8IN CAKE • PREP 20 MINS • NO COOK

175g/6oz golden caster sugar
175g/6oz icing sugar, plus extra for dusting
250g/9oz ground almonds
grated zest and juice 1 orange
1 egg
1 egg yolk

1 Sift the sugars and ground almonds together, then stir through the orange zest. Beat together the egg and egg yolk, then add to the sugar mixture, stirring well.

2 Knead briefly to ensure the marzipan is completely mixed and pliable, adding a little orange juice if the mix is too dry, or icing sugar if too wet.

PER SERVING (12) 264 kcals, carbs 34g, fat 13g, sat fat 1g, salt 0.04g

Star sparkle cake

Often the simplest idea can be so effective. Dig out your cookie cutters and ice a cake in half an hour.
Using golden marzipan adds extra contrast against the icing, but use natural or homemade if you prefer.

TAKES 30 MINS

TO COVER THE CAKE
20cm fruit cake covered with marzipan
cooled boiled water, or clear alcohol such as vodka,
    for brushing
750g/1lb 10oz white ready-to-roll or homemade
    sugarpaste icing

TO DECORATE
three 5-pointed star cutters – small, medium and large
30g pack small gold balls
approx 65cm length wide ribbon

1 Brush the sides of the marzipanned cake with water or alcohol (leave the top dry), then cover with icing and trim at the base.
2 Press star cutters gently into the icing on the top of the cake, stopping when you get to the marzipan. Pull the star shapes out with the cutter, or ease out with the tip of a knife. Stamp out a couple of small stars from re-rolled trimmings of icing and sit them inside the large star-shaped spaces.
3 Sprinkle the gold balls into the gaps and tie the ribbon around the cake.

Snowman in the garden cake

Kids will fall in love with this cute snowman in his snowy gingerbread scene.

TAKES 1 HOUR, PLUS DRYING TIME

20cm fruitcake covered with marzipan and white
    ready-to-roll, or homemade sugarpaste icing, taking
    the icing to the edge of the board
FOR GINGERBREAD TREES
75g/2½oz softened butter
50g/2oz caster sugar
½ tsp bicarbonate of soda
50g/2oz golden syrup
2 eggs yolks
250g/9oz plain flour
½ tsp each ground cinnamon and ground ginger
TO DECORATE THE CAKE
100g/4oz white ready-to-roll, or homemade
    sugarpaste icing
6 gingerbread trees
1 egg white
200g/7oz icing sugar
green food colouring
small black writing icing tube
small orange sweet, for the snowman's nose
30cm thin coloured ribbon
1m x 15mm ribbon for the base

1 Make the gingerbread trees. Heat oven to 180C/160C fan/gas 4. Beat together the softened butter and caster sugar until creamy. Stir in the bicarbonate of soda, golden syrup and egg yolks. Sift in the flour, cinnamon and ginger and bring together with a wooden spoon. Shape into two balls, knead until the dough comes together, then chill for 30 minutes. Roll out one ball at a time, to about 2 x £1 coin thickness. Stamp out trees with a 7cm cutter, then re-roll the trimmings. Lift the dough onto greased baking sheets and bake for 10–12 minutes until slightly risen and golden brown. Cool on a wire rack. (Will keep in an airtight container for up to a week.)
2 To decorate the iced cake, roll several marble-sized balls of icing. Roll two larger balls, one a little bigger than the other, to make the snowman's head and body; dry for at least 30 minutes.
3 Meanwhile, ice the gingerbread trees. Beat the egg white with the icing sugar to make a paste. Put a third of the icing into another bowl, then colour very pale green and loosen with a few drops of water. Spread over three of the trees then dry. Spoon another ⅓ icing into a piping bag fitted with a fine nozzle, or a food bag with the very corner snipped off. Pipe fir-tree-like branches over all the trees then leave to set.
4 Fix the trees and snowballs onto and around the iced cake using the remaining sugarpaste. Pipe a face onto the snowman's head and insert his nose. Fix onto his body, position on the cake, then carefully tie a ribbon scarf with the thinner ribbon. This is easiest if you start with too much ribbon, tie it, then trim with scissors. Finally, attach the ribbon around the base.

14

Desserts and puddings

What kind of pudding person are you? Chocolatey? Creamy? Or perhaps you'd do anything for a spoonful of apple crumble? From comforting Sunday lunch specials to dinner party dazzlers, we've thought of every indulgence. And there are healthy options, too – so a little of what you fancy really can do you good! Some desserts are easy as pie, and some – especially those involving chocolate, meringues, gelatine and ice creams can be more tricky – which is why we have concentrated on those topics in the intro to this chapter.

OPPOSITE Stunning summer pudding (page 359)

COOKING WITH CHOCOLATE

Dark chocolate, with 70% cocoa solids, is the most frequently called-for chocolate in this book, as it gives great depth of flavour. If you like chocolate but not the bitter flavour of a very dark bar, choose one with 50% cocoa solids instead. **Milk chocolate** contains cocoa solids, fat, and also milk or cream and sugar. **White chocolate** isn't really chocolate at all, just a mix of milk solids, cocoa butter and vanilla. That doesn't make it any less delicious.

To melt chocolate, always break it into chunks and then put it into a large, non-metallic bowl. Set the bowl over a pan of barely-simmering water, ensuring that the water does not touch the bottom of the bowl. Stir now and again until melted and smooth. Or, microwave for 1½ minutes on High, stirring halfway through cooking, until melted and smooth.

Chocolate is very temperature-sensitive and can easily 'seize' – turning thick and losing its gloss if it gets too hot. If this happens, stir in 1 teaspoon of vegetable or sunflower oil and stir until smooth. If it has turned very granular and smells bitter, discard it and start again.

Adding liquid to melted chocolate also makes it seize, so beware of drips and always use dry utensils. If melting chocolate with liquid, you'll need to have at least 1 tablespoon of liquid per 50g/2oz chocolate to ensure it stays smooth.

MAKING MERINGUES

Meringue-making is a really helpful skill to have up your sleeve, as meringue creates the base for a fabulous pavlova, the topping for a meringue pie, or even the base for some ice creams. (There's a detailed step-by-step guide on page 381); however, here are a few tips for success to absorb before you begin.

- Ensure your mixing bowl and whisks are spotlessly clean. The smallest amount of grease will make egg whites reluctant to whip up.
- Older and room-temperature eggs will make better meringues.
- Don't add any sugar until you have first whisked the whites to stiff peaks. Try not to overwhisk, as your meringues will eventually lose volume.

Overwhisked whites have a lumpy texture around the edge of the bowl.

- 'Stiff peaks' means that the whites or meringue will hold their shape firmly on up-ended whisks, without flopping over.
- Add the sugar gradually, whipping the mix back to stiff peaks each time. When ready, the egg whites should be thick and smooth with an iridescent sheen.

USING GELATINE

Gelatine gives stability and provides wobble factor. It is very temperature-sensitive; the colder it is, the firmer the set. Most gelatine desserts benefit from a few minutes at room temperature to soften a little.

Leaf gelatine needs to be soaked in very cold water for at least 5 minutes until floppy. Lift from the water, then squeeze to remove excess water. It can now be stirred into a warm or hot (never boiling) liquid until completely dissolved.

Powdered gelatine is sprinkled over cold liquid in a small bowl and left until spongy. The bowl is then left to stand in hot water until the gelatine melts (too hot and the flavour will be tainted). As a rough guide, 3 sheets of gelatine is equal to 3 teaspoons of powdered gelatine (or a 10g sachet). This will set 500ml/18fl oz liquid.

A widely available vegetarian alternative to gelatine is called **agar-agar**, made from seaweed. Use it according to the packet instructions.

ICE CREAMS

Most ice creams start life as a custard, which is then cooled and flavoured. Without churning in a machine or by hand, most ice creams (and sorbet) would freeze into a solid, icy block instead of being creamy and smooth. For food-safety reasons, custards should be cooled as quickly as possible. Do not thaw then re-freeze ice creams.

Some ice-cream makers have a bowl that needs freezing ahead of time; others you can just switch on and go. Once the ice cream is thick and smooth, it is transferred to a container and frozen.

A fabulous result is perfectly possible if making ice cream by hand – just freeze the ice cream mixture in a rigid container, removing it and stirring every 40 minutes or so until very thick and smooth. Sounds complicated?

Some ice creams helpfully don't need churning at all, such as the semifreddos on page 385, and the super-simple Maple crunch ice cream on page 383.

COOKING WITH FRUIT

With the changing seasons come all kinds of fruit that are perfect for puddings; from the first forced rhubarb, to summer berries, stone fruits, and the heavy autumn windfall of apples and pears (see page 471 for a seasonal calendar). In the winter we rely on mainly imported fruit – citrus, mango, pineapple, figs and other exotics that remind us that the sun is shining somewhere. Most fruit are simple to prepare, but there are a few that desire a little explanation.

- To prepare a pineapple, cut it into quarters along the length, then remove the paler core. Criss-cross cut the flesh down to the skin with a serrated knife, then cut along the skin to release the cubes.
- To remove the flesh from a mango, cut the two 'cheeks' away from the central almond-shaped stone. Criss-cross the flesh, cutting right down to but not through the skin, then invert the flesh so that it looks like a hedgehog. Cut away the chunks.
- Pomegranate seeds can be tricky to extract from the thick white pith that threads through them. To prepare them easily, cut the fruit across the middle and then, with your hands in a bowl of cold water, turn the flesh inside out, pushing out the seeds and pith. The seeds will sink and the pith will float.
- To segment an orange, remove the peel and the outer layer of pith with a small, serrated knife. Holding the orange over a bowl, slice down the side of each segment, between the flesh and membrane.
- Pick fruit that are heavy for their size, with unblemished skin and no soft patches.
- Except for bananas, keep ripe fruit in the fridge, but remember that all fruit tastes best at room temperature. This is especially the case with melon.
- Apples, pears and bananas will turn brown quickly once they are peeled and cut, so always toss them with a little lemon, lime or orange juice.
- If a recipe calls for zest, either buy unwaxed fruit (normally only possible with lemons) or wash it in hot soapy water before zesting. The zest is the very top layer of the skin, with a concentrated citrus flavour. Be careful not to grate the white pith below the zest, as it is very bitter.

Lemon curd and yogurt fool

Classic fool recipes are made with whipped cream and fruit. Greek yogurt is lighter yet every bit as tasty.

SERVES 4 • PREP 5 MINS • NO COOK
V

300g jar good-quality lemon curd
500g tub 0% fat Greek yogurt
200g punnet raspberries, at room temperature
1 tbsp icing sugar

1 Put the lemon curd and yogurt into a bowl. Fold together for a rippled effect. Divide the mixture between four glasses and chill.
2 Mix the raspberries and icing sugar together and gently crush, then spoon with their juices over the chilled mix and serve.

PER SERVING 299 kcals, carbs 42g, fat 9g, sat fat 5g, salt 0.66g

Banoffee trifles

A trifle cheating will still impress your friends with this made-in-moments banoffee pud.

SERVES 4 • PREP 10 MINS, PLUS CHILLING • NO COOK
V

6 tbsp tropical fruit juice (from a carton)
2 tbsp rum or brandy
2 firm bananas
8 thin slices from a bought Madeira cake
2 tbsp Belgian chocolate sauce
4 heaped tbsp dulce de leche or thick toffee sauce
225g tub mascarpone
250ml/9floz chilled ready-made custard
a block of dark chocolate (any type or size will do)

1 In a large bowl, stir the tropical fruit juice with the rum or brandy. Slice the bananas into the fruit juice mixture and toss together. Sandwich the slices of Madeira cake with the chocolate sauce, dice it into squares and pile in the bottom of 4 pretty glasses.
2 Top with the bananas and rum mixture then add a heaped spoonful of dulce de leche to make another layer. Next, beat the mascarpone and custard together until smooth, then spoon on top of the mixture. (Chill until ready to serve for up to 2 hours.) Before serving, run a potato peeler down the flat back of the bar of chocolate to make shavings and scatter indulgently on top of the trifles.

PER SERVING 786 kcals, carbs 87.5g, fat 45.2g, sat fat 26.5g, salt 0.79g

Cookie-dough crumble

With just two ingredients, hot puddings don't get much simpler than this!

SERVES 4 • PREP 2 MINS • COOK 20 MINS
V

500g bag mixed frozen fruit of your choice
350g pot fresh cookie dough (find this in the chilled aisle, near the ready-made pastry)

1 Heat oven to 220C/200C fan/gas 7. Tip the still-frozen fruit into a shallow baking dish and scatter torn pieces of the dough all over the top. Bake for 20 minutes until crisp and golden and serve with cream, ice cream or custard.

PER SERVING 457 kcals, carbs 57g, fat 24g, sat fat 13g, salt 1.2g

tip To make the crumble extra fruity, slice up a couple of pears or a cooking apple with a sprinkling of sugar and stir into the fruit.

Iced berries with hot chocolate sauce

Here's a simple and tasty pudding idea for using up a packet of frozen berries – and smart enough for weeknight entertaining too.

SERVES 4 • PREP 5 MINS • COOK 5 MINS
V

500g/1lb 2oz mixed frozen berries (blackberries,
    blueberries, raspberries, redcurrants)
FOR THE SAUCE
142ml carton double cream
140g/5oz white chocolate
1 tbsp white rum (optional)

1 Make the sauce. Pour the cream into a small saucepan and break in the chocolate. Heat gently, stirring, until the chocolate melts into a smooth sauce. Take care not to overheat or the chocolate will seize into a hard lump. Remove from the heat and stir in the rum, if using.
2 Scatter the frozen berries on 4 dessert plates or in shallow bowls. Pour the hot chocolate sauce over the fruits and serve immediately, as the fruits start to defrost.

PER SERVING 377 kcals, carbs 28g, fat 28g, sat fat 11g, salt 0.14g

Maple plum crumble

This crumble topping would be just as good over apples or pears. Make double and keep the extra in the freezer for next time.

SERVES 4 • PREP 5 MINS • COOK 25 MINS
V

8 ripe plums, halved, stone removed
4 tbsp maple syrup
50g/2oz butter, cut into pieces
50g/2oz plain flour
50g/2oz rolled oats
25g/1oz golden caster sugar
½ tsp ground cinnamon
25g/1oz flaked almonds

1 Heat oven to 200C/180C fan/gas 6. Place the plum halves, skin-side down, in the base of a large heatproof dish. Drizzle over half the maple syrup and roast for 10 minutes.
2 Meanwhile place the butter, flour, oats, sugar and cinnamon in a bowl and rub the butter into the mixture until you have rough crumbs. Stir in the almonds, then sprinkle over the plums. Drizzle the top with the remaining maple syrup and bake for 15 minutes until the top is golden. Serve with custard.

PER SERVING 325 kcals, carbs 45g, fat 15g, sat fat 7g, salt 0.21g

Fastest-ever lemon pudding

Use your microwave to the max for this tangy family favourite.

SERVES 4 • PREP 5 MINS, PLUS RESTING • COOK 4 MINS
V ❄

100g/4oz golden caster sugar
100g/4oz softened butter
100g/4oz self-raising flour
2 eggs, beaten
zest 1 lemon
1 tsp vanilla extract
4 tbsp lemon curd
crème fraîche or ice cream, to serve

1 Mix the sugar, butter, flour, eggs, lemon zest and vanilla together until creamy, then spoon into a medium microwave-proof baking dish. Microwave on High for 3 minutes, turning halfway through cooking, until risen and set all the way through. Leave to stand for 1 minute.
2 Meanwhile, heat the lemon curd for 30 seconds in the microwave and stir until smooth. Pour all over the top of the pudding and serve with a dollop of crème fraîche or scoops of ice cream.

PER SERVING 457 kcals, carbs 55g, fat 25g, sat fat 14g, salt 0.75g

Sticky cinnamon figs

 A simple and stylish nutty fig pudding, ready in just 10 minutes.

SERVES 4 • PREP 5 MINS • COOK 5 MINS
V

8 ripe figs
large knob of butter
4 tbsp clear honey
handful shelled pistachio nuts or almonds
1 tsp ground cinnamon or mixed spice
mascarpone or Greek yogurt, to serve

1 Heat grill to Medium-High. Cut a deep cross in the top of each fig then ease the top apart like a flower. Sit the figs in a baking dish and drop a small piece of the butter into the centre of each fruit. Drizzle the honey over the figs, then sprinkle with the nuts and spice.
2 Grill for 5 minutes until the figs are softened and the honey and butter make a sticky sauce in the bottom of the dish. Serve warm, with dollops of mascarpone or yogurt.

PER SERVING 162 kcals, carbs 23g, fat 7g, sat fat 2g, salt 0.06g

Pineapple and pink grapefruit with mint sugar

 Palate-cleansing and healthy, this dish is perfect after a rich Thai curry. Try the mint sugar over ripe sliced mango too.

SERVES 4 EASILY HALVED OR DOUBLED
PREP 10 MINS • NO COOK
V

1 medium pineapple
2 pink grapefruits
50g/2oz golden granulated sugar
small bunch mint, leaves only

A ripe pineapple will smell sweet and you should be able to pull the leaves from the centre easily.

1 Use a sharp knife to top and tail the pineapple, then stand it upright on a chopping board. With the sharp knife, carve the skin away and discard. Rest the pineapple on its side, then cut into wafer-thin slices. Repeat with the grapefruit, cutting away the peel and pith, then cut into slices. Arrange the fruit on a serving platter, catching any juices, and set aside.
2 Using a pestle and mortar, pound the sugar and mint together until completely blended. Scatter the mint sugar over the fruit and serve with yogurt.

PER SERVING 168 kcals, carbs 42g, fat 1g, sat fat none, salt 0.02g

Strawberries in rosé wine

 Such a simple idea that tastes heavenly.

SERVES 4 • PREP 5 MINS • NO COOK
V

400g/14oz small ripe strawberries
about ½ bottle rosé wine
4 tbsp cassis
4 sprigs mint
icing sugar, for dusting
crisp buttery biscuits, to serve

1 Halve any large strawberries. Divide the fruit between 4 wine glasses and pour over the wine and cassis. Tuck a mint sprig into each glass. Leave to soak for up to 1 hour, then dust each with icing sugar and serve with crisp biscuits.

PER SERVING 140 kcals, carbs 15g, fat none, sat fat none, salt 0.03g

Tropical fruits in lemongrass syrup

 Lemongrass adds an intriguing citrus taste and fragrance to the syrup for this exotic fruit salad, which rounds off a Thai meal perfectly. Good with a scoop of mango sorbet.

SERVES 4 • PREP 5 MINS, PLUS COOLING • COOK 1 MIN
V

425g can lychees in syrup
2 stems lemongrass, halved and bashed with a rolling pin
85g/3oz golden caster sugar
850g tubs fresh mixed tropical fruit
100g/4oz seedless red grapes
6 macaroons or coconut biscuits, to serve

1 Drain the lychees' syrup into a pan and put the lychees in a large serving bowl. Add the lemongrass and sugar to the pan, heat gently until the sugar dissolves, then boil for 1 minute. Turn off the heat and set aside – the lemongrass will add flavour as it cools.
2 Strain the syrup over the lychees and tip in the other fruits. Chill until needed. Serve with the macaroons.

PER SERVING 172 kcals, carbs 44g, fat none, sat fat none, salt 0.02g

Stunning summer pudding

 This quintessentially British pud, packed with juicy summer berries, is so much easier than it looks.

SERVES 8 • PREP 20 MINS, PLUS OVERNIGHT CHILLING COOK 4 MINS
V

175g/6oz golden caster sugar
1.25kg/2lb 12oz mixed berries and currants, washed.
    We used:
300g/11oz strawberries, quartered
250g/9oz blackberries
100g/4oz blackcurrants
100g/4oz redcurrants
500g/1lb 2oz raspberries
7 slices from a day-old, square, medium-cut, white
    sliced loaf, crusts removed
double cream, to serve

1 Dissolve the sugar in 3 tbsp water in a large pan. Boil for 1 minute then tip in all the fruit except the strawberries. Cook for 3 minutes, stirring 2–3 times until soft and juicy. Drain the juice into a bowl, cool.
2 Line a 1.4-litre basin with cling film, letting it overhang. Cut 4 pieces of bread in half, a little on an angle, each giving 2 lopsided rectangles. Cut 2 slices into 4 triangles each and leave the final piece whole.
3 Dip the whole piece of bread into the juice to coat and use to line the base of the bowl. Dip the wonky rectangular pieces and use to line the basin's sides; alternately place wide and narrow ends up. Spoon in the mixed fruit and strawberries.
4 Dip the bread triangles in juice and use to cover the fruit, – trim any excess with scissors. Keep any leftover juice. Wrap in cling film then weigh down using a small plate and a couple of cans. Chill overnight. To serve, open the cling film and turn out onto a plate. Serve with the leftover juice, extra berries and cream.

PER SERVING 248 kcals, carbs 57g, fat 1g, sat fat none, salt 0.45g

OPPOSITE Clockwise from top left Elderflower and raspberry jellies (page 363); Lemon pannacotta with blackberries (page 360); Maple plum crumble (page 356); Spiced poached pears in chocolate sauce (page 362); Lemon curd and yogurt fool (page 355); Pineapple and pink grapefruit with mint sugar (page 357).

Mango and cardamom syllabub

Delicious puds, ideal for a post-curry treat and perfect for entertaining as they can be made ahead.

SERVES 8 • PREP 25 MINS • NO COOK
V

4 large mangoes, peeled and stoned, 2 finely chopped
10 green cardamom pods, seeds removed
finely grated zest and juice 2 limes
85g/3oz icing sugar
4 tbsp brandy
600ml pot double cream
4 meringue shells, lightly crushed
mint sprigs, to serve

1 Put the flesh of 2 mangoes in a food processor and blend to a purée. Stir in almost all the finely chopped flesh of the other 2 mangoes, then spoon into the base of 8 glasses.
2 Grind the cardamom seeds to a powder, then put in a bowl with the lime zest and juice, icing sugar and brandy. Stir well, then tip in the cream and whip until it holds its shape. Fold in the crushed meringue.
3 Spoon the cream mixture on top of the mango purée, then spoon the remaining chopped mango on top. (This can be made 1 hour ahead.) Serve decorated with mint sprigs.

PER SYLLABUB 537 kcals, carbs 43g, fat 39g, sat fat 22g, salt 0.07g

tip Don't make these too far in advance – the meringue will start to dissolve. If you would rather make the syllabubs a day ahead, serve the meringues whole on the side of the syllabubs..

Lemon pannacotta with blackberries

Wow your guests with this wickedly simple twist on the Italian classic pannacotta, or 'cooked cream'.

SERVES 6 • PREP 20 MINS, PLUS OVERNIGHT CHILLING COOK 5 MINS

4 gelatine leaves
425ml/¾ pint full-fat milk
grated zest and juice 1 large lemon
425ml/¾ pint double or whipping cream
100g/4oz caster sugar, plus 1 tbsp
300g/11oz blackberries
2 tbsp crème de mûre or cassis (optional)

1 Put the gelatine leaves in a bowl of ice-cold water for 10 minutes to soften. Put the milk, lemon zest, cream and sugar in a pan then heat until it starts to bubble gently. Simmer for 2–3 minutes. Remove from the heat, then take the gelatine out of the water, shaking off any excess, and add it to the pan, stirring until the gelatine has dissolved.
2 Leave to cool, then stir again and pour into 6 ramekins, cups or individual pudding basins. Put on a tray in the fridge overnight to set.
3 Mix the blackberries with 1 tbsp each of lemon juice and sugar, then stir in the crème de mûre, if using.
4 Loosen the edges of the creams with the tip of a small knife, then turn them out onto serving plates, and scatter around the blackberries and sauce.

PER SERVING 486 kcals, carbs 27g, fat 39g, sat fat 22g, salt 0.16g

If you are nervous about turning these creams out, make them in small dishes or cups and top with blackberries and a drizzle of sauce to serve.

The secret of success with these little creams is to add just enough gelatine so they are very lightly set but turn out soft and limpid with just the barest resistance to your spoon. You need to give them plenty of chilling time, overnight if possible.

Quick summer compote

 This is equally delicious served hot or chilled, as a dessert with ice cream or perhaps with granola and yogurt in the morning.

SERVES 4 EASILY DOUBLED OR MORE • PREP 5 MINS, PLUS COOLING • COOK 5–7 MINS
V ❄ UNLESS BERRIES ALREADY FROZEN

500g/1lb 2oz mixed berries (blackcurrants, blueberries, raspberries, redcurrants, strawberries)
50–85g/2–3oz golden caster sugar
FOR FLAVOURING
1 vanilla pod
1 cinnamon stick
2–3 sprigs of fresh mint or lemon balm

1 If using strawberries, hull, halve or quarter to make them a similar size to the other berries. Tip all the fruits into a large pan with 2–3 tbsp water, sugar to taste and one of the flavourings. Bring to the boil then simmer for 3–5 mins. Don't overcook, or the fruits will not hold their shape. (Keeps in the fridge for up to 2 days, in the freezer for up to 3 months.)

PER SERVING 83 kcals, carbs 20g, fat none, sat fat none, salt 0.01g

tip If you've got a glut of fruit, make a large batch of compote and freeze it in small quantities so you don't need to defrost the whole lot at once.

Summer berry mousse cake

You can never have enough of this kind of summer dessert recipe in your repertoire – and, as it can be made ahead, it's ideal for summer entertaining.

SERVES 8 • PREP 40 MINS, PLUS CHILLING • COOK 2 MINS

FOR THE BISCUIT BASE
200g/7oz digestive biscuits
100g/4oz butter, melted
FOR THE MOUSSE CAKE
4 sheets leaf gelatine
150ml pot single cream
500g pot fromage frais
140g/5oz golden caster sugar
zest 1 small orange, plus 4 tbsp juice
400g/14oz raspberries, a few of them crushed
300ml pot carton double cream
FOR THE SAUCE
250g/9oz mixture strawberries (chopped) and raspberries
3 tbsp orange juice
2 tbsp golden caster sugar
TO DECORATE
mixture of strawberries (some halved), raspberries and blueberries
icing sugar, for dusting

1 Put the biscuits in a plastic food bag and bash to crumbs with a rolling pin. Stir with the butter until even. Tip into a 23cm springform tin and press down firmly. Chill.
2 Submerge the gelatine leaves in a large bowl of cold water and soak for 5 minutes. Bring the single cream to the boil then take off the heat. Squeeze the excess water from the gelatine then stir into the hot cream until dissolved. Leave to cool slightly.
3 Beat together the fromage frais, sugar, orange zest and juice with a whisk or wooden spoon. Stir in the cooled cream and gelatine mixture and the raspberries.
4 Whip the double cream to soft peaks, fold it into the raspberry mix then pour over biscuit base and chill for 3 hours, or overnight, until set.
5 Blitz the sauce ingredients in a food processor and chill until ready to serve. Run a knife between the mousse and the tin, lift it out of the tin and onto a serving plate. Pile the fruits on top, dust with icing sugar and serve with the sauce.

PER SERVING 607 kcal, carbs 53g, fat 41g, sat fat 24g, salt 0.76g

Roasted stone fruits with vanilla

Perfumed and delicate, this is delicious served at the end of a summer meal – just warm and with a scoop of ice cream.

SERVES 4 • PREP 10 MINS • COOK 20 MINS
Ⅴ

175g/6oz golden caster sugar
1 vanilla pod, split in two
5 cardamom pods
zest and juice 1 lime
6 apricots, halved and stoned
3 peaches, quartered and stoned
3 nectarines, quartered and stoned

1 Heat oven to 220C/200C fan/gas 8. Tip the sugar, vanilla pod, cardamom, lime zest and juice into a food processor, then blitz until blended, or mash together using a pestle and mortar. Tip the fruit into a shallow baking dish, then toss in the sludgy sugar.
2 Roast for 20 minutes until the fruits have softened, but not collapsed, and the sugar and fruit juices have made a sticky sauce. Leave the fruit to cool a little, then serve straight from the dish with ice cream.

PER SERVING 270 kcals, carbs 68g, fat none, sat fat none, salt 0.02g

Spiced poached pears in chocolate sauce

An updated version of one of the nicest pear puddings of yesteryear, poires belle Hélene. The poaching syrup can be frozen and used to poach other fruits.

SERVES 4 • PREP 15 MINS • COOK 45 MINS
Ⅴ

FOR THE PEARS
750g/1lb 10oz golden caster sugar
1 cinnamon stick
2 strips lemon zest (use a potato peeler)
1 star anise
1 vanilla pod, split lengthways
5 cloves
piece fresh root ginger, peeled and sliced
4 ripe pears, peeled
FOR THE CHOCOLATE SAUCE
200g/7oz good-quality dark chocolate, chopped
142ml double cream
150ml/¼ pint full-fat milk
pinch ground cinnamon
vanilla ice cream, to serve

1 In a pan big enough to hold the pears snugly, tip in all the ingredients except the pears. Half-fill the pan with water and bring to the boil. Simmer for 10 minutes to infuse, drop in the pears, cover and gently poach for about 30 minutes until soft. Turn off the heat and set aside. (The pears can be poached up to 2 days ahead and kept in the poaching syrup in the fridge.)
2 To make the chocolate sauce, tip the chocolate into a heatproof bowl. Bring the cream, milk and cinnamon to the boil and pour over the chocolate. Stir until the chocolate has melted. To serve, drain the pears and, holding them by the stem, dip them in the chocolate sauce to completely cover. Serve each pear with a generous scoop of vanilla ice cream.

PER SERVING 642 kcals, carbs 66g, fat 41g, sat fat 22g, salt 0.08g

Biscuity lime pie

The perfect addition to an afternoon cup of tea, this zingy citrus slice uses gingernuts for the base. To make it into a key lime pie of sorts, top with plenty of sweetened whipped cream.

SERVES 6 ● PREP 20 MINS ● COOK 35 MINS
V

300g pack gingernut biscuits
100g/4oz butter, melted
3 egg yolks
50g/2oz golden caster sugar
zest and juice 4 limes, plus thin lime slices (optional),
    to serve
zest and juice 1 lemon
397g can sweetened condensed milk

1 Heat oven to 180C/160C fan/gas 4. Tip the biscuits into a food processor and blitz to crumbs. Add the butter and pulse to combine. Tip the mix into a fluted rectangular tart tin, about 10 x 34cm (or 20cm round tin) and press into the base and up the sides right to the edge. Bake for 15 minutes until crisp.
2 While the base is baking, tip the egg yolks, sugar and lime and lemon zests into a bowl and beat with an electric whisk until doubled in volume. Pour in the condensed milk, beat until combined, then add the citrus juices.
3 Pour the mix into the tart case and bake for 20 minutes until just set with a slight wobble in the centre. Leave to set completely, then remove from the tin, cool and chill. Serve in slices topped with thin lime slices, if you like.

PER SERVING 633 kcals, carbs 85g, fat 30g, sat fat 15g, salt 0.93g

Elderflower and raspberry jellies

 You won't find this jelly at any kids party… For information about using gelatine turn to page 354.

SERVES 6 ● PREP 15 MINS, PLUS COOLING ● NO COOK

2 leaves of gelatine
4 tbsp hot water
100ml/3fl oz elderflower cordial
approx. 350 ml/12fl oz sparkling white wine
punnet of raspberries

1 Soak the gelatine leaves in cold water, then dissolve in the hot water in a measuring jug. Add the elderflower cordial and top up with the sparkling wine to make 450ml of liquid in total.
2 Drop a few raspberries into six tall glasses and fill to about a third with the elderflower mix. Chill to set completely, then add a few more raspberries and some more elderflower. Repeat again until the glasses are nearly full to the top.

PER SERVING 131 kcals, carbs 18g, fat 0.1g, sat fat none, salt 0.04g

Baked raspberry and bramble trifle with Drambuie

This wonderful pudding is based on a traditional trifle, but with a layer of creamy baked custard.

SERVES 8 • PREP 15 MINS, PLUS SOAKING AND CHILLING • COOK 1 HOUR 10 MINS
V

350g/12oz raspberries, fresh or frozen, plus extra
    to decorate
225g/8oz Madeira cake or any other light sponge,
    thinly sliced
5 tbsp Drambuie
grated zest and juice 1 large orange
1 litre/1¾ pints double cream
4 eggs
85g/3oz golden caster sugar
few drops vanilla extract
8 tbsp bramble jam or jelly
5 bought shortbread biscuits, coarsely crumbled
    and lightly toasted
icing sugar, to dust

1 The day before you want to serve, heat oven to 160C/140C fan/gas 3. Tip the raspberries into a large deep, ovenproof dish. Press down lightly with the back of a spoon to release some of the berry juices. Cover the raspberries with the slices of cake, then spoon over the Drambuie and orange juice. Soak for 10 minutes.

2 Whisk 600ml double cream with the eggs, sugar, orange zest and vanilla. Spread the jam over the sponge to cover it completely then slowly pour on the custard mixture.

3 Sit the dish in a roasting tin with enough hot water to come at least 5cm up the sides. Bake for 1 hour to 1 hour 10 minutes, or until the custard is just set, with a little wobble left in it. Leave to cool then cover with cling film and keep overnight in the fridge.

4 On the day, whip the remaining cream until it just holds its shape, then spoon it over the custard. Scatter over the raspberries and toasted shortbread and finish with a dusting of icing sugar.

PER SERVING 873 kcals, carbs 53g, fat 70g, sat fat 42g, salt 0.58g

Flourless chocolate and pear cake

This cake is as light as a soufflé and matches pears with their perfect partner –
chocolate. Try it with dollops of cream or crème fraîche.

SERVES 8 • PREP 20 MINS • COOK 40 MINS
V

85g/3oz butter, plus 1 tbsp extra for greasing
85g/3oz golden caster sugar, plus 2tbsp extra for greasing
85g/3oz chocolate, broken into pieces
1 tbsp brandy
3 eggs, separated
85g/3oz hazelnuts, toasted, then ground in a
    food processor
4 very ripe pears, peeled, cored and halved
icing sugar for dusting

1 Use 1 tbsp melted butter to grease a 25cm loose-bottomed tin, line the bottom with baking paper, then butter that too. Spoon in 2 tbsp sugar and swirl it around to coat the tin. Tip out any excess.

2 Heat oven to 180C/160C fan/gas 4. Melt the chocolate and butter together over a pan of hot water, then stir in the brandy off the heat and let cool. Whisk the yolks with the sugar until pale and thick; fold into the chocolate with the hazelnuts.

3 In a separate bowl, whisk the whites to soft peaks. Stir a spoonful of the whites into the chocolate mix, then fold in the rest in two goes. Spoon the mixture into the tin, level, then add the pears, cut-side down. Bake for 40 minutes until the cake is cooked through. Cool in the tin slightly before releasing it and cooling completely on a rack. Dust with icing sugar to serve.

PER SERVING 334 kcals, carbs 28g, fat 23g, sat fat 9g, salt 0.28g

OPPOSITE Flourless chocolate and pear cake

Chocolate truffle torte

Create a mouthwatering chocolate truffle torte – and there's no cooking necessary.

PREP 50–60 MINS • NO COOK
Ⓥ ❄

250g/9oz dark chocolate, broken into peices
2 tbsp golden syrup
600ml carton double cream
4 tsp instant coffee granules
1 tsp ground cinnamon
cocoa powder, for dusting

> Lining cake tins with plastic is a chef's trick, and gives a great smooth finish. You could use cling film, but take care to get it well into the corners of the tin as the torte will take the exact shape of the cling film, wrinkles and all.

1 Put the chocolate, syrup and 150ml cream in a heatproof bowl, then melt over a pan of simmering water until the chocolate has melted. Stir, then cool until just barely warm.
2 Meanwhile, use a clean A4 plastic folder to line the base and sides of an 18cm springform tin and 3 strips to line the sides. Or line the tin with parchment.
3 Pour the rest of the cream into a very large bowl and tip in the coffee and cinnamon. Whisk until thick but still runny, like a thick milkshake. It should hold a trail for a second or two.
4 Pour the cooled chocolate into the cream then fold together until even. The mix will thicken as you fold. Pour into the tin, level the surface then chill for at least 1 hour (overnight is ideal).
5 Unclip the tin and turn the torte out onto a plate, removing the lining. Dust all over with cocoa.

PER SERVING 331 kcals, carbs 17g, fat 29g, sat fat 18g, salt 0.09g

Light chocolate mousse

This sophisticated dessert is a great guilt-free way to finish a meal.

SERVES 4 • PREP 20 MINS • NO COOK
Ⓥ

85g/3oz dark chocolate, 70% cocoa solids, finely chopped
1 tbsp cocoa powder, plus extra for dusting
½ tsp coffee granules
½ tsp vanilla extract
2 egg whites
1 tbsp golden caster sugar
50g/2oz full-fat Greek yogurt
handful raspberries, to decorate

try this...

> ### Chocolate caramel mousse
> Melt 4 chopped Mars bars, 50ml milk and 4 tbsp cocoa powder, whisking frequently. Softly whip 3 egg whites, fold a third of them into the chocolate mix then fold in the rest until even. Pour into cups and chill until set. Serve with chocolate shavings.

1 Mix the chocolate, cocoa, coffee and vanilla with 2 tbsp cold water in a heatproof bowl. Place the bowl over the gently simmering water, and slowly melt, stirring occasionally. Take off the heat.
2 Stir 2 tbsp boiling water into the mix – the chocolate will immediately thin down and become silky smooth. Leave to cool slightly.
3 Whisk the egg whites to fairly soft peaks, then whisk in the sugar until thick and glossy. Beat the yogurt into the cooled chocolate. Fold a third of the whites into the chocolate mix using a large metal spoon, then very gently fold in the remainder until even. Take care not to over-mix or you will lose the volume of the mousse. Spoon into 4 small cups or ramekins and chill for at least hours.
4 Place each mousse on a saucer or small plate. Top with a few raspberries, then dust with a little cocoa powder. (Will keep for up to 2 days in the fridge.)

PER SERVING 167 kcals, carbs 15g, fat 10g, sat fat 5g, salt 0.12g

Chocolate and coffee truffle pots

What better way to finish a meal than rich chocolate truffles and coffee? This easy dessert combines the two.

**SERVES 6 • PREP 15 MINS, PLUS OVERNIGHT SETTING
COOK 5 MINS**
V

200g/7oz dark chocolate
100ml/3½fl oz strong coffee
4 tbsp your favourite spirit, such as rum, brandy or
    amaretto
400ml/14fl oz double cream
2 tbsp golden caster sugar
cocoa powder, to serve

1 Break the chocolate into small chunks and tip into a bowl with the coffee and alcohol. Bring 250ml of the cream to the boil, then pour over the chocolate mixture and stir until the chocolate has melted and the mixture is smooth. Divide the mix between 6 coffee cups and leave to set overnight in the fridge.
2 To serve, whip the remaining cream with the sugar until just set. Spoon the cream onto the chocolate pots and serve dusted with cocoa powder so each cup looks like a cappuccino.

PER SERVING 543 kcals, carbs 28g, fat 45g, sat fat 25g, salt 0.04g

Best-ever tiramisu

This classic no-cook pud can be made up to 2 days ahead.

**SERVES 6 • PREP 30 MINS, PLUS OVERNIGHT CHILLING
NO COOK**
V

600ml pot double cream
250g tub mascarpone
75ml/2½fl oz Marsala
5 tbsp golden caster sugar
300ml/½ pint strong coffee (dissolve 2 tbsp coffee
    granules in 300ml/½ pint boiling water)
175g pack sponge fingers
25g/1oz chunk dark chocolate
2 tsp cocoa powder

1 Put the cream, mascarpone, Marsala and sugar in a large bowl. Whisk until the cream and mascarpone have completely combined and have the consistency of thickly whipped cream.
2 Get your serving dish ready. Put the coffee into a shallow dish and dip in a few sponge fingers at a time, turning for a few seconds until they are nicely soaked but not soggy. Layer these into your dish until you have used half the biscuits, then spread over half of the creamy mixture. Using the coarse side of the grater, grate over most of the chocolate. Then repeat the layers (you should use up all the coffee), finishing with a creamy layer.
3 Cover and chill for a few hours or overnight. This can now be kept in the fridge for up to 2 days. To serve, dust with cocoa powder and grate over the remainder of the chocolate.

PER SERVING 853 kcals, carbs 44g, fat 73g, sat fat 42g, salt 0.25g

Hot chocolate soufflés with chocolate cream sauce

These soufflés melt in the mouth and make a stunning dinner party finale.

**SERVES 6 • PREP 20 MINS, PLUS COOLING
COOK 8–10 MINS**
V

FOR THE HOT CHOCOLATE SAUCE
142ml pot single cream
25g/1oz caster sugar
100g/4oz dark chocolate (70% cocoa solids), broken
    into pieces
25g/1oz butter
FOR THE SOUFFLES
melted butter, for greasing
50g/2oz caster sugar, plus 2 tbsp extra
175g/6oz dark chocolate (70% cocoa solids), broken
    into pieces
2 tbsp double cream
4 egg yolks
5 egg whites
icing sugar, to serve

1 Heat oven to 220C/200C fan/gas 7 and place a baking sheet on the top shelf. For the sauce, heat the cream and sugar until boiling. Off the heat, stir in the chocolate and butter until melted. Keep warm.

2 Brush 6 x 150ml ramekins with melted butter, sprinkle with 2 tbsp caster sugar, then tip out any excess. Melt the chocolate and cream over simmering water, cool, then stir in the egg yolks. Whisk the whites until they hold their shape, then add the 50g sugar, 1 tbsp at a time, whisking back to the same consistency. Mix a spoonful into the chocolate, then gently fold in the rest.

3 Working quickly, fill the ramekins, wipe the rims clean and run your thumb around the edges. Turn the oven down to 200C/180C fan/ gas 6, place ramekins onto the baking sheet, then bake for 8–10 minutes until risen with a slight wobble.

4 When ready, dust with icing sugar, spoon out a small 'lid' from each soufflé, then pour in some sauce. Replace the lids and serve straight away.

PER SOUFFLE 511 kcals, carbs 41g, fat 36g, sat fat 18g, salt 0.29g

White chocolate and strawberry marquise

A decadent make-ahead dessert that even the most saintly of guests won't be able to resist.

**SERVES 8–10 • PREP 30 MINS, PLUS OVERNIGHT
CHILLING • COOK 5 MINS**
V

6–8 sponge fingers
4 tbsp freshly squeezed orange juice
300g/11oz white chocolate, broken up
25g/1oz unsalted butter
200ml/7fl oz double cream
3 tbsp icing sugar
500g/1lb 2oz strawberries

1 Line a 900g loaf tin with a double layer of cling film, with some overhang. Arrange a row of sponge fingers, widthways, across the base. Sprinkle evenly with 3 tbsp orange juice. Put the chocolate in a heatproof bowl with the butter. Microwave on Medium for 1½–2 minutes, gently stirring halfway through. Whisk the cream with 1 tbsp icing sugar until it just holds its shape. Fold in the melted chocolate until evenly mixed.

2 Select 8–10 even-sized strawberries. Spoon half the chocolate mix into the tin, then put selected strawberries down the centre of the tin, pressing down gently. Spoon over remaining chocolate cream and smooth the top. Fold overhanging cling film over the marquise. Chill in the fridge for at least 24 hours, preferably 2 days, until set.

3 Roughly chop 250g of the remaining strawberries, put in the food processor with the remaining icing sugar and orange juice and blitz until smooth. Sieve to remove the seeds. Chill until needed. To serve, unmould the marquise and cut into thick slices. Serve with strawberry sauce and a few reserved strawberries.

PER SERVING 400 kcals, carbs 36g, fat 28g, sat fat 16g, salt 0.14g

OPPOSITE Clockwise from top left *Hazelnut and Baileys meringue cake (page 376); Sticky ginger pear pudding (page 371); White chocolate and strawberry marquise; Chocolate truffle torte (page 366); White chocolate berry cheesecake (page 380); Panettone pudding (page 370).*

Panettone pudding

Panettone, the fluffy Italian cross between bread and cake, is a popular gift at Christmas. If you find yourself with more than you need after the festivities, try this posh version of bread and butter pudding.

SERVES 4 • PREP 10 MINS • COOK 35 MINS
V

50g/2oz butter, softened (optional)
250g/9oz panettone (about 5 medium slices), or use
    stale bread, fruit loaf or hot cross buns
2 eggs
150ml pot double cream
225ml/8fl oz milk
1 tsp vanilla extract
2 tbsp caster sugar
icing sugar, for sprinkling
softly whipped cream, to serve

1 Heat oven to 160C/140C fan/gas 3 and butter a medium shallow baking dish. Cut the panettone into wedges, leaving the crusts on. Butter the slices lightly with the rest of the butter. Cut the slices in half and arrange them in the dish, buttered-side up.
2 In a bowl, whisk together the eggs, cream, milk, vanilla extract and sugar and pour evenly over the panettone.
3 Put the dish in a roasting tin and pour hot water around it to a depth of about 2.5cm. Bake for 35 minutes until the pudding is just set – it should be yellow inside and nicely browned on top. Dust with icing sugar and serve with spoonfuls of whipped cream.

PER SERVING 536 kcals, carbs 49.1g, fat 34.6g, sat fat 16.7g, salt 0.51g

Guilt-free sticky toffee pudding

A healthy version of the classic pudding – full of sticky dates and maple syrup.

SERVES 4 • PREP 30 MINS • COOK 1 HOUR
V ❄

175g/6oz pitted dried dates
10 tbsp maple syrup
1 tbsp vanilla extract
2 eggs, separated
85g/3oz self-raising flour
0% fat Greek yogurt and extra maple syrup, to serve
    (optional)

1 Heat oven to 180C/160C fan/gas 4. Put the dates and 175ml/6fl oz water in a pan and simmer for 5 minutes. Tip into a food processor, add 6 tablespoons maple syrup and the vanilla extract, and blend until smooth.
2 Transfer to a bowl and mix in the egg yolks, followed by the flour. In another bowl, whisk the egg whites until stiff, and fold into the date mixture.
3 Put 1 tablespoon maple syrup into each of four 200ml pudding moulds and add the mixture. Cover each tightly with foil, stand in an ovenproof dish and pour in hot water to halfway up the sides of the moulds. Cook for 1 hour, until a skewer inserted into the centre comes out clean. Uncover, run a knife around the edges, and invert onto plates. Drizzle over yogurt and maple syrup to serve, if you like.

PER SERVING 339 kcals, carbs 73g, fat 4g, sat fat 1g, salt 0.33g

Schooldays treacle sponge

Try this traditional British pud for an indulgent end to a Sunday lunch.

**SERVES 4 GENEROUSLY • PREP 30 MINS
COOK 1½ HOURS**
V ❄

175g/6oz unsalted butter, softened, plus extra
    for greasing
3 tbsp golden syrup, plus extra for drizzling
1 tbsp fresh white breadcrumbs
splash brandy (optional, but delicious)
175g/6oz golden caster sugar
zest 1 lemon
3 eggs, beaten
175g/6oz self-raising flour
2 tbsp milk
clotted cream or custard, to serve

1 Use a small knob of butter to heavily grease a 1-litre pudding basin. In a small bowl, mix the golden syrup with the breadcrumbs and brandy, if using, then tip into the pudding basin.
2 Beat the butter with the sugar and lemon zest until light and fluffy, then add the eggs gradually. Fold in the flour, then finally add the milk.
3 Spoon the mix into the pudding basin. Cover with a double layer of buttered foil and baking paper, making a pleat in the centre to allow the pudding to rise. Tie the foil securely with string, then place in a steamer or large pan containing enough gently simmering water to come halfway up the sides of the basin. Steam for 1½ hours. Turn out onto a serving dish. Serve with lashings of clotted cream or custard and a little extra golden syrup drizzled over, if you wish.

PER SERVING 763 kcals, carbs 90g, fat 43g, sat fat 25g, salt 0.71g

Sticky ginger pear pudding

*Crowned with golden stem ginger and drenched with sticky brandy syrup, this dark
gingery number would give a traditional Christmas pud a real run for its money.*

SERVES 8 • PREP 20 MINS • COOK 1½ HOURS
V ❄

85g/3oz golden syrup
175g/6oz dark muscovado sugar, plus 1 tsp extra
150ml/¼ pint milk
100g/4oz butter, plus lots extra for greasing
175g/6oz self-raising flour
1 tsp bicarbonate of soda
2 tsp ground ginger
1 tsp cinnamon
6 balls stem ginger from a jar, three halved and
    rest finely chopped
2 ripe pears, peeled
1 egg
custard, to serve
FOR THE GINGER BRANDY SYRUP
50ml/2fl oz syrup from the ginger jar
100ml/3½fl oz brandy
85g/3oz dark muscovado sugar

1 Put the golden syrup, sugar and milk into a pan, simmer to dissolve then cool. Heat oven to 180C/160C fan/gas 4.
2 Put the butter, flour, bicarbonate of soda, ground ginger and cinnamon into a food processor, then pulse to fine crumbs. Generously butter a 1.4-litre pudding basin and sprinkle 1 tsp sugar in the bottom. Put 5 ginger halves into the bowl, rounded-side down. Cut one cheek from a pear, then slice thinly, without cutting through the stalk end. Fan out amongst the ginger. Core, then thinly slice the remaining pear.
3 Tip the cooled syrup and egg into theprocessor and whizz to a batter. Take out the blade, then stir in the chopped ginger and sliced pear. Scrape into the basin, then bake for 1 hour 20 minutes until risen and dark golden, and a skewer comes out clean.
4 To finish, gently melt the syrup ingredients in a pan until the sugar dissolves, then boil briefly. Turn the pudding out of its basin just before serving, spoon over the syrup and serve with custard.

PER SERVING 457 kcals, carbs 79g, fat 13g, sat fat 8g, salt 0.99g

Apple flapjack crumble

Sweetening the apples with apricot jam and orange juice makes it twice as fruity and adding a little syrup to the oaty crumble makes great little chewy clusters.

SERVES 6 • **PREP 20 MINS** • **COOK 30–35 MINS**
Ⓥ ❄

1.1kg/2½lb eating apples, such as Cox's
3-4 tbsp apricot jam
juice 1 large orange
butter, for greasing
FOR THE CRUMBLE
140g/5oz porridge oats
100g/4oz plain flour
1 tsp ground cinnamon
100g/4oz butter
100g/4oz light muscovado sugar
1 tbsp golden syrup

1 Heat oven to 190C/170C fan/gas 5. Peel, core and thinly slice the apples and mix with the jam and orange juice. Spread evenly over a buttered ovenproof dish, not too deep.
2 Mix the oats, flour and cinnamon in a large bowl. Add the butter in small chunks and rub in gently. Stir in the sugar and rub in again. Drizzle over the syrup, mixing with a knife so it forms small clumps. Sprinkle evenly over the apples and bake for 30-35 minutes until the juices from the apples start to bubble up. Cool for 10 minutes, then serve with custard, cream or ice cream.

PER SERVING 447 kcals, carbs 75g, fat 16g, sat fat 9g, salt 0.33g

tip You could use pears, plums or a mixture of winter fruits in this recipe. A handful of blueberries is also good with the apple.

Jam roly-poly

Like most recipes that have stood the test of time, jam roly-poly is simple to make and full of ingredients you've probably got hanging around in your storecupboard, come the cold weather.

SERVES 6 • **PREP 15 MINS** • **COOK 1 HOUR**
❄ Ⓥ **IF USING VEGETABLE SUET**

50g/2oz salted butter, cold and cut into chunks, plus
    extra for greasing
250g/9oz self-raising flour, plus extra for rolling
1 vanilla pod, seeds scraped out
50g/2oz shredded suet
150ml/¼ pint milk, plus a drop more if needed
100g/4oz raspberry or plum jam, or a mixture
custard, to serve

1 Put a deep roasting tin onto the bottom shelf of the oven with another shelf directly above it. Fill the tin two-thirds full with water from the kettle. Heat oven to 180C/160C fan/gas 4. Tear a large sheet of foil and baking parchment (about 30 x 40cm). Sit the greaseproof on top of the foil and butter it.
2 Tip the butter, flour and vanilla seeds into a food processor; pulse until the butter disappears. Tip into a mixing bowl. Stir in the suet, pour in the milk and stir to a sticky dough, adding more milk if needed.
3 Tip onto a floured surface, pat together to smooth, then roll out to roughly 25 x 25cm. Spread with jam, leaving a gap along the far edge. Roll up from the nearest edge. Pinch the jam-free edge into the dough where it meets, and pinch the ends roughly, too. Lift, seam-side down, onto the paper and foil. Seal up like a loose parcel. Put onto shelf above the tin and cook for 1 hour.
4 Let the pudding sit for 5 minutes before unwrapping, then carefully open the foil and paper, and thickly slice to serve.

PER SERVING 330 kcals, carbs 45g, fat 16g, sat fat 8g, salt 0.56g

Suet consists of little shreds of hard animal fat, usually taken from the thick layer of fat around the kidneys of cows and sheep, and traditionally used in steamed puddings and pastries. Now, both vegetable and animal suet is available. A good alternative is to (carefully) grate frozen butter, which is easier to find and has a good flavour.

Creamy vanilla custard

A no-hassle custard that's far more delicious than anything made with custard powder.

MAKES 600ML/1PINT • PREP 2 MINS • COOK 7–12 MINS
V

vanilla pod, seeds scraped out
300ml/½ pint full-fat milk
300ml pot double cream
4 egg yolks
85g/3oz-100g/4oz golden caster sugar, depending
    on your taste
2 tsp cornflour (optional)

> Cornflour will prevent the custard from curdling and gives it just a little more body. To make this custard as a quick all-in-one recipe, mix the cornflour with a little milk until smooth. Put into the pan with all the other ingredients and bring up to a boil, whisking, until thickened.

1 Put the vanilla pod and seeds in a medium pan with the milk and cream. Bring to the boil slowly then take off the heat.
2 Lightly whisk the egg yolks and caster sugar (and cornflour, if you are using it) until pale and thick. Remove the pod then whisk the hot, vanilla-infused mix into the yolks.
3 Strain the custard mixture into a clean pan. Stir continuously with a wooden spoon over a medium heat, taking care to get into the corners, until the custard thickens enough to coat the back of the spoon. This can take 5-10 minutes, especially if not using cornflour. Be patient; don't let it overheat or boil or the egg will curdle.

PER SERVING (6) 393 kcals, carbs 19.7g, fat 33.3g, sat fat 17.5g, salt 0.11g

Plum, orange and almond cobbler

With a little less flour and added almonds, a scone mix transforms into a comfortingly cakey cobbler topping.

**SERVES 6 GENEROUSLY • PREP 30 MINS
COOK ABOUT 1 HOUR**
V

1.5kg/3lb 5oz ripe plums (about 14), stoned and halved
100g/4oz golden caster sugar, plus extra
1 tbsp plain flour
1 cinnamon stick, snapped in half
zest and juice 2 oranges
FOR THE TOPPING
50g/2oz ground almonds
300g/11oz self-raising flour, plus more for dusting
¼ tsp salt
1 tsp baking powder
85g/3oz cold butter, cut into cubes
4 tbsp golden caster sugar
150g pot natural full-fat yogurt
4 tbsp full-fat milk
1 tsp vanilla extract
1 egg beaten with 1 tbsp milk, to glaze
handful flaked almonds

1 Heat oven to 200C/180C fan/gas 6. For the fruit, mix the plums, sugar, 1 tbsp flour and cinnamon stick in a large baking dish. Splash over the orange juice, cover with foil, then bake for 30 minutes until the fruit has softened.
2 For the topping, mix the dry ingredients in a processor then whizz in the butter until it disappears. Tip into a large bowl, stir in the sugar then make a well in the middle. Warm the yogurt, milk and vanilla together in a pan. Tip into the bowl and quickly work into the flour mix using a cutlery knife. As soon as it's all in, stop. The mixture should be stiffish but spoonable.
3 Take the plums from the oven, uncover, then top with 6 big spoonfuls of batter. Scatter with flaked almonds and a little sugar. Bake for 30–35 minutes until the topping is golden and the fruit bubbles underneath. Scatter with more caster sugar to serve.

PER SERVING 459 kcals, carbs 73g, fat 17g, sat fat 7g, salt 0.94g

A nice rice pudding

 A low-fat rice pudding which doesn't skimp on creaminess.

**SERVES 4 EASILY DOUBLED • PREP 5 MINS
COOK 2 HOURS**
V

100g/4oz pudding rice
50g/2oz golden caster sugar
700ml/1¼ pint semi-skimmed milk
pinch grated nutmeg
1 bay leaf or strip lemon zest

1 Heat oven to 150C/130C fan/gas 2. Rinse the rice and drain well. Butter an 850ml heatproof baking dish, then tip in the rice and sugar and stir through the milk. Sprinkle the nutmeg over and top with the bay leaf or lemon zest. Cook for 2 hours or until the pudding wobbles ever so slightly when shaken.

PER SERVING 214 kcals, carbs 40g, fat 3g, sat fat 2g, salt 0.19g

Ultimate crème brûlée

Our professional tips will help you to create this crunchy-and-custardy delight.

**SERVES 4–6 • PREP 15 MINS, PLUS COOLING
COOK 40 MINS**
V

300ml pot double cream, plus 150ml pot
100ml/3½fl oz full-fat milk
1 vanilla pod, split and seeds scraped out
5 egg yolks
50g/2oz golden caster sugar, plus extra for the topping

1 Heat oven to 180C/160C fan/gas 4. Sit 4 x 175ml (or 6 x 150ml) ramekins in a large, deep roasting tin. Pour the cream, milk and vanilla into a pan.
2 Whisk together the yolks and sugar for 1 minute with an electric hand whisk until pale and fluffy. Heat the cream over a medium heat, bring just to the boil, then whisk into the beaten egg yolks. Strain.
3 Fill the roasting tin with hot water 1.5cm up the sides of the ramekins. Pour the cream to the top of the ramekins, cover the tops with a baking sheet, then bake for 30–35 minutes or until the mix is softly set. Don't let them get too firm.
4 Remove the ramekins from the tin, cool for 10 minutes then put in the fridge to cool completely – overnight is fine.
5 To serve, spread 1½ tsp caster sugar evenly over each custard with the back of a spoon, dampen the sugar with a spritz of water then use a blowtorch to caramelize it. Hold the flame just above the sugar and keep moving it round and round until caramelized. Let the topping cool and harden before eating.

PER SERVING 620 kcals, carbs 17g, fat 59g, sat fat 34g, salt 0.01g

tip It's very hard to get a brulée to crisp successfully under a domestic grill – often by the time the sugar has melted so has much of the cream beneath. A blowtorch is the best tool, as it will melt the sugar instantly.

Perfect meringues

Crisp, light and with just the right amount of chew in the middle, these are meringue perfection sandwiched with cream.

MAKES 16 • **PREP 20 MINS** • **COOK 1¼–1¾ HOURS**
Ⓥ ❄

4 egg whites, at room temperature
100g/4oz caster sugar
100g/4oz icing sugar

1 Heat oven to 110C/100C fan/gas ¼. Line 2 baking sheets with a silicon liner or baking parchment (meringue can stick on greaseproof paper and foil).

2 Tip the egg whites into a large clean mixing bowl (not plastic). Beat them on medium speed with an electric hand whisk until the mixture resembles a fluffy cloud and stands up in stiff peaks when the blades are lifted (photo 1).

3 Keep whisking, adding the caster sugar tbsp by tbsp and beating for 3–4 seconds between each addition, but don't over-beat. When ready, the mixture should be thick and glossy (photo 2).

4 Sift in a third of the icing sugar, fold in with a large metal spoon then continue to sift and fold it in, in thirds. The mixture should now look smooth and billowy, almost like a snowdrift.

5 Scoop a dessertspoonful of the meringue then, using another dessertspoon, ease it on to the baking sheet to make an oval shape (photo 3). Repeat. Or just drop them in rough rounds, if you prefer.

6 Bake for 1½–1¾ hours in a fan oven, 1¼ hours in a conventional or gas oven, until the meringues sound crisp when tapped underneath and are a pale coffee colour (photo 4). Leave to cool on the sheets or a cooling rack. (The meringues will now keep in an airtight tin for up to 2 weeks, or frozen for a month.) Serve two meringues sandwiched together with a generous dollop of softly whipped double cream.

PER MERINGUE 60 kcals, carbs 15g, fat none, sat fat none, salt 0.05g

Hazelnut and Baileys meringue cake

A fantastic combination of sweet nutty meringue, fresh cream and tart raspberries.

SERVES 6 ● PREP 20 MINS ● COOK 40-45 MINS
V

sunflower oil, for greasing
150g/4½oz toasted hazelnuts
5 egg whites
280g/10oz golden caster sugar
1 tbsp white wine vinegar
300ml pot double cream
2 tbsp icing sugar, plus extra for dusting
3 tbsp Baileys cream liqueur
200g pack fresh raspberries

tip This cake can be made up the end of Step 3 then kept in a tin for up to 3 days. Follow Step 4 to serve.

1 Heat oven to 190C/170C fan/gas 5. Line 2 x 20cm sandwich tins with foil, then lightly oil. Whizz the nuts in a processor until finely ground.
2 Whisk the egg whites in a bowl until they form stiff peaks. Whisk in most of the sugar, a spoonful at a time, until the mixture is stiff and glossy. Stir the rest of the sugar into the nuts, then fold into the meringue with the vinegar. Divide between the tins and level the tops.
3 Bake for 40–45 minutes until firm, then cool in the oven. When the meringues are cold, carefully peel off the foil.
4 To serve, whisk the cream, icing sugar and Baileys together until softly stiff. Put one of the meringues, top-side down, on a plate, then spread with the cream and scatter over some raspberries. Put the other meringue layer on top and dust generously with icing sugar.

PER SERVING 662 kcals, carbs 61g, fat 44g, sat fat 16g, salt 0.21g

Mango and passion fruit roulade

 This recipe is so rich and creamy your guests won't believe it's low in fat.

SERVES 6 ● PREP 30 MINS, PLUS COOLING COOK 30 MINS
V

3 large egg whites
175g/6oz caster sugar
1 level tsp cornflour
1 tsp malt vinegar
1 tsp vanilla extract
icing sugar, to dust
200g/7oz fat-free Greek yogurt
1 large ripe mango, peeled, stoned and diced
pulp from 4 passion fruit
icing sugar (optional) and a few physalis, to decorate
raspberry sauce, to serve (see below)

tip For a quick and delicious raspberry coulis to serve alongside, whizz 225g thawed frozen raspberries with 2 tbsp icing sugar in a blender, then press through a sieve.

1 Heat oven to 150C/130C fan/gas 2. Line a 33 x 23cm Swiss roll tin with baking parchment. Beat the egg whites with an electric whisk until frothy and doubled in bulk. Slowly whisk in the caster sugar until thick and shiny. Mix the cornflour, vinegar and vanilla extract, then whisk into the egg whites.
2 Spoon into the tin and level the surface carefully, so you don't push out the air. Bake for 30 minutes until the meringue surface is just firm.
3 Remove from the oven; cover with damp greaseproof paper for 10 minutes. Dust another sheet of paper with icing sugar. Discard the damp paper and turn the meringue out on to the sugar-coated paper. Peel off the lining, then spread yogurt over the meringue and scatter with mango and passion fruit. Use the paper to roll up the roulade from one short end. Keep the join underneath. Sift a little icing sugar on top, if you like, decorate with physalis and serve with raspberry sauce.

PER SERVING 223 kcals, carbs 45g, fat 4g, sat fat 1g, salt 0.17g

Simple strawberry cheesecake

A really easy, no-cook cheesecake that's creamy yet light.

CUTS INTO 12 SLICES • PREP 30 MINS, PLUS 1 HOUR AND OVERNIGHT CHILLING • NO COOK

V

100g/4oz butter, melted, plus extra for greasing
250g/9oz digestive biscuits
600g/1lb 4oz soft cheese
100g/4oz icing sugar
1 vanilla pod, seeds scraped out
300ml pot double cream

FOR THE TOPPING
400g punnet strawberries, halved
25g/1oz icing sugar

1 Butter and line a 23cm springform tin with baking parchment. Put the biscuits in a plastic food bag and crush to crumbs using a rolling pin. Transfer the crumbs to a bowl, then pour over the melted butter and mix until completely coated. Tip into the tin and press firmly and evenly to make a base. Chill in the fridge for 1 hour to set firmly.
2 Place the soft cheese, icing sugar and vanilla seeds in a bowl, then beat with an electric mixer until smooth. Tip in the cream and beat until smooth. Spoon over the base, smooth the top, then leave to set in the fridge overnight.
3 For the strawberry sauce, purée half the strawberries in a blender or food processor with the icing sugar and 1 tsp water, then sieve. Bring the cheesecake to room temperature, about 30 minutes before serving. Transfer the cake to a plate. Pile the remaining strawberries on top, then drizzle over the sauce.

PER SERVING 546 kcals, carbs 28g, fat 48g, sat fat 28g, salt 0.85g

Praline meringue cake with strawberries

This cake needs to be assembled just before serving – however, the meringues can be made up to a day ahead, or a month ahead and frozen.

SERVES 12 • PREP 30 MINS • COOK 1 HOUR, PLUS 1 HOUR COOLING IN OVEN

❄ V **MERINGUES ONLY**

FOR THE MERINGUE
175g/6oz whole almonds, toasted
225g/8oz golden caster sugar
225g/8oz light muscovado sugar
6 egg whites
1 tbsp cornflour
2 tsp white wine vinegar

TO ASSEMBLE
1kg/2lb 4oz strawberries, hulled and halved, or quartered if large
50g/2oz icing sugar, plus extra for dusting
568ml pot double cream

1 Heat oven to 140C/120C fan/gas 1 and line 2 flat baking sheets with baking parchment. Whizz two-thirds of the almonds in a food processor until finely chopped but not ground. Roughly chop the rest by hand.
2 Stir the sugars together. Using electric beaters, beat the egg whites until stiff, then add the sugars, cornflour and vinegar in three batches, beating back to stiff each time. Whisk until the mix is almost too stiff for the beaters.
3 Fold in the finely chopped nuts and most of the roughly chopped nuts, then spread into 20cm circles on the baking sheets. Scatter with the remaining nuts. Bake for 1 hour, then leave inside the turned-off oven for at least 1 hour.
4 Whizz 600g strawberries in a processor. Sieve, then add 2 tbsp icing sugar. Sieve the remaining icing sugar into the cream, whip softly, then swirl through two-thirds of the sauce.
5 Sandwich and top the meringues with strawberry cream. Top with strawberries, dust with icing sugar and serve the leftover strawberry sauce alongside.

PER SERVING 533 kcals, carbs 51g, fat 35g, sat fat 15g, salt 0.16g

Luscious lemon baked cheesecake

If you like your cheesecake baked to silky perfection rather than chilled, this recipe won't disappoint.

**CUTS INTO 10 SLICES • PREP 10 MINS, PLUS CHILLING
COOK 35–40 MINS**
Ⓥ ❄ **WITHOUT TOPPING**

225g/8oz digestive biscuits
100g/4oz butter, melted
250g tub mascarpone
600g/1lb 5oz soft cheese
2 eggs, plus 2 yolks
zest 3 lemons, juice 1
4 tbsp plain flour
175g/6oz caster sugar
FOR THE TOPPING
150ml pot soured cream
3 tbsp lemon curd
handful raspberries, to serve (optional)

1 Heat oven to 180C/160C fan/gas 4. Line the bottom of a 23cm springform tin with greaseproof paper. Tip the biscuits and melted butter into a food processor, then blitz to make fine crumbs. Press into the tin and chill.
2 Whisk all the other cheesecake ingredients in a large bowl until completely combined, pour into the tin, then bake for 35–40 minutes until the cheesecake has a uniform wobble.
3 Turn off the oven and leave the cake inside until cool. When it is completely cooled, remove from the tin and top with soured cream. Swirl lemon curd over the top and decorate with raspberries, if you like.

PER SLICE 705 kcals, carbs 43g, fat 57g, sat fat 34g, salt 1.08g

Double chocolate cheesecake

Cheesecake is always incredibly popular, but add chocolate and it elevates it to something with even more crowd appeal. The texture of the filling is incredibly luxurious.

**SERVES 16 • PREP 40 MINS • COOK 45–50 MINS, PLUS
2 HOURS COOLING IN THE OVEN**
Ⓥ ❄ **BEFORE DECORATING**

FOR THE BISCUIT CRUST
85g/3oz hot melted butter, plus a little extra for greasing
14 plain chocolate digestives, finely crushed
FOR THE CHEESECAKE
900g full-fat cream cheese, at room
    temperature
200g/7oz golden caster sugar
4 tbsp cocoa, sifted
2 tsp vanilla extract
3 tbsp Tia Maria
3 eggs
300ml pot soured cream
100g bar dark coffee-flavoured chocolate, melted
2–3 tbsp milk
300ml pot double cream
chocolate curls, to decorate (see below)

1 Heat oven to 180C/160C fan/gas 4. Butter then line the base of a 25cm springform tin with baking parchment. Thoroughly mix the melted butter and biscuit crumbs, then press firmly onto the base of the tin. Bake for 10 minutes.
2 Turn oven to 240C/220C fan/gas 9. Beat the cream cheese and sugar with an electric whisk until smooth and creamy, then beat in the cocoa, vanilla, Tia Maria, eggs, soured cream and half the melted chocolate. Stir enough milk into the remaining chocolate to make a sauce consistency, then set aside.
3 Pour the cheese mix into the tin and level the top. Bake for 10 minutes, then turn down to 110C/90C fan/gas ¼ for 25–30 minutes until set with a slight wobble. Turn off the oven, open the door a crack, then cool for 2 hours. Chill until ready to serve.
4 Turn the cheesecake onto a plate. Lightly whip the cream until it just holds its shape, swirl it on top of the cheesecake and drizzle and ripple with the reserved chocolate sauce. Serve with chocolate curls, if you've made them.

PER SERVING 490 kcals, carbs 29g, fat 39g, sat fat 22g, salt 0.88g

> **For chocolate curls, take a large block of chocolate and firmly run a swivel potato peeler down the smooth back of the block. Curls of chocolate will flake away from the bar. Chill until needed.**

OPPOSITE Double chocolate cheesecake

White chocolate berry cheesecake

A stunning no-cook pudding bursting with summer flavours – great for relaxed entertaining.

SERVES 8 • PREP 25 MINS, PLUS 6 HOURS OR OVERNIGHT CHILLING • NO COOK

V

oil, for greasing
600g tubs soft cheese
300ml pot double cream
50g/2oz caster sugar
2 x 150g bars white chocolate, melted
170g punnet raspberries
5 tbsp raspberry jam
85g/3oz amaretti biscuits
200g/7oz small strawberries
a few blueberries (optional)

1 Lightly oil then line a 900g loaf tin with cling film. Whisk the cheese, cream and sugar together, preferably with electric beaters, then stir into the almost-cool melted white chocolate until well combined.

2 Stir 50g raspberries with 2 tbsp of the jam. Spoon half the cheese mixture into the loaf tin, then spoon the jammy raspberries down the centre. Top with the rest of the cheese mixture, level the top, then press in the biscuits. Cover and chill for 6 hours or overnight.

3 Set aside about 6 strawberries. Warm the rest in a pan with the remaining jam until soft. Whizz in a food processor then sieve to make a smooth sauce. Add a drop of water if it seems too thick.

4 To serve, carefully turn the tin onto a plate, lift it away and strip off the cling film. Halve the remaining strawberries, then arrange on top of the cake with the remaining raspberries and blueberries (if using). Pour over a little sauce and serve the rest separately for drizzling over.

PER SERVING 667 kcals, carbs 49g, fat 50g, sat fat 29g, salt 1.01g

Frozen banana and peanut butter cheesecake

Once made, this is a great standby that can be pulled out at a moment's notice.
The combination of banana and peanut butter will impress children and adults alike.

SERVES 8–10 • PREP 30 MINS, PLUS 6 HOURS OR OVERNIGHT FREEZING • NO COOK

V ❄

3 small bananas
50g/2oz butter, melted
10 digestive biscuits, crushed to crumbs
142ml tub double cream
140g/5oz icing sugar
400g tub soft cheese
½ tsp vanilla extract
237g pot crunchy peanut butter

1 Several hours before, place 2 bananas in the freezer until the skins go black, then remove and defrost. You'll be left with really soft bananas. Peel, then mash well and set aside.

2 Mix the butter and biscuits together, then press into a 23cm springform cake tin. Whip the cream until it just holds its shape. In a separate bowl, beat the sugar, soft cheese and vanilla together until completely combined. In another bowl, beat the peanut butter to loosen it.

3 Fold the cheese mixture into the peanut butter, then tip in the mashed banana and gently fold in the cream. Spread the mix over the biscuit base and smooth the top. Freeze for several hours or preferably overnight. To serve, leave the cake in the fridge for 20 minutes, then run a knife around the side and remove the sides of the tin. Slice the remaining banana and use to decorate the cheesecake.

PER SERVING (8) 624 kcals, carbs 43g, fat 46g, sat fat 21g, salt 1.18g

Classic vanilla ice cream

Everyone will be very impressed that you've made this creamy smooth ice cream from scratch.
This recipe makes about 500g – the size of the average luxury-brand tub. First, you create the
basic mixture by making custard, then you churn it to turn it into ice cream. It's that simple.

**SERVES 6 • PREP 10 MINS, PLUS COOLING, CHURNING
AND FREEZING • COOK 20 MINS**
V ❄

1 plump vanilla pod
300ml/½ pint full-fat milk
300ml/½ pint double cream
100g/4oz golden caster sugar
4 egg yolks

1 Place a container in the freezer. Split the vanilla pod lengthways, scrape the seeds out with the point of the knife and tip into a pan with the milk, cream and pod. Bring to the boil, then remove from the heat and leave to infuse for at least 20 minutes. For the best flavour, this can be done a few hours beforehand and left to go cold (photo 1).

2 In a large bowl, whisk the sugar and egg yolks together for a few minutes until they turn pale and fluffy. Put the vanilla cream back on the heat until it's just about to boil, then carefully pour the liquid onto the yolks, beating with the whisk until completely mixed (photo 2).

3 At this point, get a large bowl of iced water and sit a smaller bowl in it. Pour the custard back into a clean pan and cook on the lowest heat, stirring slowly and continuously, making sure the spoon touches the bottom of the pan, for about 10 minutes until thickened. The custard is ready when it is thick enough to coat the back of a spoon; draw a finger through the custard – the mark left behind should last for a few moments (photo 3). It isn't essential, but if you have a kitchen thermometer, this is a good time to use it – the custard should not go above 90C.

4 Strain the custard into the bowl sitting in the iced water and leave to cool. Churn in an ice cream machine then transfer to the cold container, add chunks or ripples, if you want, and freeze. To churn by hand, put the cooled mix in a freezerproof container and, when it becomes slushy, whisk it hard or whizz with a hand blender. Place back in the freezer and repeat the process two more times, then leave to freeze until scoopable. Finally, transfer to a smaller container, adding chunks or ripples if you want. When rippling or adding chunks to the ice cream, you get a better finished scoop by 'layering up' the flavour into the ice cream, rather than folding or stirring it through (photo 4).

PER SERVING 396 kcals, carbs 21g, fat 33g, sat fat 18g, salt 0.10g

try this...

For alternative flavour suggestions turn to the next page.

Blackcurrant cheesecake ice cream

SERVES 6 • PREP 15 MINS, PLUS COOLING, CHURNING AND FREEZING • COOK 20 MINS
V ❄

1 quantity vanilla ice cream ingredients (see page 381)
150g tub cream cheese, beaten
100g/4oz blackcurrant conserve (or your favourite flavour)
5–6 shortbread biscuits, crumbled into chunks

1 Make the custard as described in the vanilla recipe and, before straining into the cold bowl, stir in the cream cheese. Churn, then sandwich layers of the ice cream in the container with large dollops of blackcurrant conserve and chunks of biscuit. Freeze until solid.

PER SERVING 587 kcals, carbs 44g, fat 44g, sat fat 24g, salt 0.48g

Chunky fudge and coffee ripple ice cream

SERVES 6 • PREP 15 MINS PLUS COOLING, CHURNING AND FREEZING • COOK 20 MINS
V ❄

1 quantity vanilla ice cream ingredients (see page 381)
3 tbsp instant coffee granules
210g pot coffee sauce
8 pieces of dairy fudge, squashed into smaller chunks

1 Make the custard as described in the vanilla recipe, then, just before sieving the hot custard into the cold bowl, stir through the coffee granules. Chill and churn, then layer the cold container with ice cream and spoonfuls of coffee sauce and fudge pieces. Freeze until solid.

PER SERVING 603 kcals, carbs 46g, fat 45g, sat fat 25g, salt 0.17g

try this...

Rich chocolate ice cream

Melt 200g/7oz dark chocolate and cool a little. Add 1 tbsp cocoa powder and the melted chocolate to the egg and sugar mixture as in the Classic vanilla recipe, before pouring on the hot milk.

Affogato

Italians love to serve vanilla ice cream with a shot of hot espresso poured over the top – and call it affogato. Kids can try it with hot chocolate.

Maple crunch ice cream

SERVES 2 WITH LEFTOVERS • PREP 10 MINS, PLUS OVERNIGHT FREEZING • NO COOK

1 tsp vanilla extract
200g/7oz light condensed milk
600ml pot double cream
4 tbsp maple syrup (strength 2, if you have the option)
50g/2oz hard caramels, crushed (see below)

To crush the sweets, unwrap, then fold them up in a clean tea towel. Bash with a rolling pin or heavy saucepan until roughly crushed.

1 Stir the vanilla into the condensed milk in a large bowl. Lightly whip the cream until it just holds its shape, then fold into the condensed milk using a metal spoon. Spoon into a 1-litre freezerproof container and freeze for about 3 hours, until softly frozen. This mix won't crystallise at the edges like most ice creams.
2 Working quickly, ruffle up the ice cream, pour over the syrup and the crushed caramels, then give another quick swirl. Freeze for another 4 hours or ideally overnight until firm. (Will freeze for up to 1 month.)

PER SERVING (8) 487 kcals, carbs 27g, fat 41g, sat fat 23g, salt 0.14g

Strawberry crème fraîche ice cream

SERVES 8 • PREP 15 MINS, PLUS FREEZING • NO COOK

500g/1lb 2oz ripe strawberries
200g/7oz caster sugar
500g tub crème fraîche

1 Remove the tops from the strawberries and put in a food processor with the sugar. Blitz to make a rough purée – a few chunky bits add texture to the ice cream.
2 Tip the crème fraîche into a bowl and stir in the strawberry purée. Churn, then freeze until solid. Remove to the the fridge for about 20 minutes to soften before serving.

PER SERVING 351 kcals, carbs 36g, fat 25g, sat fat 16g, salt 0.05g

Crunchy raspberry ripple terrine

SERVES 8 • PREP 25 MINS, PLUS FREEZING • NO COOK
V

350g/12oz raspberries
3 eggs
100g/4oz golden caster sugar
300ml pot double cream
2 meringue shells, crushed into small pieces

1 Mash 150g of the raspberries, sieve into a bowl, and set aside. Line a 1-litre loaf tin with cling film. Whisk the eggs and sugar continuously over a bowl of barely simmering water, until doubled in volume and thick. Remove the bowl from the heat. Continue to whisk until completely cool; the whole process will take about 10 minutes.
2 Whisk the cream until just thick. Fold the egg mix into the cream until completely combined, then fold in the meringue pieces. Pour the raspberry purée over the mix in a zigzag, then gently pour into the lined loaf tin. Freeze for minimum 4 hours and serve in slices with the remaining whole raspberries.

PER SERVING 284 kcals, carbs 19g, fat 22g, sat fat 11g, salt 0.11g

Coffee semifreddo

An elegant dessert that is easy to slice straight from the freezer. There's no need to churn the mix, as it's made with a very stable meringue base.

SERVES 8 • PREP 20 MINS, PLUS FREEZING • NO COOK
V ❄

1 tbsp instant coffee granules
1 tbsp Tia Maria or brandy
4 large eggs, separated
100g/4oz golden caster sugar
300ml pot double cream
100g pack honeycomb Toblerone, finely chopped
dark chocolate curls, to decorate

> *tip* To make a refreshing orange semifreddo, omit the coffee and Tia Maria and replace with the zest of ½ orange and an orange liqueur. Use dark chocolate instead of the Toblerone.

1 Oil and line a 1-litre loaf tin with cling film. Put the coffee, Tia Maria or brandy, egg yolks and sugar in a bowl and stir to dissolve the coffee. Put the egg whites in a large bowl and pour the cream in another.
2 Beat the egg whites until stiff with an electric whisk, then quickly beat the egg yolk mixture until thick and leaving a trail. Now beat the cream until it holds its shape. If you beat everything in this order, you don't need to wash the whisks in between.
3 Fold the cream into the coffee mixture, then carefully fold in the whites. Fold through the Toblerone and tip into the loaf tin. Lightly cover the surface with cling film. When frozen, overwrap in foil and freeze. (Will keep for up to 6 weeks.) You can make the chocolate curls and keep them in an airtight container or freeze them.
4 To serve, unwrap and turn out onto a platter. Strip off the cling film and serve topped with the chocolate curls.

PER SERVING 365 kcals, carbs 24g, fat 28g, sat fat 15g, salt 0.16g

Smooth chocolate sorbet

A light yet indulgent-tasting alternative to chocolate ice cream.

SERVES 4 • PREP 5 MINS PLUS COOLING, CHURNING AND FREEZING • COOK 5 MINS
V

225g/8oz caster sugar
200g bar dark chocolate, 70% cocoa solids

1 Put the sugar into a pan with 500ml water and warm until dissolved. Cool completely. Meanwhile, gently melt the chocolate over a pan of barely simmering water or in the microwave. When both the syrup and the melted chocolate are cool (this is very important), slowly combine the two in a large bowl and chill. Once chilled, churn in an ice-cream machine or by hand until frozen, then freeze.

PER SERVING 504 kcals, carbs 81.8g, fat 20.3g, sat fat 10.3g, salt 0.01g

OPPOSITE Clockwise from top left Crunchy raspberry ripple terrine (page 383); Pomegranate ice (page 386); Blackcurrant cheesecake icecream (page 382); Coffee semifreddo; Fruity coconut ices (page 386); Mango and vanilla granita (page 387).

Pomegranate ice

 Preserve the sweet flavour of juicy pomegranates by turning them into a sorbet. Ideal in wintertime, when pomegranates are most plentiful.

SERVES 8 • EASY PREP 40 MINS • NO COOK
❄ Ⅴ **LOW FAT**

450g/1lb golden caster sugar
8 pomegranates

1 Tip the sugar into a bowl and pour over 600ml boiling water from a kettle. Stir to dissolve, then set aside to cool.
2 Meanwhile, juice the pomegranates. Squeeze and press the skin of 7 of the pomegranates vigorously to crush the seeds inside. Hold the squashed fruit over a bowl, slit the skin with a knife and the juice will pour out. Mix the juice with the syrup and churn in an ice cream machine until set. If you don't own an ice cream machine, make the syrup into a granita by freezing it on a tray, then breaking up the ice crystals with a fork when it starts to turn slushy. Scoop into a plastic container and freeze. Serve the sorbet in scoops, scattered with a few seeds from the remaining fruit.

PER SERVING 305 kcals, carbs 78g, fat none, sat fat none, salt 0.01g

Fruity coconut ices

A yummy treat on a hot day.

MAKES 8 • PREP 20 MINS, PLUS FREEZING • NO COOK
Ⅴ ❄

150g/5½oz raspberries
4 tbsp icing sugar
450g/1lb Greek coconut flavoured yogurt
8 lolly moulds

1 Purée the raspberries in a food processor along with the icing sugar. Sieve to remove the seeds. Spoon half the yogurt into a bowl and stir in 2 tbsp of purée so it is stained pink. Spoon into lolly moulds, add the rest of the purée then the rest of the yogurt. Push in lolly sticks and freeze until solid.

PER SERVING 123 kcals, carbs 14.7g, fat 6.4g, sat fat 4.7g, salt 0.06g

Mango and vanilla granita

 The vanilla in this recipe is optional and certainly not essential, but it works really well when served with strawberries.

SERVES 6–8 • PREP 15 MINS, PLUS COOLING AND FREEZING
❄ Ⓥ

1 vanilla pod, split (optional)
140g/5oz caster sugar
2 large ripe mangoes
300g/11oz strawberries, sliced, to serve

 For successful granitas, switch your freezer to its coldest setting. The shallower the container, the quicker the mixture will freeze.

Always check the mixture for flavour before freezing and remember that it will taste blander when frozen. So aim for a mixture that's intense and slightly oversweet.

If you forget to fork it and the mixture freezes solid, defrost it, then start again or simply break it up in a food processor.

1 Clear a shelf in the freezer and place a sided metal tray in to chill. Tip the vanilla into a bowl with the sugar. Bring a kettle of water to the boil and pour 250ml over the sugar. Stir until completely dissolved, then leave to cool.
2 Meanwhile, peel the mangoes and cut away all the flesh, then blitz in a food processor until you have a smooth purée. Stir the purée into the syrup and fish out the vanilla pod. Freeze the purée in the tray, covered with cling film, until frozen around the edges and slushy in the middle.
3 Use a fork to break up the ice into smaller crystals. Return the tray to the freezer. Repeat the breaking up process every half hour (at least three times) until it's completely frozen and the texture of snow. Serve with sliced strawberries.

PER SERVING 163 kcals, carbs 42g, fat none, sat fat none, salt 0.02g

Vanilla yogurt ice

If you're watching your fat intake, yogurt ices make a great alternative to ice cream. Serve with sweet seasonal fruit.

SERVES 6 • PREP 15 MINS, PLUS FREEZING • NO COOK
Ⓥ

200g/7oz golden caster sugar
1 vanilla pod, seeds scraped out
2 x 500g pots natural yogurt

1 Place the caster sugar in a bowl, then rub in the vanilla seeds with your fingers so they're evenly mixed. Stir in the yogurt until the sugar has dissolved. Churn the mixture in an ice cream machine until frozen but still soft or, if you don't have a machine, pour the yogurt into a freezer-safe container and freeze for 4–6 hours, stirring thoroughly every hour or so. Meanwhile, line a 900g loaf tin with cling film.
2 Spoon the soft frozen yogurt into the tin, cover with another piece of cling film, then freeze for at least 4 hours, until firm. Take the yogurt ice from the freezer about 10 minutes before you want to serve it.

PER SERVING 265 kcals, carbs 48.5g, fat 5g, sat fat 3.1g, salt 0.34g

Christmas cooking

For many of us, Christmas starts in November (or sometimes earlier), preparing the cake and pudding then tucking them away. Then some of us – well, we're in the shops on Christmas Eve, fighting for the last bag of sprouts. Whatever kind of cook you are, the following recipes and information should help you to make this your best, and tastiest, Christmas ever.

THE TURKEY

A well-chosen turkey, cooked with the right know-how, will reward you with a truly memorable meal (and leave you wondering why you don't cook it more often). If you feel particularly daunted by cooking a turkey, then just think of this as one (albeit bigger) roast chicken. (If turkey is definitely off the menu, there are great alternatives in goose, duck, beef or vegetarian dishes in this book – and something for every party size, too.)

What size to buy

Weight (kg)	Serves	Weight (kg)	Serves
2–2.5	4–6	4–4.5	8–10
3	6–7	5–5.5	10–12
3.5	7–8	6–6.5	12–15

Do I need a whole one?

If you don't fancy roasting a whole bird or know you won't eat that much meat, go for a more compact turkey crown – this is just the breast section of the bird and can be bought on the bone, or boned and rolled. It cooks quickly and there will be no tricky bones to negotiate when carving.

Free-range

It really is worth spending a bit more on your bird for flavour and texture. Make sure it is labelled free-range or organic – 'farm-reared' or 'farm-fresh' labels don't have any legal meaning. For a fuller, denser flavour try a Bronze or Black turkey. If your budget won't stretch to free-range, look for the British Turkey Quality mark.

Fresh and frozen

Pick up your fresh turkey no more than 2 days before Christmas. Choose one with a plump breast with no tears in the skin. Remove any packaging and take the giblets out of their bag. If your fresh turkey isn't pre-packed,

OPPOSITE *Classic roast turkey (page 396).*

cover it with foil and place it on a plate at the bottom of the fridge until Christmas morning. Bring it to room temperature an hour before cooking – if you roast it from chilled, the cooking times will be longer.

Make sure the bird is completely frozen when you buy it and hasn't started to thaw. Calculate in advance how long it will take to defrost, and thaw the turkey in its packaging in the fridge or in a cool place such as a shed or garage – protected from pets or other animals. You can speed up the process by defrosting it in cold water – in a sink, or a large bucket – that is regularly changed. Once thawed, unwrap and wipe the turkey inside and out with kitchen paper. Return to the fridge or keep in a cool place.

Stuffing

The stuffing can be prepared ahead, but don't stuff the bird until it is about to be cooked. Stuff only the neck cavity, never the body cavity (as it will not cook through); this can be filled with sprigs of fresh herbs and slices of lemon or onion to infuse the meat with extra flavours.

How long in the oven?

Whatever size bird you go for, allow 40 minutes per kilo at 190C/170C fan/gas 5 (20 minutes per 450g/1 lb). Calculate cooking times for crowns and boned joints in exactly the same way. These timings and temperatures correlate with our turkey recipe on page 396; for accurate timing, always weigh your turkey after stuffing. If it's very large, you may need to use bathroom scales.

How to test if the turkey is done

Make sure the juices run clear when you pierce the thigh using the point of a knife or a skewer where it meets the body. Catch the juices with a spoon. If there is any hint of pink or streaks of blood, put the bird back in the oven for another 20 minutes, then test again.

Let it rest

Rest the cooked turkey for at least 20 minutes (ideally 30–45 minutes) before carving – this is essential for a juicy, tender result, and it makes it easier to carve, too. Don't worry about the meat getting cold while resting, just make sure you put it onto a hot platter and cover it tightly with foil. This then allows you to turn up the oven temperature to crisp your roast potatoes, if needed.

Leftovers

You can keep cold, cooked turkey in the fridge for up to 3 days. Slice it from the carcass first so it can cool quickly on a cold plate somewhere cool (an unheated room is ideal). Leftover stuffing should be cooled too. (It can be frozen for up to two months.) Make sure the stuffing is piping hot if you reheat it.

GOOSE

A free-range or traditionally reared goose will give the most tender meat and a crisp skin. A goose won't stretch as far as a turkey – a 4.5kg goose will serve 6–8 people, a 5.5kg goose will serve 8–10, and a 6.5kg goose between 10 and 12.

If you're buying a fresh goose more than 2 days ahead of roasting it, it's best to freeze it, keeping the giblets separate. Allow 24 hours for it to defrost completely in the fridge. Always unwrap the bird and keep it chilled or in a cold room. Keep giblets in the fridge as they defrost.

Stuffing, roasting and resting

Before stuffing and roasting a goose, pull out the two big lumps of fat from inside the cavity and wipe around the inside with kitchen paper. Then, using a fork or skewer, prick the goose skin (try to avoid going through to the flesh) all over, then rub over plenty of coarse sea or rock salt. As a general rule, allow 30 minutes per kilo (15 minutes per 450g/lb), plus an extra 30 minutes. Weigh the stuffed goose and then calculate the cooking times.

To check if it's done, test it with a skewer just as you would for a turkey. When removing the goose from the oven at the end of roasting, carefully tip away the excess fat from its cavity. Put on a serving platter and rest as for turkey.

Step-by-step: How to carve a turkey

Rather than struggling to carve around the legs, this clever technique lets you cut away the thighs ready to portion, leaving the breast meat easy to access.

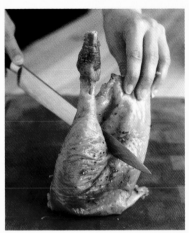

1 Remove legs Cut the string around the legs then cut through the skin between leg and body. Force the knife between the end of the thigh bone and the body; twist leg off. Do the same with the wings.

2 Separate the drumstick and thigh Slice between the drumstick and thigh until the knife hits the joint. Twist the knife through the joint to separate the drumstick and thigh.

3 Begin carving the breast Hold the turkey firmly on the board with a carving fork. Make a horizontal cut into the breast above the wing, cutting through the bone. Carve the breast meat in long downward slices (or do chunkier slices) following the curves of the bird's body until you reach the bone.

TIPS FOR SUCCESS:

• Order your turkey (or other meat) early. Ask for the wishbone to be removed from a fresh turkey, as this makes carving easier.

• Tiny oven, huge turkey? Remove the legs and roast these separately, or divide the bird up completely into legs, wings and breasts.

• Fridge space is always tight at Christmas: give meat and dairy priority in the fridge and store surplus veggies in a cool place.

• Write a timeplan for the Christmas meal so you can work out the order in which you'll need to cook everything. To make things less stressful on the day, do as much preparation as you can the day before,
such as peeling the vegetables, making the stuffing, infusing the milk for the bread sauce and making the breadcrumbs. You could even lay the table and decide which serving dishes you are going to use.

• Parboil or blanch and refresh veg to reduce the cooking time on Christmas Day. (There are get-ahead tips at the bottom of every veg recipe in this chapter.)

• Speed up the preparation time for accompaniments and save space on the hob by steaming veg in an electric steamer and warming through sauces in the microwave.

• If you're short on oven space, warm plates quickly in a washing-up bowl of hot water.

• And finally, if anyone offers to help by bringing along part of the meal – have no pride, accept their offer!

CHRISTMAS PUDDINGS

And onto dessert we go. All steamed puds, including Christmas pudding, need to be tied up before cooking to ensure an airtight seal. Check you have the right size of pudding basin as specified in the recipe, because the mixture requires space to expand during cooking.

COUNTDOWN TO CHRISTMAS

The best way to keep yourself in good spirits this holiday is to be as well prepared as possible.

October

- If making a traditional Christmas cake, do it now, ready to feed throughout the coming months.
- Book your Christmas online shopping delivery slot, if that's how you shop. They get booked up very early.
- Start to clear your freezer.

November

- Plan your menu, and place meat orders early to avoid disappointment.
- It's stir up Sunday, the last Sunday before advent, and traditionally time to make your Christmas pudding.
- Begin building up the Christmas storecupboard, eg vac-packed chestnuts. Buy wines, beers, spirits and mixers while there are good offers on.
- Make any pickles and chutneys (whether for you or for gifts) that need time to mellow before eating.

December

Week one and two

- Put a few batches of mince pies in the freezer, in case of impromptu visitors.
- And if you are planning a drinks party before Christmas, take a look at our canapé ideas on page 447 and freeze what you can ahead of time.
- Make a couple of one-pot dishes for the freezer – handy for Christmas eve or when you get home late from a long day of shopping.
- Finalise your menu and shopping lists. Make-ahead starters and desserts are best – as well as those in this chapter, you'll find many other suitable recipes throughout this book.

Week three

- Marzipan and decorate the cake, if you are making a traditional cake.
- Pick up any fruit and vegetables that will keep happily in a cool place, such as potatoes, apples and satsumas,

nuts. Also buy your cheeses, so that any that need to be eaten soft have time to ripen.
- Make bread sauce, cranberry sauce, stuffing and anything else that can be made ahead and kept in the fridge or freezer. Stash a couple of loaves in there, ready for sandwiches.
- Write a timetable for the day, so you can work out the order you'll need to cook everything.

3 days before

- Clear your kitchen surfaces of equipment you won't be using
- Brave the shops or the market for your sprouts and any other perishables.

Also check that you have:

- Extra-wide foil
- Thermometer or skewer
- Chopping board – one with a reservoir for catching juices is ideal
- Kitchen roll
- String – useful for tying up the turkey and making a handle for the pud.
- Matches – buy long cook's matches to light candles and for flaming the traditional pud.
- Washing up liquid
- Spare batteries, not only for toys, but also in case you need them in your kitchen timers or scales

23rd December

- Collect your orders from the butcher and keep in a cold garage or in the fridge if room. There's more info about storing or defrosting your turkey on page 389.
- Check that you have enough ice in the freezer.

Christmas eve

- Make the base for the gravy, wrap sausages in bacon, make stuffing if not already, peel vegetables, and part-cook some if that helps you to feel more prepared.
- Write out a full time plan of the cooking for tomorrow, allowing for resting time, during which you can turn the oven temp up and finish off roast potatoes and the gravy.
- Lay the table if that's practical.
- If serving ham on Boxing Day, cook and cool it today, ready to reheat or serve cold.

Christmas day

- If you're short on oven space, warm plates quickly in a washing up bowl of hot water.
- Tiny oven, huge turkey? Remove the legs and roast these separately.

Step-by-step: Wrapping a pudding basin

Steaming a pudding cooks it gently and gives an unbeatably moist texture. The pleat in the foil and paper is essential – without it the pudding would burst out at the seams. This method is the same for meat puddings and also steamed sponges, and can be used for cooking in the oven as well as in a saucepan.

1 Cut a length of baking parchment approximately 40cm long and the same of foil, and lay them on top of each other. Keeping the sheets together, make a pleat widthways across the centre. Cover the basin with the paper facing down and press to the shape of the bowl.

2 Cut a length of string approximately 1.5m long (stretch both your arms out when holding the string to get the right length).Tie the string under the ridge around the top of the bowl at one end of the bowl, then double it back the other way and tie a knot in it at the other end.

3 To make a handle, bring the string back across the top of the bowl and secure it to the opposite side with a knot.

4 Trim off the excess paper and foil, leaving a collar of about 3cm, then tuck the foil neatly under itself.

The traditional way to steam a pudding is in a large, deep saucepan or steamer. Steamers are straightforward to use; simply fill the bottom compartment with water and sit the basin in the top section.

When using a pan, you'll need to protect the basin from the bottom of the pan. An upturned saucer makes an excellent trivet, or you can use a squashed egg box.

Lower the basin into the pan, then fill the pan with hot water from the kettle, so that the water level reaches half way up the sides of the basin. Bring to a simmer with the lid on.

As the pudding steams, top up the water levels from time to time with more boiling water. Some cooks like to put something like a marble in the bottom of the pan – if the pan boils dry, the marble rattles and you come running.

Duck and pork terrine with cranberries and pistachios

Set aside a couple of hours and enjoy every minute of making this terrine that's ideal as a starter or part of a buffet. It will keep for a week in the fridge tightly covered with foil.

SERVES 10–12 ● PREP 45 MINS ● COOK 2 HOURS 35 MINS
❄

2 duck breasts, about 300g/11oz each, skin removed
    and reserved
200g/7oz thinly sliced streaky bacon rashers
1kg/2lb 4oz pork shoulder, cubed
2 slices bread, crusts removed
100ml/3½fl oz milk
3 shallots, roughly chopped
1 large garlic clove, roughly chopped
200g/7oz duck or chicken livers, roughly chopped
6 black peppercorns
12 coriander seeds
2 cloves
good pinch ground cinnamon
2 tbsp Cognac or brandy
2 eggs, beaten
25g/1oz shelled pistachios
50g/2oz dried cranberries

1 Heat oven to 160C/140C fan/gas 3. Put the duck breasts and skin in a shallow dish, then place in the hot oven for 20 minutes. Discard the shrivelled bit of skin that remains, then pour the fat into a bowl to cool. Roughly chop the cooked duck meat.

2 Reserve 6 bacon rashers, then roughly chop the remainder. In a food processor, blend the chopped bacon, pork and duck in batches to a coarse texture, then tip into a large bowl. Tear up the bread and soak in the milk for 5 minutes. Squeeze out the bread and put in the food processor with the shallots, garlic and livers. Process to a coarse texture, then add to the bowl, mixing well.

3 Grind the peppercorns, coriander seeds and cloves to a coarse powder using a pestle and mortar or spice grinder. Stir in the cinnamon. Add the spices to the meat along with 4 tbsp reserved duck fat, the Cognac, eggs and 2 tsp salt. Mix together very thoroughly – the best way is to use your hands.

4 Press half the mixture into a 1.5-litre terrine baking dish or similar. Scatter over the pistachios and cranberries, then cover with the remaining meat. Arrange the reserved bacon rashers over the top, tucking in the ends. Cover tightly with foil, then put in a roasting tin. Pour boiling water into the tin to come halfway up the sides of the dish.

5 Bake for 2 hours, remove the foil, then bake for 15 minutes more to brown the top. Cool completely, then wrap in fresh foil and chill. For the best flavour, let the terrine chill and mature for at least 2 days before eating.

PER SERVING 476 kcals, carbs 11g, fat 30g, sat fat 11g, salt 1.66g

try this...

Serve with Chicory and lamb's lettuce with walnut dressing.
Slice 3 chicory heads and mix in a salad bowl with 100g lamb's lettuce, a good handful coarsely chopped walnuts and 1 finely chopped shallot. Whisk together 1 tbsp sherry vinegar, a little Dijon mustard, salt and pepper. Whisk in 1 tbsp walnut oil and 2 tbsp mild olive oil and dress.

tip To get well ahead, make the terrine as stated, cool, then freeze for up to 1 month. Defrost in the fridge before serving.

Smoked salmon with beetroot and vodka crème fraîche

*This is smoked salmon Russian style, and a simple but stunning starter. Serve with
a shot of vodka, if you like.*

SERVES 6 • PREP 15 MINS • NO COOK

200ml tub crème fraîche
3 tsp vodka
2 tsp hot horseradish sauce
6 slices smoked salmon
250g pack small, cooked beetroot (not in vinegar),
    thinly sliced, then shredded
50g pot salmon caviar (optional)
few small, torn dill sprigs

1 Beat the crème fraîche with the vodka and a little
seasoning until it holds its shape, then stir in the horseradish.
Chill in the fridge.
2 Lay the slices of salmon over plates, then top with the
beetroot and a spoonful of the crème fraîche. Top with the
salmon caviar, if using, then scatter with the dill. Grind over
some black pepper and serve.

PER SERVING 189 kcals, carbs 5g, fat 15g, sat fat 9g, salt 1.37g

Grilled goat's cheese with cranberry dressing

*Wonderfully easy, this dish is always greeted with appreciative noises! As another
vegetarian dish, it works really well before most meat or fish courses.*

SERVES 6 • PREP 15 MINS • COOK 6 MINS
Ⓥ

2 red-skinned apples
3 tbsp lemon juice
3 x 100g goat's cheeses (the kind with rind), halved
    horizontally
2 tbsp cranberry sauce
2 tbsp olive oil
1 tsp clear honey
25g/1oz pecans
2 chicory heads, separated into leaves
handful radish sprouts (available from larger
    supermarkets) or watercress

1 Quarter, core, then thinly slice the apple into a bowl with
the lemon juice and 1 tbsp water. Toss well, as this stops the
apples going brown.
2 Heat grill to High, then line the grill rack with foil. Put the
cheeses rind-side down on the foil, then set aside for a
moment.
3 Drain 2 tbsp of the juice from the apple bowl into another
small bowl and discard the rest. Add the cranberry sauce,
oil and honey with some seasoning, and whisk to form a
dressing. Grill the cheeses for 4 minutes, then scatter the
nuts on and around the cheeses and return to the grill to
cook for a few minutes more – but take care that the nuts
don't burn.
4 Arrange the apple, chicory and radish sprouts or
watercress on 6 plates, then carefully top with the hot
melted cheese. Scatter over the nuts, spoon over the
dressing and serve straight away.

PER SERVING 200 kcals, carbs 10g, fat 15g, sat fat 6g, salt 0.61g

Classic roast turkey

Here's how to guarantee your turkey is succulent, full of flavour and takes pride of place on your table. Spend as much as you can afford on your turkey – the difference is well worth it.

SERVES 8-10 WITH LEFTOVERS • PREP 20 MINS COOK 3–3½ HOURS

1 onion, quartered
fresh bay leaves, to flavour and serve
4.5–5.6kg/10–12lb turkey, giblets removed
250g/9oz stuffing (see page 399)
85g/3oz butter, softened
1 whole nutmeg
10 rashers streaky bacon
glass red wine, such as Merlot

tip Since turkeys are so large, it's not advisable to stuff the cavity of the bird. It takes a long time for the stuffing to heat through which leads to the risk of salmonella. Stuff the neck end instead, and add a few fresh herbs and onions to the cavity.

1 Heat oven to 190C/170C fan/gas 5. Put the onion and a large sprig of bay in the cavity between the legs. Now pack the stuffing into the neck end, pushing it towards the breast. Secure the neck skin in position with skewers and tie the turkey legs together at the top of the drumsticks to give a neat shape. Weigh the turkey and calculate the cooking time at 40 minutes per kilo (20 minutes per lb). (You may need to use your bathroom scales.)
2 Put a large sheet of extra-wide foil in a large roasting tin, then put the turkey on top. Smear the breast with the butter, grate over half the nutmeg and season well. Cover the breast with bacon, pour over the wine, then loosely bring up the foil and seal well to make a parcel.
3 Roast in the oven, then 90 minutes before the end of cooking, open the foil, discard the bacon and drain the excess fat from the tin. Leaving the foil open, return the turkey to the oven to brown, basting with the juices several times.
4 To test whether the turkey is cooked, push a skewer into the thickest part of the thigh – the juices should run clear. If they are pinkish, cook for 15 minutes more, then test again. Transfer the turkey to a platter, cover with foil, then a couple of tea towels and allow to rest for up to 30 minutes before carving. This gives the juices time to settle back into the meat, ensuring that the turkey will be juicy. Garnish with sprigs of bay.

PER SERVING 476 kcals, carbs none, fat 19g, sat fat 7g, salt 0.69g

Easy red wine gravy

SERVES 10 • TAKES 10 MINS
❄

200ml/7fl oz red wine (we used Merlot)
3 tbsp cornflour
600ml/1 pint turkey or chicken stock, made with cubes or freshly made (see page 28)
2 tbsp redcurrant jelly
200ml/7fl oz turkey juices, skimmed of all fat (make up with stock if you don't have enough)

1 Mix 3 tbsp red wine with the cornflour until smooth, then mix in all the wine. Heat the stock in a pan, then pour in the red wine mixture and redcurrant jelly, stirring until thickened. Cover the surface with cling film to stop a skin forming. (Chill for up to 2 days.)
2 To serve, reheat in a pan until bubbling, then stir in the turkey juices and transfer to a warm gravy boat.

PER SERVING 35 kcals, carbs 7g, fat none, sat fat none, salt 0.42g

Pancetta-wrapped turkey breast with herby lemon and pine nut stuffing

Wrapped in pancetta, this rolled turkey breast will be so succulent you really won't miss the rest of the bird – or the carving. A quick white wine and cream sauce makes a change from gravy, or use the red wine gravy opposite.

SERVES 6–8 PLUS LEFTOVERS ● PREP 30 MINS COOK APPROX 2 HOURS
❄ UNCOOKED

butter, for greasing
20 rashers pancetta or thinly sliced streaky bacon
3kg/6lb 8oz butterflied turkey breast

FOR THE STUFFING
25g/1oz butter
1 tbsp olive oil
2 large onions, halved and sliced
140g pack pancetta cubes or bacon lardons
50g/2oz pine nuts
4 garlic cloves, chopped
25g pack sage, leaves only, roughly shredded
zest 2 lemons
40g bunch flat-leaf parsley, roughly chopped
100g/4oz coarse white breadcrumbs
1 egg, beaten

FOR THE GRAVY
300ml/10fl oz dry white wine
300ml/10fl oz chicken stock
150ml pot double cream
handful flat-leaf parsley, roughly chopped

1 First prepare the stuffing. Heat the butter and oil in a large frying pan, then soften the onion without colouring for 10 minutes. Tip into a bowl. Add the pancetta or bacon to the pan, fry for 5 minutes until golden, then add the pine nuts, garlic, sage and lemon zest. Fry for 1 minute more until fragrant and the pine nuts are starting to brown. Stir in the chopped parsley. Tip into the bowl with the onions, then bind with the crumbs, egg and seasoning.

2 Butter and season a sheet of turkey foil or use 2 sheets of foil crimped together to make a sheet about 50 x 60cm. Lay five long pieces of string over the foil like rungs of a ladder, ready to tie the breast together. Arrange the pancetta or bacon in a lattice over the middle of the foil, on top of the string.

3 Open out the butterflied breast, skin-side down, and slash each side several times. Cover with cling film and bash with a rolling pin until the meat is about 5cm thick all over. Trim the sides so that you have a roughly rectangular shape (but be careful not to cut the skin). Lift onto the pancetta, then fill any gaps with the trimmings. Season, then press the stuffing along the middle of the joint. Pull up the sides at one end, tucking in the short end, then tie the string tightly so that the stuffing is encased. Repeat with all the strings. Wrap up tightly in the foil, then turn the roll over so that the pancetta is on the top. (Can be left in the fridge for up to 2 days.)

4 Heat oven to 190C/170C fan/gas 5. Sit the joint in a roasting tin and roast for 40 minutes per kilo or until a skewer inserted into the middle comes out very hot and the juices run clear. Unwrap for the last 10 minutes of cooking.

5 Lift the joint onto a board and leave to rest, covered, for at least 10 minutes. For the gravy, heat the tin on the hob, then splash in the wine and any juices. Reduce by half, then add the stock and repeat. Pour in the cream and bubble to a slightly reduced sauce. Season to taste, then stir in the parsley and any resting juices.

PER SERVING (8) 850 kcals, carbs 18g, fat 43g, sat fat 16g, salt 2.96g

> A butterflied turkey breast consists of two turkey breasts taken off the bird but still joined by the skin. Ask your butcher to do this for you.

Bacon-wrapped sausages

SERVES 12 • PREP 10 MINS • COOK 20 MINS

12 rashers streaky bacon
24 cocktail sausages

1 Heat the oven to 190C/170C/gas 5. Cut the bacon rashers in half lengthways, then wrap around the cocktail sausages. Place the wrapped sausages on a baking sheet, then cook for 20 minutes until crisp.

PER SERVING 130 kcals, carbs 6.3g, fat 1.5g, sat fat 8g, salt 0.83g

Lemon and herb stuffing

**SERVES 8 PLUS 250G TO STUFF THE TURKEY
PREP 20 MINS • COOK 50 MINS
❄ V IF BAKED WITHOUT THE SAUSAGES AND BACON**

4 tbsp sunflower oil
5 onions, finely chopped
300g/11oz white bread, in chunks
small bunch curly parsley
small bunch sage, leaves only
1 tbsp thyme leaves
zest 3 lemons, juice 1
8 cocktail sausages
4 smoked, dry-cured streaky bacon rashers, halved
    across the middle

1 Heat oven to 190C/170C fan/gas 5. Heat oil in a large frying pan, then soften the onions for 10 minutes with the pan covered. Pulse the bread and herbs in a food processor to make herby breadcrumbs. Stir into the onion with the lemon zest and juice and plenty of seasoning. Set aside 250g for the turkey (see page 396), then press the remainder into a well-buttered baking tin or dish, about 20 x 30cm.
2 Wrap half a bacon rasher around each sausage. Score the stuffing in the tin into 8 rectangles, then sit a sausage on top of each. Cover with foil and cook for 20 minutes. Uncover, then roast for 20 minutes more until golden and sizzling.

PER SERVING 142 kcals, carbs 13g, fat 8g, sat fat 2g, salt 0.67g

Chestnut, bacon and cranberry stuffing

**SERVES 8 PLUS 250G TO STUFF THE TURKEY • PREP 15
MINS, PLUS SOAKING • COOK ABOUT 50 MINS**

100g/4oz dried cranberries
50ml/2fl oz ruby port
1 small onion, chopped
2 rashers unsmoked back bacon, cut into strips
50g/2oz butter
2 garlic cloves, chopped
450g/1lb sausagemeat
140g/5oz fresh white or brown breadcrumbs
2 tbsp chopped fresh parsley
½ tsp chopped fresh thyme leaves
140g/5oz peeled, cooked chestnuts, roughly chopped
1 medium egg, lightly beaten

1 Soak the cranberries in the port for an hour. Fry the onion and bacon in the butter for 10 minutes until the onion is soft and the bacon is cooked. Add the garlic and fry for 1 minute.
2 Cool slightly, then mix with all the remaining ingredients, including the cranberries and port, adding enough egg to bind. Season to taste. Set aside 250g for the turkey, (see page 396).
3 Heat oven to 190C/170C fan/gas 5. Roll into walnut-size balls then roast for 30–40 minutes, until crisp and nicely browned.

PER STUFFING BALL 123 kcals, carbs 12g, fat 7g, sat fat 3g, salt 0.65g

OPPOSITE Clockwise from top left Smoked salmon with beetroot and vodka crème fraîche (page 395); Crisp honey mustard parsnips (page 401); Pancetta-wrapped turkey breast with herb(397), lemon and pine nut stuffing; Grilled goat's cheese with cranberry dressing (page 395).

Sage, leek and onion balls

**MAKES 16 SMALL BALLS PLUS 250G TO STUFF THE TURKEY
PREP 20 MINS • COOK ABOUT 1 HOUR**

4 tbsp sunflower or vegetable oil
2 onions, finely chopped
1 leek, finely sliced into rings
2 celery sticks, finely chopped
450g pack good-quality pork sausages, meat squeezed out
20g pack sage, leaves finely chopped
140g/5oz white breadcrumbs
1 large egg
8 smoked dry-cured streaky bacon rashers, halved and
    stretched out a bit
sage sprig, to garnish (optional)

1 Heat oven to 190C/170C fan/gas 5. Heat the oil in a large frying pan, then soften the onions, leek and celery for 15 minutes with the pan covered. Put the sausagemeat into a bowl. Once the onion mix has cooled, tip onto the sausagemeat, add the sage, breadcrumbs, egg and seasoning, then mix really well with your hands.
2 Set aside 250g to stuff the turkey, (see page 396), then shape the rest into 16 balls, wrapping each with bacon. Sit these on a non-stick baking sheet, cover with foil, then bake for 15 minutes. Uncover, then bake for 30 minutes more until the bacon is golden. Garnish with a sage sprig, if you like.

PER SERVING 131 kcals, carbs 8g, fat 9g, sat fat 2g, salt 0.72g

Creamy bread and onion sauce

SERVES 8–10 • PREP 15 MINS • COOK 30 MINS

85g/3oz butter
2 onions, sliced
2 fresh bay leaves, plus extra to serve
600ml/1 pint whole milk
7 cloves
140g/5oz crustless white bread
142ml pot double cream

1 Heat the butter in a pan, add the onions and bay leaves, then gently fry with the lid on for 10 minutes until soft, but not coloured.
2 Add the milk and cloves, then simmer gently, uncovered, for 30 minutes, stirring occasionally.
3 Remove the bay and cloves, then tip everything into a processor and blitz with two-thirds of the bread until smooth. (Chill for up to 2 days.) To serve, tip the cream into a pan, add the sauce, then stir until mixed. Tear in the remaining bread. Add a little milk if necessary to thin the consistency. Season and serve warm.

PER SERVING 269 kcals, carbs 15g, fat 22g, sat fat 13g, salt 0.48g

Simple port and cranberry sauce

**SERVES 8–10 WITH LEFTOVERS • PREP 5 MINS
COOK 5–10 MINS**
V ❄

300ml/½ pint port
175g/6oz light muscovado sugar
500g/1lb 2oz fresh or frozen cranberries

1 Tip the port and sugar into a pan and bring to the boil. Add the cranberries, then cook for 5 minutes (for frozen) and 8–10 minutes (for fresh) until tender, but holding their shape. The sauce will thicken as it cools. (It will keep in the fridge for 1 week or freeze for up to 6 weeks. Thaw for 2 hours or overnight before serving.)

PER SERVING 151 kcals, carbs 29g, fat none, sat fat none, salt 0.02g

Buttered sprouts with chestnuts and bacon

SERVES 8 • **PREP 15 MINS** • **COOK 15 MINS**

1.25kg/2lb 12oz Brussels sprouts, trimmed (or if buying
   pre-trimmed, buy 1kg/2lb 4oz)
6 rashers streaky smoked bacon, cut into bite-size
   pieces (or use more, if you like)
200g vacuum-packed chestnuts
50g/2oz butter

> *tip* To get ahead, boil the sprouts, drain and cool,
> then chill in the fridge. You can also fry the bacon and
> chestnuts two days ahead, then chill. On the day, just
> finish cooking the sprouts and assemble the dish.

1 Boil the sprouts in salted water for 5 minutes. Drain, cool
under the cold tap, then drain again. Meanwhile, dry fry the
bacon in a frying pan for 10 minutes until crisp and golden.
Tip out of the pan, leaving the fat behind, then add the
chestnuts and fry over a high heat for about 5 minutes until
tinged. Tip out of the pan.
2 Add the sprouts and a splash of water, then cover and
finish cooking over a medium heat for about 5 minutes,
stirring now and again, until just tender. Uncover, turn up the
heat, then add most of the butter and sauté the sprouts for
2 minutes more. Tip in the bacon and chestnuts, season
generously, then serve with the last knob of butter on top.

PER SERVING 196 kcals, carbs 16g, fat 12g, sat fat 5g, salt 0.61g

Crisp honey mustard parsnips

SERVES 8 • **PREP 15 MINS** • **COOK 15 MINS**
Ⓥ

1kg/2lb 4oz parsnips, peeled and cut into thumb-width
   batons
2 tsp English mustard powder
2 tbsp plain flour
4 tbsp rapeseed oil
about 3 tsp clear honey

1 Boil the parsnips for 5 minutes, then drain and let them
steam-dry for a few minutes. Mix the mustard, flour and
plenty of seasoning. Toss the parsnips in the mix, then shake
off any excess.
2 Heat oven to 220C/200C fan/gas 7. Put the oil onto one
large, or even better 2, non-stick baking sheets (the parsnips
mustn't be crowded), then heat in the oven for 5 minutes.
Carefully scoop the parsnips into the fat, turn them a few
times, then roast for 30 minutes or until golden and crisp.
Drizzle honey over the hot parsnips, shake to coat then
scatter with flaky sea salt to serve.

PER SERVING 149 kcals, carbs 19g, fat 7g, sat fat none, salt 0.66g

Sticky spiced red cabbage

 SERVES 6–8 • **PREP 15 MINS** • **COOK 35 MINS**
Ⓥ ❄

1 tbsp olive oil
1 medium-size red cabbage, quartered, cored and
   shredded
1 finger-size piece fresh root ginger, finely chopped
2 onions, sliced
1 tsp ground allspice
1 tbsp mustard seeds
100g/4oz golden caster sugar
150ml/¼ pint red wine vinegar

1 Heat the oil in a large saucepan, add the cabbage, ginger,
onions, allspice and mustard seeds, then cook for 5 minutes
until just starting to wilt.
2 Scatter over the sugar and pour in the vinegar. Cover the
pan, gently cook for 10 minutes, then remove the lid and
turn up the heat to medium. Simmer the liquid in the
cabbage for about 20 minutes, stirring occasionally, then stir
continuously for the last few minutes until all the liquid has
evaporated and becomes sticky on the bottom of the pan.
You can make ahead and chill for 2 days.

PER SERVING 137 kcals, carbs 27g, fat 3g, sat fat none, salt 0.04g

Glazed orange carrots

SERVES 6 • PREP 5 MINS • COOK 10 MINS
V

600g/1lb 5oz baby carrots, or carrots cut into batons
1½ tbsp butter
3 tbsp orange juice
handful parsley leaves, chopped

1 Trim the carrots and cook in boiling water for 4–6 minutes until just tender, then drain. Melt the butter in a large frying pan, add the drained carrots, then fry over a high heat for 1 minute. Pour over the orange juice and cook for a further 2–3 minutes, bubbling the sauce and stirring to thoroughly coat the carrots. Finally, stir in the chopped parsley and serve.

PER SERVING 61 kcals, carbs 7g, fat 4g, sat fat 2g, salt 0.16g

> *tip* Make the dish up to a day ahead, tip into the serving dish and chill. Reheat in the microwave in a covered dish for 3-4 minutes on High.

Caramelized carrots and onions

 SERVES 8 • PREP 15 MINS • COOK 40 MINS
V

500g/1lb 2oz carrots, peeled and cut into long chunks
50g/2oz butter
1 tbsp olive oil
8 red onions, peeled and quartered with root intact
3 sprigs thyme
1 tbsp soft brown sugar
3 tbsp red wine
1 tbsp good-quality balsamic vinegar

1 Blanch the carrots in a pan of boiling salted water for 3 minutes, drain well, then pat dry. In a large pan, melt the butter and oil, then fry the carrots, onions and thyme over a low heat for 30 minutes until golden.
2 Stir in the sugar and red wine and bubble for a few minutes to boil off the alcohol. Add the vinegar, then continue to cook until syrupy, about 5 minutes. Remove the sprigs of thyme and serve. (Make up to 2 days ahead and store in a covered container. Tip back into a pan and reheat or use a microwave.)

PER SERVING 129 kcals, carbs 15g, fat 7g, sat fat 4g, salt 0.15g

Three-in-one braised vegetables

SERVES 4 EASILY DOUBLED • PREP 5 MINS COOK 10 MINS
V

400g/14oz ready-trimmed sprouts, halved
2 large carrots, sliced on the diagonal
1 chicken stock cube
25g/1oz butter
100g/4oz frozen peas

1 Tip the sprouts and carrots into a pan and cover with boiling water. Sprinkle in the stock cube, add the butter and bring to the boil. Simmer for 8–10 minutes until the veg are tender. Add the peas and cook a few minutes more. Drain to serve.

PER SERVING 103 kcals, carbs 12g, fat 4g, sat fat 2g, salt 0.62g

Parmesan-roasted potatoes

SERVES 6 • PREP 10 MINS • COOK 50 MINS
V ❄

1.8kg/4lb floury potatoes, cut in half, or quarters if large
5 tbsp olive oil
2 tsp plain flour
100g/4oz Parmesan, finely grated
handful parsley leaves, finely chopped
4 rosemary sprigs, leaves finely chopped
pinch grated nutmeg

1 Heat oven to 220C/200C fan/gas 7. Place the potatoes into a pan of salted water, bring to the boil and simmer for 2 minutes exactly. Drain well and toss in a little of the oil to coat.
2 Stir the flour, Parmesan, herbs and nutmeg together in a dish with a small pinch of salt and toss the potatoes in the mix until evenly coated. Heat a good layer of oil in a shallow, non-stick roasting tin on the hob or in the oven, then carefully add the potatoes to it. Turn the potatoes to coat them in the oil and roast for 40 minutes, turning once. If they feel like they are sticking to the pan, don't move them, just leave them for the full time. Roast until golden brown and crisp, and serve straight away.

PER SERVING 339 kcals, carbs 43g, fat 15g, sat fat 5g, salt 0.36g

Winter root mash with buttery crumbs

SERVES 10 WITH OTHER VEG • PREP 15 MINS COOK 1HOUR
V ❄

650g/1lb 7oz each parsnip and swede, cut into
    even chunks
150ml tub soured cream
1 rounded tbsp hot horseradish
2 tbsp fresh thyme leaves
FOR THE BUTTER TOPPING
50g/2oz butter, plus extra for greasing
1 small onion, finely chopped
50g/2oz fresh white breadcrumbs
a small handful of thyme leaves, plus extra for scattering
25g/1oz Parmesan, coarsely grated

1 Boil the parsnips and swede in salted water for 20 minutes until tender. Drain well then mash, leaving a bit of texture. Stir in the soured cream, horseradish and thyme and season to taste. Spoon into a buttered, shallow ovenproof dish.
2 Melt the butter in a frying pan and cook the onion for 5–6 minutes until golden. Mix in the breadcrumbs. Season and add the thyme then spoon over the mash. Scatter with Parmesan then bake for 35–40 minutes from cold, 25–30 minutes if not – until golden and crisp.

PER SERVING 158 kcals, carbs 17g, fat 9g, sat fat 5g, salt 0.57g

tip Scattered over with Parmesan, the dish can be made ahead to this point and kept covered in the fridge for up to a day, or frozen for up to a month.

Classic roast goose with cider gravy

*A golden goose is the chef's choice for Christmas dinner; here's our foolproof guide
to cooking one at home. Keep the fat for the best roast potatoes of the year.*

**SERVES 6–8 • PREP 30 MINS • COOK 3½ HOURS,
PLUS RESTING**

4–5kg/9–11lb 4oz oven-ready goose, trussed for roasting
6 small onions, halved
3 bay leaves
bunch thyme
2 tbsp sunflower oil
FOR THE CIDER GRAVY
1 tbsp sunflower oil
goose neck, chopped into a few pieces
2 carrots, cut into small chunks
2 onions, chopped
2 bay leaves
small bunch thyme
500ml bottle cider
1 litre/1¾ pints chicken stock
4 tbsp plain flour

1 Heat oven to 200C/180C fan/gas 6. Remove all the fat from inside the bird and use a skewer to prick the skin all over, especially under the wings. Season the inside and stuff with the onions and herbs. Rub with the oil, season generously then sit the bird, breast up, in a large roasting tin. Cover tightly with foil. Roast for 3 hours, twice using a ladle to remove all of the fat pooling around the bird and lightly basting as it cooks. Cook, uncovered, for a final 30–40 minutes until golden brown. Transfer to a large board or platter to rest in a warm place for 30 minutes. Keep the tin to finish the gravy in.

2 For the gravy, brown the goose neck in the oil, add the veg and fry for 10 minutes until just starting to catch. Throw in the herbs, then pour over the cider and boil down by about two-thirds. Skim off any froth. Pour in the chicken stock, reduce by half, then strain into a large jug and set aside. (Can be made a day ahead.)

3 Pour all but 2 tbsp fat from the goose tin, keeping in any brown juices. Place the tin on the heat, scatter in the flour and stir to make a paste; cook for 1 minute until golden. Stir in the cider stock to make a gravy. Season to taste, then strain into a jug. Serve the goose on a platter with the herby onions from the cavity scattered around.

PER SERVING (6) 956 kcals, carbs 11g, fat 65g, sat fat 20g, salt 1.40g

The timings in this recipe will give you a perfectly roasted goose of about 5kg. If your goose is larger, increase the cooking times with the foil on by 15 minutes per 450g/1lb extra, giving all birds a final 30 minutes uncovered to brown.

try this...

The Bramley apple sauce on page 165 goes really well with this recipe.

Duck two ways with spiced clementine sauce

Roast two legs, serve one, then save the second for a Peking duck wrap with hoisin sauce, cucumber and spring onions while the rest of the nation tucks into turkey sarnies.

SERVES 2 EASILY DOUBLED • PREP 10 MINS, PLUS MARINATING • COOK 1 HOUR 40 MINS

1 tsp ground coriander
1 tsp ground ginger
pinch ground allspice
6 or so thyme sprigs, left whole
zest 2 clementines, juice of 4
2 duck legs
1 large duck breast, skin slashed
FOR THE SAUCE
50g/2oz light muscovado sugar
100ml/3½fl oz sherry vinegar
150ml/½ pint good chicken stock
knob of butter

1 Mix the spices, thyme and clementine zest and rub over the meat. Leave for at least 2 hours, or up to 24 hours in the fridge.
2 Heat oven to 160C/140C fan/gas 3. Roast the legs in a small tin for 1½ hours until deep golden and crisp. Keep warm on a plate. Spoon away any excess fat. Shred the legs, using 2 forks. Keep warm.
3 Put the pan on the hob, add the sugar and melt to a dark caramel. Add the vinegar, reduce by half then add the juice and most of the stock and boil until syrupy. Whisk in the butter and season.
4 Heat a frying pan and fry the breast, skin-side down, for 10–12 minutes until crisp and the fat has run out. Turn over, fry for 5 minutes, then rest, uncovered, for 10 minutes. Spoon off the remaining fat, deglaze the pan with the remaining stock and add to the sauce.
5 Slice the breast and serve on top of piles of leg meat with sauce drizzled around.

PER SERVING 834 kcals, carbs 38g, fat 48g, sat fat 14g, salt 1.14g

Christmas poussin

With poussin taking just 40 minutes to roast, this recipe makes Christmas that little bit quicker.

SERVES 4 EASILY DOUBLED OR HALVED • PREP 5 MINS COOK 40 MINS

50g/2oz butter, softened
4 poussins
4 rashers smoked streaky bacon, halved
1 tbsp plain flour
1 tbsp Worcestershire sauce
600ml/1 pint vegetable stock

1 Heat oven to 230C/210C fan/gas 8. Smear the butter all over the poussins, season inside and out, then criss-cross the bacon over each one. Sit the poussins in a roasting tin and cook for 40 minutes until the birds are golden and the bacon is crisp. Remove from the tin, leave to rest and set the tin aside until you're ready to make the gravy.
2 About 5 minutes before you sit down to eat, make the gravy. Place the tin on a medium heat, then stir in the flour and splash in the Worcestershire sauce. Bubble together, then drain the veg over the roasting tin and stir in the vegetable stock. Bring the gravy to the boil, taste for seasoning, adding more Worcestershire sauce if needed, then pour into a warm gravy jug.

PER SERVING 701 kcals, carbs 4g, fat 52g, sat fat 19g, salt 2.09g

Roast fillet of beef with mushroom stuffing

Serve up a spectacular centrepiece of beef with a rich mushroom stuffing and creamy sauce. Ideal for New Year too.

SERVES 6 WITH LEFTOVERS • PREP 30 MINS, PLUS COOLING • COOK 1 HOUR

25g/1oz dried porcini mushrooms
400g/14oz fresh wild mushrooms
knob of butter, plus extra for roasting
2 tbsp olive oil
200g/7oz shallots, peeled and one very finely chopped
1 garlic clove, crushed
2 thyme sprigs
1.5kg/3lb 5oz beef fillet

FOR THE SAUCE

1 tbsp plain flour
3 tbsp brandy
400ml/14fl oz hot beef stock
2 tsp wholegrain mustard
2 tbsp crème fraîche
handful parsley, chopped

1 Tip the porcini into a bowl and pour over 250ml boiling water. Leave for 20 minutes then scoop out the mushrooms with a slotted spoon and finely chop. Strain the liquid, leaving behind the last tablespoon, as this can be gritty, and set aside.
2 Set aside about half the wild mushrooms, choosing those with the best shape, then finely chop the remainder. Heat a large frying pan, add the butter and 1 tbsp olive oil, then cook the chopped shallot and garlic for 3–5 minutes until softened. Tip in the chopped porcini, stir for 2 minutes then add the chopped mushrooms and thyme sprigs. Cook for 10 minutes until lightly browned and any liquid has evaporated. Cool.
3 Place the beef on a board. Slice lengthways along the fillet, about one-third of the way down, so it folds out like a book (photo 1) with one side thicker than the other. Make another lengthways cut along the thick half, so that the beef unfolds to a flat, evenly thick piece of meat, about A4 in size. Spread the mushroom mixture all over the beef (photo 2) and season generously. Tightly re-roll the beef (photo 3) then secure with about 8 pieces of string (photo 4).
4 Heat oven to 200C/180C fan/gas 6. Place a large heavy-based roasting tin over a high heat, melt more butter with 1 tbsp oil, then brown the beef all over, about 10 minutes.
5 Tip the whole shallots around the beef, toss in the fat then roast for 20–25 minutes for rare, 35 minutes for medium and 45 minutes for well done. Ten minutes before the end of cooking, stir the whole mushrooms around the pan and return to the oven. Rest the meat for 10–15 minutes and keep the vegetables warm in a serving dish while you make the sauce.
6 Place the tin back on the hob. Stir in the flour then very carefully add the brandy. Use a small whisk to stir in the brandy, scraping up all browned bits from the tin. When the brandy has nearly boiled away, add the mushroom liquid and beef stock. Bubble for 5 minutes until just thickened, then stir in the mustard and crème fraîche. Season, sprinkle with parsley and pour into a gravy boat. Cut the beef into thick slices and serve.

PER SERVING (6) 499 kcals, carbs 4g, fat 28g, sat fat 11g, salt 0.61g

1   2

3   4

tip The beef can be prepped to the end of Stage 3 a day ahead and chilled in the fridge.

Beef Wellington

Beef Wellington is an all time great way to feed a crowd. In this recipe the meat is kept deliciously moist by a layer of chopped mushrooms, or duxelles.

**SERVES 6 ● PREP 45 MINS PLUS CHILLING
COOK ABOUT 1 HR**

1 tbsp olive oil

1.15kg/2½ lb thick beef fillet, tied with string to keep its shape

1 shallot, finely chopped

100g/4oz chestnut mushrooms, finely chopped

a generous knob of butter

3 tbsp chopped parsley

500g pack frozen puff pastry

beaten egg, to glaze

2 tsp plain flour

600ml/1pint good quality chicken or beef stock

6 tbsp red wine

1-2 tbsp Dijon mustard

watercress and fresh herbs such as thyme and parsley, to serve

1 Heat oven to 220C/200C fan/gas 7. Season the beef then roast in a roasting tin for 15 mins for medium-rare and 20 mins for medium. Cool the beef and remove the string. Chill for at least 20 mins. Keep any juices. Fry the shallot and mushrooms in the butter until no juices remain. Remove from the pan then stir in the parsley and seasoning. Leave to cool.

2 Roll out a third of the pastry to a 18 x 30cm strip and place on a non-stick baking sheet. Roll out the remaining pastry to about 28 x 36cm. Sit the fillet in the centre of the smaller strip of pastry then brush the pastry's edges, and the top and sides of beef, with beaten egg. Spoon the mushrooms down the length of the meat. Using a rolling pin, carefully lift and drape the larger piece of pastry over the fillet, pressing well into the sides. Trim the joins to about a 4cm rim. Seal the rim with the edge of a fork. Glaze all over with more egg yolk and, using the back of a knife, mark the beef Wellington with long diagonal lines taking care not to cut into the pastry. Chill for at least 30 mins and up to 24 hrs.

3 Heat oven to 200C/180C fan/gas 6. Bake the Wellington until golden and crisp; 20-25 mins for medium-rare beef, 30 for medium. Leave to stand while you make the gravy. Heat the roasting tin with its juices, then stir in the flour. Stir until browned. Gradually stir in the stock and wine and let the gravy bubble to thicken and reduce a little. Stir in the mustard then serve with the Wellington.

PER SERVING (6) 679 kcals, carbs 33.6g, fat 37.g, sat fat 14.5g, salt 1.66g

Moroccan spiced pie

A vegetarian option on Christmas Day should have real presence. This flamboyant filo pastry pie fits the bill with its colourful blend of spices, nuts and dried fruit.

SERVES 6 ● PREP 1 HOUR 30 MINS ● COOK 35 MINS
V

2 tsp each coriander and cumin seeds
1 tsp paprika, plus extra for dusting
½ tsp ground cinnamon
150ml/¼ pint olive oil
900g/2lb squash, peeled and cut into small chunks
    (about 2cm)
12 shallots, quartered
4cm/1½in piece root ginger, finely chopped
140g/5oz whole blanched almonds
140g/5oz shelled pistachios
75g pack dried cranberries
6 tbsp clear honey
225g bag fresh spinach
400g can chickpeas, drained and rinsed
2 garlic cloves
1 tsp ground cumin
3 tbsp lemon juice
4 tbsp chopped fresh coriander
100g/4oz butter, plus extra for greasing
8 large sheets of filo pastry
lemon wedges and Harissa yogurt sauce (see below),
    to serve

Harissa yogurt sauce
Mix 200g Greek yogurt with 6 tbsp milk to make a
thin sauce, stir in the chopped leaves from 3 large
sprigs mint and a good handful of chopped fresh
coriander. Swirl in 2-3 tsp harissa paste and serve.

1 Heat oven to 200C/180C fan/gas 6. Dry fry the seeds briefly in a small pan over a medium heat until toasty – don't let them burn. Grind coarsely using a pestle and mortar, then mix in the paprika, cinnamon, ½ tsp salt and 4 tbsp oil. Tip the squash into a roasting tin, pour over the spiced oil and toss. Roast for 20 minutes.

2 Meanwhile, heat 2 tbsp oil in a frying pan, add the shallots and cook, stirring, until they start to brown. Stir in the ginger and 100g each almonds and pistachios. When brown, toss in the cranberries, 2 tbsp honey, and the spinach so it wilts. Take off the heat and stir into the squash when it comes out of the oven. Set aside.

3 In a food processor, whizz the chickpeas with the garlic, cumin, remaining oil, lemon juice, 2 tbsp water and seasoning to make houmous. Stir in the coriander.

4 Melt the butter in a small pan. Put a loose-bottomed 28cm tart tin on a baking sheet and brush with some butter. Keeping the filo covered with a damp cloth so it doesn't dry out, lay one sheet over half of the tin so that it overhangs by about 10cm. Lay another sheet on the other side, so it overlaps the first in the centre and hangs over the opposite edge. Brush with butter. Lay two more filo sheets in the opposite direction in the same way and brush with more butter.

5 Build up two more layers in this way, so you use a total of eight sheets of filo. Pile half the squash mixture in the centre of the pastry. Spread over the houmous and then the rest of the squash mixture. One at a time, bring the edge of each filo sheet up to the centre to cover the filling, creating voluptuous folds as you go. Brush carefully with more butter. (If making a day ahead, cover now with cling film and chill.)

6 Bake for 30–35 minutes (35–40 minutes from the fridge), until crisp and golden. Just before the pie is ready, reheat any remaining butter in the pan, tip in the rest of the nuts and fry until golden. Spoon in the 4 remaining tbsps of honey and, when it melts, take off the heat and pour over the pie. Serve with Harissa yogurt sauce and lemon wedges.

PER SERVING 987 kcals, carbs 82g, fat 66g, sat fat 15g, salt 1.64g

Christmas ham with sticky ginger glaze

With a ham this size you will have plenty left over for salads and sandwiches for the rest of the holiday – if well wrapped, it will keep in the fridge for at least a week. And don't throw away the bones – they are a great addition to a warming lentil soup.

SERVES 8–10 WITH LEFTOVERS • 30 MINS COOK 4.5 HOURS

1 uncooked ham (about 5kg/11lb), soaked according to the butcher's instructions
1 large onion, thickly sliced
5cm piece fresh ginger, sliced
small bunch fresh thyme
5 cloves
sprigs of bay leaves, to garnish

FOR THE GLAZE

175g/6oz light muscovado sugar
2.5cm piece fresh ginger, peeled and sliced
10 kumquats, thickly sliced and any pips discarded, plus extra for garnish
3 pieces preserved stem ginger in syrup, cut into small matchstick-size strips
1 tsp ground ginger
10–15 cloves

1 Heat oven to 180C/160C fan/gas 4. Weigh the ham and calculate the cooking time at 25 minutes per 500g. Scatter the onion, ginger, thyme and cloves over the base of a large, deep roasting tin. Put the ham on top and add water to 3–5cm deep. Cover the whole ham and tin with two or three layers of foil (making a tent over the ham to allow the steam to circulate), sealing the foil around the edges of the tin. Bake for 1½ hours, then reduce the oven to 160C/140C fan/ gas 3 for the remaining 2 hours 40 minutes of the cooking time. When the ham is cooked, remove it from the oven. Leave to rest for 30 minutes.

2 Now make the glaze. Put the sugar and 100ml water in a medium pan. Heat gently until the sugar melts, add the fresh ginger and simmer for 3–4 minutes. Add the kumquats and cook for a few more minutes, just until they soften. Scoop out and reserve the kumquats, discard the ginger and add the stem ginger strips. Bring to the boil, then turn down the heat and let the mixture bubble for 3–5 minutes until thick and reduced by just under half. Remove from the heat and set aside.

3 Line a clean roasting tin with foil and oil it. Unwrap the ham and put it in the foil-lined tin. Cut off the skin, leaving a layer of fat all over. Using a sharp knife, score the fat into a diamond criss-cross pattern. Turn up the oven to 220C/200C fan/ gas 7.

4 Rub ground ginger over the ham, then brush over all but a couple of spoonfuls of the glaze, evenly distributing the stem ginger strips. Scatter over the kumquat slices, studding cloves through some to secure. Drizzle over the remaining glaze. Roast for another 20 minutes or until golden and sticky and the kumquats start to colour. Serve garnished with halved kumquats and sprigs of bay leaves. If serving hot, allow to rest for 15–20 minutes before carving.

PER SERVING (8) 379 kcals, carbs 8g, fat 21g, sat fat 8g, salt 5.14g

These days, few of us have a pan big enough to simmer an entire ham, so we recommend this oven method, which entails half baking, half steaming the ham so it stays moist. Ask your butcher whether the ham needs soaking. Some modern cures don't require the long soak that traditional hams need.

OPPOSITE Clockwise from top left Chesnut, bacon and cranberry stuffing (page 399); Star-topped mince pies (page 416); Stollen slice (page 414); Cheeseboard and onion tart (page 419); Duck two ways with spiced clementine sauce (page 406); Moroccan spiced pie (page 409).

Spiced roast beef

*Ideal for Christmas eve or Boxing Day, either hot or cold. If made ahead, take the beef out
of the fridge a bit before carving, so that the flavours come back to life.*

**SERVES 6 WITH LEFTOVERS • PREP 10 MINS PLUS
MARINATING • COOK 1 HR 5 MINS–1 HR 50 MINS**

1 tbsp juniper berries
1 tbsp coriander seeds
1 tbsp black peppercorns
1 tbsp allspice berries
2 tbsp olive oil
2kg/4lb 8oz–3kg/6lb 8oz topside joint of beef – depending
   on the amount of leftovers you want

1 Combine all the spices and ½ tbsp salt together in a pestle
and mortar. Give everything a good grind, keeping a little of
its coarseness. Rub the oil and then the ground spices all
over the beef and massage in well. Cover and chill overnight
to marinate.
2 Next day, heat oven to 190C/170C fan/ gas 5. Weigh your
joint and roast for 10 mins per 450g/1lb for rare meat and 15
mins per 450g/1lb for medium, plus an extra 20 mins. Cover
and rest for 20 mins, then slice and serve. Alternatively, roast
the beef in the morning and serve at room temperature
for dinner.

PER SERVING (8) 396 kcals, carbs 1g, fat 21g, sat fat 9g, salt 0.68g

Garland sausage roll slice

This party recipe looks really special and can be made one day ahead for minimum stress.

SERVES 8–10 SLICES • PREP 35 MINS • COOK 40 MINS

18 quail eggs
650g/1lb 7oz Cumberland sausages, split and meat
   squeezed out
1 small onion, grated
1 Bramley apple, peeled and grated
small bunch flat-leaf parsley, leaves chopped
shake Tabasco sauce
1cm thick slice of ham, cut into small chunks
50g/2oz fresh breadcrumbs
500g pack all-butter puff pastry
1 egg, beaten
wholegrain mustard, to serve

1 Boil eggs for 2½ minutes, then cool slightly before peeling
and trimming each end.
2 Heat oven to 220C/200C fan/gas 7. In a bowl, mix together
the sausage meat, grated onion, apple, parsley, Tabasco,
ham and breadcrumbs. Roll the pastry out to a rectangle
about 25 x 35cm, carefully lift onto a baking sheet and brush
all over with beaten egg.
3 Press two-thirds of the sausage mix along one of the long
sides of the pastry, leaving 2cm pastry clear for sealing, and
half of the pastry empty on the other side for folding over
later. Press a line down the middle of the meat with your
finger, then lay the eggs along it. Press over the rest of the
meat. Fold the pastry over the sausage meat and press the
edges together, before trimming with a knife and sealing
well by pressing with a fork. (Can be made 1 day ahead.)
4 Brush all over with more egg and bake for 40 minutes until
golden. Leave to cool, then slice and serve with mustard.

PER SERVING 564 kcals, carbs 33g, fat 37g, sat fat 0g, salt 2.66 g

Christmas pudding with citrus and spice

Although you can buy some excellent Christmas puddings, this fruity version is worth the effort, and making your own is all part of the Christmas magic.

SERVES 10 • PREP 30 MINS, PLUS OVERNIGHT SOAKING COOK 6 HOURS

V ❄

175g/6oz each raisins, currants and sultanas
140g/5oz whole glacé cherries
50g/2oz mixed peel
50g/2oz whole blanched almonds
zest 1 orange and 1 lemon
1 medium carrot, peeled and finely grated
150ml/¼ pint brandy
50ml/2fl oz orange liqueur
175g/6oz light muscovado sugar
175g/6oz fresh white breadcrumbs
125g/4½oz self-raising flour
1 tsp mixed spice
¼ tsp grated nutmeg
175g/6oz butter, frozen
2 eggs, beaten
butter, for greasing

try this...

Orange custard cream
Whip 300ml double cream with the zest of ½ orange until it holds its shape. Fold in a 500ml tub fresh vanilla custard and serve.

1 Mix the first eight ingredients in a large mixing bowl. Cover and leave to soak overnight.
2 Mix all the dry ingredients together, then add to the soaked fruit mixture. Grate in the butter, then add the eggs and stir.
3 Heat oven to 160C/140C fan/gas 3. Grease a 1.5-litre pudding basin with butter and line the base with baking parchment. Spoon in the mixture, press down well and make a slight hollow in the middle. Cover the surface with a circle of greaseproof paper, then cover the bowl with double-thickness greaseproof paper and foil and tie at the rim with string (see page 393). Stand the basin in a roasting tin filled with water, then cover with a tent of foil and cook for 6 hours, topping up with water now and again. To store, allow to cool, then keep in a cool dry cupboard. (The pudding will keep for up to a year.)
4 On the day, steam in a pan or in the oven depending on your oven space for 1 hour before turning out. Decorate with holly and serve with extra-thick double cream, orange custard cream or a dollop of traditional brandy butter.

PER SERVING 596 kcals, carbs 92g, fat 20g, sat fat 10g, salt 0.89g

Hot little Christmas cakes

If you don't have a pudding basin or are looking for a last-minute Christmas pud, these are the perfect solution. Make this cake mix in the morning, then bake 15 minutes before you fancy dessert.

SERVES 4 EASILY DOUBLED • PREP 10 MINS COOK 15 MINS

❄

50g/2oz melted butter, plus extra for greasing
50g/2oz plain flour, plus extra for dusting
1 tsp mixed spice
¼ tsp baking powder
50g/2oz dark muscovado sugar
1 egg
zest 1 orange
small handful dried berries and cherries
vanilla ice cream and honey, to serve

1 Grease and flour 4 small ramekins and set aside. Tip all the ingredients, except the berries and cherries and ice cream, into a large jug or bowl. Using a hand blender, blend until completely combined, then stir in the dried fruit. Chill the cake mix until needed.
2 Heat oven to 230C/210C fan/gas 8. Divide the mix between the ramekins and bake for 15 minutes until puffed up and golden. Tip the cakes out onto plates, top with a scoop of vanilla ice cream and drizzle with honey.

PER CAKE 243 kcals, carbs 29g, fat 13g, sat fat 8g, salt 0.37g

Christmas pudding ice cream

A cool, creamy way to finish your Christmas meal. Can be made up to a month in advance.

SERVES 8 • PREP 15 MINS, PLUS COOLING AND FREEZING • COOK 15 MINS
❄ Ⓥ

85g/3oz each raisins, sultanas and dried cherries
100g/4oz fresh or frozen cranberries
6 tbsp brandy
2 tbsp dark muscovado sugar
FOR THE ICE CREAM
2 cinnamon sticks, snapped in half
¼ tsp each ground ginger and caraway seeds
½ tsp freshly grated nutmeg
4 cloves
600ml pot double cream
1 vanilla pod, split and seeds scraped out
3 egg yolks
100g/4oz golden caster sugar
6 gingernut biscuits, broken into chunks
zest ½ lemon and ½ orange
FOR THE CRANBERRY SYRUP TOPPING
85g/3oz golden caster sugar
2 tbsp brandy
100g/4oz fresh or frozen cranberries

1 Mix the first four ingredients a bowl, then microwave on High for 3 minutes. Stir, then leave to cool, ideally overnight.
2 Heat the spices in a pan for 3 minutes or so, stirring until fragrant. Tip in the cream and vanilla and bring to the boil. Whisk the yolks and sugar together. Whisk in the hot cream, then tip into a clean pan and cook gently for 5–10 minutes until the mix coats the back of a wooden spoon. Pour into a container, cool, then chill overnight.
3 Sieve the mix into another container, then churn in an ice-cream machine (or follow the by hand instructions on page 381). Oil a 1.4-litre pudding basin and line with cling film.
4 Drain the fruit in a sieve and mix it with the biscuits and zests, then quickly fold it into the ice cream. Tip into the basin, cover, and freeze for at least 6 hours.
5 For the topping, gently heat everything together until the sugar dissolves, then simmer for 2 minutes. Cool completely. Leave the pudding at room temperature for 15 minutes before turning out. Serve with the cranberries and sauce.

PER SERVING 675 kcals, carbs 61g, fat 45g, sat fat 24g, salt 0.15g

Stollen slice

An easy ready-rolled pastry version of traditional German stollen bread. Serve with Brandy butter.

MAKES 12 SLICES • PREP 20–25 MINS • COOK 15 MINS
❄ Ⓥ

25g/1oz mixed peel
50g/2oz pistachio nuts, chopped
50g/2oz dried cranberries
50g/2oz raisins
1 tbsp brandy or rum
375g pack ready-rolled puff pastry
flour, for dusting
200g/7oz bought or homemade marzipan
FOR THE GLAZE
4 tbsp apricot conserve or jam
2 tbsp brandy or rum

1 Heat oven to 220C/200C fan/gas 7. Line a baking sheet with baking parchment. Put the peel, nuts, cranberries and raisins in a bowl, stir in the brandy or rum and let it soak in while you make the glaze.
2 Spoon the conserve or jam into a small pan, add the brandy or rum, heat gently, then bubble briefly for about 1 minute. Push it through a sieve into a small bowl and set aside to cool.
3 Lay the pastry on a floured work surface. Scatter over the fruit and nuts and spread almost to the edges. Roll the marzipan into a long sausage so it's a bit shorter than the length of the pastry. Lay the marzipan along the length of the pastry over the fruit and nuts, about 2.5cm from one edge. Roll the pastry around the marzipan so the join is underneath.
4 Trim off the ends, then slice into 12 pieces. Lay the slices, slightly overlapping, on the baking sheet to make a ring. Bake for 15–20 minutes or until puffed and golden, then remove and brush the glaze all over. Cut through the slices to separate. Serve warm on the day it's made, or reheated the next.

PER SLICE 257 kcals, carbs 34g, fat 11.8g, sat fat 3.4, salt 0.28g

Christmas pudding ice cream

Festive mincemeat

Nothing beats homemade mincemeat with plump fruit, plenty of spice and a little alcoholic kick.

MAKES ABOUT 4 X 450G/1LB JARS
PREP 30 MINS • NO COOK
❋

300g/11oz raisins
300g/11oz currants
300g/11oz shredded suet (use vegetarian if you prefer)
250g/9oz dark muscovado sugar
85g/3oz mixed chopped peel
grating of nutmeg
pinch mixed spice
finely grated zest and juice 1 lemon and 1 small orange
1 medium Bramley apple, peeled and grated
100ml/3½fl oz whisky
4 fresh bay leaves

1 Mix all the ingredients except the apple, whisky and bay leaves in the order they are listed. Stir through the apple, then add the whisky once all the other ingredients are completely combined. Pack the mincemeat into sterilised jars. Tuck a bay leaf into each jar to scent the mincemeat, then seal. Leave for 2 weeks before using. Will keep for 6 months.

PER TBSP 93 kcals, carbs 13g, fat 4g, sat fat none, salt 0.02g

Unbelievably easy mince pies

The pastry cases and lids are pressed out by hand, so they're ideal for children to help with.

MAKES 18 PIES • PREP 20 MINS, PLUS COOLING
COOK 20 MINS
❋ **UNCOOKED**
Ⓥ **IF USING VEGETARIAN MINCEMEAT**

225g/8oz cold butter, diced
350g/12oz plain flour
100g/4oz golden caster sugar
280g/10oz mincemeat
1 small egg, beaten
icing sugar, to dust

tips For star-topped mince pies, roll out the pastry for the tops and stamp out 18 stars. Put on top of the mincemeat and bake.

• For more pie but less pastry, mix 100g frozen cranberries into the mincemeat. Scatter with a handful flaked almonds and bake. Dust with icing sugar to serve.

1 To make the pastry, rub the butter into the flour until it looks like fine breadcrumbs, then mix in the sugar and a pinch of salt. Combine the pastry into a ball and knead briefly to a firm dough. Use immediately or chill.
2 Heat oven to 200C/180C fan/gas 6. Line 18 holes of two 12-hole bun tins by pressing small walnut-size balls of pastry into each hole. Spoon the mincemeat into the pies.
3 Take slightly smaller balls of pastry than before and pat out between your hands to make round lids. Top the pies with their lids, pressing the edges gently together to seal. (The pies may now be frozen for up to 1 month.)
4 Brush the tops of the pies with the beaten egg. Bake for 20 minutes until golden. Leave to cool in the tin for 5 minutes, then remove to a wire rack. To serve, lightly dust with icing sugar. They will keep for 3 to 4 days in an airtight container.

PER PIE 222 kcals, carbs 30g, fat 11g, sat fat 7g, salt 0.26g

Little Eccles mince pies

The beauty of these Eccles cake-shaped pies is that you don't need a special baking tin.
Enjoy with a glass of mulled wine.

MAKES 18 • PREP 30 MINS • COOK 15–30 MINS
❄ IF PASTRY NOT PREVIOUSLY FROZEN

500g block all-butter puff pastry
plain flour, for dusting
450g/1lb mincemeat
1 egg white, lightly beaten
golden caster sugar

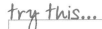

> To make Brandy butter, beat 175g soft unsalted butter,
> zest of 1½ oranges and 5 tbsp icing sugar until pale
> and creamy. Gradually beat in 4 tbsp brandy or
> Cognac. (Will keep for a week in the fridge, or it can
> be frozen for up to 6 weeks.)

1 Roll the pastry out to about the thickness of a 50p piece onto a floured surface and cut out 10cm circles, then continue to re-roll and cut out until you have about 18 circles.
2 Place 1 tsp mincemeat in the centre of each circle, brush the edges with egg white, then gather together tightly to completely encase the mincemeat. Flip the pies over so the sealed edges are underneath, then squash them with your hand so you have a small puck-shaped pie.
3 Heat oven to 200C/180C fan/gas 6. Cut two small slits in the top of each pie, brush generously with egg white and scatter with sugar. (The pies can now be frozen for up to 2 months.) Bake for 15 minutes from raw or 25–30 minutes from frozen.

PER SERVING 268 kcals, carbs 34g, fat 14g, sat fat 3g, salt 0.27g

Mulled wine

SERVES 6 EASILY DOUBLED OR MORE • PREP 10 MINS
COOK 10 MINS
V

750ml bottle red wine
3 tbsp light muscovado sugar
2 cinnamon sticks
2 star anise
1 chopped lemon (including skin)
1 chopped orange (including skin)
1 small apple, thinly sliced into rounds
handful fresh or frozen cranberries

1 Put all of the ingredients into a large pan, then bring gently to the boil. Simmer for 5 minutes then ladle into small glasses.

Mulled apple juice

1 litre apple juice
4 strips orange peel
1 cinnamon stick
3 cloves
sugar or honey, to taste

1 Simmer the apple juice with the strips orange peel, cinnamon stick and cloves for about 5-10 minutes until all the flavours have infused. Sweeten with sugar or honey to taste. Serve each drink with a little orange peel and a piece of cinnamon stick, if you like. Ideal for kids and designated drivers.

Ham, leek and potato pie

Use up every last scrap of your Christmas ham with this heart-warming family pie. If you've got a few sticks of celery hanging about, finely chop them and soften with the onions and leeks too.

SERVES 4–6 • PREP 20 MINS • COOK 45 MINS

2 tbsp butter
1 large onion, finely chopped
3 leeks, finely sliced
2 large potatoes, cut into small cubes
2 tbsp plain flour, plus extra for dusting
300ml/½ pint chicken or ham stock
100ml pot crème fraîche (or use leftover double cream)
2 tsp wholegrain mustard
200g/7oz cooked ham, shredded
4 bay leaves (optional)
375g pack puff pastry
flour, for dusting
1 egg, beaten, to glaze (or use milk)

1 Melt the butter in a large pan, add the onion and leeks, cover and soften gently for 15 minutes. Add the potatoes after 5 minutes cooking.
2 Stir in the flour, turn up the heat, then add the stock, stirring until the mix thickens a little. Take off the heat, then stir in the crème fraîche, mustard and ham and two bay leaves. Season to taste, then cool. Spoon into a large pie dish. Heat oven to 220C/200C fan/gas 7.
3 Roll the pastry on a floured surface to £1 coin thickness. Cut a strip the same width as the lip of the dish, brush the lip with egg, then fix the strip around it. Brush with egg, then lay over the remaining pastry.
4 Trim the pastry, then ruffle the cut edges with the knife blade to help the layers rise. Cut a few slits in the top, decorate with bay leaves, if you like, then brush all over the top with egg. (Can be made up to a day ahead and chilled. Bake for 30 minutes until risen and golden.)

PER SERVING (6) 499 kcals, carbs 44g, fat 29g, sat fat 14g, salt 1.84g

Sherried turkey and ham bake

This warming bake, rich with sherry and mustard, will have you looking forward to eating up the leftovers.

SERVES 4 • PREP 10 MINS • COOK 35 MINS
❄

350g/12oz cooked turkey, cut into strips
140g/5oz thickly sliced cooked ham, cut into strips
175g/6oz frozen peas
50g/2oz butter, plus a little extra for greasing
50g/2oz plain flour
600ml/1 pint milk
3 tbsp medium sherry
2 tsp wholegrain mustard
100g/4oz mature Cheddar cheese, grated
50g/2oz chopped mixed nuts, such as hazelnuts, almonds and walnuts

1 Heat oven to 200C/180C fan/gas 6. Mix the turkey, ham and frozen peas in a buttered ovenproof dish.
2 Put the butter, flour and milk in a saucepan and bring to the boil, whisking all the time, until the sauce is thickened and smooth. Stir in the sherry and mustard, season to taste and simmer for 1 minute. Remove from the heat and stir in half the cheese.
3 Pour the sauce over the ingredients in the dish. Mix the remaining cheese with the nuts and sprinkle on top. (Can be chilled for a day, or frozen for 1 month.) When ready, bake for 25–35 minutes until the topping is golden and the sauce is bubbling.

PER SERVING 633 kcals, carbs 23g, fat 37g, sat fat 18g, salt 2.16g

Cheeseboard and onion tart

You've heard of four-cheese pizza, so here's a three-cheese tart; a delicious way to use up the remains of the cheeseboard and perfect for lunch over the holidays.

SERVES 8 • PREP 15 MINS IF MAKING OWN PASTRY, PLUS CHILLING • COOK 1 HOUR 5 MINS

V ❄

FOR THE PASTRY (or use a 375g pack bought shortcrust)
250g/9oz plain flour, plus extra for dusting
125g/4½oz butter, cold and cubed
½ tsp salt
FOR THE FILLING
2 onions, sliced into rings
1 tbsp oil
2 eggs
300ml pot double cream
250g/9oz mixed cheese (we used one-third each Stilton, Brie and Cheddar)

1 Put the flour, butter and salt into a food processor, then pulse to fine crumbs. Splash in 4 tbsp cold water, then pulse to a dough. Turn onto a lightly floured surface, shape into a smooth disc, then wrap and chill for at least 10 minutes. Heat oven to 200C/180C fan/gas 6.

2 Roll pastry out on a floured surface until large enough to line a 23cm loose-bottomed tart tin. Bake blind for 15 minutes, then remove paper and beans and bake for 10 minutes more until pale golden and cooked.

3 While the pastry cooks, soften the onions in the oil over a medium heat for 10 minutes until golden. Beat the eggs and cream together, then season to taste. Crumble up hard cheeses and chop or pull creamy cheeses into small pieces. Scatter the cheese into the pastry case, add the onions, then pour in the egg mix. Turn the oven down to 160C/140C fan/gas 3 and bake for 40 minutes until set and lightly golden.

PER SERVING 603 kcals, carbs 30g, fat 49g, sat fat 26g, salt 1.18g

Bubble and squeak

Bubble and squeak should be on everyone's radar come Christmas time as a wonderful way to use up leftover mash, sprouts and cabbage. Perfect with fried eggs, or ham and piccalilli.

SERVES 4 • PREP 10 MINS • COOK 20 MINS

1 tbsp duck fat, goose fat or butter
4 rashers streaky bacon, chopped
1 onion, finely sliced
1 garlic clove, chopped
15–20 cooked sprouts, sliced or leftover boiled cabbage, shredded
400g/14oz cold leftover mashed potato or cold crushed boiled potatoes

1 Melt the fat in a non-stick pan, allow it to get nice and hot, then add the bacon. As it begins to brown, add the onion and garlic. Next, add the sliced sprouts or cabbage and let it colour slightly. All this will take 5–6 minutes.

2 Next, add the potato. Work everything together in the pan and push it down so that the mixture covers the base of the pan – allow the mixture to catch slightly on the base of the pan before turning it over and doing the same again. It's the bits of potato that catch in the pan that define the term 'bubble and squeak', so be brave and let the mixture colour. Cut into wedges and serve.

PER SERVING 212 kcals, carbs 20g, fat 13g, sat fat 5g, salt 0.89g

16

Jams, preserves and pickles

Relaxing, satisfying and in tune with the seasons, home preserving is a tradition that's worth keeping alive. With a little time and know how you'll soon be spreading your own jam on your toast and savouring homemade chutney with cheese.

MAKING JAM

The main aim of preserving is to stop bacteria or mould developing or fermentation occurring in ingredients while being stored. If prepared correctly, then sealed in sterilized containers and stored in a cool, dark place, homemade preserves should keep for up to a year. Once opened, store them in the fridge and use within the month.

Jam is a basic mix of cooked fruit and sugar. The fruit is first softened in a pan with water, then boiled, and then cooked with sugar until the jam reaches 'setting point' (see below), after which it is put into jars and left to set. A high sugar content, high cooking temperature and the acid in the fruit work together to prevent any bugs or mould spoiling the jam.

Smaller batches of marmalade and jam are more successful than big batches, so don't be tempted to double up the recipes if you have a glut of fruit to use. Large volumes take a longer time to reach setting point, which can affect flavour. Both jams and marmalades can be eaten straightaway.

Pectin is a substance that naturally occurs within fruit which, when heated with sugar, causes the fruit and their juices to set to a jelly. Some fruit have lots of it (such as lemons, apples, blackcurrants and sour plums) and will set firmly, while others have very little (such as rhubarb, peaches and pears) and set softly. Adding lemon juice, a high-pectin fruit or liquid pectin from a sachet or bottle will also boost the set of a soft jam. Choose under- or just-ripe fruits, as overripe fruit has a lower pectin level.

The setting point of jam (and marmalade) is 105C. This is most reliably measured with a sugar thermometer (see equipment on page 422), but if you don't have a thermometer, put a few saucers into the freezer before you begin. Once the jam has been boiled, drop a little of it onto a chilled saucer. Allow it to cool a little, then push your finger through the jam. If the jam parts, leaving wrinkled ripples, it is ready. If not, boil for another 2 minutes and test again.

Marmalade making follows the same principles as jam-making, but only the peel and the juice of the fruit are used. The pectin within citrus fruit is highly concentrated in the membranes and seeds, so these are included in the cooking, tied into a muslin bag.

OPPOSITE Autumn piccalilli and Balsamic pickled shallots (pages 428 and 430)

A BIT ABOUT SUGARS

- **Preserving sugar**, which has a very large grain, creates very little scum as it dissolves, giving a clear result. However, it is more expensive than granulated sugar, which does the job just as well. Avoid using caster sugar.
- **'Jam sugar'** is sugar that has extra pectin added to it, and will guarantee a good set if you are using a fruit low in natural pectin.
- Some recipes suggest warming the sugar in a low oven before adding it to the fruit, which helps the jam to reach setting point more quickly.

CHUTNEYS AND KETCHUPS

The simplest kind of savoury preserve to make, chutneys and ketchups are a cross between a jam and a pickle – sugar and vinegar are added to fruit and vegetables, together with salt and other flavourings. Imperfect and overripe fruit and vegetables are ideal for these sorts of preserves, and there is no setting point to worry about either. Most chutneys benefit from several weeks mellowing, during which time the flavours develop and become more rounded.

PICKLES

Pickles usually rely on salt and vinegar to preserve their contents. Vegetables are soaked in brine or packed in salt overnight, to draw out as much of their liquid as possible (bacteria need water to grow, so this process arrests bacterial growth). The vinegar used for pickles should be at least 5 per cent acetic acid; check the bottle before you buy. If a recipe for pickles does not involve brining, it is likely to involve cooking instead, but the end result may not have such a long shelf life. Freshly made pickles are very sharp; like chutneys, most are best left to mature before eating.

EQUIPMENT

For all basic preserving, a **large preserving pan** is the key piece of equipment. These pans are very large and, crucially, are wider at the top than at the bottom. This is particularly important for making jams and marmalades, as a wider pan helps the fruit to reach setting point more quickly, thus retaining the fresh flavour of the fruit and not overcooking it. When making chutneys, a large surface area helps the mix to reduce down more quickly. If you don't have, or can't borrow, a preserving pan, then a very large and heavy-based saucepan is the next best bet. Do not use brass, iron or copper preserving pans if your recipe uses vinegar.

For jams and marmalades, a **sugar thermometer** is extremely helpful, as it will help you to ascertain 'setting point' – the point at which your jam or marmalade is ready. These thermometers have a special hook that allows you to keep the thermometer in the pan the whole time, without it falling in.

Jars are the best thing for storing jams, marmalades, chutneys and pickles, whereas you may want to source glass pouring bottles for homemade ketchup. Choose new jam jars or re-use old jars with metal lids (recycled plastic lids won't give a good seal). It is vital that your jars and lids are sterilized before use (see below), and that jars are sealed up as soon as possible, while the preserve is still hot. Use paper jam covers or wax discs to cover the jam or preserve – this seals it and, in the case of pickles and chutneys, prevents the vinegar from eating at the metal lid.

A **jam funnel and a ladle** or a jug make transferring boiling hot preserves into a jar a whole lot easier.

STERILIZING CONTAINERS

A scrupulously clean and sterilised jar or bottle is essential for successful preserving. Firstly, wash the jars and their lids in hot soapy water, rinse them out with fresh hot water, then dry them with a clean tea towel. Place them on a baking sheet then put them in a low oven at 100C/80C fan/gas ½ for 10 minutes until completely dry. The jars will be hot, so don't put them directly onto a cold surface as they could crack. Alternatively, put them through the hot cycle of a dishwasher.

If you want to use glass, rubber-sealed jars, remove the seals, put them in bowl and cover them with just-boiled water. Sterilise the jars as above. It's not that easy to replace the rubber seals when everything is very hot, so be prepared! Remember that, once opened, larger jars still need to be eaten up as quickly as smaller ones, so smaller jars could be more economical in the long run.

Seville orange marmalade

For a darker 'Oxford'-style spread, just add one tablespoon of black treacle when you add the sugar.

MAKES 3 x 450G/1LB JARS MARMALADE, PLUS 1 x 100G/4OZ JAR • PREP 45 MINS, PLUS OVERNIGHT SOAKING • COOK 2 HOURS

4 Seville oranges (about 500g/1lb 2oz in total), scrubbed
1.7 litres/3 pints water
1kg/2lb 4oz granulated sugar

You will need:

- citrus squeezer
- string and a 20cm square piece of muslin or new white cleaning cloth, sterilised by covering with boiling water in a large stainless-steel pan. (It doesn't have to be a preserving pan, but one with a wider top than bottom is best.)
- clean rubber gloves
- sterilized glass jars with close-fitting lids and wax discs
- ladle or jug to transfer marmalade from pan to jar. (Dip the ladle in boiling water or the boiling marmalade to sterilise. A jug is easy to sterilise when you do the jars.)

Sevilles oranges are too bitter to eat but are high in pectin, the natural setting agent for jams and jellies, which makes them ideal for marmalade. Buy them as soon as they appear in the shops. If you don't have time to make marmalade straight away, they keep in the fridge for a few weeks or they can be frozen, whole, for up to six months.

Freezing reduces the pectin levels so it's a good idea to add the juice of one large lemon (naturally very high in pectin) to each 500g/1lb 2oz of fruit if making marmalade from frozen oranges.

Don't try to make too much marmalade at once. The unboiled sugar and fruit mixture should not come more than a third of the way up the side of the pan, as the marmalade rises to more than twice its original level when boiling and can boil over.

1 Halve the oranges and squeeze the juice into a large pan. Scoop the pips and pulp into a sieve over the pan and squeeze out as much juice as possible, then tie the pulp and pips in the muslin. Shred the remaining peel and its pith with a sharp knife. Add the shredded peel and muslin bag to the pan along with the water. Leave to soak overnight. (This helps to extract the maximum amount of pectin from the fruit pulp, which will give a better set, and also helps to soften the peel, which will reduce the cooking time.)

2 Put the pan over a medium heat and bring up to a simmer. Cook, uncovered, for 1½–2 hours, until the peel has become very soft. (The cooking time will be affected by how thickly you have cut the peel.) To see if the peel is ready, pick out a thicker piece and press it between your thumb and finger – it should look slightly see-through and feel soft when you rub it.

3 Carefully remove the muslin bag, allow to cool slightly and then, wearing the rubber gloves, squeeze out as much liquid as possible to extract the pectin from the fruit pulp. Discard the muslin bag and weigh the simmered peel mixture. There should be between 775–800g; if less, then top up with water to 775g.

4 Put 4 small plates in the freezer, ready to use when testing for setting point. Add the sugar to the pan, then put it over a low heat. Warm gently so that the sugar dissolves completely, stirring occasionally. Do not boil before the sugar is dissolved.

5 Increase the heat and bring up to the boil but do not stir while the marmalade is boiling. After about 5 minutes the marmalade will start to rise up the pan (it may drop back and then rise again) and larger bubbles will cover the surface (photo 1). After 8–10 minutes boiling, test for setting point. As setting point can be easily missed it's better to test too early than too late.

6 If you have a sugar thermometer, setting point is reached at 105C, then take the pan off the heat and allow the bubbles to subside. To test without a thermometer, take a plate from the ▶

A really vigorous rolling boil is needed to get a good set – with large quantities it can be difficult to achieve this at home. It is not advisable to make more than double the quantities in the recipe here.

Granulated sugar works perfectly well for marmalades, but if you prefer, use preserving sugar instead; the larger crystals reduce scum and make a clearer preserve. Jam sugar has extra pectin added, but as oranges are high in pectin, you won't need it.

If you have a bought a lot of fruit, it's best to make several batches rather than one big one as the fresh flavour of the fruit will diminish the longer you boil the mixture to get the set.

freezer, spoon a little marmalade onto the plate, then return to the freezer for 1 minute. Push the marmalade along the plate with your finger; if setting point has been reached then the marmalade surface will wrinkle slightly and the marmalade won't run back straight away (photo 2). If it's not at setting point, return to the heat and boil again for 2 minutes before re-testing. Repeat until setting point is reached.

7 Leave the marmalade to stand for 10 minutes or until starting to thicken. If there's any scum on the surface, spoon it off. Transfer the marmalade to sterilized jars (see page 422). Cover with a wax disc (wax-side down) and seal. When cold, label the jars and store in a cool dark cupboard. The marmalade should keep for up to a year.

PER 10G SERVING 28 kcals, carbs 7g, fat none, sat fat none, salt none

'Flexible' jam

This simple recipe can be used for summer and autumn fruits that don't require extra pectin to set. Choose your fruit, then follow the chart below for the recommended amounts of liquid and timings.

MAKES ABOUT 4 X 450G/1LB JARS

900g/2lb fruit (prepared weight)
900g/2lb golden granulated sugar
knob of butter

1 Put the fruit and the recommended liquid additions (see box below) into a preserving pan or large heavy-based saucepan, then bring to the boil. Lower the heat and simmer until the fruit is soft.
2 Tip in the sugar and stir over a very low heat until it has completely dissolved. Raise the heat, bring to a full rolling boil, then boil rapidly for the suggested time – don't stir, though – until a sugar thermometer reads 105C.
3 Remove from the heat, skim off any excess scum, then stir a knob of butter across the surface (this helps to dissolve any remaining scum). Leave for about 15 minutes so the fruit can settle. Pour into sterilized jars, label, and seal. Store in a cool dark place and refrigerate once opened.

Fruit	Simmering time	Boiling time	Additions
Blackberries	15 minutes	10–12 minutes	50ml water plus 1½ tbsp lemon juice
Plums, halved and stoned	30–40 minutes	10 minutes	150ml water
Raspberries	2 minutes	5 minutes	None
Strawberries, hulled and lightly crushed	5 minutes	20–25 minutes	3 tbsp lemon juice

OPPOSITE Clockwise from top left Rhubarb and vanilla jam (page 426); Red onion marmalade (page 427); Fragrant mango and apple chutney (page 431); Pickled pears (page 430); Apple and cranberry chutney (page 426); Seville orange marmalade (page 432)

Rhubarb and vanilla jam

A seasonal treat – make a batch when you see the first flush of rhubarb in the shops.

**MAKES 3 X 450G/1LB JARS • PREP 10 MINS, PLUS
COOLING TIME • COOK 25–30 MINS**

1kg/2lb 4oz rhubarb, weighed after trimming, cut into
    3cm chunks
1kg/2lb 4oz jam sugar (or 1kg caster sugar plus
    1 x 8g sachet pectin)
2 vanilla pods, halved lengthways
juice 1 lemon

1 Put a small plate in the freezer. Put the rhubarb into a preserving pan or your largest saucepan with the sugar and halved vanilla pods. Heat gently, stirring, until all the sugar has dissolved, then squeeze in the lemon juice and increase the heat.

2 Boil for about 10 minutes, skimming off the scum as you go (the fruit should be soft). When ready, a sugar thermometer will read 105C, or test for setting point as on page 423.

3 Once the jam is ready, ladle into warm sterilised jars and seal. (Store in a cool, dark place for up to 6 months. Refrigerate on opening.)

PER LEVEL TBSP 44 kcals, carbs 12g, fat none, sat fat none, salt none

Apple and cranberry chutney

Make this a few months ahead so that the flavours mellow together, ready to serve with Christmas cheeses and cold meats.

**MAKES 4 X 450G/1LB JARS • PREP 20 MINS
COOK 1 HOUR 10 MINS**

1kg/2lb 4oz cooking apples, peeled and chopped
    into small chunks
500g/1lb 2oz eating apples, peeled and chopped
    into large chunks
450g/1lb onions, sliced
50g/2oz fresh root ginger, finely chopped
1 tsp peppercorns
500g/1lb 2oz granulated sugar
250ml/9fl oz cider vinegar
500g/1lb 2oz cranberries

1 Place all the ingredients except the cranberries into a preserving pan or your largest saucepan, then gently heat, stirring, until the sugar dissolves. Bring to the boil, then reduce the heat and simmer, uncovered, for about 50 minutes, stirring regularly until the apples and onions are tender, the mixture has thickened and no watery juice remains.

2 Add the cranberries, then cook for a further 10 minutes or so until the berries have just softened but not burst.

3 Spoon the hot chutney into sterilised jars and seal. Store in a cool, dark place. (Store in a cool, dark place for up to 6 months. Refrigerate on opening.)

PER SERVING (25G) 35 kcals, carbs 9g, fat none, sat fat none, salt none

Red onion marmalade

You'll love this with terrines, cold meats or cheese, sausages, or on the side of a ploughman's. Try adding a few tablespoons to gravy, too.

MAKES 4 X 450G/1LB JARS • PREP 20 MINS COOK ABOUT 1 HOUR 20 MINS
Ⓥ ❄

140g/5oz butter
4 tbsp olive oil
2kg/4lb 8oz red or regular onions, halved
    and thinly sliced
4 garlic cloves, thinly sliced
140g/5oz golden caster sugar
1 tbsp fresh thyme leaves
pinch chilli flakes (optional)
750ml bottle red wine
350ml/12fl oz sherry or red wine vinegar
200ml/7fl oz port

1 Melt the butter with the oil in a preserving pan or your largest saucepan over a high heat. Tip in the onions and garlic and stir until well glossed with butter. Sprinkle over the sugar, thyme leaves, chilli flakes, if using, and some salt and pepper. Stir, reduce the heat slightly then cook, uncovered, for 40–50 minutes, stirring occasionally. The onions are ready when all their juices have evaporated, they're really soft and sticky and smell of caramelising sugar. They should be so soft that they break when pressed against the side of the pan.

2 Pour in the wine, vinegar and port and simmer everything, still uncovered, over a high heat for 25–30 minutes, stirring every so often until the onions are a deep mahogany colour and the liquid has reduced by about two-thirds. It's done when drawing a spoon across the bottom of the pan clears a path that fills rapidly with syrupy juice. Leave the onions to cool, then scoop into sterilized jars and seal. (Keeps in the fridge for up to 3 months.)

PER SERVING (25g) 40 kcals, carbs 4.2g, fat 2g, sat fat 1g, salt 0.03g

Sweet chilli jam

This has a kick but it won't blow your head off, and goes well with any selection of cold cuts of meat.

MAKES 4 SMALL JARS • PREP 20 MINS • COOK 1 HOUR

8 red peppers, deseeded and roughly chopped
10 ordinary red chillies, roughly chopped
finger-size piece fresh root ginger, peeled and roughly
    chopped
8 garlic cloves, peeled
400g can cherry tomatoes
750g/1lb 10oz golden caster sugar
250ml/9fl oz red wine vinegar

1 Tip the peppers, chillies (with seeds), ginger and garlic into a food processor, then whizz until very finely chopped. Scrape into a preserving pan or large heavy-bottomed pan with the tomatoes, sugar and vinegar, then bring everything to the boil. Skim off any scum that comes to the surface, then turn the heat down to a simmer and cook for about 50 minutes, stirring occasionally.

2 Once the jam is becoming sticky, continue cooking for 10–15 minutes more, stirring frequently so that it doesn't catch and burn. It should now look like thick bubbling lava. Cool slightly, transfer to sterilized jars, then leave to cool completely. (Store in a cool, dark place for up to 3 months. Refrigerate on opening.)

PER JAR 857 kcals, carbs 220g, fat 1g, sat fat none, salt 0.34g

Homemade tomato chutney

Preserve the sunshine flavour of summer tomatoes right through the year.

**MAKES 2 X 450G/1LB JARS • PREP 30 MINS
COOK 1 HOUR 10 MINS**

500g/1lb 2oz red onions, finely sliced
1kg/2lb 4oz tomatoes, chopped
4 garlic cloves, sliced
1 red chilli, chopped (optional)
4cm piece fresh ginger, peeled and chopped
250g/9oz light muscovado sugar
150ml/¼ pint red wine vinegar
5 cardamom seeds
½ tsp paprika

1 Tip all the ingredients into a preserving pan or large, heavy-based pan and bring to a gentle simmer, stirring frequently. Simmer for 1 hour, then bring to a gentle boil so that the mixture turns dark, jammy and shiny. Pour into sterilized jars and allow to cool before covering. (Store in a cool, dark place for up to 3 months. Refrigerate on opening.)

PER SERVING 35 kcals, carbs 9g, fat none, sat fat none, salt 0.02g

Autumn piccalilli

Eaten immediately, this pickle will have a punchy tang that's perfect with strong cheeses, but by winter the flavours will mellow, making it ideal with sliced ham.

**MAKES 5 x 450G/1LB JARS • PREP 20 MINS, PLUS SALTING
OVERNIGHT • COOK 15 MINS**

2 small cauliflowers, cut into small florets
400g/14oz silverskin or pearl onions
600g/1lb 5oz courgettes, cut into small chunks (about 2cm pieces)
6 firm pears, cored, and cut as the courgettes
100g/4oz flaky sea salt (not fine salt)
1.7 litres/3 pints cider vinegar
finger-length piece fresh root ginger, grated
2 tbsp coriander seeds
3 tbsp brown or black mustard seeds
300g/11oz golden caster sugar
8 tbsp cornflour
5 tbsp English mustard powder
3 tsp turmeric

1 In a bowl, mix together the vegetables, pears and salt with 2 litres of cold water, then cover and leave overnight.
2 The next day, drain the brine from the vegetables, rinse briefly, then tip into a preserving pan or large saucepan with the vinegar, ginger, coriander seeds, mustard seeds and sugar. Bring to the boil and simmer for 8–10 minutes until the veg is just tender but still has a little bite. Drain the vegetables, reserving the liquid, and set aside while you make the sweet mustard sauce.
3 In a large bowl, stir together the cornflour, mustard powder and turmeric, then gradually pour in the hot vinegar, whisking all the while until you have a lump-free, thin yellow sauce. Return it to the saucepan and bubble over a low heat, stirring constantly, for 4 minutes until smooth and thickened.
4 Stir in the veg and spoon into sterilized jars while hot, then seal. Once cool, enjoy straight away or store in a cool dark place for up to 3 months. (Refrigerate on opening.)

PER SERVING 31 kcals, carbs 6g, fat 1g, sat fat none, salt 1.01g

OPPOSITE *Autumn piccalilli*

Balsamic pickled shallots

Crisp shallots in a sweet spiced vinegar – perfect with cheese.

MAKES 4 x 450ML/1LB JARS • PREP 1 HOUR, PLUS 3 DAYS STANDING • COOK 30 MINS

1.5kg/3lb 5oz small shallots or pearl onions
1 litre/1¾ pints white wine vinegar
150ml/¼ pint olive oil
600ml/1 pint water
140g/5oz golden caster sugar
1 tbsp salt
1 tsp black peppercorns, cracked
2 handfuls basil leaves
100ml/3½fl oz balsamic vinegar

1 Tip the shallots into a large bowl, pour over a kettleful of boiling water, leave to stand for a minute, then drain. When cool enough to handle, peel the shallots.
2 Set the peeled shallots aside and place all the other ingredients except the balsamic vinegar into a preserving pan or large saucepan. Bring to the boil, lower the heat, then simmer for 3 minutes. Drop the shallots into the pan and simmer for 8-10 minutes until just tender. Use a slotted spoon to scoop the shallots and basil out into sterilized jars, then boil the liquid vigorously for 5 minutes.
3 Turn off the heat, stir in the balsamic vinegar, then pour over the shallots to cover. Seal the jars and leave for at least 3 days. (Will keep in a cool, dark place for up to 3 months. Refrigerate on opening.)

PER SERVING 25 kcals, carbs 3g, fat 1g, sat fat none, salt 0.26g

Pickled pears

These gorgeous spiced pears look so stylish and taste great spooned out of the jar with a little of the syrup to enjoy with cold meats, cheeses, savoury tarts or pies.

MAKES 3 X 450G/1LB JARS • PREP 30 MINS • COOK 35 MINS

1 lemon or orange
10 cloves
2 tsp black peppercorns, lightly crushed
1 tsp allspice berries, lightly crushed
5cm piece fresh root ginger, sliced
1 litre/1¾ pints cider or white wine vinegar
2 cinnamon sticks
1kg bag caster sugar
2kg/4.4lb small pears

1 Pare the zest from the lemon or orange and put in a preserving pan or large saucepan with the cloves, peppercorns, allspice berries, root ginger, vinegar, cinnamon sticks and sugar. Squeeze the juice from the lemon or orange and add to the pan. Stir over a gentle heat until the sugar has dissolved.
2 Peel, core and halve the pears, then add to the pan and simmer for 15 minutes until the pears are tender. Remove the pears with a slotted spoon and put in a colander to drain. Meanwhile, increase the heat under the syrup and boil rapidly for 15 minutes until the syrup has reduced by about a third and is slightly thickened.
3 Pack the fruit into sterilized jars and pour over the hot syrup to cover. Seal, label and store in a cool dry place for a month before using.

PER JAR 4553 kcals, carbs 1203g, fat 2g, sat fat none, salt 0.74g

Homemade tomato sauce

Once you've tried this ketchup you'll be hooked on the homemade version!

MAKES 400ML • PREP 10 MINS • COOK 45 MINS
Ⓥ ❄

1 tbsp olive oil
2 onions, chopped
1 thumb-size piece fresh root ginger, finely chopped or
    grated
2 garlic cloves, crushed
1 red chilli, deseeded and finely chopped
800g/1lb 12oz tomatoes, briefly whizzed in a food
    processor or finely chopped
100g/4oz dark brown sugar
100ml/3½fl oz red wine vinegar
2 tbsp tomato purée
½ tsp coriander seeds

1 Heat the oil in a large deep pan, then fry the onions, ginger, garlic and chilli for 10–15 minutes until soft. Add the remaining ingredients and some seasoning, then boil for 30 minutes, stirring occasionally, until the mixture has thickened and is sticky.

2 Cool slightly, then whizz in a blender or food processor until smooth. If the sauce is a bit thick for your liking, stir in a dribble of boiling water. Sieve, then funnel into a sterilized bottle or jar while still hot. Cool completely before serving. (Will keep for 3 months in the fridge.)

PER TBSP 28 kcals, carbs 6g, fat 1g, sat fat none, salt 0.02g

Fragrant mango and apple chutney

Cooking apples, like Bramleys, form a lovely pulpy base to the chutney while not overpowering the flavour of the mango. The result is heady with fresh ginger and aromatic spices – delicious.

MAKES ABOUT 4 x 450G/1LB JARS • PREP 30 MINS COOK 1½ HOUR

3 large ripe mangoes, about 1kg/2¼lb
2 tbsp sunflower oil
2 onions, halved and thinly sliced
thumb-size piece fresh root ginger, peeled and
    cut into thin shreds
10 green cardamom pods
1 cinnamon stick
½ tsp cumin seeds
½ tsp coriander seeds, lightly crushed
¼ tsp black onion seeds (nigella or kalonji)
½ tsp ground turmeric
2 Bramley apples, about 500g/1lb 2oz, peeled, cored
    and chopped
1 large red chilli, deseeded and finely chopped
375ml/13fl oz white wine vinegar
400g/14oz golden caster sugar
1 tsp salt

1 Cut away the fleshy cheeks from the mangoes then cut criss-cross slices in the flesh, taking care not to cut the skin. Turn each half inside out, then cut away the chunks of mango. Peel and chop the flesh left around the stone too.

2 Heat the oil in a large, deep frying pan, add the onions and fry for a few minutes until starting to soften. Stir in the ginger and cook, stirring frequently, for about 8–10 minutes until the onion is golden. Stir in all of the spices, except the turmeric, and fry until smelling fragrant.

3 Stir in the turmeric, add the apples and 500ml water, then cover and cook for 10 minutes. Stir in the mango and chilli, cover and cook for 20 minutes more until the apple is pulpy and the mango is tender.

4 Pour in the vinegar, stir in the sugar and salt, then simmer uncovered, for 30 minutes, stirring frequently (especially towards the end of the cooking time) until the mixture is pulpy. Spoon into sterilized jars.

PER TBSP 17 kcals, carbs 4g, fat none, sat fat none, salt none

17

Merry Xmas x

Gifts to make

Of course, no one needs to make homemade chocolate truffles, or stamp out oatcakes for the cheeseboard, or spend an afternoon making panettone, but when the love of cooking has really got you in its grips, there's no better way to say 'Happy Christmas' or 'Thank you' than with a thoughtful, handmade gift that gives you as such pleasure to make as it does to give.

No one will want to admit it out loud, but making your own gifts can be thrifty too. The cost can really creep up when presents have to be given en-masse to, say, teachers or neighbours, but a few batches of chocolate florentines or stained-glass biscuits will go a long way when prettily wrapped, and will be a welcome change to the chocolates and smellies they normally receive. If you're planning or helping to plan a wedding, why not make the favours yourself? Or you could have a crack at some homemade fudge for trick-or-treaters.

MAKE IT PERSONAL

The real fun starts when you cook for someone special; a cheese-lover, maybe. Why not bake some oatcakes and wrap them up along with their favourite cheese and put them in a festive hamper with a bottle of red? Or, for that chocoholic in your life, present them with handmade truffles and perhaps some cleverly chosen coffee for an after-dinner treat. There's a hamper for everyone – all it takes is a little imagination.

PRESENTING YOUR GIFTS

When giving handmade presents, their packaging is important. High-street cook shops sell cellophane bags which are perfect for stacks of biscuits or sweets when tied with a little ribbon. Staple doilies into cones; cover jam jars with festive fabric; and use shoeboxes as hampers, covered with thick brown paper and filled with raffia. All easily done, but at little expense.

And if you're short of time but still like the sentiment of giving a handmade gift, some of the following recipes (such as the Mulled wine kit on page 441) don't even need cooking. Now that's what we call a good idea.

OPPOSITE Melting middle truffles (page 435), Spanish fig and almond cakes (page 438) and Sweet chilli jam (page 427).

Melting middle truffles

Get these made and in the freezer up to a month ahead. Once they've defrosted, the caramel middles will be melty and the outside truffle just firm.

MAKES 40 • PREP 45 MINS, PLUS COOLING AND FREEZING • COOK 5 MINS

❄

½ x 450g jar dulce de leche caramel toffee
100g/4oz dark chocolate (70% cocoa solids), chopped
oil, for greasing
2 x 200g bars milk chocolate, chopped
150ml pot double cream
1 tsp vanilla extract
about 85g/3oz cocoa powder, to coat

tips You may have some filling left over, but it's best to be on the generous side. What's left can be gently warmed and served over ice cream…

• Latex gloves are a great help when rolling truffles, as they stop your hands from melting the chocolate.

1 Make the middles first. Heat the caramel in a pan for 1 minute until warmed and runny, then stir in the chopped dark chocolate and leave to melt. Stir until smooth. Cover a dinner plate with cling film, oil the cling film well, then tip the mix onto it. Cool, then freeze for 2 hours or until very firm.
2 Put the milk chocolate into a bowl. Bring the cream to the boil in another pan, then pour it over the chocolate. Leave for 2 minutes, then add the vanilla and stir until smooth. Cool, then chill until set.
3 Peel the caramel from the cling film, then snip into thumbnail-size pieces (wet kitchen scissors work best). Spread cocoa powder over a large baking sheet. Take a heaped teaspoon of the truffle mix then, with cocoa-dusted hands, poke in a caramel chunk. Squash the mix around the caramel to seal, then roll into a ball. Put onto the sheet and shake to coat in the cocoa. Repeat with the rest of the mix, then freeze, or chill if making less than 3 days ahead.

PER TRUFFLE 112 kcals, carbs 12g, fat 7g, sat fat 4g, salt 0.05g

Orange and ginger stained-glass biscuits

Get into the festive spirit and make your own edible tree decorations.

MAKES 14 • PREP 15 MINS • COOK 15–20 MINS
❄ **RAW DOUGH, UP TO A MONTH**

sunflower oil, for greasing
175g/6oz plain flour, plus extra to dust
1 tsp ground ginger
zest 1 orange
100g/4oz butter, cold, cut into chunks
50g/2oz golden caster sugar
1 tbsp milk
12 fruit-flavoured boiled sweets, crushed in their wrappers
icing sugar, to dust
about 120cm thin ribbon, to decorate

1 Heat oven to 180C/160C fan/gas 4. Grease 2 large non-stick baking sheets with oil. Whizz the flour, ginger, orange zest and butter with ½ tsp salt to fine crumbs in a food processor. Pulse in the sugar and milk, then turn out and knead briefly onto a floured surface until smooth. Wrap in cling film, then chill for about 30 minutes.
2 Flour the work surface again, then roll the dough to £1 coin thickness. Use 7cm cutters to cut out shapes, then use 4cm cutters to cut out the middles. Re-roll trimmings. Make a hole in the top of each biscuit, then carefully lift onto the baking sheets.
3 Tip out enough of the crushed sweets into the middles of the biscuits to be level with the top of the dough. Bake for 15–20 minutes or until the biscuits are golden brown and the middles have melted.
4 Leave to harden, then transfer to a rack to cool. Thread with ribbon through the hole, then dust with icing sugar. (Will keep for a month, but best eaten within 3 days.)

PER SERVING 160 kcals, carbs 23g, fat 8g, sat fat 5g, salt 0.14g

OPPOSITE Orange and ginger stained-glass biscuits

Coconut ice squares

Who could resist a bag of nostalgically pink and white coconut ice? With no cooking involved, it's ideal for kids to make by themselves or with a little help.

MAKES ABOUT 30 PIECES • PREP 15 MINS

200g/7oz sweetened condensed milk
250g/9oz icing sugar, sifted, plus extra for dusting
200g/7oz desiccated coconut
pink edible colouring (optional)

1 Stir together the condensed milk and icing sugar in a large bowl. It will get very stiff. Work in the coconut until well combined; use your hands if you like.

2 Split the mix into two, then knead a very small amount of colouring into one piece. Dust the surface with icing sugar, shape each half into a smooth rectangle and place one on top of the other. Roll with a rolling pin, re-shaping with your hands every couple of rolls, to a rectangle of coconut ice about 3cm thick.

3 Transfer to a board and leave to set overnight. Cut into squares and pack into bags or boxes. (Will keep for 1 month in an airtight container.)

PER SERVING 91 kcals, carbs 12.3g, fat 4.6g, sat fat 3.8g, salt 0.02g

Cherry and coconut Florentines

Instead of making individual biscuits, make one big traybake then stamp out the star shapes - leaving lots of bits to nibble!

MAKES 24 EASILY DOUBLED • PREP 30 MINS, PLUS CHILLING • COOK 20 MINS

140g/5oz light muscovado sugar
100g/4oz clear honey
200g/7oz salted butter
100g/4oz desiccated coconut
140g/5oz flaked almonds
300g/11oz glacé cherries, sliced
4 tbsp plain flour
250g/9oz dark, milk or white chocolate, or a mix

1 Heat oven to 200C/180C fan/gas 6. Put the sugar, honey and butter in a large pan and gently melt together until the sugar dissolves. Stir in the coconut, flaked almonds, sliced cherries and flour.

2 Line a large baking sheet with baking parchment and spread the Florentine mixture out to a thin layer. Bake for 10–12 minutes until a rich golden colour, then cool completely.

3 Melt the chocolate(s) all in separate heatproof bowls over gently simmering water. Line a second large baking sheet or board with baking parchment and carefully flip the cooled Florentine onto it. Peel away the lining. Spread with melted chocolate, leave to set, then stamp out shapes using star cookie cutters. (Will keep for up to a week, kept cool)

PER SERVING (24) 247 kcals, carbs 26g, fat 15g, sat fat 9g, salt 0.15g

OPPOSITE Clockwise from top left Peppermint lollipops (page 441); Orange and ginger stained-glass biscuits (page 435); Spice lovers' mix (page 441); Cherry and coconut florentines; Coconut ice squares; Cranberry and white chocolate panettone (page 440)

Chocolate and vanilla fudge

Creamy and soft, this fudge keeps fresh for 2 weeks. Take extra care if children are in the kitchen as you make this; the mix is dangerously hot.

MAKES 28 PIECES • PREP 5 MINS, PLUS 1 HOUR COOLING • COOK 15 MINS

125g/4½oz butter, cut into cubes, plus extra for greasing
170g can evaporated milk
450g/1lb golden granulated sugar
1 tsp vanilla extract
100g/4oz plain chocolate, broken into squares

1 Butter then line the base and sides of an 18cm square tin with baking parchment. Put everything but the chocolate into a saucepan and add 4 tbsp water. Put over a gentle heat and stir with a wooden spoon until the sugar is melted and no longer feels grainy against the pan. Bring to a boil.

2 Adjust the heat until the mix bubbles without getting too near the top of the pan. Boil for 10 minutes, then take off the heat. Cool for a few minutes then carefully tip in the chocolate and mix until even.

3 Tip into the tin then cool completely. Mark into squares, then package up or keep in an airtight tin until needed.

PER PIECE 124 kcals, carbs 20g, fat 5g, sat fat 3g, salt 0.10g

Spanish fig and almond cakes

Our festive version of Pan de Higo, a dried fig cake traditionally eaten with cheese in Spain. Particularly good with a chunk of manchego.

MAKES 6 • PREP 20 MINS, PLUS DRYING TIME • NO COOK

100g/4oz whole almonds, toasted
500g pack dried whole figs, hard stalk and centre of base removed
85g/3oz dried apricots, chopped into small pieces
50g/2oz dried cranberries
1 tbsp brandy
1 tbsp clear honey
1 tsp ground cloves
100g/4oz sesame seeds, toasted

1 Whizz the almonds in a food processor until most are finely chopped, then tip into a large bowl. Roughly chop the figs, then whizz to a smooth sticky paste. Scrape onto the almonds then, using your hands, mix together well with the dried fruit, brandy, honey and cloves.

2 Divide the mixture into 6 and roll into balls (or make them smaller if you like). Tip the sesame seeds onto a baking sheet, then roll the balls in them until covered. Cover the sheet loosely with a clean tea towel, then leave the fig balls to dry for a week before packaging. (Will keep in a cool place for 2 months.)

PER BALL 306 kcals, carbs 24g, fat 20g, sat fat 2g, salt 0.05g

Stilton and poppy seed sablés

Sablé is French for sandy, which explains the crumbly texture of these little biscuits - given extra crunch by the addition of polenta.

MAKES 30 BISCUITS • PREP 15 MINS, PLUS CHILLING COOK 10–15 MINS

V ❄

100g/4oz plain flour, plus extra for dusting
85g/3oz cold butter, diced
small pinch mustard powder
small pinch cayenne pepper
1 tbsp polenta (optional, but does give crunch)
1 tbsp poppy seeds
100g/4oz Stilton, crumbled, plus extra
    to top the biscuits

1 In a large bowl, rub together the flour, butter, mustard powder, cayenne, polenta (if using), poppy seeds, Stilton and a pinch of salt, until the mixture forms a pastry. Knead briefly until smooth and very lightly speckled with cheese.
2 On a lightly floured surface, roll the dough into a sausage about 25cm long, then wrap and chill for at least 1 hour.
3 Heat oven to 190C/170C fan/gas 5. Slice the dough into rounds just under 1cm thick. Space out on lined baking sheets, top each with a little more cheese and bake for 10-15 minutes, until golden at the edges. Cool. (Will keep for 2–3 days in an airtight container.)

PER BISCUIT 61 kcals, carbs 3g, fat 5g, sat fat 3g, salt 0.2g

Walnut and raisin oatcakes

Delicious with cheese, or as a sustaining alternative to biscuits, these oatcakes have interest in every bite.

MAKES 40 • PREP 20 MINS • COOK 15 MINS

❄ **DOUGH ONLY**

¼ tsp baking powder
4 tbsp milk
175g/6oz soft butter
100g/4oz caster sugar
300g/11oz rolled oats
140g/5oz wholemeal flour, plus extra for dusting
50g/2oz raisins, roughly chopped
50g/2oz walnuts, finely chopped
oil, for greasing

1 Heat oven to 180C/160C fan/gas 4. Dissolve the baking powder in the milk. Beat the butter and sugar until pale and creamy, then mix in the oats, flour, raisins, walnuts and milk to make a stiff dough.
2 Tip the dough onto a lightly floured surface and roll out until about 1cm thick. Cut into circles with a 5cm pastry cutter, place on an oiled baking sheet, then bake for 15 minutes until lightly golden. Leave to cool, then serve with cheese or wrap as a gift. (Will keep for up to a week in an airtight container.)

PER OATCAKE 94 kcals, carbs 11g, fat 5g, sat fat 3g, salt 0.08g

Cranberry and white chocolate panettone

A classic Italian gift for friends and neighbours at Christmas time.

CUTS INTO 8 SLICES • PREP 3 HOURS, INCLUDING 2½ HOURS RISING • COOK 45–50 MINS
❄

500g/1lb 2oz plain flour, plus extra for dusting
2 x 7g sachets fast action yeast
100g/4oz golden caster sugar
200ml/7fl oz milk, warmed to hand hot
3 eggs, beaten
1 tsp vanilla extract
200g/7oz butter, softened and cut into pieces
175g/6oz dried cranberries
100g/4oz candied peel, finely chopped
85g/3oz white chocolate, chopped into chunks

TO FINISH
1 egg, lightly beaten
2 tbsp flaked almonds

1 Mix the flour, yeast, 1 tsp salt and the sugar in a food processor fitted with a dough blade. Tip in the milk, eggs and vanilla then work for 2 minutes to a soft dough. Leave in the machine until doubled in size, about 1 hour.
2 Add the butter, pulse until incorporated then leave for another hour to rise again. Add the cranberries, peel and chocolate, then pulse until evenly mixed.
3 Butter and line a deep 20cm cake tin, making a 10cm collar with double thickness baking parchment around the sides. Tip the dough onto a lightly floured surface and knead to a smooth ball using floured hands. Drop into the tin and leave to rise for 30 minutes. Heat oven to 180C/160C fan/gas 4.
4 Brush the dough liberally with beaten egg and scatter with almonds. Bake for 45–50 mintes until well risen and deep golden. Turn out of the tin and cool on a wire rack. (Package as a gift, keep well-wrapped for 2 weeks, or freeze on the day of making for up to 1 month.)

PER SERVING 681 kcals, carbs 95g, fat 30g, sat fat 17g, salt 0.65g

tip Don't have a food processor? Just knead the dough by hand on a lightly floured surface until smooth and elastic.

Starry toffee cake squares

Great for kids to make, with a little help from a grown-up.

MAKES 24 SQUARES • PREP 15 MINS • COOK 40–50 MINS

200g/7oz butter, plus extra for greasing
200g/7oz golden syrup
300g/11oz self-raising flour
200g/7oz light muscovado sugar
3 medium eggs, beaten
2 tbsp milk
4 tbsp icing sugar
225g/8oz yellow marzipan, split into three balls
red and green food colouring

1 Heat oven to 160C/140C fan/gas 3. Butter a Swiss roll tin, about 32 x 23cm, then line with baking parchment. Gently melt the butter and syrup together, then cool for 15 minutes.
2 Mix the flour, sugar and 1 tsp salt in a large bowl. Beat in the cooled syrup mix, eggs and milk until smooth.
3 Pour into the tin and tap gently on the work surface to level it. Bake for 40–50 minutes until risen and golden. Cool for 10 minutes, trim any cake that has come over the sides then tip onto a cooling rack. Once cold, slide onto a board, trim, then cut into 24 squares.
4 Mix 2 tbsp icing sugar and a drop of warm water. Mix to a thick paste. Set aside. Colour one piece of marzipan red and one green. Dust worktop with icing sugar then roll out and stamp 24 stars. Fix a star onto each square using a little icing.
5 Dust the cakes with icing sugar, then put in pretty boxes. (Will keep in an airtight container for up to a week.)

PER SQUARE 217 kcals, carbs 34g, fat 9g, sat fat 5g, salt 0.37g

Peppermint lollipops

MAKES ABOUT 40 EASILY DOUBLED OR MORE
PREP 30 MINS • COOK 20 MINS

500g/1lb 2oz granulated sugar
1 tsp cream of tartar
200ml/7fl oz water
2 tsp peppermint essence
green food colouring
40 plastic lollipop sticks or wooden skewers cut into
short lengths

1 Put the sugar, cream of tartar and 200ml hot water in a saucepan. Gently dissolve the sugar over a low heat, then boil until the mixture reaches the 'hard crack' stage on a sugar thermometer (or a small spoonful dropped into cold water sets hard). Remove from the heat immediately and swirl in the peppermint essence and a drop of colouring.
2 Cover a heatproof surface with baking parchment. Using a metal spoon, carefully spoon blobs of peppermint syrup onto the paper – roughly ½–1 tbsp per lolly. Push a lolly stick into each. If the syrup becomes too thick, reheat the pan briefly. If too runny, set aside to cool for a minute. Leave the lollies to set hard then tie them in cellophane.

PER SERVING 50 kcals, carbs 13.3g, fat none, sat fat none, salt 0.07g

Mulled wine kit

MAKES 1 KIT • PREP 25 MINS • NO COOK

25cm/10in square butter muslin (available from
department and hardware stores)
85g/3oz demerara sugar
1 tsp ground ginger
½ tsp ground nutmeg
750ml bottle red wine (a smooth Shiraz is good for this)
1 cinnamon stick
8-12 cloves
1 orange

1 Put the muslin on a flat surface and tip the sugar, ginger and nutmeg into the centre. Tie into a pouch with fine string and tie to the neck of the wine bottle. Attach the cinnamon stick to the wine bottle neck with raffia or ribbon.
2 Stick the cloves into the orange and pack into a box lined with raffia or shredded paper with the wine.
3 Tie a label to the wine, saying: 'Tip the contents of the muslin bag into a pan with the wine, orange, cinnamon stick and 300ml water. Simmer for 5 minutes and serve.' (Keeps for 1 week with the orange, 6 weeks without – add the orange later if you want to get ahead).

Spice lovers' mix

MAKES 8–10 SMALL BAGS EASILY DOUBLED OR MORE
PREP 5 MINS • NO COOK

25g/1oz black peppercorns
50g/2oz fennel seeds
50g/2oz coriander seeds
50g/2oz cumin seeds
2 tbsp brown or white mustard seeds
2 tbsp crushed chillies

1 Simply mix all the spices together in a bag or large bowl, then pack into paper cones or little bags or boxes. On the label suggest transferring the mix to a pepper mill to grind over meat, fish or veg before barbecuing, or adding straight into curries.

18

Cooking for crowds

Whether it's a few nibbles with drinks, a barbecue in the garden or even a home-catered wedding, you don't need to be a domestic god or goddess to throw a good party. But, if you're entertaining the idea of a get-together, then you will need to use a little organisation. Within this chapter you will find practical information, advice and ideas that will help your gathering go smoothly, plus the perfect nibble, drink, picnic and barbecue recipes to get everyone in the party mood.

BEFORE THE FUN STUFF, SOME PRACTICALITIES
- Will you have enough space to seat everyone around the table? If not, then buffet-style would be a better option.
- Do you lack worktop space? In that case choosing a meal that can be served up at the table is a good idea.
- Don't cook out of your comfort zone, it will only cause you stress.
- It's your meal too, and you want to enjoy hosting your friends or family. Unless you want to spend all night away from it all, choose a prepare-ahead starter and dessert and don't try to make too many courses. This is home, not restaurant, cooking after all. Serve drinks with dips and nibbles instead of a starter if it's a casual get-together.

Planning your menu

Keep the meal to one cuisine, or at least don't massively mix things up – a curry followed by traditional apple crumble, for example, would be odd. This also makes wine matching more tricky, too. It's also fun to have a themed menu – choose a theme to suit your guests or a particular occasion. Below are a few menu ideas using the recipes that appear in this cook book:

Budget but brilliant (Serves 4): Asian aubergine and pork hotpot, Perfect fluffy rice, Pineapple and pink grapefruit with mint sugar
Bistro-style (Serves 6): Blue cheese, bacon and walnut salad, Confit of duck (increase quantity by half), Dauphinoise potatoes, Dressed green beans and Tangy lemon tart
Family food (Serves 4-6): Proper beef, ale and mushroom pie, Perfect mash, Quick braised cabbage and Apple flapjack crumble
Freeze ahead (Serves 6): Smoked salmon soufflés with dressed leaves, beef bourguignon, Chocolate truffle torte
Girls' night in (Serves 4): Pea and mint soup, One pan salmon with asparagus (double it) and Iced berries with white chocolate sauce
Just the two of us (Serves 2): Lobster salad with fennel and lime, Steak with sticky red wine shallots and Light chocolate mousse (make half quantity)

OPPOSITE Summer sausage rolls (page 451)

Supper in 20 mins (Serves 4): Pasta with lemon butter prawns and Affogato

Curry night for friends (Serves 6-8): Prawn, mango and spring onion pakoras, Ginger chicken curry, Makhani dhal and Toasted cumin raita, Perfect fluffy rice and Mango cardamom syllabubs

Meat-free Moroccan (Serves 4): Lemon and coriander houmous, served with flatbreads and olives, Vegetable tagine with almond and chickpea couscous and Sticky cinnamon figs or Pomegranate ice

Best-ever barbecue (Serves 8): Sticky barbecue ribs, Lime and coriander chicken (double quantity), Carrot and sesame burgers (double quantity), Barbecue-baked sweet potatoes, Cheesy garlic bread (make two), Stunning summer pudding

Summer picnic (Serves 6-8): Really easy lemonade, Tomato, basil and Parmesan quiche, Roast chicken with couscous and pine nut stuffing, Tuna, asparagus and white bean salad, Raspberry layer cake

Bonfire night (Serves 8): Butternut squash soup with chilli and crème fraiche (small cups), Bonfire bangers and beans, Garlic and rosemary wedges (double quantity) and Homemade toffee apples

Christmas eve drinks (10): Mulled wine cocktail, Thyme potatoes with Camembert fondue, Little chestnut and leek pasties, Prawn and pancetta skewers and Easiest ever mince pies

New Year's supper (Serves 6): Smoked salmon with prawns, horseradish and lime vinaigrette (triple quantity), Beef Wellington, Wild mushroom and potato cake, green beans and Spiced poached pears with chocolate sauce (use 6 pears)

Burns night (Serves 8): Warm salad of scallops and bacon, Succulent braised venison, Roast sweet potato, squash and garlic mash (double quantity), Buttered leeks and Baked raspberry & bramble trifle with Drambuie

Chinese New Year (Serves 6): Chicken noodle soup (double quantity), Crispy pork and vegetable spring rolls, Seabass with sizzled ginger, chilli and spring onion, Tofu, greens and cashew stir-fry and Perfect fluffy rice (use Jasmine rice)

Wedding party (Serves 20): Lamb cutlets with herb relish, Foil-poached salmon with dill & avocado mayo, Spinach and artichoke filo pie (make two), Ratatouille (make two batches), Mustard potato salad, Dressed leaves and Orange berry wedding cake

Tips for success:
- Food should reflect the season and weather – and ingredients cooked in season will always taste best. Heavier dishes are a better option when it's cold outside, lighter when it's hot.
- Try not to repeat ingredients or sauces within your menu; for instance a pastry tart for a starter and a pie for dessert.
- Keep textures varied – don't follow creamy pasta with custard.
- Give some thought to the colour and visual appeal of your menu as well as its flavour.
- Think about who you're feeding. Check if there is anyone who might be vegetarian or vegan, and be sure about allergies. Are they adventurous, or more traditional in their tastes?
- Remember that buffet dishes need to be easy to scoop or pick up, or be eaten without too much work with a knife and fork.
- If you plan to serve cheese, do this after the main course to allow your guests to enjoy it with their wine, and to give yourself a little breathing space to organise dessert.
- It's not a crime to use shop-bought elements, if you like. For instance, order naan breads and poppadums from a curry house to go with your home-made curry, or finish dessert with some luxury ice cream.

Getting ahead

Preparing ahead is something restaurant chefs have down to an art; they call it mise-en-place, or 'putting into place'. Unlike chefs, not many of us have an army of hands to do our prep, but we can use their tricks to make life easy.

- Cook dishes ahead, either in part or completely, and freeze or chill them. (We have clearly marked the recipes here where this is possible.) Slow-cooked dishes often taste better the next day.
- Chop, peel and even part-cook vegetables in advance Green veg can be blanched and refreshed, potatoes par-boiled.
- Make gravies and sauces beforehand, then add the meat resting juices later.
- Poach eggs ahead of time then keep them cold (page 32).
- Prepare elements of a salad and keep the dressing separate.
- Scoop ice cream into balls earlier in the day and return them to the freezer on a flat baking sheet.

The real key is organization. Write a detailed plan of the meal or event well in advance, listing what can be made ahead and what needs doing at the last minute, plus the required oven temperatures and timings. This will highlight any clashes before they happen and help things to run smoothly.

Quantities

All of our recipes are labelled with a number per serving, and a great many of them can be doubled or halved depending on what you need. It's best not to change quantities when it comes to baking, but most savoury dishes are easily scaled up or down. If scaling down meat recipes that are roasted, remember to adjust the cooking times. These won't change for stews and braises, but if scaling these down or up, always make sure that the meat is just-covered with liquid or your dish will be too dry or liquid.

BIG EVENTS

Preparing for a really big event like a wedding can be daunting, so break down all the tasks into chunks, making a list of what needs to be done, and when, and ticking them off as you go.

- Fridge space is crucial. Clear your fridge as much as you can and hire an extra fridge, if needed.
- Beg, borrow or hire platters and serving dishes and a cake stand, if needed.
- The same goes for jugs, cutlery, tables and table linen, etc. Arrange for anything hired to be sent back unwashed, for ease.
- Buy large, plastic buckets to use as giant ice buckets for cooling wine and Champagne. Put the bottles upright in the buckets and half-fill with a mix of ice and water.
- Work out a plan of where the tables will go and where the food and drink will be served to try to avoid bottlenecks.
- Clear away unnecessary furniture and fragile ornaments.

Have a chat with your wine supplier or supermarket as they will be able to recommend wines to go with your menu. Buy a small selection and have a wine tasting to determine your choice before buying in bulk on sale or return. Buy soft drinks, cocktails and beers too.

BRINGING A DISH

Bring-a-dish parties are a great way to feed lots of people, as the load is shared by everyone. Covered cooking dishes in which the food can also be served are ideal. Pack dressings and salads separately. If you are running the party, set out rough guidelines for each guest to prevent recipe repeats and make sure there is enough room to reheat/finish off dishes on the hob or in the oven.

CANAPES AND NIBBLES

- A good canapé will be small enough to eat in one bite – or two as long as biting it won't cause it to fall apart.
- Choose make-ahead recipes that can be served straight from the fridge or oven – the less fiddling for you, the better.
- It's very hard to hold a plate and a glass and stand and eat, so make sure that there are plenty of napkins in strategic places and plates to drop used cocktail sticks. Make a point of placing different plates of food around the room or taking them round to guests so that everyone gets a good choice of what's on offer.
- Provide a varied selection of veggie, fish, meat, hot and cold options.
- As a general guide, for a two-hour party serve 6–8 nibbles per person; for a four-hour bash, 8–10 nibbles per person; and for an all-evening event, serve 10–12 nibbles per person. Canapés are fairly labour intensive, so be sure you have enough prep time before sending out the invites.

PICNICS AND BARBECUES

When the sunshine season starts, thoughts turn to outdoor eating, and in particular barbecues and picnics. It is of utmost importance to cook and store barbecue and picnic food correctly, as warm temperatures are a green light for harmful bacteria to multiply rapidly. Oh, and if the sun stops shining on your barbecue, don't worry, we've included 'if it rains' instructions on each recipe too.

Top picnic tips:

- The number one rule is to keep food cold – a cool bag or box is your picnic's best friend. Make sure you remember to put cool packs in the freezer the night before. Unless you're picnicking nearby, make sure that you pack food that has been well chilled before transporting.

- Avoid high-risk ingredients such as raw or lightly cooked eggs, cream, or shellfish.
- Keep food covered to protect it from insects, birds and pets, and pack antibacterial hand wipes.
- Invest in some airtight plastic containers, to avoid spills.
- Pack heavier items at the bottom of the cool bag; lighter ones at the top.
- Take a knife, a small, light chopping board and plenty of kitchen paper.
- The easiest way to transport homemade tarts and pies, etc is to leave them in their baking tins and wrap them well in foil or cling film.
- Keep salads separate from dressings until ready to eat.
- Don't put leftovers back in the fridge – it's always safest to throw away food that has been warming in the sun.

Top tips for barbecuing:

- Make sure the charcoal is at the right temperature before you start to cook food on the grill. After 25–30 minutes the coals should be ready, glowing red and with pale grey ash. Gas barbecues need 15 minutes to heat.
- Invest in long-handled tongs and a long-length, heat-resistant mitt to allow you to turn food comfortably without any fear of getting near the heat.
- If the heat gets too high on the barbecue, spray the coals with a little water.

- Scrape off excess marinade from food – too much will cause the flames to flare and burn the outside of the food before the middle is cooked.
- Metal skewers are best, but if you want to use wooden skewers, soak them in water for 30 minutes before use.
- Never rush cooking on a barbecue. Make sure that all food, particularly chicken, is well cooked. Don't assume that if something is charred on the outside it will be cooked inside. To test if chicken is cooked, insert a skewer into the thickest part of the meat – the juices should run clear and there should be no sign of blood. Cut open burgers and sausages and check them carefully.
- Keep raw and cooked foods apart to prevent bacteria from raw meat contaminating cooked items. Use separate equipment for raw and cooked foods, including chopping boards, tongs, knives and plates and wash hands in between touching raw meat and other food. Never put any cooked foods on a plate or surface that has been used for raw meat. (For more information, see page 133.)
- Don't leave food out in the sun. Keep it in the kitchen, then transfer it to the barbecue just before cooking or store it in a cool box.
- If there are any leftovers, throw them away or put them in the fridge as soon as you can.
- The best way to clean a barbecue is to use long tongs and a ball of foil, which you should rub up and down the grill rack while it's still warm.

Little Stilton and chestnut pasties

MAKES 20 • **PREP 30 MINS, PLUS COOLING COOK 35 MINS**

2 leeks, trimmed and finely sliced
2 tbsp olive oil or butter
85g/3oz peeled cooked chestnuts, chopped
25g/1oz walnuts, chopped
100g/4oz Stilton, crumbled
100g/4oz ricotta
1 tbsp finely chopped parsley or thyme
500g pack shortcrust pastry
plain flour, for dusting
1 egg, beaten

1 Heat oven to 190C/170C fan/gas 5. Gently cook the leeks in the oil or butter for 4–5 minutes until soft. Cool.
2 Mix the chestnuts, walnuts and Stilton with the ricotta and parsley or thyme. Season to taste and stir in the leeks.
3 Roll out the pastry thinly on a lightly floured surface and cut into 9cm rounds. Brush the edges with beaten egg and place a heaped teaspoon of filling in the centre of each round. Bring the sides up and pinch then crimp in the middle to seal, leaving the ends open. Place on a baking sheet, then brush with beaten egg. (Can be prepared up to a day ahead.) Bake for 30 minutes or until golden. Serve warm or at room temperature.

PER PASTY 154 kcals, carbs 12g, fat 11g, sat fat 4g, salt 0.18g

Prawn and pancetta spears

 MAKES 20 EASILY DOUBLED • **PREP 30 MINS COOK ABOUT 5 MINS**

10 slices pancetta or prosciutto
20 whole raw prawns, peeled but tails left on
2 tbsp extra virgin olive oil
FOR THE DIP
1 tbsp finely chopped preserved lemon or grated zest 1 lemon
1 tbsp lemon juice
1 tbsp finely snipped chives
4 tbsp mayonnaise
20 short wooden skewers, soaked in water

1 To make the dip, combine the preserved lemon or lemon zest, juice, chives and mayonnaise. Chill.
2 Heat grill to High. Cut the pancetta or prosciutto in half and wrap a piece around the middle of each prawn, still showing some prawn at either end. Thread each prawn onto a skewer and lay on a baking sheet with a rim. Mix the olive oil with salt and pepper then brush over the prawns. Chill until ready to serve.
3 Grill for 3–4 minutes on one side until the pancetta is crisp, then turn and grill 1 or 2 minutes more until cooked through. Serve hot or warm with the lemon mayonnaise for dipping.

PER SKEWER 58 kcals, carbs 0g, fat 5g, sat fat 1g, salt 0.32g

Smoked mackerel-loaded leaves

SERVES 8 EASILY DOUBLED OR MORE PREP 15 MINS • **NO COOK**

200g/7oz smoked mackerel fillets, skin removed and flaked
4 tbsp crème fraîche
juice and zest ½ lemon
small bunch chives, snipped
small handful dill, chopped
1 small radicchio, separated into leaves
1–2 chicory heads, separated into leaves

1 Gently mix the mackerel flakes with the crème fraîche, lemon juice, half the herbs and some pepper (but no salt – smoked mackerel is salty enough). Chill until ready to serve.
2 Spoon a generous amount of the mixture into each leaf, then arrange on plates. Sprinkle each 'scoop' with the remaining fresh herbs and a pinch of the lemon zest, then serve.

PER CANAPE 121 kcals, carbs 1g, fat 11g, sat fat 4g, salt 0.48g

Satay shots

Give your party a shot of Thai style with these satay canapés.

MAKES 36 • PREP 30 MINS • COOK 10 MINS
▦ CHICKEN IN MARINADE ONLY

4 skinless, boneless chicken breasts
3 tbsp soy sauce
1 heaped tbsp crushed chillies from a jar
2 garlic cloves, crushed
1 tbsp vegetable oil
1 heaped tbsp light muscovado sugar
415g jar ready-made peanut satay sauce
1 lime, cut in half
12 lime slices
36 wooden skewers, soaked in water

1 Cut the chicken breasts into 36 thin strips and put them into a bowl with the soy sauce, chillies, garlic, oil and sugar. Mix together until the chicken is coated, then thread each strip onto a bamboo skewer. Get the skewers lined up on a baking sheet and keep covered in the fridge until ready to cook.

2 Heat oven to 190C/170C fan/gas 5. Put the sheet in the hottest part of the oven for 10 minutes. Meanwhile, warm the satay sauce in a pan, then spoon a little into each of 12 shot glasses or small tumblers.

3 When the chicken is done, remove the sheet from the oven and squeeze the lime juice over the chicken. Pop 3 skewers in each shot glass and a slice of lime on to each rim. Serve warm or cold – they're nice either way.

PER SERVING (12) 72 kcals, carbs 2.3g, fat 1.8g, sat fat 0.4g, salt 0.49g

Mini chilli beef pies

Mini comfort food bites, perfect for a wintry get together.

MAKES 24 EASILY DOUBLED • PREP 25 MINS, PLUS
COOLING • COOK 1 HOUR
▦ CHILLI AND MASH, SEPARATELY

450g pack ready-rolled shortcrust pastry sheets
FOR THE QUICK CHILLI
1 tbsp sunflower oil
1 small onion, chopped
2 tsp each hot chilli powder and ground cumin
250g/9oz beef mince
85g/3oz tomato purée
150ml/¼ pint beef stock
large pinch ground cinnamon
200g/7oz kidney beans, drained and rinsed
FOR THE MASH
1 large floury potato (about 250g/9oz), peeled and cut
    into chunks
3 tbsp soured cream
2 tbsp chopped chives

1 To make the chilli, heat the oil in a pan and fry the onion for 5 minutes until soft. Add the spices and fry for 1 minute. Stir in the beef and cook for a few minutes. Add the tomato purée, stock and cinnamon. Give it a stir, bring to the boil, then simmer for 15-20 minutes until very little liquid is left. Add the beans 5 minutes before the end of cooking. Check seasoning and cool.

2 Heat oven to 200C/180C fan/gas 6. Unroll the pastry and, using a 7cm pastry cutter, stamp out 12 circles. Use to line a 12-hole mini muffin tray, prick the bases of the pastry tarts with a fork, and bake for 10 minutes. Remove from the oven and cool on a wire tray. Repeat with remaining pastry.

3 Meanwhile, cook the potato in boiling water until tender. Drain, mash with the soured cream and seasoning, then stir through the chives. Spoon 1–2 tsp of chilli mix into the pastry cases and top with a teaspoon of mash. Ruffle the mash with a fork; return to the oven for 15 minutes or until golden.

PER SERVING 137 kcals, carbs 13g, fat 8g, sat fat 3g, salt 0.33g

10 Quick party nibbles

With a few simply ingredients cleverly put together, these speedy recipes demonstrate just how easy it can be to prepare your own party fare.

1   **Cucumber salmon** Cut 1 large cucumber into 20 thick slices and scoop out the seeds, leaving a dip. Mix 200ml crème fraîche with the zest of 1 lemon and freshly ground black pepper, then spoon 1 tsp into each dip. Top with a piece of smoked salmon, some more lemon zest and some black pepper.

2   **Goat's cheese on toast** Roughly mash 250g goat's cheese with 2 finely chopped shallots. Toast 5–6 slices of sourdough and stamp out 20 small circles. Spread each circle with some cheese, top with a small blob of chilli jam (you'll need about 3 tbsp) and scatter with snipped chives.

3   **Little caviar jackets** Put 20 small new potatoes on a baking sheet. Drizzle with olive oil and season. Roast for 25 minutes at 200C/180C fan/gas 6, then cool to room temperature. Cut a small cross in the top of each one, push open a little and top with 1 tsp crème fraîche and some caviar or keta.

4   **Stuffed prosciutto balls** Mash 100g feta with ½ finely chopped chilli, 2 tsp chopped mint and the zest and juice of ¼ lemon. Roll into 24 small balls. Quarter 6 prosciutto slices lengthways, then wrap each prosciutto strip around a feta ball.

5   **Pesto bites** Take 20 small crackers or 20 homemade crostini. Spread 1 tsp pesto onto each cracker, top each with a piece of mozzarella from a 125g ball and sprinkle with basil leaves.

6   **Mini chorizo kebabs** Slice 32 finger-thick slices from a large chorizo sausage, then fry until crisp. Skewer 2 slices each onto 16 mini skewers, alternating with 16 chunks of roasted pepper from a jar and 16 cubes of feta. Serve on a platter, scattered with rocket.

7   **Falafel scoops** Cook 16 ready-made falafels according to the pack instructions. Stir ½ bunch chopped mint into 100ml natural yogurt, then season. To serve, sit each falafel into a small Baby Gem lettuce leaf, drizzle with a little of the minty yogurt and decorate with some mint leaves.

8   **Bloody Mary shots with horseradish** Mix 700ml tomato juice with 50ml vodka, the juice of 1 lemon and a good splash Tabasco and Worcestershire sauce. Season, then chill. To serve, pour into 10 shot glasses, add a thin cucumber stick to each as a stirrer, and top with a small spoon of creamed horseradish.

9   **Quails' eggs with sesame dukka** Toast 1 tbsp each cumin and coriander seeds and 85g hazelnuts, then whizz in a food processor until finely chopped. Mix with 50g sesame seeds and salt to taste, then serve in small bowls with 24–36 hard-boiled quails' eggs, halved, alongside for dipping. Good with flatbread and extra virgin olive oil too.

10   **Little chicken poppadums** Arrange a 75g tub of mini poppadums on a plate and slice 85g cooked chicken so there's 1 piece per poppadum. Mix ½ tsp curry powder, 100ml crème fraîche and the zest of ½ lemon, put 1 tsp in each poppadum with ½ tsp mango chutney. Finish with a slice of chicken and some chopped coriander. Best assembled just before serving.

Summer sausage rolls

These little bites are a much lighter choice than pork sausage rolls, but every bit as tasty.

**MAKES 20 EASILY DOUBLED • PREP 20 MINS
COOK 20 MINS**
❄ **RAW**

2 large skinless chicken breasts
1 garlic clove, crushed
3 rashers streaky bacon, thinly sliced
4 sun-dried tomatoes, chopped
handful basil leaves, chopped
375g pack ready-rolled puff pastry
plain flour, for dusting
1 egg yolk, beaten
25g/1oz sesame seeds

1 Whizz the chicken and garlic in a processor until the chicken is minced. Tip in the bacon, sun-dried tomatoes and basil. Pulse for 5 seconds to just mix through. Season well.
2 Roll the pastry sheet on a lightly floured surface and cut in half lengthways. Spread half the chicken mixture along the middle of one of the pastry strips, then roll up the pastry, pinching the ends together to seal. Using a sharp knife, cut into 2.5cm long pieces. Repeat with the remaining pastry strip. (Can be frozen, uncooked, for up to 1 month.)
3 Heat oven to 200C/180C fan/gas 6. Place the rolls on a large baking sheet. Brush with the egg, then sprinkle with the seeds. Bake for 20 minutes until golden.

PER ROLL 119 kcals, carbs 6g, fat 8g, sat fat 3g, salt 0.38g

Lamb and feta burgers with minty yogurt

Delicately spiced morsels with a cooling yogurt dip, ideal for making a head. Serve in halved mini pitta pockets if you want to serve something more substantial.

**MAKES 16 EASILY DOUBLED • PREP 20 MINS
COOK 15 MINS**
❄ **BURGERS ONLY, RAW**

500g/1lb 2oz lamb mince
2 tsp ground coriander
2 tsp cumin seeds
1 red chilli, deseeded and finely chopped
handful parsley, chopped
2 rosemary sprigs, leaves stripped and chopped
good splash Worcestershire sauce
1 egg, lightly beaten with a fork
100g/4oz feta, cut into 16 cubes
1 tbsp sunflower oil
FOR THE DIP
200ml/7fl oz natural yogurt
small bunch mint, leaves chopped

1 First make the dip by mixing together the yogurt and mint with a little seasoning, then chill until ready to serve.
2 Tip the lamb mince into a big bowl with the spices, chilli, herbs, Worcestershire sauce and egg. Season, then get your hands in and mix well. Divide the mixture into 16. Shape into burgers, pushing a cube of cheese into the centre of each and sealing in. Chill until just before your guests arrive (or freeze for up to 1 month).
3 Heat oven to 200C/180C fan/gas 6 and heat the oil in a frying pan. Fry the burgers for 1–2 minutes until brown on each side, then transfer to a baking sheet. Put in the oven for 5–10 minutes until cooked through and piping hot. Pile onto a big plate and serve with the dip on the side.

PER CANAPE 100 kcals, carbs 1g, fat 7g, sat fat 3g, salt 0.33g

OPPOSITE Clockwise from top left *Rosemary and olive drop scones with goat's cheese (page 452); Satay chicken burgers (page 448); Mini chilli beef pies (page 448); Lamb and feta burgers with minty yogurt; Layered houmous, tabbouleh and feta picnic bowl (page 455); Little Stilton and chestnut pasties and Prawn and pancetta spears (page 447).*

Prawn, mango and spring onion pakoras

MAKES 24 EASILY HALVED • PREP 20 MINS • COOK 20 MINS
❄ **PAKORAS ONLY**

140g/5oz gram flour or plain flour
2 tsp garam masala
1 tsp turmeric
3 green chillies, deseeded and finely chopped
1 small mango, peeled and chopped
4 spring onions, finely sliced
200g bag raw peeled prawns, chopped
vegetable oil, for deep-frying
mango chutney for dipping, or Cumin raita (opposite)

1 Tip the flour into a large bowl and stir in the spices and chillies and a large pinch of salt. Make a well in the middle, then gradually pour in 100ml water, whisking well until you have a smooth but very thick batter, similar in consistency to toothpaste. Mix in the mango, spring onions and prawns.
2 Heat the oil for deep-frying, then drop in spoonfuls of the mix. Fry four at a time for 3–4 minutes, until crisp and lightly golden. Drain on kitchen paper and keep warm in a low oven until ready to serve. Serve with mango chutney or Cumin raita.

PER PAKORA 97 kcals, carbs 5g, fat 7g, sat fat 3g, salt 0.05g

Rosemary and olive drop scones with goat's cheese

MAKES 24 EASILY DOUBLED • PREP 15 MINS
COOK 30 MINS
Ⓥ ❄ **BASES ONLY**

200g/7oz self-raising flour, sifted
1 tsp baking powder
2 eggs, beaten
200ml/7fl oz milk
1 sprig rosemary, leaves removed and finely chopped
handful black olives, stoned and chopped
sunflower oil, for frying
175g/6oz firm goat's cheese, cut into small pieces
200g punnet cherry tomatoes, halved
extra virgin olive oil, to serve (optional)

1 Mix the flour, baking powder and seasoning in a bowl. Pour in the eggs and a splash of milk then whisk until smooth. Stir in the rest of the milk, rosemary and olives.
2 Heat a little oil in a non-stick frying pan. Fry tablespoons of batter for 2 minutes until you see bubbles on the surface and the bottoms are golden. Flip over, fry for another minute.
3 To serve, heat grill to High. Spread the scones over a baking sheet. Top each with a piece of cheese and a tomato half. Grill for 5 minutes until the cheese has melted. Serve with a grinding of black pepper and a drizzle of olive oil, if you like. (Can be made up to a day ahead.)

PER SCONE 66 kcals, carbs 7g, fat 3g, sat fat 2g, salt 0.31g

Crispy pork and vegetable spring rolls

MAKES ABOUT 30 • PREP 40 MINS • COOK 5 MINS
❄ **RAW**

2 tbsp cornflour
50g/2oz thin rice noodles
100g/4oz minced pork
1 garlic clove, finely chopped
1 carrot, grated
50g/2oz oyster mushrooms, finely chopped
2 tbsp finely chopped coriander
2 tbsp light soy sauce mixed with 1 tsp sugar
7–8 spring roll wrappers, each cut into 4 squares
vegetable oil, for frying
sweet chilli sauce, to serve

1 Cover the noodles with boiling water and leave for 3 minutes. Drain. Cool under running cold water, drain, then snip into short lengths with scissors. Meanwhile, mix the cornflour and 3 tbsp cold water to a paste.
2 Mix the noodles with the pork, garlic, carrot, mushrooms, coriander, soy sauce, sugar and ½ tsp pepper.
3 Put a heaped teaspoon of filling onto one side of each wrapper square, brush the sides with cornflour paste, fold over the ends, then the two sides and roll up. Repeat. Cover and chill.
4 Heat 3cm oil in a deep frying pan, fry the rolls in batches until crisp and golden, about 2–3 minutes. Drain on kitchen paper then serve with sweet chilli sauce to dip.

PER SERVING 307kcals, carbs 36g, fat 16g, sat fat 2g, salt 2.11g

10 Delicious dips

1 **Tzatziki** In a bowl combine 250g pot Greek yogurt, ½ cucumber, peeled, deseeded then coarsely grated, 1 crushed garlic clove, 3 tbsp chopped dill, 2 tsp white wine vinegar and a pinch of sugar. Season with salt, then mix well. Chill for 1 hour, if time permits, letting the flavours infuse.

2 **Smoky pepper salsa** Heat grill to High. Grill 2 red peppers, halved lengthways, skin-side up, until the skins are black. Put into a bowl and cover. Leave until cool, then peel the skins away. Scoop out and discard the seeds from 6 ripe tomatoes. Put the tomatoes into a food processor with 1 crushed garlic clove, the juice of 1 lime, 1 tbsp oil and 2 tsp chipotle paste. Add the peppers, then pulse until chunky. Stir through 1 finely chopped red onion and small bunch chopped coriander, then serve.

3 **Lemon and coriander houmous** Drain 2 x 400g cans chickpeas, put into a food processor with 2 fat garlic cloves, roughly chopped, 3 tbsp Greek yogurt, 3 tbsp tahini, 3 tbsp extra virgin olive oil and zest and juice 2 lemons. Whiz to a fairly smooth mix. Scrape down the sides of the processor if you need to. Season generously then add a small bunch coriander and pulse until roughly chopped. Drizzle with more oil, then serve.

4 **Best-ever chunky guacamole** Use a large knife to pulverize 1 large ripe tomato on a board, then tip into a bowl. Scoop in the flesh 3 ripe avocados, then add the juice of 1 large lime, a handful of chopped coriander, 1 finely chopped small red onion and 1 finely chopped red chilli. Season, then roughly mash.

5 **Toasted cumin raita** Put 1 tsp cumin seeds in a dry frying pan, then toast for about 2 minutes, making sure you don't burn them. Stir into 500g tub Greek yogurt and chill until ready to serve. Sprinkle with paprika or cayenne before serving, if you like.

6 **Smoked aubergine purée** Heat grill to very hot. Slice 2 aubergines in half lengthways, then grill for 25 minutes, turning occasionally, until soft inside. Cool, score the flesh, then scoop out into a bowl. Mash with a fork to a thick pulp. Beat in the juice of 1 lemon, 2–3 crushed garlic cloves, 150ml thick yogurt and a small bunch of dill, chopped. Season and serve while still warm.

7 **Low-fat garlic and herb dip** Mix 100g light soft cheese with 50g fat-free bio-yogurt, then stir in 1 crushed garlic clove, a handful of snipped chives, a little lemon juice and fresh ground pepper.

8 **Creamy salmon and dill dip** Mix 100g soft cheese with 50g fat-free bio-yogurt, then stir in 1 crushed garlic clove. Stir 125g pack chopped smoked salmon and a few sprigs of chopped dill through the dip.

9 **Tangy roast pepper and walnut dip** In a pan, heat 1 tsp each ground cumin and smoked paprika in 6 tbsp olive oil until fragrant. Combine 100g walnuts, 225g roasted red peppers from a jar, 1 tbsp tomato purée, 1 garlic clove, crushed, and 2 tbsp pomegranate molasses in a food processor and season. With the motor running, slowly pour in the spiced oil. Add 1 tbsp of water if it's too thick.

10 **Artichoke, caper and lemon dip** In a food processor, combine a drained 280g jar marinated artichokes, 1 garlic clove, 50g toasted pine nuts, the zest and juice of 1 lemon, 3 tbsp grated Parmesan, a small bunch of flat-leaf parsley and 3 tbsp extra virgin olive oil. Purée until fine, season, then scrape into a bowl. Sprinkle with extra pine nuts to serve.

Best-ever crab sandwiches

Great for a smart afternoon tea, too.

MAKES 4 DEEP-FILLED SANDWICHES • PREP 20 MINS NO COOK

8 hand-cut slices best-quality brown or granary bread
unsalted butter, for spreading
1 lemon, in wedges, to serve
FOR THE CRAB PASTE
About 125g/4½oz brown crabmeat from a large
      brown crab
1 tbsp mayonnaise
1 tsp tomato ketchup
juice ½ lemon
1 tsp Dijon mustard
big pinch cayenne pepper
few drops brandy (optional)
FOR THE WHITE MEAT
250g/9oz white meat from the same crab
small handful chopped mixed herbs, such as parsley,
      dill, tarragon, chervil and chives
juice ½ lemon
2 tbsp olive oil

1 Make the crab paste: mix the ingredients together in a bowl and season, then set aside. In a separate bowl, mix the white meat with the herbs, lemon juice, oil and seasoning.
2 Spread the bread lightly with butter, then spoon and spread the crab paste over 4 of the slices. Pile the white meat over, then top with the remaining bread. Cut the crusts off, if you like, and serve halved or in small triangles or squares with lemon wedges on the side.

PER SANDWICH 529 kcals, carbs 41g, fat 28g, sat fat 9g, salt 2.65g

Pan bagnat

 Pan bagnat is a loaf stuffed with most of the ingredients you'd find in a salade niçoise.
Unlike a normal sandwich, it will improve for several hours as the flavours work together.

CUTS INTO 8 SLICES • PREP 20 MINS, PLUS SOAKING NO COOK

1 long, country-style loaf
4 tbsp olive oil
1 tbsp white wine vinegar
2 garlic cloves, chopped
500g/1lb 2oz ripe vine tomatoes
1 tbsp capers
2–3 tbsp chopped stoned black olives
8–10 anchovies (leave out for a vegetarian version)
handful basil leaves

1 Split the loaf in half lengthwise. Drizzle both cut surfaces with olive oil and scatter the vinegar and garlic on the bottom half. Sprinkle both cut sides with salt and pepper.
2 Roughly chop the tomatoes and spread over the bottom half, then sprinkle over the capers and olives. Lay the anchovies on top, scatter with basil leaves and press everything down lightly.
3 Cover the filling with the other half of the loaf and press down firmly. Wrap tightly in foil or greaseproof paper and place a weight on top for at least half an hour, longer if you have the time (4 hours maximum). Unwrap and cut into thick slices.

PER SERVING 246 kcals, carbs 38g, fat 8g, sat fat 1g, salt 1.47g

Layered houmous, tabbouleh and feta picnic bowl

This salad combines delicious meze-type dishes and a layering of several Greek- and Middle Eastern-inspired flavours that marry together as they sit in the fridge.

SERVES 4 • PREP 20 MINS • COOK 15 MINS

400g/14oz houmous
400g can chickpeas, rinsed and drained
200g pack feta, broken into chunks
handful pitted black olives
1 crisp Romaine heart
flatbreads, to serve
FOR THE TABBOULEH
85g/3oz bulghar wheat
large (80g) bunch mint, leaves finely chopped
large (80g) bunch flat-leaf parsley, leaves finely chopped
2 large ripe tomatoes, deseeded and chopped
1 red onion, finely chopped
zest and juice 1 lemon
4 tbsp olive oil, plus extra for drizzling

1 First, make the tabbouleh. Tip the bulghar into a saucepan, cover with water, season with salt, then simmer for 15 minutes until tender. Drain in a sieve, rinse under cold running water, then drain over the pan. Mix the mint and parsley with the tomatoes, onion and drained bulghar. Whisk the lemon zest and juice and oil together with seasoning, then toss with the bulghar.

2 Spoon the houmous into the bottom of a portable picnic bowl (or use a large plastic mixing bowl, as you can cover it tightly with cling film later). Scatter with chickpeas, then sprinkle with seasoning and drizzle with a little oil. Spoon the tabbouleh on top. Now top with the feta and olives, then tear over the lettuce leaves.

3 Cover the bowl tightly. Put a little more olive oil in a sealed container to take with you, then chill for up to 24 hours.

4 To eat, drizzle the olive oil over the leaves, then scoop onto serving plates, making sure everyone gets a bit of each layer. Serve with the flatbreads.

PER SERVING 768 kcals, carbs 41g, fat 58g, sat fat 13g, salt 2.85g

Tuna, asparagus and white bean salad

 This is a classic spring salad that makes the most of home-grown asparagus – and it also travels very well.

SERVES 4 • PREP 10 MINS • COOK 5 MINS

1 large bunch asparagus
2 x 200g cans yellowfin tuna steaks in water, drained
2 x 400g cans cannellini beans in water, drained
1 red onion, very finely chopped
2 tbsp capers
1 tbsp olive oil
1 tbsp red wine vinegar
2 tbsp tarragon, finely chopped

1 Cook the asparagus in a large pan of boiling water for 4–5 minutes until tender. Drain well, cool under running water, then cut into finger-length pieces. Toss together the tuna, beans, onion, capers and asparagus in a large serving bowl.

2 Mix the oil, vinegar and tarragon together, then pour over the salad. Chill until ready to serve.

PER SERVING 275 kcals, carbs 26g, fat 5g, sat fat 1g, salt 1.28g

Cold meatloaf with squashed tomato and pepper salsa

Thickly slice this meatloaf and serve in rolls or on its own as a tasty and economical cold cut.

SERVES 6 • PREP 20 MINS • COOK 1 HOUR 10 MINS
❄ **MEATLOAF ONLY**

500g pack beef mince
500g pack pork mince
1 onion, finely chopped
2 eggs
50g/2oz stale breadcrumbs
handful oregano sprigs, leaves roughly chopped,
     or use 1 tsp dried plus extra for scattering
handful thyme sprigs, leaves roughly chopped,
     or use 1 tsp dried
2 rosemary sprigs, leaves picked
2 garlic cloves, 1 crushed, 1 thinly sliced
2 tbsp olive oil, plus extra for greasing
bread rolls and rocket leaves, to serve
FOR THE SALSA
2 red and 2 yellow peppers, deseeded and thickly sliced
½ tsp dried crushed chillies
300g/11oz ripe tomatoes, quartered
2 tsp balsamic vinegar
1 tsp caster sugar
handful basil leaves

1 Heat oven to 180C/160C fan/gas 4. Put the mince, onion, eggs, crumbs, 1 tsp salt and ½ tsp black pepper into a large bowl. Add the chopped herbs and crushed garlic, then mix very well with your hands. Grease a 900g loaf tin with a little oil, then press in the mince, leaving the top a little mounded. Scatter with more thyme leaves and drizzle with a little oil.
2 Toss the peppers with the remaining garlic, 2 tbsp oil and chillies in a large roasting tin. Put the meatloaf and peppers into the oven, with the peppers on the shelf below. Roast for 30 minutes.
3 Stir the tomatoes, vinegar and sugar into the peppers, then cook for 40 minutes more. The meatloaf should be hot in the middle (test with a skewer), and the tomatoes soft and juicy.
4 Pour excess fat and juice away from the meatloaf, then cool. Squash the tomatoes into the peppers with the back of a fork, tear in the basil and season. Put into a container. Wrap the meatloaf and its tin in foil and keep chilled for up to 2 days.

PER SERVING 472 kcals, carbs 17g, fat 29g, sat fat 10g, salt 0.57g

Picnic pie

Served with pickles and salad, this big pork pie will take some beating.

SERVES 6 • PREP 25 MINS • COOK 50 MINS
❄ **COOKED**

butter, for greasing
500g block puff pastry
175g/6oz sausagemeat or skinned sausages (a pork
     and apple variety works well)
1 apple, peeled, cored and grated
1 onion, grated
1 tbsp thyme leaves
8 thick slices cooked ham, fat trimmed from edge
2 tbsp Dijon mustard
1 beaten egg, to glaze

1 Heat oven to 190C/170C fan/gas 5. Butter a 20cm springform tin. Cut one-third of the pastry from the block. Roll out the smaller piece, then cut a circle to make the top of the pie – use the tin base as a template. Use the rest to line the tin, leaving a good overhang.
2 Mix the sausagemeat with the apple, onion and thyme. Line the pie with 4 slices of ham and spread over 1 tbsp mustard. Press in half the sausagemeat then repeat the layers.
3 Put the pastry lid on top and brush with beaten egg. Fold the excess pastry over and press gently. Trim off any thick bits to make the lid look as attractive as possible. Brush again with beaten egg and cut a steam hole in the centre. Bake for 50 minutes or until a skewer pushed in through the steam hole comes out very hot. Cool for 15 minutes, then release the sides of the tin (but leave on the base) and cool completely on a rack.

PER SERVING 631 kcals, carbs 35g, fat 44g, sat fat 18g, salt 3.39g

OPPOSITE *Picnic pie*

Spicy tiffin eggs

A vegetarian take on Scotch eggs, these are mildly spiced and perfect for packing up with mango chutney and a salad.

MAKES 6 • PREP 20 MINS • COOK 15–20 MINS
V

7 large eggs
2 tbsp olive oil
1 onion, chopped
250g/9oz grated carrot
2 heaped tbsp korma curry paste
200g/7oz granary breadcrumbs
85g/3oz roasted cashews, finely chopped

1 Put 6 of the eggs in a pan of cold water and bring to the boil. Boil for 5 minutes, then cool quickly in cold water. Carefully remove the shells.
2 While the eggs are cooling, heat the oil, fry the onion for 5 minutes, then add the carrot and cook for 10 minutes more until soft. Stir in the curry paste and fry for a few minutes more. Stir in the breadcrumbs, then, when the mixture is cool, beat the remaining egg and stir in with seasoning to make a paste.
3 Divide the mixture into 6 and flatten with your hands (wetting them makes this a bit easier), then use to wrap round each egg – the mixture will seal well as you press it together. Roll in the cashews and chill until ready to cook. (The prepared eggs can be kept in the fridge overnight.)
4 Heat oven to 190C/170C fan/gas 5, then bake the eggs for 15–20 minutes. Cool for 5 minutes, then carefully cut in half using a very sharp knife.

PER EGG 340 kcals, carbs 24g, fat 21g, sat fat 4g, salt 0.77g

Orzo and mozzarella salad

Pasta salad packed with flavour.

SERVES 4 EASILY DOUBLED • PREP 10 MINS • COOK 8 MINS
V

350g/12oz orzo (see tip, below)
small bunch basil
4 tbsp extra virgin olive oil
25g/1oz Parmesan, finely grated, plus more to serve (optional)
1 garlic clove, very roughly chopped
50g/2oz toasted pine nuts
290g pack bocconcini (baby mozzarella balls)
100g/4oz semi-dried tomatoes, very roughly chopped
50g bag wild rocket

1 Boil the orzo for 8 minutes until tender, then drain and cool under cold water. Drain again, then tip into a large bowl. Meanwhile, tear the basil, stalks and all, into a food processor. Add the oil, Parmesan, garlic and half the pine nuts, then whizz to a thick pesto-like dressing.
2 Stir the dressing through the orzo, then season. The dressing will seem quite thick, but keep stirring and it will eventually coat all the grains. Add the bocconcini, tomatoes and scatter with the remaining pine nuts and a little more Parmesan, if you like. Top with the rocket, then toss through when ready to serve.

PER SERVING 742 kcals, carbs 71g, fat 40g, sat fat 13g, salt 1.25g

tip Orzo is a very small pasta shape, with each piece resembling a long, fat grain of barley (orzo means barley in Italian.) If you can't find it, the dish will work with any other tiny pasta shape, such as stelline (small stars) or rice-shaped pasta called risoni.

Roast chicken with couscous and pine nut stuffing

Delicious hot or cold and perfect for a picnic, this stuffed chicken will be a real family favourite.

**SERVES 8 • PREP 40 MINS, PLUS CHILLING
COOK 1 HOUR 10 MINS**

16 rashers streaky bacon
6 skinless chicken breasts
FOR THE STUFFING
100g/4oz couscous
175ml/6fl oz boiling chicken stock
1 onion, finely chopped
1 garlic clove, crushed
50g/2oz butter
100g/4oz pine nuts, toasted
140g/5oz dried apricots, roughly chopped
large handful parsley, roughly chopped
2 tbsp mint leaves, roughly chopped
juice ½ lemon
1 egg, beaten

1 Put the couscous in a large heatproof bowl, pour over the stock, then cover with cling film for 5 minutes. Soften the onion and garlic in 25g butter for 5–8 minutes until soft, cool, then mix with the couscous and other stuffing ingredients.
2 Using the back of a knife, stretch the rashers to 1½ times their original length. Overlap them on a large sheet of foil to make a rectangle. Slash the thickest part of each chicken breast, put between sheets of cling film then bat out until 1cm thick. Lay the chicken over the bacon, leaving no gaps, but leaving a bacon border around the longer sides.
3 Spoon the stuffing over the chicken along one long edge. Using the foil to help, roll the bacon and chicken around the stuffing like a log. Wrap tightly in foil, twisting the ends to secure, then chill for 2 hours or up to 1 day.
4 Heat oven to 180C/160C fan/gas 4. Place chicken, join-side down, in a roasting tin. Cook for 30 minutes, then unwrap and brush with the remaining butter. Cook, uncovered, for 20–30 minutes more until cooked through (a metal skewer inserted into the middle should come out hot). Cool and wrap in fresh foil to transport.

PER SERVING 348 kcals, carbs 16g, fat 20g, sat fat 7g, salt 1.32g

Satay chicken pieces

*Everyone has had tikka or tandoori chicken before, so how about going a little Thai with
a satay marinade instead? Perfect with sweet chilli sauce or mango chutney.*

**SERVES 6 • PREP 10 MINS, PLUS MARINATING
COOK 1 HOUR**

6 skinless chicken drumsticks and 6 skinless
    chicken thighs
zest and juice 1 lime
2 lemongrass, very roughly chopped
2 thumb-size chunks ginger, very roughly chopped
3 garlic cloves
2 tbsp peanut butter, crunchy or smooth
½ tsp each turmeric and ground cumin
160ml can coconut cream
small bunch coriander, plus extra to serve (optional)
a little oil, for greasing

1 Slash several deep cuts into each drumstick and thigh, then put into a large, non-metallic container. Put the lime zest and juice, lemongrass, ginger, garlic, peanut butter, spices, coconut cream and 1 tsp salt into a food processor, then whizz until it's as smooth as you can get it. Roughly chop the coriander leaves and finely chop the stalks, then add to the mix. Pour the marinade over the chicken, massage it into the meat with your hands, then leave to chill for at least 2 hours, or up to 24 hours if you have time.
2 Heat oven to 190C/170C fan/gas 5. Line 1–2 large baking sheets with foil and grease with a little oil. Spread out the chicken over the sheets, skin-side up, and roast for 1 hour, or until the chicken is cooked through and the coating golden and slightly charred in places. Cool, then chill well and pack in a container, ready to transport. Scatter with a few more coriander leaves to serve, if you like.

PER SERVING 302 kcals, carbs 3g, fat 17g, sat fat 10g, salt 0.4g

Seared steak with chimichurri dressing

A big steak for two to share, with a tasty fresh Argentinian sauce.

**SERVES 2 • PREP 15 MINS, PLUS MARINATING
COOK 8 MINS EACH**

300–400g/11-14oz piece lean rump or sirloin steak
FOR THE DRESSING
1 tsp cumin seeds
½ tsp fennel seeds
small bunch flat-leaf parsley, leaves chopped
1 red chilli, deseeded and finely chopped
1 tsp thyme leaves
5 tbsp olive oil
2 tbsp red wine vinegar

tip If it rains… Heat a griddle until very hot and cook the steak for the same timing as above.

1 To make the chimichurri dressing, toast the seeds in a small non-stick pan for 30 seconds or so, until they smell fragrant. Tip into a small bowl and stir in the chopped parsley, chilli, thyme, oil and vinegar. Season well with pepper – you can add salt just before serving.
2 Put the steak onto a plate and rub over about a quarter of the dressing. Leave the steak marinating at room temperature for about 30 minutes. (If you're making ahead, chill for up to 2 hours, then bring out of the fridge about 30 minutes before you want to cook it.)
3 Light the barbecue and allow the flames to die down until the ashes have gone white with heat. Season the steak and dressing with salt, then cook the steak for 2–3 minutes on each side, depending on the thickness and how you like you meat cooked. Serve on a board, then slice into thin strips as you eat – spooning over the remaining dressing.

PER SERVING 452 kcals, carbs 1g, fat 34g, sat fat 7g, salt 0.22g

Barbecued pork with sage, lemon and prosciutto

A super-tasty way to turn good-value pork into something really special.

SERVES 8 • PREP 30 MINS • COOK 15 MINS

85g/3oz prosciutto
3 lemons
3 tbsp roughly chopped sage leaves, plus extra sprigs
    to serve
3 x 350–450g/12oz–1lb pork tenderloins, trimmed of any fat
oil, for brushing
50g/2oz butter, chilled and cut into thin slices

tip If it rains… Griddle or grill the pork for the same cooking time as above.

1 In a food processor, whizz together the prosciutto, zest from all the lemons and juice from half, the chopped sage and plenty of seasoning until blended to a thick paste. Reserve the remaining 1½ lemons.
2 Cut each tenderloin lengthways down the centre, but not all the way through. Open out the meat and flatten slightly. Make about 10 deep slashes in each tenderloin, then rub the paste over the meat and into the slashes. Light the barbecue and allow the flames to die down until the ashes have gone white with heat.
3 Brush the tenderloins with oil, then barbecue, paste-side down, for 6–8 minutes. Turn and cook for a further 6–8 minutes until tender and cooked through.
4 Transfer the pork to a platter and, while hot, top it with the butter. Leave for a minute to melt, then squeeze over the reserved lemon halves. Scatter with sage sprigs and serve cut into thick slices.

PER SERVING 255 kcals, carbs 1g, fat 14g, sat fat 6g, salt 0.62g

Sticky barbecue ribs

You can use this BBQ sauce with any meat, or with chicken or sausages.

**SERVES 6 • PREP 10 MINS, PLUS MARINATING
COOK 20–30 MINS**
❄ **RAW**

2kg/4lb 8oz meaty pork spare ribs
1 bunch spring onions, roughly chopped (green stems
    and all)
1 Scotch bonnet chilli, seeded and finely chopped
4 garlic cloves, roughly chopped
6 tbsp dark rum
6 tbsp demerara sugar
6 tbsp dark soy sauce
6 tbsp clear honey
6 tsp Dijon mustard
1 tsp ground allspice

1 Tip the ribs into a big non-metallic bowl and throw in the spring onions, chilli and garlic. Now spoon all the remaining ingredients over the ribs and sprinkle with salt and pepper. Get your hands in the bowl and turn the ribs over and over again until they're coated in the sauce. (You can keep the ribs uncooked – tightly covered – in the fridge for up to 3 days or freeze for 2 months.)
2 Light the barbecue and allow the flames to die down until the ashes have gone white with heat. Cook the ribs for 20–30 minutes, depending on their size, turning them over frequently and brushing with sauce each time. The turning and brushing is important, so that all four sides of each rib get encrusted with the sauce, which builds up like a lacquer. If you have any leftover sauce at the end, boil it up in a pan and pour it over the ribs just before serving.

PER SERVING 484 kcals, carbs 32g, fat 22g, sat fat 8g, salt 3.09g

tip If it rains… Heat oven to 220C/200C fan/gas 7. Put the ribs in a large shallow roasting tin and roast in the top of the oven for 1 hour 15 minutes, turning and basting frequently.

Sticky chicken drumsticks

Finger-licking chicken that kids will love.

**SERVES 4 • PREP 5 MINS, PLUS MARINATING
COOK 35 MINS**
❄ **RAW**

8 chicken drumsticks
2 tbsp soy sauce
1 tbsp honey
1 tbsp olive oil
1 tsp tomato purée
1 tbsp Dijon mustard

1 Make 3 slashes on each of the drumsticks. Mix together the soy, honey, oil, tomato purée and mustard. Pour this mixture over the chicken and coat thoroughly. Leave to marinate for 30 minutes at room temperature or overnight in the fridge.
2 Light the barbecue and allow the flames to die down until the ashes have gone white with heat. Cook for 30 minutes, basting with the marinade now and and again, until tender and sticky.

PER SERVING 267 kcals, carbs 4g, fat 14g, sat fat 4g, salt 2.04g

tip If it rains… Heat oven to 200C/180C fan/gas 6. Tip the chicken into a roasting tin and cook for 35 minutes, turning occasionally, until the chicken is tender and glistening with the marinade.

Lime and coriander chicken

Barbecued chicken on the bone cooks and tastes so much better if you make slashes in the meat first.

**SERVES 4 • PREP 30 MINS, PLUS MARINATING
COOK 40 MINS
🔲 RAW**

1 medium chicken (about 1.6kg/3lb 8oz)
FOR THE MARINADE
3 garlic cloves
2 tbsp black peppercorns
juice 2 limes, plus 1 lime cut into wedges, to serve
bunch coriander, a few nice sprigs reserved,
    the rest finely chopped

1 First, spatchcock the chicken so that it will sit flat on the barbecue. All this means is using a pair of kitchen scissors or a sharp kitchen knife to cut down either side of the parson's nose to completely remove the backbone. Now place the chicken, breast-side up, on a chopping board and push down hard to flatten with your hands. Use a sharp knife to make lots of deep slashes in the chicken, about three in each breast and two in each leg.
2 In a mortar and pestle, crush the garlic and peppercorns together to a grey, mushy paste. Stir in the lime juice and chopped coriander. Put the chicken in a dish and massage the marinade into the chicken. Cover and chill for at least 2 hours or ideally overnight.
3 Light the barbecue and allow the flames to die down until the ashes have gone white with heat. Lay the chicken on the bars, skin-side up, and sprinkle with salt. Leave it there for 25 minutes, without moving it, then flip onto the skin side and give it 10 minutes more to crisp up and finish the cooking. Remove to a board and leave for a few minutes.
4 Carve or chop up the chicken then pile up on a platter and serve scattered with fresh coriander and lime wedges.

PER SERVING 415 kcals, carbs 4g, fat 27g, sat fat 9g, salt 0.43g

tip If it rains… Heat oven to 220C/200C fan/gas 7 and roast the chicken, skin-side up in a roasting tin, for 40 minutes until crisp and cooked through.

Thai-style prawns

 Leave the prawns in their shells (with the heads off) for this recipe. The shells will protect their meat from the intense heat of the barbecue, and trap any tasty juices.

SERVES 4 • PREP 5–10 MINS • COOK 5 MINS

600g/1lb 5oz jumbo king prawns
4 stalks lemongrass, bruised
FOR THE MARINADE
1 large red chilli, seeded and finely chopped
1 tbsp olive oil
2 tsp Thai fish sauce or soy sauce
2 fat garlic cloves, crushed
2 tsp grated ginger
1 tsp ground cumin

1 Light the barbecue and allow the flames to die down until the ashes have gone white with heat. Mix the marinade ingredients and add to the prawns. Leave for 5 minutes. Thread the prawns on metal skewers. Put the lemongrass across the bars in the centre of the barbecue then place the prawns on top. Cook for 2–3 minutes, turning once, until opaque. Discard the lemongrass before eating.

PER SERVING 132 kcals, carbs 1g, fat 2g, sat fat 1g, salt 0.97g

tip If it rains… Heat a griddle pan to very hot. Put the prawn skewers and lemongrass on for 2–3 minutes, turning once – don't overcook.

Stuffed peppers on the barbecue

Serve these peppers as a summer vegetable dish or with barbecued meat and fish.

SERVES 6 ● PREP 10 MINS ● COOK 30 MINS
V

2 tbsp olive oil
50g/2oz pine nuts
140g/5oz long grain rice
2 garlic cloves, chopped
350ml/12fl oz vegetable stock
1 bunch spring onions, sliced thinly
140g/5oz cherry tomatoes, halved
150g ball mozzarella, chopped
140g/5oz gorgonzola
handful each parsley and basil, chopped
3 red and 3 yellow peppers
kitchen string, for tying

tip If it rains… Heat oven to 180C/160C fan/gas 4, Put the peppers into a roasting tin, drizzle with a little oil then roast for 30–40 minutes.

1 Heat the oil in a medium pan with a lid and fry the pine nuts until lightly toasted, then add the rice and stir for 1 minute. Stir in the garlic and stock, boil, then cover and simmer for 10 minutes, until the rice is tender. Off the heat, stir in the spring onions, tomatoes, cheeses and herbs. Season well then cool.
2 Cut around the stalk of one pepper, and set aside. Make a slit down the length of the pepper and open out gently. Remove the seeds and membrane. Spoon in some filling. Take 1m string and wrap the centre point several times around the pepper stalk, tying it firmly. Top with the stalk and wrap the ends of the string several times around pepper to secure filling. Secure with a knot. Repeat with the other peppers.
3 Light the barbecue and allow the flames to die down until the ashes have gone white with heat. Cook for 15–20 minutes, turning gently until evenly browned.

PER SERVING 378 kcals, carbs 31g, fat 21g, sat fat 8g, salt 1.4g

Barbecued mackerel with ginger, chilli and lime drizzle

Asian flavours work fantastically with oily fish. Try this with sardines too.

SERVES 4 ● PREP 15 MINS ● COOK 8 MINS

3 tbsp extra virgin olive oil
4 small whole mackerel, gutted and cleaned
FOR THE DRIZZLE
1 large red chilli, deseeded and finely chopped
1 small garlic clove, finely chopped
small knob of fresh root ginger, finely chopped
2 tsp clear honey
finely grated zest and juice 2 large limes
1 tsp sesame oil
1 tsp Thai fish sauce
small handful coriander leaves, chopped

tip If it rains… Heat oven to 220C/200C fan/gas 7. Roast the fish in a roasting tin for 15 minutes or until the flesh flakes easily near the bone, then spoon over the drizzle.

1 Light the barbecue and allow the flames to die down until the ashes have gone white with heat. Make the drizzle by whisking 2 tbsp olive oil and all the other ingredients together in a small bowl, adjusting the ratio of honey and lime to make a sharp sweetness. Season to taste.
2 Score each side of the mackerel about 6 times, not quite through to the bone. Brush the fish with the remaining oil and season lightly. Barbecue the mackerel for 5–6 minutes on each side until the fish is charred and the eyes have turned white. Spoon the drizzle over the fish and allow to stand for 2–3 minutes before serving.

PER SERVING 406 kcals, carbs 3g, fat 31g, sat fat 6g, salt 0.49g

Lamb, lemon and dill souvlaki

Try varying the meats for these classic Greek skewers, with chicken, pork, beef and fish –
just remember to adjust the cooking times accordingly.

SERVES 4 • PREP 20 MINS, PLUS MARINATING
COOK 6 MINS
⊞ RAW

2 garlic cloves, finely chopped

2 tsp sea salt

4 tbsp olive oil

zest and juice 1 lemon

1 tbsp finely chopped fresh dill

700g/1lb 9oz lean lamb such as neck fillet or boneless leg,
      trimmed, then cut into large chunks

pitta or flatbread, to serve

tip If it rains… Heat the grill to High or have a hot
griddle pan ready, and cook the lamb for the same
time as before.

1 Pound the garlic with sea salt in a pestle and mortar (or
use a small food processor), until the garlic forms a paste.
Whisk together the oil, lemon juice and zest, dill and garlic.
Mix in the lamb and combine well. Cover and marinate for at
least 2 hours or overnight in the fridge. If you're going to use
bamboo skewers, soak them in cold water first.

2 Light the barbecue and allow the flames to die down until
the ashes have gone white with heat. If you've prepared the
lamb the previous day, take it out of the fridge 30 minutes
before cooking. Thread the meat onto the soaked or metal
skewers. Cook the skewers for 2–3 minutes on each side,
basting with the remaining marinade. Heat the pitta or
flatbreads briefly, then stuff with the souvlaki. Try serving
with Greek salad and Tzatziki (see pages 41 and 453).

PER SERVING (4) 457 kcals, carbs none, fat 35g, sat fat 14g, salt 0.27g

Tikka-style fish

Cooking a whole fish feels special, but is pure simplicity. So go on, bring a little Goan
beach barbecue to your back garden.

SERVES 6 • PREP 10 MINS • COOK 12–16 MINS

2 whole sea bream or red snapper (about 900g/2lb each)

2 tbsp finely grated fresh root ginger

4 garlic cloves, finely grated or crushed

6 tbsp plain yogurt

2 tbsp olive oil

2 tsp turmeric

2 tsp mild chilli powder

3 tsp cumin seeds

tip If it rains… Heat oven to 220C/200C fan/
gas 7 and roast the fish for 20 minutes or until the
flesh flakes easily near the bone and the marinade
is starting to char.

1 Slash the skin of the whole fish on each side with a sharp
knife. Mix the ginger and garlic, season with salt, then rub all
over the fish.

2 Mix the yogurt with the oil, spices and seasoning. Use to
coat the fish inside and out, then chill until ready to cook
(can be made a few hours ahead).

3 Light the barbecue and allow the flames to die down until
the ashes have gone white with heat. Cook straight on the
bars (or on foil if you are afraid of it sticking) for 6–8 minutes
each side.

PER SERVING 266 kcals, carbs 4g, fat 11g, sat fat 2g, salt 0.67g

OPPOSITE Clockwise from top left Barbecue baked sweet potatoes
(page 466); Carrot and sesame burgers (page 468); Cold meatloaf with
squashed tomato and pepper salsa (page 457); Lamb, lemon and dill
souvlaki; Barbecued mackerel with ginger, chilli and lime drizzle (page
463); Seared steak with chimichurri dressing (page 460)

Grilled sweetcorn with chermoula butter

SERVES 4 • PREP 10 MINS • COOK 10 MINS
V

4 cobs sweetcorn
FOR THE CHERMOULA BUTTER
175g/6oz butter, softened
1 tbsp ground cumin
2 tsp ground coriander
zest and juice 1 lemon
½ tsp paprika
2 garlic cloves, crushed
2 handfuls coriander, finely chopped

1 Make the chermoula butter by beating together all the ingredients. Wrap the butter in cling film and roll it into a log shape, then chill to harden. (The butter will keep in the fridge for up to a week or frozen for a month.)
2 If cooking outdoors, leave the corn in the husk. Light the barbecue and allow the flames to die down until the ashes have gone white with heat. Grill the corn for 10 minutes until charred on all sides. Carefully remove the husk and silk, then smear the butter over the hot corn.

PER SERVING 448 kcals, carbs 20g, fat 39g, sat fat 23g, salt 0.7g

Barbecue-baked sweet potatoes

SERVES 8 • PREP 15 MINS • COOK 30 MINS
V

8 medium sweet potatoes
4 tsp olive oil
4 tbsp Greek yogurt
1 spring onion, sliced

tip If it rains…Heat oven to 200C/180C fan/gas 6 and bake the potatoes for 45 minutes.

1 Rub each potato with a little oil and salt, then wrap in a double layer of foil.
2 Light the barbecue and allow the flames to die down until the ashes have gone white with heat. Put the potatoes directly onto the coals, cook for 15 minutes, turn with tongs, then cook for 15 minutes more. Remove one, unwrap, and check it is cooked through.
3 Peel back the top of the foil from each potato, split open and top with a spoonful of yogurt and a few spring onion slices.

PER SERVING 153 kcals, carbs 32g, fat 3g, sat fat 1g, salt 0.42g

Fully-loaded Cajun chicken burgers

SERVES 4 • PREP 20 MINS • COOK 15 MINS

4 skinless, boneless chicken breasts
2 tbsp olive oil
4 rashers smoked bacon
2 avocados, sliced
4 ciabatta rolls, split and toasted
4 thin slices of your favourite cheese
mayonnaise, to serve
4 small handfuls baby spinach leaves
FOR THE CAJUN SEASONING
1 tbsp ground cumin
1 tbsp ground coriander
1 tbsp paprika

1 Mix the seasoning ingredients with salt and pepper. Light the barbecue and leave until the ashes are white with heat. On a board, flatten out the chicken slightly, then drizzle with oil and toss in the seasoning to coat. Barbecue or grill the chicken for 5 minutes on each side, until cooked through. Cook the bacon on the bars too.
2 To assemble the burgers, spread the buns with mayonnaise, top with spinach, then bacon, then alternating slices of avocado and chicken and a slice of cheese.

PER SERVING 721 kcals, carbs 51g, fat 36g, sat fat 10g, salt 2.84g

Classic beef burgers

To turn these into cheeseburgers, add a slice of Cheddar to each patty after they have been turned. The cheese will melt on top while the burger finishes cooking underneath.

**MAKES 4 • PREP 20 MINS, PLUS CHILLING
COOK 15 MINS**
❄ **UNCOOKED BURGERS**

500g/1lb 2oz good-quality minced beef
1 small onion, finely chopped
1 egg
1 tbsp vegetable oil
4 burger buns, halved
any combination of sliced tomato, beetroot, lettuce, red onion, mayonnaise and ketchup, to serve

1 In a bowl, mix the beef with the onion, egg and plenty of seasoning. Divide the mixture into 4 and lightly wet your hands. Carefully roll each piece into rough tennis-ball shapes. Set in the palm of your hand and gently flatten into even patties about 3cm deep. Put on a plate, cover with cling film and leave in the fridge to firm up for at least 30 minutes.
2 Light the barbecue and allow the flames to die down until the ashes have gone white with heat. Lightly brush 1 side of each burger with oil, then place the burgers, oil-side down, on the rack. Cook for 5 minutes until lightly charred – don't move them – then turn over using tongs. Don't press down on the meat, as that will squeeze out the juices. Cook for about 5 minutes more, or until the burgers are done to your liking.
3 Toast the buns on the rack for 1 minute until golden, then pack with a burger and your favourite accompaniments.

PER BURGER 402 kcals, carbs 25g, fat 19g, sat fat 7g, salt 1.04g

> *tip* If it rains… Heat a griddle pan or the grill to very hot and cook the burgers as above.

Spanish-style burgers

Mix 500g/1lb 2oz pork mince with 50g/2oz chopped chorizo sausage, the onion and egg. Cook until well done, then serve with some rocket and roasted red peppers.

Sticky sausage burgers with blue cheese

Mix the meat from 6 large sausages (450g/1lb) with 50g/2oz breadcrumbs, 2 tbsp caramelized onion chutney and 1 tbsp chopped sage. Poke a small chunk of blue cheese into the middle of each burger then cook for 20 minutes until well done. Serve with more chutney.

Kofta burgers

Mix 500g/1lb 2oz lamb mince with the onion and egg, 1 crushed garlic clove, 3 tbsp garam masala and 1 tbsp chilli sauce. Cook as above then serve in pittas with shredded cabbage, tomatoes, red onion and dollops of natural yogurt.

Spiced turkey burgers

For a low-fat choice, mix 500g/1lb 2oz turkey mince with the onion and egg, 1 crushed garlic clove, 2 tsp curry powder and a handful of chopped coriander. Cook until well done then serve topped with mango chutney.

Carrot and sesame burgers

These creative burgers beat anything you can buy. Make sure that you chill the mix thoroughly,
as this will help them hold together as they cook.

MAKES 6 • PREP 30 MINS • COOK 20 MINS
V ❄ UNCOOKED

400g can chickpeas, rinsed and drained
1 small onion, roughly chopped
2 tbsp tahini, plus 1 tsp to serve
1 tsp ground cumin
1 egg
750g/1lb 10oz carrots, peeled and grated
3 tbsp olive oil
100g/4oz wholemeal breadcrumbs
zest 1 lemon, plus 1 tsp juice
3 tbsp sesame seeds, toasted
natural yogurt, buns, rocket, avocado and chilli sauce,
    to serve

1 Put the first 5 ingredients into a food processor with a third of the grated carrot. Whizz to a paste, then scrape into a large bowl. Heat 1 tbsp oil in a large frying pan, then cook the remaining carrot for 8–10 minutes, stirring until softened. Add to the paste with the crumbs, zest and sesame seeds. Season and mix with your hands.
2 Using wet hands, shape into 6 burgers. Cover and chill for 30 minutes. Mix the yogurt with the remaining tahini and lemon juice.
3 Barbecue the burgers for 5 minutes on each side, until golden and crisp. When ready, spread the toasted buns with the yogurt then stuff with avocado, burgers and salad. Finish with a drizzle of chilli sauce.

PER SERVING 284 kcals, carbs 27g, fat 16g, sat fat 3g, salt 0.5g

> *tip* If it rains…Heat a non-stick frying pan and cook for the same time as above.

Tangy tuna burgers

It might sound unusual to chop tuna steak but this is really worth trying. The meat creates deliciously
juicy burgers with a fraction of the fat of beef mince.

MAKES 2 • PREP 20 MINS • COOK 5 MINS

200g/7oz fresh tuna steaks (choose sustainably sourced
    tuna, preferably yellowfin)
1 garlic clove, finely chopped
small knob of fresh root ginger, finely chopped
1 tbsp soy sauce
handful coriander leaves, chopped
1 tbsp sunflower oil
burger buns, lettuce leaves, sliced tomato and avocado,
    to serve

1 Chop the tuna into small chunks, then carry on chopping until roughly minced. Tip into a bowl, then mix with the garlic, ginger, soy sauce and coriander. Shape into 2 burgers, place on a plate, cover with cling film, then freeze for 10 minutes to firm up.
2 Heat the barbecue and brush the burgers with oil. Cook for 1–2 minutes on each side or until done to your liking. Toast the buns on the rack, then stuff with the burgers, lettuce, tomato and avocado.

PER BURGER 97 kcals, carbs 1g, fat 5g, sat fat 1g, salt 0.74g

> *tip* If it rains…Heat the oil in a non-stick frying pan and fry for 1–2 minutes on each side.

Top drinks

Unleash your inner mixologist and surprise your guests with something other than wine, beer or juice.

1 **Black velvet** Half-fill champagne flutes with Guinness, then slowly top them up with chilled champagne.

2 **Peach sparker** Mix 100ml ready-made peach purée with 4 tsp orange liqueur and pour into 6 glasses. Top up each glass with Prosecco or dry sparkling white wine.

3 **Drivers' punch** Mix together 300ml cloudy apple juice, 300ml lemonade and 100ml cranberry juice. Add some ice, some thinly sliced apple and a few fresh cranberries, then pour into 8 glasses.

4 **Cranberry mojitos** Put 140g fresh or frozen cranberries, a handful mint and 2 tbsp brown sugar in a bowl. Crush with the end of a rolling pin, then add a couple of handfuls of crushed ice and stir to mix. Add a shot of vodka to 6–8 tall glasses, divide the cranberry crush between them, then top up with cranberry juice and sparkling water.

5 **Mulled wine cocktail** Put 100g light muscovado sugar in a pan with 1 star anise, 1 cinnamon stick, 4 cloves and 150ml water. Bring slowly to the boil, stirring to dissolve the sugar. Simmer for 2 minutes, then pour into a large jug and leave to cool. Add 1 lemon and 2 clementines, both thinly sliced, to the jug along with 150ml Cointreau and 750ml light red wine, such as Beaujolais. Stir well, then chill and serve over ice. If you'd like to serve a traditional warm mulled wine, there's no need to chill – simply warm it through without boiling and serve in heatproof glasses. Serves 6–8.

6 **Bitter orange and cardamom** Bash 6 cardamom pods in a pestle and mortar until they split. Melt 6 tbsp Seville orange marmalade in a pan, then whisk in 400ml (14fl oz) vodka. Add the crushed pods and warm the mixture for a few minutes, but don't let it boil. Leave to infuse off the heat for 20 minutes, then strain the liquid into a jug. Add 125ml (4fl oz) Cointreau, 4 tbsp lemon juice and chill (or store in the freezer). Pour into 6 glasses with a little more marmalade in the bottom, some ice and a whole cardamom pod floating on top.

Kitchen know-how

WHAT'S IN SEASON?

Buying seasonal produce will ensure you get maximum flavour from your ingredients. Here's an at-a-glance guide to what you should look out for in the shops and at markets throughout the year.

VEGETABLES

KEY: **x** = at its best **o** = coming into season

	Jan	Feb	Mar	Apr	May	Jun	Jul	Aug	Sep	Oct	Nov	Dec
Asparagus				o	x	x	x					
Aubergine					o	x	x	x	x	x		
Beetroot				o	x	x	x	x	x	x	x	x
Broccoli							o	x	x	x		
Broad bean						o	x	x	x	x		
Brussels sprout	x	x							o	x	x	x
Cabbage							o	x	x			
Cauliflower	x	x	x	x							o	x
Cavalo nero						o	x	x	x	x		
Celeriac	x	x	o	x					x	x	x	x
Celery	x	x					o	x	x	x	x	x
Chicory	x	x	x									o
Courgette and cucumber					o	x	x	x	x			
Fennel bulb					o	x	x	x	x			
Garlic						o	x	x	x	x		
Globe artichoke					o	x	x	x	x	x		
Jerusalem artichoke	x	x	x							o	x	x
Kale	x	x						o	x	x	x	x
Lamb's lettuce				o	x	x	x	x	x	x	x	
Leek	x	x	x					o	x	x	x	x
Lettuce				o	x	x	x	x	x	x	x	x
New potatoes			o	x	x	x	x					
Parsnip	x	x	x						o	x	x	x
Peas				o	x	x	x	x	x	x	x	
Pepper		o	x	x	x	x	x	x	x			
Potato	x	x				o	x	x	x	x	x	x
Pumpkin									o	x	x	x
Purple sprouting broccoli	o	x	x	x								
Radish				o	x	x	x	x	x	x		
Spinach			o	x	x	x	x	x	x			
Spring Greens			o	x	x	x						
Swede	x	x							o	x	x	x
Sweet potato	x	x	x						o	x	x	x
Sweetcorn							o	x	x			
Swiss chard						o	x	x	x	x	x	
Turnip	x	x							o	x	x	x
Watercress			o	x	x	x	x	x	x			

FRUIT

KEY: **x** = at its best   **o** = coming into season

	Jan	Feb	Mar	Apr	May	Jun	Jul	Aug	Sep	Oct	Nov	Dec
Apple	x	x							o	x	x	x
Apricot			o	o	x	x	x	x	x			
Blackberry				o					x			
Blackcurrant						o	x	x				
Blueberry						o	x	x				
Bramley apple									o	x	x	x
Cherry						o	x	x				
Clementine										o	x	x
Cranberry									o	x	x	x
Damson								o	x			
Fig							o	x	x	x	x	
Gooseberry				o	x	x	x	x				
Lemon	x	x	x									o
Melon					o	x	x	x	x			
Peach						o	x	x	x			
Pear	x							o	x	x	x	x
Plum							o	x	x			
Quince									o	x	x	x
Raspberry					o	x	x	x	x			
Redcurrant						o	x	x	x			
Rhubarb (forced + outdoor)		x		x	x	x	x	x	x			x
Strawberry				o	x	x	x	x	x			
Tomato					o	x	x	x	x	x		

STORECUPBOARD ESSENTIALS

A well-stocked storecupboard should have a few basics that you can add to speciality items or fresh ingredients when you need them.

A few notes on storing

Many dried ingredients come in plastic packets that can split easily. Lidded containers are good alternatives for avoiding spillages, but carefully opened packets can also be secured with rubber bands or clips.

- Keep herbs and spices in a cool, dry place to get the longest life out of them.
- Fresh herbs will last up to a week if they are removed from their bags, wrapped in damp kitchen paper, sealed into a food bag and kept in the salad drawer of the fridge.

EVERYDAY ESSENTIALS

Canned plum tomatoes Chopped tomatoes contain more flesh per can than whole plum tomatoes.

Canned pulses A great convenience food. Dried are better value, but they need soaking and therefore the recipe requires advance planning; having a few cans of the ones you use most often will mean you can make supper in minutes.

Honey Clear, runny honey can be drizzled over meat for an instant glaze or added to sauces, dressings and marinades for sweetness. Ideal for baking and puds.

Sugar Light and dark muscovado, plus golden caster are the most useful types.

Mustards Dijon and wholegrain are milder than English but it's worth having a selection. Use English mustard powder as a dry seasoning when roasting beef, lamb or pork.

Pasta There are so many shapes to choose from, so pick your favourite. However, it's a good idea to keep a long pasta, such as spaghetti, and a chunkier shape, such as penne. (For more info, see page 54.)

Rice Risotto and long grain are essential for everyday cooking; basmati will give fragrant and fluffy mounds.

Stock Even if you make your own it's still handy to have a bought version in the cupboard. Vegetable bouillon powder is the most versatile.

Wine vinegar A bottle of either red or white can cover most dishes and dressings, and balsamic is good for drizzling. Save malt vinegar for shaking over your chips.

Oils A bottle of a flavourless oil, such as sunflower or vegetable, is best for frying and a mild olive oil is ideal for general usage. Keep extra virgin olive oil and flavoured oils, such as walnut, for dressings and finishing dishes.

Dried herbs Oregano, thyme and mixed herbs are the most useful. They are much stronger in flavour than fresh, so use 1 teaspoon dried herbs to every tablespoon of fresh if you want to substitute in a recipe.

Dried spices Black pepper, chilli flakes or powder, ground cinnamon, coriander, cumin and paprika will all come in handy. Don't buy large quantities of dried herbs and spices, though, as they lose their pungency over time.

Salt Flaky salt is the best choice, for its pure flavour and because you use less of it. Grind it down for baking.

Flours and raising agents Self-raising, plain and cornflour are best for baking, thickening, and coating before frying, to name a few uses. Bicarbonate of soda and baking powder will come in handy if you bake regularly.

Vanilla extract is a great everyday alternative to more expensive vanilla pods.

Don't forget that the fridge can be an extension of your storecupboard. Stock it with long-lasting flavour-makers such as bacon, Parmesan, tomato purée, olives, capers, lemons and limes and you'll have even greater choice without shopping from scratch every night.

If you particularly enjoy cooking one kind of cuisine, then why not stock up on its classic ingredients? In addition to the list above, buy in the following:

Caribbean Key ingredients include jerk seasoning or jerk paste, desiccated coconut or canned coconut milk, kidney, pinto and black-eyed beans, allspice, thyme and Scotch bonnet chillies.

Chinese Add noodles and toasted sesame and chilli oil to your list. Rice vinegar, soy sauce (dark and light), five-spice powder and hoisin sauce are commonly used too.

Greek Fresh ingredients simply prepared are the basis of modern Greek cuisine, so add feta, yogurt and lemons to your list, along with good extra virgin olive oil, olives, and also dried or canned butterbeans.

Indian In addition to those spices listed above, garam masala, turmeric, cardamom pods and cinnamon sticks are often used. To get maximum flavour, buy whole spices then toast and grind them yourself, or invest in jars of paste. Stock up on dried curry leaves, tamarind paste, coconut milk, lentils and cashews for sprinkling.

Italian Pick up anchovies, capers, fennel seeds, dried mushrooms, olives, pine nuts and chargrilled vegetables in oil.

Mexican Choose canned black beans, chipotle chilli paste, coriander, pickled jalapeños, limes, tortillas and taco shells.

North African Go for chickpeas, preserved lemons, almonds, olives and dried apricots, dates or prunes. Harissa paste adds a chilli and garlic kick.

Spanish Put chickpeas, chorizo, pine nuts, sherry and sherry vinegar, smoked paprika and saffron in your trolley.

Thai Go for roasted peanuts and peanut butter, Thai sweet chilli sauce, jasmine rice, rice noodles, Thai curry paste and coconut milk and fish sauce.

Vegetarian The core ingredients to healthy vegetarian food are the protein powerhouses of beans, nuts and tofu. Vegetarian food lends itself to the spices in Indian cooking and Japanese condiments, such as tamari, mirin, miso paste and hot wasabi. Add carbs with beans and pulses, and stock up on dried red, green, brown and Puy lentils. Brown rice, wild rice, bulghar wheat, quinoa and couscous are storecupboard standards.

FOOD SAFETY

Being conscious of food safety goes hand in hand with good cooking. Many foods contain harmful micro-organisms which can cause food poisoning. Pregnant women, the elderly, young children and anyone with an impaired immune system should avoid dishes containing raw eggs and unpasteurised dairy products.

Buy fresh food from suppliers you trust, and follow these guidelines:

Avoid cross-contamination

- Wash hands before cooking or touching food and after handling raw meat, fish and eggs.
- Keep cloths and surfaces clean and wash these, plus knives and utensils. as soon as possible after touching raw meat, poultry or eggs.
- Keep separate chopping boards for raw and cooked foods.
- Don't wash raw meat, you'll just splash germs around the kitchen.

Chilling

- Make sure your fridge is set to between 0C and 5C.
- Cool hot food quickly. Spread it out thinly to speed cooling, then pack it away. This is especially important for recipes involving lightly cooked eggs (such as custard) and meat.
- Keep raw meat and fish away from ready-to-eat food, and below it in the fridge.
- Keep food out of the fridge for as short a time as possible.

Cooking and reheating

- Always cook and reheat food until piping hot, with the exception of joints of meat (not pork) and steaks. These can be served rare, as long as the outside has been well seared.
- All poultry, sausages, burgers and anything containing mince should be cooked through.
- Be particularly careful with rice; cool it quickly, chill it, and if you reheat it, make sure it is piping hot.

Best-before and use-by dates

'Best-before' dates are more about quality than safety – as long as the food smells and looks fine, it is safe to eat food past the best-before date. Don't, however, use food after its 'use-by' date – even if the food looks and smells fine.

FREEZING

There are three golden rules for food safety:

- Cool foods quickly before you freeze them.
- Avoid re-freezing anything that's been frozen, unless you have cooked it again completely. So, for instance, frozen minced beef cooked into bolognese sauce can be refrozen. Always reheat to piping hot. Use your common sense and don't do this with anything containing eggs or seafood.
- Contrary to what many people think, freezing doesn't kill bacteria, so don't take any chances with food that looks or smells anything less than fresh.

Ingredients that freeze well

- Butter and margarine – up to 3 months.
- Grated cheese – up to 4 months.
- Bread and cakes – up to 3 months.
- Bacon – up to 2 months.
- Milk – up to 1 month (defrost in the fridge.)
- Raw pastry and bread doughs – up to 6 months.
- Double cream – up to 4 months, if softly whipped first.
- Raw egg whites and yolks (separately) – up to 6 months.
- Stocks and gravies – up to a year.
- Hard herbs and flavourings (such as bay leaves, kaffir lime leaves and grated ginger) – up to 3 months. Chopped herbs frozen in a little water in ice-cube trays will do for emergencies.

And those that don't:

- Raw eggs in their shells. Hard-boiled eggs will go rubbery.
- Salad veg and other veg with a high water content (e.g. beansprouts).
- Soft herbs, such as parsley, basil and chives.
- Jam and gelatine desserts.
- Emulsion sauces, such as mayonnaise.
- Plain yogurt, low-fat cream cheese, single cream and cottage cheese.

Freezing to get ahead

There are a great many recipes that can be made ahead and defrosted to enjoy cold, or to be reheated. For hot dishes, best results generally come from defrosting in the fridge overnight, then cooking as if from fresh. Recipes in this book that can be frozen are labelled with this symbol:

Cooking from frozen

Some dishes can be cooked from frozen, but remember this will take longer than cooking from fresh and some non-lidded dishes can over-colour or dry out on the top before the middle is hot. To prevent this, cover with foil towards the end of cooking. Dishes that cook well from frozen include: soups, stews, casseroles, braises and saucy dishes – such as bolognese sauce, bakes, gratins and potato-topped pies, thin fish fillets, small fish, sausages and burgers, and seafood, if added to the end of a hot dish. Do not cook raw poultry and large joints of meat from frozen.

Thawing

Thaw food in the fridge in a container that will catch any juices or moisture from the food. Always thaw meat and fish at the bottom of the fridge, so that juices can't splash onto food below. Microwaves are good for thawing but should only be used if the food is to be cooked or reheated straight after being defrosted.

Freezing fresh produce

When properly frozen, fruit and vegetables retain all their flavour and nutrients. To freeze small, or small chunks of green veg, boil a large pan of water then cook a handful at a time for 30 seconds. Using a slotted spoon, scoop them out into a bowl of heavily iced water. Once chilled, drain the veg and scatter it onto a tray lined with kitchen paper. Freeze on the tray then transfer them to a freezer bag.

Fruit can be frozen as whole small fruit or in chunks. Again, first freeze it flat on trays, then pack it into boxes.

Freezing – tips for success

- **Freeze as quickly as possible** by freezing in small quantities, in shallow containers, or by 'open freezing' – which means freezing food unwrapped, then wrapping and labelling it. Never put hot or warm food into the freezer.
- **Wrap food properly** or put it into sealed containers, otherwise your food can get freezer-burn (dry and discoloured patches).
- **Label everything**, as lots of foods look the same when they're frozen. Mark the container with the date, too, so you can track how long it has been in there.
- **Portion control** Freeze food in realistically sized portions.

You don't want to have to defrost a stew big enough to feed eight when you're only feeding a family of three.
- **Don't freeze old food;** the point of freezing is to keep food at its prime.
- **For an efficient freezer, defrost it regularly** and keep it full.
- **In a power cut**, don't open the freezer door. Foods should remain frozen for about 24 hours, leaving you time to sort out the problem.

YOUR KITCHEN KIT

Every cook needs a basic 'batterie de cuisine', plus a few gadgets to make life easier. Check out our guide to help you decide what will be the most useful items in your kitchen.

Pans

Casserole Large, flameproof, with a heatproof handle and a lid – for hob-to-oven cooking.

A large frying pan About 24cm across. An ovenproof handle is worth paying more for.

A smaller omelette pan is also helpful.

A deep sauté pan Again with an ovenproof handle. Ideal for browning meat and cooking paellas, pilaus and stews.

Saucepans One large, one medium, and one small.

A griddle pan Heavy and with deep ridges for clear griddle marks.

Wok Not essential, but worth buying if you make a lot of stir-fries.

Tins, trays and dishes

Baking tray Approx 30 x 40cm for biscuits, roulades and for grilling.

Pair of sandwich tins 20cm, loose-bottomed, for sandwiched cakes.

Deep, round cake tin 20cm, for large cakes and deep pies.

23cm springform tin, easy to release for delicate desserts.

A muffin tin for muffins, deep cupcakes and individual Yorkshire puds.

Small roasting tin, approx 20 x 30cm for traybakes, toad in the hole and more.

900g/2lb loaf tin for loaf cakes, bread and terrines.

Baking sheet with a lip on one edge, to help pull it from the oven.

Large roasting tin, sturdy enough not to warp and as large as your oven will allow.

Shallow tart tin 23cm, with sides about 3cm deep, for tarts and quiches.

Metal pie plate for traditional sweet and savoury pies.

Large baking dish for lasagnes, shepherd's pies, etc.

Shallow baking dish for gratins and grills.

Baking

Mixing bowls One large, one medium, and a small – glass is the best all-round material.

Piping bags with wide nozzles for piping choux pastry and meringues, small nozzles for icing cakes and biscuits. Disposable bags are very handy.

Set of cutters for cookies and scones. Plastic ones won't rust.

Sieves A little one (or tea strainer) for dusting icing sugar, a large one for flour, etc.

Rolling pin A long one is best. Ceramic stays cold for pastry work and is easy to clean.

Balloon whisk for beating batters and sauces, egg whites and cream.

Wire racks Stacking ones are useful if you do a lot of baking.

Baking parchment Siliconized paper, for lining non-stick tins. Greaseproof tends to stick.

Hand-held beaters for whisking and beating – a labour-saving device well worth the money, even if you only bake occasionally.

Flexible rubber spatula for scraping out cake mix.

Palette knife for smoothing frostings and fillings.

Individual metal pudding moulds for mini steamed puds.

Ceramic 1.5-litre pudding basin for steamed puds and bombes.

Ramekins 150ml size, for crème brulées, mini puds and bakes.

Baking beans Heavy ceramic balls that will keep pastry cases in shape.

General

Knives For information see page 478.

Chopping boards Plastic won't hold flavours or odours and are cheap to replace. Good wooden boards won't blunt knives, but are expensive and can warp if left in water.

Colander for draining pasta and veg. Choose one with lots of holes and two handles to balance over a large pan.

Graters A box grater is a good all-rounder, but a fine microplane is best for zesting and grating nutmeg.

Peeler Y-shaped peelers are great for speedy veg prep and for making Parmesan or chocolate shavings.

Kitchen scissors Choose a robust-looking pair.

Kitchen string for tying roasts and puddings.

Citrus juicer One with a base will catch the pips.

Also: Fish slice, ladle, slotted spoon, wooden spoons, tongs, potato masher, wooden or metal skewers, plastic lidded containers and freezer bags for storage.

Measuring

Measuring spoons Narrow ones that fit into jars are most helpful.

Scales Digital ones are most accurate.

Oven thermometer Make sure your oven is as hot as it says it is. Some are meat thermometers too – these are ideal for roasting.

Kitchen timer One with a string to go around your neck – then you'll always hear it.

Jugs Choose heatproof glass – a 600ml jug is most useful, as it has smaller increments marked on it.

A little help...

If there are tasks that you do regularly in the kitchen, it makes sense to invest in a bit of serious kit to make life easier.

Food processor Invaluable if you cook from scratch or in bulk and saves time and effort. Buy a good-quality model, but don't worry about getting one with all the gadgets, you probably won't use them.

Ice cream maker Self-freezing machines are very expensive; ones where you freeze the bowl yourself do the job perfectly.

Table-top mixer Especially worthwhile if you make bread or bake a lot as it will knead while you do something else.

Blender Useful if you make soup regularly or love smoothies – they often come as an attachment on a food processor.

Hand blender Ideal for small blitzing jobs, such as blending soups, and so much easier to clean.

Steamer A stacking bamboo steamer is the economical option, and sits on top of a similar-sized pan. If you steam a lot, a special steamer pan with metal inserts will be useful.

KNIFE SKILLS

Basic knife skills

Many recipes begin with chopping an onion, so it's a skill well worth honing. The benefit? Evenly-sized pieces of onion that will all soften at the same speed. This technique also applies to finely chopping shallots.

1 Sit the onion on a board and cut a thin slice off the stem end (leave the root end to hold the onion together). Halve lengthways through the root end, then peel off the outer skin. Place the onion cut-side down on the board and, following its natural lines, make evenly spaced slices almost up to the root end (photo 1).

2 Make a couple of horizontal cuts through the onion's width, keeping the root intact (photo 2).

3 Holding your fingers like a claw at the root end, slice vertically and evenly across the width of the onion so it falls into dice (photo 3).

Chopping other veg

Slicing and chopping are the basic skills for everyday cooking, but some recipes may suggest batons (thick sticks), julienne or matchsticks (very thin slices), dice (small cubes) or chiffonade (thin ribbons).

The common way to describe a good chopping motion is 'rock and chop'. When chopping, keep the tip of the knife in contact with the board as you lift it up and down to chop, using the full length of the blade. If you're not feeling confident about chopping, buy some cheap mushrooms – they have the perfect texture to practice on.

To prevent your board sliding around while chopping, place a damp cloth underneath it.

Batons Cut veg lengthways into slices, then lengthways into batons (photo 4). For perfectly angular batons, first trim away the rounded edges of carrots and other veg. It's not essential, but leaves a neat rectangular chunk that's easy to cut into even slices. Make sure you keep the trimmings and use them for stock or soup.

Dice Start with batons, then 'rock and chop' across them to make even cubes (photo 5).

Julienne or matchsticks 'Rock and chop' each slice lengthways into very thin slices (photo 6).

Chiffonade Lay several leaves of a vegetable (such as cabbage) on top of each other, roll them up like a fat cigar, then 'rock and chop' so they fall into thin ribbons (photo 7).

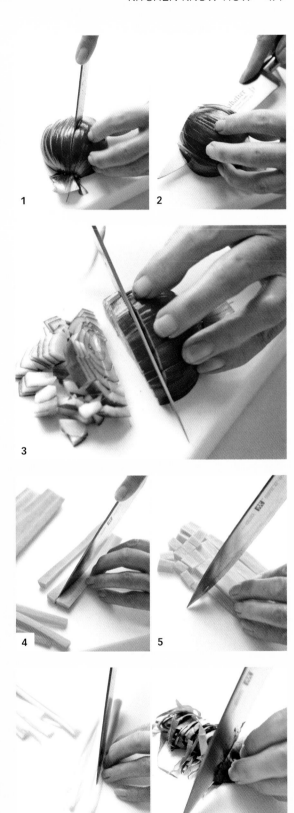

1   2

3

4   5

6   7

What about herbs?

Most recipes will call for fresh herbs to be torn or roughly or finely chopped. Mint and basil in particular are better torn than chopped, as cutting bruises the leaves and causes them to blacken. Other 'soft' herbs, such as coriander, flat-leaf parsley, tarragon and dill are best roughly chopped at the last minute (unless otherwise specified in the recipe) to preserve their flavour and scent. So-called 'hard' herbs, such as thyme and rosemary, need to be chopped more finely. Holding the knife handle in one hand, rest the fingers of your other hand on the tip of the blade. 'Rock and chop' from side to side in a continuous motion over the pile of herbs (photo 8). Keep gathering the herbs back into a pile as you chop.

8

BASIC KIT

Cook's knife The essential kitchen knife – available in several sizes. 15cm or 20cm knives (this refers to the length of the blade) are good starter sizes, or you may want both, to cover smaller and larger jobs. Choose a size and weight that feels comfortable for you. Choose the best chef's knife you can afford, as this will be the main workhorse in the kitchen.

Paring knife Essential for smaller jobs; a serrated blade is best for slicing anything fibrous or with a slightly tougher skin (such as citrus fruits and tomatoes), and a straight blade for smoother veg such as mushrooms.

Serrated bread knife For slicing bread and cakes.

Caring for your knives

Wash them carefully by hand in warm, soapy water, then dry well. Don't put them in the dishwasher – the chemicals used in the machine will eventually corrode the knife, plus the heat of the dishwasher can damage and dull the blade.

Keep knives out of drawers (but safely in a block or, better still, on a magnetic rack), as this will easily blunt them.

Keep it sharp

Rather than testing the sharpness of a knife blade with your thumb, use a tomato. If it is sharp enough, your knife will cut through the tomato skin with the bare minimum of pressure from you.

- A blunt knife is a dangerous knife, as it is far more likely to slip.
- A steel or knife sharpener is worth the investment – or use a sharpening service.
- Never sharpen serrated knives.
- Don't scrape food from chopping boards with the blade of your knife – always use the back of the knife.

Glossary

Acidulated water Water with lemon juice or vinegar added, to preserve the colour of certain fruit and veg that quickly turn brown when peeled/sliced.

Al dente Translates from the Italian as 'firm to the tooth'. Used to describe cooked, but still slightly firm pasta, gnocchi and vegetables.

Bake blind To bake an empty pastry case, weight it down with ceramic beans to stop the base rising. Recipes may state that you should remove the beans and cook the case further to dry the bottom out. Both helps avoid soggy bases once filled and cooked.

Bain-marie Half-fill a roasting tin with water, set a dish in the water and the food inside will cook gently. This expression also refers to placing a bowl over a pan of simmering water when melting chocolate, for example.

Basting Spooning cooking juices and fat over meat during cooking, to keep it moist and to add flavour.

Blanch and refresh To briefly boil a vegetable, then stop the cooking process by plunging it into ice-cold water. This preserves its colour and texture and cuts cooking time later.

Blood temperature The temperature when a heated liquid matches that of your body's normal temperature: 37C/98.6F.

Bouquet garni A bunch of fresh herbs, usually parsley stalks, bay leaf and thyme sprigs tied to celery stalks.

Braise To cook gently in a sealed pan with stock or other liquid until tender.

Clarified butter Butter melted, then separated into clear butter and milk solids. The clear yellow butter is used, and is less likely to burn and spoil.

Coating consistency When liquid coats the back of a spoon evenly.

Confit To cook slowly in fat.

Deglaze Adding liquid, such as stock, wine or water to a hot pan to loosen the crusty, cooked bits from the pan.

Deseed Remove the seeds from a fruit or vegetable by first cutting it in half then scraping out the seeds with a spoon or the tip of a knife.

Devein Use a knife to make a slit in a prawn, gently pull out the thin intestinal tract, which runs down its length.

Dropping consistency Mixture that drops slowly from a spoon rather than pouring off or sticking to it firmly.

Emulsify Mixing two substances together vigorously to form an even suspension; for instance, salad dressing.

Fluff up Loosening and separating the grains of rice or couscous once cooked, using the tines of a fork.

Game Rabbit, venison, pheasant, partridge or other wild birds or animals that have been killed for cooking.

Infuse Flavouring a liquid by adding an aromatic ingredient such as bay leaf, vanilla or onion, then bringing it to the boil before leaving it to cool with the flavouring still in.

Knock back To punch, or knead, the air from risen dough, ready for shaping.

Marinade A liquid that is used to flavour meat, fish or vegetables. Cover the ingredient in the marinade and leave to marinate for a set amount of time.

Meltingly tender Usually refers to meat cooked in a braise until tender enough to cut with a spoon.

Papillote Wrapping food in a parcel of greaseproof paper or foil before cooking. The food steams within the parcel.

Pin bone Plucking out fine bones in fish with tweezers or the tip of a small, sharp knife.

Pulse Turning a food processor on in short sharp bursts to chop ingredients together without blending them completely.

Reduce Rapidly boil a liquid to reduce its volume, to give it a concentrated flavour and to thicken it.

Score Cutting into flesh to allow marinades to penetrate, or to reduce cooking times. The key is to not cut too deep.

Seize When chocolate thickens and turns grainy, normally due to overheating or water getting into the bowl.

Skewer test A useful way to test if a sponge-type cake is cooked. Insert a skewer into the middle of the cake. If the skewer comes out with wet cake mix on it, return the cake to the oven and check again in 10 minutes. If it comes out clean or with a few damp crumbs, the cake is ready.

Sweat To cook vegetables in oil or butter over a low heat until softened but not coloured.

Well A hole hollowed out of a mound of flour, into which liquids are added.

Zest Citrus fruit has a thin layer above the white pith that can be grated to add flavour to dishes.

Recipe index

One-pots

Quick and easy

Index

Picture credits

BBC *Good Food* magazine and BBC Books would like to thank the following people for providing photos. While every effort has been made to trace and acknowledge all photographers, we should like to apologise should their be any errors or omissions.

Prelims: 1 Elisabeth Parsons; 2 Kate Whitaker; 4 , Elisabeth Parsons; 6 (clockwise from top left) Myles New, Elisabeth Parsons, Elisabeth Parsons, Myles New. *Soups*: 12 Gareth Morgans; 21 (clockwise from top left) Philip Webb, Philip Webb, Miles New, Philip Webb, Yuki Sugiura, Elisabeth Parsons; 26 Myles New. *Eggs and cheese*: 30 Elisabeth Parsons; 39 (clockwise from top left) David Munns, Philip Webb, Simon Wheeler, Simon Walton, Myles New, Elisabeth Parsons; 43 Myles New; 49 (clockwise from top left) Myles New, Jean Cazals, Elisabeth Parsons, Jean Cazals, Maja Smend, Philip Webb. *Pasta*: 54 Elisabeth Parsons; 63 (clockwise from top left) Simon Walton, Myles New, Roger Stowell, Peter Cassidy, Rob White; 69 David Munns; 75 (clockwise from top left) Kate Whitaker, Debi Treloar, David Munns, Elisabeth Parsons, David Munns, Myles New; 76 Geoff Wilkinson; 78 Elisabeth Parsons. *Pulses*: 80 David Munns; 89 (clockwise from top left) David Munns, Gareth Morgans, David Munns, Elisabeth Parsons, Yuki Sugiura, Elisabeth Parsons; 98 (clockwise from top left) Yuki Sugiura, Elisabeth Parsons, Yuki Sugiura, Elisabeth Parsons, Dean Grennan, Elisabeth Parsons. *Poultry*: 102 David Munns; 105 Myles New; 111 (clockwise from top left) Elisabeth Parsons, Myles New, Elisabeth Parsons, Elisabeth Parsons, Elisabeth Parsons, Gareth Morgans; 117 (clockwise from top left) Peter Cassidy, Philip Webb, Philip Webb, Dawie Verwey, Elisabeth Parsons, Jean Cazals; 120 Tim Evans; 125 Yuki Sigiura; 129 (clockwise from top left) David Munns, David Munns, Will Heap, Philip Webb, Philip Webb, Philip Webb. *Meat*: 132 David Munns; 141 (clockwise from top left) Gareth Morgans, Elisabeth Parsons, Myles New, Dawie Verwey, Myles New, Philip Webb; 146 Gareth Morgans; 152 (clockwise from top left) Peter Cassidy, Myles New, Elisabeth Parsons, David Munns, Philip Webb, Elisabeth Parsons; 160 Roger Stowell. *Fish*: 166 Elisabeth Parsons; 171 David Munns; 172-173 Myles New; 174 Lisa Linder; 179 (clockwise from top left) Myles New, Gareth Morgans, David Munns, Gareth Morgans, Philip Webb, Myles New; 186 (step) Marie-Louise Avery, (plated oysters) Philip Webb; 188 Myles New; 191 Debi Treloar; 196 (clockwise from top left) Elisabeth Parsons, Kate Whitaker, Yuki Sugiura, David Munns, Elisabeth Parsons, Myles New; 199 David Munns. *Vegetables*: 200 Elisabeth Parsons; 207 (clockwise from top left) Peter Cassidy, David Munns, Roger Stowell, Simon Walton, Simon Wheeler, Myles New; 216 Elisabeth Parsons. *Children*: 220 Gareth Morgans; 227 (clockwise from top left) David Munns, Marie-Louise Avery, Gareth Morgans, Gareth Morgans, Gareth Morgans, Myles New; 233 (clockwise from top left) Philip Webb, Elisabeth Parsons, Noel Murphy, Myles New, Elisabeth Parsons, Marie-Louise Avery; 239 Philip Webb. *Bread*: 244 David Munns; 247 Cameron Watt; 252 Elisabeth Parsons, Cameron Watt, Marie-Louise Avery, Simon Wheeler, Cameron Watt, David Munns; 256 David Munns; 258 Elisabeth Parsons. *Pastries*: 260 Philip Webb; 263 Roger Stowell; 264 Elisabeth Parsons; 271 (clockwise from top left) Debi Treloar, David Munns, Philip Webb, Simon Wheeler, Myles New, Roger Stowell; 277 Philip Webb; 284 Myles New, Roger Stowell, Jean Cazals, Philip Webb, Jean Cazals, Myles New; 286 Philip Webb. *Cakes*: 288 Peter Cassidy; 292 David Munns; 299 (clockwise from top left) Elisabeth Parsons, Jean Cazals, David Munns, Philip Webb, Elisabeth Parsons, Philip Webb; 303 Maja Smend; 314 (clockwise from top left) Peter Cassidy, William Lingwood, Philip Webb, Roger Stowell, Gareth Morgans, David Munns; 320 Myles New. *Celebration*: 324 (clockwise from top left) Philip Webb, Elisabeth Parsons, Philip Webb, Marie-Louise Avery; 332-333 Myles New; 334-338 Myles New; 339-341 Roger Stowell; 342-344 Marie-Louise Avery; 349 (clockwise from top left) Simon Walton, David Munns, Myles New, Myles New, Myles New, Myles New; 350 (marzipan steps) Peter Cassidy, (icing) Lis Parsons. *Desserts*: 352 David Munns; 358 (clockwise from top left) Elisabeth Parsons, David Munns, Will Heap, Simon Walton, Gareth Morgans, Gareth Morgans; 364 Philip Webb; 368 (clockwise from top left) Myles New, Lis Parsons, Maja Smend, Simon Wheeler, Philip Webb; 375 Simon Wheeler; 379 Philip Webb; 381 Yuki Sugiura; 384 (clockwise from top left) Simon Walton, Philip Webb, David Munns, Elisabeth Parsons, Craig Robertson, Jean Cazals. *Christmas*: 388 Simon Walton; 390 Simon Walton; 393 David Munns; 398 (clockwise from top left) David Munns, Myles New, David Munns, David Munns; 405 David Munns; 407 Myles New; 410 (clockwise from top left) Marie-Louise Avery, Myles New, Philip Webb, Elisabeth Parsons, Philip Webb, David Munns; 415 Myles New. *Jams*: 420 Philip Webb; 423 Philip Webb; 425 (clockwise from top left) Philip Webb, David Munns, Peter Cassidy, Peter Cassidy, Elisabeth Parsons, Philip Webb; 429 Philip Webb. *Gifts*: 432 Philip Webb; 434 Philip Webb; 437 Maja Smend, Philip Webb, Maja Smend, Elisabeth Parsons, Elizabeth Zeschin, Peter Cassidy. *Crowds*: 442 Gareth Morgans; 450 (clockwise from top left) Elisabeth Parsons, Myles New, Elisabeth Parsons, Elisabeth Parsons, Roger Stowell; 456 Myles New; 465 (clockwise from top left) Debi Treloar, Elisabeth Parsons, Myles New, Gareth Morgans, Myles New. *Know-how*: Philip Webb; 477-478 Simon Wheeler. Page 470: Roger Stowell. Page 480: Philip Webb.

10 9 8 7 6 5 4 3 2 1

Published in 2011 by BBC Books, an imprint of Ebury Publishing.
A Random House Group Company
Photographs © BBC Magazines 2011
Recipes © BBC Magazines 2011
Book design © Woodlands Books Ltd 2011

The Random House Group Limited Reg. No. 954009

Addresses for companies within the Random House Group can be found at www.randomhouse.co.uk

A CIP catalogue record for this book is available from the British Library.

978 1 849 90151 2

The Random House Group Limited supports the Forest Stewardship Council (FSC), the leading international forest certification organisation. All our titles that are printed on Greenpeace approved FSC certified paper carry the FSC logo. Our paper procurement policy can be found at www.rbooks.co.uk/environment

Commissioning editor: Muna Reyal
Project editor: Laura Higginson
Designer: Kathryn Gammon
Copy-editor: Helena Caldon
Proofreader: Emily Hatchwell
Production: Helen Everson

Colour origination by Dot Gradations Ltd
Printed and bound in China by C & C Offset

To buy books by your favourite authors and register for offers, visit www.rbooks.co.uk